Wm. E. Caldwell.

THE

WAY OF SALVATION

ILLUSTRATED IN

A SERIES OF DISCOURSES.

BY

ALBERT BARNES.

PHILADELPHIA:
PUBLISHED BY PARRY AND M'MILLAN,
(SUCCESSORS TO A. HART, LATE CAREY AND HART.)
LONDON: KNIGHT AND SON.
1855.

Printed by T. K. & P. G. Collins

PREFACE.

THERE are two classes of Sermons. One is composed of those which enter into the permanent literature of a nation, and which take their rank with its most pure and elevated writings, as enduring monuments of argument and of style. The English language is, perhaps, more rich in this species of literature than any other. For lucid statement; for profound argument; for richness of imagination; for copiousness of illustration; for beauty of style; for just views of morals,—the sermons of Barrow, and Tillotson, and Jeremy Taylor, and South, have taken their place with the best classical writings in our language.

The other class is composed of those which are of a less exalted and permanent character, and which are adapted to meet only a local or a temporary, though it may be a very important purpose. They are addressed mainly to the passing age. They are adapted to meet some peculiar state of public opinion, or some prevailing phase of error. They are designed to illustrate the doctrines and duties of religion in the language and style of that age. They, perhaps, have some temporary and local advantage from the name of the author, or from the relations which he sustains to a particular congregation. They accomplish an important purpose on a limited scale, and then pass away, with much of the literature of past ages, to be recalled and remembered no more.

The volume of Sermons now submitted to the public does not aspire to the dignity of the former class, nor is there any hope or expectation that it will occupy that elevated rank. All the hopes cherished in respect to it will be accomplished, if it has a place of temporary usefulness among the other class of sermons referred to, and if it may be made a means, to any extent, of meeting the wants of any portion of the passing generation.

This work has been prepared at the suggestion and the request of the English publishers. As it seemed desirable that there should be some unity of design which might be expressed by an appropriate title, "THE WAY OF SALVATION" has been selected as indicating, in the main, the purpose and character of the volume; and though not properly a *treatise* on that subject, yet it will be found, I trust, that all the Sermons have a bearing more or less direct upon the theme, and that each one will help to remove some obstacle, to explain some difficulty, or to throw some light on the points on which one inquiring how man can be saved, might desire information.

The volume is not an argument for the truth of revelation, nor is it designed formally to meet the objections of infidels, the difficulties of honest sceptics, or the sneers of cavillers. The man whom I have had in my eye in the preparation of the discourses—as I have usually had in my preaching on these and kindred topics—is not he who disbelieves because he *chooses* to do so; nor he who *prefers* to be a sceptic; nor the mere caviller, who, because he *can* laugh at death and the judgment, seeks to satisfy his conscience that it is right to do so; nor he who *desires* to find difficulties in religion because he is unwilling to submit to its claims and its restraints:—but I have had in my eye a class of minds, much larger than is generally supposed to exist, which see *real* difficulties in religion which they would not be *unwilling* to have explained. They are minds so constituted that they see the *difficulties* in believing as well as the *facilities* for it—the things which tend to *hinder* it, as well as those which tend to *promote* it. In all communities there are probably many of this class of minds. They should not be regarded as confirmed in infidelity, and still less as disposed to cavil; but they see real difficulties in Christianity and in the plan of salvation, and they would be gratified, not offended, to find a rational solution of them. It is in vain to deny that there *are* such difficulties; and though he who has a mind so constituted as never to have seen them may be regarded as in some respects in a very enviable situation, yet he greatly errs in regard to human nature, and greatly underrates the magnitude of the subject of religion, who supposes that to all contemplative minds, even to candid minds, the subject appears to be free from perplexity and doubt. A perceived difficulty in the doctrines of religion—a difficulty so great as to lead to weighty and perplexing doubts—is not *always* proof of a depraved heart.

I may be permitted to remark, perhaps, as explaining the general character of the Sermons in this volume, that from the native tendencies of my own mind, from my early cherished habits of thought, and from my early reading, I have had this class of minds more frequently in my eye, in preaching, than any other. It has not been by avowedly meeting the arguments and difficulties of such minds; it has not been by a formal defence of the doctrines of Christianity against the objections of infidels; it has not been by an open reply to the objections of sceptics or cavillers, *but as a secret guide to my line of argument and thought*, that I have had such minds almost constantly before me. My own mind has suggested what I have supposed they would suggest; and in meeting difficulties which have occurred to me, I have supposed that I have also met those which would occur to them. I cannot here repress the acknowledgment of the debt which, in this respect, I owe to "Butler's Analogy"—a work which has met more difficulties in my own mind, and aided me more in preaching, than any other work of uninspired composition. A careful reader of these Sermons will perceive that, in their preparation, I owe to that great work even much more than can be expressed by such a general acknowledgment.

These remarks may suffice to explain the pervading character of this volume of Sermons. In their general arrangement, they begin with a consideration of the claims of the Bible as a guide on the subject of religion (Sermon I.), and with an effort to show (Sermon II.) that the acknowledged obscurities in that book should not deter us from accrediting its claims; with a statement (Sermon III.) of the claims of Christianity, and an attempt to show (Sermon IV.) that the condition of man could not be benefited by the rejection of Christianity, and that the same difficulties precisely would remain, with no known method whatever of relief. The next object (Sermon V.) is to show that Christianity reveals the true ground of the importance attributed to man in the plan of salvation; that the earth is fitted to be a place of probation (Sermon VI.), and that man is actually on probation (Sermon VII.); and that in religion, as in other things, he should accommodate himself to what are the actual arrangements of the Divine government (Sermon VIII.) The next object is to explain the condition in which the Gospel FINDS man—as an actual state which Christianity did not originate, for which it is not responsible, and which is a simple *matter of fact* in which all men are equally interested, whatever system of religion may be true or false (Sermon IX.); a state which naturally prompts to the inquiry what must be done in order to be saved—an inquiry which springs up in the heart of man everywhere, and in reference to which man pants for an answer (Sermon X.) This is followed (Sermons XI.—XIV.) by a description of the struggles of a convicted sinner—and by an attempt to show what is *necessary*, in the nature of things, to give peace to a mind in that condition. To meet the case, the mind thus anxious is directed to the mercy of God (Sermon XV.), and the effort is made to show that it is only an atonement for sin that can give permanent peace to the soul conscious of guilt (Sermons XVI., XVII.) The doctrine of Regeneration, or the new birth, is then considered (Sermons XVIII.—XX.); an attempt is made to vindicate and explain the *conditions*—repentance and faith—which are made necessary to salvation, and to show not only their place in a revealed system of religion, but their relation to the human mind and the circumstances in which man is placed (Sermons XXI.—XXVIII.); and the whole series is closed (Sermons XXIX.—XXXVI.) by a consideration of the nature of justification, or the method by which a sinner may be just with God.

It will be seen that these topics embrace the most material and important inquiries which come before the mind on the question *how man may be saved;* and if a correct representation is given of them, they will furnish to an inquirer after truth a just view of the way of salvation.

I commit this volume to the public with the hope that it may be found to be a safe guide on the most momentous inquiry which can come before the human mind. I have abundant occasion for gratitude for the manner in which the volumes that I have published heretofore have been received by the British public, as well as by my own countrymen; and I would hope that this volume may contribute something to the diffusion of the knowledge of the great principles of religious duty and doctrine which it has been the labour of my life to illustrate and defend.

ALBERT BARNES.

PHILADELPHIA,
May 19, 1855.

CONTENTS.

THE

WAY OF SALVATION.

SERMON I.

THE BIBLE.

Psalm cxix. 105.—"Thy word is a lamp unto my feet, and a light unto my path."

My wish, in illustration of this text, is to call your attention to the Bible. It is not to pronounce an eulogy on it, or to enter into an argument for its Divine origin, or to state and defend its doctrines; but it is to urge its claims to attention, particularly as laying the foundation for the only true knowledge of the Way of Salvation.

When a man, especially one who has cherished sceptical views and feelings, sits down to read the Bible, there is a class of thoughts that bear upon his mind wholly different from such as exist when he peruses any other book. When he sits down to the study of the Iliad, he is conscious that he is perusing the most celebrated poem of the world. It has come down from a very remote antiquity; it has been read by millions, and always with increasing pleasure; it has commanded the admiration of the most eminent scholars of all ages. He feels, therefore, that his perusal of it will be attended with no discredit anywhere; and it will excite no feeling of shame in his bosom should it be known by all his friends that he is engaged in that employment. Substantially the same feeling exists when he reads the Paradise Lost. To admire it, is an evidence of good taste; and an intimate acquaintance with it will be a passport of some value to the good esteem of others, and will never suffuse his cheek with a blush. The same remarks might be made of Herodotus and Xenophon; of Hume and Gibbon; of Seneca and Bacon; of the Spectator and the Rambler. No young man could be found who would think it necessary to practise any concealment in reading them; no one would close them if surprised in their perusal; no one would feel the blood mounting to his cheek as if he were engaged in an occupation which he would rather should be unknown. On the contrary, he knows that he will rise in the estimation of others in proportion to his familiarity with such productions of genius and taste, and is furnishing evidence that he is worthy of esteem.

But when he sits down to read the Bible, he is surrounded by a new set of influences, and is conscious of a new train of emotions. Unless he is a Christian, he enters upon it as if it were some deed that is to be done when alone. He would feel some revulsion at being surprised in the employment. He would expect that it would excite remark—perhaps a playful remark—if he were to select this book for perusal from a collection of annuals and poems on a centre table. He would be apt to close it if he was found reading it when he had laid down his Homer or his Virgil, his Addison or Shakspeare or Byron, for this purpose. His first feeling is, that it is a book of RELIGION, and that to read it will be understood to be indicative of seriousness, and, a purpose to become a Christian. He is intimidated also by a somewhat antiquated style, and by what seems to him an uncouth phraseology; and, perhaps, he would be also by its denunciation of some passion that reigns in his heart; by its frequent reference to death and the judgment; and by the serious and solemn tone which everywhere pervades it. It is a book which he does not mean wholly to neglect, but its perusal he intends to defer until that somewhat remote period when it will be necessary to prepare for the future state, and when he purposes, as preliminary to that, to become religious.

The consequence of such feelings is, that the Bible is a book greatly neglected. Many are quite familiar with a considerable part of the range of ancient classic learning, who have almost no acquaintance with the sacred Scriptures. Many are familiar with the whole range of fictitious literature to which this age has given birth, who are strangers almost wholly to the Book of God, except in name. Many see exquisite beauty in the poets of modern times, who see none in the "sweet psalmist of Israel;" and many find pleasure in copious draughts from the fountains of Helicon, who have no relish for the "gently flowing" waters of Siloam. I may add, too, that the people in a nominally Christian community are distinguished pre-eminently for the neglect of the oracles of the religion which prevails in their own country. The Mussulman reads the Koran with profound attention, and without any consciousness of doing anything that should excite a blush; the Shasters and Vedas of the Hindoos are read by the worshippers of the gods with anxious care; but how few are there, except professed Christians, who are in the regular habit of reading the Bible! How few young men are there who could be seen reading it without some consciousness that they were doing that which they would rather not have known!

I will, therefore, proceed to suggest some considerations designed to urge upon you the study of the Bible; and shall deem it a sufficient reward for my labour if I can induce but one to commence and continue the practice through life.

I. In the first place, *it is the oldest book in the world.* Of course you will not understand me as saying that the entire Bible is more ancient than any other book. I know that some parts of it were written since the time of Hesiod and Homer; of Xenophon and Herodotus; of Demosthenes and Plato. But what I mean is, that some portions of it stretch far back beyond the records of classic literature, and before the dawn of well-authenticated profane history. He who sits down to read the book of Job may do it with the moral certainty that he is perusing the most ancient written poem in the world; and he who reads the book of Genesis is certain that he is perusing a history that was penned long before any Grecian writer collected and recorded the deeds of ancient times. Take away the history of the past which we have in the Bible, and there are at least some two thousand years of the existence of our race of which we know nothing—and that too the *forming* period, and in many respects the most interesting part of the history of the world. Begin, in your investigation of past events, where ancient profane history begins, and you are plunged into the midst of a state of affairs of whose origin you know nothing, and where the mind wanders in perfect night, and can find no rest. Kingdoms are seen, but no one can tell when or how they were founded; cities appear, whose origin no one knows; heroes are playing their part in the great and mysterious drama, but no one knows whence they came, and what are their designs; a race of beings is seen whose origin is unknown, and the past periods of whose existence on the earth no one can determine—a race formed no one can tell for what purpose, or by what hand. Vast multitudes of beings are suffering and dying for causes which no one can explain; a generation in their own journey to the grave tread over the monuments of extinct generations, and with the memorials of fearful changes and convulsions in the past all around them, of which no one can give an account. Begin your knowledge of the past at the remotest period to which profane history would conduct you, and you are in the midst of chaos, and you cannot advance a step without going into deeper night—a night strikingly resembling that which the oldest poet in the world describes as the abode of the dead:—"The land of darkness and the shadow of death; a land of darkness as darkness itself; and of the shadow of death, without any order, and where the light is as darkness." Job x. 21, 22. And thus in reference to the darkness of the past—the history of our race in its by-gone periods—beyond the reach of all other guides—the Bible is "a lamp unto our feet, and a light unto our path."

Now there is some interest, at least, in the fact that we have in our possession the most ancient book which was ever written. We should feel some interest in seeing and conversing with a man who had lived on earth during all that time, and had looked on the sun, and stars, and earth before the time of Hesiod and Homer; who had lived amidst all the revolutions of past kingdoms and empires—while proud Assyria spread its conquests and fell; while Babylon rose and declined; while Rome carried its arms around the world and sank:—if he had lived on while seasons walked their rounds, and had seen fifty generations buried, and had come to us now with the ancient costume and manners, to tell us what was in the days of Noah or Abraham. We contemplate with deep interest an "ancient river;" and no one ever looked on the Mississippi or the Ganges for the first time without emotion. So of a venerable elm or oak that has stood while many a winter storm has howled through its branches, and while the trees that grew up with it have long since decayed. So with an ancient bulwark or castle; an ancient monument, or work of art. Whatever stands alone, and has lived on while others have decayed, excites our admiration. The pyramids of Egypt, and the tombs of the kings of Thebes, and the pillar of Pompey, thus attract attention. Any lonely memento of the past has a claim to our regard, and excites an interest, which we feel for nothing when surrounded by the objects amidst which it rose. In the wastes of Arabia, between the Nile and Mount Sinai, there stand some half a dozen or more headstones in an ancient burying-place. There is not a town, or city, or house, or tent, or fertile field near. They are the lonely memorials of a far-distant generation. All else is gone,—the men that placed them there; the towns where they dwelt; the mouldering ashes, and the names of those whose last place of sleep they mark. So the Bible stands in the past. All is desolation around it. The books that were written when that was, if there were any, are gone. The generations that lived then are gone. The cities where they dwelt are gone. Their tombs and monuments are gone; and the Bible is all that we have to tell us who they were, why they lived, and what occurred in their times. Had the Bible to this day been unknown, or were it suddenly discovered in some venerable ruin and authenticated, who would not hail such a monument of what occurred in the past periods of the world?

The circumstance here referred to of the antiquity of the Bible derives additional interest from the attempts which have been made to destroy it. No *book* has excited so much opposition as this; but it has survived every attack which power, talent, and eloquence have ever made on it. Now, we do and we should feel an interest in anything which has survived repeated attempts to destroy it. The remnant of an army that has survived a battle, and that has successfully resisted great numbers in the conflicts of war; the tree that has stood firm when all others in its neighbourhood have been prostrated; the ancient castle that has sustained many a siege, and that remains impregnable; the solid rock that has been washed by floods for centuries, and that has not been swept away—all excite a deep interest. We love to contemplate these, and we should deem ourselves destitute of all right feeling if we should pass them by without attention. But no army ever survived so many battles as the Bible; no tree has stood so long, and weathered so many storms; no ancient bulwark has endured so many sieges, and stood so firm amid the thunders of war and the ravages of time; and no rock has been swept by so many currents, and has still stood unmoved. It has outlived all conflicts, survived all the changes in empires, and come down to us notwithstanding all the efforts made to destroy it; and while the stream of time has rolled on, and thousands of other books have been engulphed, this book has been borne triumphantly on the wave. It has shown that it is destined to be borne onward to the end of time, while millions of others shall sink degradedly to the bottom.

II. The second consideration which I suggest is, *that the Bible contains the religion of your country.* Chillingworth uttered a sentiment which contains as much meaning as can be well condensed into a few words, when he said, that "The Bible is the religion of Protestants." In a similar sense, we may say that the Bible is the religion of our country. The ancient religion of Persia is in the Zendavesta; the religion of India is in the Shasters; the religion of Turkey is in the Koran; the religion of *our* country is in the Bible. We have no religion in this land, and can have none, which is not in the Bible. Throughout the length and breadth of this great nation there is not an altar erected to an idol-god; nor in all our history has a molten image been cast, or a carved block received the homage of an American citizen. Not a temple has been reared in honour of a pagan divinity, nor is the knee bent anywhere to adore the hosts of heaven. It is a remarkable, but indisputable fact, that they who reject the Bible in our country have no altar; no temple; no worship; no religion. They offer no sacrifice; they have no incense; they have no books of praise or of prayer—no hymn-book, and no liturgy; they are emphatically living without God in the world. No religion will be sustained in this land which does not appeal to the Bible; and if that is driven away, we shall be a people without any religion. The religion of this nation is to be the Christian religion or none; and when an American is asked what is his religion, he can only refer to the Bible.

We have, indeed, our different opinions. We are divided into sects and denominations, with peculiar views and modes of worship, yet with a good degree of common sympathy and of fraternal feeling; and we all harmonize in the sentiment, that whatever religion there is in this land is in the Bible, and that that is the rule of faith and practice. Our religion is not in creeds and confessions; in catechisms and symbols; in tradition and the decrees of synods and councils; it is IN THE BIBLE. To that, as a common standard, we all appeal; and around that we all rally. Much as Christians differ from each other, *all* would rush to the defence of that Book when attacked, and all regard it as the fountain of their opinions and the source of their hopes.

There is, moreover, among Christians in this country a *growing* conviction that the standard of all religion is the Bible. There is less and less confidence in the deductions of reason; less reliance on creeds and confessions and tradition; less dependence on the judgment of man, and a more simple dependence on the word of God. It is, and it is to be, a great principle in this nation, that the Bible contains our religion.

Now, if this be so, then the reasons why the Bible should be studied are very obvious. One is, that any man must be destitute of a very essential part of valuable knowledge if he is ignorant of the foundation of the religion of his own country. Its institutions he can never understand, nor can he ever be fully prepared to discharge his duty in any calling in this country without an acquaintance with the sacred Scriptures. As connected with the history and institutions of his country, and as here destined to exert a controlling influence over millions of the most free minds on the earth, it demands his profound attention. I confess I feel a deep interest in the Koran, though I never expect to be subject in any way to the laws of that book; and though I have never been able to read it though, often as I have resolved I would read it, and have attempted to do it. But I feel an interest in *any* book that has power to hold one hundred and twenty millions of the human race in subjection, and to mould the institutions and laws of so large a portion of mankind. I feel far more interest in that than I can in the power of Alexander, who subdued the world by arms; or of the Autocrat of the Russias, who rules a vast empire by hereditary might; or even of Napoleon, who held nations in subjection by a most potent and active will. For in such cases there is living power, and there are vast armies, and frowning bulwarks, and long lines of open-mouthed cannon prepared to pour sheets of flame on all who dare oppose. But the dominion of the Koran is THE DOMINION OF A BOOK—a silent, still, speechless thing, that has no will, no armies, no living energies, no chain-shot, no cannons;—and yet it exerts a power which the monarch and the conqueror never wields. It lives, too, when monarchs and conquerors have died. It meets advancing generations, and subdues their wills too. It moulds their opinions, leads them to the temples of worship, and controls their passions with a power which monarchs never knew. So it is with the BIBLE. That, too, is a book—a silent, speechless book. But in our own land, twenty millions acknowledge its right to give laws; and in other lands, one hundred millions confess its power; and in past times, many thousand millions have been moulded by its precepts, and I would not be ignorant of that which exerts a control so near Omnipotence over so many human minds.

Again: No man should be a stranger to the religion of his country. At some future period of life, and that not far distant, these questions may be asked of some young man here, for aught you know, on the shores of India, or in the islands of the Pacific, or in the heart of the Celestial Empire:—'What is the religion of the United States? On what is it based? What are the doctrines of the Book which is the acknowledged authority there? By whom, and when, and where was it written? And why is it there received as of Divine origin?' How many a young American may have been asked these questions, who was as unable to answer them as he would be similar inquiries respecting the Koran or the Shasters! How strange to an intelligent foreigner would it seem that one from a land like this could give no account of the religion of his own country!

There is another thought here, which I wish to express with as much deference for the elevated classes in our land as possible. Some who read these pages may possibly yet occupy places of influence and power in the councils of the nation, or be called as professional men to appear in conspicuous stations before their countrymen. Now the idea which I wish to express is, that the uses which are made of the Bible, and the allusions to it, by men in public life, are sometimes such as may admonish those who are coming on to the stage of action to become familiar with it, and such as are anything but commendatory of the knowledge which they have of the one Book which, more than any other, controls this nation. Shakspeare shall not be inaccurately quoted; and Byron and Burns, and Homer and Virgil shall be referred to with classic elegance; but a quotation from the Bible shall show that with whatever other learning the orator may be endowed, his familiarity has not been with the inspired records of the religion of his country; and the words of David, Isaiah, and Paul, and even of the Redeemer, shall be miserably mangled, and made almost unintelligible. Many a young man now entering on life will yet be placed in circumstances where it will be discreditable to him not to be acquainted with the Bible. No one can be placed in circumstances where that knowledge would be disreputable or injurious.

There is one other thought under this head. It is this:—The Bible has gone deeply into our institutions, customs, and laws, and no one can understand the history of this country who does not understand the Bible. It has made us, directly or indirectly, what we are. Our own ancestors, in our father-land, once were wild barbarians, and sacrificed human beings to idols. The oaken groves of England witnessed many a Druid superstition; many a now well-cultivated spot in that land was a place where men, woven in wicker-work, were consumed as an offering to the gods! I need not say that the change in that country from what it *was* to what it *is*, was brought about by the influence of the religion which is taught in the Bible. That religion banished superstition and idolatry; raised Christian temples in the places where stood the groves of the Druids; introduced civilization, intelligence, and social order; made immortal Alfred what he was; laid the foundations of Cambridge and of Oxford; and moulded the literature and the laws of our ancestors.

Still more directly has it gone into our own institutions. We have derived our origin in great part from the Puritans, a people to whom Hume said was to be traced whatever of civil liberty there was in England. I need not recall any of the events of our early history. I need only remind you that with the Puritan, the axe was not a more needful or inseparable companion than the Bible. It went with him into the deep forest; comforted him when the war-whoop of the savage sounded in his ears; prompted him to build the church, the school-house, and the college; entered into his literature, and constituted his laws; was the foundation of his civil rights, and the platform of his views of government. It contained the lessons which he taught to his children; and his parting counsel to them, when he lay on a bed of death, was, that they should always love it. Phidias so wrought his own name into the shield of the statue of Minerva at Athens, that it could not be removed without destroying the statue. So the precepts and truths of the Bible have been inwrought into all our institutions. They are not *interwoven*—as if they were separate warp and woof. They are not *laid on*—as plates of gold may be on a carved image. They are *fused in*—intermingled—and run together—as the gold and silver and brass of Corinth were in the great fire which burnt down its statues of silver and gold and brass—forming the much-valued compound of antiquity, the Corinthian brass. They cannot be separated; and it is too late to trace their independent proportions and influence. We have no institutions, no laws, no social habits, that are worth anything, and no learning, no literature of any kind, no liberty, which have not been moulded and modified by the Bible. No man can write our history who is a stranger to the Bible; and you will NEVER understand it, if you are ignorant of that Book. The man who enters on public life ignorant of the influence of this book in our history, is liable to perpetual mistakes and blunders in regard to the institutions of his own country. He will perpetually come in contact with opinions and habits which he cannot understand. He will never be acquainted with the public mind in this nation. He will be mistaken in regard to the course which the popular feeling will take on any subject. He will run counter to what he will esteem mere prejudice, but what in fact is conscience; and he will suppose that he meets mere popular feeling, when he encounters that which enters into every principle of our liberty. There is nothing on which foreigners who come among us are more liable to misunderstand us than on this point; and nothing which to them appears more inexplicable than that religion is propagated and maintained by voluntary efforts, and without an alliance with the State. The secret of the whole is, the hold which the Bible has on the public mind, and the fact that that Book is allowed to influence so extensively the opinions, the laws, and the customs of the land. It is now in almost every family, and we intend it *shall be* in every family. It is read every day by millions; and hundreds of thousands of children and youth are taught every week in the Sabbath-school to reverence it. A great National Society is in existence whose business it is to see that that Book is placed and kept in every family in the land; and though the press teems with novels, and romances, and poems, and books of science, yet the book that is most frequently printed, and on which the art of the printer and the binder is most abundantly lavished still, as a private enterprise, is the Bible. And in reference to our own most interesting history as a people, and to the nature of our institutions, civil and religious, as well as in reference to all the past, the Bible is the only certain "lamp unto our feet, and light unto our path."

III. A third consideration is, *that the Bible has such evidences of Divine origin as to claim your attention.* I do not assume that it is given by inspiration—for my purpose now does not require this, nor am I about to detain you with any proofs on that point. But I would show you that there are such presumptive proofs of its being a revelation from God, as to demand study and inquiry; such that it is ill-becoming the young man, or any man, to neglect it; and such that to reject it without examination, is no mark of an elevated understanding, or of true manliness of sentiment. The considerations which I would suggest under this head are these:—

(1.) The friends of the Bible have been among the most sober, calm, and thoughtful of mankind. They have been such men as are accustomed to look at evidence, and to weigh arguments before they embrace them. That some of its neglectors and adversaries have had this character I have no occasion to deny; but that the mass of them have been of this stamp no one will venture to affirm. But a book which has commended itself to the faith of millions of thinking and intelligent men as of Divine origin, is not to be treated with contempt, or rejected without a hearing. No man recommends his own intelligence or wisdom by a contemptuous rejection of such a book.

(2.) Again, a considerable part of those who have embraced the Bible as of Divine origin, have done it as the result of examination. I admit that *all* have not done it from this cause.

Many have been trained up in its belief, and have never doubted of its Divine origin; but a considerable portion even of this class, when they have arrived at mature age, have instituted an examination on the subject, and have satisfied their own minds that it is from God. But many an hereditary infidel has yielded his opposition to the Bible by the force of evidence, and embraced it as true; many a scoffer has become a believer by the force of the argument, and admitted that it was from God. Meantime all its friends, whether hereditary friends—if I may so call them—or the friends made such by argument, have been willing to submit the evidence of the Divine origin of the Scriptures to the sober reason of mankind. They have asked them to examine the question. They hold themselves ready at any moment to give the book to any man who *will* examine it. They invite discussion, and they always consider it a point gained, and a very probable indication of the conversion of an infidel, if he can from any motive be induced to examine the Divine origin of the Scriptures. And so scoffers and infidels feel when one of their own number is induced, from any cause, to read the Bible. From the moment when he takes the book in his hands, they regard his conversion to Christianity as more than half certain. They anticipate, almost as a matter of course, that if he is led to investigate this question he is lost to their cause. And so all feel. Many a man is deterred from reading the Bible, and from examining its claims, under a belief that, if he does it, he will become a Christian. Yet what a state of mind is this! And what a tribute is thus unwittingly paid to the Bible! And how clear is it, that, if this be the case, the Bible has such evidence of a Divine origin as to demand your attention!

(3.) Again, its effects on the world are such as to show that it has sufficient claims to a Divine origin to demand attention. As a mere matter of curiosity, if there were no better motive, one would suppose that an interest would be felt in the Book which displaced the ancient systems of philosophy; which changed the whole form of religion in the Roman empire—overturning altars, closing temples, disrobing priests, and revolutionizing laws; which abolished slavery in all the ancient world; which has elevated the female sex from the deepest degradation; which has everywhere been the promoter of good morals; which banished the barbarous sports of the amphitheatre; which has led to the foundation of colleges, and the erection of hospitals, and the diffusion of universal education; which has curbed the tiger-passions of many a man, and made him like a lamb; and which has transformed the intemperate, the licentious, and the profane, in millions of instances, and made them pure and holy men. Now a book which can do this has such claims of a Divine origin as to demand attention, and to be worthy of perusal.

(4.) And again, the class of men whom it has satisfied of its Divine origin is such as to show the same thing. They have been, in many instances, men most eminent in all departments of science and learning, and who stand, by common consent, at the head of the race. I need not tell you who they are. In our most rich English literature there is scarcely a man of eminence who has not bowed to the authority of the sacred Scriptures. Who, in teaching the laws of morals, was superior to Johnson? Who better understood the beauties of the English tongue than Addison? Who was a sweeter poet than Cowper? Who more majestic and grand than Milton? Who has controlled more human minds by stating its laws than Locke? Who has seen farther into the distant heavens than Newton? What individual of our race is by common consent at the head of any department of learning, who has not acknowledged the Divine authority of the Bible? I by no means say that this proves that it is of Divine origin. I say only, that it demonstrates that there are claims to such an origin which demand examination. I add one other thought under this head—

(5.) That the same thing is shown by the fact that the Bible has outlived all the attacks which have been made on it, and has nearly or quite weathered out the storm of conflict. It was penned in a remote age; in a little corner of the world; among a people without science, and without any other literature; when the rules of poetry and history were unwritten, and when the human mind was comparatively in its infancy. That a book so written, and with such pretensions, should be attacked was not wonderful. Accordingly, every science, I believe, has been made the occasion of an assault on the Bible. Astronomy, and history, and antiquities, and geology, and chemistry, all have had their turn; and all have in their turn alarmed the friends of revelation. But the war from these quarters has nearly ceased to rage. Every gun has been spiked, or turned on the foe—except in the matter of geology—and the friends of revelation may safely leave that until the geologist will tell us precisely what his own settled opinion is. In the year 1806 the French Institute counted more than eighty theories in geology hostile to the Scripture history, not one of which has lived to the present time (*Lyell*). The argument from astronomy was demolished by Chalmers. The argument from the high antiquity of the sacred books, and the history of India, has been abandoned by infidels themselves. Point after point has been yielded, and the Bible still lives; and it advances in its power over the human mind just as science advances, and at the moment when I am writing has a control over the intellect of the world which it never had before. It will have a greater control to-morrow; and will continue to extend its empire to the end of time. It is speaking now in an hundred and fifty languages more than it was fifty years ago, and there is nothing more fixed pertaining to the future than that the period is not distant when it will speak in all the languages of the world. It is destined to be the book which shall ultimately model the laws, and direct the worship of the race; the book which is to displace the Koran, the Zendavesta, and the Vedas; and the book which is to be found in every living language when the great globe shall dissolve. Now I do not say that this proves that the Bible has a Divine origin. I say only, that it demonstrates that such a book is not to be treated with contempt, that it has sufficient claims to a Divine origin to demand perusal and study. He gives no evidence of extraordinary talent or independence who can neglect or despise such a book; he who studies it is at least associated in *one* thing with the minds that have done the most to honour our race, and who have secured the widest respect among mankind. And in reference to the whole range of investigations that come before the human mind, to the actual developments of the human powers, and to the changes that have occurred on earth, and to all our inquiries respecting the future, as well as in reference to the past history of nations, and to our own history as a people, it may be found to be true that the Bible is the only certain "lamp unto our feet, and light unto our path."

IV. The fourth consideration which I urge is, *that the Bible reveals a way of salvation*—a method by which a sinner may be conducted to happiness and to heaven. I here mean only to *state* this—not to attempt to *prove* it. Nor is it necessary for my purpose now to prove it. All that my purpose demands is to bring the fact to your notice, and to state that such a plan is revealed, and in such circumstances as to demand your attention. That it professes to reveal a way by which a man may be saved, no one can doubt;—for this is the leading design of the book. That it is a simple and intelligible way, is demonstrated by the fact that it has been embraced by millions of our race who had no special claims to superior intellectual endowments, and no superior attainments in science. That it is a safe way has been demonstrated, as far as such a fact could be, by its sustaining power in those circumstances which most certainly test the truth and value of our principles—the circumstances which attend our departure from the world. But while commending itself to minds in humble walks, and in the lowly condition of life, it has also so commended itself to minds most elevated and cultivated; has so met their wants, and so imparted peace, and so sustained them in the day of trial, as to show that it has a claim on the attention of all mankind. To such minds it has commended itself as simple, satisfactory, and rational; as adapted to the condition of fallen man, and as imparting the true peace, for which a soul conscious of guilt seeks. It claims, too, to reveal the *only* way by which a sinner can be saved, and urges this on the attention of the race by all its proofs of its being a communication from heaven—by its miracles, and its prophecies, and its purity of doctrine, and its elevated rules of morality, and its influence on mankind. He is not, he cannot be wise, who turns away from a book that comes with such evidence of a heavenly origin as the Bible has, and that has satisfied so many minds of its truth. He is not, he cannot be wise, who in such circumstances refuses to examine the claims of a book that professes to disclose the only method by which man can be saved.

V. The fifth and last consideration which I shall suggest is, *that the Bible is a book whose consolations and counsels you will need on a bed of death.* Instead of detaining you with an *argument* on this point, I will just advert to one fact which will have more weight with many whom I address than anything which I can say; and with this I shall close this discourse. A few days before the death of Sir Walter Scott, there was a lucid interval of that distressing malady which had for some time afflicted him, and to remove which he had travelled in vain to London, to Italy, and to Malta. He was again in his own home. In one of these calm moments of reason, "gentle as an infant," says his biographer, when the distressing aberrations of his mind had for a time ceased, he desired to be drawn into his library, and placed by the window, that he might look down upon the Tweed. To his son-in-law he expressed a wish that he should read to him. "From what book shall I read?" said he. "Can you ask?" Scott replied; "THERE IS BUT ONE." "I chose," says his biographer, "the fourteenth chapter of St. John's Gospel. He listened with mild devotion, and said when I had done, Well, this is a great comfort; I have followed you distinctly, and I feel as if I were yet to be myself again" (Life of Scott, vi. 288). I need not enlarge on the dying testimony of this eminent man in favour of the Bible. On the bed of death, "there IS but one" book that can meet the case. Not his own beautiful poems; not his own enchanting works of fiction, were his comforters there. He had come to a point where fiction gave way to reality; and we can conceive of scarcely any scene of higher sublimity than was thus evinced, when a mind that had charmed so many other minds, the most popular writer of his age, if not of any age, in the solemn hour when life was about to close, gave this voluntary tribute to the solitary eminence of the Bible above all other books. Would that his dying declaration could be imprinted on the title-page of all his works—that wherever they shall be read, his solemn testimony might go with them, that a time is coming when BUT ONE BOOK can have claims on the attention of men, and BUT ONE BOOK will be adapted to guide their steps and to comfort their hearts! May I suggest to the readers of novels and romances that the time is coming when, one after another, these books will be laid aside; when the romance of life will be exchanged for the sober reality of death; and when the most gorgeous and splendid illusions of this world will give place to the contemplation of the realities of that everlasting scene which opens beyond the grave. Then you will need, not fiction, but truth; not gorgeous description, not the enchanting narrative, not the wizard illusions of the master mind that can play upon the feelings and entrance the heart; but the word—the eternal word of that God who cannot lie, and the sweet consolations of that "ONE BOOK" whose beauties, after all, as much transcend the highest creations of genius as its truths are more valuable than fiction. We may *live* amidst gorgeous scenes; amidst splendid illusions; amidst changing clouds; amidst vapours that float on the air, and then vanish; but when we *die* we shall wish to plant our feet, not on evanescent vapours and changing though brilliant clouds, but on the Eternal Rock;—a position which shall be firm when the rains descend, and the floods come, and the winds blow (Matt. vii. 25). And in reference to that dark valley which we must all soon tread—that valley that appears so chilly and dismal to man—along which no one has returned to be our conductor and guide, whatever may be said of the value of the Bible in regard to the past history of our race, or our own history in particular, or the various inquiries which have come before the human mind—it is indubitably *then* to be the only certain "lamp unto our feet, and light unto our path."

Let me, in conclusion, ask of each one individually, Is there force enough in my argument to induce *you* to read the Bible?

If there is, let it be done. I ask you not to lay aside your Homer, your Cowper, your Dryden, your Milton. I ask you not to burn your Addison, your Johnson, or your Burke. I ask you not to throw away your Galen, or your Davy—your Coke, or your Hale; but I ask you to give THE SUPREME PLACE in your life to that ONE BOOK which the greatest of all writers of fiction gave on the approach of death—to THE BIBLE.

SERMON II.

THE OBSCURITIES OF DIVINE REVELATION.

PSALM xliii. 3.—"O send out thy light and thy truth: let them lead me; let them bring me unto thy holy hill, and to thy tabernacles."

PSALM xxxvi. 9.—"For with thee is the fountain of life: in thy light shall we see light."

PERHAPS no one ever studied the Bible as a professed revelation from God who has not had such questions cross his mind as the following:—Why is there so much in this book that is obscure and unintelligible? Why is not more information given on great and important questions about which the human mind has always been perplexed? Why is no more light thrown on the subject of moral government; on the question why sin and misery were allowed to enter the world; on the nature of the happiness of heaven; on the reasons why the wicked are to suffer for ever? Why are so many subjects left in total darkness in a professed revelation, and others left with only such a feeble glimmering of light as almost to make us wish that there had been none?

These questions produce increased perplexity and embarrassment when such thoughts as the following occur, as they will be very likely to do, in connexion with them:—First, it seems that it would have been so easy for God to have removed all difficulty on many or all of these subjects. There can be no darkness or obscurity with Him in relation to them, and he could readily have taken away all our perplexity by a simple explanation, almost by a single "stroke of the pen." Secondly, such an explanation seems to have been demanded in order to clear up his own character and dealings. There are many dark things about his government; many things which give occasion to hard thoughts, to aspersions, and to reflections on his character, which his friends cannot meet, and to difficulties which they cannot solve; and, instead of removing all these, he has so left the matter as to perplex the good, and to give occasion for the unanswered reproaches of the evil, when a simple explanation might have saved the whole difficulty. Thirdly, such an explanation seemed to be demanded as an act of benevolence on his part, in order to remove perplexity and distress from the human mind, even if he was willing that his own character and the principles of his government should rest under a cloud. Man by nature is in darkness. He is perplexed and embarrassed with his condition and prospects. He struggles in vain to obtain relief by the unassisted efforts of his own mind. A revelation is proposed; but on the most important and perplexing of his difficulties it seems only to tantalize him, and to leave him as much in the dark as he was before. And, fourthly, all this difficulty is increased when he reflects how much of this same book is occupied with histories which have lost their interest; with names and genealogical tables now of little or no value; with laws pertaining to rites and ceremonies long since obsolete, and always apparently pertaining to trifling subjects; and with narratives often of apparently little dignity, and of slight importance. The thought will cross the mind, Why were not those portions of the book occupied with statements which would have been of permanent value to man? Why, instead of these, did not God cause to be inserted there important explanations respecting his own character and government; the condition of the heavenly world; the reasons why sin and woe came into the system; and why the wicked must be punished for ever? Disappointed, and troubled, and half feeling that he is trifled with, many an inquirer after truth is tempted to throw the book aside, and never to open it again with the hope of finding an answer to the questions which most deeply agitate his soul.

These are *bold* questions which man asks, but they will come into the mind, and it is important to meet them, and to calm down the spirit which would ask them, if we can. To obtain a rational view of this matter, there are two inquiries:—

I. What is the measure of light actually imparted in the Bible? and,

II. Why is there no more?

In the answer which may be given to these two inquiries, we may find something, perhaps, to soothe the feelings and calm the mind, in reference to the perplexities referred to.

I. The first inquiry is, What is the measure of light actually imparted in the Bible? I do not, of course, intend to go into detail here—for this would involve an enumeration of all the points embraced in the system of Christian theology,—but I purpose only to suggest the *principles*, if I may be allowed the expression, which guided the Divine Mind in giving a revelation to man. It is evident that in giving such a revelation, the question must have occurred, whether light should be imparted on these points referred to; whether all should be communicated that could be; whether care should be taken to explain every question that might ever arise in the human mind; whether the whole subject of moral government should be unfolded, or whether some other rule should be adopted, and some other object should be aimed at. Now, the principles which seem to have guided the Divine Mind, admitting for the time that the Bible is a revelation from God, so far as we can judge from the manner in which the revelation was actually given, are the following:—

(1.) First, to leave many subjects, and among them some of those on which the mind is most inquisitive, *perfectly in the dark*. It was intended that not a ray of light should be shed on them; that there should be nothing which could constitute a basis of even a plausible conjecture. It was clearly the design of God to fix an outer limit to human knowledge so far as this world is concerned, in reference to those points, and to leave the race totally and designedly in the dark. This principle is involved in the declaration, "Secret things belong to the Lord your God, but things that are revealed to you and your children."

A few remarks in relation to this outer limit, or this boundary, will apply equally to reason and revelation; and while they may do something as an explanation of the general principles of the Divine proceedings, they may, at the same time, do something to reconcile us to the fact that it is found in a book of professed revelation.

(*a*) There is a limit to the human faculties—a point beyond which man, in this world, cannot go in inquiring into the various questions which may occur. That point may not yet have been reached on any one subject; but clearly there *is* such a point, beyond which all is dark. Occasionally a bright genius arises—some one endowed with almost superhuman powers—who seems to secure, almost by intuition, all that man had before discovered, and who is prepared, at the beginning of his own career, to start where others left off, and to penetrate the deep profound where mortals never before have trod—to open the eyes on new regions of thought, and new worlds of matter; but even *he* soon comes to the outer limit of the human powers, and will always feel, as Newton did at the close of his life, that the great ocean of truth is still unexplored. "I do not know," said he, "what I may appear to the world; but to myself I seem to have been only like a boy playing on the sea-shore, and diverting myself in now and then finding a smoother pebble or a prettier shell than ordinary, while the great ocean of truth lay all undiscovered before me." * Whatever may be the attainments which man may make in the general progress of society, and whatever light may be shed on objects before obscure by the few men of transcendant genius whom God raises up from age to age, there is an *outer limit* to all such progress—a point beyond which all is involved in Cimmerian darkness. The ancients, in their ignorance of the true structure of the world, supposed that the earth was surrounded by interminable seas, and that whosoever should venture out in a right line from the land would soon enter regions deepening in darkness, till not a ray of light should be visible; and they feigned one such voyage, in which the mariner stood boldly for the west, until, terrified and affrighted by the increasing darkness, he turned the prow of his vessel, and sought again his native shores. What to them pertaining to the structure of the earth was fable, is true on the point before us in regard to higher subjects. There is an outer limit beyond which there is no light. We cannot penetrate it. We have no faculties, as men ordinarily are made, to penetrate it; and no genius arises so superior to the ordinary human endowments as to be able to carry the torch of discovery into those unexplored regions.

(*b*) In like manner, as in regard to our natural faculties, so it was clearly the design of God that there should be many subjects on which not a ray of light should be thrown by revelation. There are many points on which no statement is made; on which no hint is given that would relieve the anxiety of a troubled mind. Far on the hither side of what we would like to know, the line is drawn, and the whole book is closed at what may, without irreverence, be called—or which, whether irreverent or not, expresses our natural feelings—*a provoking point*, just at the point where we would be glad to ask questions, and where we by no means feel our minds satisfied with what we possess.

(*c*) As a matter of fact, therefore, whatever conclusions may be drawn from it, there is a great variety of subjects, many of them of great interest to the human mind, which are left totally in the dark, and on which the utmost efforts of ingenuity,

* Brewster's Life of Newton, pp. 300, 301.

employed in endeavouring to make the Bible speak out, have been utterly ineffectual. The silence of the Bible is, in this respect, somewhat like the silence of the dead about their condition, and about the future world. If they live, why do they not return? Why do they not come and tell us what it is to die?—whither man goes when he dies?—and whether they are happy or not, and how we may be? Why do they keep their countenances so fixed and grave; and why do the lips once so ready to impart knowledge now keep themselves so close on the very points on which we would be glad to have them speak?

As a believer in revelation, and a friend of it, I am constrained, therefore, to admit that there are many important points on which not a ray of light is shed. I am, for one, willing to concede that among these points are the questions why moral evil was admitted into the system; why misery ever found its way into the empire of an infinitely benevolent and almighty Creator and moral Governor; and why the period will never arrive when sin and woe shall everywhere come to an end. On these, and on many kindred topics of great interest to man, I confess I have never seen a ray of light cast by any human speculation; and that though I have been *silenced,* I have not been *convinced.* Other men think they see light here; I see none.

Just here, however, one remark should be made, to guard this observation from abuse. It is, that as we cannot allow the darkness attending the subject of moral evil to disprove *the fact* that it exists—for no one can dispute the fact—we should not allow the darkness in relation to future punishment, even though it should be eternal, to lead us to doubt or deny *that fact.* Our ignorance in the one case does not disprove the fact—how can it in the other?

(2.) A second principle on which revelation seems to have been given, similar to the one just mentioned, is, to state nothing *merely* to gratify curiosity. In the large book which constitutes what we call the Bible, embracing as it does a vast variety of histories, of apophthegms, of laws, of parables, of proverbs, of poetry, of eloquent appeals, it would be difficult, if not impossible, to fix the attention on a single thing that seems to have been revealed merely to gratify curiosity, or which would not have been recorded in the absence of such design. It was remarkable, in particular, how steadily the Saviour refused to gratify this spirit, or to answer questions based on this, when it would have been so easy to have responded to the questions proposed. I say "so easy to have responded to them," for, on the supposition that he was what he claimed to be, and had actually come down from heaven, the information which was asked could have been readily given; and on the supposition of the infidel that he was an impostor, nothing would have been more easy than to give *some* answer—since no one could prove that it was wrong; and I may add, that nothing would have been more unnatural than that, with that assumed character, he should have attempted *no* answer. But he never attempted it—never gratified such an inquiry. Thus, when he was asked, "Lord, are there few that be saved?" he gave no hint to gratify the spirit of curiosity, but directed those who propounded the question to "strive to enter in at the strait gate." When the mother of James and John came to him requesting that her two sons might sit the one on his right hand and the other on his left hand in his kingdom, he said "it was not his to give, except for those for whom it had been prepared by his Father." When, after his resurrection, he was asked by his disciples whether he "would at that time restore the kingdom to Israel?" he said it was "not for them to know the times or the seasons, which the Father had put in his own power." Thus Paul also, in the most explicit manner (Col. ii. 18), condemns those deceivers, one of the characteristics of whose teaching was, that they "intruded into those things which they had not seen." And so throughout the Bible, nothing seems to be done *merely* to gratify curiosity. If we go to it to learn what is duty; to obtain principles of conduct to guide us; to discover some promise that shall support us in temptation and trouble; to learn in what way we may acceptably worship our Maker; to know what we should *do* in the relations of husbands and wives, of parents and children, and of masters and servants; to ascertain what we should do for the poor, the ignorant, the prisoner, the oppressed; to learn what we must do to be saved, we never consult the oracle in vain. If we go with a question of mere curiosity; with a desire to obtain some response that shall be of no practical advantage, that shall flatter our self-esteem, or inflate us with a vain conceit of knowledge, we are sure to return with not even the respect that would be involved in the most ambiguous and unmeaning response that was ever uttered at Delphi.

(3.) The third and vital principle, therefore, that seems to have directed the Divine Mind in giving a revelation was, to furnish knowledge *enough* to be a safe guide to heaven. The principle seems to have been to give us so much information that we may learn the way of life if we will, and so as to keep the mind in a healthful exercise in investigating truth. It is never forgotten that we are moral agents; that we have powers to be disciplined and cultivated; and that our grand business here is not to gratify our curiosity, but to secure our salvation. Would not all the essential purposes of a revelation be answered if it would enable us to secure the salvation of our souls? Should it be a serious objection to it, if, while it did this, it did not also cast light on a thousand other points, however interesting and important they might be? And should we reject it and spurn it because there are many things which it leaves in the dark—many questions which are unanswered? Revelation to us is not like the broad and clear sun that sheds down its rays on the spread-out landscape covered with smiling fields, and flocks, and hamlets; disclosing each tree, and hill, and house, and the winding course of each rivulet:—it is, to use an illustration suggested by another, like the lighthouse that gleams on a dark and stormy coast to reveal the haven to the ocean-tossed mariner. "It shines afar over the stormy ocean, only *penetrating* a darkness which it never was intended to expel." The mariner can see that light clearly. It guides him. It cheers him when the tempest beats around him, and when the waves roll high. It shows him where the port is. It assures him that if he reaches that spot he is safe. It is all that he wants from that shore now, amid the darkness of the night, to guide him. True, it is not a sun; it does not dissipate all the darkness; "it is a mere star, showing nothing but itself—perhaps not even its own reflection on the water." But it is enough. There it stands, despite the storm and the darkness, to tell the mariner just what he wishes to know, and no more. It has saved many a richly-freighted bark, and all that he needs is that it will save his own. It tells him there is a haven there, though it leaves him all uninformed about everything else. Beyond the distance where it throws its beams, all is midnight. On a thousand questions, on which curiosity might be excited, it casts no light whatever. "The cities, the towns, the green fields, the thousand happy homes which spread along the shore to which it invites him, it does not reveal." On a calmer sea curiosity would be glad to know all about the land on which that light stands, and to anticipate the time when, safe from danger, the feet might range over those fields "beyond the swelling flood." And so, too, "all is dark in reference to that stormy expanse over which the mariner has sailed," and all around him, as well as on the land to which he goes; but shall he therefore reject the aid of that light because it discloses no more? Shall he refuse its assistance in guiding his vessel into port because it does not disclose to him all that there is in that land, or shed a flood of day on the heavens above him, and on all that stormy ocean on which he is embarked?

So it is in respect to the Gospel. Man, too, is on a stormy ocean—the ocean of life, and the night is very dark. There are tempests that beat around us; under-currents that would drift us into unknown seas; rocks that make our voyage perilous. The Gospel is a light "standing on the dark shore of eternity, just simply guiding us there." It reveals to us almost nothing of the land to which we go, but only the way to reach it. It does nothing to answer the thousand questions which we would ask about that world, but it tells how we may see it with our own eyes. It does not tell us all about the past—the vast ocean of eternity that rolled on countless ages before we had a beginning; about the government of God; about our own mysterious being; but it would guide us to God's "holy hill and tabernacle," where in his "light we may see light;" and where what is now obscure *may* become as clear as noonday.

If these are correct views, then it follows that the Bible, as a revelation from God, was not designed to give us *all* the information which we might desire, nor to solve all the questions about which the human mind is perplexed, but to impart enough to be a safe guide to the haven of eternal rest.

II. Our second inquiry is, Why was no *more* light given? Why was no more done to dissipate the darkness on those points on which we are now so much perplexed; to answer the questions which we are so ready to ask, and which we feel it is proper for us to ask?

It would be presumptuous to attempt to assign with certainty the reasons which influenced the Divine Mind in adopting the principles which have been suggested in making a revelation, and all that is proper for man to *attempt* to do in the case is to show that revelation is not liable to any well-founded objection on that account, and that, grateful for the light which *has* been given us, we should not murmur because we have no more—as the appropriate feeling of our mariner would be *gratitude* that that bright and clear, though little light is kept burning on that stormy coast to guide every vessel that may chance to come into those waters, not of complaint that it does not reveal the hills, and vales, and cities, and hamlets of that land.

In endeavouring, therefore, to show you that this is the appropriate state in which the mind should be, or to calm down the murmurs that rise in our souls because God has told us no more, I would submit the following remarks:—

(1.) First, our essential condition on earth is one of *discipline* and *probation*. But this supposes that, while there shall be light and truth enough to make our condition *safe*, if we choose to have it so—that is, that it shall be a practicable thing to secure our salvation—there shall be enough also to exercise our powers in the best manner; to secure their most healthful development; to determine whether we are *disposed* to exert ourselves and to make inquiry; while there shall be enough in reserve to furnish occupation for the mind ever onward. Now it is certain that while many of the points suggested may furnish material for inquiry and thought, and while in advancing years in our own lives, or in the progress of society, light *may* be thrown on many subjects which are now dark, yet their solution is not necessary to our salvation, and perhaps would in no manner promote it. To recur once more to our illustration. Desirable as it might be, on many accounts, to know all that there is in that land on which the light stands that is to direct the mariner, yet the knowledge of that would not aid him in guiding his vessel into port. That it was a land of peace and plenty; that it was the place of his fathers' sepulchres; that it was the home of his wife and children; that it opened rich fields for commerce or scientific research, might indeed stimulate and animate him amidst the billows, as our hope of heaven does in the storms that beat around us, but the most minute acquaintance with that country would not materially aid him in guiding his vessel into port.

Now, if we would search our own minds we should probably find that the questions in reference to which we are most disposed to complain because they are not solved, are not those which really embarrass us in the matter of salvation, or which, being solved, would aid us, but those in reference to which our salvation may be equally safe and easy whether they are solved or not. When a man finds himself struggling in a stream, it does nothing to facilitate his escape to know how he came there; nor would it aid the matter if he could determine beyond a doubt why God made streams so that men *could* ever fall into them, and did not make every bank so that it would not crumble beneath the feet.

In the condition of man, therefore, regarded as in a state of discipline and probation, all that seems really to be demanded is, first, to furnish so much light in regard to the future that the salvation of the soul shall not *necessarily* be endangered—as in the case of our lighthouse; and, secondly, to bring before it so many unsolved, but important questions, as to furnish a healthful exercise of its powers:—to place the mind in such a state that there may be *progress*, but not exhaustion; to leave to the soul the stimulus derived from the fact that there are boundless fields of thought and inquiry before it, not to leave it to the imbecility and inaction resulting from the fact that all has been explored, and that there are no new discoveries to be made, as Alexander is said to have sat down and wept because there were no other worlds to be conquered.

Accordingly, this is the way in which God everywhere deals with the human powers. Youth is stimulated to make attainments in literature and science because there are vast fields yet unexplored, and to a noble mind it is all the better if not a ray of light has ever been shed upon them; nor would a generous-minded youth thank even his Maker to stop the career of noble thought and the path of discovery by pouring down a flood of light on all those regions, so that no more was left for the efforts of honourable ambition. The explorer of unknown lands is cheered because a vast and inviting field is before him which the foot of man has never trod; and as he passes on in his obstructed way through fields of flowers new to the eye of man, and ascends streams on which man has never glided, and climbs the mountain top on which a human being ever before stood, and looks abroad on rich valleys that still invite him, he is cheered and excited by the fact that all this has been unknown; nor would he thank even his Maker to disclose all this at once to the world, and bid him sink down to supineness and inaction. It was this which animated Columbus when his prow first crossed the line beyond which no ship had ever sailed, and plunged into unknown seas. Every wave that was thrown up had a new interest and beauty from the fact that its repose had never been disturbed before by the keel of a vessel; and when his eyes first saw the land, and he prostrated himself and kissed the earth, his glory was at the highest, for he saw what in all ages was unknown before. So we are everywhere stimulated and animated by the unknown; by what is before us and may be gained; by the fields of new thought which man has never explored. But for this, which arises from the very nature of discipline, how flaccid and supine would be all our powers! *

* "Avia Pieridum peragro loca, nullius ante
Trita solo; juvat integros accedere fonteis;
Atque haurire—"

LUCRETIUS.

And here, I will just say in this connexion, to those whose minds are perplexed because God has revealed no more; to those who find a thousand questions crowding upon them which they cannot solve; and especially to those who are in the beginning of their Christian way, in whose minds there rise sceptical, or murmuring, or even blasphemous thoughts against God, and around whom, on the most important subjects, there seem to be the shades of the deepest midnight, that in a few years, as the result of calm examination and of maturer reflection and observation, most of these difficulties will disappear. Light steals in gradually but certainly on a man's soul when he "watches daily at the gates of wisdom, and waits at the posts of her doors" (Prov. viii. 34), and not many years will elapse when either these questions which are started in connexion with revelation will be solved, or will take their place with those that pertain not to the Bible peculiarly, but to the government of the world as actually administered, and, therefore, are questions with which the Christian is not peculiarly concerned.

"In the early part of my biblical studies, some thirty to thirty-five years ago," says the most distinguished professor of biblical learning in this country, "when I first began the critical investigation of the Scriptures, doubts and difficulties started up on every side, like the armed men whom Cadmus is fabled to have raised up. Time, patience, continued study, a better acquaintance with the original scriptural languages, and the countries where the sacred books were written, have scattered to the winds nearly all those doubts. I meet, indeed," says he, "with difficulties still, which I cannot solve at once, with some where even repeated efforts have not solved them. But I quiet myself by calling to mind that hosts of other difficulties, once apparently to me as formidable as these, have been removed, and have disappeared from the circle of my troubled vision. Why may I not hope, then, as to the difficulties that remain?"*

(2.) The second thought which I suggest as a reason why no more was imparted to man on these great questions is, that it is not absolutely certain, it is not even probable, that we *could* comprehend any statements which could be made on those points which now perplex us. "If I have told you earthly things," said the Saviour to Nicodemus, "and ye believe not, how shall ye believe if I tell you of heavenly things?" (John iii. 12). If one should undertake to explain to an ordinary child of four years of age the views which governed Canning in some great

* Prof. Stuart on the Canon of the Old Testament, p. 18.

act of diplomacy, or all the bearings of the positions assumed by the different contracting powers at the peace of Tilsit, the difficulty would not be so much in the explanation, or in the thing itself, as in the immature powers, the want of knowledge, the feeble grasp of comprehension of the boy that he should seek thus to instruct. A few years may do wonders for that boy. He may then possibly grasp these principles more clearly than even Canning could, or might perhaps conduct a negotiation for peace with more talent than either of the great powers of Russia, France, or Prussia. The following specifications under this head may do something further to explain this, and to relieve the difficulty:—

(*a*) One is, that though up to a certain point—a point which depends on the measure of our faculties, our age, and our attainments, a thing may be clear to us as the sunbeam, yet beyond that it is impossible to convey any idea. The mind is confused and overpowered. It falters under the great and incomprehensible subject, and no matter how much you may *say* with a view to imparting instruction, not a new idea is conveyed to the soul. Thus, for example, up to a certain extent, we comprehend what is meant by *distances*. We know the length of the journey that we have made; we have an idea of distances as measured on the surface of the earth; we form a conception of what is the distance from Philadelphia to London, or to Canton; we have a faint conception of the distance of some of the planets from the earth. But beyond that, though you may use figures and language, you convey no distinct idea. When you speak of the planet Herschel as one thousand eight hundred millions of miles from the sun, and, still more, when you speak of the nearest fixed star as certainly more than twenty billions of miles from the earth, though you use words, and are capable of conducting an investigation by the figures before you, you form no distinct idea of so amazing a distance. So it is of *magnitude*. Up to a certain point, all may be clear. The magnitude of a mountain, or of the earth, or even of the planet Jupiter, you may form some conception of; but what distinct conception have you of the magnitude of the sun? And what idea is conveyed when you are told of one of the fixed stars, that it is fourteen millions of times as large as our sun? Still more, what conception have you of the extent of the visible universe? After a short distance in the description, you are lost, and there is no power that could convey the great idea to a finite mind. So it is of *velocity*. The fleet horse, the wind, the fast-sailing ship, the railroad car, the bird, perhaps the earth in its orbit, we may conceive of in regard to velocity; but what idea have you of the velocity of a substance that flies at the rate of twelve millions of miles every minute, like light? So of *heat*. Of melted iron, or burning lava, you may form some conception; but what idea is conveyed to the mind, when you are told of the comet that approaches so near to the sun, that it is several thousand times hotter than red-hot iron? Men may indeed use *words* on such subjects, and they may be founded in truth, but they convey no idea to the human soul.

Now, how do you know but that it may be so on those great subjects which pertain to the moral government of God that give you so much trouble? You understand something—but after all how little—of the government of a family or a school; you may have a clear idea of the principles which regulate civil government in its ordinary administration; perhaps you might embrace some of the views that would influence such a mind as that of Metternich; but are you certain that you could comprehend the high principles of the Divine administration, even if they were stated to you? Do you believe that the views of Metternich could be understood ordinarily by a boy of four years old; or that any statements on the subject would convey any clear conceptions to his mind, or that the perplexities which might arise in contemplating those complicated views of government and diplomacy *could* be made clear to such a mind? And, "Canst thou by searching find out God? canst thou find out the Almighty unto perfection? It is as high as heaven; what canst thou do? deeper than hell; what canst thou know? The measure thereof is longer than the earth, and broader than the sea," Job xi. 7—9.

(*b*) Again, reflect how little of the future and the unseen can be known by *description;* how faint and imperfect a view you can get of anything by a mere statement; how little you know of a landscape, a waterfall, a picture, by any description that can be given. Especially must this be so of objects which have no resemblance to anything that we have seen. Who ever obtained any idea of Niagara by a description? Who, say to the most polished Greek and Roman mind, could have conveyed by mere description any idea of the printing-press, of a locomotive engine, of the magnetic telegraph? Who could convey to one born blind an idea of the prismatic colours; or to the deaf an idea of sounds? And when you think how meagre in the Bible is the description of heaven; when you think how easy it would have been to furnish a more minute explanation, are you certain that human language could have communicated to you the great and bright conception; or that, if words could have been found, they would have conveyed to you any exact idea of a state so different from what is our condition here? If the comparison is not too low, may we not for a moment suppose the gay and gilded butterfly that plays in the sunbeam, endued with the power of imparting ideas; but to its companions of yesterday—low and grovelling worms—could any adequate idea be furnished of that new condition of being into which the chrysalis had emerged?

I have spoken of what grows necessarily out of the fact that we are in a state of discipline as regulating revelation, and of the difficulty of conveying any ideas to the human mind beyond a certain point. I add

(3.) A third thought. It is, that we are in the very infancy of our being; that we have but just opened our eyes upon this wonderful universe, which in its structure demanded all the wisdom, and goodness, and power of an infinite God! Very few of us have lived through the period of seventy revolving suns; a majority of us not fifty; many not twenty. We have but just learned to speak, to handle things, to talk, to walk. But yesterday we were at our mothers' breasts. We knew not anything. We knew not that a candle would burn our finger if we put it there. We knew not how to distinguish one sound from another, nor whence any sound came. We knew not the use of the eye, or ear, or hand, or foot. We knew not the name of one rock, or plant, or human being—not even what is meant by *father* and *mother*. We could neither walk, nor stand, nor creep. By slow degrees we first learned to creep. Then, sustained by the hand of a parent, we began to stand. Then, assuming boldness, to the delight of father and mother, we ventured off half a dozen steps alone. We began to utter sounds that were kindly construed into language. We lisped, and hesitated, and then achieved a great victory in mastering a few simple monosyllables. And now, forsooth, we wonder that we do not know all about God, and these worlds, and the moral government of the Most High. We sit in judgment on what our Maker has told us. We complain that anything is left dark. We murmur that we do not know why he permitted sin to come into his system; why he allowed misery to enter his universe; why he does not check and remove it altogether. We complain that he has not told us all about heaven, and that there is even *one* subject to which the human mind can apply itself that is not as clear as noonday. We are sullen and silent; we repress our gratitude; we throw back his Bible in his face; we have no songs and no thanksgivings, because we are not told all about this earth, and these skies—about heaven, and about hell, and about the God that made, and that rules over all!

Hoping that these views may do something to calm the murmurs that rise up in our souls; to reconcile us to the manner in which the book of revealed truth has been given; to make us grateful for the measure of light which we have; to bear without complaining the trials involved in mystery that are brought upon us; and to lead us to look forward to the developments of the Divine government in future times and worlds, I will now close the consideration of the subject with two additional remarks.

(1.) First, in the view of our subject, we may be prepared to see the beauty of the passages of Scripture which speak of heaven as a world of light. Standing in the midst of our darkness, in a world where there is so much mystery, where we see so few things with any degree of clearness, we may learn to prize more the descriptions of that world to which we go—the declarations respecting heaven with which the sacred volume so appropriately closes:—"And the city had no need of the sun, neither of the moon, to shine in it: for the glory of God did lighten it, and the Lamb is the light thereof. And the nations of them which are saved shall walk in the light of it,—and there shall be no night there.—And there shall be no more curse: but the throne of God and of the Lamb shall be in it; and his servants shall serve him.—And they need no candle, neither light of the sun; for the Lord God giveth them light: and they shall reign for ever and ever," Rev. xxi. 23—25; xxii. 3—5.

In view, too, of such future light and glory, and in view of our darkness now on a thousand subjects on which we pant to be informed, how appropriate for man is the language of our text—"O send out thy light and thy truth: let them lead me; let them bring me unto thy holy hill and to thy tabernacles. For with thee is the fountain of life: in thy light shall we see light."

(2.) The second and last remark is, what a glorious career is before the Christian. All this darkness shall yet be dissipated; all that is now obscure shall be made light. Destined to live for ever and ever; capable of an eternal progression in knowledge; advancing to a world where all is light; soon to be ushered into the splendours of that eternal abode where there is no need of the light of the sun or the moon, and where there is no night, we may well submit for a little time to the mysteries which hang over the Divine dealings, and with exulting feelings look onward. In a little time—a few week or days—by removal to a higher sphere of being, we shall doubtless have made a progress in true knowledge, compared with which all that we have gained since we left our cradles is a nameless trifle; and then all that there is to be known in those worlds that shine upon our path by day and night; all that is to be known in the character of our Maker and the principles of his moral government; all that is to be enjoyed in a world of glory without a cloud and without a tear; all that is beatific in the friendship of God the Father, of the ascended Redeemer, of the Sacred Spirit, and of the angels; all that is blessed and pure in the goodly fellowship of the apostles and martyrs; and all that is rapturous in reunion with the spirits of those we loved on earth, and the friendship of the "just made perfect," is before us. Let it be dark, then, a little longer; let the storm a little longer beat around me, and the waves arise; let even the heavens be overcast so that I can see neither sun nor star, I will neither murmur nor complain—for I see the light burn clearly that stands on the shores of Eternity, and that invites and guides me there.

SERMON III.

THE CLAIMS OF THE CHRISTIAN RELIGION.

1 PETER iii. 15.—"And be ready always to give an answer to every man that asketh you a reason of the hope that is in you with meekness and fear."

EVERY man has a moral right to ask me what reason I have to hope for eternal life—for salvation is a matter of common interest. He has as much concern in the question about future happiness as I have, and if I have a well-founded hope of heaven, he may also have such a hope. As he has a right to ask this question, I am bound to give him an answer. As one cherishing such a hope, I ought to be able to state the grounds of it; and as I may be presumed to have a benevolent regard for the welfare of others, I ought to be willing to impart to him whatever knowledge I have on the subject: for if I have knowledge of so great a truth as that there is a way by which man may be happy for ever, I am not at liberty to withhold from another what may be to him of so much value.

The inquiry which one might make of another respecting the hope that is in him, might relate to two points. It might be either in regard to the hope which Christianity as a system holds out to man; or to the hope which in particular *he* entertains of reaching heaven. This latter inquiry would involve so much reference to personal feeling and experience that there might be some delicacy and hesitancy in replying to it; and yet, if proposed in a serious and candid manner, and with a sincere desire to know what true religion is, a Christian would not feel himself at liberty to withhold the information. Such an answer would be appropriate to a serious and anxious inquirer on the subject of religion; the reply to the question in the other form would be appropriate at all times. The one is that which would properly be stated in the free, confidential intercourse of friendship; the other is that which is appropriate to the public instructions of the pulpit or the press.

Whenever we come before you in any public manner, it is in some way to set forth the claims of the Christian religion.

Either by illustrating detached portions of its doctrines and duties, or by a formal argument in its defence, we seek to show you that it has a claim upon each one of your hearts, and that it furnishes a ground of hope for the life to come. It is not improper, on some occasions, to consider ourselves as giving a distinct answer to one who should make an inquiry of the reason of the hope that is in us, or what there is in Christianity which satisfies the mind that it is proper to cherish that hope. Such a position I desire to regard myself as occupying at this time, and I propose, therefore, to set forth the claims of the gospel in this way.

This religion has been in the world, inspiring these hopes, eighteen hundred years. At this period of the world, and after it has existed so long upon the earth, what is there to be seen in the system which makes it proper to cherish the hope of eternal life based on its promises? What is there, in the view of an intelligent Christian, on which the system rests as justifying hope in his own case, and as furnishing an argument to be used in addressing others to induce them to repose on it with the same measure of confidence?

I suppose that a man who is *not* a Christian, if called upon to give reasons *why* he is not, in the public manner in which I am to show why I am, would arrange his thoughts under some such heads as the following:—the deficiency of the evidence of the Divine authority of the Bible; the ambiguity and uncertainty of the alleged prophecies, and the intrinsic difficulty in believing in miracles; the difficulties in the Scriptures, and in the doctrines which they have revealed; the fact that in the pretended book of revealed truth there are many questions which are unsolved; the bigotry, wars, persecutions, and wrongs to which it would be said Christianity has given rise; the little influence which it has on the lives of its professors, and the general character of the church.—Whether these would be the true reasons, or whether there are reasons lying *back* of these in the state of the heart, is not of importance now to be considered. All that I wish to say just here is, that it is not to be assumed by the friends of Christianity that these reasons, as they might be drawn out, have no force; and as little is it to be assumed by its enemies that they who embrace the Christian system do not see their force, and are not capable of appreciating it. It is a circumstance of some importance that not a few who are Christians were once infidels themselves; and it is not fair to assume that they have never looked at these arguments as attentively as other men.

Cecil, once himself an infidel of a most decided character, after his conversion made this striking remark: "I have read," said he, "all the most acute, and learned, and serious infidel writers, and have been really surprised at their poverty. The process of my mind has been such on the subject of revelation, that I have often thought Satan has done more for me than for the best of them; for I have had, and could have produced, arguments that appeared to me far more weighty than any I ever found in them against revelation" (Life and Remains, p. lxxxix.) "It is the registered saying of a man, eminent alike for talent and piety, that he never found such strong arguments against the Bible, in all writings of infidels, as had suggested themselves to his own mind" (Melville, Sermons, vol. i. p. 276).

Without impropriety I may be permitted to say, that in my investigations I have found things that have seemed to me to have much greater strength *against* the truth of the Bible, and that have given me much more perplexity than anything which I have found in the books of infidel writers; and that now, if I were to assume the position of an advocate of infidelity, I could draw out an argument that would seem to me to have more force than is found in any book that I could recommend to you. If you will suffer these remarks to pass without an imputation of vanity, I will proceed to state why, notwithstanding these facts, a man may see reasons why he should be a Christian. I will suggest several considerations, which together may perhaps furnish an answer to *both* the aspects of the question referred to in the beginning of this discourse.

I. The first is, *because the Christian religion has such claims of a Divine origin that they* MAY *convince and satisfy the mind.* I do not mean here such as to *compel* the assent of the mind; nor would I say such as to satisfy every mind in every state. I mean such as may satisfy a mind in a healthful state; a mind in the best condition for looking at evidence; a mind that shall reason on the subject of religion as men reason on other things. There is but one kind of evidence that *compels* assent—that which is found in the pure mathematics, and that embraces but a small part of the subjects that come before mankind. In morals; in law; in medicine; in mental philosophy; in political economy; in the mechanic arts; in history, we are content with another kind of evidence—that which *convinces*, not *compels*. The word *convinces* expresses the idea exactly—that which *overcomes*, or which gets a *victory* over difficulties and objections; which *subdues* the opposition of the mind to the truth; which furnishes evidence to remove the pre-existing reasons for doubt, and which, as by a victory, secures the assent of the understanding. Now religion, from the nature of the case, belongs to this class of subjects; that is, it rests on the same basis on which are placed most of the other great interests of mankind.

I suppose that it can hardly be deemed necessary for me to attempt elaborately to prove the truth of my proposition—that the Christian religion has such evidences of a Divine origin that they *may* convince and satisfy the mind. If there is no inherent impossibility in that, it would be fair to suppose, unless the contrary can be shown, that this *does* occur, and that a man is a Christian *because* his mind is thus satisfied, and that this is the first reason which he would allege why he is a Christian.

Yet I have a few remarks to make in regard to this attitude of the mind, viewed in its relation to the evidence of the Divine origin of the Christian religion now after a period of one thousand eight hundred years. They may be numbered in their order, though it must be without illustration: (*a*) First, then, as already shown, the mind *may* become convinced and satisfied. This has been done in many millions of instances; this is now constantly occurring in the world. There are now great numbers of believers who have embraced Christianity only because they are convinced of its truth—for there is no other motive to explain this; and the arguments which have convinced *them* are the same which have convinced the millions that have gone before them. (*b*) Secondly, the evidence in the case has stood through the severest *tests* which could be applied; and Christianity exists now simply because the world cannot be convinced that its claims are delusive and false. Whatever may be inferred from this one way or the other, no one can doubt that it lives, and is carrying on its great movements among the nations, because the attempts which have been made to satisfy mankind that it is an imposture have not been such as to convince the world. The severest tests have been applied to it that can be—those derived from reason, ridicule, contempt, power, persecution; and whatever *else* may befall it, he who is a Christian rests in this certainty that his religion will never be removed from the world by reasoning, by ridicule, by contempt, by power, by persecution. If it is to lose its hold on the minds of men, it is to be by some agency which has not yet been employed; yet what that is to be, the mind finds it difficult to imagine. (*c*) Thirdly, it has passed, it may be supposed, what it had really to apprehend as the *great crisis* of its fate. For the great crisis was not, as is commonly supposed, in the time of persecution; it was to meet the developments of science.

Itself originated in a rude age and land, its great encounter was to be not so much with *power* as with *knowledge;* not so much with *princes* as with *philosophers;* not so much with Nero and Diocletian as with Bacon, Cuvier, and Davy; not so much with the powers of darkness as with the floods of light that would be poured upon the world, when the danger was that it might be found in error as all false religions are, and might, by excess of light, become eclipsed. That danger may be regarded as now passed. If it can retain its hold on the intellect of the world at the present hour, it may be presumed to have little to fear in the future. (*d*) Fourthly, it has shown that it has power to control the intellect of men, and to maintain its dominion there. That dominion it has set up now over the best, and the most highly cultivated intellect of this age, and it *loses* none of its hold by the progress which society makes in science and in the arts. It is undoubtedly a fact that the period has never been when Christianity had such a hold on the intellect of the world as it has at the present time, or when so many cultivated minds would come forth to its defence; and it has shown its power by securing that ascendency just in proportion as the mind of the world is developed and cultivated, and just in proportion as the best *type* of intellect becomes uppermost in the control of human affairs. For not only has it maintained its ascendency as the sciences have advanced, but, if I may be allowed the expression, it has shown a singular affinity for the mind that appears to be destined to be the ruling mind of the world, and that is more closely identified than any other with all that tends to promote the progress of human affairs—the Anglo-Saxon mind. (*e*) Fifthly; just one other thought under this head: it is, that the claims of the Christian religion are such as to command the assent of the conscience and the heart of men. After all, it makes its practical way in the world rather by appeals to the conscience and the heart than by appeals to the understanding. When men become Christians, they feel that they are doing right, and the conscience and the heart acquiesce in what is done, and they have no misgivings about it. Not so if they are not Christians. They feel that they are resisting claims which may be urged upon them at least with a considerable show of reason. They feel that it requires no little ingenuity to evade the arguments which are advanced for the claims of religion, and no little ingenuity to invent excuses for not becoming Christians. To become a Christian is a straightforward work, where a man is following the leadings of his own judgment, and conscience, and interest, and duty, and which requires no ingenuity to apologize for; to refuse to become one is a task, where a man has to meet the claims of argument, and conscience, and interest, and duty, and to reconcile his refusal with these claims in the best way he can.

II. In the second place, *I embrace this hope because, if I reject it, I do not get rid of the difficulties which press upon my mind on the subject of religion.* I will frankly state to you that I see great difficulties on the whole subject of religion, whether the Bible be embraced or not. Far beyond what ought to be the state of a man's mind who undertakes to defend a system with earnestness, and which cannot be supposed often to exist when a man pleads a cause at the bar, or in the Senate House when his country is in danger, a minister of the gospel may be conscious of obscurities and difficulties in the high subjects of the Divine nature; the introduction of moral evil; the actual government of the world; the apparent contradictions in the Bible; the mode of the Divine revelation; the obscurity of the whole system of doctrines, and the nature and duration of future punishment; and, however others may feel, *I* can easily conceive of a man's being in such a state of mind on these matters that he is in no condition to preach properly at all. The state of mind to which I refer cannot be more strongly expressed than in the language of Dr. Payson. Said he in a letter to a friend long after he began to preach, "My difficulties increase every year. There is one trial which you cannot know experimentally. It is that of being obliged to preach to others when one doubts of everything, and can scarcely believe that there is a God. All the atheistical, deistical, and heretical objections which I meet with in books are childish babblings compared with those which Satan suggests, and which he urges upon the mind with a force which seems irresistible. Yet I am often obliged to write sermons and to preach when these objections beat upon me like a whirlwind, and almost distract me" Works, i., 379, 380.

But, on the other hand, looking at the subject as a candid man, I do not see that I am relieved, or that I get rid of these difficulties by rejecting the Bible. The main difficulties on the whole subject lie *back* of the Bible and of Christianity, and have nothing to do with the one or the other, and I am in no manner relieved if I reject the Old and the New Testaments. I rather fall back on the difficulties with no explanation and no relief, and then I am prepared to appreciate the perplexities of Socrates, and the trouble of Cicero, and the difficulties of Zoroaster and of Mani, and the anguish of Augustine before he became converted. For I find the same difficulties press upon me, and that without light or relief. They are difficulties growing out of the Divine character; and the principles of the Divine administration; and the introduction of moral evil; and the treatment which men receive at the hand of God; and the fearful impending prospects hereafter. I get rid of no one of them by rejecting the Bible, and I am not only not relieved, but I deprive myself of all the explanation which I can now find in the Bible on these subjects, and at the same time of the bright light which shines on a thousand topics which otherwise would be as dark to me as *they* are—the light which would guide me safely to a better world.

III. In the third place, *I embrace this hope because it meets the wants of my nature, and furnishes me such a religion as I need.* On the subject of religion there are certain things which my nature and my circumstances demand; and a religion to be such as religion should be, must meet those demands. The Christian system, though it does not yet answer all the questions which I would ask, does substantially meet those demands, and does set the mind at rest. It is, of course, impossible in a single head of a discourse to do anything more than to give some *hints* of what I here refer to, and which must appear bald and dry because there is no time to illustrate them. But I will just refer to some of them: (1.) Man wants a God, and has always been looking out for the Infinite One, to discern him amidst his works, or to obtain by revelation some knowledge of his existence and perfections. The Bible reveals such a God, clothed with every glorious attribute, and infinite in his perfections, and spiritual in his nature, and pure in his government, and benignant in his character, and so vast, and great, and glorious that he is seen to be worthy of universal adoration and praise. (2.) Man wants *faith.* He wants some being in whom he may confide, and who has all power; some one on whom he can rely; some one to whom he can go in trouble; some one on whom he can repose in the hour of death. A state of scepticism is an unnatural state, and therefore a miserable state. The mind never finds rest till it finds a God in whom it can confide, and it is constantly going out in restlessness and anxiety and discomfort till it finds such a God. (3.) Man needs a knowledge of the way by which sin can be forgiven, and no system of religion can meet our condition which does not reveal such a method. That man is a fallen being is perfectly plain, and no one can deny it; and that a system of religion that does not recognise that fact and provide for it, is false and defective, is apparent at a glance. Indeed, the consciousness of sin has been the principal source of trouble in this world, and the profoundest and most anxious inquiries of men have been to find out some way by which sin can be pardoned. One thing is certain, that man cannot look calmly forward to eternity, as a sinner, without some knowledge of a way of pardon; some evidence that his sins are forgiven. Somehow, conscience has a power which man dreads, and sin, after being long committed and apparently forgotten, has a way of reviving in its power by the aid of memory which he would not meet beyond the grave. The world needs the knowledge of a way by which sin may be forgiven, and individual man needs the knowledge of such a way, or he cannot find peace. The gospel has revealed such a method. It has done two things in this respect—one of which was *necessary* to be done, and the other of which was *not* necessary, and which is, therefore, a matter of mere favour: it has proclaimed the *fact* that sin may be pardoned; and it has disclosed the *method* by which it is done; and in both these the mind fully and joyfully acquiesces. Man finds in the gospel, in this respect, that which quite meets the case, and which puts the mind to rest. He finds a method of pardon revealed which displays the character of God in a most lovely manner; which does all that can be done, and all that is needful to be done, to maintain the honour of the law of God; and which is adapted to give entire peace to a troubled conscience. (4.) Man needs a knowledge of a way by which the soul may be made holy; by which he may be defended in the day of temptation; by which he may be supported in the time of trial; by which he may find peace in the hour of death—and he finds all this amply in the gospel. And (5) he needs a revelation of a future state—some assurance about the immortality of the soul—something more than vague conjecture, and loose and uncertain analogies, to assure him that his soul is immortal. I need not say that men have sought this everywhere and at all times, nor need I remind you how loose and unsatisfactory have been all their reasonings on this subject. To the classic scholar I need not say that if I should here adduce the reasonings of Plato in the Phaedo on the immortality of the soul, those reasonings which Addison makes Cato pronounce to be so well founded, there is not a man here present who would feel himself convinced by them, or who would not feel, if this were all, that the subject was left in utter and most distressing doubt: perhaps no one who would not feel that I was insulting his understanding by insisting on these arguments —certainly no infidel who would not ask me if I had no *better* reasons than those for believing in the immortality of the soul. Of this work, and of Plato's reasonings in it, Cicero, in his Tusculan Questions, most feelingly and strikingly remarks: "I do not know how it is, but when I read I assent; but when I lay down the book and begin to reflect by myself on the immortality of the soul, all my assent glides away."[—Nescio quo modo, dum lego, assentior; cum posui librum, et mecum ipse de immortalitate animorum cœpi cogitare, assentio omnis illa elabitur.] But, as a matter of simple fact, this result does *not* follow from the faith reposed in the New Testament. The hope of immortality becomes a fixed and ruling principle of the nature, just as certain and determinate in its influence on the life as the belief that the sun will continue to rise, and that the laws of nature will remain unchanged. On the whole, and in a word, I look at my nature in reference to its capabilities and wants, and to the question whether the gospel meets those capabilities and wants, and I can see no deficiency—nothing which it has not provided for. Man is endowed with reason;—it meets his reason in the evidence of its truth, and in the nature of its revelations. Man has a conscience;—it discloses the way in which it may have peace. Man has sinned;—it reveals a way of pardon. Man pants to live for ever;—it tells him he will. He is made to be influenced by hope;—it has set the highest conceivable hopes before him. He has duties to perform;—it has told him what they are, and how to perform them. He is to be governed by motives;—it has told him what they should be. He is in a world of trials;—it tells him how to bear them. He has an imagination;—it sets before him objects most brilliant—compared with which the most splendid descriptions of genius die away. He sees in himself *some* evidences that he has an immortal soul;—it confirms them, and raises this beginning of hope from a state of uncertainty and doubt when it produced no influence on his life, to most certain assurance, and makes it the most influential of all the principles of action.

IV. In the fourth place, *I cherish this hope, and embrace this system, because of its undeniably happy influence on all the interests of man.* I am aware of the objection which some may start here, and do not forget that I might be referred to the wars, and crusades, and persecutions, and horrors of the inquisition, and the miserable superstition in pilgrimages and the rules of the monastic life, which it would be said have grown out of Christianity. But I trust I need not argue this point. I am speaking of pure Christianity; not of Christianity perverted and abused. I am speaking of what every man knows will be its influence if an individual, or a family, or a larger community, comes under its power. These things to which I have just referred are no part of the proper effect of true religion, and I presume that they who would urge the objection know that as well as I do. Every man knows what the effect of pure Christianity is; and when its professed friends evince any of these things, its enemies are not slow to remark that they do not "live up" to the requirements and the spirit of their religion. But let a few simple facts be submitted under this head in the form in which I am conducting this argument—that is, stating reasons why I cherish the hope that is in me. We who are professed Christians, then, look (*a*) at the influence of that gospel on our own character. None of us who are Christians have anything of which to boast, and there is not one of us that is not sensible of serious defects in his character, and of errors and follies over which he mourns in secret. But, as far as we can trace the influence of that gospel on our minds and hearts, it has not been a *bad* influence, or an influence of which we should be ashamed. We have found it giving us the victory over low and debasing propensities and passions; furnishing a check, in numerous cases wholly effectual, on what were before unbridled appetites; elevating our views, and expanding our conceptions, of the dignity of our nature, and of the objects for which we should live; raising us in the scale of being, and teaching us to aspire to fellowship with the more exalted intellects before the "throne;" removing the acerbities, and destroying the unevenness of our temper; making us willing to forgive our "enemies, persecutors, and slanderers," and to pray that God would "change their hearts;" giving us cheerfulness, peace, and "minds contented with our present condition;" purifying our hearts, subduing the stubbornness of our will, and making us submissive in trial; disposing us to kindness and affection in the various relations of life, and inclining us to look with an eye of tenderness and pity on the oppressed, the fatherless, and the sad. (*b*) We look again at the effects of the gospel on the minds of our friends—living and dead—and we find there, too, only the same purifying and happy influence. It has given the chief virtues to our living friends; it has done more than all things else to hallow the memory of those who are dead. A father, a mother, a wife, a daughter, a sister, has none the less claim to affection by becoming a Christian; and we feel that whatever may be their native amiableness, there is not a virtue which will not be brightened, not a lovely trait which will not be rendered more lovely, and not a defect which will not be lessened or removed, by the influence of the gospel. No man believes that his wife will be made less pure, kind, virtuous, chaste, faithful, by being a true Christian; no man supposes that his son or daughter would become a more ready prey to corrupt influences and evil passions by being brought wholly under the influence of the gospel of Christ. As far as we can trace that influence on the character of any of our friends now living, or on the character of those who have departed, it has been a happy influence. We fear not that it will injure the cherished memory on earth of those who have left the world, or hinder their salvation in the future state; nor do we fear its proper influence on the life and heart of any living friend. When the sailor-boy leaves his home for a seafaring life; when a son embarks on a vessel to go to a distant land for scientific purposes, to perfect himself in some liberal art, or for commerce, we do not feel that he will be injured by any fair influence of religion on his soul. We sleep not the less calmly at night when the storm howls and we feel that he is danger; nor are we the less serene when we think of the temptations to which he is exposed in a distant land, nor when the thought crosses our minds that perhaps we may never see him again. It is not a record which we are unwilling to have made on the stone which marks the grave of a friend that he lived and died with the Christian hope; it is not one which would dishonour us if it should be at last cut on our own. (*c*) The same remarks, expanded, might be made respecting a neighbourhood or a nation; respecting the relation of Christianity to the progress of society, to civilization, to learning, to the arts, to schools, to social customs, to human liberty. Look around you, and ask what injury the Christian religion has done in the institutions of our own land; or rather ask what we have here which has not been originated or improved by the influence of the Christian religion. What is there in this land now that is valuable that it does not preserve; what is there that has cost so much blood and treasure, and that now so much excites the hopes of humanity everywhere, that would not soon become corrupt and worthless if it were not for the influence of the gospel of Christ? I confess that I feel that it elevates my nature to cherish a hope derived from a religion that has scattered blessings in every age and every land; that has been connected with human progress everywhere; that has been identified with the best notions of liberty and civil government—with the progress of learning—with institutions of charity—with the sweetest virtues and enjoyments of domestic life—with all that gives support in trial—and with the only real consolation that is ever felt on the bed of death.

V. I had intended to have dwelt at some length on a fifth point as a reason for cherishing this hope, but perhaps all that I could say might be condensed into a sentence or two, and, at any rate, must be now: it is this, *because I feel assured that I shall most prize this religion when I come to lie upon the bed of death.* You will not understand me to imply that I think the dying moment the most favourable time to form a correct judgment on any subject, but that the judgment which will then be formed will be in accordance with the views which I have been endeavouring to set forth. I am certain that when I come to die, my sense of the truth and the value of this religion will not be diminished, and that I shall not then regret my having cherished this Christian hope. I am not accustomed to see men die sorrowing that they are Christians, nor have I found, in the books which make record of the last thoughts of the dying, expressions of regret from the lips of saints and martyrs that they had too early in life embraced the hope inspired by the gospel of Christ. I think we cannot be more firmly assured of anything than that when we come to die, we shall not find the Christian hope valueless, or wish that we could recall and change that hour in our lives when we gave ourselves to the Saviour. I give this, then, as a reason—last, but not least—why we cherish this hope, that when the final hour of our lives shall come, and "our eyes shall be turned for the last time to behold the sun in the heavens," when all the plans and hopes which we have ever cherished shall be ended, and we shall give the parting hand to the friends, few or many, that affection shall summon around our beds, we shall prize the hopes of the gospel of Christ more than we do now—more, infinitely more, than we shall all other things. We shall see the whole subject rise with a dignity and value which we cannot now estimate, and the brightest earthly crowns will be baubles then, compared with the crown of righteousness laid up for us in heaven. I would that you all could see in these considerations reasons why you should embrace and cherish this hope also, but, whatever may be the effect on you, they are the "answer" which we are required to "give to any man that asketh us a reason of the hope that is in us."

SERMON IV.

THE CONDITION OF MAN NOT BENEFITTED BY THE REJECTION OF CHRISTIANITY.

JOHN vi. 68.—"Then Simon Peter answered him, Lord, to whom shall we go? thou hast the words of eternal life."

ANY system of religion which has had a wide and permanent influence in the world, must be founded on some principles of plausible or solid philosophy. There must be something in human nature, or in the relations of things, which furnishes a basis for it on which to rest, and by which it may be made to *appear* to the human mind to be true. It may be doubted whether the mind can long cherish error, knowing it to be such, and whether the arguments from supposed interest can be so magnified, and rendered so plausible, that the race would long adhere to what is known to be false. It may be presumed, then, that the great mass of those who have embraced an erroneous system are the victims of delusion; and yet, that the delusion is kept up by something which deserves the name of philosophy. There is as real philosophy at the basis of the views of the heathens now, as there was in the speculations of the Greeks; there is much adaptation to certain wants and laws of human nature in the religion of Mohammed; there are at the basis of the Roman Catholic system those profound views of man, of his wants, and of his passions, which have been ascertained by the keen investigations of more than a thousand years; and neither of these systems is to be overthrown by declamation, or denunciation, or by arguments drawn from superficial views of the nature of man. I would not despise any system of belief which has held on its way amidst fierce discussions and in the face of violent opposition for ages; which has lived while empires have arisen and decayed; and which draws to itself with mighty power the minds of succeeding millions of the race.

It is supposed by many persons now, as it was by those who turned away from the Saviour, that by not embracing Christianity, certain difficulties are avoided which are regarded as inseparable from that system, and that thus dissociated from it they will have nothing more to do with those things which are considered as most perplexing and repulsive. It is supposed that the religion of Christ is encompassed with difficulties from which it is desirable that the human mind should escape, and from which it will escape if the system be rejected.

It is important to institute an examination in regard to this, and to see whether it is so. It cannot be denied that there are certain embarrassments in Christianity, or in things usually associated with it, from which it would be desirable to escape. Can they be avoided by rejecting this system, and embracing any other? This question I propose to examine, by showing, that there are common evils under which the race labours, and which were not originated by Christianity; that there are common principles which lie at the basis of all systems of religion, and on which all the race must act; and that the rejection of Christianity does not relieve us of those evils, or enable us to act better in accordance with those principles; or, in other words, that we cannot improve our condition by rejecting the Christian system. "Lord, to whom shall we go? thou hast the words of eternal life."

I. There are common evils under which the race labours, and which were not originated by Christianity. I mean, that they are simple matters of fact which are in no way affected, so far as their existence is concerned, by the solution of the question whether Christianity be true or false. They as much pertain to the system of the Mussulman or the Pagan as to that of the Christian, and the deist and the infidel are as much concerned to explain them as we are. Christianity did not originate those evils, nor has it so modified them, or incorporated them into its system, as to make it particularly incumbent on its friends to explain them. Those evils are no part of religion of any kind, nor can any form of religion be held responsible for them.

Great injustice is often done to religion, and to the Christian religion in particular, by reasoning as if it were responsible for all the evil that there is in the world, and especially as if it had originated sin, and woe, and death. Men seem to feel that these things are indissolubly connected with Christianity, and that that system is to be held answerable for the whole doctrine respecting the fall of man, and the depravity of the race, for the introduction of moral evil, and for the exposure of the race to final ruin. There is a disposition often manifested to throw whatever is odious in these doctrines on the Bible, and to group them and the doctrines of redemption together, as if they were parts of one system, and to regard them as having no claim to the attention of any who may choose to reject the Christian system.

Now, I will not say that there is always *designed* injustice in this, though I shall endeavour to show you that the injustice is *real.* There is an illusion about it which I do not doubt affects the minds of many persons who would by no means do injustice to any system of religion, or its friends. The illusion arises from this fact, that *all* religion, in our world, has much to do with these painful things—the fall, sickness, death, the grave. In other worlds religion may be a materially different thing—the pure and delightful service of a holy God without one gloomy association, for there is no sin there, no sick-bed, no grave. But here, religion must be essentially a remedial system. It will answer no purpose if it is not. It must propose some way for the pardon of sin; some relief in calamity; some consolation in bereavement and death; and it must shed some light on the grave. It seems to be demanded that it should do something to tell us how it was that man came into his present condition; what, in fact, the condition is, and how it bears on his prospects for the future world. It of necessity, therefore, has much to do with the doctrine of depravity, and with the subject of death—just as the practice of medicine has much to do with diseases and sick-beds. Now, by a very obvious law of mind, we fall into a delusion, and unconsciously do injustice to the system. We group all these things together; regard them as part and parcel of the same system, and think that they must stand or fall together. But nothing can be more obviously unjust than such a course. It is as if we should associate the science of medicine and the diseases which it proposes to remedy together, and hold that science responsible for having introduced pleurisies and consumptions into the world, and for all the evils connected with them. It is as if you should suppose that by banishing the science of medicine from the earth, you would at the same time deliver yourselves from pain and death. The truth is, though we seldom fall into the delusion there to which I am adverting in religion, that the healing art is solely a remedial system, and is to be judged *as* such a system alone. It *finds* disease already existing; it does not create it: and whether the proposed remedial system turns out to be of value or not, the great original fact on which it is based remains the same. It is altogether isolated; a fact with which every other man is as much concerned as the disciple of Galen.

Or to use another illustration. It is as if the statesman were held responsible for all the original evils of the social system which he proposes to remedy; and as if, instead of judging of the constitution which he proposes merely as a remedial system, we group that and all the evils which he proposes to correct together, and by rejecting his system suppose that we get rid of all concern about those evils. Or, still further, it is as if we were to hold the historian responsible for the crimes and calamities of which he makes a record, and to suppose that by denying the credibility of his statements, the *facts* which he has recorded cease to be true. A large part of the Bible, in introducing the account of the remedial system, is occupied in a mere statement of *facts* about the fall and depravity of man. But the sacred historian did not originate the fall or the depravity of man, any more than Livy or Hume did the wars with the Sabines, or the contests between the red and white roses; nor should the Bible, or the system of religion which it reveals, be held responsible for those facts any more than Gibbon should be for the character of Nero and Caligula, or than the Father of history should for the plague at Athens. A history should be held answerable only as a record of facts. The facts are independent things, and remain the same, whether recorded or not. A remedial system should be held answerable only as such, and not at all for the evils which it proposes to remedy. Those evils are independent things, having no immediate connexion with that system, and are evils in which others are as much concerned as its friends. It should be held answerable, not for the introduction or the existence of the evil, but only for what it proposes to do, and for the fair inferences which follow from its influence on a system already existing.

With these indisputable principles before us, I now remark, that Christianity did not originate the evils of our race, and is no more responsible for them than infidelity is. They are matters of simple FACT, whether Christianity be true or false—as it is a fact that there is disease in the world, and that men suffer and die, whether the remedies proposed answer the purpose or not. The atheist, the deist, the man of the world, the man of science, the historian, the moralist, the epicurean, and the stoic, have as much to do with them as the Christian, and are as much bound to explain them. We meet on common ground here, and in the development of our different systems *we start together*.

Let us look a moment at some of those facts:—

(1.) Man is a fallen being; a sinner. Can there be any difference of opinion on this point? The Bible records the fact; and do not Livy, and Sallust, and Hume, and Gibbon, and

Baronius, and Alison do the same thing? Is there *any* historical record which describes man as any otherwise than as a sinner? The accounts of the perfection or perfectability of man are in philosophical speculations, not in historical records. The Bible describes man as prone to evil. And does not every man so regard the race? What mean the laws made to restrain men? What mean prisons, and padlocks, and securities against fraud and dishonesty? Is there a merchant who would repose quietly on his pillow if there were not a strong and skilfully constructed lock on his store? Is there a vault of a bank that could be safely left open for a single night? Is there a man who does not make it his business to guard against the fraud, duplicity, cunning, and violence of every other man *as if* he would do wrong?

Now, about the *fact* of the depravity of man there surely can be no manner of doubt. The fact exists, whatever remedy is proposed; whatever statement is made of its origin; or however you may account for it. It no more pertains to the Christian, or to his theory of religion, than it does to the theory or religion of any other man. Men do not get rid of it by denying Christianity; they do not make it any worse by embracing it. It belongs to the race *as such*, and we must make the best of it. Whether Christianity be true or false, the evil is the same, and all men will continue to act *as if* the doctrine were true. We may differ in our explanations about the way in which man became a sinner; we may speculate in a different manner in regard to the time when he begins to go astray; we may have different views about the condition of the infant mind; and we might not agree as to the exact connexion between facts which now exist, and the act of the progenitor of the race, but the material facts pertain to one system as much as to another. Revealed religion is in no way peculiarly concerned about it, except that it has offered an explanation of the manner in which sin has come into the world, and it is responsible only for that *explanation*.

(2.) The same is true in regard to sickness and suffering. Man is a sufferer, whatever system of religion be embraced or rejected. The earth is a vale of tears, and no art of man can drive sickness, care, bereavement, or pain from it. That the race suffers is a great fact which is in no way affected by the question whether this or that form of religion be true or false, except as religion may in some way mitigate sorrow. We may differ as to the cause of suffering. We may have our different theories in explanation of the question how it is consistent with the government of God. We may inquire whether sin is the cause, proximate or remote, or whether it is to be traced wholly to some physical laws; but the fact remains the same, and it pertains no more to the Christian system than to any other. Christianity has originated no disease. It has not generated the malaria of the Pontine marshes; it does not give birth to the plague in Cairo or Constantinople, nor has it caused the cholera which sweeps over the plains of India. There is not a disease to which the human frame is subject that has been either increased or aggravated by the Christian religion, or for which the Christian religion, or any other religion, is responsible. There is not one of them that would be healed by burning the last Bible on the earth, or by driving the last vestige of religion from the world.

(3.) Thus, too, it is with the *mental* sorrows to which the race is subject. The illusion to which I have adverted operates with more power here than it does in regard to the point just referred to. There is no one who would directly charge Christianity with being the cause of a cancer or of consumption; but there is many a one who would suffer the illusion to play around the mind that it is the cause of the *mental* sorrows to which we are subject, and that those sorrows are parts of this system of religion. There has been a steady effort, though not always open and avowed, to connect these sorrows and Christianity together, and to lead men to suppose that by casting off the restraints of religion they free themselves from mental griefs. The reason of this illusion I have already adverted to, and the injustice of the feeling may be seen at a glance. An effort has been made to make it appear to a world that seeks to be gay, that somehow the alarms of conscience, the dread of death, and the apprehension of the world to come, are the creation of Christianity, and that religion is responsible for their existence in the soul. But is this so? Can it be so? Do these things exist nowhere else? Are they found under no other system of religion? Are they never found where there is no religion of any kind? And is it true that by casting off the Christian religion a man obtains a guarantee that he will never be troubled by the remembrance of guilt; that he will escape from remorse of conscience; that he will not be overborne by the fear of death? He must have studied the world very imperfectly who can suppose that these things are the creation of religion, or that they have any peculiar relation to religion of any kind whatever. The truth is, they belong to us as men. They are the operation of great laws of our nature. They lie back of all religion, and would not be affected, except by being deepened, if you were to sweep every Bible and every Christian church from every land.

(4.) The same thing is true in regard to death. Here, too, the illusion to which I have adverted constantly operates. There is a feeling somehow that death, always a painful subject of reflection, peculiarly pertains to religion, and a serious contemplation of death, or a remark made about it as a personal matter, is somehow regarded as an omen that one is becoming religious. But what has religion particularly to do with the subject of death? Did it introduce it into the world? Has it aggravated its pangs? Do religious people only die? Can a man, by becoming an infidel or an universal sceptic, avoid dying? Will it drive death from the world to laugh at religion; or would it if it could be proved that all religion is imposture? The truth is—and it is a truth so obvious that it would hardly be proper formally to state it if it were not for the illusion already referred to—that death pertains to our race, whether Christianity be true or false. Religion did not introduce it, and is in no way responsible for it; nor is death in any way modified, whatever opinions may be entertained of Christianity, or of any other system of religion. We may differ in our explanations of it. I may have my theory about the cause, and you may have yours, and still the *fact* remains the same. Death approaches with the same steady pace, and with the same repulsive aspect, whatever may be the nature of our speculations. Religion does not quicken his pace, nor does infidelity retard it; and he is just as likely to come into the ball-room, or among a company of savans speculating on its cause, or among a company of revellers blaspheming all religion, as into the church of the living God. We are all brothers here, and we all have an equal interest in this matter. The entrance of death into our world was prior to the entrance of Christianity, and if Christianity should take its everlasting flight from the earth, the angel of death would linger here, glad of her departure, for he could make the pains of death more terrific than they are now.

If these things are so, then all men have the same interest in them. They lie apart from all religion as indisputable FACTS, and they pertain as much to the infidel as the Christian; as much really to the scientific lecture-room as to the pulpit. Religion *finds* these things in existence; it does not create them, and is in no manner responsible for them. Christianity found them upon the earth, as Galen and Hippocrates found disease, and for their existence there is no more responsibility in the one case than in the other. Here we begin our investigations together, having the same facts to deal with, and with the certainty that the adoption or rejection of any particular form of religion does not materially alter them. The point now illustrated is, that the Christian, the infidel, and the scoffer, are equally concerned in these facts, for they pertain to man whatever form of religion he has, or whether he has any religion or none. This leads me,

II. In the second place, to observe, that as there are evils pertaining to our race which lie back of religion, and in which all men have a common interest, so there are certain *principles* which pertain to all men; principles *supposed* to be true by the Christian religion, but which are in no way affected by the question whether Christianity be true or false; principles which are better *met* by that system than by any other. My limits will not allow me to illustrate them at length; and all that I can do is to advert to them in the most summary manner. Among those principles are the following:—

(1.) That man is a moral agent, and in this respect differs from the whole brute creation beneath him. I say that this pertains to man as such, for it cannot be pretended that the Bible, or the Christian system, has so altered the nature of man as to *make* him a moral agent. He is so under every system of religion, and is equally so whether Christianity be true or false. It would be easy to show that the Bible recognises this, and adapts itself to it better than any other system of religion.

(2.) That he is under a moral government. I mean that there are marks of a moral government over the world entirely independent of Christianity, or that there is a course of events which tends to the punishment of vice and the reward of virtue. It is possible to make out the great principles of this government without the aid of revelation, for it was seen and understood when there *was* no revelation. The course of events in the world is such that, as a great law, one course of conduct will be followed by life, health, happiness, and a good name; another by disease, poverty, wretchedness, disgrace, and a dishonoured grave. Innumerable facts in the world, and long observation, show what *is* the course which will tend to the one or the other, and so clearly that it may be the basis of counsel to those who are entering on the career of life. These principles accord with those in the Bible, and have received an additional sanction *from* the Bible, but they exist independently of any particular form of religion, and are those on which men must act. They are met and carried out better by Christianity than by any other system, for the whole arrangement is one that is designed to exhibit ultimately the perfection of moral government.

(3.) Man's future condition will in some way be determined by his present conduct. This, too, is a principle on which all men act by nature, whether they have, or have not, any religion, or whether any particular form of religion be true or false. Every young man admits it as one of the things which spur him on to great or noble efforts, and which encourage him in study, in resisting temptation, or in laying his plans of life; and every man who has reached mature life or old age, sees that it has been so in regard to himself. He can trace the esteem in which he is held, or the health which he enjoys, or the property which he has accumulated, to his conduct and plans far back in life, and can see how the one is but the development of the other. This principle is indeed an essential one in Christianity; but it is not peculiar to it, nor has it been originated by it. It is in the world everywhere, and the man who rejects religion acts on it as certainly as he who embraces it.

(4.) It is a principle which is held in common by all, that the conduct of the present life *may* affect that which is to come. This is but carrying out the principle just stated, for why should the operation of this law terminate at death? What is there in death to check it? Why should the act of dying arrest this course of things any more than the slumbers of a night? For, as the conduct of yesterday travels over the interval of the night-watches, and meets us in its results to-day, why shall not the same law operate in reference to the shorter night—the sleep of death? Here is a uniform system of things, that our conduct at present affects our future destiny; uniform as far as the eye can run it backward into past generations; uniform, so as to become the foundation of laws, and of the entire government of the world; and uniform so far as the eye can trace the results of conduct *forward* in all the landmarks set up along our future course. Why should it be arrested by so unimportant a circumstance as death—death that less suspends human consciousness and action than a night's sleep; death that no more interrupts identity, and arrests the course of events in regard to an individual, than a passage from one land to another, or than the crossing of the conventional boundary of a kingdom? And as crime here meets its results after we have crossed oceans, and snows, and sands; as punishment, in remorse of conscience, in the storm, in the siroc, in the ocean, may follow us when far from country and home, in lands of strangers, where no eye may recognise us but that of the unseen Witness of our actions, why shall not the results of our conduct meet us beyond the little rivulet of death? That the conduct of this life is to be followed by results appropriate to it in the world to come is not a peculiar principle of Christianity; it pertains to the almost universal faith of man, and enters into all the religions of man. It is one of those great principles on which man must act whether Christianity or any other particular form of religion be regarded as true or false. And yet there is no provision made to meet this principle fully in any other system of religion but the Christian.

(5.) It is an original principle pertaining to man as such that a future state of existence is desirable. The language of Addison, which we so much admire, is not mere poetry. He utters the feelings of all men, when he says—

> Whence this secret dread and inward horror
> Of falling into nought? Why shrinks the soul
> Back on herself, and startles at destruction?
> 'Tis the divinity that stirs within us;
> 'Tis Heaven itself that points out an hereafter,
> And intimates eternity to man.—CATO, Act V.

Man has this desire everywhere, and a large portion of his reasonings from the earliest days downward has been designed to show that it was proper for him to cherish it. It is not created by the Christian religion. It lies beyond that, and exists in the soul, with all its intensity, whether Christianity or any other particular form of religion be true:—but what other system of religion so fully meets it as this?

(6.) It is somehow a great law of our nature that we need an atonement for our transgressions—that some sacrifice or oblation should be made that will appease the wrath of God, and do honour to a violated law, and open a way of pardon to the guilty. This is not originated by Christianity, nor is it peculiar to it. It is found in every land, among all people, and in every age. The evidence of it is seen on every bloody altar, and in the creeds of nearly all forms of religion. But where is this so fully met; where is there any form of atonement by which its demands are so fully accomplished, as in the sacrifice made by Christ? That meets *all* that we think the law demands; does all that can be done to repair the evils of the apostasy; and leaves the mind wholly at rest as to the necessity of any other sacrifice for the sins of the world.

(7.) And a well-founded, or seventh principle is equally universal. It is, that this world does not furnish all the happiness of which we are capable. Our nature pants for something more; it looks on to something still future. We partake of the happiness which this world can give, but there is still a "void" in the soul which is not filled. We look into the future. We try to lift the veil which hides the invisible world. We believe, in spite of ourselves, that if the soul is ever satisfied it must be by something there. *This* desire, too, is not the creation of the Christian religion. It lies back of that religion in the soul of man, and exists in the human bosom whether that religion be true or false.

Such are some of the evils under which the race groans, and such some of the principles on which the race must act. They are evils and principles which exist independently of any system of religion, and yet which demand some arrangement to meet them, and in reference to which every scheme of religion has been originated. We are led here to our

III. Third general inquiry—to what system can we go where there are fewer perplexities; where these evils are better met; and where these principles are better consulted, than in the Christian system? "Will ye also go away?" said the Saviour to his disciples. "Lord, to whom shall we go?" asked Peter; "thou hast the words of eternal life?" To what teacher should they repair who would be better qualified to instruct them? To what Jewish party should they apply, that they might better learn the way to heaven? To what sect of philosophers should they go, that they might find more consolation in the ills of life, be better supported in its trials, and find a more satisfactory answer to those questions which their very nature prompted them to ask? Difficulties there might be in the Christian religion, but where would they find fewer? Mysteries there might be, but where could they go where there were none?

And where will a man go now to find a system that is better fitted to meet the evils of the present world, or to carry out and satisfy the great original principles on which he must act? For you will remember that the question is not, whether by rejecting Christianity he may avoid these evils, or whether the race will cease to act on these principles. Those points are settled; and whether Christianity be embraced or rejected, they pertain to the race. The question is, whether he can improve his condition in regard to these things by rejecting this revelation, and turning to some other system? This is a fair question, and one which it becomes every man to answer for himself. It *should be* answered. Christianity proposes a remedy for these evils, and a way by which these great principles of our nature may be met and carried out. It does not originate these things, and should not be held answerable for them. It is in all respects, and in every aspect of it, a remedial system, and should be examined and judged only *as* such. Man by nature, sunk under sin, and exposed to pain and death, seeks some system which shall meet his sad condition, and alleviate his sorrows. He looks around for some way by which his sin may be forgiven ; by which a propitiation may be made for his offences ; by which he may obtain consolation in the prospect of dying. The gospel comes, and proposes a method of meeting his case, and declares that sin may be forgiven through the atonement made by the Son of God, and opens upon him the prospect of a resurrection and a glorious immortality. Now is not this just what he wants, and can he find a system that will better answer the end than this? For you will remember, I repeat it, that the question is not whether by rejecting this system you can avoid sin and pain and death. That point is so settled as not to admit of debate. But do not these things which Christianity has revealed meet the case? Can sinful, suffering, and dying man *find* a system that will better meet his condition? Where will he turn to find a better system? Will he go to heathenism? But would he find any sacrifice there for sin which for purity, and dignity, and efficacy would compare with that of the Son of God? Will he, then, consent to blot out all that Christianity has done for society, and place the race again in the condition of the Caffrarian or the Bushman? Does he suppose that the evils of the world would be mitigated by a return to that condition in which man was before the light of Christianity dawned on it? Will he turn to the ancient philosophers? And does he suppose that they can explain the mysteries of his being, and provide a better deliverance, than has been done by Him whom the Father has sent into the world? Let him become an Epicurean or a Stoic. Does he escape from the perplexities which he has been accustomed to associate with Christianity? Do not the Epicurean and the Stoic sin and suffer and die; and do not men sin and suffer and die all around them? Will he turn to the modern philosopher, or the modern infidel? Do they propose a better way by which a guilty conscience may become calm ; by which life's sorrows may be borne, and by which the pangs of death may be more patiently or triumphantly endured? Or does he escape from any of the mysteries and perplexities which encompass this subject when associated with Christianity? Do no other men but Christians die? Do they have no trouble of conscience? Are they never sick? Did not Paine, and Volney, and Hume die? And have they left any *recipe* by which death can be more calmly met and *better* borne than it was by Stephen, and Paul, and Halyburton, and Baxter, and Payson?

Oh, what *is* this world when we have turned away from the cross of Christ, and from the instruction which God has given us in his word? Man is seen upon the earth a strange being, playing a strange part, and encircled by mysteries. He has been created he knows not by whom, or when, or for what purpose. He begins to sin as soon as he begins to act, but he knows not why. He finds himself prone to evil by some mysterious law for which there is no explanation. He suffers, he knows not why. He lives, he knows not for what end; and when he dies he goes into another world, he knows not whither or why. He can do nothing to stay the progress of the plague which sweeps away the race, and he can only stand and weep over the grave which he digs for his pale brother, and which he himself must soon enter. He stretches out his hands to heaven *as if* there might be help there, but none appears. "His eye poureth out tears" as it is lifted toward the skies; it gazes intensely for light, but not a ray is seen. His nature pants to live for ever, but no response is given to the aspirings of his soul; nothing tells him that he *may* live. He is a poor, ignorant, degraded, and dying being, seeking for a guide, and panting for a system of religion that will meet the wants of his nature, and raise him up to God. Revealed religion comes and tells him who made him, and why; explains the way in which the race sank into this melancholy condition, and how it may be recovered; proposes promises adapted to him as an immortal being; reveals a brighter world, and explains to him how it may be his own. It originates no new form of disease; dips the arrow of death in no new poison; creates no new darkness around the grave; robs the sufferer of no consolation, and creates no new danger. *Then why, oh why should he go away?*

SERMON V.

THE IMPORTANCE OF MAN.

PSALM viii. 3, 4.—"When I consider thy heavens, the work of thy fingers, the moon and the stars, which thou hast ordained; what is man, that thou art mindful of him? and the son of man, that thou visitest him?"

THIS language is such as would have been prompted at any period of the world by a contemplation of the starry heavens. Even to the naked eye, they are so vast and grand that man dwindles into insignificance in comparison with them, and it seems wonderful that God should stoop from the contemplation of works so sublime to notice the affairs of a creature like man.

The language of the Bible is adapted by the Spirit of inspiration to express the emotions of piety in all ages; and though in the time of the psalmist the language of the text was fitted to express the feelings of deep devotion, yet two circumstances have contributed to give it in our times increased force and significance. One is, the greatly enlarged views which have been obtained of those "heavens" contemplated by the psalmist, by the discoveries of modern astronomy. The other is, the almost equal enlargement of conception of what God has done for man, and of the importance attached to him in his estimation, in the disclosures of the plan of redemption. These have not indeed entirely kept pace with each other, but together they give a greatly increased significance to the language of my text. With all the disclosures of modern astronomy before us, and in full view of what God has done for man in the work of redemption, one may well say, "When I consider thy heavens, the work of thy fingers, the moon and the stars, which thou hast ordained; what is man, that thou art mindful of him?"

There are two somewhat opposite methods of estimating man, both of them having much that is erroneous. One is, so to speak of his godlike nature, his achievements in council, in arts, and in science, his susceptibilities for progress, and the progress which he has actually made, as to conceal the degradation of his nature, and to fill him with pride and self-elation. This has been much the manner of poets and philosophers; of the writers of fiction, and of those systems of religion in which it is forgotten or denied that the race is in ruins. The other is, so to dwell on the circumstances of his wretchedness and sinfulness, on his foibles and crimes, and on the brevity of his life, and his comparative insignificance among the sublime works of God, as to make us feel that the race is wholly beneath the Divine notice. This is the view of the disappointed, of the sour, of the morose, of the haters of the species; and it is as far from the truth as the former.

Is there any way in which what is true in these views may be united? Is there anything fitted to give us elevated conceptions of the dignity of man, and yet to clothe us with humility; anything that makes man a proper object of special Divine notice, and yet anything that makes us wonder that he has attracted so much attention? In answering these questions, I may direct your attention to two points:—

I. In what way God has magnified man, or shown that he regards him as of special importance; and,

II. Why he has done it.

I. *In what way has God magnified man, or how has he shown a special interest in him?* My purpose, under this head, demands only a very brief statement—my main design being to show *why* man has attracted so much attention in the universe, as it is said in the Scriptures that he has.

What God has done for other portions of the universe we have only slight means of knowing; and it is not important for us to understand. Probably if we were admitted to a knowledge of what he has done for intelligent beings in other worlds, we should find proofs of his care and attention not less striking than those which are exhibited in our own. But, for obvious reasons, revelation is silent in regard to them.

The *peculiar* interest which has been shown in man—the interest apart from that which he has shown in creation and providence towards all intelligent creatures—according to the sacred Scriptures, consists in the following things:—

(1.) A plan of redemption has been formed for him. This was laid far back in eternity, and was contemplated from far distant ages. This plan, according to the sacred Scriptures, was one of special interest to the Divine Mind, and in accomplishing it, God was willing to institute a train of measures elsewhere unknown, and submit to sacrifices which to us would have been deemed impossible. According to that plan, he designed to make on the earth one of the most sublime manifestations of his glory, and to perform a work here that should interest in a peculiar manner the inhabitants of all other worlds, "to the intent that now unto the principalities and powers in heavenly places might be known, by the church, the manifold wisdom of God," Ephes. iii. 10.

(2.) For man, in the execution of that purpose, he sent his Son to become incarnate, and to die. Such was the interest which he felt in our race; so much has he magnified man, that a work has been performed which requires the highest measure of our faith to believe it true now that it has been done, and which we should have deemed incredible or impossible, could it have been submitted beforehand to our sense of probability. It resulted in the formation of a perfect union between the Divine and human nature in the person of the Son of God, and in his sacrifice as an offering for the sin of the world on a cross. This event stands by itself. There is no reason to suppose that a transaction of this nature has occurred in any other part of the universe. The more we contemplate it, the more we are amazed; and the more impressively does the question come home to us, "What is *man*," that such a plan should be formed for his redemption? It overpowers us. The mind sinks under the burden of the great conception that there should have been an incarnation of the Deity; that that incarnate Being should submit to be reviled and treated with scorn; and that he should, by his own sufferings and death, make expiation for human guilt. What is there in man that should lead such a being down to earth to suffer, to bleed, to die? Even in all our vain glorying; in all that has been said of the godlike dignity of the human powers; in all the dreams of philosophy and poetry about what man is, or is to be, what is there that would seem to make it proper that God should be thus "manifest in the flesh?" I wonder not that men pause with amazement, and hesitate before they admit the great idea to be true; nor that they feel tasked, and burdened, and overpowered by the claim which Christianity makes on their faith in the announcement of this truth.

(3.) For man the Spirit of God is sent down to the earth. He comes to enlighten, to arouse, to awaken, to renew, to sanctify. Of so much importance is man, that this Great Agent begins a special work in the heart of each one that is to be saved, and performs the distinct and definite achievement of changing the current of feeling, and the principles of the soul. He is the chief and the crown of all those agencies and influences intended to bring man back to God, and win him to heaven. A train of means has been employed designed to arrest his attention; to convict him of sin; to convert his soul; to open his eyes on the fields of heavenly glory; to send the current of spiritual life through the heart dead in transgression; to awaken the consciousness of an immortal nature in the lost soul; to make of the alien a friend—of the apostate an heir of heaven. As if there were some special importance in recovering *man;* as if his restoration would be worth all which it would cost in the institution of the most numerous and expensive measures, a train of operations has been commenced, all expressive of the intensest interest in the Divine Mind, for the accomplishment of this result. Why is this? Why does He who made and who rules these vast heavens feel so deep an interest in the recovery of a creature like man?

(4.) For man, we are told, there is intense interest felt among the inhabitants of heaven. There is joy among the angels over *one sinner* that repenteth. They, we are told, desire to look into the things connected with redemption; and the entire sacred history leads us to believe that celestial beings have been ready at all times to wing their way to the earth to watch the progress made in redemption; to relieve the wretched, and to comfort the dying; and that they hail with fresh rapture the coming of each ransomed spirit to the skies. Though man is insignificant in himself, yet there is *somehow* such an importance attached to him that angelic beings are willing for a season to vacate their happy seats if they can be helpers of his salvation.

(5.) God manifestly attaches great importance to each individual of the species. No matter how ignorant, or poor, or downtrodden he may be, the Divine dealings have an individuality in relation to him as if he were the only dweller upon earth. God never overlooks him. He sends his messengers of mercy to him—his prophets, apostles, and ministers of religion; he repeats the message when rejected, and urges it upon his attention with all the arguments which can be adduced—as though it were a matter of immense moment that *he* should repent, believe, and be saved. When we look upon enfeebled age, or upon a child; when we contemplate the downtrodden and ignorant tribes that dwell upon the earth—many of them but little above the brutes; when we see how frail and helpless man is at the best, and how soon he will vanish away, and his name be forgotten; and then, when we look up at these heavens in the light of modern astronomy, we can hardly help asking, as the psalmist did, "What is man, that thou art mindful of him?" Why does God treat him as if he were of so much consequence? Of what importance can it be to God where his location shall be? Why does he follow him so constantly, and why does he so earnestly press upon him compliance with the terms of his favour? In one word, why is this vast array of plan and motive, and eternal decree, and celestial influences, and heavenly interest, and solemn mandate, and fearful threatening, brought to bear on a frail, erring, dying, evanescent creature like man?

II. These questions it is my design, in the second place, to answer. I shall suggest four considerations in answer to the inquiry. They will show the importance of man, but they will be such as will be adapted to humble us. They will be fitted to avoid the self-glorifying of the philosopher—showing that the importance of man arises, in the main, from causes which should have *any* effect rather than to inflate us with pride; and they will be such as to avoid the other extreme of regarding man as so degraded and so unworthy of notice, as to leave on the mind, in the contemplation of him, the feeling of contempt or misanthropy.

(1.) I observe, first, that the attention which God bestows on man is in strict accordance with his universal providential care. In his empire, nothing is overlooked; nothing is forgotten. The Redeemer has told us that not a sparrow falls to the ground without his notice, and that even the hairs of the head are all numbered. Everything is treated as if it were of consequence; everything shares in the superintendence of the Most High. There is not an insect or a blade of grass whose structure does not appear as perfect as though the whole of the Divine wisdom had been exhausted to form it; there is not a rose that is not made with as nice a degree of attention and skill as though God had nothing else to do; there is not an emerald or an amethyst that does not seem to have combined all there is in infinite wisdom in its formation. The leaf; the flower; the particle of blood; the dewdrop; the forming crystal of the snow—all, taken singly, appear to be objects of special Divine attention, as if each were the solitary production of the infinitely wise and powerful God. We know not, we cannot conceive how this is. *We* become soon distracted with the very few objects that pass under our notice. We narrow down those that demand our attention; and from necessity pass over the infinitude of objects that are around us. We cannot conceive how it is that any one Being can direct his attention to countless millions of things at the same time:—at the same instant holding worlds and systems in their place; restraining the raging floods of the deep; directing the lightning; controlling armies engaged in the conflict of battle; and with gentle hand in the summer morning opening the rosebud, and at silent evening letting down the dewdrop on the spire of grass. Yet so it is; and such is God. And when we speak of the importance of man as evinced by the Divine care and attention, you are to remember the care that is bestowed on the poor worm on which you tread, as well as yourself; the care bestowed on the shaking leaf, as well as on the rolling world.

(2.) The second reason to which I refer is, that man, in his immortal nature, is a being who has all the importance which has ever been attributed to him. He has an intrinsic worth that renders proper all the care that God has shown for him; all the interest manifested for him in the eternal councils of heaven; all the value implied in the incarnation and atonement of the Redeemer for his salvation. Great as has been the sacrifice made for him on the cross; inconceivable as were the sufferings of the Son of God in his behalf, his salvation is worth all which it has cost, and will be an adequate and ample return to the Redeemer for all his pangs, and toils, and blood: for "he shall see of the fruit of his wearisome toil, and *shall be satisfied,*" Isa. liii. 11.* The Redeemer estimated man as of unspeakable value. He regarded his recovery as worth all which he would endure in becoming incarnate, and dying on the cross. The glory which the ransomed sinner would have in heaven, and the honour thence resulting to the Saviour, he deemed of sufficient worth to induce *him* to leave the heavens and to die. It is for the honour of Christ that we should feel and know that redemption is worth all which it has cost; and that the scheme of recovery is one that is based on a just view of the relative importance of things. The price, indeed, was infinite. Silver, gold, diamonds, pearls, all the treasures of kings, do not furnish us with the means of estimating its value. The blood of patriots, of prophets, of martyrs, of confessors, scarcely furnishes us with the means of comparison by which to measure the worth of the blood shed by the Redeemer. Still we hold that the Redeemer sought a prize in the redemption of man worth all which it cost him, and which will "satisfy" him for all his humiliation and toils.

Do you ask what was that prize? I reply, *It was the immortal soul.* Its value is estimated by the fact that man, so degraded, so sinful, so blind, so lost to his own interests, is IMMORTAL. Men see not this, nor feel it, for they *will* not be convinced that they are immortal, or that the soul is to have an infinite duration beyond the grave. Were you to be thrown into a dungeon

* Lowth's translation.

on earth, to live and linger on *for ever* in darkness, you would realize something of what constitutes immortality. If in that gloomy dungeon, nor father, nor mother, nor sister were to see you more; if the light of heaven were to greet you no more; if sleep were to visit your eyes no more; if harsh sounds and groans were to grate for ever and ever on your ears; if neither cord, nor pistol, nor assassin's hand, nor murderous phial could close your conscious being, you might form some idea of what it is to live for ever and ever.

To be immortal! The very moment you attach the idea of *immortality* to a thing, no matter how insignificant it may be otherwise, that moment you invest it with unspeakable importance. Nothing can be mean and unworthy of notice which is to exist for ever. An eternal rock, an eternal tree, plant, river, would impress our minds with the idea of vast sublimity, and make us feel that we were contemplating an object of unspeakable moment. Affix, then, to it the idea of eternal consciousness, though of the lowest order, and the mind is overwhelmed. The little humming-bird that in a May morning poises itself over the opening honeysuckle in your garden, and which is fixed a moment and then is gone, is lovely to the eye, but we do not attach to it the idea of great importance in the scale of being. But attach to that now short-lived beautiful visitant of the garden the word IMMORTALITY—and you invest it at once with an unspeakable dignity. Let it be confined *for ever* in a cage—or let it start off on rapid wing never to tire or faint beyond the orbit of Neptune, or where the comet flies, or where Sirius is fixed in the heavens, to continue its flight when the heavens shall vanish away, and though with most diminutive consciousness of being, you make it an object of the deepest interest. The little, lonely, fluttering, eternal wanderer! The beautiful little bird on an undying wing, among the stars! Who can track its way? What shall we think of its solitariness and eternal homelessness?—What, then, shall we think of an immortal soul? A soul to endure for ever! A soul to which is attached all that is meant by the word ETERNITY! A soul capable of immortal happiness or pain!—My careless, thoughtless reader, that soul, immortal and eternal, is yours. You feel it not. I was about to say you *know* it not. But Christ knew it, and felt it; and hence he came and died. The stamp, the seal of eternity is on you—and you must live for ever. And is your redemption not *worth* his death—not worth more than all these material suns and stars? Christ felt this when he said, "What shall it profit a man, though he gain the whole world, and lose his own soul?" And when we think of its immortality, and attempt to track its wondrous way on its eternal journey, we find an answer to that which so much perplexed the psalmist:—"When I consider thy heavens, the work of thy fingers, the moon and the stars, which thou hast ordained; what is man, that thou art mindful of him?"

(3.) Man is of peculiar importance as *a guilty being*. He has sinned; and has thus exalted himself into a melancholy notoriety such as he might never otherwise have had. A transgressor of law, no matter where, becomes at once a being of importance. A thousand questions are at once asked in reference to him which it would not have occurred to have asked if he had not sinned, and which would have been impertinent and improper if he had remained upright. A man who commits murder, becomes at once one who attracts attention. Before he did this, he may have been unknown; he may have been a stranger; he may have been a down-trodden slave; but the moment he imbrues his hands in the blood of his fellow, that moment the eyes of the community are turned towards him with the deepest interest. His name is gazetted and blazoned abroad; his person is described; his former course of life becomes a subject of interesting history; his feelings, views, destiny, all become a matter of consequence. A mark on his person is exalted into a thing of importance, and his death will attract the attention of thousands. His melancholy conspicuity he owes to his guilt; and but for that, he might have lived and died unknown. This would be more especially true, if the crime were one committed against a prince, a nobleman, a benefactor of his species, or the saviour of his country. To what a degree of importance would the lowest man in our country have exalted himself if he had assassinated La Fayette or Washington!—A vessel may cross and recross oceans, and attract almost no attention. Her coming and going shall be recorded only among the numbers that are alike undistinguished. But let it be rumoured that she was fitted out with knives, and dirks, and pistols, and guns, and that she has hoisted a false flag, and all at once she rises into conspicuity. The world begins to feel an interest in her as she roams on the ocean, and in all that pertains to her. Everything relating to her course, her colour, her form, her complement of men, becomes a matter of the deepest concern, and a nation feels that her capture is worthy of its attention. Her importance arises from the criminal intention, and the purpose to make war on the peaceful commerce of the world.—A child in a family that has done wrong at once attracts peculiar attention, and many a question is asked in the little community of which he is a member. Every eye is turned toward him. What will be the consequence of his offence? is the immediate inquiry. Will he be punished? Will his father forgive? A train of deeply interesting emotions also at once passes through the bosom of the distressed and afflicted parent. His attention is diverted from his other children to the offender. Can he safely pardon him? If not, what is the kind and measure of punishment which will be necessary? How can he so dispose of the painful occurrence as to secure the observance of his laws hereafter, and to turn the affair to good account in the government of his other children? The *guilt* of the offender has given him temporary and painful consequence in that circle, and has attracted towards him a degree of attention which but for that would never have been excited.

Such is man—one of the apostate children of the great family of God. Not having any peculiar claims to the Divine notice and attention from his original dignity and importance; not being of rank superior to other intelligences, he has raised himself into notice among immortal beings, as Richard III., and Cesar Borgia, and the Duke of Alva did among mortals, by guilt more than by talent; by eminence in crime, more than by exalted rank. He has, by his apostasy, given occasion to many a question of deep interest in regard to him which could never have been asked had he not revolted, and is raised to this bad eminence by his rebellion against the Most High. And *though* man is but the creature of a day, and crushed before the moth, yet when we look upon the numbers of the guilty—upon the aggravated nature of their crimes—the apostasy of *a world as such*—one entire province of the mighty empire,—we are not to wonder that they have attracted attention in heaven, and that great questions are pending there about the disposition which shall be made of the rebel race.—The importance of man now arises in no small degree from the fact that he is a sinner. We do not excite notice in heaven by our talent or learning; by our skill or accomplishments; by our beauty or strength. We can never make our names known there by our eloquence, our valour, our wealth. We are known as guilty men; as wanderers; as criminals; as having foolishly and wickedly gone away from God, and as being in rebellion against the Most High. It is the eminence of guilt, the fame of depravity, the notoriety of rebellion that distinguishes us in other worlds; and though we have become of so much importance as to attract attention there, yet the fact is one fitted not to fill us with pride, but to sink us low in the dust. It is true that the remark now made might be made of rebel angels, and would be correct in regard to them, and that this would SEEM to be a reason as strong in their case why they should be objects of special Divine notice as in ours—and so they may be in their own way, or in some method that shall as clearly show that the Divine attention is directed to them as if a plan of redemption had been provided for them: but there may have been reasons unknown to us, why the Divine notice of them as guilty was not manifested in the same way as towards us—that is, why they should not be redeemed.

(4.) Man is of importance as a *sufferer;* as actually now a sufferer; and as being exposed to deep and prolonged sorrows in the future world. A *sufferer* is always a being of importance, no matter what may be the cause of his woes. That interest is in proportion to the tenderness of the ties which bind him to others, or to the benevolence of those by whom he is surrounded. Who is the object of deepest interest in the family? Who is the one around whom most anxieties cluster? Look on that little afflicted daughter. All are ready to do anything for her; to carry her, to fan her, to bathe her temples, to watch with her during the long night. The reason is, simply, that she is a sufferer. She has now an importance, and attracts a degree of attention, which she could never have done had she lived in the enjoyment of health. Her pains, her sighs, her fading cheek, her sunken eye, exalt her into importance; and when she dies, you regard her as the most lovely of your children, and feel for the moment that you have laid your pride and your hopes in the grave.

It matters little—though I admit it does something—what is the *cause* of suffering, whether it be misfortune or guilt. The son that has been dissipated, and that lies on a bed of death as the result of his folly, is not cut off from our sympathy by his crimes. And especially if he has been led into temptation by others; if by their arts he has been seduced from virtue, our interest is excited in his behalf, perhaps not less than if he were innocent. Rare is it, if it ever happens, that a *mother's* heart is cold and repellant towards a suffering daughter, though she has been frail, and led away by a seducer.

If suffering is long, or is likely to be long, the importance of the sufferer is proportionally increased. Attach the idea of *eternal suffering* to anything, and you at once exalt it into unspeakable magnitude. It matters not how insignificant the sufferer may be, the idea of its suffering *for ever* gives it a magnitude which words can never express. Allow me to advert to my former simple illustration—the case of the little beautiful humming-bird. Suppose it—small as it is—transfixed with a tiny dart, and yet deathless; suppose the little arrow to pierce its heart, and the death struggle to continue on till the heavens shall waste away and the earth be no more, and then that it be removed to a place where it would struggle on with the quivering dart fixed there for ever—what would you not do to rescue such a sufferer? Tell me, ye rich and benevolent men, would you not give the last cent of your property to extract that tiny dart, and make that little beautiful being happy? What then is man, immortal man, if he is destined to eternal suffering unless redeemed? Why should we wonder that such a being becomes an object of interest in heaven; why that the angels regard him with emotion; why that the Redeemer came to die for him; why that God looks upon him with intensest feeling? No words can estimate the importance of man exposed to infinite suffering in the future world; and nothing but the fact that he is a sufferer here, and that he is in danger of eternal suffering in the world to come, is necessary to solve the question in the text:—"When I consider thy heavens, the work of thy fingers, the moon and the stars, which thou hast ordained; what is man, that thou art mindful of him?" How *could* a benevolent God but be mindful of one who might suffer for ever?

In view of our subject, I may suggest the following remarks:—

1. We may see the propriety and fitness of the plan of salvation by the incarnation and death of the Son of God. It was indeed amazing. It seems almost to surpass the limits of possibility that it should have occurred. Yet when we think of what man is; of his own immortal nature; of his magnitude of guilt; of the severity and duration of suffering due to him as a sinner; and of the numbers of the guilty and the dying, it is impossible to over-estimate his importance among the creatures of God. All about our subject is great. God is great; and the human soul is great. The plans of God are great; and the interests of man are great. The incarnation of the Son of God was great; and the object for which it took place was great. His sufferings and his agony for sin were great; and the sorrows of hell from which he came to redeem us were great. There is a fitness between the one and the other; and great as were the pangs of Jesus Christ, I see in the whole plan that beautiful harmony which I delight to trace in all the ways and works of God. "The redemption of the soul is precious." *It is worth all which it has cost.* The gain to the universe is to be an ample compensation for all those sufferings; and when the Redeemer shall see

all the purchased of his blood around his throne, he will not feel that in the garden of Gethsemane, or on Calvary, he endured one pang too much.

2. Our subject should teach us humility. Insignificant as creatures when compared with angelic beings, and infinitely so when compared with the great God, we have exalted ourselves into melancholy conspicuity by our guilt, and by our exposure to suffering as the result of our guilt. Distinguished though we are, and though we attract notice and attention from the heavenly hosts, yet the effect on us should be anything but to make us proud. Our crimes magnify us; but it is not a matter of self-exaltation when guilt attracts attention, and when the principal claim to notice is criminality. Though the gospel, therefore, reveals the interest which is felt in us by distant beings, it does it in such a way as not to fill us with pride; it does it so that the cardinal virtue in our bosoms which it produces is *humility*. And when you are in danger of being proud that God and Christ and holy angels feel a deep interest in you, and that for you an eternal plan has been formed, and for you the Son of God has become incarnate, remember that it was your crimes that attracted this attention, and that your peril on account of sin moved heaven to notice you. Go and see the crowd gather towards the cell of the pirate, or the throng that accompanies the man on the way to the block, and forget your pride.

3. If so much interest is manifested for man; if heaven is moved with compassion on his behalf; if angels look down with deep anxiety, solicitous to aid and save him, we cannot but be struck with the indifference of man himself to these great truths. Of all beings he is usually most unconcerned in the great events that contemplate his salvation, or that hasten his ruin. His eye is not attracted by the glories of the incarnation; nor does he feel alarmed at the preparations for his final woe. Much I have meditated on this; and much I have wondered at it, and still wonder. I have sought out arguments and words to rouse those whom I am called to address; but usually in vain. I can scarcely get the ear, or the eye—much less the heart—to contemplate the amazing interest felt in heaven based on man's guilt; those wonders of compassion in the cross that was reared that man might be saved. I see a parallel to it sometimes on earth—but where my philosophy equally fails me—in the guilty wretch about to die for his crimes, himself the most thoughtless of the throng, and with the utmost coolness walking up to the instrument of death, while every other heart shudders. Why it

is, I know not, I cannot explain it. But our subject makes yet another appeal to you. There *is* interest felt for you in heaven—in God's bosom—in the Redeemer's heart. There was interest felt for you in the eternal plan which contemplated redemption. There was interest felt for you on the plains of Bethlehem, when the angelic host sang "Glory to God in the highest, and on earth peace, good will toward men." There was interest felt for you in the garden of Gethsemane, and on the cross. There is interest felt for you still. Your God desires your salvation. Your Redeemer desires it. Your pious wife desires it. Your Christian daughter desires it. Your child that is a Christian desires it. All feel your danger but yourself. All pray for your salvation but yourself. All eyes but your own weep when they survey your eternal doom.

(4.) Finally, our subject shows us that the sinner cannot escape the notice of God. His sins have given him a bad eminence, and he will not be forgotten. "There is no darkness nor shadow of death where the workers of iniquity can hide themselves." He that has sought the redemption of the guilty by giving his Son to die, will not suffer him to escape if he neglects it. Sin makes the rebel of too much importance in a government like that of God; and the offender cannot escape. Human penalty you may escape. You may have never deserved it. But the penalty of the Divine law cannot be evaded; nor can the sinner plead his own insignificance when he stands before his Maker. Insignificant a man *may* have been till he became a murderer—but not then, nor ever onwards. Insignificant *you* may be as a creature, but never henceforward as a sinner.

I know, my hearer, that you and I shall die and moulder back to dust. I know that your name and mine will soon be forgotten among men. The traces of our existence on earth will be like the marks in the sand on the sea-shore which the next wave washes away. Yet we shall not be altogether forgotten. One Eye will be upon us; and we cannot escape it. There is One who will remember us, and who will never forget us. Dying—deathless man! What is to be your doom beyond the grave? Oh, think one moment, I beseech you, what it will be to live for ever; to suffer for ever; to be driven away for ever from God, and from heaven!—And then think what it *would be* to live for ever in heaven—for ever, for ever, oh, for ever, amid the songs of redeeming love—to have to all eternity the importance attached to you of being among the redeemed, and of being admitted nearer the throne than you might have been had you never fallen. Then, when you shall see these heavens rolled together as a scroll, and the stars fall from their places, and the light of this sun fade away; then, when you see a bright and glorious eternity before you, you will understand in its fulness the subject which so much perplexed the psalmist, why such importance was attached to man. Redeemed in those heavens, and for ever blessed, what will be the fading and dying splendours of all those material worlds compared with the bliss of your own ransomed soul?

SERMON VI.

THE EARTH A PLACE OF PROBATION.

ACTS xvii. 26, 27.—"And hath made of one blood all nations of men for to dwell on all the face of the earth, and hath determined the times before appointed, and the bounds of their habitation; that they should seek the Lord, if haply they might feel after him, and find him."

THIS passage teaches the following things: First, that men have a common origin, being made of one blood or family, and having the same Creator; and, therefore, that notwithstanding their diversity of language, of complexion, and condition, they are essentially equal, and have equal rights. Secondly, that God is a sovereign, and has fixed the various habitations of men according to his own pleasure, and as he saw would be best fitted to subserve the ends which he had in view in the creation of the race. And, thirdly, that the grand design for which they were made, and for which they have been distributed as they have been over the earth, was, that they might seek after the knowledge of their Creator; trace the evidence of his existence, and learn the character of his attributes in his works. He designed that the earth should be occupied by moral and responsible agents; and to the different branches of the one great family he has fixed the bounds of their dwelling; ordained the periods and the circumstances of their changes, and so arranged all things in regard to them as best to determine the question whether they are disposed to seek after him, and to serve him. This is equivalent to saying that they have been placed here on probation with reference to the knowledge, the service, and the favour of God; and that the circumstances of their probation have been intentionally arranged by the Creator with reference to that end. The general sentiment of the text then is, that the earth is fitted to be a place of probation. This sentiment I propose to illustrate.

The conjecture—for it can be little more than conjecture—is not improbable that all the intelligent creatures of God pass through a period of probation. It is in this world, as far as our eye can trace events, a universal law in regard to all advancement to a higher degree of existence; and the analogy would lead us to suppose that it is so in regard to all moral agents. Yet the *mode* of this may be different in different worlds. It must be adapted to the rank, the intellectual endowments, and the degree of light of the individual, or of the race that is to be tried. It may have been one thing for the angels; another for the inhabitants of distant worlds; and another still for man. In all, however, the grand purpose is the same—to furnish evidence, by proper trial, of a disposition to obey the will of God. In man at first the trial was made with reference to his willingness, in obedience to the command of his Maker, to abstain from a specified kind of fruit; in man now the same trial is made with reference to a law, or test, adapted to his fallen condition.

Probation on earth is a common thing. Every child is on probation in respect to what he will be in subsequent life; every youth in respect to the rewards of health, property, office, or honour, which the world may have to bestow; every student of divinity, law, or medicine; every clerk, or apprentice; every aspirant for office, in regard to the degree of esteem which he may have in the pulpit, of reputation at the bar, or in the practice of medicine, or of glory which may encircle his name when death comes. The world does not bestow its rewards except when there has been a trial. It does not commonly withhold them when the result of the trial has shown that the rewards were deserved. In a college, it is contemplated that he who shall receive the first appointment in his class, shall obtain it as the result of a fair trial or probation; in the learned professions, that he who shall bear the palm shall have shown that he was entitled to it; in respect to subsequent life, that he shall be most honoured who in the trying junctures that test the character shall have shown that he resisted temptation, and adhered to the laws of virtue; in the bestowment of the offices in a commonwealth, that no one shall receive them but he who has shown in appropriate situations that he has an established character for ability, patriotism, and virtue. If there are departures in any case from these principles, they are departures from what is admitted to be the true theory of the system.

It is essential to probation, in all cases, that there shall be freedom to act as we please; that the test applied shall be adapted to our capacity; that the conditions on which it depends shall be known, or such as may be easily ascertained; that the inducements to virtue shall be sufficiently strong to excite us to an effort to secure the reward; and yet that there shall be sufficient exposures to a contrary course to show that we are *disposed* to resist evil. He who has never resisted the temptations to indolence, vice, ambition, avarice, or sensuality, cannot be said yet to have a tried character for virtue. He who has never been in circumstances where he was called to *decide* whether he would be temperate or intemperate; industrious or indolent; pure or impure; a patriot or a traitor; a companion of the good or the evil—if there could *be* such a case—could not be said to be tried. He knows not what he *is*. He knows not what he *might be* in some new situation. He cannot be said to be in a state where it would be appropriate to reward him.

The question now is, if these are the conditions of probation, what arrangements are there in this world to adapt it to be a suitable place of trial for eternity? Are there things here which contemplate this, and which can be accounted for on no other supposition? Are they wisely arranged? Can we find in them the hand of a Father contemplating our own welfare, and adapting us to the world, and the world to us, in such a way as best to promote the grand object of a probation for a future state? We repine and murmur much at our lot; we wonder often at the mingling of light and shade, and good and evil, in our condition. Let us inquire whether, with reference to the great purposes of our being, we cannot find matter for hope, contentment, adoration, and praise.

I. The first thing that occurs to us as suggesting the idea of probation is, *the unsettled state of things in this world*. Nothing seems fixed, determined, ended. Everything looks forward. Light struggles with darkness; truth with error; good with evil; happiness with misery. There is no place of sunshine which may not be soon overshadowed with a cloud; no smooth sea where there may not be a hidden rock, or a whirlpool near; no highway that man travels where there are not paths branching off that lead astray; no plan in the "full tide of successful experiment" which may not be blighted; no reward that man can gain that seems fixed and abiding.

This is a remarkable world, and is probably unlike all the others that God has made. It is a most beautiful world, which, after all that sin has done, has still many of the features of the Eden where man first dwelt. The sun, for anything that appears to the contrary, shines as bright as it did then; the moon and the stars are as beautiful; the stream purls as gently; the ocean is as grand, and the rose and the magnolia are as fragrant. Man, if he were himself to *select* a place of probation, could not well *imagine* a world more full of beauty than this—for most of his ideas of beauty are drawn from this very earth. It is a world replete with proofs of the wisdom and the goodness of God; and whatever there may be in other worlds, here are depths of skill and benevolence which none have been able to fathom, and which seem as inexhaustible now as they did when the first created being bent with admiration over the beauty of a flower, examined the structure of the insect's wing, or looked upon the stars at night.

Yet how is all this intermingled with evil! There is darkness; there is sin; there is temptation; there are things that fill the mind with perplexity and doubt; there are evil beings as well as good abroad upon the earth, "both when we wake and when we sleep;" there are enticements to *wrong* as well as allurements to *right;* there are mighty means and influences to draw the mind to virtue, and there are mighty means and influences to draw it to vice.

Everything is *unsettled,*—just as it must be in a state of probation. There is as yet no certain or fixed reward. There is no crown which is unfading. There are no title-deeds which can make property sure. There is no happiness of whose continuance there can be certainty. Everything seems to partake much of the nature of *experiment* or *trial.* The whole subject of medicine, and finance, and agriculture, and mechanics, and even *morals,* seems to have partaken much of this character. Man is *on* trial, and he is constantly *making* trial for the future. Youth is on trial for manhood, and manhood for old age, and one generation for the next; and all for eternity. In all conditions there is a looking out of the human mind for the future. At any one stage of being there is an impatient longing for the next. There is an instinctive feeling that the destiny of the next stage is to be determined by the character of the present. And there is, in all and above all this, an instinctive feeling that *all* these stages on earth are preliminary to a higher, fixed stage beyond. Man is so made that he must look onward and upward, and must feel that the eternal condition is to be determined by the character formed in this life.

Then there is here a mingling together of influences from other worlds designed for the trial of man. There are seductive influences to evil. There are fallen spirits that have access to man. There are powerful appeals which they are able to make through our senses; by the objects of light, and taste, and touch; by suggestions made to our desire of knowledge, our pride, our vanity, our ambition; by the arts acquired by long experience in temptation, and by the aids which they can derive from the advocates of error, and the panders to guilt which they have already enlisted under their banners. And on the other hand, there are holy influences from above. There is the ministry and the solicitude of angels. There is the fact that the Son of God became incarnate and died in our world to win and save us. There is the ministration of the Holy Ghost to encourage those who wish to be confirmed in goodness, and to reach the rewards of heaven. There are the counsels and entreaties of the friends of virtue; the instructions and pleadings of the ministers of a holy religion; the admonitions of parents; the lessons of history—all leading the mind to virtue and to God. Such mingled things show that this is a world of probation, or is designed to *try* men with reference to what is to be their lot in the future stage of their existence; and they at the same time show the wisdom and goodness of God in the arrangement. It is the *kind* of a world which it *should be, if* it is designed as a place of trial. For what characteristics could it have as a world of probation, if the sun were withdrawn, and the moon and the stars shone no more, and no flower bloomed, and no Saviour had died, and no sacred Spirit came to aid men, and there were no living friends to help the weak and the ignorant on to God? What if all the comforts which we have were withdrawn, and the earth were converted into a dark prison, or were made a lurid meteor, bearing its wretched inhabitants through chilly regions of night farther and farther from the sun? It would then answer no purpose as a world of probation. See what the great prison-house of the universe, *hell*, is. Who has been reformed there? Who has been prepared there for a higher stage of being? See what a prison is. Man shuts his fellow out from the light of the sun, and the moon, and the stars. He closes dark, massive doors upon him. He takes him away from wife, and children, and friends. He clothes him in coarse raiment; feeds him on coarse fare; spreads for him a couch of straw; forbids him to look upon the face of man; deprives him of the balmy air; guards him with unslumbering vigilance when he wakes, or when he sleeps, perchance, binds his quivering limbs in fetters of iron. Who is made the better by this? Who is reformed? Who supposes that *that* would be an appropriate place of probation for a youth? None are reformed there—unless you can introduce an *independent* influence of goodness and mercy—the light of the glorious gospel—the voice of a friend of virtue—the offer of salvation—the hope of heaven. And if God had made *this* world as man makes *his* prisons, vain would have been the hope of securing a fair trial of what man *is* or *might be*, or of preparing him for a higher stage of existence. But he has not made it so. He has not attempted to *drive* man to the pursuit of virtue or the performance of duty, by the clanking of fetters, the sound of the lash, or the gloom of a dungeon. He has another method. He places man, though a sinner, in a world apparently as beautiful as it can be made; surrounds him with all that can appeal to his gratitude and his sense of right; tells him of eternal love, and of infinite sacrifices in his behalf; sends divine ministering spirits to aid him in his efforts to secure salvation; gives him a Saviour; comes and dwells with him; raises him up when he is bowed down; and, amidst his sorrows, as he struggles with darkness and sin, points him to a world where these struggles shall cease, and where there shall be no intermingling of light and shade, but where all shall be a sea of glory. How different this from the clanking of fetters, and the chilliness of a dungeon! A prison, as man makes it, is a different thing from this world as God has made, and as he preserves it. The one is *designed* primarily as a place of *punishment*, and all the arrangements for *reformation* are things superinduced; the other is primarily a place of *probation*, and all that looks like *punishment* here is designed to contribute to the great plan of preparing for the retributions of another state.

II. A second feature illustrating the condition of the world as a state of probation is, *that the offered reward*—the inducement to good—*is commensurate with such an object.* Here we need not be detained long. The rewards proposed should always be such as to constitute a fair probation. They should be sufficient to a life of virtue. The rewards of industry, soberness, integrity, scholarship, proposed to a youth should be sufficient to be a reasonable stimulus, or to make them worth striving for. They *are* so in the present life—even if there were no bearing of these things on the life to come. Apart from every consideration drawn from another world—real or imaginary—the rewards which may be secured in this world by early virtue and industry are worth all which they cost. Take one instance as an illustration of the whole. The influence of diligence in the acquisition of knowledge by a student on his future happiness, if his life is spared, is worth all which it will cost him to make the highest attainments possible. The effect in giving him a desirable reputation, to which no virtuous and sensible man will be indifferent; the effect in gratifying his friends; the effect in introducing him into successful and prosperous business; and the effect in opening before him rich sources of enjoyment in the hours of leisure, and in old age—an effect so often and so beautifully described by Cicero when speaking of philosophy—are ample rewards for all the sacrifice which is required in order to be a good scholar.

The same remarks may be made of everything good in regard to which a young man may be considered to be on probation.

Is this so in regard to the rewards proposed to man considered as on probation for eternity? Open your Bibles; or cast the eye upward and onward, and see whether the rewards proposed are not commensurate with the highest measure of sacrifice, and self-denial, and holiness on earth. What could be *beyond* these? What *higher* offering of reward could stimulate man to pursue that course which will be connected with the eternal crown? It may be doubted by some, but with those who have made the trial it will not be a matter of doubt, whether virtue and religion do not carry their own rewards with them; and whether if there were no future state whatever, there would not be an ample recompense for all that religion costs a man on earth. This can hardly be questioned in regard to the peace, and happiness, and joy, of a self-approving conscience when virtue is subjected to no extraordinary trial. Many a man finds within his own bosom an ample recompense for what a deed of charity costs him; and it is not to be doubted that Howard felt himself abundantly repaid for all the property which he expended, and all the time which he devoted, to alleviate the condition of the prisoners; and that Wilberforce and Clarkson, when it could be said that the moment any person trod the soil of England he was free, found an ample recompense for their extraordinary toils, in securing this result. But the assertion, though it may be deemed extravagant by many, *may be* nevertheless true, that even Paul and Silas in the prison at Philippi, and Bunyan in a British dungeon, and Latimer and Ridley at the stake, MAY have enjoyed *even there* a degree of holy joy which *they* would have regarded as an ample compensation for all that they had been called to endure in the cause of religion.

But not to dwell on this. The question which our subject demands to be answered is this:—Are the rewards proffered to men in heaven such as it is proper should be offered to those in a state of probation to induce them to walk in the ways of religion? Are they such as *fairly* to put man on his trial, and to be all the inducement of this kind which can be reasonably asked to lead him to be what he should be? The only answer that is needful here is, that the rewards offered to man as the result of a successful probation are the highest that man can himself conceive. They are the crown incorruptible; immortality; a resurrection to glory; perfect freedom from sin, pain, and tears; the highest happiness, and the purest friendship, and the most exalted intelligence and moral worth of which our nature is capable, and all this continued for ever. When you have affixed the idea of *immortality* or *eternity* to anything which is regarded as a good, you have gone to the utmost limit which the human mind is capable of conceiving. If man will not be won by *that* to a life of virtue, what is there to influence him? Beyond this, it is not possible to conceive that even God himself can go. What can *even He* offer more?

III. It is equally true that there are sufficient exposures or solicitations to evil to determine what the character is, and in all respects to fit this to be a world of probation. No confidence is to be placed in untried character. We want some evidence which will enable us to judge how a young man will *act* before we admit him to form a matrimonial connexion with a daughter; before we entrust him with our keys; before we make him a cashier in a bank, or a treasurer of the county or the commonwealth. We wish to know how he *has* acted in circumstances where men are liable to go astray, and where we know that the integrity of many has shown itself too feeble to resist evil. We would not *lead* him into temptation, nor would we place allurements to evil before him; but we wish him to have had some experience in a world which we know to abound with temptations, and to see in what manner he meets them. We judge of his virtue by the evidence that he has come unscathed from scenes where many have fallen. If never tried, we know not what he would be; if tried, and if the result has been successful, we take him as a partner in our business, or admit him to our friendship.

It will not be denied that this world has all the characteristics in this respect which can be considered proper in order to a just probation. No one is compelled to do wrong; but there are abundant exposures to evil to show whether man is disposed to do right. It is a world sufficiently full of the allurements of ambition, and gain, and sensuality, and vanity; sufficiently filled with attractive crimes, and false opinions, and "evil men and seducers" that wax worse and worse, to bring out everything that there is *in* man, and show what his true character *is*, and what he *would* be in other worlds. It in fact answers the purpose. The disposition of every man becomes *tested* before he reaches the grave, nor does one who acts on this theatre of being enter eternity in such a way that there can be any reasonable doubt about his character. Under the operation of this principle of the Divine administration, Satan fell; Adam fell; and millions have since fallen. Youths, trained to other things, fall to rise no more; men whose character was supposed to be matured by long and steady virtue, under the influence of some new form of temptation, fall, and reveal what was the secret character of the heart; clergymen supposed to be of tried virtue are suffered to fall, disclosing, perhaps, a long career of secret iniquity. But it is not wrong that the test should be applied. It was not wrong that it should be applied to Adam. It is not wrong that it should be applied to a youth; an officer of a bank; a candidate for a high office of the state; a minister of the gospel, or man at large—considered as a probationer for eternity. If there is secret iniquity in the heart it is well that it should be developed; and I do not see how we can conceive of a world better fitted to show what man *is*, and yet furnishing more helps to a virtuous life, than this. If so, it is adapted to be a state of probation.

IV. The conditions of trial are sufficiently plain and easy. The conditions of trial should be adapted to the capacity. You would not apply the same test to man and to angels; nor to a child and to an aged and experienced statesman or financier. To Adam a simple test was applied, perfectly easy to be complied with; adapted to the condition of one who had just opened his eyes upon a world of which as yet he knew nothing. Compare that simple prohibition with the form in which temptation approached the Son of God (Matt. iv.), and the way in which the virtue of the prospective Redeemer of the world was assailed. The test was adapted to each. The one fell; the other was incorruptible, and there, after success in a greater or less degree everywhere else, Satan was foiled.

It is essential to the trial that the test be adapted to the capacity; that it be practicable to be complied with; that it shall be such as to bring out the character. It would be no proper condition of probation for man to make his salvation depend on his creating a world, or guiding the chariot of the sun in the heavens, or directing the comet's flight, or converting the sea into dry land; for all these are beyond any power with which he is endowed.

What, then, *is* the point of probation for man now? The true issue always is *obedience* to the will of God; the question is, whether man is disposed to *obey*. This may be modified according to circumstances. In Adam it related to the forbidden fruit. Among the angels it may have been quite a different thing. In man *now* it might have been perfect and uninterrupted compliance with the holy law of God through life; but who then would be saved? Or it might have been a pilgrimage to a distant tomb; or the maceration of the body by fasts and vigils; or a certain number of genuflexions; or the wearing of a garment of a peculiar form or colour. Any one of these would have answered *some* purpose as a test, and however senseless or stupid they might be in other respects, they would have illustrated the question whether man was *disposed* to obey. But none of these things are chosen; and it would be easy to show that none of them would be adapted to the condition of man as he is on trial for eternity.

What, then, *is* man to *do* in order that his probation may be successful? He is perpetually doing *something*, and every man has his own views as to what constitutes the real nature of the trial. One makes it to consist in a form of religion; another in a pilgrimage; another in fastings; another in honesty; another in kindness to the poor; another in the upright discharge of his duties as a merchant, a bank officer, a father, or a friend. He stakes his eternal destiny on the manner in which these duties are discharged. What is the truth about it?

Our text says that the substantial point of trial is, whether men will "feel after God and find him;" that is, whether they will seek to know him, and to become practically acquainted with him; for "this is life eternal, to know thee the true God, and Jesus Christ whom thou hast sent," John xvii. 3. In the Bible, the true issue is always put on such a ground as this. It is to know whether man will seek for, and return to his Maker; whether he will embrace the instruction which God gives, and accept that Great Teacher as his guide who alone can lead back to God; whether man, regarded as an apostate being, will cease from his wanderings, give up his opposition, and return to his Creator; whether he will surrender his heart to the claims of him who made him; lay down the weapons of his rebellion; accept of the pardon proffered through the merits of the Redeemer, and thenceforward yield obedience to the holy law of his God. You will perceive, then, that this makes the issue of a peculiar character, and is fitted to be such a trial as is required in probation. It makes the true test of probation, not the acquisition of property, or learning, or accomplishment; not external morality, grace, beauty, or strength; not a pilgrimage, or a sacrifice; but *the surrender of the heart to God, a return from sin, a willingness to be saved, an acceptance of the Lord Jesus as a Saviour*.

A subject of a government—say a baron under the feudal system—rebels against his sovereign. He is in possession of a strong castle, and has entrenched himself there. Guilty of treason, he is liable to the penalty of death in its most fearful form. If now that castle is besieged and its outworks are taken; if he is closely pressed, and a demand is made on him to return to his allegiance, and if there is a disposition on the part of the sovereign to show him clemency, what would be the terms of the surrender, or what would be the true point of *trial* in the case? It would not be any impracticable thing, such as ascending the heights of an inaccessible mountain, or making himself wings to fly. It would not be that he should lacerate his body, or emaciate himself by fasting. It would not be primarily that he should honestly pay off those in his employ, and do justice to those under him whom he might have wronged. All these things might or might not be proper in their place, but they would not be the real point at issue. That would be, whether *he would give up that fortress;* whether he would lay down his arms and pull down his flag; whether he would return to allegiance to his lawful sovereign; whether he would give hostages as pledges or promises that would be satisfactory for his future good behaviour. So the true matter in issue with *man* is, whether he will yield the citadel of his heart to his lawful sovereign; whether he will lay down the weapons of his rebellion; whether he will leave the service of the enemy; whether he will accept of pardon for the past on the conditions proposed, and whether by oath and covenant made over the blood of the Great Sacrifice, he will solemnly pledge himself to rebel no more. This issue is to be tried in the present life; and to determine this, man lives in this world of probation, and the terms are constantly submitted to him. These terms are easy. They have been embraced by millions of all classes and ages. They are no more difficult to be complied with than it is for the rebel baron to lay down his arms and open the gates of his castle; and they are such that God *must* insist on them in regard to every one found in this position; that is, to every human being. It is a *fair* test; and it *must be applied.*

V. The time allotted to man is long enough as a season of probation. In the case just referred to, the time *need not* be long for the rebel baron to determine whether he would surrender. His character, his disposition, his views would be fully tested even if the time allowed him were but a single day. If he surrendered, that would settle the matter; if he refused, that would determine it with equal certainty. The very position in which he was found—in arms, with the flag of rebellion floating on his ramparts, leagued, perhaps, with a more powerful foe, and barring his gates against the approach of his lawful sovereign, would determine what he was *then;* the terms of surrender now proposed, even if respite were given but a day, would furnish sufficient trial of what he was disposed to be.

Our life is very short. It is a vapour; a breath; a summer cloud; a morning mist. But it is long enough to answer all the purposes of probation for eternity. Let a proposal of surrender be sent to this rebellious baron, and if he pays no attention to it, it shows what he is. If sent again, and he is still sullen and indifferent; or if he coolly and with outward respect sends it back; or if he scourges the messenger and then sends him back; or if he hurls back defiance; or if he crucifies the messenger, and suspends him on the walls in the sight of him who sent him, can there be any doubt about his character? Would it be wrong to proceed to a sentence on the ground of this? To man—short-lived, and found in rebellion against God—an offer of mercy is sent. If he is indifferent; if he turns away; if he closes his ear; if he meets it with contempt, mockery, and reproaches; if he seizes the messenger and incarcerates him or crucifies him, is there any doubt about his character? Is it necessary to a fair and equal probation that our supposed baron should have an opportunity of doing this repeatedly? Would you say that equity required that his sovereign should patiently wait, "rising up early" and sending his messengers to be despised, rejected, or crucified, until the moss of years should overspread the walls of that castle, and the keeper should become grey with age? I tell you, my friends, as *you* would say in that case, that this is *not* necessary; that if God makes you an offer of salvation so that you fairly understand it; if he sets life and death before you, and life be despised, there is a fair trial. Justice and judgment might then proceed apace; and though you be cut down at twenty years of age, the character is determined. Life even in such a case is long enough for this purpose, and the probation is a fair one.

There are several other thoughts which might be suggested in order fully to illustrate my subject; but I may not trespass on your attention by dwelling on them. I have stated some views which seem to me important to give us just conceptions of what life is, and to reconcile us to our condition. There is one other thought, however, which cannot be omitted without leaving the subject incomplete. I can do little more than name it.

VI. It is this:—that there is just uncertainty enough about all the objects of life, and about its close, to make this a proper world of probation. All things are uncertain—life, health, property, friends, office, honour. When these things are gained, they satisfy no one. The mind is uneasy, restless, discontented. The thoughts stretch onward still; nor, in our weary journey, do we all find a resting-place. A palace or a cottage, a city or a village, a feudal castle or an Arab's tent, are alike unfit to be the permanent abode of man. He wants another home—one more fixed, one more adapted to his nature—the "house not made with hands, eternal in the heavens."

And amidst this general instability, the close of life itself is just so uncertain as to show that this is a proper world of probation. If human life were fixed uniformly at fifty years without the variation of a day, and if the manner of death were in all circumstances the same, it is not difficult to see what would be the effect in regard to a preparation for eternity. Who can be ignorant of the disposition in man to defer preparation for a future state as long as possible? And who can be ignorant how prone men are, even with all the uncertainty about the *manner* of death, still to defer preparation to the very hour of departure? What, then, in reference to a preparation for a future state, would be the condition of things if all men knew the day, the hour, the moment, the circumstances of death? God has ordered this better. You may live on yet many years, or this day's sun may be the last that you will ever behold. What is better fitted to lead man, if he would be wise, to think of another world, and to make a timely preparation for it, than this uncertainty when his probation will close? What *could* there be that would be more adapted to crown all the other arrangements of probation, and to bring the mind to make preparation for heaven? Probably in all other worlds there has been no arrangement better fitted to secure the end in view than this; and the fact—the sad and mournful fact—that a candidate for eternity remains unconcerned in these circumstances, shows the inexpressible wickedness and folly of man.

SERMON VII.

MAN ON PROBATION.

GAL. vi. 7, 8.—"Be not deceived; God is not mocked: for whatsoever a man soweth, that shall he also reap. For he that soweth to his flesh, shall of the flesh reap corruption; but he that soweth to the Spirit, shall of the Spirit reap life everlasting."

THE literal truth of what is here affirmed no one can doubt. He that sows wheat shall reap the same; he that sows rye, or barley, or cockle, or tares, shall reap the same. Wheat that is sown will not produce tares; nor will tares produce wheat. So in morals. He that sows to the flesh, or cultivates the depraved and corrupt appetites of his nature, will reap only what those depraved and corrupt appetites can produce—wretchedness, corruption, and woe. He that cultivates the affections produced by the Spirit of God, shall inherit life everlasting. God is not mocked. He is no more imposed upon by any art of man, so that happiness is the result of sin, than he is in respect to grain that is sown. Eternal life can no more be made the fruit of fleshly appetites than a harvest of wheat can be made to grow in a field sown only with tares.

The doctrine then is, that man is on trial or probation with reference to his future state; and that the destiny in the eternal world will depend on the character formed in this life. This truth I propose to explain and to defend.

In the explanation of the doctrine, I would observe, that I do not use the word *probation* as implying that man is not fallen, or that he is on trial in the same sense in which Adam was when created. Considerable exception has been taken to the use of that word, as if it implied that in all respects the condition of man now is the same as before the fall. But this idea is not necessarily conveyed by the use of the word. Nor is it meant that man does not come into the world with a strong and universal tendency to sin—a tendency uniform in its nature and effects, except when arrested by the grace of God.

The essential idea in the term is, that future happiness and reward are dependent on present conduct and character. Adam was in the strictest sense of the word on probation. He was created, indeed, holy. But it was important, for purposes which need not now be referred to, that his holiness should be tested. A single act would do that as well as many acts—just as a man's character now may be fully tried if placed in some extraordinary circumstances of temptation. God, therefore, forbade a specific act on pain of death; with, it is commonly supposed, an implied promise that if he obeyed, he should be confirmed in obedience, and be rewarded with eternal life. He acted; fell; involved his posterity in ruin; and died. The probation was complete; the trial was passed. His virtue was not proof to the temptation. As the head and father of the race, he sinned and fell; as his children, we inherit the consequences of the unsuccessful probation.

Man is not now on probation in the same sense in which Adam was; nor will he ever be again. He is not in the same circumstances; he has not the same character; he does not begin life as he did. No man can now secure immortal temporal life, as Adam might have done, as the fruit of obedience; none can stretch out his hand and take hold of the crown of glory, as he might have done, as the reward of personal obedience. The affairs of the race are placed on a different footing; and this idea is never to be lost sight of when we speak of the probation of fallen men.

The following remarks will explain what is meant when we make use of this word:—

(1.) The essential thing in all probation or trial is, that the happiness or misery of the future is determined by the conduct of the present. Man acts with reference to that which is to come; and his conduct draws on a train of consequences in that future period. His actions do not terminate in the immediate pleasure or pain in committing them, but they constitute that by which his happiness is to be determined hereafter.

(2.) The great thing contemplated always by probation is still set before the human family. The same heaven is to be secured, and the same hell avoided, as when man was made in the image of God. If man succeeds in reaching the rewards of heaven, they will be the same rewards which would have been obtained had Adam not sinned; if he sinks to hell, it will be the same hell to which *he* sunk for his sin, unless he repented and was pardoned.

3. The same *character* is demanded of man as that which would be required if man had never sinned. Heaven will be made up of holy beings—possessing holiness of the same kind

whether it be by those who never fell, or those who are recovered by redemption. There will not be two kinds of holiness in heaven; and it is as necessary now that man should be holy in order to enter it, as it was that Adam should be, or any one of the angels.

(4.) While the main thing before man now is the same, and the holiness required is of the same nature, the *mode* by which heaven is to be reached now is different, and the question now before man, and on which he is to be tried, is changed. Man is not now to obtain eternal life, as Adam might have done, by personal obedience and by unsullied holiness. That is now out of the question in a world where all are born prone to sin, and are certain to sin. The question *now* is, not whether you will obey perfectly a pure and holy law—for no man could be saved if that were the question—but whether you will repent of your sins, embrace the offer of pardon through a Redeemer, and submit to a process of sanctification under the Spirit of God, designed to fit you for heaven. In regard to this, I would observe further, that it is as simple a question as can be submitted to man, or ever was. The question solemnly proposed to each successive mortal as he comes on to the stage of being, whether he will repent and believe in the name of the Saviour, is as intelligible, and as plain, as was the question proposed to Adam whether he would abstain from the forbidden fruit. It is a question adapted in all respects to his powers, and one the answer to which may as reasonably affect and determine his destiny hereafter. Bear in remembrance, therefore, that the question on which man is tried, and is to be tried; the question which is to be determined by your living on earth, and the only very material question is, whether you will embrace the Lord Jesus and depend on his atonement for salvation. It is not whether you are beautiful—for heaven cannot be made to depend on that; it is not whether you are rich, or learned, or accomplished—for it would obviously be absurd to make the bliss of a holy heaven depend on that; it is not whether you deserve to be praised, flattered, or caressed, or whether you can clothe yourself in fine linen and fare sumptuously every day; it is not whether you are externally moral, and a man of truth and honesty; it is, whether you comply with God's commands in embracing the gospel of his Son, and are willing to be pardoned and saved through him. "For he that believeth and is baptized shall be saved, and he that believeth not shall be damned." If you sow to the flesh, you show that you are not willing to be saved in that manner; if you sow to the Spirit, you show that you are disposed to embrace him, and shall reap everlasting life.

(5.) The theatre of probation is this narrow world where we are placed. The time of probation is the present life—that narrow, pent-up, short and shortening period in which we are to dwell on earth;—that life which the Bible calls a vapour;—those days which the Scriptures say are like a handbreadth, and a weaver's shuttle. It is all confined to that unknown portion of existence which constitutes *our* life; or rather to that uncertain period lying between the present moment and death. We can fix the outer limits—and then draw them gradually nearer to us. We can say it is *not* a thousand years; it is *not* five hundred years; it is *not* one hundred years; with many it is certainly *not* fifty, with some not half that;—with some here it is morally certain it is not *one* year; with any one of you, it may not be a week! Yet there lies the question of probation. There the character is to be determined. How much like sowing seed on the margin of an ocean—all along whose borders a thick mist lies which no eye can penetrate; and where, for aught you know, the next wave may break over you and sweep all away!

(6.) One other remark respecting probation. It is, that God holds in his hand the prerogative of closing it when he pleases. Of the particular period when it is to cease he has given no indication in the book of nature or of grace. The question of probation, like that proposed to Adam, does not require much *time* to settle it. It may be done in an instant, as well as in a hundred years. It may as certainly be determined of a young man at fifteen or twenty, whether he is willing to embrace the gospel and to sow to the Spirit, as at eighty or a hundred years. It may be determined by the simple offer of the gospel to-day, as well as by repeated offers for many years. No man can control God in this, or prescribe to him *how long* the probation is to continue; no man can determine by any act when it shall close; no man can tell in what circumstances it will end. No one can ascertain, in reference to himself, whether it would be agreeable to God that he should plead for pardon on a death-bed, when he has a thousand times rejected it in health; no one can ascertain whether God will not visit him with delirium or stupor on a bed of death; no one whether he will not cut him down so instantaneously that he may not utter the short cry, "Lord, have mercy on me," when he comes to die.—The end of life to all is hidden. The death of each one comes up in its proper place—unknown to him till his turn arrives. The wheels of nature roll on; and as God advances his vast plans, the individual whose turn is next, dies. Not a moment is given him if he is unprepared. To us it seems to be irregular—but an invisible finger touches the springs of life: like the skilful finger that runs apparently so irregularly over the piano, yet the *proper* key is touched—and to God all is harmony. Probationers die when according to his views they *ought* to die; and when that time comes, no created being can for a moment put back the gentle touch which reaches the heart-strings. You cannot know, if you would, where is the outer limit of your life; you need not be deceived by supposing that it is far off. If your eyes were open, you might see the hideous gulph yawn even now at your feet.

With these explanations, I proceed to show that the present *is* a state of probation. I desire to show you that your eternal destiny is to be determined by your character in this life, and particularly by the question whether you will or will not embrace the Lord Jesus Christ.

(1.) I begin, in the first place, with that which is most obvious, and which settles the general principle. It is, that our conduct at one period of our lives determine the destiny of the future. With this truth all are familiar; and it is not necessary to dwell on it. As a general law, industry, sobriety, and honesty in youth are the pledge of health, competence, and esteem in old age. On the other hand, vice in youth conducts, as a general law, to poverty, shame, the penitentiary, and the gallows. On this principle the world acts, and must act. Every young man is on trial with reference to the future. Every apprentice, or student, is thus a probationer. No one *presumes* that a young man is worthy of unlimited confidence until he gives proof of it; no one is disposed to withhold it when he *has* furnished that proof. Thus it is everywhere. The man that sows, reaps. The man that labours has a competence; the idle and dissipated have not. The young man that has moral principle enough to pass a gaming-room when it allures—or to pass a tavern when it tempts him—or to refuse to go near either when invited,—which is the probation that fixes the doom, temporal and eternal, of many a young man,—may have a *tried* virtue which will ultimately secure the confidence of the world. The professional man that is attentive to his business is appropriately rewarded. He that toils not, that wastes his youth in idleness or dissipation, or that is a mere *hanger-on* in his profession, will ultimately drop into deserved insignificance and contempt.

So well settled is this law, that were a man certain that he would live through a period of eighty years, and be favoured with ordinary health, he could almost draw out a chart of his course, and determine the measure of his wealth and honour in that distant period. And were my object at this time to convince those whom I now address that *their* future lives here would be determined by their present character and conduct, I might now close, for my work would be done. Indeed, I should do no more than state to you the principle on which you yourselves act every day, and repeat the lesson which you have heard from the very cradle. We can easily convince any young man that his prospect of eminence in his profession, or of wealth in future years, depends on his character and conduct now. Nay, I should not despair of being able to convince a young man in danger of falling into habits of dissipation, that he is dependent on his good conduct now for esteem, and health, and property, and even life, in future years. Were this the only object of my preaching, I should in every discourse carry my readers with me, and satisfy every mind.

Yet when I attempt to carry the mind across that very narrow but most cold and turbid stream which divides the present from the unseen world—*death;* when I attempt to carry the argument though but the smallest distance into eternity, and to survey the landmarks set up along our future being there, and to show that men are on probation for that state as well as for old age, I part with, alas! the most of my hearers. They seem to suppose that at death their interest in all things stops; that there is a final pause of being; and they feel no concern in inquiring whether the probation for future years on earth may not run on into the higher probation for an eternity beyond. There they stand near the brink, interested in all that is this side the Jordan; wholly uninterested in all that is beyond. My hearer! *I ask you for once to forget that you are to die*—a thing which I need not commonly ask you to do. It is not commonly remembered too much—but I ask you to FORGET IT for a moment, and to look just at one point—THE CONTINUANCE OF EXISTENCE —as if there were no death; no grave. I ask you to remember that death suspends not your existence; changes not your nature; affects not your character;—that your souls will live on IN death, and will *live on* BEYOND for ever.

You are now a probationer for future health, reputation, property, office. This you know; this you will not deny. Your character and conduct now is to affect all your course ever onward in this world. Young man, you are on trial every day with reference to future years, and you expect that your destiny in this life will be determined by the character you form now. I have now to ask you, why should this state of things stop at death? Why should the course of events be arrested then? Why should affairs beyond be carried on on a new and independent principle? Tell me, what is death? Is it annihilation? Is it the destruction of any mental power? Is it the loss of consciousness? Is it a change in the nature of the soul? Oh no. Not so much as one night's sleep. For in sleep our senses are locked up; we become unconscious, and sink into forgetfulness; and the intercourse with the living world is suspended; and to us it is as if it were not. Yet, when we wake, we find the actions of yesterday determine our destiny to-day. We walk amidst the results of the plans and deeds of the past; and we have brought over with us the character which we formed then—nor can we separate it from us. The man who toiled yesterday sees his fields to-day ripening and waving in the sun; the professional man of industry and skill yesterday finds to-day his way thronged by those attracted by the character he has formed; the man of temperance rises strong as in the dew of youth from healthful repose; and each one meets the *rewards* of the probation of yesterday. So the man of idleness, and intemperance, and vice, and crime, meets to-day the consequences which have travelled with him through the disturbed slumbers of the night; and he reaps the recompense of the conduct of the preceding day. Why should not the same thing go through the sleep of death—that sleep which we speak of as long, and quiet, and undisturbed—but which may not be, and which *is* not probably *a moment?* Why not rather? Death is not even sleep. It suspends nothing; arrests nothing. The unslumbering soul, in the fulness of its immortal energies, breaks from its clay tenement, and wings its way to God. Not one of its powers is annihilated; not one of its faculties sleeps. It goes a complete moral agent, with the character formed here, up to the bar of God; and while the living convey the body to the grave, and speak of *the sleep of death*, that immortal spirit has soared to higher regions, and is fully awake to sleep no more.

(2.) A second consideration showing that this is a state of probation is derived from the fact, that rewards and punishments here are not equally distributed. This fact is well known, and needs scarcely more than a passing remark. The force of the argument, I admit, proceeds on the supposition that God is a *just* Being—a fact which must here be taken for granted. If he is, nothing can be clearer than that there must be a future state, where virtue will be rewarded, and vice punished. The *fact* in regard to the point now before us is this:—The affairs of men are arrested *in the midst of their way.* The righteous are not always rewarded with health and happiness; nor are the wicked always punished. It may be true, that if men were to *live long enough* on earth, things would come near to adjusting themselves to what is right; but they are arrested. Had Paul, for example, lived to the present time, his name would have been clothed with all the honour which he could desire. Had the early martyrs lived, or had they been raised from their ashes to life again, all the honour which has clustered around their names—and it is all that any man could wish—might have gathered around them. But as it was, they died amidst contempt and scorn. So the world over. Virtue is often despised, persecuted, and neglected; vice triumphs, and riots, and revels, unrebuked and unpunished. Profaneness occupies a splendid dwelling; profligacy is elevated to office; perfidy and meanness and sensuality lie on a bed of down. Now all this looks to something future, and must be adjusted in some future world. No man can believe that under the government of a just God this state of things is to continue always; nor that those various characters either are to be, or should be, treated alike in the future world. The state of things on earth is *just such* as to keep before us as impressively as possible the truth that this is a world of probation, and it must be such, or the government of God is incapable of vindication.

(3.) The whole arrangement in the Bible, and in the plan of salvation, regards man as in a state of probation. It is but varying the mode while the same great object is kept steadily in view. Our first father, indeed, by a most rash and wicked deed, for ever prevented the possibility of reaching heaven by works. On that plan, we have reason to suppose, the angels stood, and were confirmed in bliss. But that single deed for ever prevented our race from obtaining heaven in *that* way. Still, the object was too great to be abandoned; and another mode is proposed in the gospel. The same object is in view—heaven; the same holiness is demanded; the same conformity to the will of God is required. The plan is varied—not abandoned. God plucked no jewel from the crown of glory; he abridged none of the joys of heaven; he dried up none of the fountains of life. He did not offer to man a tarnished crown, or diminished and faded joys. It is the same heaven still, in the fulness of its glory; the same crown; the same light; the same river of life; the same freedom from pain and woe. *The way of reaching it only is changed.* He proposes a new question—adapted to the new circumstances of man; but still as simple, and as easy of compliance as possible. It is, *whether men will repent and accept of heaven now as a gift;* whether they will believe the record which God has given of his Son, and embrace life without money and without price.

This is the question which is now before men. And this is the question which God is constantly pressing on their attention. By the preaching of the gospel; by his Spirit; by his providence; by all the means that can be devised, he is bringing this question home to the minds of men, and demanding a reply.

But is this state of things to continue always? Is this probation to be lengthened out and varied in some future world, or is it finally to close when the sinner leaves this state of being? An essential idea in the notion of probation is, that it is not to continue *always;* that it is to give place to *retribution,* and that present conduct is to *determine* the future destiny. Now, is the arrangement of the plan of redemption made on this supposition, or is it on the supposition that the state of things in which we now are, or a state of things similar to that, is to continue for ever? Is God again to send his Son to the lost and ruined, after the lapse of many ages, to be crucified again, and to make another atonement for sin? Is he to fill up eternity by ineffectual appeals and remonstrances, and by repeating invitations to be for ever rejected? Is he to send down his Spirit to strive *always* with men in this world and the next, and to be grieved and resisted for ever? No. This strange state of things must cease. There is to be no other sacrifice for sin. There is to be no other world where the Spirit of God will strive with men. There is not to be an eternal preaching of the Gospel—an eternal succession of appeals and remonstrances on the part of God. The period *must,* in the nature of things, come when this will cease, and the affairs of the world will be wound up. There is but one Great Sacrifice for sin; and when that has been fairly and fully presented to the mind according to the Divine purpose and arrangement, and has been rejected, the probation *must* then end. All the arrangements of the plan of redemption contemplate such a close; and the affairs of earth are moving on to such a consummation.

(4.) The doom of man may, with evident propriety, be fixed at the close of this life. What better world of probation could there be than this? What stronger inducements to holiness could be presented than are here set before man? What more simple and easy tests could be furnished than are furnished in the gospel? And though life is short, yet that "life is long which answers life's great end;" and the great end is to prepare for heaven. Though it *is* short, yet it is long enough to repent of sin, to embrace the gospel, and to secure an interest in the world of glory. Not the age of Methuselah is needful for that; for the child may embrace it, and the man of years might have embraced it a thousand times. His life has been long enough to reject the plan; and a life which is long enough to reject it, is long enough to embrace it. In regard to the reception or the rejection of the gospel, and in regard to the whole character of man, the question is fully tested by this life. What further trial is necessary for a man who has lived for eighty, or sixty, or fifty, or forty years; who has a thousand times been offered salvation; and who has as often rejected it? Why should it be necessary for him to live another eighty years to know what he is? What would be gained, either in justice or propriety, if that period were doubled or quadrupled? What would be gained if the same thing were to be rejected till time itself shall end? Is there any doubt about his character?

Here bear in mind one truth which all men are prone to forget. It does not require many years, or many deeds, to test the character, and show what man is. The prisoner in the cold dungeon condemned to die, that would treat the offer of pardon with scorn, if you can suppose such a case, does he not by that single act show what he is? Is it needful to go again and again, to submit to repeated neglect or insult in order to ascertain what he is? So of man. If pardon and heaven are fairly offered and are rejected, it is enough. It settles the question, and determines what the man is. And when the character is thus settled, why should not man die, and his eternal doom be fixed according to the deeds done in the body?

(5.) Lastly, I observe, that God regards men as on probation, and treats them accordingly. He offers them salvation; he treats them as moral agents; he sets life and death before them; he places them in circumstances where they must develope their character, and then he removes them to another world. What the nature of *that* world is, he has told us. As the tree falls, so it lies. He that is holy shall be holy still, and he that is filthy shall be filthy still. The one part shall go away into everlasting punishment, the other into life eternal. In all the volume of revelation, there is not the slightest hint on which ingenuity has ever fastened that intimates that there will be any other world of probation; not a hint that the Redeemer will again bleed, or that pardon will be offered there in virtue of his atonement made on earth; not an intimation that the sacred Spirit will ever be again sent to purify a polluted heart. As man dies, he is to continue for ever; and as his character is formed in this life, so must be his final doom.

My point I regard as established. It remains only, before I conclude, to entreat those whom I now address not to be deceived. God is not mocked, and he cannot be under any delusion in regard to what you are. He will judge you according to your true character; a character which is to be ascertained by the manner in which you treat his offer of mercy through Jesus Christ. No man need deceive himself on this point; no man need be lost. Nothing is plainer than the gospel of Christ; nothing more clear than what God requires you to do. It is, to repent and believe the gospel; to embrace the terms of mercy, and lead a holy life. To do that is to sow to the Spirit; not to do that is to sow to the flesh. And if instead of doing that, my fellow-sinner, you choose to pursue the ways of licentious and sensual pleasure; to give the reins to corrupt and corrupting passions; to make provision only for this life, I forewarn you that God will not be mocked in this thing; nor will he suppose that such a course *can* entitle you to reap everlasting life. You will reap corruption. You will gather the appropriate harvest of such a course. You are here for a little time—yet time long enough with reference to a future world; and you are every day, and hour, and moment, forming a character for that future world. Soon you will be there. Soon you will give up your account for *all* the deeds done in the body. To apprize you of that fact I now address you, with one more message announcing to you that you must soon give up your account, and assuring you once more that the great question which your Creator designs shall be settled, is not whether you are accomplished, or learned, or beautiful, or rich, or honoured; but whether you have embraced the offer of mercy through a Redeemer, and have truly repented of your sins. On the grave's brink you stand, and soon this question will be settled for ever; and I conjure you to act *for* eternity. For soon the harvest will be passed, and the summer ended—whether you are or are not saved.

SERMON VIII.

THE NECESSITY OF ACCOMMODATING OURSELVES TO THE ARRANGEMENTS OF THE DIVINE GOVERNMENT.

MATT. xxv. 26, 27.—"Thou knewest that I reap where I sowed not, and gather where I have not strawed: thou oughtest therefore to have put my money to the exchangers, and then at my coming I should have received mine own with usury."

THIS is a part of a parable; and its design is to illustrate the views which men who neglect religion have of the government and plans of God. The man who had failed to improve his one talent alleged as a reason that he who had committed it to him was unjust and severe in his exactions; and not being satisfied with the arrangements, he had buried it in the earth. The illustration evidently refers to those who fail to improve the talents committed to them; and who, when the Judge shall come to reckon with them, will be found to be unprepared.

The reason why they do this is some secret dissatisfaction with the government of God. They are not pleased with his law, his plan of salvation, or his requirements, and they make no effort to be prepared to meet him, and to give up their account. God's administration they regard as one where he reaps what he has not sown—a government severe, harsh, tyrannical. The answer of the man who had committed the talent to him who made the complaint was, that *knowing* what were the principles on which his affairs were administered, he OUGHT TO HAVE accommodated himself to them, and then he would have been rewarded like the others. We are not to suppose that the Saviour meant to admit that the charge which men bring against God is *just*, or that God is severe, harsh, or capricious in his requirements; but the idea is, that since men understand what are the principles of his government, and on what terms he will bestow favours, it is wise to comply with those terms, and not neglect their salvation:—"Thou knewest that I reap where I sowed not,—thou oughtest THEREFORE to have put my money to the exchangers!" You know what are the principles of the Divine government; you know on what terms God bestows salvation; you know that he is inflexible in those terms, even so much so as to seem stern and severe; you ought, therefore, with so much more anxiety to endeavour to comply with those terms, and to be prepared for your strict and solemn account.

In illustrating this sentiment, I shall,

I. In the first place, show what are the grounds of complaint among men about the government and plans of God; and,

II. That it is wise to comply with the actual state of things, and to seek his favour in the way which he has prescribed.

I. *What are the grounds of complaint among men about the government and plans of God?*

There are men who think the government of God, as described in the Bible, to be harsh and severe, who yet do not *mean* to regard God himself as a tyrant. They have no belief of the truth of the Bible, but suppose they have a view of the Divine government much more conformable to truth than that which is there represented. Yet these men do not *mean* to be regarded as infidels. They are known externally as respecters of religion; but the religion which they respect is not the religion of the Bible, but the semi-deistical system which they have formed in their minds;—that sentimental religion which floats before the fancy; the religion of nature which they think to be the true, the beautiful, and the reasonable, rather than that severe and harsh religion which denounces punishment, and which sternly requires repentance and faith on the penalty of being lost for ever. Yet even such men are not altogether free from regarding the government of God, contemplated under any view, as harsh and severe. There are some facts in the world which are about as difficult to manage as any of the doctrines of revelation; and even when man has rejected revelation, he is sometimes as much embarrassed in grappling with those facts as he would be with the doctrines of the Divine administration as developed in the Bible. Men do not get away from difficulty by rejecting Christianity.

The mass of men, whether they are among the speculative believers in the truth of the Bible or not, at heart are *complainers* in regard to the principles of the Divine administration. They are not satisfied with the government of God. They regard it as harsh and severe. And instead of accommodating themselves to what are undeniable facts, or to what is revealed as certainly true, they suffer the mind to accumulate complaints against God; to be chafed and soured by the operations of his government; and to cherish such views of him that it is impossible for them to love him. Before they can be reconciled to God it is necessary to remove those accumulated complaints and dissatisfactions; to show them that God is worthy of their confidence, and that he is qualified for universal empire; and this is often a more difficult task than it would be to clear away the rubbish from Babylon or Nineveh to find a place to lay a foundation on which to rear a wall or a dwelling.

Now the views which men actually cherish of the plans and government of God are something like the following:—

(1.) That his *law* is needlessly severe and stern. "I knew thee that thou art an hard man" was the language of the complainer in the text. A law of some kind they would not object to; but the law that condemns all sin; that attempts to control the feelings; that takes cognizance of the motives; that frowns on the most trivial offences; that makes no apology for the infirmities of men, and for the strength of passion, and for an original propensity to a certain course of thought or life, they feel is needlessly severe. That God should hold them answerable for each idle word, and for the roving of a wanton eye, and for the least stain of pollution on the heart, and for the slightest wandering of the fancy from pure objects, they hold to be unreasonably hard and stern.

(2.) That the law of God should have such a penalty as it has. To some penalty they would not object; for they see it appended to all laws. But the penalty which denounces eternal death for every offence; which dooms a sinner to infinite and unending pain without respite and without hope; which never speaks of mitigation or end, seems to them to be horrible, and they do not scruple to cherish the feeling in their hearts, though they for various reasons would not choose to express it openly, that a being who can deliberately affix such a penalty to his law is wholly unworthy of the confidence of the universe.

(3.) Men suppose that his government is arbitrary. That he governs by will,—not by reason; that he has formed an eternal plan and ordained an unchangeable decree, and then attempts to treat men and to punish them as though they were free—though he knew that they could not do otherwise if they would.

(4.) That he requires much more of them than they can perform; that he requires them to love him and serve him with a perfect heart, when he does not give them the grace to enable them to do it. This, perhaps, is the leading thought in the text: "Thou art an hard man, reaping where thou hast not sown, and gathering where thou hast not strawed." The idea is, that God does not give grace, and yet exacts as pure and perfect love as that of the angels; that "the tale of bricks is not diminished aught though no straw be given," Exod. v. 7, 8. *Some* service they would be willing to render to God; but to demand a service of entire obedience where no grace is given—a service of perfect love, when God confers none of the influences needful for it, which they regard as the nature of his government—they consider as a tyranny.

(5.) That he requires them to forsake pleasures which are harmless, and to practise austerities which are needless; that he demands a separation from the common pursuits in which men are engaged, which is required by no dictates of reason; that he insists on a devotion to religion of time, and property, and influence, and feeling, which interferes with the real happiness of men; and that he claims from the heart and the life a slavish devotion to his cause which would interfere much with rational enjoyment and solid happiness. To the rendering of an external service they would have little objection; to the bowing of the knee at stated times they would have no reluctance; to a devotion to the interests of religion which would be consistent with the ordinary and accustomed pleasures of life, they would not seriously demur; but when the demand comes for the *whole* body, soul, and spirit to be employed in his service; for the consecration to God of the "*talent*," though single, to him only, they object as being needlessly unreasonable and severe, and they say of him that they "know that his government is hard—he reaps where he has not sown, he gathers where he has not strawed."

(6.) The same thing is felt in regard to the terms of salvation. It is a "hard" administration, they feel, that they are not permitted to rely on their own morality, and that even the most amiable and upright life is to go for nothing in the matter of justification before God. To *some* conditions of salvation they would not object; and any service which an amiable disposition, or an honest life, or a fair character would confer, they would not be unwilling to render. But why should repentance be demanded of him who feels that he has nothing, or almost nothing, of which to repent? Why make this an indispensable condition to him who has been upright and fair all his life? And why require faith as the sole condition of salvation of him who feels that he really deserves some other doom than that of inextinguishable fires? Why must he come and be saved in the same way with the most vile of the species, and confess his dependence on the merits of the Redeemer in a manner as absolute and entire as the most degraded son or daughter of Adam? That all his morals, his amiableness, his integrity, his self-culture, his self-discipline, his temperance, his purity, his reputation, his character acquired by a life of many years of steady virtue, should go for nothing in the matter of salvation, seems to him "hard," and he is ready to accuse the government of God as being unreasonable and severe.

(7.) He has another difficulty still. The government of God, he feels, is arbitrary in the dispensation of favours. To one he gives five talents, to another two, to another one. On one he bestows great endowments, and from others he withholds them. To one he gives his Holy Spirit, from another he withholds this gift. The mind of one he makes tender, and that of another he leaves as hard as adamant. One is converted by his almighty power, and another is left in his sins. One is chosen to life, and another is passed over and doomed to death. To one he gives grace to become a Christian, and to another not; and yet of all it is said he requires the same service, demands in all the same faith, and condemns to woe in all cases where he affords no help to avoid it. This, says he, is a "hard" government; this is a hard master to serve. It is "reaping where he has not sown, and gathering where he has not strawed," and the talent is hid in the earth. No effort is made to improve it; no desire is felt to comply with the requisition of such a government—and many secretly go back from this view to that to which I have already adverted—to what seems to them a more plausible and rational system—the system of semi-infidelity—a system of religion which every man forms for himself.

At this stage of the argument it is not improper to pause and ask you, my friends, whether I have given an account of any feelings which you will recognise as your own. I have intended not to do injustice to the objection which is felt—*felt* rather than avowed. Can you not discover here some of the operations of your own minds, as if some one had been reading what you had supposed to be hidden thoughts in the chambers of your own souls? That there are such feelings there I have no doubt; that they are feelings which ought not to be cherished *you* would show by your unwillingness to avow them. But *if* there, they are standing in the way of your salvation, and you will not become Christians, whatever else you may be, till they are removed. I propose to meet these feelings in what I have yet to say, and I shall do you an essential service if I can contribute anything towards removing them.

There are two questions about the plans and government of God. The one is, whether his arrangement is a wise and good one; the other is, whether, being what it is, it is not wise and best for us to accommodate ourselves to it, and avail ourselves of the arrangements which actually exist, even though we cannot exactly see that they are the best. The latter is the point now before us.

II. My second proposition is, *that it is wise to fall in with the actual state of things, and seek the favour of God in the way which he has prescribed.* "Thou knewest that I reap where I sowed not,—thou OUGHTEST THEREFORE to have put my money to the exchangers." Let us paraphrase this:—'Thou knowest that God has given a law which is holy, and strict in its requirements; thou knowest that he has appointed the penalty of eternal death on its violation; thou knowest that he requires a holy and obedient life; thou knowest that he bestows salvation only on the conditions of repentance and faith; and thou knowest that he dispenses his favours only according to his sovereign will. Even if this *seems* severe and stern, yet, knowing that these are the unchangeable laws of the Divine administration, thou *oughtest* THEREFORE to comply with them, and be prepared to meet him and render up thy account.' This sentiment I shall illustrate by several considerations, which I trust will not only close the mouth of the objector, but carry conviction to the understanding and the heart.

(1.) The first is this:—It is the way in which you act in other things. In those things you act without complaint, and yet complaint would be as reasonable there as here. The whole of life indeed is little else than this:—finding out what are *in fact* the laws on which the affairs of the universe are administered, and then complying with them. We find out what will support life, and then we go to work and raise the fruit and the breadstuffs needful for that support. Do men complain that they have to do it even by the sweat of their brow? We ascertain what are the laws of health, and then we make use of the means to preserve or restore it. Do men prefer to die because they are not satisfied with those laws, or because they do not understand them? A company of men wish to construct a railway or a canal. What do they do? They estimate the expense, and the difficulties, and the advantage. They take the level and look out for the best route, and *accommodate* themselves to the condition of the country. If there is a hill, instead of complaining, they level it; if a valley, they fill it up; if a stream, they build a bridge; if a fen or morass, they go across or around it. But why not sit down and complain that God did not make railroads and canals, and that he made hills and vales and rivers and morasses? A merchant needs the produce of distant lands. What does he do? He *finds out* the laws of navigation, and seeks to understand the theory of currents and winds and storms, and *accommodates* himself to them. He builds a ship fitted to the navigation of distant seas, and seeks to get within the influence of favourable gales, and prepares for the billows and tempests that he has reason to suppose he must encounter. But why not complain that God made such wastes of waters, and that he raises up a storm or makes the billows roll? A man purposes to become a farmer. The piece of land which he buys is covered with the forest, where the sunbeams have never looked down through the thick foliage on the soil. What does he do? He *accommodates* himself to the case, shoulders his axe, and tree after tree is laid low; and he ploughs and fences his land and gathers out the stones, and ascertains the nature of the soil and adapts the seed to it, and raises cotton on that which will produce cotton, and wheat on that which will produce wheat, and lentiles on that which will produce lentiles. We dread the lightning. What do we do? We find out what its laws are, and accommodate ourselves to them, and the rod conducts it harmless to the earth. So in lands where earthquakes are feared, what do men do? They build their houses low, they put them where they will be safe, and they *accommodate* themselves to the laws of nature. Thus men act in food and raiment, houses, commerce, agriculture, and the arts. The man in Greenland, who builds his house of ice, and he in Kamskatka, who makes his in the earth, and he at the Equator, who seeks a shelter at noonday behind some cool projecting rock, all *accommodate* themselves to the laws of nature. Our whole life is little else. This is all our philosophy; all our practical wisdom in living; all that distinguishes the refined from the savage portions of the world. It is simply that, knowing what are the laws of nature or of God, we accommodate ourselves to them—and we have learned that it is as well to do it without complaining. All that is asked now is, that the same thing should be done in religion. Why should it not be?

(2.) My second observation is this,—that we cannot change the arrangements of Providence, and that, knowing what they are, it is the part of wisdom to accommodate ourselves to them. A wise man will comply with what he cannot help, unless it can be shown to be wrong to do so. To refuse to do this is to make himself miserable to no benefit, and life will be spent in the employment of "gnawing a file." If men by resistance could *change* the actual order of things; if they could reverse what are now facts, and substitute what would meet their views in place of what actually occurs, the case would be different. But if they can do none of these things, what is the way of wisdom?

A man is dissatisfied that there are tempests and head winds on the ocean. Will his displeasure calm the billows or still the storm? He is dissatisfied that there are hills, and morasses, and floods, and earthquakes on land. Will his displeasure change any of these things? What is the path of the wise in such cases? Is it not to act *as if* these things were so, and to accommodate ourselves to them; and since there are tempests and storms on the deep, to act as if it were so, and build our ships so as to be safe in them; and on the land to act as if there were hills and rocks and streams, and when they cannot be removed make the best of actual circumstances? So a man grows old, and his head becomes white—blossoming for the grave. The course of events is onward, and he cannot make one white hair black again, or roll back the wheels of life a day or an hour. What is the path of wisdom? It is to act as if he were to be old, and to accommodate himself to this fact? Will his displeasure at it change the fact? So in regard to the laws of property. They are settled laws. If a man wishes to be prospered in the world, as a general thing the way is by industry, and temperance, and honesty, and straightforward dealing. This is so well understood that it may be regarded as settled. What is the way of wisdom? Is it to *brave* this settled law, and set himself against the course of events, and attempt to be rich and happy, and at the same time idle, and intemperate, and dishonest, and crooked in his dealings? Men do not act thus; and though it may require much self-denial and many hardships, yet they submit to the settled course of events, and are industrious and sober and upright *in order* to be rich and happy. If they do *not* choose to accommodate themselves to the course of events, those events will move on still; man cannot change them. Seed time and harvest, summer and winter, cold and heat succeed each other just as though the complainer had no existence.

So in the case before us, there are settled principles in the Divine administration. There are certain facts. There is a course of events which we cannot change. There is a revealed way of salvation. Are these things changed if men oppose them, or refuse to act as if they were so? Not one of them. Men are dissatisfied that sin is in the world, and murmur that God permitted it. Is the fact changed at all? Is it not just as mighty and loathsome and ruinous in your soul as if it were admitted that God was right in all that he had done? Men think the law of God harsh and severe. Is the course of events under the administration of that law changed? You deny that there is a judgment. What effect has this on the *fact* of the judgment? Is the judgment-seat likely to be swept away because you do not choose to believe what is said of it? You think it hard that there is a hell. And what then? Are its fires extinguished because you choose to think so? You doubt the truth of the Bible. And what then? Is it any the less true? And suppose you could prove that it were false, what would follow then? Would it change the fact that man is a sinner, and that he is miserable, and that he is to die, and that eternity is to be dreaded, and that the apostasy has filled the world with griefs and tears? Not one of them. The Bible has created none of these woes. They are sad, melancholy *facts*, whether the Bible be true or false, and your destroying the Bible would make no change in regard to these facts. Now what is wise in such a case? It is to accommodate ourselves to these facts, and act as if they were so. The course of nature must bend, or we must. But can we stand up against the course of events and act as if they were not so?

(3.) The third consideration is, that there is no reason to believe man can be saved in any other way than by compliance with the plan which God has prescribed, and it is wise, therefore, to conform to his terms. God has, for illustration, told the farmer how he may have a harvest. It is by a proper cultivation of his soil, by seasonably ploughing, and sowing, and tilling his fields. But if he choose to spend the time of ploughing and sowing in bed, or in the place of dissipation, nothing prevents his doing it; but will God work a miracle to accommodate his love of idleness or dissipation, and give him a harvest? God has told a young man how he may become learned. It is by patient and persevering study. But if he chooses to waste the time of study in sleep, or with the idle, nothing prevents his doing it; but will God work a miracle and make him by inspiration a Parr or a Porson? He has told us how we may, as a great law, enjoy health. It is by temperance in eating and drinking, by exercise, by a good conscience, by avoiding the excesses of passion, and guarding from needless exposures. But if we choose to neglect these salutary rules, and pursue a life just the opposite, will God work a miracle for our accommodation? So in all things, God has appointed certain conditions of his favour in health, morals, reputation, property, salvation. Man, a free agent, can neglect them all. But will God bend the laws of the universe to us? Will he work a succession of miracles to accommodate our indolence, our selfishness, our sensuality, our pride, our distrust of his wisdom and goodness?

No. The fixed laws of nature and of grace move on, and if, by our conforming ourselves to them, they do not bear us to affluence, and virtue, and reputation, and heaven, they will sweep us on to poverty, and rags, and disgrace, and the drunkard's grave, and to hell. And knowing what they are, we ought THEREFORE to accommodate ourselves to what we know is to be the result.

Now, in regard to the particular matter before us, many have been dissatisfied with the Bible, and have rejected it. Have they therefore been safe, and have they gone to heaven? *That remains to be proved.* Neither the heaven nor the earth; neither God nor angels; neither their own lives nor their death-beds have given any evidence of it. What *is* the proof that they were saved? Is it such that you and I can feel that our immortal interests are safe if we do the same thing? Many have refused to repent and believe the gospel, and have lived and died thus. What is the evidence that they have not been 'lost,' as the Saviour said they would be? Is it such that we can feel ourselves safe in doing the same thing? Many have been living in the neglect of religion, and have died thus. They were opposed in heart to the law of God and to its penalty. They doubted the wisdom of his administration. They hardened themselves when the gospel was preached and when salvation was proclaimed. What is the proof that they were saved? Where, where shall we look for it? Is it such that it would be safe to risk the welfare of our souls upon it? What sign is there in the sky which says that they are there? Has a new star appeared, as it was said there did when Cæsar died, to show that they are gone to heaven? Has an angel come forth and written their names among the constellations? Think not this extravagant. If I am to be safe if I am an infidel, an impenitent sinner, a wicked man, a neglecter of prayer, and a despiser of the cross, I wish to have some evidence that they who have done the same thing before me were safe and are now happy. I look about for the proofs. They are not in the sky. I see no sign there; I hear no voice. I go to their graves. I see no reason to credit the flattering epitaph on their gravestones that they went to heaven. I see them not coming back from the world of glory to tell me they are blessed. I ask, where is the evidence, where on a dying bed, at their graves,—in all the universe, where is the evidence that *I* may live thus and be safe? I see none; I hear none; I am told of none, even by those who are expecting to be saved in the same way. And then you ask me what evidence *I* have that the man who repents and believes will be saved. I *have* evidence. It may not seem strong to you; it is clear to me; and yourself being judge, it is better than none. It is in the promises of the Bible; in the voice of inspiration; in the resurrection of the Redeemer; in his assurance that his people shall be with him; and nothing yet has occurred in regard to the influence of his gospel, to the living virtues or the dying peace of his friends, to shake my belief that it *will* be so. I see them die just *as if* they were going to heaven—so peaceful, so calm, so happy, that I cannot doubt that they are safe. Knowing what are the terms on which God bestows eternal life, they have conformed to those principles, and their lives and death have been all that could be demanded on the supposition that they were going to heaven.

(4.) My fourth consideration is, that the arrangements by which God proposes to save men are not unreasonable, or such as to throw any insuperable barrier in their way, and they should therefore conform to them. It was no impracticable thing that was required of the man with the one talent. Was it beyond his power to put the money to the exchangers? So we say of the terms of salvation. Are they impossible to be complied with? Are they so stern, so severe, so much beyond the human powers as to put eternal life beyond our reach? I could make a long argument on this point, but I shall not enter now upon it. I will settle it by two or three questions:—Who are they that believe and are saved? Children; the ignorant; slaves, as well as the learned and the great. Is that impossible for you which may be done by your child?—that, beyond your power, which has been done by many a poor, benighted heathen, by the savage, by the man in bonds? What does God require of you? Does he say, Go on a pilgrimage over oceans to visit some far distant shore? No. He says, "Come unto me!" Does he ask money? No. "Come without money and without price." Does he ask painful penance? Just as much as you do of your child, when he has done wrong, that he will confess and forsake it. Does he demand a hard service? He asks confidence in the great and glorious Saviour; a pure heart and life; a meek, gentle, holy walk; hands free from bribes, and a heart without covetousness and sensuality; a spirit of kindness, and forbearance, and forgiveness; love, pure, glowing, steady to himself and to all mankind. Is this hard? Is it stern? Is it severe?

We are conducted to these conclusions:—

(1.) Religion requires humility. It demands of us that the intellect should be bowed and the will subdued. *We* must bend, and not God; our hearts must yield, and not his principles of government; we must accommodate ourselves to the settled course of events, and not require them to be accommodated to us. As the first thing in religion, therefore, we may say that humility is required, and we might go on to say of it, as Demosthenes said of *action*, that it is the *second* thing and the *third* thing. And yet it is no more than is required anywhere else. It is the condition of our being—the law of our nature. We must yield to the settled course of events on our farms, in commerce, and in our health, and why should we not in religion? Why pause and hesitate only here?

(2.) Yielding must be wholly on our side. God will not yield, nor should he. His terms are settled and understood, and he will not depart from them, nor should he. The universe would not be safe should he depart from the great principles of his administration, nor is there any reason why he should do it. If we have any safety, it is in the assurance that he does not change, and that the principles of his government are always the same.

(3.) Finally, the sum of the whole matter is this:—We must comply with the terms which he has provided for salvation, or be lost. Those terms must be met exactly, and nothing can be substituted in their place. He demands of us repentance, and faith in the Lord Jesus. He solemnly assures us that "he that believeth not shall be damned," and has said, "Except ye repent ye shall all likewise perish." There is, therefore, my friends, a simple question before your minds at this time—a question as I believe of vital interest to your souls. It is, whether, knowing the principles of the Divine government, and the terms on which God will save men, you are willing to accommodate yourselves to those terms and be saved, or whether you will, dissatisfied and murmuring, bury your talent in the earth. That question is now before you for decision. That it is a momentous question I need not say. Believing, as I do, that on it depends the eternal weal or woe of every one who hears me now; that the decision is to enter into all that there is of joy or woe beyond the grave; that we are sinners, lost, ruined, and condemned, and that these are the terms of pardon, and these only, how can I neglect to urge it upon you with affectionate entreaty? The great, the momentous subject I leave with you. Above us is heaven and immortal glory, to be obtained by us only on certain conditions, which God has made known. Beneath us is the world of despair, to be avoided only on certain terms, which God has prescribed. Just before us is the grave, where there is no work, and in which no offer of life and salvation is made on any terms, and where the everlasting doom is sealed for ever. Dying friends, oh how soon shall we be there!

SERMON IX.

THE STATE IN WHICH THE GOSPEL FINDS MAN.

MATT. xviii. 11.—"The Son of man is come to save that which was lost."

ALL men, with exceptions too few to be taken into the general account, have some scheme of salvation. The exceptions relate to the very few cases where individuals are in a state of despair; or where, either from physical disease, or from some perverted view of the truths of religion, they have abandoned all hope of happiness in the world to come. With these very few exceptions, there are none who do not expect to be happy beyond the grave. The proof of this is plain. It is found in the composure with which men look at eternity; the indifference which they manifest when warned of a coming judgment; the cool and unperturbed spirit with which they pursue the things of this life, whether they are serious things or mere trifles; the unconcern which they evince when told of eternal sorrows. It requires the utmost strength of human hardihood when a criminal looks with no paleness of the features, and no trembling of the limbs, on the gibbet where he is soon to be executed; and no man *could* look on eternal sorrow with a belief that it is to be his own, and be unmoved. When we see men, therefore, wholly unconcerned about their eternal state; men, though professing to believe that there *is* a place of future woe, wholly unalarmed and unmoved, the fair inference is, that not one word of the statements about future woe is believed, and that they have some secret scheme by which they hope to be saved at last. Either by works of righteousness which they have done; or in virtue of the native amiableness of their character; or because they have done no injury to others; or because they believe that it would be wrong for God to consign them to an eternal hell; or because they confide in what they regard as the illimitable compassion of God, they expect to be saved, and, therefore, give themselves no trouble about it. It is not, it cannot be human nature to believe that eternal pain is to be our portion, and still to sit unmoved. Still less can men believe this and be cheerful and gay. Every man, therefore, must have some secret scheme by which he hopes to be saved.

Yet, there can be but one method of salvation that is true. If the Christian plan is true, then all others are false; if they are true, then that is false. If there are other schemes by which man can be saved, then there was no need of the Sacrifice on the cross, and the scheme proposed in the gospel is an imposture. The admission, then, that the Christian religion is true—an admission which sinners often so readily and so thoughtlessly make—is a condemnation of all other systems, and shuts out all who are not interested in the plan of the gospel from all hope of heaven.

On this account, if on no other, therefore, it cannot but be a matter of importance to know what the plan of salvation proposed in the gospel is. The previous discourses have been designed, in part, to prepare the way for this by considering certain states of the mind in regard to religion; by removing certain difficulties felt by men on the subject, and by stating certain presumptive claims which Christianity has on the attention of men. It seemed proper to do this before attempting to show specifically what the plan of salvation revealed in the gospel is; and having done that, the way is now prepared for a more definite statement of the scheme of salvation proposed in the gospel, or the mental process through which a sinner passes when he embraces the plan. In doing this, I wish to take out this scheme from all others, and to show what it *is*, so that a man who asks what he shall do to be saved, may understand what, according to this scheme, is to be done; what is required of him; what hindrances he will meet, and what encouragements will be held out to him: what, in one word, according to this scheme, is the method by which God proposes to bring a sinner to heaven.

I begin, of course, with a consideration of the state in which the gospel finds man; and the general statement which I make on this point is, that God's plan of saving men is based on the fact that the race is by nature destitute of holiness. If this were not so, there would have been no necessity for the scheme. Men would have possessed full capability of saving themselves. If men before or since the promulgation of this plan had any elements of holiness in their character, or any traits which could by their own skill be wrought into a texture of righteousness; or if there was remaining in the human soul any *germ* of goodness which could by culture be developed into holiness; or if there was any slumbering spark of piety that needed only to be uncovered and fanned into a flame, then the design of interposing in the manner revealed in the gospel would have been unnecessary, and would not have occurred. For then all that would have been needful would have been to leave the race to themselves, with only such moral encouragement as would stimulate them to effort, or with such aid as would enable them to unfold the germ of piety in the soul, as they now cultivate the intellectual powers, or as they cultivate a plant from a seed sown in a garden. This is very far from being the gospel scheme.

But it is of the last importance that we should understand what is meant when it is said that God's plan of saving men is based on the fact that the race is destitute of holiness. There are things which men try to do in religion which they cannot do, and are, therefore, not required to do; there are instructions given to men seeking to be saved, which the nature of the human mind forbids any one to follow, and which ought not to be followed; there are statements made on this point which no man can believe to be true, hard as he may try to think them true, and much as he may endeavour to blame himself because he does not; there are acts for which a man thinks he ought to condemn himself, when after all his struggling he cannot work himself up to feel one particle of guilt; and there are doctrines which men are sometimes taught that they ought to believe, which are so obviously and palpably false, that in trying to believe them they become disgusted with the entire system, and renounce the whole together. After all the efforts which men make to credit absurdities, there are things which the human mind can believe, and those which it cannot; there are things which we can repent of, and those which we cannot. In a certain state of mind, and under a certain kind of teaching, a man often works himself up into a belief that he *ought* to feel guilty, when he cannot; and often blames himself in this respect, when he ought to feel that he is acting perfectly right. And so, on the other hand, there are cases where a man resists the conviction of guilt when he ought to feel it, and does just as much injustice to his own nature by refusing to be penitent, as he did in the other case by trying to repent. How, then, is a man who wishes to be saved to regard himself on this point? What is he held to be guilty of? what not?

In the answer to these questions, I shall, first, state to you what you are not to regard yourselves as guilty of; and then, secondly, what is to be regarded as the real state of the soul by nature in respect to God and religion. I can most conveniently, and with no want of respect for you, use the style of direct address.

(1.) First, then, you are not held to be guilty of the sin of Adam, nor is repentance for that, in any proper sense, to enter into your repentance if you are saved according to the way of salvation provided in the gospel. I do not mean by this that you are not involved seriously in the consequences of his apostacy—for, except in the notion of personal guilt in the matter, I would go as far as any man in holding that you are so; but that you are not to regard yourselves as personally *blameworthy* on account of what he has done, and that you need not try to feel, and that you are not to reflect on yourselves if you cannot feel that you are. If a man ever *does* work himself up into the belief that he is guilty, or blameworthy, or responsible for the sin of Adam, it is simply a *delusion* of his mind: harmless in some respects, but hurtful so far as he supposes that any *piety* grows out of it—for no true religion grows out of a falsehood, and so far as it tends to modify his views of the character of God. In a sound and healthy state of the mind, it is impossible that a man should feel guilty or blameworthy for any sins but his own. He may be affected in his person, character, happiness, or property, and in some sense in his reputation, by the sin of another; he may greatly regret it, and may weep over it as a calamity, and may feel himself humbled by it on account of his relation to the offender; but he can never feel in regard to it as he does in regard to his own sins; he can never weep for it as he does in view of his own personal guilt. God, in the constitution of the human mind, has fixed bounds on this subject more impassable than are those which restrain the ocean. You feel guilty for your own sins; you do not, you cannot for the sin of another. The feeling with which you regard your own sin, and the feeling with which you regard the sin of another, are as distinct as any two classes of feeling possible, and they can never be confounded, and they are not to be intermingled in a plan of salvation. I believe that the Bible does not hold you to be blameworthy, or responsible, or in the proper sense of the term *guilty*, for the sin of Adam, or of any other man. I am certain that your conscience does not hold you thus guilty. It is a simple matter of fact that you cannot *make* yourself feel guilty of that, however much you may try to, and however often you may be told that you must. The act was *his* act, not yours; the disobedience was his, not yours; the responsibility was his, not yours. It took place nearly six thousand years before you were born: you were not there; you had no agency in it whatever—and you cannot make yourself feel personally guilty for it, and are not to try to do so in the matter of salvation. You may lament it—may feel its effects—may weep over those effects; but you are not to lament this, to feel this, to weep over this, as a personal crime—

for you cannot do it. That is a separate feeling—limited and bounded as distinctly as any feeling which the mind ever has, and never going outside of the consciousness of personal criminality. I shall endeavour to show you that you have enough to lament and weep over, without attempting to burden yourself with this. Settle it, then, as an elementary principle in the way of salvation, that repentance must be limited to personal guilt, and that you can feel condemned only for your own sins—not for the sin of another.

(2.) You are not to suppose that it is necessary in order to salvation, that you should feel that you are as bad as you can be. I am saying that the plan of salvation in the gospel is based on the idea that the race is destitute of holiness:—but I am not saying that it is based on the idea that the sinner is as bad as he can be, or that it is necessary to true repentance that he should suppose that he is. I do not know that it could be affirmed of any one of our race that has yet lived, that he was in all respects, at all times, and in all his relations, as wicked a man as he could have been, any more than it can be affirmed of any one, the Saviour excepted, that he was in all respects, and at all times, as good as he could be. I am sure that this is not true of the great mass of those to whom the gospel is preached, and who do exercise true repentance: and I do not mean to say to you, therefore, that in order to be saved, it is necessary that you should feel that you are as bad as you can be. It is simply *not true.* You might be much worse. You might be more profane, more sensual, more proud, more irritable, more covetous. You might have deeper feelings of malignity against God, and deeper hatred for man. You might be openly corrupt as well as corrupt at heart; and you might be more corrupt at heart than you are. There are in the soul of the most abandoned man some remains of decency—I do not say of holiness—that might be obliterated, so that he would be worse than he is; there is in the most debased and wretched female, now an outcast, some lingering of a generous and noble feeling—I do not say of love to God—that might be quenched, so that she would be more depraved than she is. It is true that under deep conviction—under very highly wrought feeling—and when the floods of remembered guilt come rolling over the soul, the sinner does sometimes feel that he has been as bad as he could be, and that all the past in his life has been the blackness of the deepest criminality with nothing to relieve the picture. But this is the prompting of feeling—perhaps an unavoidable feeling in the case;—it is not the conviction of the sober judgment. And it is true, perhaps, that convicted sinners *try* sometimes to make themselves feel so, and suppose that they *ought* to feel so; but they should be told that it is not *true*, and that all real piety is based on *truth*, not on pious falsehood. It is true, indeed, that under the deepest conviction which an awakened sinner ordinarily feels, it may with propriety be told him that he is worse at heart than he really supposes himself to be; that there is a depth of depravity in his soul which has not yet been seen or developed, and that he might dread the revelation of the truth; but it is not true that it is *necessary* in order to be saved that he should work himself up into the belief that he is as bad as he can be, or that he should charge upon himself sins of which he has never been guilty.

Nor, for the same reason, is it necessary that you should regard yourself as worse than all others. It is true that Paul felt that he was "the chief of sinners," and it is true that a similar conviction *may* come over the minds of others. But this is not necessary to genuine repentance, simply (*a*) because it is not *true* in the case of the great mass of those who become really penitent; and (*b*) because it is not necessary to true repentance that we should compare ourselves with others in any respect. Genuine repentance, and a just view of ourselves, are not based in any degree on such a comparison with other men, but must arise from the contemplation of our own character as compared with the law of God.

(3.) When we say that the plan of salvation in the gospel is based on the supposition that the race is destitute of holiness, it is not meant that in any of its arrangements it is implied that the sinner is guilty for not doing that which he had no power to do. The sense of guilt is, by the constitution of the human mind, as accurately limited in this respect as it is in the cases already referred to. A man can no more feel guilty for not doing that which he had no power to do, than he can for what is done by another. In all cases where there is, in the common sense of the term, a want of ability, there is no obligation, and there can be no sense of guilt if the thing is not done: and no method of *reasoning* can change this conviction of the human soul. There is no way by which you could convince a man that he is under obligation to create a world, or to remove a mountain, or to raise the dead; or by which you could convince him that he is guilty if he does not do it. And so, for the same reason, and to the same extent precisely, there is no method of reasoning by which you can convince a man that he is under obligation to believe if he cannot believe, or to love if he cannot love, or to repent if he cannot repent, or to obey if he cannot obey; or by which you can make him feel the genuine compunctions of guilt if, under these circumstances, he does *not* believe, repent, love, and obey.* He may profess to be convinced, but he is not convinced; he may fancy that he feels guilt, but he does not feel it. The human mind was not so made as to be approached in that manner, and religion makes its advances in the world in accordance with the laws of the mind, and not against them. Obligation is limited by ability; and the consciousness of criminality is always bounded by the feeling that we have omitted to do what we might have done, or have done what we had the power of abstaining from doing.

(4.) When we say that the gospel plan of salvation is based on the fact that the race is destitute of holiness, we are not to be understood as teaching that there are no amiable qualities in the minds of sinners, or that there is nothing that can in any sense be commended. Of the Saviour it is said respecting a young man who came to him, and who afterwards showed that he had no real piety, that "beholding him, he *loved* him" (Mark x. 21); and with all the real, and genuine, and ardent piety of John, there is no reason to believe that it was solely on this account that the Saviour loved him. It is not improper to suppose that Peter, and some of the other apostles, had as sincere love to the Saviour as John had, and that they were willing to make as many sacrifices for him as the "beloved disciple" would, and that they as cheerfully laid down their lives for the Master as he would have done; but it is not improper to suppose—indeed we cannot help believing—that there was a native modesty, gentleness, meekness, amiableness in the character of John that bore a strong resemblance to these traits in the mind of the Saviour himself, and that made him peculiarly the object of endearment. So it may be, so it is, of others. It is not asserted by the friends of the Christian religion, that there is no morality, no parental or filial affection, no kindness or compassion, no courteousness or urbanity, no love of truth, and no honest dealing among unconverted men. The friends of religion cannot be blind to the existence of these qualities in a high degree in society, nor are they slow to value them, or to render them appropriate honours. Yet they suppose that all these things may exist, and may diffuse a charm over society, and promote many of the ends of social life, and still that there may be an utter destitution of all right feeling toward God. They suppose that it is possible that a man may be very kind to the poor, and

* The reference here, perhaps it need hardly be said, is to *natural* and not to what is called *moral* inability. My views on this subject are more fully given in a subsequent discourse.

very just in his dealings with others, and still have a heart of pride, and selfishness, and envy, and be an entire neglecter of God; that a man may be upright in his intercourse with his neighbours, and have no right feelings towards his Maker; that a youthful female may be very accomplished, and very gentle, and very winning in her manners, and yet never pray, or in any proper way acknowledge God. Yet, when the heart is under the deepest convictions for sin—when crushed and broken by the consciousness of guilt, as that of the most amiable and gentle person may be, whether male or female—it is not necessary that the mind should be blind to these qualities, or that the convicted sinner should "write bitter things against himself" on account of them. He is no *worse* for having possessed them, and if they will not *save* him, they will at least not be charged against him as a fault.

With these necessary metes and bounds on the subject, which it seemed proper to state, I proceed now to illustrate the general statement that, in the plan of salvation, God regards men as destitute of holiness. The remainder of this discourse will be occupied with a statement showing in what respects this is true.

The foundation and the sum of all that I have to say is, that you are *destitute* of true piety towards God. Whatever else you may have, there is nothing that can be construed as holiness of heart; nothing that is properly the Divine image in the soul. But, lest you should suppose that I am using a mere theological technicality, I would explain this as meaning that there is in your heart no real love to God; no true desire to honour him; no just appreciation of his character; no confidence in him as your Creator; no proper regard for his will; no pleasure in the principles of his government; no desire to please him. This view does not deny to you the possession of much that is amiable and kind in other respects; it simply denies that there is in you "any good thing towards the Lord God of Israel."

It is undeniable that it is on this view that the whole plan of salvation is based, and that that plan has grown out of this view, and is *adjusted* to it. If it had been supposed that man were not fallen, no plan of salvation would have been provided, for none would have been necessary any more than for the angels of heaven; if it had not been supposed that the race is by nature entirely destitute of holiness, then the plan, if one had been formed, would have been wholly different from what it is now. If it had been presumed that there was any *germ* of goodness in the soul, then the plan would have been to *develop* that germ—as we now seek to expand the intellectual powers by education. If it had been supposed that the amiable qualities of the mind were in any sense of the word true piety, or could be transmuted into piety, then the plan would have been to *attach* these qualities to religion, or to embody them in some form of religion. If it had been supposed that there were some remains of piety dormant in the soul—some slumbering and almost smothered spark of goodness—that needed only to be brought out and fanned to a flame, then the scheme of salvation would have been simply a device to accomplish that object. But it is not so: it is impossible to explain the plan of salvation on the supposition that it is so. The way of salvation in the gospel does not contemplate that. You may take the supposition that man is destitute of holiness, and that he is so regarded by the Author of the scheme, and you can explain every part of the arrangement as having grown out of that supposition—just as you can explain the science of the healing art on the supposition that man is liable to disease, and can explain it on no other. If you do not admit that supposition in regard to the character of man, you can explain nothing in the gospel; you can see no propriety in any of its arrangements. By a simple glance at the subject, you can see what I shall more fully explain hereafter, that on this supposition all that is said in connexion with that plan about the atonement—the new birth—the work of the Holy Spirit—the doctrine of justification by faith, has a place and a meaning: what place what signification, have they on any other supposition? The way of salvation, as revealed in the gospel, is *adjusted* to the idea that the race is destitute of holiness, and to no other view of the character of our race. I lay this, therefore, at the foundation. If this is not so, the whole plan is uncalled for and unmeaning, and, therefore, having taken a wrong view of human nature in the starting point, is false throughout. You can never make anything of Christianity on any other supposition than that this is a fallen race, and that the race is wholly destitute of holiness; but *on* that supposition it has at least the merit of being an admirably adjusted scheme, as it will be easy to show you hereafter. You can never hope to see the beauty or the fitness of Christianity *as* a way of salvation until you admit and feel that whatever else you have, you have by nature no true love towards God.

In the expansion and application of this view there are several things which follow, and which it is important to state in order to put the mind into possession of the exact truth, and to confirm what has been just said.

First. In the way of salvation it is assumed that your morality is not holiness. It was not in the case of the young ruler whom, on that account, Jesus loved; it was not in the case of Saul of Tarsus, who said of himself, referring to his character before his conversion, "touching the righteousness which is in the law *blameless*," Phil. iii. 6. It is not in your case. It is another thing altogether than religion. Your morality relates to man; not to God. It has, in your own mind, even, no reference to God. It leads you to no act of devotion to him; to no prayer, to no desire to learn his will, to no worship in your family or in your closet. You do not yourself, even, pretend on this account to be a *religious* or *pious* man. You do not profess to be; you do not ally yourself to those who are pious; you do not expect to be ranked among their number; you would be surprised if you were—either by man or God. You would either receive it as a witticism if you were called a *saint*, or would regard it as intended to be an insult. You have never pretended to perform the proper act of a *religious* man; and you would be greatly surprised if a religious man should address you as a brother believer. Your morality is very valuable in some respects, but it has a very limited sphere considering all your relations; and, though amiable in itself, it may exist in connexion with other things that are far from being amiable. Will you suffer me to show you, by a very plain illustration, how this is? A company of boys are playing on a common. They are blithe, merry, happy. They are kind to each other, and true to each other, and faithful to each other. If one falls into danger, all are ready to help him; if one is unfortunate, all sympathize with him; if one is prospered, all rejoice. They do not steal from each other; they do not slander each other; they do not cheat each other. If one makes a promise to another it is faithfully kept; if a bargain is made, the most scrupulous rules of honesty are observed. *But they are all truants.* They have broken away from the restraints of home; are there contrary to the wishes of their parents, and in direct violation of their commands. They refuse to return home at the time when they are commanded to; and if at home they manifest no regard for a parent's will or comfort. What do you think of them? Does their system of morality among themselves prove that they love their parents, or are entitled to the favour of their parents? Does it prove that they are not to be regarded as *truant*, and treated accordingly? Suppose that one of them is charged with disobedience to his parents. 'Oh,' says he, 'we are very kind, and honest, and truthful among ourselves. I have injured no one of my playmates; I am esteemed to be honourable and upright; I am among them strictly moral.' Exactly so; but how does this prove that he is not guilty of crime against a parent? Just as much, fellow-sinner, as your morality proves that you are not a sinner in the sight of God—and no more.

Second. In the way of salvation in the gospel, it is assumed that your amiable traits of character are not holiness, and that they cannot be construed as religion. Why should they be any more than the innocence of the lamb, or the gentleness of the dove? They have no more reference to religion in your own mind; they do nothing to *make* you religious. They do not lead you to prayer, or to a religious life, or to the worship of God, or to the love and imitation of the Saviour—more meek, and gentle, and amiable by far than you can pretend to be; nor do they lead you to prepare for the world to come. Besides, you may not be as amiable as you think you are. Others may see things in you which you do not see; and God may see more than all. Your real character may have been little tested, and you may yet be in circumstances where you yourself may be surprised to find how much pride, and envy, and irritability, and perverseness, and petulance, and selfishness, there was lurking in your own soul.

Thirdly. In the way of salvation in the gospel, it is assumed that your personal accomplishments are not religion; and that they do not prove that you have any holiness of heart. It assuredly does not demonstrate that you are a child of God, whatever praises it may elicit from men, if you can sing well, or dance well, or play well on an instrument of music; if you are fitted to adorn the most polished circles, or if by the grace of movement, or the charms of conversation, you attract the admiration of all. Some of these things are well in their way, and are desirable; but why should any one deceive himself in regard to them? They are not religion; they cannot be made *to be* religion.

Fourthly. It is assumed in the way of salvation in the gospel, that there is no native germ of goodness or holiness in your heart; that there is none implanted by baptism that can be so developed or cultivated as to become religion. Holiness, if it ever exists in the human soul, is to have a *beginning* there. It is not there by nature. You may cultivate your intellectual powers, but the result will not be religion; you may cultivate amiableness of temper, but it is not religion; you may cultivate gracefulness of manner or of person, but it is not religion; you may cultivate morality, but it is not religion. And so of baptism. It has its advantages, and they who have been baptized should bless God for it; but it is not given to man, whether clothed in sacred vestments or not—to man, though ministering at the altar, and in the name of God, to implant a principle of grace, or a germ of piety in the soul. God's Spirit alone creates life there; and it is done through the instrumentality of truth, and not by an outward ordinance. Baptism has imparted nothing to you that can be certainly cultivated into piety, or that will *grow* into the love of God.

And, *fifthly*, then it is assumed in the way of salvation in the gospel, that your heart is evil. It has by nature no religion. It has nothing which can grow up into religion; nothing which can be a substitute for it. It is proud, selfish, vain, worldly, polluted, wicked, unlike God.

This may seem to be a dark picture, but it lies at the foundation of the way of salvation as revealed in the gospel; and on this sad fact the whole plan is based. All men, as is supposed in this plan, have failed to yield obedience to the reasonable requirements of the law of God. The violation of that law is held to be the first act of a child when he becomes a moral agent; the continued act of his life, unless he is renewed; the last act on his dying pillow. His whole career is regarded as one act of rebellion, because he is selfish, neglects God, is proud, is cherishing enmity against his Maker, and is opposed to all efforts to produce better feelings. In innumerable instances, this want of holiness, this destitution of love to God, goes forth in acts of falsehood, impurity, blasphemy, theft, murder, adultery, oppression, and implacable individual and national war. In support of this view of the character of man, the sacred Scriptures assert the naked fact, claiming to be the testimony of God. The Bible has, moreover, recorded, under Divine guidance, the history of the world for more than two-thirds of its continuance, and presents no exception to this melancholy account of men. Profane writers, with no reference to any theological debate, and nine-tenths of them with no expectation that their testimony would ever be adduced to settle questions of divinity, have presented the same fact. Not one solitary historian, though coming from the midst of the people whose deeds are recorded, and designing to give the most favourable representation of their character, has exhibited a nation bearing any marks of holiness—an individual that is like God. The world, the wide world, is apostate; and he must be worse than blind that would attempt to maintain that man by nature is fit for the kingdom of heaven.

On this broad fact, wide as the world, and prolonged as its history, the Christian way of salvation is based. Here is an apostate province of God's empire. Rebellion has come upon the earth, though not as it came among the ranks of heaven. There it cut off a fixed number, all mature in wisdom and in strength. It would not spread; it could not be extended to successive tribes. Here it poisoned a fountain. It was amidst God's works at first, but a little spring, pouring into a rill, but soon swelling to creeks, to rivers, to lakes, to oceans. An incalculable number would descend from the first pair of apostates, and with prophetic certainty it could be foretold that not one of their descendants would escape the contagion to the end of time, however long the apostate world might stand. To all ages it would be the same. On each mountain, in each valley, in each cavern—on each extended and fertile plain—in all lands, barbarous or civilized—under every complexion in which man would appear—white, black, copper, olive, or mixed,—it would be the same. Crime would be heaped on crime; whole nations would bleed; whole tribes would wail; one generation of sinners would tread on another generation, and then themselves expire—and all die as enemies of the God that made them.

We need not embarrass ourselves by inquiring how this came upon us, or why this is so. It is the *fact* with which we are concerned, not the *mode*. The grand question is not *why* this is so; or *why* this was permitted; or *how* we can reconcile it with the goodness of God, but *how shall we escape?* When a man is struggling in a current of mighty waters, it does nothing to facilitate his escape to be able to determine how he came there; nor would it help him if he could satisfy his own mind on the question why God ever made streams so that men could fall into them, and did not make every bank of granite or iron so that it would not give way.

The grand question is, how shall we escape? You will not escape if you remain in your present condition. Indifference is not safety; and unconcern is not salvation. It is not the way to be saved to give one's self no concern about it, or to suffer things to pass on as they are. If you remain as you are with a sinful and depraved heart—with no love to God—what *can* befall you but ruin? Without holiness you cannot be fit for heaven. For what world *are* you preparing?

It will not save you to murmur and complain at your lot, or to find fault with the Divine arrangements, or even reverently and devoutly to call these things mysterious. Scepticism saves no one from danger; murmuring saves no one; a sneer saves no one; contempt saves no one; nor does it save any one to call a truth a *mystery*. None of these things make you a better man;

none do anything to fit you for heaven; none will make the sorrows of perdition more easy to be borne.

It will not save you to cultivate the graces of manner, or the accomplishments of life; to become more learned in the sciences, and a better critic of the productions of art; to make yourself more moral before men; to break off your external sins, or to put on the "form of godliness without its power." You may cultivate a bramble, but it will not be a rose; a rose, but it will not be a bird of Paradise; a bird of Paradise, but it will not be a gazelle; a gazelle, but it will not be a beautiful woman. You may polish brass, but it is not gold; and may set in gold a piece of quartz, but it is not a diamond:—and just as certain is it that none of the graces of native character which you can cultivate will ever become true religion. The evil lies deeper than this, and must be healed in another way. How this is may be explained hereafter. My point now is gained if I have shown you that the Christian way of salvation justly assumes as its basis that our race is by nature destitute of holiness; and if you are convinced, as I would wish you to be convinced, that it is not by works of righteousness which you have done that you can be saved.

SERMON X.

THE INQUIRY, WHAT MUST I DO TO BE SAVED?

ACTS xvi. 30.—"What must I do to be saved?"

IN the last discourse I endeavoured to show that God's plan of saving men is based on the fact that the race is by nature destitute of holiness. I illustrated this by showing that it is *not* meant that the race is held to be guilty of the sin of Adam; or that it is necessary in order to salvation to suppose that the sinner is as bad as he can be; or that he is guilty for not doing that which he has no power to do; or that there are no amiable qualities in the minds of men by nature, or that there is nothing that may, in any way, be commended. I showed that it *is* meant that there is in the heart by nature no real love to God; no just appreciation of his character; no pleasure in the principles of his government; no desire to please him.

This is the condition, I suppose, in which the gospel finds man; this certainly is the assumption in regard to man in the way of salvation revealed in the gospel. This being supposed, the Scripture plan has, at least, consistency and meaning; this being denied, it has no consistency and no meaning. You can make nothing out of the gospel except on the supposition that "Christ Jesus came into the world to save *sinners*;" except, in his own language, it be admitted that he "came to seek and to save that which was *lost*." He is not, then, in the path of salvation who does not feel and admit that he is a sinner, and who is not prepared to receive salvation as it has been provided for sinners.

We advance a step, then, at the present time, by considering the state of mind which exists when one, impressed with these truths, begins to feel that something must be *done* to save his own soul; the condition when one enters on the inquiry *what he must do to be saved.* I may not be able to state *all* that will be necessary on this part of the subject in this discourse, but I would hope to be able to show you that this inquiry is at least rational and proper, and that it starts questions not beneath the attention of any.

To give some general order to the remarks which I propose to make, I shall endeavour, in the first place, to describe the state of mind to which I refer; shall then state some of the causes which produce it; and then notice some of the perplexities and embarrassments which the mind in that condition experiences.

That is an epoch in a man's life when, from a former condition of carelessness and unconcern, he is first led to ask the question *what he must do to be saved?* A new inquiry has come before him, evidently in every way worthy of his attention as a man, and yet in some respects as difficult as it is momentous. It is evidently a great subject, and may involve great changes in his character and plans of life, and it lies far without the range of the ordinary inquiries which come before the minds of men. The word "*saved*" suggests thoughts which do not enter into his ordinary investigations; the word "*how*" starts questions which have not entered into other matters which have occupied his attention. How a man may accumulate property; how he may gain honour; how he may become learned, accomplished, influential; how he may ward off the attacks of disease, and how he may defend himself if in danger, are points which he may have often considered, and on which he may have definitely-formed opinions. How he is to be *saved* is another inquiry altogether. For this is a different question from that about becoming rich, graceful, or honoured; and the knowledge which he has gained on one of these points does not afford him any clue in his inquiries on the former topic. For how shall the knowledge of the best way of acquiring property aid a man in answering the question how he shall be saved?

The state of mind which I am describing is that which exists when this inquiry first comes up for consideration. It may be characterized by the single word *seriousness;* or by the phrase *a disposition to thought and reflection.* There may be as yet a very slight sense of personal sinfulness, and almost or quite none of danger; but there is the feeling now that religion is of importance, and that it is at least worthy of *inquiry*—inquiry as to its truth, and as to the method of salvation which it proposes. There is a conviction hitherto unfelt of the worth of the soul, and a feeling that that *should* have a degree of thought and attention not before bestowed upon it. Religion somehow occupies more of the attention; it is suggested more frequently; it is not so easily disposed of; it is more likely to return after the mind has by a slight effort been diverted from it to other things; it seems to come before the mind with more importunate claims than it has done before.

The power of reflecting on the past, the present, and the future, is one of the highest endowments of man, and nowhere is that power more appropriately exercised than on the subject of religion. We think on the past, and derive valuable lessons from what we have seen and experienced, and from what has occurred to others, to guide us in that which is to come; we think on the present—on what we are—on our characters, duties, and relations, and inquire what we should be in those relations; we think on that which is to come, and inquire what we are yet to be. Thought has no limit. The past, the present, and the future; the distant, the vast, and the incomprehensible; the real and the imaginary; time and eternity; death and life; earth, hell, and heaven; God, angels, devils, and men; the living, and the dead; nature and grace; sin and redemption; man here and man hereafter,—all are within the proper range of thought, and all may suggest thoughts about our personal salvation.

Thought gives birth to new plans, new hopes, new prospects in the lives of men. It leads to permanent revolutions of character; to the exchange of wild and visionary schemes for those of soberness and reality; to corrections of follies, to enlargement of views, and to the formation of generous and noble purposes. No man is likely to be injured by calm and serious reflection; none can be by the questions which true religion suggests.

There are inquiries pertaining to religion which are worthy of thought, and which have been so regarded by the profoundest thinkers of our race. Some of the most careful and laboured investigations to which the human mind has given birth have had reference to religion; suggested by the single inquiry how a man can be saved. Much of the profound reasoning of Socrates, Plato, Cicero, Seneca, Bacon, and Locke, like all that we have of Paul's writings, had reference to *religion*. More minds have been employed on this inquiry than on any other one subject in which men have been interested, and the inquiry has been pursued with a zeal and ardour such as has been felt on no other. The inquiries which religion suggests are sufficiently various, dignified, and important, to be worthy of the most careful reflection of every man. Is there a God? Is there an hereafter? Is the soul immortal? Is there a way by which sin can be pardoned, and by which a sinner can be saved? Has God devised a plan by which a sinner can be justified, and are there conditions on which the benefits of that plan are proposed to men? Does the Bible contain the record of the way by which a sinner may be saved; or if not, where may such a record be found? Is the Christian religion true? If so, what are its claims, hopes, privileges? What is the way of salvation which is revealed, and how may one be assured that he is walking in that way?

And there are *personal* questions which demand thought. What has been the character of our lives? What are our hopes for the future? How are we regarded in the view of the holy law of God; how by the Author and Administrator of that law? Are we living in accordance with the purpose for which we were made? Are we prepared for our exit from this present life? Have we done all that we ought to do; all that our consciences require us to do; all that we have ourselves deemed it desirable to do, that we may be ready for our departure?

The state of mind which I am endeavouring to describe is that in which these inquiries begin to assume something of their proper magnitude. This will not always, indeed, be manifested by assuming the position of an avowed *inquirer* on the subject of religion. It will be rather, perhaps, in some such ways as these:—conscious seriousness when the subject of religion is alluded to, accompanied with a feeling of its importance such as has not been usual in the mind; a willingness to examine the arguments in favour of religion, and a growing interest in them as addressed to the understanding; an increasing conviction that this world is not a satisfactory portion for the soul, and a disposition to inquire whether the universe has not something better in reserve; a disposition to reflect on the past life—more now on its faults than on its virtues—more on the neglect of duty than on the performance of duty—more on the internal feelings than on the external conduct—more on the thoughts and the motives than on the outward deeds—more on the treatment of God than on the treatment of men—and more on the now conscious want of holiness towards God than on personal amiableness and morality. You seem to be far less perfect than you supposed you were. You see more errors of judgment; more aberrations from what your conscience tells you you should be; more things in which the motives were doubtful or wrong; more cases in which there was an improper indulgence of passion and criminal desire. Your temper has been less amiable; your treatment of your father less respectful, and of your mother less kind; your compassion for the suffering and the sad less tender; your charities less generous; your principles of life less scrupulously exact than you had supposed. You begin to feel, as you have not heretofore done, that you are a sinner; and the inquiry is springing up in your mind as one that claims attention, *What must I do to be saved?* Religion begins to appear to your mind to be the most important of all subjects; and you feel that, whatever may be the inclination of the heart in regard to it, it *ought* to be attended to. It is beginning to be seen to be a subject that pertains to you as a personal matter; and the inquiry, "What must I do to be saved?" is one that begins to have a place among those in which your own mind is deeply interested. It may be, as yet, merely an *awakened* interest in religion; or it may be that there is deep and pungent "conviction" for sin —an overwhelming sense of past guilt—such as the jailer in the text seems to have had, when all the sins of a past life are brought to the remembrance, and the intensest interest is thrown into the question, "What *must* I do to be saved?"

This state of mind is necessarily connected with the way of salvation as revealed in the gospel, and, to a greater or less degree, always exists before the fitness and the beauty of that plan of salvation are perceived by the mind. Christ came to save sinners; and the whole plan of salvation is adjusted to the supposition that it is *for* sinners, and there is inwoven into the scheme an arrangement for making men feel that they *are* sinners as preliminary to, and indispensable to, a revelation of mercy through the Saviour. It is supposed that men would feel this, and ought to feel this sense of guilt, and there is a special agency appointed in the gospel to secure this state of mind in the case of all who become Christians and are saved. No man, according to the plan of salvation in the gospel, can be saved who has not a just view of himself as a sinner, and who does not come, as such, to the cross of Christ.

It is very important, therefore, to inquire what is done, under the Christian plan of salvation, to produce this state of mind. This is the next point which I proposed to illustrate.

I do not design to say to you that the feeling of thoughtfulness or solicitude is in all cases the same in intensity or in duration, or that it is always to be traced to the same causes. From the nature of the case it must vary with the time of life; with the temperament of the individual; with the general character; with the amount of education and the power of self-government; and with the causes which produce the serious reflections. In some cases the seriousness may be the slow growth of many years; in others, the result of some visitation of Providence, or some message of truth coming suddenly to the soul. In some the mind may fasten on a single great sin that shall occupy all the attention, and fill all the field of vision; in others it may be a calmer view of all the past life. Among youths it may be calm, serious thought, apparently the result of early training, and when the seed sown in childhood seems to spring up and ripen as gently and as noiselessly as the grain in the harvest field does under the gently falling dew and the noiseless sunshine; in the man of strong passions, and infidel opinions, and great wickedness, it may be with the violence and commotion of the winds when they sweep along the hills, and when in their rage they twist off the gnarled oak, or tear it up by the roots. In the educated and disciplined mind it may be apparently mere calm contemplation and profound reflection; in the uneducated and undisciplined a genuine work of grace may be going on, under all the outcries and outbreaks of what seems the wildest fanaticism and disorder. Under the steady preaching of the gospel it may be one thing, in the storm of adversity and affliction it may be another; here the Spirit of truth may seem to approach the conscience through the understanding, and there through the emotions. No one would expect precisely the same feelings in John, the meek and gentle friend; Peter, the bold, the impetuous, and the rash; and Saul of Tarsus, the zealot and the bigot, when they passed through the stages preliminary to conversion; no one would expect precisely the same feelings in the heathen jailer at Philippi, and in the conversion of a youth trained now in the Sabbath school. In certain great features we should expect indeed to find similarity or identity; in the intensity of the feeling, the amount of anxiety, the duration of this state of mind, or the causes which produced it, we might expect to find every imaginable variety. To show this I will now enumerate some of the causes which tend to produce the state of mind referred to.

First, it is produced, in some cases, by a growing sense of the unsatisfactory nature of worldly pursuits and enjoyments. With all the love which there is in the human soul for these things, there is a constant tendency to become dissatisfied with them, and to feel that they are not what the soul needs. They pall upon the senses, and there is need of new excitements and new forms of attractiveness to make them interesting. It requires much effort to keep up an interest in worldly things, and much variety and novelty to prevent a growing distaste for them; for there are wants of the soul which no brilliancy, change, and novelty in those pursuits can meet. Solomon made a designed experiment on this subject, under all the advantages which any human being can hope for, and reached results which all would reach in similar circumstances:—"I made me great works; I builded me houses; I planted me vineyards: I made me gardens and orchards, and I planted trees in them of all kind of fruits: I made me pools of water, to water therewith the wood that bringeth forth trees: I got me servants and maidens, and had servants born in my house; also I had great possessions of great and small cattle above all that were in Jerusalem before me: I gathered me also silver and gold, and the peculiar treasure of kings and of the provinces: I gat me men singers and women singers, and the delights of the sons of men, as musical instruments, and that of all sorts.—And whatsoever mine eyes desired I kept not from them, I withheld not my heart from any joy; for my heart rejoiced in all my labour: and this was my portion of all my labour. Then I looked on all the works that my hands had wrought, and on the labour that I had laboured to do: and, behold, all was vanity and vexation of spirit, and there was no profit under the sun," Eccles. ii. 4—11. And who, in similar circumstances, has not had similar reflections? How difficult is it always to prevent such reflections from springing up in the mind as the following:—'To what purpose is all this? Is this the end for which man should live? Is this the way in which God designs that rational creatures should be happy? Will this save me? Will this prepare me to die? Will this fit me to dwell in a holy heaven? Is there, after all, no better portion for man than costly viands, and gay apparel, and splendid equipages, and music, and dancing? Has man been formed for no nobler end than to eat and drink and be merry, and can he obtain nothing that shall be substantial and permanent? Is there nothing—nothing in this world or in any other—that can meet the deep desires of our nature—the aspirations of the undying mind for substantial good?' These reflections *may* occur in a ball-room; in a brilliant party of pleasure; in a palace; on a bed of down; and when the incense of the flattery that we have long sought is wafted around us. And these reflections are often aided much by the chagrin and mortification, the neglect and the coldness, the jealousies and heart-burnings experienced in the world; and, chafed and oppressed by these, the mind begins to inquire whether there is no world that will furnish substantial good,—to reflect soberly, and to ask, What must be done to be saved?

Secondly, there are, in other cases, or in these, the secret, silent workings of the conscience, prompting to the inquiry, *What must be done to be saved?* Conscience is sometimes armed with a terrific power—a power that rives the soul as the lightning does the gnarled oak; but it is not that to which I now refer. It has also a comparatively milder and more humble office; a gentler power; a stiller voice. It silently reminds the soul of the obligations of religion, and gently and kindly awakens it to reflection, and stimulates it to the performance of long-neglected duty. It becomes a friendly counsellor, makes kind suggestions, urges us to pray, keeps before us the remembrance of some duty that is unperformed, or some sin which we strive in vain to forget. It leads us to "think on our ways," to "ponder the paths of our feet," and opens to us reflections of the deepest interest in regard to that which is past and that which is to come, and thus leads the mind along gently to the inquiry, "What must I do to be saved?"

Thirdly, there are in other cases the recollected instructions of earlier years, now strangely and mysteriously brought to the memory. The father, the mother, the pastor, the Sabbath school teacher, the friend, may be dead, or may be far far away. But their lessons of virtue and their counsels may come with freshness and power to your minds as you stand in calm contemplation near their graves. Or, roaming in a distant clime, far away from the home of your childhood, in the land of strangers, where no one seems to feel an interest in you, and you feel an interest in no one of the multitudes around you, you may think of the counsels of a parent, of the family Bible, of the morning and evening sacrifice in your father's house; and the question, which may scarcely have occurred to you for years, may spring up anew in your mind, "What shall I do to be saved?" Or, even in the dense and crowded city, a stranger amidst the jostling multitudes that care neither for you nor for one another; where you know no one, and no one knows you; where no one of all that crowd along the thronged avenue greets you with a kind look, or would care if you should die; where no one sympathizes with your sorrows, or would miss you if you were never seen there again,—in the unutterable sense of loneliness which a strange youth feels in such a city,—your home, and your father, and your mother, and the influence of religion there, and the sweet and calm peace which religion produces there, or the calm peace which it shed on the last hours of some loved one, may come to your memory, and the involuntary question may arise, "What shall *I* do to be saved?" Or perhaps, having long forgotten these lessons, now on the deep, or in a distant land, or remote from the scenes of childhood in your own country, you may take up the long-neglected Bible, and the first passage which may greet you may be one that shall start the inquiry, "What must I do to be saved?"

Fourthly, there is another class in whose minds the inquiry may be started by some of the scenes of nature—some of the works of God, that may fix the roving thoughts, and lead the mind upward and onward. Creation is full of God, and his voice may be heard in everything round about us. When, weary with the toils of the day, the merchant comes to his dwelling; when the "ploughman homeward plods his weary way;" when the seaman in a calm sees his sails hang loosely, and his "ship like a painted thing upon a painted ocean;" when in the still evening the zephyr gently breathes, God speaks often in tones *as* gentle to the soul. Then the mind is calm, and the passions are hushed, and nature is still, and all in and around prompts to serious thought, and leads the soul to the contemplation of the world to come. And so when the thunder-peal breaks on the hills, or over the dwelling in the silence of the night; when the tempest sweeps along, and the oak is prostrated on the mountain, God often speaks to the soul and awakens solemn thought. Luther was awakened to a sense of sin and danger, and led to ask the question, "What must I do to be saved?" by the terrors of the tempest, and God made the lightning and the storm the means of arousing his mind to do the great work which he had for him to accomplish. He was then twenty-two years of age. He was on his way from his home to the academy at Erfurth. On his journey he was overtaken by a violent storm. The thunder roared. He threw himself upon the ground on his knees. His hour he apprehended had come. Death, judgment, and eternity were before him in all their terrors, and spoke with a voice which he could no longer resist. "Encompassed," as he said, "with the anguish and terror of death, he made a vow that, if God would deliver him from this danger, he would forsake the world and devote himself to his service." * That event changed the course of his life—changed the destiny of nations. And who, in conscious danger, has *not* felt the inquiry cross the mind, as Luther and the jailer did, "What must I do to be saved?"

Fifthly, there are others in whose minds the inquiry is started by the dispensations of Providence. The providence which embarrasses you in your business; which throws unexpected obstacles in your way when you are grasping the world, and living for this world alone; which strips away your property by causes which you could not foresee and could not surmount,—how much adapted is it to show you that there is a Presiding Being over the affairs of men; to lead you to inquire *why* he placed these obstacles in your path; to lead you to ask the question

* D'Aubigné.

whether there are not higher ends for which you *should* live? The providence which takes away your health, and lays you for weeks on a bed of languishing, *appears* to be designed to lead you to reflect on the feebleness of your frame; on the uncertain tenure of the hold on life; on the higher scenes which await man in the future world; and to lead you to ask on that bed of languishing, "What must I do to be saved?" The providence which takes away a lovely child, how much fitted is it to lead the mind to sober thought! Yesterday it was blithe and playful, and your home was happy; to-day it lies pale and cold in death, and you cannot but feel that God has designed that you should pause in your career, and reflect on death and the coming world.

And, *Sixthly*, there are those, in great numbers, who are led to reflection and to inquiry by the warnings of his word. The preaching of the gospel is God's great ordinance for awakening the attention of men to the subject of religion, and arousing them to thought and solicitude in regard to their immortal welfare. To secure this is one of the great ends contemplated by the institution of the ministry of reconciliation; and it is every way adapted to the end in view. Of those who become Christians, by far the largest portion are awakened to a sense of their sin and danger under the preaching of the gospel; and more frequently the inquiry is started, "What must I do to be saved," in this manner than in all other methods combined.

I might go on to speak of many other methods by which the attention of the sinner is arrested, and by which he is brought to serious reflection:—his own solemn thoughts when alone; the conversation of a stranger; the counsel of a friend; the Bible that he casually opens; the tract that is laid in his way; the book that he has been induced by a friend to read; the deep feeling that sometimes pervades a community in a revival of religion; or some secret, silent influence of the Eternal Spirit on his mind that he is never able to trace to any secondary cause. One thing cannot but strike you in all this: it is the variety of methods—the numberless ways—in which God makes his appeal to men; the countless modes of access which he has to the soul, prompting to the great inquiry, "*What must I do to be saved?*" And yet, in all cases, with all the endless variety of means employed, and all the variety of emotions and feelings produced, arising from age, and temperament, and diversity of education, and the manner in which the appeal is brought to the mind—the general character of the feeling is the same: it is awakened interest in religion; it is a growing conviction of its importance;

it is calm reflection; it is a sense of danger and insecurity in the present state; it is a feeling that *something ought to be done* in order to be saved.

At this stage, however, everything seems to be full of perplexity. Doubts arise on the whole subject of religion. What is to be believed as true and what is to be done, are alike points on which the mind is often in the utmost perplexity. Amidst the thousand opinions entertained in the church, which is to be believed? Who shall tell us what is true? Who shall guide us into the path of peace? And another thing is equally perplexing—what is to be *done*. Something, it is clear, should be done; but *what* shall it be? In this state of feeling, the jailer came to Paul and Silas to know what should be done; in a similar state of feeling many would give worlds if some one would tell them with certainty what they should do.

I desire now, in conclusion, to suggest a few thoughts, by way of counsel, applicable to this state of mind.

(1.) The first is, *Cherish* the disposition to reflection. Be *willing* to think on your ways; to ponder calmly and seriously so important a subject as religion. Be *willing* to think it all over—the past, the present, the future; your character, your hopes, your dangers, your duties, your privileges, and your destiny. Be willing to think on the question whether religion is true; what it is; whether its hopes may be yours. He is not far from the kingdom of God who is *willing to think* on the subject of religion, and in all honesty to follow out the result of his own reflections. Need I urge any more reasons for this counsel? It is a subject *worthy* of thought. Assuredly, if there is anything that can properly claim the attention of the human mind it is this. What are all things else in respect to us, compared with the salvation of our own souls? And who is *injured* by calm and careful thought? Who is made the poorer, or the less worthy to be respected, by sober reflection? What merchant is more likely to fail by reflecting carefully on his business; what youth endangers his reputation by considerate reflection on his character and plans; what student is retarded in the attainment of knowledge by attentive thoughtfulness on his studies; what physician is injured by a close application of his mind to the symptoms of disease and the right methods of healing; what lawyer by close attention to the law and the evidence in the case entrusted to him? But again, what interests are there which are *not* jeoparded by recklessness and want of thought? How often is fortune squandered; is health ruined; is the opportunity of preparing for honour and usefulness lost; is life itself the forfeit of a want of reflection! How many bankrupts are there who might have been saved by timely thought; how many drunkards who might have been happy and useful by proper reflection; how many are there now useless to the world, who would have been ornaments to society if in early years they had reflected calmly on their privileges, and thoughtfully pursued the paths of learning or business! I counsel you, therefore, to cherish every serious thought that passes through your minds on the subject of religion, and to be willing to follow where sober thought would lead you.

(2.) I counsel you to avoid the scenes which would be likely to dissipate your serious reflections. You may be less ready to follow me in this than in the former, and yet this is essential if you would secure the salvation of the soul. But do not misunderstand me. I do not counsel you to immure yourself in a cloister. I advise not a useless and a gloomy asceticism. I ask you not to be morose, sour, dissocial, melancholy. All these I regard as infinitely far from religion, alike in its beginnings in the soul, and in its highest progress towards perfection.

But there *are* scenes which are unfavourable to serious reflection, and which tend to dissipate serious thought, and which one must consent to leave for ever if he would serve God and follow the Saviour. The theatre, the ball-room, the circles of gaiety, the places of revelry—how can they be made to be favourable to serious thought; how are they consistent with an earnest desire to be saved? Between those scenes and the calm and serene spirit of the gospel—between the spirit which reigns there, and that which reigned in the bosom of the Saviour, there is such a contrast that the one cannot live where the other does; and if you make up your mind to have the one, you must make up your mind *not* to have the other.

I am sensible that, even to a mind under the degree of thoughtfulness which I have now been endeavouring to describe, it is one of the most difficult things that I can exhort you to do, to follow the counsel which I am now giving. So fascinating is that gay and brilliant world; so many of your friends find pleasure there; so entirely may you seem to be shut out from all society if you withdraw from that; so many ties bind you to it by a network so interlaced and so strong; and so much would you dread to have it whispered around to "lover and friend" that you are becoming *serious*, that I do not wonder at the difficulty of breaking away. Yet, there is no option. If you would be a Christian, if you would find the way of salvation, you must make up your mind, if need be, to bear the frowns, the sneers, the ridicule of the world—for the path to heaven and to glory lies not through scenes of vanity and of sin.

(3.) I counsel you to *pray*. For what is more appropriate than prayer in the state of mind which I have described? Where should one go who is asking what he shall do to be saved, if not to God? You are just beginning to grapple with great questions that are too much for the unaided human mind. You are beginning to think about themes on which the profoundest human intellects have been employed, and which are the subject of the contemplation of angels and seraphs. You are beginning to reflect on the past, and the future; the distant, the grand, the infinite, when every thought takes hold on eternity. You are commencing an inquiry which has never been continued long, and which has never been conducted to a happy issue without prayer. To your mind all is dark, and in this inquiry you need above all things the guidance of the Father of lights, and you will never find the path to heaven till "in *his* light *you* see light." What, then, can be more appropriate for a human being in these circumstances than prayer?

Are there any of you whose minds are in the condition described in this discourse—serious, thoughtful, pondering the question, What shall I do to be saved? Go to your closets. Pray. Alone with the God that made you—with the Father of lights—with him who hears prayer—ask *him* this great question, What must I do to be saved? If your Maker has never heard the voice of prayer before come from your lips, this night, ere you slumber, let him hear the humble, fervent cry for knowledge, for mercy, for salvation.

SERMON XI.

CONVICTION OF SIN.

PSALM li. 4.—"Against thee, thee only, have I sinned, and done this evil in thy sight; that thou mightest be justified when thou speakest, and be clear when thou judgest."

THE plan of salvation is designed for sinners. None are saved by that plan who are not regarded as such. The gospel has no significancy unless it be supposed that men are violators of the law of God. It has no peculiar adaptation to men except on that supposition. It seeks to excite the conviction that he is a sinner in the bosom of every man whom it addresses, and it is certain that no one will appreciate its provisions, or be saved by it, who does not feel and admit that truth in regard to himself. If there is, therefore, any one who is unwilling to admit, in the proper sense of the term, that he is a sinner, he should not entertain the hope of being saved by the gospel, and should not feel himself specially addressed in any of its communications. It is indispensable that a man, if he would be saved, should be convinced of sin. The two preceding discourses were, respectively, on the state of man as the gospel finds him, and on the condition of the mind when it begins to reflect on the subject of religion. We advance a step further in unfolding the way of salvation by considering the state of the mind when under conviction for sin. I shall explain what is meant by the term; consider the law of our nature in accordance with which conviction for sin is produced; and show what it *is* that the sinner is convinced *of* in that state, or what constitutes genuine conviction of sin.

I. What is meant by the term *conviction of sin*. The short and perhaps the sufficient explanation of this is, *being convinced of sin so as to feel and acknowledge that we are sinners*. The term has, however, somewhat of a technical and theological signification which makes it necessary to explain it somewhat further; and unfortunately, also, it is so associated in the minds of many with what they would be pleased to regard as cant or fanaticism—with Calvinism, or Methodism, or Evangelism—that it seems necessary, if I can, to do something to remove this impression, and to show you that it is possible that sensible men may, without compromising their own dignity, become convinced that they are sinners. I would, then, submit to you the following remarks:—

(*a*) There is a state of mind, very common, which results from being convinced by *argument*. A course of reasoning may be so conclusive that there can be no doubt on the subject. A mathematical proposition may be so demonstrated; an historical fact may be so established; a truth in morals may be so clearly proved; a jury may be so satisfied; a point in theology may be so defended, that no one can have any doubt on the truth of the point under consideration. And thus a man may be so thoroughly convinced that our race is fallen, and that he, as one of the race, has come into the world with a corrupt nature, that his mind may be as fully satisfied on this subject as he is of the truth of a mathematical proposition. Yet it is clear that, though thus convinced, this latter truth may be held in such a manner as to make no more impression on his conscience and his heart than the mathematical demonstration had done. Though pertaining to itself, yet the mind has the power of looking at it as a mere abstraction; and nothing is more common than for a man to be able to prove that he is himself a sinner, or to listen to an argument clearly demonstrating it, without emotion.

(*b*) Again, a man may not only look at this as an abstract argument, but he may have a very distinct *recollection* of wrong doing, and yet have no compunction, no remorse. By knowing or supposing that the fact is concealed; or by a cultivated habit of severe mental discipline; or by the hardening effect of many acts of guilt on his own soul; or by some perverted views of mental philosophy, morals, or theology, he may have succeeded in keeping his mind calm and undisturbed, though he *is* conscious that he has done wrong. The mind may be in such a state as to contemplate its own past acts of depravity as calmly as it does the depravity of others, and with as little compunction. This is the state of mind which men commonly seek; and in this they are frequently, for a time at least, eminently successful.

(*c*) Again, there is a kind of conviction of guilt from the *testimony of others*, which may produce as little impression on the soul. There is a difference, in this respect, between the use of the word in theology and in the courts. A man is convicted, or found guilty, by a jury, and is so regarded and treated by the court. But he may or may not be convinced of the crime himself, or be sensible of guilt in the matter. He may be a hardened wretch, so steeped in crime as to be apparently beyond the possibility of feeling; or he may be perfectly innocent of the crime, though he has been adjudged to be guilty by the jury, and is so held up to the public by the sentence of the court. But, in either case, the verdict of the jury and the sentence of the court have done nothing to convince him that he is guilty. He is *convicted*—not *convinced*. The verdict of the jury and the judgment of the court may or may not tend to convince him that he is guilty. That is a private, personal matter, with which the jury and the court have nothing to do. Even *if* guilty, the process in the court-room may have made no practical impression of his own criminality on his mind. He may have watched the evidence that has been adduced against him with the utmost attention, and may have no doubt when the verdict of the jury finding him guilty is rendered, that it is according to the testimony, and according to truth, and yet neither the evidence nor the verdict may have made any practical impression of guilt on his own mind.

(*d*) Again, there is a state of mind in which one who has been guilty of crime may, in the proper sense of the term, be *convinced* of it,—convinced neither as an abstract proposition, nor by the finding of a jury, nor by the judgment of a court, but as a personal matter and in the proper sense of the term, so as to produce a *sense* of wrong doing—*distress* in view of the past, and *apprehension* in view of what is to come. This is *conviction of sin.*

This, if not sufficiently plain already, can be made plain by a reference to the case already adverted to. A man on trial for his life has been convicted by a jury. We will suppose it to be a case where he before knew that he had committed the crime, but he was a hardened offender. For the crime when committed, or subsequently before the trial, or during the trial, he had had no compunction. He had so disciplined his moral and his physical frame as to obliterate all the natural expressions of criminality, and even so as to suppress all feeling of guilt. He went through the whole process of the trial with an unperturbed spirit, scarcely feeling any emotion, and betraying none. His was such an intellectual, and, to a great degree, such an abstract employment in watching the progress of the trial—in estimating the weight of the testimony—and in contemplating the skill of the counsel, that, in union with his former hardened character, and with the hope of escape, he may scarcely have had during the trial a single compunctious visitation of remorse. When the trial is over, however, and he is remanded to his lonely prison, and the darkness of the night in his cell draws on, and he has opportunity to reflect on the past, a kind of *conviction* may occur very different from that which has been found by the court and jury. Then it is of no use longer to dissemble. Then there is no hope of concealment. Then the mind is no longer diverted from its own criminality by watching the evidence, or by observing the intellectual conflicts of the counsel, or by indulging the hope of escape from conviction. Then nature acts, and the proper effect of guilt is felt in the soul. Then there comes to his soul the recollection of the nature and claims of the law which he has violated; the evil motives which actuated him; the base passions which controlled him; the wrong which has been done to an individual or to the community; the sight of the suffering victim; the dishonour which he has brought upon himself or his family; the shame of the public death which he is to suffer; the better instructions which he had in his childhood, and of the better life which he might have led: and all these topics now find their way to his heart and conscience. This state of mind is quite different from what is meant by the conviction implied in the verdict of a jury. That is a declaration that he is guilty at the bar of his country; this, that he is guilty at the bar of conscience and of God.

This is what I mean by conviction of sin. It is not merely that which is produced by argument; it is not merely that which arises from an intellectual process convincing one in general that he, as a man, is a sinner, as all other men are; it is that which exists when he sees and feels personally that he is guilty before God, and when the feeling is attended by the distress, trouble, apprehension and alarm, which, by the laws of our nature, are the proper concomitants of the consciousness of guilt.

I have only to say further, under this head, that this conviction of sin is, under the Divine government and in the plan of salvation, preliminary to, and necessary to, pardon. In a human government it may or it may not be. An executive in pardoning a convict from the penitentiary may not require this; or may not act in view of it, if it does exist; nor would he feel bound to extend pardon in any case where it did exist—for pardon, under any human government, is not founded on this. The pardoned man, there *may be* still a hardened offender, or he may have been innocent all along, and in either case may have never felt any of the compunctions of guilt. It might contribute much, indeed, in a given case, to dispose an executive to pardon an offender if he was satisfied that he was truly penitent, but he would not feel bound on that account to pardon him if it were so, or to withhold pardon if it were not; nor would pardon ever be extended on that sole ground at all. Not so in the Divine administration. There the genuine conviction—the feeling of personal guilt—is an indispensable preliminary to pardon; and there, wherever and whenever it truly exists, by an arrangement in the plan of salvation it secures forgiveness.

II. My second object was to consider *the law of our nature in accordance with which this conviction of sin is produced.*

(*a*) That law, when nature acts freely, is simply this,—that when we have done wrong we *feel* guilty, or distressed on account of it. The mind itself decides that wrong has been done; the conscience rebukes and troubles us for having done it. This is an internal feeling; it springs up in the mind itself; it is the result of its own mysterious mechanism; it may be conceived of as existing apart from any apprehension of what is to come, and apart from any outward expression or manifestation whatever. It is simple self-condemnation of the act—a sense of wrong-doing—a sense of ill-desert. In the actual arrangements, however, it is connected with two things which serve to characterize it: (1) one is, the apprehension of punishment in the future—for the soul is so made as to feel that, if guilty, there is a Supreme Being whose wrath is to be feared; and (2) the other is, that, in our present bodily organization, it has a proper outward expression or sign. When nature acts freely, guilt is indicated by the blush of shame, the trembling limbs, the averted or downcast eye, the suspicious and suspecting look, the disposition to withdraw from the presence and the gaze of men. The God of nature, as he made man, *intended* that guilt should thus express itself, and it would always do it if the laws of our being were acted out.

(*b*) The *design* of this law of nature is threefold, and it is as beneficent as it is marvellous; it could have been devised only by a God who is at the same time *just* and *good*. It is (1), to deter us from committing crime by this consciousness of wrong—by the fear of this terrible rebuke—the dread of this self-condemnation; (2), to induce us to repair a wrong that has been done, since under the regular law of our being we can never find peace unless confession is made and the wrong is repaired; and (3), to be a means of recovering us from an evil course, and saving us from future suffering and sin, when we have done wrong. It is thus a great moral means of governing the world, and is thus also connected with a scheme of recovery from sin—*inwrought* into the whole plan of salvation. If man would always regard this he would be deterred from sin; were it not for this, he, having sinned, could never be redeemed and saved. As it is, the plan of salvation will yet be seen to be based on great laws of our nature, and to be in great measure their development.

(*c*) But this great law of our nature, I need not remark, is not always operative. The instances already referred to, and thousands of well-known cases in the world, sufficiently illustrate this. The reasons why it is not so are too numerous to be specified here, and are not immediately necessary to the purpose which I have in view. I have said that if nature were true to herself, or rather if we were true to nature, the act of crime would be always and immediately followed by the convictions and by the indications of guilt,—the blush of conscious criminality; the trembling of the frame; the apprehension of the wrath of God. But crime is committed often under the influence of strong passions, and the passion lingers after the act is done, and does not immediately leave the mind clear and free to act. Or, we dread the convictions of guilt, and try to vindicate ourselves, and by perverted reasoning ward off the consciousness of criminality. Or, we fear the shame of the manifestation of conscious guilt, and learn to discipline our frame so that it shall not betray us. Or, we have a fancied interest in the evil course, and by becoming absorbed in it turn the mind from the contemplation of the real guilt. Or, we bring ourselves under another law of our being—that by constantly practising iniquity we become less sensible of the evil; we acquire a confirmed habit; we make the conscience less susceptible and less quick in its decisions; we blind the mind to nice moral distinctions, and we harden the heart to the enormity of evil. In this way we learn to commit iniquity without blushing, without shame, and without remorse. The eye becomes fixed, and the hand steady, and the frame firm, even when doing conscious wrong. Men learn even to command the blood so that it shall not mantle the cheek to betray them, and learn to make the forehead smooth and cloudless. They go coolly into the work of crime and steep their hands in blood, or practise iniquity for years, with no sense of remorse, no rebuke of conscience. The cheek of the harlot, where the last blush of modesty has long since disappeared; the steady hand of the assassin; the calm step of the midnight robber; the cool purpose of the seducer of innocence; the "seared conscience" of the impenitent sinner; the unperturbed spirit of the man that neglects his God and Saviour, show how effectual may be this effort on the part of the guilty, and how the benevolent intentions of this law of our nature may be frustrated. Thus the brethren of Joseph, without compunction or remorse, pursued coolly their purpose toward their younger brother—a helpless, inoffensive, and lovely boy—first in proposing to kill him, then in thrusting him into a deep pit, and then in selling him to be exposed in a slave market in a distant land, and to be subjected to all the unknown evils of perpetual bondage there. Thus David, apparently with as little compunction or remorse at the time, was guilty of an enormous wrong to a highly meritorious officer in his army, and a devoted patriot, by first destroying his domestic peace, and then seeking to kill him: having done him one wrong, laying a plan to do him another by plotting his death, and giving his instructions to that effect with a spirit as cool and undisturbed as if he had been giving an ordinary order about storming a fortress. Thus Judas Iscariot seems to have made the bargain for the betrayal of his Lord with as calm and unperturbed a spirit as he would have made a contract in the most common matters of trade, nor did the enormous *guilt* of the act which he was doing seem even to occur to his mind. I need not say that men often show that they have this power of extinguishing all the natural marks of guilt, and stifling for years all its convictions, in committing crime, or in the practices of vice. The conscience is "seared as with a hot iron;" the soul becomes lost to all the feelings of guilt, shame, modesty, decency, self-respect. The great law of nature, so wise and so beneficent, so essential to the good of society and to the individual himself, is well nigh obliterated, and, for a time, may cease to act altogether.

(*d*) But there are arrangements in the soul itself, in society, under the Divine government, and in the plan of salvation, for *reviving* that law, and giving it its true place, and it is under that arrangement that men are convicted of sin. Those arrangements need not be adverted to now at length. They embrace all the devices for calling past sins to remembrance; for quickening the power and the decisions of conscience; for bringing the nature and the degree of guilt before the mind, and for arousing the souls of the guilty with the apprehensions of the wrath to come. There may be, from some cause, a mysterious recalling of those long-forgotten sins to the memory in such a way that their guilt may be deeply felt. The tumult of the mind which existed when the crime was committed may have subsided; the passion which blinded the soul may have passed away; the companions and associates of guilt may have gone to other lands or other worlds; you may have leisure to think of the past, and may be in circumstances strongly fitted to recall the past to your remembrance:—in solitude; in the silence of the night-watches; in affliction and trouble; under the admonition of a friend, or under the preaching of the gospel, or by the silent influences of the Divine Spirit on the soul, these forgotten sins may rise to the remembrance, and the soul be overwhelmed with the consciousness of criminality. A brief allusion to the cases already referred to, will illustrate the operation of this law, and at the same time do something to show the nature of genuine conviction of sin.

Joseph's brethren had sold their innocent young brother to a company of travelling merchants. They appear to have divided the money, and to have supposed that that was an end of the matter. They invented the most plausible falsehood they could devise to deceive their aged father, and they gave themselves no more concern about it. Years passed away. A sore famine came upon their land. They were constrained to go to a distant country to buy food. There they were accused and arrested as spies. A strict inquiry was made of them respecting their family, their father, their younger brother at home. Everything was dark to them. A series of calamities had come upon them which they could not account for. They began to think of their former conduct and of God; and the wrong which they had done to their brother, though long forgotten, flashed upon their minds. "And they said one to another, We are verily guilty concerning our brother, in that we saw the anguish of his soul when he besought us, and we would not hear; therefore is this distress come upon us," Gen. xlii. 21. David, little impressed, as it would seem, at first, with the enormity of his crime, soon forgot it altogether. The faithful officer, the patriot, the husband who might have given him trouble, was out of the way—having fallen, as he intended, under the arrows of the Ammonites. The beautiful wife of that officer, David's partner in crime, he had taken to his home, and the crimes of adultery and murder appear to have been forgotten. But a man whom the monarch was accustomed to hear, and who spake in the name of God, came to the palace, and by one of the most beautiful and touching parables ever uttered, arrested the attention of the man of guilt, so that in a moment all the blackness of his crime stood before him, and broken-hearted he prostrated himself before his offended God, and pleaded for pardon. Judas seems to have taken his thirty pieces of silver, the price of treachery, and to have borne them off calmly, if not exultingly—having accomplished a leading purpose of his whole life in obtaining money, and being little troubled at the wrong that he had done. He expected, perhaps, that he who had so often evaded his enemies, and who had foiled their attempts to seize him, would do it again. But, contrary to these expectations, the Saviour had suffered himself to be taken. He was bound, he was tried, he was condemned, he was about to be crucified—and in a moment all his own guilt flashed in his face. He threw down the ignominious price of blood at the feet of his employers, and, stung by remorse, he went out and closed his life.

This, as I understand it, is the law of our nature under which conviction of sin is produced, and all that is done when a sinner *is* convicted is in accordance with this law, and is but carrying out an arrangement designed to deter him from the commission of crime, and to check and recover him to virtue, if it has been committed. It is under this law that the arrangement is made in the plan of salvation, that no man shall obtain pardon who does not feel that he is a sinner, or who is not truly convicted of sin.

Yet it is evident that there may be a false, as well as a genuine conviction; a conviction that shall arise from the mere dread of punishment, as well as that which arises from the intrinsic evil of sin; a conviction which will, as in the case of Judas, lead a sinner to the act of self-murder, as well as that which will lead, as in the case of the jailer at Philippi, or Saul of Tarsus, to true repentance.

III. It remains, then, in the third place, to state *what is implied in genuine conviction of sin.* Of what is the sinner convinced or convicted in this state of mind? This question I answer by a few specifications.

(1.) It is *his own sin* of which he is convicted, and no other. It must be limited to his own; he cannot be convicted of the sins of another. We are not carelessly made in this respect. We are so formed that the sense of guilt or blameworthiness can arise in the mind *only* in view of our own sins. We may have *many* emotions in view of the sins of others, and be concerned in them in most important ways, but we never have in regard to them the feeling of *guilt,* and it is no part of the way of salvation that we should have it. Over the sins of others we may indeed weep on account of their folly; as a consequence of their faults we may suffer; for their sins we may be affected with shame and confusion of face, if they are the sins of those to whom we are united by the ties of blood or friendship, but we never have the sense of guilt or blameworthiness on account of them. You cannot have it. You can no more have this feeling on account of the sin of a father than on account of the sin of a stranger whom you have never seen before; on account of the sin of an erring son or daughter than on account of the folly of the son or daughter of your neighbour or of a stranger; on account of the sin of Adam than on account of the sin of Judas Iscariot. You may, indeed, be affected by the one in a way in which you will not be by the other; you may be made poor, and begin life under disadvantages, in consequence of the sin of a father, which you would not incur by the sin of a stranger; you may be clothed with shame, and filled with sorrow, by the sin of your own son or daughter, as you would not be by the folly of others; you may have been—and you have certainly been—affected by the sin of Adam as you have not been by the sin of Judas—for to him we trace the origin of all our woes—the fact that we are fallen, that we have a depraved nature, that we are to die—and by his sin we *may* be affected for ever; but you no more feel *guilt* in the one case than in the other. You cannot if you try. You ought not if you could. It is not required of you in order to be saved; and if you imagine that you *do* feel guilty for his sin, or the sin of any other man but yourself, it is simply an hallucination of the mind. No man ever yet *did* feel it; no man ever can. The rocky shores of ocean are not fixed so firmly as this barrier in regard to the consciousness of guilt; the stars will fly from their spheres, before this law is changed—that the consciousness of guilt is attached to personal criminality, and to nothing else. You have no genuine conviction of sin but that which arises from your own guilt.

(2.) Genuine conviction of sin is a sense of its evil considered as committed against God. It is not a feeling produced by the fact that it has exposed us to shame, to disadvantage, or to punishment; or that our fellow-men may have been wronged by us; or that it will blast our reputation, or will overwhelm those who are dear to us with disgrace. That one or more or all of these classes of feeling may be connected with genuine conviction of sin, there can be no doubt; but it is equally clear that there may be genuine and deep conviction where not one of them may exist, and that all these combined would not of themselves be such conviction; for a man may have a deep apprehension of shame, of disgrace, and of punishment, and still never have felt that he was blameworthy. This idea which I am now presenting is the prominent one in my text:—"Against thee, thee only, have I sinned, and done this evil in thy sight." It was true that David had committed an enormous wrong against a fellow-man; it was true that he had been guilty of an atrocious evil against society, and against good morals; but still, all this evil terminated on God, and the evil considered as committed against *him* was so vast and overwhelming that every other aspect of it was absorbed and lost. Whoever else was wronged, he was most wronged; whoever was injured, the great evil in the case consisted in the violation of his law; and whatever wrong had been done to an individual or to society, the grand evil in the case consisted in the fact that God had been disobeyed, and his law set at nought. So sin in all cases, whatever may be its form, and whoever may be affected by it, is a violation of the law of God, and its grand evil is to be found in that fact. Approved by men or disapproved; followed with honour or disgrace; punished or not punished; known to the world or unknown, it has an intrinsic evil in its nature as a violation of the Divine law; and it is that evil which is always contemplated, and which is the source of the sorrow in genuine repentance. It is, then, in the view of the mind, an evil and a bitter thing. If you conceal it, it does not alter its nature; if you could assure the penitent that it would be for ever unknown to any human being, and would never be followed by either shame or punishment, it would not essentially change the nature of his feelings towards it. He is sad at the remembrance of the fact that he *has* committed it; he feels himself degraded, and mortified, and debased that he has ever been guilty of violating the law of his God.

(3.) Though the fear of shame and punishment may not be the leading idea in genuine repentance, and may not even enter into it at all, yet there *is* a feeling *always* that it *deserves* punishment. This is inseparable, in the constitution of our minds, from the conviction of guilt. The guilty child feels that it would be *right* in a parent to punish him; the man who has violated the laws of his country, and who has any proper sense of the evil of his course, feels that a penalty affixed to the law is right; the man who is sensible that he has sinned against his God feels that it is *right* that God should manifest his displeasure, and that the guilty should suffer. He may not be able to determine the *amount* of punishment that is due to his act, nor may he see clearly as yet that his sin deserves *eternal* punishment, or that it should throw him beyond the reach of mercy and hope,—but it is of the nature of *all* true conviction of sin to feel that punishment is deserved, and that he who inflicts it is right and just. Thus David in the text says, "That thou mightest be justified when thou speakest, and be clear when thou judgest." A man cannot feel genuine conviction of sin and not feel that he *ought* to be punished. Hence men, under the pressure of this conviction, come and confess an act of murder, and give themselves up to be punished. And hence sinners, when under genuine conviction of sin, look forward to punishment in the future world, and dread it, not so much because it is *said* that they will be punished, as because guilt always supposes that it will be so, and that it is right that it should be so.

These three things, therefore, I think will always enter into true conviction of sin,—that it is our own sins, and not those of another, on account of which we feel guilty; that the primary and principal reason of our conviction is the fact that sin is itself an evil as committed against God; and that there is involved essentially the feeling that it *deserves* the expression of displeasure on the part of Him whose law has been violated. How deep these convictions may be; how long they may be continued; how pungent and distressing our feelings under them; and how the distress is to be relieved, are other points of inquiry which it is not necessary now to consider. There are two or three remarks, however, which seem necessary to complete the just view of the subject, and with these I shall close.

(1.) These laws of our nature, on which conviction of sin is based, will be likely to operate in the future as well as in the present; in the world beyond the grave as well as in the land of the living. Why should they not? There is to be no change in our essential constitution; and far on in the most distant portion of eternity to which we can now look forward, we shall be under the administration of the same God, and the laws of our being will be essentially the same. Past sin, though long forgotten, may be called to remembrance. Time, distance, new circumstances, do not change or diminish its power over the soul. After the lapse of ten or twenty—of a hundred or a million of years, it may rise to the mind with all the freshness which it had at the time of committing the deed, and inflicting the same keen and fearful tortures, and exciting the same deep and dreadful alarms in the prospect of the future, which it ought to have caused then. He gains nothing, then, who succeeds in stifling conviction now; he has secured no permanent peace who has, for the present, wholly forgotten his past crimes.

(2.) It accords with my general subject, and with this part of my general plan, to say that in a way of salvation adapted to man, it is necessary that there should be something that will meet this law of our nature—that will be founded on the fact of its existence—and that will prevent the effect to which I have adverted in the future:—that is, that shall recognise the fact that man is a sinner, and that he is liable to be convicted of sin; and that will so *dispose* of sin that it shall not produce distress and anguish in the future periods of our existence—at some time in our present life, on the bed of death, or beyond the grave. This must be done, and done in a way that shall accord with the proper method of dealing with sin and with the conscience. It will not do this to teach men to forget it—for they cannot always forget it; it will not do it to teach them that sin is a trifle—for God will not let them always feel that it is a trifle; it will not do this to introduce them into the circles of vain amusements—for men cannot always be engaged in vain amusements; it will not do it to teach them some false system of religion that shall be a present opiate to the conscience—for we are going to a world not of falsehood, but of truth.

(3.) It seems to follow from the view taken that the only way by which this can be done is by some system of effectual *pardon.* If sin is pardoned—if it is freely and fully forgiven, all is done that can be done to meet those laws of our being, and to place the soul in the condition in which it would have been if it had not sinned. If sin is pardoned, of course there is nothing to be dreaded as to punishment in the future; if sin is pardoned, the offender is placed essentially in the circumstances in which he was before he had sinned. A scheme of salvation, then, that is adapted to man, *must* embody and express some way by which a sinner may be forgiven.

(4.) Peace in such a case can be found only in connexion with *confession* of sin,—confession made not to a third person, but to the One whose law has been violated. All genuine conviction of sin prompts to this, and David was but acting out the law of our nature when he said, "I acknowledge my transgressions, and my sin is ever before me. Against thee, thee only, have I sinned;" Job, when he said, "Behold, I am vile; what shall I answer thee? I will lay my hand upon my mouth;" the prodigal son, when he said, "I have sinned against heaven and in thy sight;" and the publican, when, not being able to lift up his eyes to heaven, he said, "God be merciful to me a sinner." "He that covereth his sins shall not prosper: but whoso confesseth and forsaketh them shall find mercy." You cannot find permanent peace by attempting to stifle the conviction of sin. You cannot by endeavouring to cover and conceal your offences. You cannot by suffering them to pass from your remembrance. You cannot by confessing your sins against God to man—though robed in a priestly vestment and consecrated with holy oil. You must go to God—a poor penitent—laden with the conviction of guilt—renouncing all attempts to justify yourself—admitting the full truth that you are a sinner—not attempting to cloak or conceal *one* of your transgressions; saying substantially, as David did, "Have mercy upon me, O God, according to thy loving-kindness; according unto the multitude of thy tender mercies blot out my transgressions. Wash me throughly from mine iniquity, and cleanse me from my sin. For I acknowledge my transgressions, and my sin is ever before me. Against thee, thee only, have I sinned," Psa. li. 1—4. So pleading, by faith in the blood that cleanseth from all sin—the blood of the Redeemer—your "sins will be blotted out as a cloud, and your transgressions as a thick cloud," Isa. xliv. 22. So pleading, you will hear the voice which so often gave relief to the troubled soul when the Redeemer walked on the earth, "Thy sins be forgiven thee, go in peace!"

SERMON XII.

THE STRUGGLES OF A CONVICTED SINNER.

MARK x. 22, 23.—"And he was sad at that saying, and went away grieved; for he had great possessions. And Jesus looked round about, and saith unto his disciples, How hardly shall they that have riches enter into the kingdom of God!"

MATT. viii. 21, 22.—"And another of his disciples said unto him, Lord, suffer me first to go and bury my father. But Jesus said unto him, Follow me, and let the dead bury their dead."

LUKE ix. 61, 62.—"And another also said, Lord, I will follow thee; but let me first go bid them farewell which are at home at my house. And Jesus said unto him, No man, having put his hand to the plough, and looking back, is fit for the kingdom of God."

EVERY one who has become a Christian has been conscious of a *struggle* of greater or less intensity, and of longer or shorter duration, before he found peace in believing. This struggle arises from the conviction of duty and the sense of guilt and of danger, on the one hand, and the love of the world and of sin, in some form, on the other. The intensity and the duration of this struggle will be varied much by the character of the individual; will be modified much by his time of life or by the kind of instruction which he receives; will be intense as his love of sin may be intense and his conviction of its guilt may be intense, and protracted as the love of sin and the world has been made strong in his heart.

The cases to which I have referred in opening this discourse are, each of them, an illustration of this thought:—a few of the many to be found in the New Testament, and all of them having a counterpart in the application of the gospel to the hearts of men in every age. The first is that of a rich young man—a man full of ardour, of many amiable qualities, and a sincere inquirer on the subject of religion—whom the Saviour required to give up his wealth, and consecrate it to God if he would follow him; and the struggle in his case was between his conviction of the necessity of religion and his love of his possessions. The second was that of a man whom the Saviour called to follow him, but who asked that he might first go and bury his father; and the struggle in his case was between his conviction of a duty which he owed to Christ and a desire to be saved, on the one hand, and a strong domestic tie—one of the strongest that can be conceived of—and a supposed pressing duty, growing out of that, on the other. The third was a similar case—that of a man who expressed a *willingness* to follow him, but who merely asked a *delay* that he might go, before he gave himself up to be a follower of Christ, and take a proper leave of his own friends and family connexions:—a parting struggle between his love of those friends and the love of the Saviour. In all these you will perceive essentially the same conflict of mind:—the command of Christ, his invitations and appeals, a strong sense of duty, a conviction of the necessity of religion, on the one hand; and some form of earthly attachment, some worldly engagement, some desire of respite and delay, some yet unsundered tie binding to the world, on the other. This is the subject to which, at the present time, I propose to ask your attention: in other words, I wish to describe the struggles of a sinner under conviction of sin before he yields to the claims of the gospel. I shall endeavour to describe that struggle, and to show the reasons why a sinner in that state is not converted. In doing this, I shall seek to point out the nature of the struggle; the causes which produce it; and some illustrations of it as a mental operation, and as preventing the conversion of the soul to God.

The struggle may be described, in general, in one word. It is a conflict between a conviction of duty, and an unwillingness to do it; between a sense of what is right, and an inclination to do wrong; between a feeling that God ought to be obeyed, and the love of sin and of the world which prevents obedience. It is a conflict which shall have the mastery—conscience or pleasure; benevolence or selfishness; religion or the world. The person referred to is sensible of the evil of the course which he is pursuing, but is not prepared to abandon it; he is convinced that he is a sinner, but is not willing to forsake his sins; he is unhappy in the pursuit of the world, but is not wholly ready to become a Christian; he feels in some degree the force and the reasonableness of the commands of Christ, and has some desire to be his follower, but he loves the world, as the rich young man did his possessions, or he has some strong worldly tie which he cannot yet sever, as he did who pleaded that he might go and bury his father, or he who asked that he might be suffered to bid farewell to those at his house. Two opposite things, both very powerful in their nature, are brought into conflict, and produce an agitation of the soul, as when counter currents of air meet in the sky, driving the clouds on each other and causing fierce tempests and storms, or as when a mighty river rolls down into the ocean, and meets the ebbing tide when driven onward by a mighty wind. Thus we have seen the clouds meet together on the hills, driven from the east and the west, heaving in wild commotion. And thus, too, it is at the mouth of some great river, as navigators tell us of the river Oregon, where on the one side a vast and rapid volume of waters is rolled toward the ocean, and on the other the mighty sea rolls its waves in towards the descending volume. They meet on the bar, and then occurs the strife of contending currents. Rarely are the waters so smooth that a vessel may enter the mouth of the river safely, and often the mariner, unable to enter, is compelled to turn the prow of his vessel and stand again out to sea. So often in the soul of man. There are contending passions. There is in each an unwillingness to yield. There is a long and fearful struggle before either gives way, and the soul finds peace.

The *causes* of this struggle or conflict may all be resolved into the one fact, that there is now a deeply-felt conviction of duty and of danger coming into conflict with passion, pride, selfishness, worldliness, and the conscious opposition of the heart to a holy God.

On the one hand, there is the strong conviction of duty, and a sense of sin and danger more or less deep. The nobler powers of our nature, long torpid, are awakened into energy, and demand that the world and sin shall be abandoned, and that God shall be obeyed. Those powers of the soul that were designed to prompt to duty, and to lead to the service of God, had been long inactive. The conscience had become insensible to the obligations of religion. Duty was neglected without exciting compunction. The lessons of early piety were forgotten. The Bible was disregarded; the Sabbath was devoted to business, to light reading, to amusement, to sin; the sanctuary was entered reluctantly, and only by constraint of parental authority, if at all, or in accommodation to the wishes of a wife or mother, or from respect to the decent proprieties of life; the gospel was heard without feeling and without interest; its solemn warnings were unheeded, and its invitations slighted; and the great interests of the soul were wholly neglected. The world was pursued as the grand end of living; plans of gain were formed and pressed earnestly to their completion; or the life was devoted to gaiety, without any fear of death, any apprehension of the coming judgment. In such a state, sin and the world had gained a victory, and the soul was held in the chains of a servitude that was loved, and where the great powers of our nature had even ceased to struggle. Sleep, like the sleep of death, had crept silently over these faculties, and all was calm, and "Satan led the sinner captive at his will."

But these slumberings are now broken. The eyes have been opened on the reality of things. The spell has been dissolved. The voice of God is heard addressing the soul, and the aroused conscience now demands that attention shall be given to that voice. A new class of thoughts are summoned before the mind, and they come in such a way that the soul cannot but regard them. The law of God, forbidding all sin, with its severe and terrible sanctions; the demands of conscience; the evils of ingratitude; the dreadful condition of a heart that is as hard as adamant; the fearful state of one living without God and without hope; the terribleness of a death without religion; the guilt of having disregarded God, and of having trampled on the blood of his dying Son; the crime of having grieved the Holy Spirit, and of having slighted the means of grace; the memory of violated sabbaths and abused mercies; the sins of the past life—pride, selfishness, envy, lust, sensuality; the guilt of having disobeyed a parent, or of having ridiculed his religion,—these and kindred topics now occupy the attention, and the mind can no longer calm them down as it did in past years, for some mysterious, invisible agency is pressing them upon the soul.

But, on the other hand, there are antagonist feelings as numerous, and, at present, as strong. There is the love of sin and of the world. There is the reluctance to be known to be serious. There is the dread of derision. There is the innate distaste for religion, and the long-cherished contempt for the gospel, and hatred of the name of Jesus. There is the pride which makes one unwilling to be seen by others reading the Bible, and the pride which makes one unwilling to pray, though alone. There is some fondly cherished plan pertaining to the world, which has been long in maturing, and which is now in the process of speedy completion. There are habits of sin which have been long indulged, from which it is now not easy to break away. There are associations of friendship or business pertaining to this world which it is difficult to sunder. There are bonds which unite to the world of gaiety and vanity, which it would require much moral courage, and much strength of resolution, and, I will add, much of the grace of God, to dissolve.

Hence the struggle—the warfare. The command of God; the sense of duty; the conviction of guilt; the apprehension of the wrath to come; the pleadings of the gospel; the love of Christ;

the dread of death; the feeling that the heart *ought* to be given to God, on the one hand:—on the other, the love of sin, of the world, of vanity—the power of sinful passion long indulged, the friendship of the gay and the worldly, the love of ease, the pleadings for delay, and the dread of shame—these coming into conflict with the others, and keeping up the struggle in the soul;—now one almost seeming to gain the ascendancy, and now the other;—at one moment, and under the pressure of truth, the soul "*almost*" ready to surrender and yield to God, and, at another moment, the world and sin *near* to getting the ascendancy, and the soul *almost* free from anxiety and from serious thoughts;—now "almost persuaded to be a Christian," and now about as near being persuaded to give up the subject altogether, and to become a thorough infidel or atheist.

This occurs when a sinner is pondering the question whether he shall become a Christian or not. I speak of the great features of the struggle, without meaning to say that the conflict is always thus strongly marked, or that it is always fierce and protracted. I am saying that with greater or less intensity, or with greater or less duration, such a struggle must exist between the claims of God and sin—between the love of the world, and the duty of giving the heart to God.

I may be speaking to some, however, who would call all this the language of "cant" and mysticism, and who, not finding this laid down in the books of mental philosophy that they have studied, and not having experienced it in their own lives, may be ready to say with a sneer, that such a conflict must be *peculiar to our holy religion;* that is, as they in such a case would use the phrase, that it evinces a disordered state of mind; or a mind not well balanced; or a disturbed condition of the nervous temperament; or a process which no well-disciplined intellect would go through with; a state to which no soul that is manly, independent, self-controlling, would submit. It may be useful, therefore, to offer a few illustrations, to show that this is neither the result of weakness nor disease; and that a man, when he becomes a Christian, is acting under mental laws in reference to religion with which we are familiar everywhere.

In referring now, as was proposed, to some *illustrations* of this struggle, I would observe—

(1) It may occur, substantially, among the heathen. Wherever there is a human being, there may be a conflict between a sense of duty on the one hand, and the love of sin on the other; between conscience and passion; between the claims of religion, and the love of the world. Araspes the Persian, as described

by Xenophon, said, in order to excuse his treasonable designs, "Certainly, I must have two souls; for plainly it is not one and the same which is both evil and good; and at the same time wishes to do a thing and not to do it. Plainly, then, there are two souls; and when the good one prevails, then it does good, and when the evil one predominates, then it does evil." So also Epictetus says, "He that sins, does not do what he would; but what he would not, that he does." So Ovid, "Desire prompts to one thing, but the mind persuades to another. I see the good, and approve it, and yet pursue the wrong." These were heathen minds. Araspes and Ovid certainly had never heard of Christianity; and though Epictetus *might* have heard of it, yet he was a heathen still, and there is no evidence that the sentiment which he uttered was shaded or modified in the slightest degree by any reflex influence of Christian truth. And yet, can any one fail to see the same laws of mind working, and the same developments of the state of the soul, as in the passages from an eminent Christian which I will now copy? "That which I do, I allow not; for what I would, that do I not; but what I hate, that do I." "It is no more I that do it, but sin that dwelleth in me." "To will is present with me; but how to perform that which is good, I find not," Rom. vii. 15, 17, 18. Had Araspes, Epictetus, Ovid, been seated as learners at the feet of the apostle Paul? No; they had been seated as learners at the feet of Nature, and had contemplated the human soul as it is under all forms of religion, and experienced a conflict in their own minds—a struggle between sin and duty, which may exist anywhere. That conflict is more common and more decided under Christianity, only because the light of truth there is more intense and more widely diffused. But can you fail in these extracts to see the same laws working which exist where the sinner is convicted of sin, and is struggling with the question whether he shall yield to the claims of duty and of God?

Under the influence of such conflicting feelings, I doubt not that the struggle of mind which I am describing may exist at all times extensively in the heathen world. It is the acting out of human nature—the development of man, a fallen being, yet a moral agent, under the government of a holy God,—and is an important means everywhere of restraining him at least from sin, if it does no more for him. We cannot doubt that, constituted as man is, there was in many an ancient Grecian, Persian, or Roman youth, and is now in the bosom of many a young man in China, in Arabia, and even in the islands of the South Sea, and in Caffraria, a long and arduous conflict between the low and gross passions of the soul, and the claims of morality, justice, honour, and truth—the claims of God still speaking to the conscience and the heart.

(2) But this occurs not only among the heathen: it occurs in Christian lands among those who never become truly converted, and who, indeed, do not regard the struggle as having any connexion with religion. There are few of the young in whose bosoms there is not such a struggle. It occurs when the question is asked by a young man whether he shall obey the nobler powers of his nature, and be virtuous, respected, and honoured, or whether he shall surrender himself to some base passion that is gaining the ascendancy in his soul, and that threatens to make him the miserable victim of vice. It occurs between every virtue that can reign in the human bosom, and that can adorn human nature, and every vice that can establish itself in our nature, and render us debased, degraded, brutalized, besotted, poor, and dishonoured. Take a single instance—alas, how common and how sad often the issue of the conflict! It relates to the way in which habits of intoxication are contracted. Can any one ever become a victim of intemperance without going through such a conflict—often a long and fearful struggle—between his convictions of duty; his self-respect; his early anticipations and hopes, and the fearful passion that is striving so successfully to gain the mastery over him? There is a point in the lives of those who become confirmed inebriates, in which this question comes fairly before the mind, and in which the struggle is fearful. The love of the intoxicating cup—that unnatural yet fascinating propensity—has begun to be formed. Habits have been commenced which it is difficult to abandon. Friendships have been contracted for those who meet to indulge in the social glass, which it would not now be easy to dissolve. These habits and these friendships are now becoming stronger and stronger, and the prospect of their being firmly rivetted on the soul is daily becoming more and more certain. It may be perfectly clear that a little further indulgence will be followed with certain ruin. There is, on the other hand, the impending ruin of reputation; the dread of poverty and disgrace; the apprehended loss of peace;—there are the rebukes of conscience; the solemn commands of God; the counsels and entreaties of parents and friends;—there is the dread of the drunkard's death, and the fear of the retribution beyond the tomb,—all these, in the sober moments, come with power to the soul, and often produce a fearful struggle. I believe that no man, young or old, is perfectly safe from the danger and the horror of intemperance, but

he who wholly and absolutely abstains from the intoxicating bowl—for there has been no class of human virtues hitherto that has constituted a perfect security where there has been indulgence;—but still, it is true, that just at the point of conflict now under consideration any man might be, if he would, saved from danger; but if he yields here, he may be gone for ever. On the great river that flows west of the Rocky Mountains to the ocean—the river already referred to—there is a place where the waters are compressed into a narrow channel, and where the river suddenly falls many feet, pitching and tumbling over the rocks. This passage, though not wholly free from danger, is, however, not unfrequently made with safety in a small boat. But then commences the danger. The boat, having shot down that narrow passage, is often seen to stop suddenly, and to lie without motion on the bosom of the waters. It neither goes forward, nor backward, nor towards either shore. It seems for the moment to be consciously *deliberating* whither it shall go. Soon it begins to move, at first so gently that the motion is scarcely perceptible, not forward, but in a circular direction—so gently, however, that one who knew not the perils of the place would feel no alarm. But then commences the fearful struggle. Every oar is plied; every nerve of the oarsmen is stretched; every effort possible made at the bow and the stern to turn the boat from that fatal current. But always in vain. It goes round, and round, and round, in spite of death-like exertions, increasing in rapidity as the circle grows smaller, until, having reached the centre, in an instant it disappears for ever. Rarely is it that a fragment of the boat is seen afterwards, or that a body that is lost is recovered. So there is a point in a man's life where there seems to be, and where there may be, calm deliberation, and where safety is yet possible—where the man in danger may pause and reflect, and be saved. Though there have been temptations, yet you would hardly say that there was a tendency now in any direction of ruin; you would say that the man might be safe. But soon that point is past, and there is a movement, slight at first, and then the current sweeps on to ruin. Do not suppose that they who perish by intemperance—or by any other vice—perish without a struggle. It is after many a struggle, when too late; it is after many a conflict, when the power that sweeps them in is too great to be resisted. Men perish by this vice, and by other vices, after many anxious moments; after many resolutions formed to abandon the course; after many tears; after many wakeful nights; for the enemy has laid hold on them with a strong grasp—like the sweeping whirlpool—and they cannot now escape.

I refer to these cases to show that all mental struggles and conflicts, all anxieties of soul, are not confined to the subject of religion. It is in every portion of the world, in reference to every vice and every temptation. There are more struggles in respect to worldly matters—more mental conflicts—more distressing agitations of the soul, than occur on the subject of religion; and rarely does any man perish under the control of any vice, who has not at some period had a most fearful conflict with his passions, and felt most deeply that he was in danger, and cried most earnestly for help.

(3) But such a struggle *does* occur on the subject of religion; and to illustrate this was the design in referring to these cases. It occurs, as I remarked in the outset of the discourse, in the case of all those who become the children of God, and who find ultimate peace in the gospel. The great question comes up for final decision, whether the gay world, so fascinating and alluring, shall be pursued or abandoned; whether the desire of worldly honour and ambition shall be exchanged for a good conscience and the hope of heaven; whether the paths of vice shall continue to be trod, or shall be forsaken for better paths; whether the voice of reason, of conscience, and of God, shall be obeyed, or whether all the solemn dictates of truth shall be disregarded. This is no slight struggle. It is often one of the most fearful in which the soul ever engages, as it is the most important in its issues of any in which man is ever concerned. Before the minds of youthful females the question *does* come up, under the influences of the Spirit of God, not whether they shall abandon the world in the sense of taking the veil, and immuring themselves in a nunnery—for the gospel never asks a human being to agitate that question;—but whether the gaieties of the world shall be exchanged for the sober pursuits of piety; the love of outward adorning, for the ornament of a meek and quiet spirit; a desire to be admired on earth, for a desire to appear in the robes of salvation on the banks of the river of life; a wish to be loved by friends here as the great end of existence, for a wish to be loved by the Saviour of the world. Before the minds of young men the question *does* come up whether the pursuits of gain, of pleasure, or ambition, shall be exchanged for the pursuits of religion; whether the passions which have reigned in the heart shall be sacrificed to the principles of the gospel; whether all that is attractive to the youthful eye and heart shall be made subordinate to the self-denying duties of the cross, and

whether this world shall be made subordinate to the world to come. It is *not* a question whether this world shall be abandoned in the sense that life shall be spent in a monastery, or in caves and solitudes—for the gospel never proposes that question to any class of men; but it *is* a question whether the world shall be abandoned as the great object of pursuit, and the soul be devoted sincerely and wholly to God; whether all forms of vice shall be forsaken; whether all associations contrary to the gospel shall be broken up; whether the understanding and the heart shall be subjected to the teachings of the Saviour; whether God shall be all in all. That is a question which *does* come before the mind; and that question *must* be decided in one way, and one only, by all who become true Christians; it *is* decided in another way by all who do not.

I have thus endeavoured to describe the struggle or conflict in the mind of the convicted sinner. The reasons why such a sinner is not converted, or the obstacles which hinder his conversion, are plain and apparent. All the facts in the case can be explained by a reference to the love of sin; to the power which the world has on him; to the strength of some mighty passion; to the influence of companions; to the dread of shame; and to an unwillingness to renounce the world, with its vanity and lusts. The sinner himself, in that state, might perhaps, in certain moods of mind, be disposed to attribute the fact that he is not converted to God himself; to say that he could convert him if he would; to resolve the matter into the Divine sovereignty and decrees; and to seek peace in the reflection that he has nothing to do, and that, as the whole matter is in the hands of God, if he is to be saved he will be; or if not, no efforts of his own can be of avail. It is not necessary now to consider the points which arise out of such suppositions; for, whatever may be the truth in regard to them, it is needless to advert to these, for there are other causes amply sufficient, as we have seen, to explain the fact that the sinner in that state struggles long, and is not converted.

A very interesting inquiry, on which there is no time now to enter, presents itself here. It is, in what way can an agitated and struggling mind, such as I have described, find peace? What do the laws of our mental constitution *demand* in order that these agitations should be calmed down, so that there may be permanent happiness? And what has the gospel plan of salvation devised and presented to men as adapted to meet these laws of our being, and to *give* peace to the mind in such a state? This inquiry will open some very interesting views about the laws of our mental structure, and introduce us at once to the provisions made in the gospel to give peace to a soul troubled and agitated by the remembrance of sin,—a soul struggling between the conviction of duty on the one hand, and the lingering and powerful love of the world on the other. The inquiry cannot be entered on now. There are a few reflections which follow from what I have said, which I desire to suggest in conclusion.

(1) One is, that we may learn why it is that a sinner is ever so long under conviction of sin before he is converted. The old theologians, with little elegance of phrase I admit, but endeavouring to express what they regarded as a valuable thought—though it was, in fact, in some respects, a practical error and illusion—speak much of what they call a "*law-work* on the soul:" by which they seem to have meant a protracted period of painful and distressing conviction of sin—a long season of gloom, and sadness, and conflict—before the heart is converted; and they appear to have supposed, not only that this was *necessary* from the nature of the mind and of religion, but that the conversion would have evidence of genuineness, and the religion of the soul itself be valuable and thorough, just in proportion to the depth of this gloom, and the severity and duration of the struggle. But never was there a greater delusion. There is no occasion for gloom at all in such a case, for the offer of pardon meets a sinner the moment he is willing to accept of it; and the only occasion for the conflict and struggle which I have described—be it longer or shorter—is, that the sinner *will not* surrender to the convictions of duty, and yield himself to God. The struggle arises from his pride, and selfishness, and obstinacy, and love of the world; the gloom is only that which the mind *must* feel when it will not submit to plain and manifest truth and duty. There is no *value* or *moral worth* in any such conflict, any more than there is in any other conflict with conscience and a sense of duty; and this struggle no more enters into religion, or gives a value to religion, than the obstinacy of a child enters into the character of obedience to a parent. There is no necessity for such a protracted and gloomy struggle in becoming a Christian. Yield at once, as the apostles on the banks of the sea of Galilee did when the Saviour called them; yield as the jailer at Philippi did when told what he must do to be saved; yield as Saul of Tarsus did when the Saviour called him in the way to Damascus, not "conferring with flesh and blood;" yield as a frank and open-hearted child who has done wrong submits to the authority of a father,—and this long and dreaded "law-work" on the soul, this

season of deep melancholy and gloom, would be unknown. But treat the commands of the Saviour as the rich young man did who had great possessions, and who was unwilling to abandon them; or let your love for the world be so strong that you cannot part with it, and beg to be permitted to return to it, as he did who asked that he might go and bury his father before he gave himself to the Saviour, or he who asked that he might go *first* and bid them farewell at his house—and, unless your serious convictions of sin and duty pass away altogether, such a conflict is inevitable, and it will be continued *until* there is a surrender of the soul unconditionally to God.

(2) Another thought is this: that if the views which I have submitted to you are correct, then undoubtedly not a few would long since have been true Christians if they had offered no resistance to the clear convictions of duty. Many a time have your consciences checked and rebuked you. Many a time have you had serious thoughts. Many a time have you felt that you *ought* to be Christians. Many a time have you felt that the world was vanity, and that sin was an "evil and bitter thing." And many a time have you been on the very borders of the kingdom of God—in such a state that the Saviour would have said of you, as he did of one in his own time, "Thou art not far from the kingdom of heaven;" and that you would have said, as Agrippa did, "*Almost* thou persuadest me to be a Christian." An influence has been setting in upon your souls, which would long since have brought you into the kingdom of God, if you had yielded to it, and had honestly done what you felt to be right. God addressed you; Christ appealed to you; your conscience summoned you to forsake your sins; your parents, your pastor, your wife, your child, your bosom-friend tenderly admonished you; darkness, solitude, morning, evening, midnight—memory, hope, fear—the obligations of gratitude, the desire of happiness, the dread of death, and the fear of the dark unknown world,—all, under the Divine Spirit, pressed the subject of religion upon your attention, and summoned you to the service of the Redeemer. Others were thronging into the kingdom of God, and your conscience urged you to follow them, and as they found peace by yielding, so might you have done also. That you are not now a Christian is not to be traced to any such fact as that there is no mercy for you, or that God is not willing to save you, or that Christ did not die for you, but to the fact that to all these things you have offered a steady resistance. When perhaps eight years of age, you would have been a Christian, if you had yielded even to those childish convictions of duty,

and had prayed to the Saviour; when twelve, fifteen, or twenty, there were considerations enough pressed upon your attention to induce you to be a Christian, and you often struggled against your convictions; at thirty, at forty, perhaps up to seventy, there have been times when your mind has been troubled, and when your conscience has urged the claims of religion, and when if you had simply *yielded* to what you knew and felt to be right, you would have found the peace which the gospel gives.

(3) Another thought is this: It is a hard and difficult thing, in many respects, for a sinner to destroy his own soul. A great work has to be done before a sinner can be sent down to eternal ruin. The path which he treads to the world of woe is a path of conflict, not a path of peace. The life of a sinner is a warfare. God means to throw obstacles in the way to his ruin. He means to check, restrain, and rebuke him; he means to set his duty and interest before him; he means that the appeals of reason and conscience, of heaven and earth, should ring loud, and long, and constant in his ears. We speak much of the *Christian* conflict, and of the struggle in the Christian's soul, and we describe not a fictitious, but a real warfare. But there is a conflict as real and as fierce in the sinner's soul before he can be lost. The Christian makes no war on himself, on his conscience, on his parents, on his pastor, on his God and Saviour. The sinner does *on all.* He fights his way down to hell. He wages a warfare on his reason, on his conscience, on his God, on his Saviour, on his pastor, on his father, mother, sister, wife, on his own convictions of what is right and of what is for his interest, and must achieve a dreadful victory over them all before he is sent to hell. God will not suffer him to be lost without such a conflict, and when he goes down to eternal woe it is as the result of a most miserable triumph—binding his brow not with the laurel, but with the deadly nightshade—a triumph over conscience, and reason, and every noble principle of his nature. How strange that men will engage in such a conflict, that they will not yield at once to conscience and to God, and find peace!

(4) Another, the last thought, is this: If a sinner is finally lost, he has but himself to blame. I assert that his own conduct will account for it irrespective of anything else. I assert that the *reason* why he will perish is not that no provision was made for his salvation; that no interest was felt for him in heaven; that he was never apprized of his duty or his danger; that he was never in a state in which he could have been saved,—but that

he resisted the conviction of duty; that he struggled against conscience and against God; that he trampled on the precious blood of the atonement, and that he "resisted the Holy Ghost." Sinner, when you perish—oh, may God avert that!—but when you perish, if you do, nor God, nor men, nor angels, will bear the blame. The dreadful responsibility will rest for ever on your own soul, and the word that may yet give you the most deep and lingering agony in the world of woe is the word—SELF-DESTROYED!

SERMON XIII

A WOUNDED SPIRIT.

PROV. xviii. 14.—"A wounded spirit who can bear?"

A WOUNDED SPIRIT:—we inquire naturally what it is; what causes produce it; what makes it difficult to bear it; and what, if any, are the remedies for it. To these four points your attention will now be directed.

I. *What is meant by a wounded spirit?* A few words only will be necessary to explain this to those who have not experienced it, if there are any such; to those who have, no explanation is necessary. We are so made that we are capable of experiencing two kinds of pain—that of the body, and that of the mind, the soul, the heart. With the former we are more conversant, not perhaps because there are more sufferers, but because the symptoms are more apparent; the sufferer is more willing that the disease should be known; the remedy is more easily applied. These sufferings lay the foundation for the skill of the physician, who professes to have little to do with the mind, and who in fact refers to this much less frequently than the perfection of his own art would require. The pains of the body and the soul are distinct in their origin and their nature; they differ in their symptoms, and they differ as much in their remedies. It is true that such is the intimate connexion between the body and the soul—the one often travels over into the department of the other, and the sorrows of the mind prostrate the powers of the body; or a diseased nervous system makes a war of desolation on the healthful operations of the soul; but still these diseases and remedies pertain to different departments of our nature, and are designed to be distinct expressions of the Divine displeasure against the crime of the apostacy.

I am concerned now, as Christian ministers mainly are, with the latter—the disease of the mind. I have no concern with the former—the diseases of the body—except to suggest considerations which will teach submission when they come upon us; to show why they are sent upon men; and except so far as the influence of the gospel may keep from the vices that engender disease, and which lead to pain and death.

When we speak of a wounded spirit, and especially as contrasted, as it is in our text, with "infirmity,"—"the spirit of a man will sustain his infirmity, but a wounded spirit who can bear?"—we refer to the sickness of the heart; the disease of the soul; the anguish which *mind* can be made to suffer; the mental derangements, the sorrows resulting from disappointments, and losses, and chagrin, and remorse, and the numerous kindred woes to which the soul is subject.

Between these sufferings and those of the body, we may remark the following points of difference as more clearly illustrating their nature. (1.) Much of the suffering of a wounded spirit is almost unavoidably concealed. It lies deep in the soul, while a disease of the body may be so apparent in a prostrate frame, in a sunken eye, in pallid features, or in the flush of fever, that it cannot be hidden. God has given to the soul no such certain indications of the existence of its diseases as he has to the body. The body may be healthful, and everything may indicate the appearance of a man sound in body and in soul, even when the mind is in anguish. (2.) Much of the pain and anguish of the soul is concealed of design. We would not have all the world know what we suffer in the soul, or all the pain that the heart feels. What we feel from disappointed affection or ambition; from abortive plans and frustrated hopes; from chagrin, neglect, and slander; and especially what we feel from recollected guilt, we would not have the world at large know, and there is much of that which we suffer in regard to which we do not choose to invite the sympathy of a friend. We should have a strong reluctance, it may be, to let our most intimate friends know how much we suffer by being slandered, and what is the actual pain we experience when a rival has been more successful than we have. We feel that our own self-respect is involved in not *appearing* even to our friends to suffer, and in bearing up under *such* trials as though they produced no effect on us. It is not so with the pain of the body. We feel that there is no disgrace in the headache, in the pain of pleurisy, or in the hectic on the cheek, or in a raging fever; but that such sufferings rather have a *claim* to sympathy, and we are willing that they should be known. (3.) A third remark is, that the sufferings of the soul often force themselves upon the body, and prostrate its powers, and reveal themselves when we have sought to conceal them. The eye not sufficiently disciplined in guilt will betray him who has done wrong. Or the bloom of beauty leaves the cheek, and the youth pines away apparently without disease, and dies as the result of a wounded spirit. Or the anguish of disappointment, and chagrin, and guilt, become too great to bear; and the sanguinary deed of a moment shows that the fires had long raged within, and that the wounded spirit could no longer be endured, and the sufferer rushes to evil that he "knows not of."

These remarks are, I trust, all that is needful to explain what is meant by a wounded spirit, in order to prepare the way for what I have yet to say. The amount of what I have said is, that the sorrows of a wounded spirit are such as result from disappointment, ingratitude, losses, slander, chagrin, and remorse; from things which go to make the *mind* sad and prostrate, or to overwhelm it with the recollections of guilt.

II. I proceed, in the second place, to state more particularly the causes of this—*the things which operate to produce a wounded spirit.* Probably the idea of wrong done to us, or of our having done wrong to others, is always connected with the sorrow of a wounded spirit; or the essential cause of it is *wrong* that has been in some way perpetrated, and that is leaving its bitter results on the soul. But this idea operates most subtilly, and we often allow ourselves to be influenced *as if* wrong had been done when none such existed, or was intended. A rival outsteps us, and we feel as if he had done us wrong; or as if the community had, by bestowing honours on him which we sought for ourselves. We are disappointed in business; we fail in our plans and expectations; our fields are blasted, or our vessel sinks in the deep, and we allow ourselves almost to feel as if the floods and streams and waves had conspired against us to do us wrong, and with a wounded spirit we sink into sadness and complaining. With this general explanatory remark we may observe, that the causes of a wounded spirit are such as the following:—

(1.) Long cherished, but ungratified desire; or deep, but disappointed affection. We seek honour, but it is withheld; we desire the reciprocal affections of friendship or love, but they are not bestowed; we fix our hopes of happiness on the attainment of some, to us, endeared object, and we cannot grasp it; there is some one whose friendship we deem to be essential to our welfare, but it is a prize which we cannot make our own. The smile that we sought gladdens the hearts of others, but not ours; the presence of the object diffuses happiness on all else except on our desolate souls. To all others there are warm beams of sunshine in the presence of the object; to us there is the coldness and darkness of an eclipse. Unrequited and unreciprocated affection makes the heart sad. "Concealment, like a worm in the bud, feeds on the damask cheek."

The heart "pines in grief," and the wounded spirit sinks in melancholy. There is a secret feeling that a *wrong* has been done; that such ardour of love should have met with a response, and that there was a claim to reciprocal affection.

(2.) Disappointment in business, or in the pursuits of ambition. We enter on the career of life with many others. We start together from the goal. They have no advantage in the time of starting, or in the smoothness of the way, or in the cheering plaudits of those who are lookers on at the race, or in the favour of those who are to distribute the prizes. But soon we begin to lag in the rear, and their success stimulates them to new efforts, and our want of success depresses us. A rival outstrips us. He has better health or better talents, or finds better friends; or facilities of success are open to him which are denied to us; or the world seems partial to him, and we begin to feel that it is disposed to do us injustice. We even feel almost that *he* has done us some injustice, and we begin to envy him and to wish him out of the way, as disappointed and sad, we suffer under the tortures of a wounded spirit. Disappointment thus meets many an aspirant after fame, wealth, and pleasure. It occurs in all professions and callings of life, and in every attempt to find pleasure in objects that are not designed by the Great Author of all things to produce it. No one can gather up and record the disappointments that have been met in the career of ambition, or in the social or in the festive circle. No one can record the secret sighs that have been heaved when pleasure has been sought in vain; or write down the account of the tears that envy, and chagrin, and mortification have caused the sons and daughters of gaiety to shed when they have gone from their places of amusement to sad and sleepless pillows. So we seek more intimacy with a friend than we have a right to look for or expect; we calculate on attentions to which we have a very slender claim; we attempt to make our way into society where our presence is not particularly sought, and are not successful, and the spirit is wounded. There are the mingled feelings of mortified pride, and chagrin, and disappointed ambition; the feelings resulting from neglect, and from the rebuke which the coldness of others has given us,—and we feel that *wrong* has been done us, and the soul pines in sadness.

(3.) The spirit is wounded by attempts to injure our name. Our richest inheritance is a good name. To a man in private life it is his comforter and joy; to a man in professional or public life it is his capital, his all. To each one of us it is the best inheritance which we expect to leave to our children—an inheritance which we believe will be to them of more value than if we could leave them the gold of Ophir; nay, we feel that it would be a worthless inheritance could we bequeath to them the wealth of Crœsus, if it descended with a name covered with infamy. There is no one of us but would wish to have some kind word cut on the humblest stone that may mark the place where we sleep, or that would not wish the stranger to hear that our character was upright, if perchance he should walk where we slumber in the dust.

Now there is nothing that pierces so deep into the soul as slander, " whose breath outvenoms all the worms of Nile." The robber may take my purse, but he has taken only " trash, which *was* mine, *is* his, and *has been* the slave of thousands. But he who takes away my good name, robs me of that which not enriches him, but makes me poor indeed." When a man charges me with a base and dishonourable action; when he accuses me of dishonesty or falsehood; when he perseveres in the accusation even in the face of a life of undisputed integrity; when he expresses no doubt about its truth, and he has the power of making many others believe that what he says is true; and when—as may happen—I may lack just the kind and degree of evidence which I need to make all clear, I need not say that then a deeper wound will be made in the spirit than would be made by the loss of property, or the death of a friend. If to all this there should now be added the circumstance that he formerly enjoyed my friendship; that he ate at my table, slept under my roof, was in my family, heard me speak in the openness of unreserved confidence, and was permitted to look into my very soul, he does me a deeper wrong. He adds not only to cruelty the sin of ingratitude—a sin that pierces deeper than any other; but he adds the power of doing me a deeper injury—for he speaks as one who may be supposed to know. Such were the wounds of the soul which David, and after him He who was " the root and offspring of David," experienced. " Mine own familiar friend in whom I trusted, which did eat of my bread, hath lifted up his heel against me," Psa. xli. 9. " It was not an enemy that reproached me; then I could have borne it: neither was it he that hated me that did magnify himself against me; then I would have hid myself from him: but it was thou, a man mine equal, my guide, and mine acquaintance. We took sweet counsel together, and walked unto the house of God in company," Psa. lv. 12—14.

(4.) The spirit is wounded by the recollection of guilt—of the wrong which we have done in days that are past. Probably this is the main, as it is the most important idea in the text. God has endowed us with a conscience; and it is a part of his arrangement that man shall be self-punished, and shall bear about with him the means of self-correction and rebuke. The severest of all the punishments, therefore, which visit the sinner, are those which spring up from the soul itself, and the torture which man is constrained to inflict on his own heart. It consists of sin brought to recollection, though long since forgotten; of the pangs of remorse; of the remembrance of injuries which we have done, over which years have rolled away, and on which many, many a sun has risen and set. I will not say that there is anything like caprice in the manner in which these sins are brought to the recollection; I will not say that it is by no regular law that it is done—for all the operations of the Spirit of God on man are in accordance with settled law; but there is much in the manner in which it is done that strongly resembles power exerted without rule, or acting by laws which we cannot trace. Now you remember some word spoken, or deed done, that injured one long since dead, and of which a voice from the tomb almost seems to remind you. Now sins that seemed to have faded from the memory, or whose lines were so obliterated that you could hardly trace them, revive, and all the faded colours are restored, and they stand out to view as if written in letters of "living light." Now one single sin seems to stand before the mind black as night. You see it everywhere. It meets you in every pathway, and in every place of solitude. You go to your counting-room, and it is there; you awake at night, and it is before you. The ghost of a murdered man is not apparently more omnipresent; nor the stain of blood on the hand more visible to a guilty eye, and you wonder what has given that prominence to that single sin just now. And now sins come in groups and clusters, and all the evils and errors and follies of your whole life stand out to view, and face you every step you take. Your spirit is wounded,—you have the feelings of a guilty man. It is not so much that you are in danger,—it is that you have done wrong—that your life has been a life of guilt. There is no effort then to cloak or conceal the offences of the past life. They are seen and confessed to be wrong. There is no attempt to ward off the appeals of truth,—to palliate the neglect of prayer or religion,—to excuse unbelief or impenitence,—or to substitute the claims of external morality for what God requires. In the most absolute and unqualified sense the soul confesses its guilt, and feels that dust and ashes become one whose whole life has been wrong. This is that state of mind which is characterized in the Bible as "a broken and a contrite heart," or as a "bruised reed"—the state of mind which David experienced when there was brought to his remembrance his great acts of guilt, when he said, "A broken and a contrite heart, O God, thou wilt not despise," Psa. li. 17. It is this sadness which is felt at the remembrance of guilt that the gospel is designed to heal, and this wound of the soul to a greater or less degree always precedes true conversion to God.

(5.) There is a wound of the spirit which only the children of God feel; or such as is found among those who give to others, if not to themselves, every evidence that they are sincere Christians, and are heirs of eternal life. It may assume with them the form of recollected guilt; or the form which exists when they see no evidence that their sins are pardoned; or the form of the hiding of the Divine countenance; or the form arising from the feeling that they are forsaken both by God and man—a form which exists when everything seems to be against us, and disappointment sits gloomily, like an ill-omened bird, on all that we undertake. This is often charged on religion itself when it should not be, for such cases often arise from the want of religion, and because the soul fears that it has no religion; and in the seasons of deepest sadness which such persons feel, as in the case of David Brainerd and Payson, religion, "instead of being the cause of gloom, is the only refuge from its overwhelming effects." This is often made an objection to religion by scoffers and revilers, and the sorrows of the soul in religion are made the subject of unseemly merriment; but with a heart of true sensibility, no matter what the source of sorrow, it will not be so—for,

"With a soul that ever felt the sting
Of sorrow, sorrow is a sacred thing."

"There are minds so delicately strung that they cannot escape the most distressing attacks of melancholy. Friendship, philosophy, and even religion, as it exists in imperfect man, cannot oppose a complete barrier to its influence." With those who feel it most, as in the case of Cowper, there are united often some of the most delicate and lovely traits of character; a warm-hearted philanthropy; a humanity that would not needlessly "set foot upon a worm;" a general cheerfulness of manners; an exquisite humour; a disposition to find pleasure anywhere and everywhere,—in a flower, with a pet rabbit, with children, in the quiet walks of nature, and above all, in sweet communion with God. But you cannot argue against nerves; you cannot heal the maladies of the body by moral influences; you cannot guard the sufferer who has such a temperament from the sorrows which may thus find their way to the soul. "The best of men have occasionally groaned under this pressure. It made Job 'weary of his life;' and that pensive, tender-hearted prophet who seems to have been made to weep says, 'When I would comfort myself against sorrow, my heart is faint within me.'" It is not fancy; it is not imagination; it is not that such persons are worse than others; it is not that they have no true piety—no amiable traits—no cheerful hours: it is to be traced often, perhaps always, to something else than moral causes, and the blame of it should not be thrown upon religion, nor should they who are thus afflicted suppose that they have no true piety.

> "'Tis not as heads that never ache suppose,
> Forgery of fancy, and a dream of woes;
> Man is a harp whose chords elude the sight,
> Each yielding harmony, disposed aright;
> The screws reversed (a task which, if he please,
> God in a moment executes with ease),
> Ten thousand thousand things at once go loose,
> Lost, till He turn them, all their power and use.
> No wounds like those a wounded spirit feels,
> No cure for such, till God, who makes them, heals."

If there is a soul that should meet with sympathy on earth, it is such a soul; if there is one that does meet with sympathy in heaven in its sufferings, it may be presumed to be such an one. Yet there is often sorrow without sympathy; anguish of spirit which no one understands but he who feels it; a depth of distress for which no balm is found in human things; and an exquisiteness of mental woe which,—while it is looked upon with indifference by men, or excites their smile, or provokes their reproaches, as if the subject of this sorrow were cast off by God, or as if religion were to bear all the blame for what human nature ever suffers,—can be met only by the Great Healer of the spirit—by that Redeemer who sympathizes with all forms of grief. How little sympathy is often felt for it; how true to the life is the manner in which it is met, is described by one who experienced it as keenly as man ever did:—

> "This, of all maladies that man infest,
> Claims most compassion, and receives the least;
> Job felt it when he groan'd beneath the rod,
> And the barb'd arrows of a frowning God;
> And such emollients as his friends could spare—
> Friends such as his for modern Jobs prepare.

Blest—rather curst—with hearts that never feel,
Kept snug in caskets of close-hammer'd steel;
With limbs of British oak and nerves of wire,
And wit that puppet prompters might inspire,
Their sovereign nostrum is a clumsy joke,
On pangs enforced with God's severest stroke."—COWPER.

That all these sorrows of the spirit are to be traced, in one way or other, to sin, there can be no reason to doubt; for how can we conceive of suffering that is not somehow connected with this? But let not a man write "bitter things against himself" on account of these sorrows of the spirit; let him not say in his heart that "God has cast off for ever; that he has forgotten to be gracious; that he has in anger shut up his tender mercies; that he will be favourable no more." Let him not say that there is no "balm in Gilead, and no physician there." Let him not say that no good can ever come out of this to his own soul. What a bright day rises after the darkness of midnight; what a beauty there is in nature after a tempest; what a charming bow of the covenant there is bent on the departing cloud; what exquisite happiness there is after pain; what a sense of the value of redemption after the night of gloom passes away; what qualifications for usefulness are given to those who pass through fiery trials; what a bright home is that heaven where there shall be no tears; and what comfort can that God impart of whom it is said by Elihu in the book of Job, with so much beauty, "He giveth songs in the night!" Job xxxv. 10.

III. The third general remark to which I proposed to direct your attention was, *that it is difficult to bear the afflictions of a wounded spirit.* The text is, "The spirit of a man will sustain his infirmity: but a wounded spirit who can bear?" The meaning of this is, that when the *body* is pained, the mind, if sound and pure and healthful, will enable us to sustain the sorrows of bodily sufferings as a faithful ally. It can uphold the sinking frame. It is a helper that may be relied on then. But if the *mind itself* be wounded, *all* support is gone. What will sustain that? The body cannot be depended on to come to the rescue, and the man sinks in despair. This is the point which is now to be illustrated.

Of one fact here adverted to, that, if the mind be sound and the heart whole, bodily pains can be borne, the world has furnished abundant illustrations. We know that disease and pain can be endured without murmuring; and the history of the church has furnished not a few beautiful illustrations of the fact that the pains of the rack, the horrors of impalement, and the agony of flame at the stake, can be all endured with a calm and tranquil spirit. A good conscience; a belief that we are right; a conviction of duty; unwavering confidence in God the Saviour, and the aid of his Holy Spirit, enable the suffering martyr to endure all that the malice of men can inflict on the human frame.

But when the *mind* is diseased—when the spirit is wounded, the case is changed. Then the prop is taken away, and the anguish of such a spirit who can bear? In illustrating this, I may observe, (1.) That this anguish of spirit often occurs when the body is feeble and prostrate. A disordered nervous temperament; or a tendency to depression and sadness; or a succession of external calamities, may prepare the way for the inexpressible tortures which the mind may be made to endure. *Then* a mental sorrow; an unkind remark of one who ought to be a friend; an unguarded and almost unmeaning word used by him who is really your friend; an instance of neglect or the want of due attention; the detraction of a slanderer; or ingratitude in a child or in one who should be your friend, comes with a force which would scarcely be felt if the body were sound, and the nervous system braced to bear the rebuffs of life. (2.) It is intolerable, because suffering from this quarter strikes at all a man's comforts and hopes. A man has a reputation. It has been to him the fruit of many a hard year's toil. It is worth more to him than all the wealth of Ophir; and there is not a monarch so rich that the brightest gem in his diadem could purchase it, or make him willing to part with it. It is all his capital, his hope, his stay, and the only inheritance that he is likely to leave to his family. The cold, unfeeling slanderer; the false friend; the rival; the man that you have befriended, and that you would befriend again, strikes the envenomed fang into that character, calumniates your name, prostrates your reputation as far as he can; and who can bear it? Far from me and my friends be a spirit that would not feel on such an occasion—a heart which would not bleed. (3.) Again, a spirit wounded by the remembrance of guilt, who can bear it? Many an illustration has the world furnished of this, and will still furnish. The remembrance of wrong done, of duty neglected, of privileges abused, of mercies disregarded; the remembrance of the days when the imagination gave loose to the reins of impure conceptions, or the tongue to words of blasphemy; the remembrance of the times when the mercy of God was disregarded, and the appeals of eternal love slighted, comes with withering power over the soul, and rests like a horrid incubus upon the crushed and tortured spirit; and who can bear it? All the wrong that the soul ever did; all the forgotten deeds of night; all the long-concealed transgressions of other days; all the visions of an impure and licentious imagination that had seemed to have flown away for ever, seem now to come back and arrange themselves before the eye of the soul,—a dark and horrid brood, and the eye can neither close itself on them, nor can it turn away. This is conviction of sin,—the anguish which the wounded spirit feels at the remembrance of past deeds of guilt. (4.) This agony of spirit has one of two issues. In one case it leads to the true source of relief,—the balm of Gilead—the blood of the Redeemer,—and the soul is made whole. The state of anguish becomes so intolerable that the soul can bear it no longer, and it gladly flees to pardoning blood. In the other case it leads to despair and to death. The anguish of remembered guilt becomes insupportable, and the wounded spirit, ignorant of a way by which peace can be found, or unwilling to accept of the peace which the gospel furnishes, seeks to fly from life as if to escape from the guilt that haunts it by day and by night. Under this heavy pressure the man closes his own life, and the wounded spirit rushes uncalled into the presence of God.

IV. It remains only, in the fourth place, to inquire *whether for the wounded spirit there is no relief*—whether a merciful God has appointed nothing which shall serve to relieve the anguish. Medicine is provided by his hands for the pains of the body; is there no medicine thus provided for the deeper sorrows of the soul? Long since this question was asked with deep solicitude by suffering man. Cicero, in the Tusculan Questions,* inquires with earnestness "why it is that since so much care has been shown to heal the body, a like care has not been evinced to discover some remedy for the soul—for the diseased, the enfeebled, the troubled mind?" He attempts to answer the inquiry. "*Philosophy*," says he, "is the medicine for the soul." This is, indeed, the best answer that the world, unaided by revelation, could furnish, but *we* know that it does not meet the case. Philosophy may teach me to blunt my sensibilities, but that is not to impart consolation, or to heal the "wounds which sin has made" in the soul. I want some security that the wound is healed; I want something that shall make the wounded part *live*, not that which shall consign it to the torpor of death.

What, then, are the remedies for a wounded spirit? How shall we be taught to bear it? With reference to the somewhat

* Lib. iii. § 1.

mixed causes of a wounded spirit, to which I have referred, I shall suggest in conclusion, and by way of a practical application, a few of those remedies, or a few considerations to those who thus suffer.

(1.) I have spoken of the wounds which the spirit feels from the envenomed tongue of slander, the efforts of others to injure our character and blast our reputation. To meet this, I need only suggest the following considerations:—(*a*) God will ultimately take care of a man's character, and give him the reputation which he *ought* to have, if he aims to do right, and to keep a good conscience. (*b*) It is possible for a man to have such a character that the calumniator cannot well injure it. A man who has been known for a dozen or twenty years in a community as a man of truth, and honesty, and industry, and straightforward dealing, and piety, is not likely to be permanently injured by the voice of detraction. The world does not judge thus hastily of the character of a man; and the community regards his character as too valuable to be sacrificed by the voice of a slanderer. I can tell you what man is likely to be injured by a slanderer, or what character is likely permanently to suffer by evil reports. It is the man whose life is one of crooked policy; who is timeserving and changeable; who is inconsistent in his walk; who makes a profession of religion, but who gives slender evidence of sincerity and piety; who is never seen in connexion with religion but at the communion table; who indulges in double-meaning and inuendoes in his conversation; who stands aloof from the cause of temperance, and speaks of the over-heated zeal of the friends of that cause; who can partake of a social glass with the world with as much joyousness and hilarity as those who make no pretensions to serious piety; and who is unsettled, unsteady, and vacillating in his plans. Such a man is just the one for the slanderer. The community is half prepared to believe the first suggestion of a departure from honesty and purity of life; and there is no way by which such a man can live down the calumny. But there are men against whose character you would not believe a word if an angel from heaven should proclaim it, and become the accuser. Have *such* a character, and your spirit need not be wounded by the voice of the slanderer.

(2.) I have spoken of those whose spirit is wounded by neglect and disappointment; by receiving a smaller measure of public favour and regard than they supposed themselves entitled to; by not being elevated to offices which they wished; by not receiving praises and commendations and appointments which they desired;

and by seeing laurels which they wished to entwine around their own brows encircle the heads of others. I admit that there is sometimes real cause of pain here, and that the world is sometimes slow to bestow the due measure of reward on those who deserve its smiles. But the remedy for a wounded spirit here is easy and simple. It is to be found in the consciousness of doing right; in an effort to please God. I may add further, it is to be found in a subdued frame of mind, and in moderated desires. He that will be willing to occupy the place for which he was designed by his Creator, content with the small measure of notice which is due to an individual, and willing that all others should occupy the place which God designed, will not usually find the world inclined to do him injustice. Water finds its proper level, and so does man. To be willing to occupy the place which God in his providence assigns us, however humble or low that place may be, is one of the ways to heal a spirit wounded by mortified pride.

(3.) I have spoken of the wounds which sin has made in the soul; of remembered guilt; of a troubled conscience. Compared with this, all other wounds are trifles; and for this, and for all other sorrows of the soul, arising from disappointment, and chagrin, and envy, and slander, the gospel has provided a remedy. I need not here state as a matter of *information* what this remedy is; it is alluded to only to persuade the wounded in spirit to apply to it. It is the mercy of God in the Redeemer; the healing balm of the gospel of peace; the forgiveness of sins, and the health and life that flow in upon the soul, so beautifully expressed in the language of Jeremiah: "Is there no balm in Gilead? Is there no physician there? Why then is not the health of the daughter of my people recovered?" Jer. viii. 22. It is this of which the Saviour spake when he said, "The Spirit of the Lord God is upon me; because the Lord hath anointed me to preach good tidings unto the meek; he hath sent me to bind up the broken hearted, to proclaim liberty to the captives, and the opening of the prison to them that are bound; to proclaim the acceptable year of the Lord, and the day of vengeance of our God; to comfort all that mourn; to appoint unto them that mourn in Zion, to give unto them beauty for ashes, the oil of joy for mourning, the garment of praise for the spirit of heaviness," Isa. lxi. 1—3. It is this that is referred to when it is said of him, "A bruised reed shall he not break, and the smoking flax shall he not quench," Isa. xlii. 3. It is this of which David sang when he said, "Bless the Lord, O my soul; and all that is within me, bless his holy name:—who forgiveth all thine iniquities; who healeth all thy diseases," Psa. ciii. 1, 3. "He healeth the broken in heart; he bindeth up their wounds," Psa. cxlvii. 3. To many, perhaps very many of my readers, I need not say one word to describe the way by which healing is thus imparted to a wounded spirit. They who are Christians will recognise what they themselves have experienced in the language of one who keenly felt the wounds which sin has made in the soul:—

"I was a stricken deer, that left the herd
Long since. With many an arrow deep infix'd
My panting side was charged, when I withdrew
To seek a tranquil death in distant shades;
There was I found by One who had himself
Been hurt by the archers. In his side he bore,
And in his hands and feet, the cruel scars.
With gentle force soliciting the darts,
He drew them forth, and heal'd, and bade me live."
COWPER, *Task*, b. iii.

Wounded spirit! that same soft and gentle hand can remove every poisoned arrow with which sin has smitten thy soul, and that great Healer of mankind can make you also live. Nor have I any other remedy to mention,—nor do I believe you would elsewhere find it. There are wounds in the soul made by sin, by conscious guilt, by remembered ingratitude and evil affections, which nothing earthly can heal, and which can be remedied effectually and for ever only by the healing balm of the gospel of Christ.

"Deep are the wounds which sin has made;
Where shall the sinner find a cure?
In vain, alas, is nature's aid—
The work exceeds all nature's power.
And can no sovereign balm be found?
And is no kind physician nigh,
To ease the pain and heal the wound
Ere life and hope for ever fly?
There is a great Physician near,—
Look up, O fainting soul, and live;
See in his heavenly smiles appear
Such ease as nature cannot give.
See in the Saviour's dying blood,
Life, health, and bliss, abundant flow;
'Tis only this dear sacred blood
Can ease thy pain, and heal thy woe."—STEELE.

SERMON XIV.

WHAT WILL GIVE PERMANENT PEACE TO A SOUL CONVICTED OF SIN.

JER. vi. 14.—"They have healed also the hurt of the daughter of my people slightly, saying, Peace, peace; when there is no peace."

LUKE vii. 48—50.—"And he said unto her, Thy sins are forgiven. And they that sat at meat with him began to say within themselves, Who is this that forgiveth sins also? And he said to the woman, Thy faith hath saved thee; go in peace."

WHAT will restore peace to a guilty conscience? This is a great and grave question in philosophy and in religion. It is a question which there is abundant occasion to ask in our world; a question of interest to every man—for every man is a sinner. The answer to this question will introduce us to the provisions made in the gospel, and to the harmony of those provisions with the laws of our mental operations.

The immediate question before us now is, What will give permanent peace to a soul convicted of sin? That is, What is demanded by the laws of mind in order that a soul disturbed and agitated with the remembrance of guilt, and apprehensive of punishment, should find peace? This might be prosecuted as a mere inquiry of mental philosophy. It is my business, however, while I shall be compelled to regard it, in some measure, in this light, to prosecute it mainly with reference to the provisions made in the gospel to meet the case.

The natural division of the subject is this:—I. On what do men naturally rely in that state of mind to obtain peace? And, II. What is necessary in any true system of religion to furnish permanent peace? The consideration of the first will make it necessary to show the *inefficacy* of the methods resorted to by men without the gospel. The consideration of the second will prepare us to show that the gospel has revealed a plan which accords with the laws of our nature, and which is effectual. The first of these points is suggested by the text from Jeremiah: "They have healed the hurt of the daughter of my people slightly, saying, *Peace, peace; when there is no peace.*" The second by the text in Luke—the case of the penitent female who came to the Saviour, and washed his feet with her tears, and to whom he said, "Thy sins are forgiven; thy faith hath saved thee: *go in peace.*"

The case which we are to consider is that of a convicted sinner; and the first inquiry relates to the methods which are commonly employed to obtain peace, and the inefficacy of those methods. In prosecuting this inquiry, we may lay out of view the two following things, as matters which cannot be affected by *any* plan:—

(1.) The *fact* that the sin has been committed cannot be *changed.* That is to remain historically true for ever. The murder has been done; the property has been stolen; the act of seduction has been perpetrated; the words of blasphemy have gone out of the mouth; the feeling of pride, envy, malice, hatred, lust, ambition, has been in the heart. Nothing now can change the *fact*, whatever may be done in regard to it, or however it may be disposed of. There it is in history, and there it will be for ever. No plan of salvation, human or Divine, can change that; not even God can make it otherwise than it is.

(2.) The sin cannot be so *forgotten* as to make that a ground of peace. It may indeed have never been known to many; and it may pass away from the recollection of many who do know it. But by Him who is most interested in it—the "Lord of the conscience"—it is not, and cannot be forgotten; and we can never find permanent peace in any plan which proceeds on the presumption that he will not remember it, or that it is not recorded in his book. And as little can we find permanent peace in any plan which presumes that *we ourselves* shall forget it. We cannot flatter ourselves with any such hope or assurance, for it remains yet to be proved that *any* sin that man has ever committed is permanently effaced from his own memory, or that he may not be in circumstances in which it may be recalled with all its original power.

Laying these, therefore, out of view, the inquiry returns as to the methods to which men sometimes resort to give peace to the mind when troubled with the recollection of guilt.

Those methods may be reduced to the following classes:—

(1.) To regard the mind, when in such a state, as morbid or diseased, and to apply remedies rather of a physical nature to *heal* it, than of a moral nature to make it *pure.* The mind is contemplated rather in its relation to the nervous system than to the moral law, and the thing to be done is to restore health to the physical frame, and through that by sympathy to the soul, rather than to adopt any measures to give peace to a troubled conscience or to a guilty mind as such. The *account* given of one in that state by himself would be, that he is low-spirited, dejected, and sad, rather than that he is guilty; and the aim would be the restoration to health of the bodily functions rather than the treatment of a guilty conscience.

(2.) To divert the mind to other than gloomy thoughts:—the thoughts of sin, of death, and of the judgment. The pleasant scenes of nature, poetry, romance, travel, social enjoyments, gaiety—any or all of these would occur as adapted to calm the troubled soul, and to turn the thoughts to objects of more pleasant contemplation.

(3.) To *conceal* the convictions, with the hope that time, which "does wonders," will restore the mind to peace. It is hoped that these troublesome thoughts will gradually die away; perhaps that by assuming a cheerful external manner there will be a reflex influence on the soul itself, and that it may be restored to peace—that thus by the cheerfulness of the countenance the heart may be made less sad.

(4.) To suppress these convictions by a direct mental effort; to assume the attitude of self-government, and to resolve to be one's own master. A direct warfare is thus made on the sources of trouble, and the mind summons to itself all the power of an "iron will," and resolves *not* to be serious—*not* to yield—*not* to be converted.

(5.) To these methods a fifth may be added—which is, that of embracing some views of religion which affirm that the soul need not be alarmed; which teach that sin is not so great an evil as it is represented to be; and which suppose that there is no ground for apprehension in regard to the world to come: that God is so merciful that he will not punish hereafter, or rather, as the doctrine is embraced in the view of the mind, that he is so *just* that he will not send one of his creatures to a world of woe, and that, therefore, there need be no alarm.

I proceed now to consider these things with reference to the inquiry whether they can give permanent peace to a soul agitated with the conviction of guilt. I do not deny that they may give *temporary* peace, and that often under their influence the agitations of the soul subside, and that the mind becomes again for a time calm, joyous, gay. But that is not the question which I wish to consider; that is not a question which it is of much importance to consider. The true inquiry is, What is the proper and effectual way of meeting the convictions of guilt in the mind; what is the way to produce *permanent* peace? Are these the true methods?

Now, in reply to this question, I have the following remarks to make:—

(1.) This is not the high and honourable method which a man should take in regard to his own sins. If a man is to be saved, he should be saved in a manner consistent with a due self-respect, and so that he can feel that he has met the great questions which have come before him in an open, frank, manly, and dignified manner. But it does not accord with this to attempt to conceal his true character; to regard the conviction of guilt as the fruit of imbecility, or of a morbid state of mind: to attempt to divert the mind to other subjects as if this were not worthy of his attention; to assume an aspect of gaiety in order to conceal what is within; or to embrace an opinion merely to evade the necessity of a frank acknowledgment of what is true. Sin should always be dealt with as a serious matter, and a man —one who is worthy the name of a man—should always be willing to look candidly at his own real character and condition. Crime is not to be treated as a disease—for it is not a disease; conviction of guilt is not to be regarded as a nervous excitement, or as morbid melancholy—for it is neither. When a man is made to feel that he is a sinner before God, the fact is *worthy* of his profound attention, for it may have higher bearings than he can yet understand. There is nothing that is more *likely* to be followed with important results than a conviction of guilt, and no question can be more important for him to settle than this:—how can a man in that state find permanent and solid peace?

(2.) My next remark is, that none of these methods furnish any security of *permanent peace*. I say "*permanent* peace," for 'hat is what we are inquiring after; that is what any *true* system of religion must furnish. And by permanent peace I mean such a disposal of guilt that it shall not rise up hereafter to trouble or annoy us; that we shall be free from all the penalties which it incurs; and that the mind can contemplate that very act of guilt without the harrowing feeling of remorse, and without the apprehension of the wrath of God. Now I say that none of these methods give such peace to a troubled conscience. The reasons for this affirmation I can present in such a manner as to be applicable to each and all of them.

(*a*) One is, that this very method of meeting the case may be itself a source of great misery to the mind. Nature, as we shall see, demands that when a wrong is done it should be confessed —that the burden should be thrown off by acknowledgment— and that relief should be sought by repairing the wrong done, or by seeking forgiveness from the offended party. To conceal guilt in the mind; to attempt to evade these laws of our nature; to refuse to make these acknowledgments, is often a source of the keenest torture, and the burden by that very means often becomes intolerable. Who knows not how the concealed consciousness of guilt may prey upon the soul—a gangrene ever eating—destroying the health and spirits—taking away the fire from the eye, and the colour from the cheek, and filling the whole soul with sadness? And who knows not that, however successful such an attempt may sometimes be, the pressure *may* become so great as to make life a burden, and compel the guilty man to go and make confession, *whatever* may be the result, whether pardon or death? We have a striking illustration of this thought in the experience of the author of one of the Psalms. It relates to an attempt which he made to suppress his convictions of sin, and to the result of a long refusal to make acknowledgment. "When I kept silence," says he, "my bones waxed old through my roaring all the day long. For day and night thy hand was heavy upon me, my moisture is turned into the drought of summer. I said"—that is, *then* I said—"I will confess my transgressions unto the Lord; and thou forgavest the iniquity of my sin. Thou art my hiding-place; thou shalt compass me about with songs of deliverance," Psa. xxxii. 3—7. If a man wishes to make himself miserable he has only to make war on his own conscience, and to repress his convictions of guilt by a violation of the laws of his own nature.

(*b*) Another reason why this course will not secure permanent peace is, that the things which trouble the mind when under conviction for sin are of a *permanent* character, and the distress may be revived at any moment. By the methods referred to you may *allay* the distress for a time, and may give to the mind temporary peace, but there is no security that all this anguish may not in an instant revisit the soul. Conviction of sin grows out of the laws of our nature when we have done wrong, and all which contributes to produce that conviction is of a permanent character. The law of God which condemns the sin is permanent, and always sustains the same relation to sin. Conscience is a permanent part of our moral nature, and though for a time it may be silenced, yet it is never *to die out*, and its rebukes may be as scathing and blasting at any future period as they are now. The Spirit of God is always the same, and at any period of your future being may call up the recollection of crime as well as now. Memory in all the future is to do its work as well as now, and it may as faithfully recall your sins at any period hereafter as it does now. You are at some time, and at no distant period, to die; and *when* death approaches, the grave may appear as gloomy, and the judgment-bar as formidable, as they do now. The fires of hell are not extinguished because men choose not now to think of that dreadful world, and in a moment on a bed of death all the horizon may be lighted up with lurid flames flashing from the lake of fire. To turn away from these truths; or to refuse to think of them; or to render the conscience callous to the appeals of truth, changes none of these things, and can give no permanent peace to the soul. Sooner or later all the questions which grow out of sin, and its relations to God, are to be met, and it does not dispose of the matter to attempt to forget it or to drive it from the mind.

(*c*) And another reason why this does not give permanent peace, and should not be relied on, is, that these thoughts which now give so much trouble to the sinner may revive in circumstances in which you will be much less *able* to calm them down than you may be at present. As you cannot prevent their returning at *some* time hereafter, so you cannot prevent their returning at any time, and at a season when you will be least of all capable of grappling with them. They will be quite as likely to return when you are lying on a sick bed, as when in the enjoyment of vigorous health; when standing on the verge of the eternal world, and when the affairs of this life are over, as when occupied with great questions of business or ambition. The mind then—when the body is prostrate with disease—will be in a condition less favourable to calm down these feelings than it is now, and in that state all the pressure of this terrible conviction of guilt may come back more heavily upon the soul. Then, too, not improbably, all the attempts which you now make to persuade yourself that conviction of sin is connected with a nervous temperament; or that sin is a trifle not worth regarding; or that the sinner has no reason for alarm under the administration of a benevolent God; or that the mind may find permanent peace in driving away its serious thoughts, will be seen to have been "refuges of lies." If a man is to grapple with the convictions of guilt; if he is ever to take hold of the great question how an immortal soul, conscious of depravity, may find peace, it is better that it should be done when he is in health than when he is enfeebled by disease; in the days when he can take up such a question calmly, and in the exercise of his best powers, than in the hour when he feels that he has but a few moments more to breathe, and when his soul is riven and agitated with the thoughts of the coming judgment.

Such are some of the reasons why the methods resorted to by men to give permanent peace to a conscience troubled by the remembrance of guilt must be inefficacious. The sum of what I have said is this:—These methods do not dispose of the subject. They do not meet it as so great and grave a question should be met. They do not consult the laws of our nature. They do not put the matter to rest. They do not give security that all the anguish arising from conscious guilt may not, and will not revisit the soul, and in circumstances in which it will be more difficult to meet it than now. Guilt loses none of its power by distance, or by age, or by circumstances; and none of these methods tend to diminish its permanent power, or to furnish permanent security to the soul.

You may apply these remarks, if you wish an illustration, to *any* case of guilt. You may see their force, for instance, in a case of murder. The crime that has been committed is a fact that cannot now be changed. Whatever disposal is made of it, it is to remain true for ever that the guilty man *did* imbrue his hands in the blood of a fellow-mortal, in violation of the law of God. That fact can never be forgotten by him who preserves the record of human deeds; it is never to be forgotten by him who has committed the crime. And it does not meet the case to treat the trouble and anguish which the mind feels in view of it as the effect of nervous excitement, or to attempt to divert the mind from the subject by the business or the amusements of life; or to conceal the convictions of guilt with the hope that they will die away; or to attempt to discipline the soul so as to banish serious thoughts; or to adopt the opinion that the murderer has nothing to fear under the government of a benevolent God; or to suppose that amends may be made by a correct life afterwards; or to flee to distant lands with the hope of going out of the reach of these convictions; or to hope that age will calm down these troubles, and that time, that "does wonders," will wipe the blood from the hand, and the memory of the deed from the soul. None of these things meet the case. No matter where the murderer wanders or rests—no matter what is his condition or employment, there is a record made on high of the deed; and though he flees over sea and land, and crosses deserts or snows, and though he should live far on beyond the age of the oldest man that has walked the earth, or become like the fabled "wandering Jew," the crime would never be forgotten or changed; but the hand of justice would be stretched out to strike, and in the ends of the earth, and in the most distant years, the act of guilt would have lost none of its freshness in its power to torture the soul. Guilt lives and lingers, and the sinner can never go beyond its power.

These things which I have considered are the methods of human wisdom and philosophy, and beyond these human wisdom cannot go in calming down the convictions of guilt.

II. I proceed, then, in the second place, to consider the great question, What is *needful* to be done to meet the case, and whether the plan proposed in the gospel is such as the case demands? The first great inquiry is, what is *necessary* in the case—and this inquiry is large enough and important enough to occupy the remainder of the present discourse. I shall state, in as few words as possible, what the laws of our mental constitution demand.

In securing permanent peace to a guilty conscience, then, it seems clear to me that the following things are indispensable:—

(1.) The laws of our nature must be understood and consulted in that plan. No plan proposing peace can be effectual which is not based on a sound mental philosophy, and which would not be adapted to produce the effect in all ages, among all people, and in all lands. It must be adapted to man as he is—endowed with reason, and conscience, and memory, and the faculty of anticipating the future. If those laws are not consulted, the plan would be what one prophet so significantly calls "daubing with untempered mortar" (Ezek. xiii. 10, 15), or what another, as in my text, calls crying "Peace, peace; when there is no peace." The great defect in all human schemes of salvation has been that those laws have not been consulted, or that, if known, it has been impossible for man to devise a method that should meet what they demand.

It would detain us too long from points more immediately bearing on the subject, if I should in this place enter on any attempt to prove to you that what I have now laid down is correct. These laws are permanent. They exist everywhere. They are found in all men, in all lands, at all times. Amidst all the variety of character, of language, of rank, of colour, of condition on earth, men feel *guilt* in the same way, and the same thing is necessary to restore peace, and any true system of religion must be adapted to the laws of our being, and must consult them. Further: every true system must come from God; and he, the Maker of the soul, must consult the laws of the soul which he has made. A true system of religion, therefore, must be in accordance with correct views of mental philosophy; and although no mere system of philosophy can *suggest* what is necessary in imparting peace to a guilty mind, yet a true system when suggested will be seen to be in accordance with the laws of our mental nature. They to whom a system of religion, therefore, is proposed, have a right to *demand* that it shall meet the real wants of their nature; that it shall be in accordance with their conscious mental structure; and that it shall be such that, in accordance with the laws of the soul, it shall be fitted to impart permanent peace. On this principle any proposed system of religion may be tested, and whatever might be supposed to be its external evidence, it could not be from God, and therefore not true, unless it accorded with the laws of our being. Keeping this obvious remark in view, I observe,

(2.) That in order that a guilty conscience may find peace, there must be a frank and open *confession* of sin,—confession made to the One who has been wronged, or whose law has been violated. This is a law of our nature—a law which cannot be departed from in any true system of religion. The mind is so made that it *cannot* find permanent peace by any device, unless the wrong which has been done is acknowledged, or while there is an attempt to "cloke or conceal our offences," or any effort to excuse or palliate them. We feel instinctively that we have not done what we *ought* to do, when we have not made a full and open acknowledgment of the wrong which we have done, whether against God or against men.

It requires but little experience in the world, and but little knowledge of human nature, to understand the relief which is furnished when we have done wrong, if we make confession of the wrong. All of us who have in childhood done wrong to father, mother, brother, sister, playmate—and who of us has not?—or, who in riper years have done wrong in some way to others, whether friends or foes—and who of us has not?—have known something of the anguish, and corrosion, and trouble of heart which is produced by an attempt to conceal the offence; to gloss it over with a low and lame apology; or to shelter ourselves under a miserable refuge of prevarication and falsehood. And all of us who have done wrong, and who have gone to him whom we offended, and made a frank and full acknowledgment, have known the peace which flows from such a confession. We have felt, in the one case, that a law of our nature has been violated; in the other, that that law has been complied with: and in the latter case, whatever may be the result of the confession—whether we obtain forgiveness or not—we feel that we have done right, and we have relieved ourselves of an intolerable burden. Even should nothing more be done; should he whom we have injured coldly turn away; should he utterly refuse to forgive us, or even to speak to us again, yet in the very act of confession we have found a relief which could never have been obtained by concealment, or by an attempt to apologize for the offence.

This law of our nature demands that the confession should be made to no third person, but to the one who has been offended. When a child has sinned against his father, it will not do for him to go and make confession to the son of a neighbour, or to his own brother, or even to his own mother. It would not have met the case for the prodigal son to resolve to go home and make humble acknowledgment of his folly to *his* own brother, or even to *his mother*. Nature prompted him to go as he did to his injured *father*, and to say, "Father, I have sinned against heaven, and in *thy* sight, and am no more worthy to be called *thy son*." So, when we have sinned against God, it will not do to go and make the confession to any *man*, whoever he may be, or whatever robes he may wear. I know that this great principle may be perverted, as all the laws of our nature may be. I know that if this strong prompting of a guilty soul to make confession can be put under the control of a priesthood; if instead of making the confession to that God whose law has been violated, the right is claimed of having it made to men consecrated to the sacred office, that no higher power can be wielded than that. And I know that this power may be so seized upon, and that there may be such confidence reposed in one invested with the priestly office, that temporary peace may be imparted to the guilty; but this is not to comply with the laws of our nature. This does not give permanent peace. The power of receiving a confession of sins committed against God has never been delegated to any one of his creatures, and all claim of such a right is a usurpation of the prerogative of the Almighty. The Being who has been offended alone can pardon, and he only can receive the confession on which pardon can be based.

It was necessary in any true system of religion, that provision should be made for producing peace in the soul *by* such confession made to God. Hence, in the Bible, we have such statements as these: "He that covereth his sins shall not prosper; but whoso confesseth and forsaketh them shall have mercy," Prov. xxviii. 13. "If we say that we have no sin, we deceive ourselves, and the truth is not in us. If we confess our sins, he is faithful and just to forgive us our sins, and to cleanse us from all unrighteousness," 1 John i. 8, 9. "I will go and return to my place, till they acknowledge their offence, and seek my face," Hos. v. 15. "While I kept silence, my bones waxed old through my roaring all the day long.—I said, I will confess my transgressions to the Lord, and thou forgavest the iniquity of my sin," Psa. xxxii. 3, 5. "Against thee, thee *only* have I sinned, and done this evil in thy sight," Psa. li. 4. And in accordance with this it is said, "With the mouth confession is made unto salvation," Rom. x. 10.

(3.) The law of our nature demands that in order that peace may be imparted to a guilty conscience there should be forgiveness. A partial and temporary peace may, indeed, be found by confession, as we have just seen; but full and permanent peace can never be found except by pardon.

We have seen that the *fact* of the guilt can never be changed. That is always to remain historically true. We have seen that it can never be forgotten:—forgotten by the God whose law has been violated; forgotten by him who has violated it. But though it cannot be historically changed, and cannot be forgotten, it may be *forgiven;* and the inquiry now is, how that can give *peace.* I do not now inquire how it may be *known* that it is forgiven—that may be a subject of inquiry hereafter; but how it is that pardon produces peace, and why it is indispensable that there should be forgiveness in order to permanent peace.

What shall be done with *sin* when it is committed, is always a great and grave question—a question too great to enter on now. What I wish now to say is, that pardon is essential to the attainment of peace.

(*a*) The laws of our nature demand this; and by the laws of our nature, when an offence is forgiven, we have peace. The feelings of a man who is *pardoned* will not, indeed, be precisely the same which he would have if he had never done wrong. In the one case there is a calm, approving conscience; a steady and undisturbed joy; an habitual tranquillity;—in the other, it is a peace which follows a troubled state of mind:—the one, the calmness of nature in a May morning, when the dew lies undisturbed on the grass—the other, the beauty of nature after the tempest has passed by and the sun breaks out from behind the dark, retiring cloud. But in each instance there is the appropriate kind of peace; and when a man has done wrong, the peace which flows from pardon is all that he can hope for, and is all that in fact he needs. It may be less calm, and steady, and uniform, than that which results from the consciousness of having always done right; but it may be more intense, and rapturous, and thrilling. The ocean is more sublime when its waves subside after a storm, than it is when its placid waters have not been disturbed by a tempest.

(*b*) When an offence is *pardoned*, all is done in regard to it which *can* be, and all which *need* to be, to give peace to the mind. It is true that as an historical *fact* it cannot be changed; it is true that it may never be literally *forgotten* by him against whom the offence was committed, or by him who committed it, but all has been done that can be to dispose of it. He against whom it was committed, and who pardoned it, is *satisfied* in regard to it. He has no wish to retain the recollection of it. The fact of our having sinned against him is not henceforward to affect his feelings towards us. The offence is not to be recalled for purposes of punishment, or to separate us from his favour and friendship, or to mortify and humble us. The child that is forgiven by a parent is to be treated in all respects *as* a child; the friend *as* a friend; the enemy *as if* he had not been an enemy. We may be humbled, indeed, at the memory of the sin which we have committed, but it will not be because he against whom we sinned has a pleasure in reminding us of it; we may still feel the natural effects of a former evil course of life, but they will not be the direct infliction of a *penalty*. Peace results necessarily from the fact that the sin is forgiven; and if it is *not* forgiven, and forgiven by him against whom the offence was committed—for no one else can forgive it—it is impossible that the mind ever should find peace.

In the life of our Saviour, as is recorded in one of the passages on which this discourse is founded, it is said that on one occasion he went into the house of a Pharisee, at his invitation, to "eat with him." As he reclined at the table, a female, whose life had been eminently depraved, came near him weeping, and washed his feet with her tears, and wiped them with the hairs of her head. She poured out before him the strong expressions of penitence and love, and the Saviour had compassion on her, and said, "Thy sins, which are many, are forgiven. And they that sat with him at the table began to say, Who is this that forgiveth sins also? And he said to the woman, Thy faith hath saved thee; *go in peace!*" *Go in peace* she would when these gracious words fell on her ear, for that was all that was wanted to give peace to her troubled soul. Need we speak of the peace of the man who has been sentenced to death for crime, and who, trembling in view of his own guilt, and of the awful death before him, sees the doors of his cell thrown open, and himself permitted to go forth to life and freedom? Need we speak of the joy of an offending child, whose father has frankly forgiven him? All over the world there is no more certain method of imparting happiness, than to declare to an offender the fact that he is forgiven; to say to the guilty that his sins shall be remembered no more. When that is done, the soul that was before like the troubled ocean, "whose waters cast up mire and dirt," settles down into calm repose—as the waves of the sea of Tiberias did when the Saviour rose from his pillow in the storm, and said, "Peace; be still."

(4.) There is one other thing that is to be provided for in any system that shall give peace to a conscience troubled by guilt. It is, that the act of pardon shall be consistent with the honour, and the truth, and the justice of him who grants it. It is not to be obtained by a bribe; it is not to be in any way connected with dishonour. A man with any just views and principles would not *wish* to be pardoned, or could not find peace if he were pardoned, if the act were to break up the government, or weaken the authority of law. It may be said, indeed, that this is not commonly an element taken into consideration by one who is applying for pardon. This may be: and yet there *are* cases in which it *would be* taken into consideration, and there are cases where it *must be;* and in all it would materially affect the views which we have on being forgiven. The heart of a child, though he *were* forgiven, would be deeply grieved, if in his case the act of pardon should bring his father into disgrace: if, for example, his father were a magistrate, and if pardon should be extended at the expense of justice, and at the sacrifice of all the claims of law. And still more true is this in the matter of salvation. Much as we desire to be forgiven and to be saved, we do not wish to enter heaven over a prostrated law, or over an humbled government;—in any way in which law, and truth, and justice will be disregarded; in any way in which the honour of God will not be promoted. Joy and peace there would be in pardon; but that joy and peace would be greatly augmented if we could see that, in the very act of forgiveness, all had been done that was needful to be done to maintain the Divine truth and justice unimpaired, and if, while God forgave, his justice and his truth only shone forth more gloriously by the very act.

These things, it seems to me, are essential in any plan for restoring peace to a conscience troubled by guilt. Whether they are to be found provided for in the way of salvation revealed in the gospel, will be a subject of future inquiry.

The sum of what I have said now, so far as it may be of practical value to one in the state of mind which I have supposed—that of a sinner troubled with the remembrance of guilt—can be expressed in few words:—

(*a*) Peace is not to be found by an attempt to change the historical fact that you have sinned, or by forgetting it.

(*b*) Peace is not to be found by driving serious impressions from your minds.

(*c*) Peace is not to be found by mingling in gay scenes, and by attempting to divert the mind from the contemplation of such subjects as sin, death, the grave, eternity.

(*d*) Peace is not to be found by embracing any false views of religion, or any doctrines which deny the fact of human guilt and danger.

(*e*) Peace *is* to be found only by making a simple, honest, frank, and full confession of sin to the God whose law has been violated, and against whom the wrong has been done.

(*f*) Peace *is* to be found by obtaining from him a full and free pardon: from *Him*—not from any *man* pretending to speak in his name.

(*g*) Peace *is* to be found in some way in which it can be seen that pardon is not inconsistent with justice—that mercy is not at war with truth—that compassion for the sinner is not inconsistent with hatred of his sin—and that the forgiveness and salvation of any number of offenders is not inconsistent with the stability of just government, and the maintenance of the honour of law.

All these conditions, we think, meet in that plan revealed in the gospel by which "God can be just, and the justifier of him that believeth in Jesus;" and to him who is penitent, and who believes in that gospel, the Saviour, not in mockery, but in sincerity, says now as he did to the penitent female, "Thy sins are forgiven; *go in peace.*"

SERMON XV.

THE MERCY OF GOD.

PSALM ciii. 8.—"The Lord is merciful and gracious, slow to anger, and plenteous in mercy."

THE subject which is brought before us in this text, is the mercy of God; and my object in considering it will be, I. To show what is meant by the mercy of God; and, II. To prove that God is a merciful Being.

I. My first object is, *to explain what is meant by the mercy of God.* In order to a correct understanding of this, and to show the exact place which the doctrine of the Divine mercy occupies in a system of revealed religion, there are several preliminary remarks which it is proper to make.

Mercy is favour shown to the undeserving. It is benevolence, tenderness, pity, compassion, clemency, evinced towards offenders. It is an essential idea in mercy that he to whom a favour is shown is guilty, and has no claim to it. If he has any claim that is commensurate with the favour bestowed, the act is one of justice and not of mercy. *Grace* is a more general term than mercy, as it relates to the bestowment of favours without so special a reference to the idea of criminality. Grace bestows favours in general; mercy pardons and forgives, and it is that of which we particularly think when we speak of mercy.

Mercy has been spoken of as the "darling attribute of God;" a phrase which has no authority in the Bible, nor in any just views of the Divine character; for that character is to be regarded as a whole, and in every respect worthy of adoration and praise. It has been the theme of eulogium by all classes of men, and there is no attribute of the Almighty on which they speak with more confidence, or to which they refer with more apparent satisfaction. It has usually been regarded as so clear that God is a merciful Being, that it might be taken for granted without formal proof; and so clear, also, that it is supposed to be a ground of confidence for all classes of men. Men of all characters, and in all conditions of life, profess to rely on that mercy; and even when they profess to have no Christian hope of heaven, they take refuge on a dying bed in what they flatter themselves is the illimitable compassion of God. It is the favourite theme of the moral man, of the infidel, of the universalist—the favourite theme of the man destitute of virtue and religion, as well as of the Christian; and there is no one subject on which men seem more disposed to mingle their congratulations than on the fact that their Maker is a God of mercy. Yet an analysis of their views and hopes would perhaps show that the apprehensions of these different classes of men are often very indefinite, and that in their professions they are not always aware of their own real feelings.

When you ask an infidel what evidence he has that God is merciful, you may wait in vain for a reply. He does not profess to have any revelation to tell him so. He cannot be permitted to use the Christian argument, for that he avowedly rejects. He cannot refer with certainty to the course of events under the Divine administration in this world, for there have been as clear indications that God is just, and that he means to punish the guilty, as there have been that he is merciful, and is disposed to pardon them. He cannot refer to his own feelings on the subject, for how can mere feeling, or opinion, or hope, without a promise, be regarded as an argument to demonstrate what God intends to do? If the real truth were reached in the case, it would probably be found to be that he does not believe that his sins *deserve* the punishment of hell; and that he would regard it as unjust in God to punish him for ever; that is, that he is to be saved by the *justice*, and not by the *mercy* of God; and, after all, he has no idea that there is occasion for the exercise of mercy in his case, or that he is to be indebted to mercy for salvation. When we put the same question to a man who is expecting heaven on the ground of his morality, and ask him definitely what are his conceptions of the mercy of God as bearing on his own case, we shall in the same manner wait in vain for a reply. If we question him about his views of himself and his hopes, the reluctant truth will be at last arrived at, that he does not believe that he *deserves* eternal death; so that in his apprehension it would be *wrong* in God to punish him in the future world; he also is depending on the *justice* of God for salvation, and has no belief that there is in his case occasion for the exercise of mercy. The universalist, too, is loud—more loud than any other man—in his commendations of the mercy of God. And yet he stoutly, and on principle, maintains that it would be *wrong* for God to cast men into an eternal hell, and exhausts all his powers of argument and eloquence to show how horrible and unjust such a punishment would be: and thus he, also, is depending on the justice of God; and the idea of mercy, after all that is said of it, does not enter into his scheme. Men are saved, according to his view, because it would be a wrong done to them if they should not be saved; because infinite injustice would be done if they should be cast off for ever. So that it happens, that although the attribute of mercy is the favourite theme of men, and is often in the mouths of the impenitent and the wicked, they have no real belief in its necessity, if in its existence, after all, and their expectations of heaven would be the same if God were possessed of no such attribute, but were only severely and sternly *just*. Real dependence on the mercy of God for salvation, is the characteristic only of the man who feels and confesses that he is a sinner; who acknowledges that no injustice would be done him if he should not be saved. True dependence on that mercy will, in fact, be found only among those who look for salvation as revealed through a Redeemer.

In all governments there are great difficulties in the exercise of mercy. Some of those difficulties are the following:—one relates to the effect which would occur if pardon were never exercised, and if no mercy were ever shown. It is easy to conceive that this might be, and that the administration of the law would be pure, and the government just. But it would be stern and unfeeling in its character. It would become the object of mere dread, not of love and confidence. Justice then would drive its decisions over some of the finest feelings of our nature, and over all the sympathies of society, for there are cases in which we all know that it is desirable that pardon should be extended to the guilty, and in which all the benevolent wishes of a community are gratified by the extending of forgiveness. So clear is this, that in all governments, except those of tyrants, the power of pardon has been lodged in the hands of the executive and the judges. And yet there is another difficulty. Pardon, in any case, does just so much to weaken the strong arm of the law. It is a proclamation that the sentence of the law may be too severe; or that it is not certain that its penalty will be inflicted; or that it would be too stern if the penalty were in all cases executed; and is so far a proclamation, and will be so interpreted, that crime may be committed in some cases with impunity. If in one case, why may it not be in others? And this difficulty which exists when pardon is extended under the best arranged safeguards, and with the wisest precautions, always becomes greater in proportion as acts of forgiveness are granted freely. If pardon is often exercised, law loses its terror. If it were always extended to the guilty, the law and the penalty would be a nullity. If all prisons were thrown open; if in every instance in which a jury should find a man guilty, an officer of the executive should be present, entrusted with the pardoning power, and instructed to exercise it, what would be the use of the trial by jury, of the organization of a court, of the effort to convict the offender? The penalty of the law would be a bugbear, and the process of trial a farce. And why should not the same difficulties exist in the Divine administration?

When we say, therefore, that God is a merciful Being, we do not mean to affirm that he will in fact bestow indiscriminate mercy on all,—that none in fact will be punished, or that all the guilty will be saved. It is not true that he thus shows mercy without any metes or bounds, or without any rules by which he regulates its dispensation. It is a simple matter of fact that men do suffer punishment in this life—that there are calamities which come upon the violators of the Divine laws which cannot be regarded otherwise than as expressions of the Divine displeasure against sin, and as proofs that God is just, and will inflict punishment on the guilty. No one has been able to explain these facts on any other supposition, or to resolve them all into expressions of mercy. It is no less certainly a fact, according to the Bible,—and no one can show that that contradicts the regular tendency of events,—that many will suffer in the world to come, and that large numbers will be unpardoned for ever. I do not mean to maintain, therefore, that the mercy of God will in fact be bestowed on *all men*.

Nor do I mean to say, or to admit, that man has any *claim* on the mercy of God. If he had a claim it would not be *mercy*, but *justice;* for it is the nature of mercy that it is not a claim which can be enforced. The moment when it begins to be urged as a matter of claim or right it ceases to be mercy, and supposes that some wrong would be done if it were not granted; in other words, if man were saved in that way, it would be by justice and not by mercy. Guilt has no claim to favour; and if God is merciful, it is only to those who are guilty, not to those who have a claim to favour.

Nor can it be maintained that God will bestow mercy in any other way than that which he has provided and proposed to men. If he has revealed one plan, that method is in fact an exclusion of all other methods; for it cannot be supposed that he would propose a new method, if there were already many ways of obtaining his favour, or that he would, by revelation, designate one when there were others equally good known without a revelation. We reason thus about other things. If he has laid down rules and laws by which he dispenses his favours, the business of men is to find out what those rules and laws are, and to act accordingly. It is not our business to make *these* laws, nor, if we are dissatisfied with them, can we suppose that he will change them to accommodate our feelings, our caprice, or our pride. If he has made wealth dependent on industry, and health on temperance, and reputation on virtue, those are the laws by which we are to obtain these blessings; nor can we suppose that he will change them to accommodate our indolence, our love of strong drink, or our philosophy. If he has appointed, as a great law, that the industrious farmer shall have a harvest, and the farmer chooses to spend the time of sowing or of reaping in idleness or dissipation rather than in his field, God will not accommodate his love of idleness or dissipation by working a miracle, nor will he change the great laws by which he bestows blessings on men. And so in regard to pardon and salvation. If God has said that these may be obtained by repentance and by faith in the Lord Jesus Christ, the revelation of that method is an exclusion of all methods of man's devising. The hope of man in obtaining salvation in that way is the same, in principle, as the hope of obtaining property, health, and reputation, by industry, temperance, and virtue; and we may expect that the rule will be as certainly adhered to in the one case as in the other. If men dislike this method, and choose to disregard it, it cannot be expected that God will work a miracle to accommodate their self-righteousness, their pride, their love of sin, any more than he will in the case of a man who is seeking property or reputation. It will still be found to be true that he bestows pardon only in the way which he has revealed; and whatever may be the consequences to men, his great laws will be observed. And when we maintain that God is a merciful Being, we mean to maintain that his mercy is imparted to men only on the condition of repentance and faith in the Lord Jesus, and that its exercise is limited to those who repent and believe the gospel.

Nor do we hold that God shows mercy any otherwise than as a Sovereign, bestowing it on whom he pleases, according to the good pleasure of his will. We do not mean, indeed, that he is arbitrary in the sense that he has no reason for what he does, or that what he does is to be resolved into mere *will;* but that the reasons which influence him are not always disclosed, and that he must determine on whom, and in what circumstances, and on what conditions, salvation shall be bestowed. In all governments the pardoning power must have some such limitation;

for as pardon is not a matter of claim, it must be left to him whose law is violated, or to whom the wrong is done, whether forgiveness shall be granted; and in all cases there are circumstances bearing on the subject which can be known only to him who makes and who administers the laws. There are great interests to be looked at, which the guilty are little qualified to understand. Whether any may or may not be pardoned; whether in particular cases they have such a character that it will be safe and proper to pardon them; whether they have or have not complied with the conditions of pardon, if any are proposed,—are points which must be left to the discretion of the executive. We cannot suppose that God will exercise mercy in any other way than as a Sovereign, dispensing pardon as he judges will be best for the interests of the immense empire over which he presides.

With these necessary metes and limits, we suppose that the character of God is essentially that of a merciful Being. We suppose that he is benevolent not only towards the innocent, but towards the guilty. We suppose that it is his nature to be inclined to show compassion. We suppose that in order to show this compassion he has been willing to stoop to any sacrifice but that of truth and justice. We suppose that he has made ample provision by which he can consistently offer pardon to the guilty children of men; that none of our race, however guilty, are excluded from the offers of salvation, and that he is ready to bestow forgiveness to any extent on the members of the human family, if they return to him by true repentance, and by faith in the blood of his Son. We suppose that none who have applied to him in this way have been rejected and cast off, or ever will be.

II. It was my second object *to prove that God is such a Being.*

I have four classes of arguments to refer to under this head, each one of which would be in itself ample proof. It is not so much for the sake of the proof that I refer to them, however, as it is to bring in varied forms and points of view before our minds one of the most glorious and momentous truths that have ever dawned on our world—a truth of deepest interest to every guilty heart.

(1.) The first argument is derived from the express declarations of the Bible,—God's own testimony about his character and purposes. From a book whose leading design is to reveal the doctrine which we are considering, it will not be possible now to adduce all the passages that might be referred to; from a book where the declarations are so unambiguous in their meaning, it will not be necessary to adduce many. Let the following suffice. Exod. xxxiv. 6: "And the Lord passed by before him, and proclaimed, The Lord, The Lord God, merciful and gracious, long-suffering, and abundant in goodness and truth, keeping mercy for thousands, forgiving iniquity and transgression and sin." So in Deut. vii. 9: "Know therefore that the Lord thy God, he is God, the faithful God, which keepeth covenant and mercy with them that love him and keep his commandments to a thousand generations." So in the Psalms: "All the paths of the Lord are mercy and truth." "The earth is full of the mercy of the Lord." "Mercy and truth are met together; righteousness and peace have kissed each other." "The Lord is good; his mercy is everlasting, and his truth endureth to all generations," Psa. xxv. 10; xxxiii. 5; lxxxv. 10; c. 5. So in Neh. ix. 17: "Thou art a God ready to pardon, gracious and merciful, slow to anger, and of great kindness."

Of the same nature, and still more to our purpose, are all those passages scattered over the Bible, so bright and so numerous as to cover all its pages with living light, which offer salvation to men—to all men—with the assurance that all may come and live. Thus Isaiah: "Ho, every one that thirsteth, come ye to the waters, and he that hath no money; come ye, buy and eat; yea, come, buy wine and milk without money and without price." "Though your sins be as scarlet, they shall be as white as snow; though they be red like crimson, they shall be as wool." "Let the wicked forsake his way, and the unrighteous man his thoughts: and let him return unto the Lord, and he will have mercy upon him, and to our God, for he will abundantly pardon," Isa. lv. 1; i. 18; lv. 7. And so the Saviour: "Come unto me, all ye that labour and are heavy laden, and I will give you rest. Take my yoke upon you, and learn of me, for I am meek and lowly in heart, and ye shall find rest to your souls." "If any man thirst, let him come unto me and drink," Matt. xi. 28, 29; John vii. 37. And so those gracious words with which a volume designed to reveal the mercy of God to man so beautifully and so appropriately closes: "And the Spirit and the bride say, Come. And let him that heareth say, Come. And let him that is athirst come: and whosoever will, let him take the water of life freely," Rev. xxii. 17.

If there were any doubts on this subject, these plain and positive passages of the Bible would put those doubts to rest. No language could be more clear. I need not add that the Bible is full of passages of a similar character. Indeed, as already hinted, the leading design of the Bible is to reveal this great truth, that God is a merciful Being, and to disclose the terms on which he will impart mercy, and the way in which it may be done consistently with the honour of his law and the good of the universe:—the way in which he may do it so as to avoid the difficulties to which I adverted in the former part of this discourse. If we were to attempt to characterize the Bible as distinguished from all other books, I do not know that we could give a better account of it than this. One other remark, however, should be made here. It is, that the mercy offered in the Bible to men is offered only on definite and carefully-guarded conditions. It is mercy only through a Redeemer; mercy imparted where there is repentance toward God, and faith in the Lord Jesus Christ. Every offer of mercy is limited to that method; within that limit, it is freely and fully offered to all mankind.

(2.) My second argument is, that this world is evidently under a dispensation of mercy, or that the facts existing on the earth can be accounted for only on the supposition that God is a merciful Being. The facts to which I refer are these:—that while God is able to detect and punish all the guilty, while he has nothing to fear though all the wicked should be cast into hell; while all sin is the object of his abhorrence; and while he might justly cut men down and consign them to woe, he spares them, gives them opportunity for repentance, and encompasses them with innumerable blessings.

It is clear that this is not a world of perfect and unmixed justice. In such a world, under the government of an Omniscient and Almighty Being, guilt and punishment would never be separated. The moment when crime was committed the hand of justice would be raised to strike, nor would it be possible for the offender to elude the blow. Hand in hand they would travel over the earth; nor should we ever see them separated by long intervals of time, or by large tracts of land or ocean. Such, we have reason to believe, was the case with the apostate angels, sent at once to hell without interval, without reprieve, and without hope. Such, too, was the letter of the threatening addressed to man: "*In the day* thou eatest thereof thou shalt surely die"—a sentence that would in like manner have been executed at once but for the interposition of mercy. And such would be the infliction of all law, unless justice were delayed by the intermingling of mercy. The convicted murderer or traitor would be executed at once, unless the pleadings of mercy were heard that the offender might have an opportunity to obtain the Divine forgiveness when human law extends no hope.

This world bears all the marks of delayed justice and suspended wrath, for the purpose of showing the mercy of God, and in order that the guilty man may have the opportunity of obtaining that mercy. Crime and punishment are, by long intervals of time or tracts of land or ocean, separated. The guilt of childhood or of youth is often unpunished even in manhood and old age. Long intervals of country may have intervened between the *places* where the crime was committed, and where the offender now lives. He may have crossed oceans. He may have committed the crime in one part of the world, and be roaming at large in another; one who has committed an offence in America may be now roaming on the plains of India; an offender in India may be living in affluence and splendour in a gay capital of Europe. He may have been a licentious, a dissipated young man, and in middle life, or in advanced age, all the blessings which every clime can yield may have been poured upon him. Guilt often treads flowery paths, and goes up the heights of honour. It reclines on a couch of ease; rests on a bed of down; puts on robes of adorning; sits at a table laden with the bounties of all climes; is admired in the gay circle; is encompassed with children and friends; is surrounded with the blessings of civilization, liberty, and art; is permitted to live amidst the hallowed institutions of religion. And why is this? Why does the blasphemer live? Why courses the vital blood in the veins of the abandoned and the profligate? Why does the seducer walk the earth, and why does the scoffer riot on the goodness of God? Why does the sun shine on the dwellings of the ungodly; and the rains and the dews of heaven descend on the fields of the prayerless; and the winds bear into port the rich cargo of the man that lives regardless of his Maker? Why is the sinner preserved from the pestilence that walketh in darkness, and the destruction that wasteth at noonday? Why is the sound of music and joy heard in his dwelling? Why hears he the sound of the viol rather than the sighings of despair; why the voice of mirth, rather than the groanings of the world of woe? It is not because he *deserves* these things. It is not because it would be wrong to cut him off, and remove him from them all. There is another reason why these things are so. It is because "the Lord is merciful and gracious, slow to anger, and plenteous in mercy."

And does not this whole world bear marks of being under a dispensation of mercy? The sun is as bright as it was over Eden; the moon and the stars keep their place as they did before man sinned; the music is as sweet in the groves; the air is as pure; the stream purls as gently; the mountain and the ocean are as grand. Nature, in all her main movements, pursues her steady course, as though the race had not sinned; and even those scenes where man suffers are tempered with mercy. Man suffers, indeed, and dies—for God is just, as well as good. But how different the scene of sorrow now from what it would be if there were no mercy; how different from the pains of hell. Around the sick bed, science and skill, and love and tenderness, are doing all they can to alleviate suffering, and to mitigate pain. Man lies indeed—often long after he began to sin, often after an aggravated life of guilt—on a bed of death. But there is the patient mother to wipe away the cold sweat of death; there is the tender wife; there is the soft hand of a much-loved daughter; there is the consoling sympathy of a friend; there is the mild and sweet voice of religion—religion that tells of a world where there shall be pain and death no more, and where all tears shall be wiped away from every eye.

We often can approximate to just views only by comparing great things with small. Bear in remembrance that this is a world of sin, and that God might have excluded us from hope, and consigned us to woe. Then ask whether this world is such an abode as man himself fits up for his guilty fellow, the offender against his own laws. Go to the dungeon—the dark, damp, cold, sepulchral place, where man confines his guilty fellow-man. He shuts him from the light of the sun; binds his limbs in chains; secludes him from society; drags him away from wife and children and home; feeds him on coarse fare; lays him on a cold bed of earth or straw; and bids him there prepare to die. I went into one of the best constructed and the best arranged prisons in our land. There were confined within its walls more than six hundred men. Those walls were high and massive, and designed to prevent all return to the world. I went through iron gates bolted and barred with all the skill that man can use. I saw on the walls men stationed to shoot down any who should attempt to escape. I saw the cells of those imprisoned criminals. They were small, and dark, and chilly. I saw those men at work. They were sad and sorrowful men. They had no communication with each other; they had none with any human being, save at distant intervals with their chaplain. I saw the father there removed probably for ever from his children; the husband from his wife; the brother from his sister; the man from his neighbour; and though surrounded by hundreds, they had become isolated beings, and the last cord which bound them to the living world seemed to have been snapped asunder. They were sullen, and sunken, and sad; for they had no hope of pardon; and there was an eye of vigilance always upon them, and there was the deep consciousness of disgrace among them, and they were held up to the community as unworthy the enjoyments of a home and of domestic comforts and liberty, and the sight of green fields and of the light. Such is the prison that man makes for man. Then I look on the offender against God, and I see him roaming at large in a world beautiful as Eden, breathing a pure air, enjoying the light of the sun, fanned by the breezes; surrounded with wife, and children, and friends; in the midst of luxuries; and crowned with the blessings which every clime can furnish to minister to his wants, gratify his appetites, and cheer him in his days of sickness and despondency.

(3.) My third illustration will be drawn from the fact that God has sent his Son into our world to die. How ample would this be as an argument if we had no other. What father would give his own son to die for the guilty? What monarch has there been who would give his only son to suffer a shameful death in order to sustain the honour of his own law, and in order to save even a whole province of rebels? And where is the man on a bench of justice in this land who, to save the guilty, would give up to the same death a much-beloved, an only son? The man has not yet lived in this land, rich as it has been in examples of virtue and benevolence, who would be willing to do it. Yet " God so loved the world that he gave his only-begotten Son, that whosoever believeth in him might not perish, but have everlasting life." And this gift was the proof of mercy; the mere expression of mercy; the sacrifice which mercy makes to save the guilty. For, it is not held, it cannot be held, that the sufferings of the Redeemer made any change in God. It is not held, and it is not true, that he was originally stern, and inflexible, and unmerciful; and that he has been *made* mild and forgiving by the death of his Son. It is not meant, it cannot be true, that those sorrows have made God different from what he was, or made a stern and severe Being mild. He gave his Son to die, not that he might *be made* merciful, but as *the expression* of mercy; not that his mercy might be bought, but because he was originally so merciful that he was willing to submit to anything, even the ignominy and death of his own Son, that man might be saved. A father standing on the shore of a deep and rapid river sees his child suddenly fall into the waters. The child struggles with the current, but is borne farther out into the stream, and is sinking to the bottom. The father will instinctively plunge into that stream, at the peril of his own life, to save that of his drowning child. But neither the danger of the child, nor his piercing cry, *makes* the father compassionate and kind. No; he loved his son so much that he is willing to throw himself into the torrent to save his life. A country is invaded. A father lays his hand on the head of his only son, and sends him forth with his blessing to the field of strife and of death. Does that invasion, that peril, *make* the father love his country—transform an enemy of its institutions to a friend? No. He so loved his country that to save it he was willing to part with his only son, if need be, that he should pour out his blood like water in its defence. So the Father of mercies looked on men. So he loved the world; so he pitied the race; so he desired its welfare, that, to save us, he was willing to give up his Son to death. And such a death! What are all the strugglings of a drowning child; what all the privations of a camp, or the perils of the field of battle; what all the pains of sickness, the tortures of the rack, the severities of flame, compared with the sufferings of Jesus Christ? They stand alone. Nowhere has there been ignominy so great, torture so keen, and pain so bitter as the Son of God endured. No other spectacle has been witnessed like that when the Son of God was nailed to a cross. And when he had been waylaid and persecuted; when he had been rejected and spurned; and when he had been mocked, and reviled, and nailed to the tree; when he had been crowned with thorns, and a spear had reached his heart, mercy still prevailed, and the murderers of the Son of God—the perpetrators of that great crime which outpeers every other deed of human guilt—were told that even *they* might be pardoned. And from that cross the proclamation has gone forth that all, no matter what their guilt, may be saved. Here flows blood so rich, so pure, so precious in the sight of the eternal Father, that it is sufficient to atone for the sins of the whole world, and all who are now penitent, and who believe on his name, may enter heaven.

(4.) There is one other source of evidence which might be insisted on at much greater length than were now expedient; and that is, the fact that sinners of all classes, and ages, and grades of guilt *have* found mercy. The proof is this:—They have gone to God confessing their sins; they have gone borne down with a deep sense of their guilt; they have gone with a troubled conscience; with an agonized spirit; with true repentance, and have in fact found peace. In their lives they have given all the evidence which could be given that their sins have been pardoned by a gracious God; in the peace and the triumph of their dying moments they have furnished all the proof which could be furnished that they have been restored to the Divine favour.

The world has been full of instances of this kind. Your own minds will instantly advert to such cases as the following:—David, after a crime which for ever dimmed the lustre of his name, and stained his memory, sought and obtained forgiveness. Saul of Tarsus, an infuriated persecutor, and regarded by himself as the chief of sinners, received forgiveness. Peter, after a most awful denial of his Lord, was pardoned. The thief on the cross was forgiven in the hour of his death, for he pleaded that he might be remembered by the Lord Jesus when he should come in his kingdom. The poor publican who smote upon his breast and said, "God be merciful to me a sinner," "went down to his house justified." Every class of men finds its representative in these and in other individuals who are described in the Scriptures as having obtained mercy. These cases at once furnish a proof that God is a merciful Being, and a warrant for all of like character with them to go to him and plead for pardon.

To the long list of Scripture characters, how easy would it be to add a catalogue of unlimited extent of others who have obtained mercy. When Augustine, after an early life of wretched dissipation, is reformed; when the Earl of Rochester, after a life of abandoned and gross sensuality, repents and obtains mercy; when Col. Gardiner in the very act of contemplated wickedness is arrested, warned, and saved; when John Newton, a slave-dealer, is changed and becomes a herald of salvation; when John Bunyan, a very model of profaneness and a proverb for blasphemy, is pardoned and made to instruct almost the whole world by his "Pilgrim," why should any sinners despair of mercy? If such men obtained pardon, is not the proof clear that God is a Being of compassion, and that he is ready to forgive?

Yet the proof does not stop here. Many thousands, nay, many millions, not less guilty, have been pardoned, purified, admitted to the favour of God, translated to heaven. Thousands, and ten times ten thousand, in the dark hour of conscious guilt, when despairing of being able to save themselves, and when an impenetrable gloom has settled on their souls, and when darkness covered the present and the future with a funeral pall, have come to the throne of mercy and found there forgiving love. How many are there at the present moment who could bear witness for God that he is merciful, and slow to anger, and ready to forgive! How many are there in all the churches in this land, and in other lands, now on their way to heaven, who had profaned his name, his sabbaths, and his word; who had been sunk in sensuality, or hardened in infidelity; who had been the companions of the dissipated and the vile; who long resisted the appeals of mercy, and slighted and despised the blood of the Redeemer, but who are now "in their right mind," and prepared to testify that he is merciful, and that his throne is accessible to the broken-hearted, returning prodigal! The earth—blessed be his name!—contains millions of living witnesses that he is merciful, and the heavens are filled with those who have been pardoned by his grace. Is God merciful? Let the ransomed saints on high speak—that blood-washed throng, now with harps in their hands in heaven. Is God merciful? Let those now on earth, redeemed by the same blood, speak—the bands of Christian pilgrims, pardoned sinners on their way to the skies. Is God merciful? Let the Christian speak from the bed of death—now, with evidence of pardoned sin, and peace in his soul, pluming himself for his eternal flight, and about to join the ransomed hosts beyond the swelling flood. Is God merciful? The church below, and the church above; the pardoned penitent, exulting and rejoicing; the dying saint,—all proclaim that he is compassionate and kind, and ready to forgive. Not one has gone to him penitent and been rejected; no sinner, however great his sins, has gone with a broken heart to the throne of mercy and been sent empty away.

Such are some of the reasons why we deem it to be right to come to the throne of our Maker with the feeling that he is a merciful Being, and that, however great and aggravated may have been our sins, it is right to hope for pardon and salvation. In conclusion, let us learn that there is ground, then, for hope. There is all the ground that, as sinners, we need—all that we could ask for. There is all that we could desire in the assurances which God gives respecting his own character; in his dealings with our world; in the sacrifices which he has made in order that he might consistently pardon; in his treatment of those who have gone to him and confessed their sins. No one could desire more plain assurances; more earnest invitations; more encouragement from the success of those who have gone before him and besought his favour. But let us learn, also, that there is no room for presumption. Mercy is indeed bestowed on the guilty, but it is only in an appointed way, and on carefully specified conditions. They who trust in God's mercy are authorized to do it to an unlimited extent in the manner which he has revealed; to no extent in any other way. For he has other attributes than that of mercy. He is true, he is holy, he is just, he is righteous, as well as long-suffering; and our hope of his favour is limited to the way which he has specified and revealed. On his mercy in that way we may rely with the fullest assurance to any extent; apart from that we have no promise, nor has he furnished evidence that he will save.

And let us learn, also, that even in this way his offer of mercy, in regard to us, will soon close. Death is its outer limit. The offer extends not beyond the grave; the evidence that it is granted lies wholly this side the tomb. Who can show us a promise that a sinner will be pardoned in the eternal world? Who can furnish evidence that one has been there forgiven? No:—the forbearance of God will soon be ended, and the sinner will soon be in a merciless world. Here the sinner may be forgiven. Here the Father invites, and the Saviour pleads, and the Holy Spirit draws the heart. Soon all this will be ended. To-day mercy may be found; to-morrow it may be too late. To-day heaven and earth, God and angels, pious parents, pastors, and friends entreat; to-morrow you may be in a world where mercy never has been found, and where the assurance that it could be found, now so much unheeded, will never fall on the ear.

SERMON XVI.

THE ATONEMENT AS FITTED TO GIVE PEACE TO A CONVICTED SINNER.

1 JOHN i. 7.—"The blood of Jesus Christ his Son cleanseth us from all sin."

IN the previous discourses we have been conducted to the great inquiry respecting the gospel,—What are its provisions and arrangements to save the guilty? The gospel is a system *to save sinners*. This is its grand peculiarity; with reference to this all its arrangements are adjusted, and all other things that are connected with it are subsidiary to this, or collateral to it. The question, we are to suppose, which was before the Divine Mind in originating this scheme was, *How may arrangements be made to save the guilty?* This is the position which a speculative inquirer ought to take when he examines the gospel; this the point from which a convicted sinner ought to look at the gospel; this the point from which infidels and Christians should regard it.

The inquiry relates now, not so much to the speculative philosopher, the infidel, or the Christian, as to the convicted and guilty sinner. When *he* looks into this revealed plan, what does he see to meet his case? He turns away from all other things as furnishing a hope of salvation; he despairs of every other method; he is condemned by the law of God and by his own conscience; he feels that he is to die, and that there is a God of justice before whom he must soon appear; he looks out tremblingly on a dark and dreaded eternity; and he comes to the Bible, as a professed revelation from God, to find something that will meet his case. What *is* the way of salvation which it reveals for a lost sinner?

Foremost in all its revelations he sees Christ and his cross. All the great statements in that book arrange themselves around one truth—that a Saviour has died; that an atonement has been made. Every promise of pardon is originated there; all the assurances of Divine mercy have their sources there; all that is said of justification and sanctification is founded on that work; all the invitations, encouragements, and assurances of favour in the book are based on that. Everything that is said in the book about the salvation of a sinner may be regarded as concentrated and embodied in my text:—"The blood of Jesus Christ his Son cleanseth us from all sin."

What can be more important for us sinners than to consider this? Yet I do not propose to discuss the doctrine of the *atonement*, as such, as I should feel myself called upon to attempt to do if I were addressing myself to infidels and philosophers. I should then regard myself as bound to endeavour at least to vindicate the doctrine from objections; to demonstrate its consistency with law; to show why it is not found in a scheme of human administration; to exhibit the defects of all human governments without it; to prove that man has everywhere shown that he has felt his need of it; and to convince such men that it, in fact, maintains the harmony of justice and mercy in a moral government. But these, however great and important in themselves, would be points foreign to the present position to which we are brought in the progress of this discussion. We are now to look at the atonement as *a revealed arrangement to meet the condition of a convicted sinner.* The inquiry is, how *that* meets his case; how that will lay the foundation for restoration to peace.

To see the real point of this inquiry, you are to recollect the state of the sinner as it has been illustrated. The following points, then, are to be borne in remembrance:—(1.) He has violated the law of God, and is in fact, and in feeling, a guilty man. (2.) He cannot now *change the fact* that he has sinned, for that is to remain historically true for ever, whatever may be the consequences. (3.) He cannot repair the wrong done to a violated law; the wrong done to society; the wrong done to his own soul and to his Maker. (4.) He cannot, by any act of his, now remove the penalty—for that has a connexion with the violation of the law which the offender cannot himself dissolve. (5.) He cannot urge any *claim* to pardon—for pardon is never a matter of *claim*, and a violator of law is dependent on sovereignty.

The inquiry then is, What does the death of Christ—the atonement—do to meet this case? It is my wish, as well as I am able, and as simply and plainly as possible, to explain this. There are substantially but two inquiries:—I. What is meant by the atonement? And, II. What is accomplished by it in the salvation of a sinner?

I. The first inquiry is, *What is meant by the atonement?* What is the idea when it is said that the blood of Jesus Christ cleanseth from all sin? What in all those passages which speak of him as "a propitiation" for sin; as giving himself a "ransom for many;" as dying in the place of sinners; as being "made a curse for us;" as "bearing our sins in his own body on the tree;" as being our "peace," and as "reconciling us to God?" What may we suppose Paul preached among the Corinthians when he resolved to "know nothing among them but Jesus Christ and him crucified?"

It seems proper, in order to a clear understanding of this, to state, first, what the atonement is *not*, or what we should *not* expect to find in it,—for the hope of heaven, so far as based on the atonement, or on anything else, should not be founded on *falsehood*, but on *truth*. No false view on any subject will be of value to a man on his final trial.

We have seen, by an incidental remark already made, that there are *some* things in regard to sin and the sinner which cannot be done by the atonement or by any other arrangement. They are, that the historical fact of the commission of sin cannot now be changed; that it will always remain true of the sinner that he *has* violated the law of God, and is a guilty man; that the wrong cannot now be repaired, since there is a wrong done by the very act of sin which nothing subsequent can entirely remove, however it may be overruled; and that nothing can now be done by which the offender can urge, in any proper sense, a *claim* to pardon.

In addition, I wish now to state the following things as points not contemplated by an atonement, and which the sinner is not to expect to find *in* the atonement. I state them because they are sometimes supposed by an inquirer to be a part of the atonement, and because there are sometimes representations made by the friends of Christianity as if they were; and because the enemies of the atonement sometimes evince a desire to represent these things as constituting a part of it.

(*a*) The atonement, then, does not *change* God, or make him a different Being from what he was. He is in nowise, now that the atonement is made, a different Being from what he was before, or from what he would have been if the atonement had not been made; he will never be a different Being from what he now is, and always has been, whatever may be the destiny of man. He is no more benevolent, no more disposed to show mercy now, than he was before the atonement was made; he was no more disposed to do justice then, or to punish offenders, than he is now, and always will be. It is a great principle in all correct views of God that he is, in all respects, unchangeably the same, "without variableness or shadow of turning;" and this principle is to be held in all its integrity in relation to every doctrine of natural or revealed religion.

(*b*) Similar to this, and growing out of it, is a second thought, that the atonement is not designed, so to speak, *to buy God over to mercy;* to make a Being before harsh and stern and severe, mild; or to melt a heart, naturally hard, to compassion. I do not deny that there have been representations by even the friends of Christianity which would bear the interpretation that this is their belief; and I do not deny that some of the language of our sacred poetry is liable to this construction. Thus such language is found in our own Watts, whose devotional poems are in general so correct in sentiment, and so well adapted to express the feelings of true piety:—

"Rich were the drops of Jesus' blood,
That *calm'd his frowning face;*
That sprinkled o'er the burning throne,
And *turn'd the wrath to grace.*"

In this language the representation undoubtedly is, that God was originally stern and unforgiving; and that he has been *made* mild and forgiving by that "blood" of atonement which "calmed his frowning face." It cannot be denied that such representations as this would be conveyed by the language used sometimes in the pulpit; or that there *are* views of the death of Christ prevailing in the Christian church which would justify such a construction.

But these views *cannot* be correct; and those who use such language must do it, as Watts seems to have done, under the influence of warm poetic or devotional feeling, where the language conveys more than it was possible in their soberer moments to believe to be true; or else they hold views of the atonement which can in no way be vindicated. God cannot change. He cannot be a different Being from what he always has been. He cannot be bought over to mercy by blood. He never has been a stern and inexorable Being, and then made mild and forgiving by the death of his Son. The human mind is so made that it cannot believe that doctrine; and no man can be required to go and proclaim such a doctrine to mankind. The true statement on this point will be seen from another part of this discourse. It is, in a word, that God was always merciful, benevolent, and kind; but that, in his government, as in all governments, there existed obstacles to the pardon of the guilty lying in eternal justice, and in the necessity of maintaining the authority of law;

that until these were removed he could not consistently make a proclamation of mercy; that in order to remove them, he gave his Son to die; and that the gift of his Son, therefore, was just an expression of the eternal benevolence of his character; a proof, not that he was originally stern and severe, and that he was *made* mild and forgiving by the atonement, but that he was *so* mild and benevolent that he was willing to stoop to any sacrifice, but that of truth and justice, to save a lost world.

(*c*) A third thought sometimes supposed to be a part of the doctrine of the atonement, but not properly connected with it, is, that Christ died to endure the strict and proper penalty of the law. But it is equally plain that this cannot be, and that men cannot be required to believe it; and that when they profess to believe it, they either have no clear ideas of what they profess to believe, or use language without any definite signification. The penalty of the law in the case of transgression is what the law appoints as an expression of the evil of the offence, and as designed to give sanction to the law and to maintain it. The proper penalty of the law can be borne by the offender only, and cannot be transferred to another. A substitute may bear something in the place of the penalty, or something which shall answer the same end; but when a man offends, the law threatens *him*, and no other. It was not true, either, that the law which man had violated ever threatened, as its specific penalty, a death on a cross; and it was not true that the Saviour endured *on* that cross what properly enters into the notion of the penalty of the law. It was not true that he suffered remorse of conscience; it was not true that he suffered eternal death; it cannot be believed that, in those short hours, he endured as *much* pain as all the wicked for whom he died would have endured in the horrors of an eternal hell. And, moreover, if he *had* endured the literal penalty of the law, no small part of the glory of the *atonement* would have been taken away. If this had been so, the short account of the whole transaction would be, that the entireness of guilt and punishment were transferred from the guilty to the innocent, and that there had been no gain to the universe, since all the punishment originally threatened had been rigidly inflicted, not indeed on those who deserved it, but on One who did *not* deserve it.

Laying these things, therefore, out of view, as not necessary in any just conceptions of the atonement, and as inconsistent with any proper view of that great work, the simple statement of it is, that it is an arrangement designed, by the substituted sufferings and death of the Lord Jesus Christ, to make the exercise of mercy towards the guilty consistent with justice and the honour of law; or an arrangement which will make it proper for God to exercise the original mercy of his nature consistently with a due regard to the stability of his government, and a due expression of his hatred of sin. The origin of the atonement is the *benevolence*, not the *justice* of God; the object aimed at is the manifestation of that benevolence consistently *with* justice; it would not have been resorted to, if benevolence towards the guilty could have been properly exercised without it.

II. We are led, then, in the second place, to inquire *what it in fact accomplishes in the plan of salvation.*

I look upon it, so far as it comes before the mind of a sinner convinced of guilt, and inquiring how peace and salvation may be found, as having two great features. First, it is an expression of the willingness of God to pardon the guilty; and, secondly, it is a device for removing the obstacles to pardon, so as to make the forgiveness of sin consistent with justice and truth.

First. It is an expression of the willingness of God to pardon the guilty. It is in this light that a sinner convicted of sin will naturally look at it; it is with reference to this that he will study it. The grand question which he wishes now to be solved, and which *must* now be solved, if he ever finds peace, is this:—whether he may hope that God will be *willing* to forgive offenders against his law. It is not whether he is benevolent in general; or whether he is just and true; but it is specifically whether he is willing to forgive the sin which now gives the inquirer so much trouble, and to receive one conscious of guilt to his favour. This is the question which the child asks respecting a parent whose law he has violated; this is the question which the offender against a human law asks when he confesses his guilt, and throws himself upon the mercy of his country; this is the question which is asked all over the heathen world, when the worshippers there, conscious of guilt, come with bloody sacrifices to their altars; and this is the question which the sinner everywhere asks, when convicted of sin, and when he feels that he deserves to be banished to the abodes of despair.

Now a simple and single declaration on the part of God *might* have settled that question for ever, and put the agitations of a troubled soul at once to rest, even if nothing were said about the *way* in which such a declaration could consistently be made.

But that is not the method which has been in fact adopted. What I beg your particular attention to is the fact, that all the offers of pardon in our world, and all the assurances of the Divine mercy to the guilty, have come through the sufferings and death of Jesus Christ—through the atonement.

(*a*) If you go *outside* of that, or look anywhere else, where will you see *evidence*, where will you find an *assurance*, that God is willing to pardon the guilty? If you go to the heathen of ancient or modern times, none of their oracles give any assurance that pardon can be obtained from an offended God; from not one of their priests could a response be obtained that would give peace to a troubled conscience. If you go to an infidel, *he* has no communication that will give peace to such a conscience. All the assurances in the Bible he on principle rejects, and he professes to have none that can be a substitute in their place. If you open the Koran, the Shasters, the Vedas, the Zendavesta, you meet no assurance on which you can rely as a communication from Heaven, that God is willing to forgive the violator of his laws. If you ask the philosopher, he has nothing to say on this point, but will rather endeavour to convince you that you do not *need* pardon,—that you should attempt to discipline your own soul to meet the trials of this life, and to be ready for the future, and not to trouble yourself about feelings that spring up from the indulgence of the passions implanted in you by your Maker. As to *pardon*, in the proper sense of the term,—as to *forgiveness*, such as a convicted sinner feels that he needs,—all these oracles, priests, and philosophers, are dumb.

(*b*) But how is this matter presented in the atonement made by Christ? The inquiry of the mind is, whether God is willing to pardon him who has violated his law, and who is troubled at the remembrance of the past, and in anticipation of the future.

There is much, it would be idle to deny, that is mysterious in the incarnation of the Son of God, and in the atonement made by Him: and what *is* there that comes before the minds of mortals that is divested of mystery? There are many questions which the sinner, in the state of mind in which I am supposing him to be, is not yet able to solve, if he ever will be in this life, or *ever afterwards*. But, in reference to the *main* matter,—to the great inquiry which perplexes him—to the question whether God is *willing* to pardon a sinner—to the disclosure of the character of God with this view, made by the gift of a Saviour and by his death on the cross,—the following things are so plain in the Bible that there can be no doubt of them in his mind, and they are of such a nature as just to meet his case:—

(1.) The atonement is, on the part of God, an expression of mere *benevolence*—a gift of love: "God so loved the world *that he gave* his only-begotten Son." He did not give him because there was a claim on him; he did not give him that he might in some mysterious way *be made* merciful;—nor did the Saviour come that he might change the character of his Father, and make an inexorable being mild and kind; or that he might *buy him over* to mercy by his sacrifice;—but God gave him *because* he loved the world, and as the *expression* of his original and eternal benevolence.

(2.) It is the *highest possible* expression of benevolence. For, to use human language, what higher expression of love can there be than for a father to give an only, a much-beloved son? And when has there been in a human soul benevolence of so high an order as to be *willing* to give up a son to die for such an object? What earthly monarch has ever occupied a throne who would be willing to give up a much-beloved son to death, to save his guilty subjects from deserved punishment? In our own land—rich as it has been in examples of benevolence and self-sacrifice—what judge has ever been seated on the bench who, to save the convicted murderer at his bar, much as there might be in his youth, or beauty, or high connexions, or endowments, to excite sympathy, would be willing to give an only son to occupy his vacated place on the gallows? Who would give up his child to save an enemy; who, even to save a friend? His own life he might give for his friend; but who would give *himself* for his *foe?* "For scarcely for a righteous man will one die; yet peradventure for a good man some would even dare to die. But God commendeth his love toward us, in that, while we were yet sinners, Christ died for us," Rom. v. 7, 8. And when the trembling and anxious sinner looks upward toward the eternal throne, and asks for a proof of love—for some intimation that God is willing to pardon—for something that shall soothe his feelings with the assurance that God is a God of mercy, and is slow to anger, and is not willing that the sinner should die,—here he sees it—sees all that the soul can ask—sees all that it can conceive of as a high expression of love.

(3.) Contemplating the death of Christ with reference to the question of so much interest to him, whether God is willing to pardon the guilty, he meets the assurance everywhere in the Bible that the sacrifice of Christ was made for all men. "God loved *the world.*" "One died *for all.*" "By the grace of God he tasted death for *every man.*" "If I be lifted up from the earth, I will draw *all men* unto me." "He is the propitiation for our sins, and not for ours only, but also for the sins *of the whole world.*" He came that "*whosoever* believeth in him should not perish, but have everlasting life."

Nothing is plainer in the Bible than that the atonement was, in some proper sense, made for all mankind. That it is so is stated in language so plain that it would seem not possible to mistake it; in language *as* plain as any found in the creeds of those churches which profess to believe the doctrine; in language *as* plain as any ever employed by those who wish to defend the doctrine; in words so plain that if it be admitted that it *was* intended to teach it, it would not be possible to do it in human language unless that actually employed in the Bible teaches it. It was an offering made for the race. It was a gift for a fallen world. It had respect not so much to *individuals* as to the *law*, the *perfections*, and the *government* of God. It was an opening of the way of pardon; a method of making forgiveness consistent; a device for preserving truth; a scheme for "magnifying the law and making it honourable;" an arrangement—such as has been wanted in all human governments, but which has been found in none—by which he who *forgives* can be at the same time strictly *just.* It is, therefore, as applicable to one individual as to another; for, having made arrangements for securing these great interests in the salvation of *one* soul, the arrangement is necessarily one that may be extended to all.

The full benefit of this atonement, therefore, is offered to all men—to each and all of the human family. God makes the offer; and he makes it in sincerity and in good faith; and he expects that his views and feelings in this will be respected and honoured by all who presume to speak in his name. He has never commissioned any class of men to make a partial offer of salvation; to limit the invitation to any favoured class—few or many—of mankind; to show any special respect in this matter to any rank, to any complexion, to any kindred or tongue. He has commissioned his servants to go and preach the gospel to "every creature;" that is, the good news that salvation is provided for *them*—for in no other sense would it be *the gospel* to them. He that does not do this; that goes to offer the gospel to a part only; to elect persons only; or that teaches that God offers the gospel only to a certain portion of mankind, violates his commission, practically charges God with insincerity, and makes the language which God has used with such apparent plainness, delusive, ambiguous, or unmeaning. It is never to be forgotten that the offer of salvation is not made by *man*, but by *God.* The offer stands recorded in his own word; the business of the ambassador is to go and proclaim that, and that only. It is the risen Saviour's commission—his solemn charge, when he was about to ascend to heaven—that the offer of salvation should be made to every creature. It is not the fault of his commission, or to be traced to any limitation in the merits of the atonement, that all that dwell upon the earth have not heard it:—that every Hindoo, African, and Islander has not long since been told that he might be saved through a Saviour's blood.

I assume the free and full offer of the gospel to all men to be one of those cardinal points of the system by which all other views of truth are to be determined. It is the corner-stone of the whole edifice; that which makes it so glorious to God, and so full of good-will to men. For one, I hold no doctrines, and never can hold any, which will seem to me inconsistent with the free and full offer of salvation to every human being, or which will bind my hands, or palsy my tongue, or freeze my heart, when I stand before sinners to tell them of a dying Saviour. I have no fellow-feeling for any other gospel; I have no "right hand of fellowship" to extend to any scheme that does not teach that God sincerely offers all the bliss of heaven to every child of Adam—be he a Caffrarian, a Hindoo, a Laplander; a beggar, or a king; a man of wealth, learning, and respectability, or an abandoned wretch;—to the man that, by the grace of God, will ultimately reach heaven, and to the man that by his own fault will wander for ever as an outcast on the plains of despair.

This scheme of salvation I regard as offered *to the world*, as freely as the light of heaven, or the rains that burst on the mountains, or the swellings of broad rivers and streams, or the bubblings of fountains in the desert. And though millions to whom it is offered do not receive it, and are not savingly benefited by it, though in regard to them the provisions of the plan may be said to be, in a certain sense, in vain, yet this result does not stand alone in the arrangements of God. I see in this the hand of the same God that pours the beams of noonday on barren sands, that sends showers on desert rocks, and that gives bubbling springs where no man is—to *our* eyes, but not to *his*, in vain. It is the overflowing of benevolence, the richness of the Divine mercy; the profusion of the gifts of the Creator, the fulness of compassion, that can afford thus to flow over all the earth—even on wastes and solitudes; for the *ocean* of love which supplies all can never be exhausted or diminished.

I have thus endeavoured to show that the atonement made by the Saviour meets the awakened and convicted sinner as a practical expression of the willingness of God to pardon the guilty; as answering a question which the mind *must* ask in that state, whether it is right for men to hope in the mercy of God, or whether there is mercy for the lost.

Second. The other aspect, as I remarked, in which the atonement is presented in the Bible, is, that it is a device or scheme, on the part of God, for removing the obstacles under a moral government to the exercise of pardon, and for making the forgiveness of a sinner consistent with the maintenance of the honour of the law, and with justice and truth. This will open before us these inquiries:—What are the obstacles in a government to the exercise of pardon; what devices are resorted to in human governments to meet these difficulties; and how the atonement removes the difficulties, and makes it consistent for God to pardon the guilty?

It was my intention to enter on this inquiry, and to complete it in this discourse; but I must reserve it for the ensuing.

In conclusion, and as a proper application of this part of the subject, I beg leave to ask your attention to one particular point; it is this:—that this view of the atonement meets an anxious inquiry which has always been made by the human mind, and which must continue to be one of the important questions before our race. It is, whether God is willing to pardon the guilty; whether those who are conscious of having violated his law may come to him with the hope that he will forgive them. Now, taking the race at large—embracing the ancient Hebrew people, the ancient and modern heathen world, and the multitudes who have resided, and do reside in Christian lands—I do not know that there is any *one* question that has interested so many minds, or interested them so deeply, as this. I admit that there have been many in all these lands who have felt no immediate interest in it, and whose attention could not be awakened to it; I admit that there are many who profess to look upon the inquiry as superfluous, and many who profess to consider it a question which could not be answered; I admit that it is not a question which has been extensively considered in the books of philosophy; and I admit that there have been other inquiries that have excited a more immediate, and, for the time, a deeper interest in many minds than this. But I am speaking of the race at large; and what I am saying is, that there is no one question that has, in one way or another, excited so deep an interest as this. It was the origin of all the sacrifices of the Hebrews. It lies at the foundation of all the bloody rites of the heathen. It is the source of all the pilgrimages and penances—the fastings and scourgings—the self-torture by uncomfortable postures, by iron beds, and by hair-cloth, among the Papists. It is the explanation of swinging on hooks, and holding the hand in one position till the muscles become immovably rigid, and walking on sharp spikes, and sacrificing children, among the heathen. And it is the cause of the anxious inquiry of the man convinced of sin in Christian lands, and under the full light of science and religion, how he may be saved. No man can be convinced that he is himself a sinner, and not ask this question; and there is no man who *may* not be convinced that he is a sinner; no one, I believe, who at some time *will* not be. It is a question which men ask in solitude—in the shades of evening, in the gloom of midnight, when the remembrance of long-forgotten guilt comes stealing over them; it is a question which men ask when in sudden danger, and when they feel that they are soon probably to be called into the presence of an offended God; it is a question which men ask when, under the preaching of the gospel, their sins are plainly set before them; it is a question which is asked with the deepest possible interest when the Spirit of God descends with power on a community in a revival of religion; it is a question which a man who has been careless, and worldly, and wicked in his life, asks with the intensest interest on the bed of death. *Can the Maker of the world show mercy?* is the great inquiry—the leading, prominent inquiry—that has stood before the minds of men. Will he pardon a transgressor of his law? Can a guilty being trust in his compassion? May one who is conscious of deep criminality, and who is soon to stand before him in judgment, hope for his favour? Can the past be forgiven? Can peace be restored to a soul, when conscience is doing its fearful work? Oh! where shall an answer be found to these questions? From what hidden recesses; from what shrines, and oracles; from what sacred groves; from what deeps of earth or of the blue ether; from what lips of the living, and from what whisperings of the "pale and sheeted dead," shall the answer come?

I believe that the answer—the sole and sufficient answer—to all these questions is found in the Cross of my Redeemer. I see there—in the gift of such a Saviour; in the avowed design of his coming; in the wonderful work of the atonement which he performed—an assurance that God loves a guilty race, and that he is ready to pardon. What more do I need than the assurance of the Son of God? What other confirmation of it do I demand than what I have in his agony and bloody sweat, his cross and passion? Mystery still there may be on a thousand questions pertaining to the Divine administration; and a thousand questions I might wish to ask even about *this* work, but the main inquiry is answered. I am assured there that God loved the world. I am assured that my Redeemer died, that God might show his willingness to pardon. I am assured that he tasted death for every man. I am assured that whosoever will may take the water of life freely. The agitations of my soul die away; my mind settles down into peace; my fears subside; I can look calmly up to God, calmly to the grave, calmly to the eternal future;—for the great question in which I feel more interest than in all others is answered—whether I, a sinner, may hope in the mercy of my God!

SERMON XVII.

THE ATONEMENT AS IT REMOVES THE OBSTACLES IN THE WAY OF PARDON.

COL. i. 20.—"Having made peace through the blood of his cross."

IN the last discourse I entered on the consideration of the *atonement* as an arrangement, under the Divine administration, for giving to a mind troubled with the consciousness of guilt a sound and permanent peace. I stated that the atonement is a device in the Divine government by which God designs to evince the benevolence of his nature in the pardon of the guilty, while at the same time he manifests a due regard to law, to truth, and to justice. The atonement, as then remarked, is founded primarily in the *benevolence*, and not in the *justice* of God; or it is a way by which benevolence can be manifested without impairing or endangering the interests of justice. As viewed by one who is condemned by his own conscience, and by the law of God, by one who feels that he is exposed to the Divine displeasure, and who is conscious of the need of pardon, which is the true point of view from which to contemplate the sacrifice made by the Lord Jesus Christ, the atonement has two aspects:—one, as it shows a sinner that God is willing to pardon; the other, as it removes the obstacles in the way of pardon.

The former of these points was then considered. I showed, (1,) that it is the expression of *mere* benevolence—guilty man having no *claim* to any such interposition; (2,) that it is the *highest* proof of benevolence which God could furnish; and, (3,) that it is benevolence shown to the *whole* race, and that, therefore, any and every sinner is free to avail himself of all the benefits of it.

I proceed now to consider the atonement in the other aspect mentioned, as removing the obstacles to pardon. It is important to our purpose to keep in remembrance this point, that we are considering the case of a sinner conscious of guilt and danger, and inquiring whether he may be pardoned and saved. Such a man wishes the assurance that he may be forgiven; he desires to understand how it is that the atonement avails to secure his pardon. He wishes to know that God is willing to forgive; he wishes to see how it is consistent for a God of truth and justice to do it. The former inquiry is answered by the fact of the gift of a Saviour, and by the Divine invitations; the latter is the point that now presents itself for our consideration.

In this inquiry there are two points:—I. What are the hindrances to the pardon of a sinner? and, II. How does the atonement remove those hindrances, and give peace to the mind of the guilty?

I. The first inquiry is, *What are the hindrances to the pardon of a sinner?*

I have already, in the former discourses, said enough to show you that those hindrances, whatever they may be, do not consist of any unwillingness on the part of God to pardon the guilty; and that, whatever may be the effect of an atonement, it is not intended to change God; or to make him a different Being from what he was before; or to buy him over to mercy; or to make a Being—before stern, inexorable, and unforgiving—mild, gentle, merciful, and kind. If any such ideas were involved in the atonement, I do not see how it would be possible for the human mind to embrace it.

Laying all such ideas out of view in contemplating the atonement, I will proceed, in as plain and simple a manner as is possible, to state what *are* the real hindrances to the pardon of a sinner.

They are such as arise from the nature of moral government, and are found under all forms of administration. In all governments there are great difficulties in regard to *pardon*, and more embarrassment is felt in adjusting it aright, than perhaps on any other subject. It is supposed, indeed, in all governments but those of tyrants, that there would be cases where pardon would be desirable; where the law, if suffered to take its course, would seem to be severe; where the real welfare of the community would be promoted, as well as the promptings of humanity obeyed, by extending forgiveness to the guilty; and where it would be desirable to leave a discretionary power on this subject to the executive officer of the government—to the sovereign power whose law has been violated. But it has never been found practicable to adjust this satisfactorily under any human administration, or to free the subject from difficulties.

The difficulties in the case—and in stating these, I am stating what exist under *all* forms of government, parental, civil, and Divine—are such as I will now refer to. (1.) One is, where pardon is *never* exercised; where it is a settled and unchanging maxim of the law, that no offender, under any circumstances, is ever to be forgiven. This *might* be, although I am ignorant that even under the darkest forms of tyranny any such principle has been avowed as the settled maxim of the administration, however it may have been practically acted on by some, as under the government of Draco, or under some forms of Oriental despotism, or by the Papal communion in the times of the Inquisition. But still it is conceivable that it *might be*, and such a government, without any mixture of the element of benevolence, would be severely and sternly and wholly just. But almost any form of tyranny would be less dreadful than this; for justice would establish its dominion at the expense of some of the finest feelings of our nature, and violate some of the plainest dictates of our moral being. There *are* cases, even cases of undoubted violation of law, where pardon is desirable; where all the benevolent feelings of a community would be gratified by forgiveness; and where all the tender feelings of humanity would be outraged if pardon were *never* extended. In the case of a single individual offender in Great Britain, thirty thousand signatures were easily obtained asking for the pardon of a man who had, in a single case, committed an offence against the laws of the land: in all communities there are cases in which the purest and best citizens are willing to unite in such petitions. All communities, as already remarked, entrust a pardoning power to the executive or the judges. As human nature now is, no man would wish to live under a government where it was an assumed principle that pardon was *never* to be extended to the guilty; no man would contribute his influence to organize a government under which *no* guilty person might ever hope to be forgiven. This difficulty is one that would arise under a government that was severely and sternly *just*. (2.) A difficulty not less, but of an opposite character, would exist if it were an admitted principle that *all* the guilty were to be pardoned; that every offender against the laws was to be forgiven, and was to be permitted to go at large. This too *might* be; but all can imagine what would be the effect of such an administration. This, not less than the former, would violate deep principles of our nature; this, more than that, would endanger the welfare of a community. For, if there are principles in our nature which would make it *desirable* that some should be pardoned, there are principles which *demand* that some shall be punished. If all were pardoned, if all the guilty were suffered to go at large, what man's property would be safe—what man's reputation—what man's life? What would be the condition of things in this or in any community, if all jails and penitentiaries were thrown open, and if all convicted and unconvicted felons were sent forth upon the community? Who would lie down calmly at night? Who would not gather up his property and flee from such a land? Law would be a bugbear; and every form of crime would be committed under the sanction of a spurious and wretched benevolence. *This* difficulty would arise if justice were *never* executed, and all the guilty were pardoned: and as a case has never occurred where it was an assumed maxim that *none* were to be pardoned, so in our world the case of a government has never occurred where it was an assumed maxim that pardon is to be extended indiscriminately to *all*. Yet, (3), there is another difficulty still. It is this: pardon in all cases does so much, even under the best arrangements that governments can make, to weaken the strong arm of the law. The influence in every case where it can be exercised is to lessen the moral power of the law; to diminish the public respect for its sanctions; to make offenders cease to dread the punishment which it threatens; and in general to produce a want of respect for the law in a community. It is of the nature of a public proclamation that crime *may* be committed in some cases with impunity; and as the cases are not specified, and as no one is excluded, the practical effect must be that each offender, whatever crime he may commit, will feel that *he* may be among the number of those who will escape the infliction of the penalty. Two things operate widely in every community to induce men to feel that the laws may be violated, and that crimes may be committed without the danger of punishment:—one is, the hope that so generally prevails among that class of men, that they will escape detection; the other,—a feeling, perhaps, as effective in producing conscious security,—is the hope that, if the crime is brought home to them, they *may* be pardoned.

What is needed in the case is, some arrangement that shall prevent this effect, and yet make pardon practicable and proper; that is, something that shall do honour to the decisions of the law, and that shall at the same time meet the promptings of benevolence; in other words, that shall secure respect for the law and the government, and yet shall make it consistent, practicable, and safe, to pardon an offender. This effect will be secured if the sanctions of the law—considered as designed to express the views of the lawgiver as to the evil of the offence, or as designed to restrain from sin, or as designed to reform offenders, or as calculated to subserve any other purpose contemplated by the infliction of penalty—can be secured, while at the same time the government is free to indulge the promptings of humanity, and to release an acknowledged offender from the infliction of the penalty. These objects, so different in their nature, have never been blended in a human administration. As the one or the other has prevailed, government has manifested a character either of severity or weakness; of tyranny or feebleness; of blood, like that of Draco, or of imbecility, where there is neither respect for the law, dread of punishment, nor restraint on crime.

In all human governments hitherto—and what has been true heretofore in this respect will be true to the end of time—there have been substantially but *two* cases in which the executive is entrusted with the power of pardon. The one is, where the sentence of the law may be regarded as *too severe;* that is, where, to use the words of Blackstone in reference to the provisions of a court of equity—"Since in laws all cases cannot be foreseen or expressed, it is necessary that when the general decrees of the law come to be applied to particular cases, there should be somewhere a power vested of defining those circumstances, which, had they been foreseen, the legislator himself would have expressed."—*Com.* i. 62. Such cases occur under all forms of human government, and under the best administration of the laws, for there are mitigating circumstances which could not have been foreseen in framing the laws; and as law is general in its nature, and not framed with reference to particular cases, the well-known maxim of the law, *Summum jus summa injuria est,* is often illustrated in the actual administration of justice. There is a propriety, therefore, that a power of remitting the penalty—improperly called a *pardoning* power—should be lodged in the hands of the executive in a state. And yet it is to be observed that this is not, in any proper sense of the word, *pardon.* It is simply a declaration, made under the authority of law, that the sentence in the case was too severe; that the penalty appointed should *not* be inflicted; that, in fact, no such crime as that of which the alleged offender has been convicted has been committed; and that of right he *ought* to be discharged. It might be true that *some* offence has been committed, and that it would have been right to have inflicted a lighter penalty, but the so-called act of pardon in this case is a proclamation that *this* penalty has not been deserved, and therefore it is clear that there has been no act of pardon as such. It is simply an acknowledgment of the imperfection of the best forms of human administration, and an act at the same time setting the government right, and the alleged offender right, before the community. Whatever honour is done to the law in the case is not in connexion with *pardon*, but it is a declaration that the law has made arrangements, so far as practicable, by which undeserved penalties shall not be inflicted.

The only other case of pardon in a human government occurs where an undoubted crime has been committed; where the offender has been tried, convicted, and sentenced; where it would be right to inflict the penalty of the law, and where, notwithstanding this, the law has entrusted the exercise of pardon to the discretion of the executive. Such cases, it must be admitted, often occur. Men of acknowledged guilt, after conviction as the result of a full and fair trial, and long before the term of sentence expires, are discharged from prison and turned upon the community practically unpunished according to the just notion of the law, and without the slightest evidence that the punishment, as far as inflicted, has had any reforming power. Nothing is done to prevent the effects of pardon noticed before; nothing is done, so far as the pardon is concerned, to maintain the authority of law; nothing is done to reform the offender; nothing is done to deter others from the commission of a similar offence. It is simply a proclamation that crime *may* be committed with impunity. To whatever it may be traced, whether to the weakness of the executive, or to the prevalent sentiments in a community demanding the frequent exercise of pardon; or to what may be regarded as the promptings of humanity or benevolence; or to a weakened sense of justice—to a feeling that punishment is essential tyranny, and that all punishment is a violation of the dictates of humanity—it is, in fact, a public proclamation that crime may be committed without the dread of punishment—a practical relaxation of all laws, and a practical invitation to all men to commit the crimes to which their passions or their supposed interests may prompt.

In all the devices of human wisdom; in all the forms of administration originated by man; in all the history of the world hitherto, it has never been found practicable to introduce an arrangement like that which is contemplated by the atonement. In no court of justice has such an arrangement ever been attempted, and no legislator has introduced it into the administration of the laws. Sensible as legislators and judges have been of the defects in the administration of law just noticed, they have never attempted, as a fixed and permanent arrangement, to introduce a device like that of the atonement. A *debt* may indeed be paid, and the obligation will be discharged; but no provision has been made by which respect may be shown to the penalty of law, and yet pardon be extended to acknowledged offenders. Whether it has been that legislators have been insensible to the evils now adverted to; or whether they have been disposed to make an experiment to see whether those evils might not be avoided; or whether they have despaired of finding any means by which due honour may be done to the law while the guilty man is acquitted, it is not material now to inquire. The fact is undoubted. No such arrangement has ever been made. History furnishes no traces of such a provision, and no court of justice has ever resorted to it in the administration of law. No one has been appointed, as a permanent legal arrangement, to suffer in the place of another; nowhere does law contemplate the acceptance of substituted sufferings in the place of those incurred by the guilty. The *only* things done by a human government in the case are the two already referred to: to wit, where an offender is pardoned, as it is termed, because the sentence was too severe; and where one guilty of undoubted crime, and deserving the infliction of the penalty, is discharged without any attempt to maintain the authority of law.

Now it is clear that in the Divine administration pardon can never be extended in either of these forms. It cannot be supposed that in an act of pardon the all-wise Legislator would practically acknowledge that the sentence of the law was too severe—that is, that it was *unjust*,—and that the offender would be discharged on that ground; nor can it be supposed that an acknowledged offender would be acquitted without any respect shown to the law, or any arrangement to prevent the effects on the individual himself, or on the community, of acquitting the offender. It cannot be supposed that God would make either a practical proclamation that his own law was stern and severe, and that its penalty *ought* not to be inflicted; nor can it be supposed that he would make a practical proclamation that his law is to be disregarded in his own mode of administering it, and that it may become an understood maxim that crime may be committed under his administration with impunity. To suppose this would be to charge on the Divine administration all that has been found to be weak, defective, inefficient, if not partial, in human governments. Whether we may be able or not to see how this difficulty is met, and how these evils are prevented, we may be certain that in a perfect government the difficulties *will* be met, and that some arrangement will be devised by which the evils may be prevented. This leads us,

II. In the second place, to inquire, *How the atonement meets the difficulties referred to*—or how it removes the hindrances to the pardon of a sinner.

This inquiry is practically whether the atonement so meets the claims of justice, or so evinces respect to the law, that the great ends of moral government can be secured when the penalty is remitted, or when the sinner is pardoned. If these ends *can* be secured, it is clear that the offender may with propriety be pardoned; and clear also, that, if this is done, his agitated and troubled mind may be at peace. If by the atonement God can as certainly and as fully evince his hatred of sin, and his respect for law, and prevent the evil effects of sin, as he could by the punishment of the sinner himself, then it is plain that the great purposes contemplated by the law and by the appointment of a penalty are accomplished. There are, then, in connexion with this, two subordinate inquiries:—What is shown by punishment? and, Can this be shown by the atonement?

(*a*) What, then, is shown by punishment? What is contemplated by the appointment of penalty? What, in respect to moral government, is secured when the penalty of law is inflicted? In what light does it represent the lawgiver, and what light does it throw on his purpose in appointing the penalty? To these inquiries the brief and obvious answer is, *that the penalty affixed to a law expresses the view of the lawgiver in respect to the evil of the offence.* So far as it is penalty, its design is to convey that idea, and nothing else. It is simply the *measure* of his estimate of the nature and desert of the crime. The penalty must be appointed, moreover, by the lawgiver himself, and must express *his* sense of the nature and desert of the act of transgression. No one can control him in this; no one can properly estimate the justice of the penalty, unless he is able to comprehend the nature and tendency of the offence as truly as the lawgiver himself; and no creature therefore, in respect to the Divine administration, can possess the qualifications which *may* be requisite to judge of the propriety of the penalty affixed to law. Much indeed of the design and the effect of punishment may be seen, but there may be depths in regard to it which no created intellect can as yet fathom, and there may be collateral purposes to be accomplished by it which a creature cannot comprehend. The main and central idea however is, that it shows the sense of the lawgiver in respect to the evil of transgression. It is an illustration and a declaration of the view which he takes of it from the stand-point which he occupies as the head of the government, or as presiding over the interests of those who are subject to his administration. The security that the penalty will be just and equal—that it will not be severe or partial—that it will be commensurate merely with the desert of the offence—that it will not be too intense in degree, or too prolonged in duration—is to be found, not in any control which the subject of the law has over it, but solely in the wisdom, the equity, and the benevolence of him who appoints it. It is plain that if the view thus entertained of the evil of transgression can be evinced either by the sufferings of the offender himself, or by anything substituted in the place of those sufferings that shall convey the same practical impression, the great ends of penalty will be accomplished, and the infliction of the penalty on the offender himself may in the latter case be remitted.

(*b*) This leads, then, to the only remaining inquiry, whether the evil of sin as designed to be expressed by the penalty of the law can be so evinced by the substituted sufferings of another, or by the atonement, that in respect to the offender himself penalty may be properly remitted; and so remitted that he himself can feel that the same testimony has been borne to the value of law, and to the evil of sin, which would have been furnished by his own personal sufferings. In other words, is it practicable or possible for an offender troubled with the remembrance of personal guilt, and realizing that he is justly exposed to the penalty of a broken law, to feel the same calmness and composure, or the same freedom from apprehended punishment, which he would have felt if it had been possible for him to bear the penalty himself, or which he would if the offence had never been committed? If sin were a *debt* in the literal sense, it is easy to see how this effect might follow;—for it is conceivable that a debt might be so paid by another as to meet all the claims of justice, or to discharge the entire pecuniary responsibility, so that the debtor himself would feel that there was no claim of the law upon him, and so that there would be created in his bosom the highest sense of obligation to him who had interposed to relieve him of a claim which he was unable to meet. It is to be admitted, however, that sin is not precisely of the nature of a debt; and it is to be admitted that there must be other elements in an atonement than those which are involved in the payment of a debt. Can the great end contemplated by the appointment of a penalty, or by the infliction of punishment—to wit, the expression of the Divine view of the evil of sin—be so accomplished by the substituted sufferings, that I, a guilty man—a helpless sinner—an acknowledged violator of law—one feeling that he deserves the infliction of such a penalty as the Lawgiver shall judge to be necessary for the maintenance of moral government—can feel that the great purpose of penalty in respect to me has been accomplished, and that I may now be properly treated as if I had not offended?

As this inquiry pertains to the very essence of the Christian scheme, as it bears on the feelings of the guilty, and relates to a question which must always occur to the mind of the guilty, it is proper to refer to a few facts and principles which may tend to illustrate and answer it.

(1.) As a matter of fact, under the Divine administration, the evil of sin or crime is perhaps more frequently seen by the effects produced on those who are innocent than by any direct and immediate effect on the guilty themselves. It is somehow a great principle under the Divine government, that the effects of our conduct often pass over from the offender himself to those who are associated with him; and that when we undertake to estimate the *evil* of the offence, or to obtain a just *measure* of the crime, we more naturally look to those effects than to anything which has as yet occurred to the offender himself. Nay, the mind of the offender himself *may* be more deeply affected as to the evil of the crime committed by the sufferings which he perceives that his conduct has caused to others than by any pain or privation which he himself has endured. Society is full of instances of this kind, and perhaps in the case of a large portion of the crimes committed in a community, the actual amount of suffering endured by the offender himself is small, if it might not even be said to be trifling, as compared with the sufferings which the offence has brought on others. The man who suffers in a penitentiary, solitary and alone, perhaps learns to bear the punishment inflicted with patience, or sinks into insensibility or stupidity, or invents some mitigation of his own sufferings; but while thus insensible comparatively to the effects of his own crime, and to the evil of the offence, his conduct may have brought the grey hairs of a father or a mother to the grave, or the sorrows of a broken-hearted wife, sister, or daughter, may be the public testimony to the evil of the offence, and may do more to impress a sense of that evil on the community than all that he endures in the loneliness and forgetfulness of his dungeon. Now, if we suppose that it had been designed beforehand to make an arrangement which would most deeply impress upon the community the evil of the offence committed, we should say that apparently the design was to show that evil to the largest extent by the collateral and incidental sufferings that would come on the innocent. The point now is not to inquire into the reason of this arrangement, or to show its justice; but simply to advert to the fact that the evil of transgression may be seen in a very high degree, and so as possibly to affect the mind of the offender himself by the sufferings which a certain course of conduct would bring on the innocent. If we suppose that those sufferings were in any sense voluntarily assumed, the principle would not be varied; for still the whole effect *might* be in some way to illustrate the evil of the offence, or to divide with the offender the sufferings produced by his crime.

(2.) The great doctrine of the Christian atonement is, not that there was any natural connexion between the sinner and the Redeemer; not that, as in the case above supposed, the consequences of the sinner's offence passed over by any natural law to the Saviour, so as to involve him in poverty, pain, and death, but that by a voluntary arrangement he was willing so to take the place of the offender that, as in the case of natural relationship, the evil effect of transgression should be illustrated, and the Divine sense of the nature of sin should be manifested by his sufferings as if they had been endured by the sinner himself. In other words, such an amount of suffering was appointed, and was submitted to, as would to the sinner himself, and to the universe at large, be a just measure of the Divine sense of the evil of transgression, and in this respect accomplish the same effect as if the sinner had himself endured the penalty of the law.

(3.) In the work of the atonement as viewed by the sinner under conviction for sin, looking at the Redeemer as suffering in his stead, the great idea which is presented to his mind is still that which is manifest in the personal sufferings produced by sins, and in the voluntary or involuntary sufferings endured by others on our account—to wit, *the connexion between sin and suffering*. It is seen there, as elsewhere, that the only cause of suffering is sin. The Redeemer suffered from no other cause. There was no other conceivable reason why he should suffer. There is no statement made—no intimation whatever—that he *did* suffer from any other cause. No reason can be given, drawn from any views of the Divine government which we can obtain, why the sufferings of the garden and the cross came upon him, unless it was from some connexion with sin. Without such a connexion, and without some design of evincing the nature of sin by his sufferings, it would be impossible to vindicate the Divine character in permitting these sufferings to come upon the only Being in our world who has been in all respects perfectly innocent. The Scripture statement, moreover, everywhere is, that he *did* thus suffer on account of sin:—that he "died the just for the unjust;" that he was the "propitiation for our sins;"

that "the chastisement of our peace was upon him;" that "the Lord laid on him the iniquity of us all;" that "by his stripes we are healed;" and that "he died for our offences, and was raised for our justification." The point of the remark now made is, that this may be so perceived by the mind itself to be the design of the Saviour's sufferings, that one who is conscious of guilt may see that *in* those sufferings there has been a real expression of a Divine sense of the evil of sin, intentionally made, an expression *as* real, though it may not be in the same form, as if the sinner himself had endured the same sufferings as a part of the penalty of the law.

(4.) One other remark only it seems necessary to make to complete the statement of the effect produced by the atonement in giving peace to a mind troubled with the consciousness of sin: it is, that the sufferings endured by the Redeemer in the place of the sinner are fitted to make a deeper impression on the universe at large than would be produced by the punishment of the sinner himself. If a sinner is lost, he is so in more senses than one;—lost not only to hope and happiness, but also in the sense that his individual sufferings may make little, if any, impression on the universe at large. He has in himself no such rank, or dignity, or exaltation, and he sustains no such relations, as to attract attention beyond a very limited sphere. The *aggregate* sufferings of the guilty may, indeed, make a deep and wide impression; but the sufferings of an individual must be limited in the sphere of their influence, and the moral effect will be comparatively unfelt. Few of all the creatures that God has made will be aware of his suffering, and even on those few the impression produced will be comparatively slight. None of these remarks, however, apply to the sufferings of the Redeemer, considered as endured in the place of sinners. His exalted dignity as the Son of God; the adoration paid him by the angelic hosts; his rank and office as Mediator; the changes that may have been produced in heaven by his incarnation; his poverty and lowliness of estate on earth; his life of weariness and toil; and pre-eminently his sufferings on the cross, were all fitted to attract the attention of the universe at large, and to produce a deep impression on distant worlds. Far as those wonderful events were known,—and if he was, indeed, the incarnate Deity, they would be known throughout all worlds,—the inquiry must have occurred, why he stooped to so low a condition; why he endured so many sufferings in his life; and why, as a malefactor, and between malefactors, he died on a cross. Whether the design of that death was known to other worlds at the time it occurred, cannot indeed now be ascertained; but it will be ultimately known that it was intended to express, to the utmost degree possible, the Divine sense of the evil of sin—the very object which would be accomplished by the punishment of the sinner himself. Throughout the universe, therefore, an impression would be made by the atonement of the evil of sin, more deep and lasting than would be produced by the natural course of the administration of justice; and if that impression is secured, it is clear that every obstacle to the pardon of the sinner is removed, and that he may be forgiven without any of the incidental evils against which it has been impossible to guard in the exercise of pardon by human governments.

If this is so, the troubled conscience may have peace. All has been done that *can* be done to show the evil of transgression, and to prevent the consequences which would flow from the exercise of pardon were it granted without an atonement. All has been done that *needs* to be done to express the Divine sense of the value of law, of the ill-desert of transgression, and of the magnitude of an offence against the government of God. God has shown that while he pardons he is not indifferent to the claims of his own law, and that while he "justifies the ungodly," he has a supreme regard for truth and holiness, and will maintain the interests of justice at all times, and at every sacrifice. The pardoned sinner, therefore, may have peace. He is not only assured of pardon, but he is assured that it is extended in such a way that the honour of God is maintained, and the great interests of the universe secured. He can *see* that the obstacles which existed to the exercise of pardon have been wholly removed, and removed in such a way that every interest of justice is safe. Sunken, degraded, and lost as he is; conscious of deep depravity and of ill-desert; feeling that his appropriate place would be with the lost; and feeling too—for that can never be forgotten—that he will always retain the recollection of his having been a violator of law, and that he can occupy only a very humble place before the throne,—yet he may feel also that God is glorified by his salvation, and every attribute of the Deity illustrated and magnified by his admission into heaven. He enjoys the favour of God, not because God disregards law, but even while he shows his respect for it, and magnifies it. He becomes an heir of glory, not by any favouritism that is regardless of justice and of the rights of others, but while the rights of others are as much respected as his own, and while they are rendered still more secure by the method of his own salvation. He enters heaven over no prostrate law; he dwells there not in defiance of the claims of justice; he wears a crown of glory not tarnished by the conviction that it is bestowed in violation of right; but while associated for ever with unfallen beings, with the angels that have not left "their first estate,"—he feels that he is there in virtue of a righteousness not *less* glorious than theirs, for it is the righteousness of the Son of God. The atonement has thus removed the obstacles to the way of pardon; the agitations of guilt in the soul die away; light, hope, and joy break in upon the mind, and the sinner finds peace.

SERMON XVIII.

THE NECESSITY OF REGENERATION.

JOHN iii. 3.—"Except a man be born again, he cannot see the kingdom of God."

I PROPOSE, from this verse, to show the necessity of regeneration, or the new birth. The only introductory remark which it is necessary to make before we enter on the argument is, that the Saviour in the text asserts, with great earnestness and emphasis, that the new birth is indispensable for *every one* who would enter into his kingdom:—"Verily, verily, I say unto thee, Except a man"—in the Greek, *any one*—"be born again, he cannot enter into the kingdom of God." My argument will be directed solely to this point, that it is necessary for *every one* to be renewed, or regenerated, in order to be saved.

With reference to this argument, mankind may be conveniently divided into two great classes. The line, perhaps, may not be in all respects very definite, and there may be a middle region of character of considerable extent such as to leave us in doubt where to place many individuals; but it is sufficiently definite for our present purpose, and will not lead us into error in the argument. The two classes are these:—First. The openly wicked, abandoned, sensual, scoffing, profane. Secondly. The moral, the amiable, the upright, the sincere, the accomplished. The former are commonly designated as vicious; the latter as virtuous. The former are destitute of virtue and religion together; the latter lay claim to virtue without religion. The former attempt no divorce between virtue and piety, but abjure both together; the latter attempt a divorce, and seek to hold the one without the other. The former are willing to be excluded from good society on earth as well as from heaven; the latter mean to retain their rank in the goodly fellowship of this world, whatever may be the fact about their admission into heaven. The former take a decided stand against religion and all its appearances and pretensions; the latter desire to occupy a position somewhere on the confines of religion—and if they have not Christian piety, they intend to have something that they hope will, on the whole, answer just as well in the future world.

Now the difficulty in regard to the subject before us is not at all in reference to the former of these classes. It will be conceded on all hands that it is necessary that *they* should be renewed in order to enter into the kingdom of heaven. Had the Saviour so modified his declaration, affirming the necessity of the new birth, as to have embraced only that portion of mankind, scarcely any doctrine would have met with more favour. The only embarrassment in the case has arisen from the fact that he so shaped his remark as to include Nicodemus and all that class of men under it, so as to make it just as necessary for *them* to be born again as for the openly abandoned and profane. It is a difficulty arising from the fact that in one respect—not in all respects—he has put them on a level, and affirmed that, whatever else might occur, they would be alike excluded from the kingdom of God unless they were "born of water and of the Spirit." Leaving the former of these classes, therefore, at present out of view, as those about whom there can be no debate, and as not probably among those who may read these pages, I shall direct your thoughts entirely to the question about the latter class—the amiable, the moral, the upright. The subject will have then this advantage at least, that it is one that pertains to your own case, and is one in which you will feel yourselves personally concerned.

It falls in with my design, and with my convictions also, to concede to you all that you would claim on the score of morality, amiableness, courtesy, and kindness. Of these virtues you could mention none which my argument would not allow me to concede; of none who might set up the claim would I be disposed to call it in question. I do not see that the Redeemer was disposed to deny the existence of these virtues in Nicodemus; I am certain he did not in the young man who came to him and told him that he had kept all the commandments from his youth up, and whom the Saviour told that he lacked but one thing in order to be perfect, and whom he "loved," Mark x. 21. Yet here lies the solemn declaration of the Saviour in our path, affecting alike the case of Nicodemus, and the amiable young man, and all who are like them:—"Except any one be born again, he cannot see the kingdom of God." Why did he make such a declaration? On what was it based? What were the views of man which lay in the Redeemer's soul that justified this remark? We may not be able exactly to answer *these* questions, but we may state some considerations which show that the declaration is true, or that there *are* reasons why it was made. To that task I now proceed.

I. The first consideration which I state is, *that the heart by nature, or when unrenewed, is not in a proper state for the employments and enjoyments of heaven.* I speak now of the human heart as such, without any special reference to the openly wicked and profane. I speak of the unrenewed heart in its best state, and under the best discipline and cultivation. I speak of it where there may be all the charms of accomplishment; all the beauties of native amiableness; all the courtesy of refined breeding; all that is attractive and valuable in unsuspected virtue.

There are two sources of evidence in regard to this:—the Bible and your own consciousness.

The testimony of the Bible is so clear that no one, I presume, will be disposed to doubt it, and this point need not detain us long. That testimony bears directly on the point before us, that the human heart, as such, is evil, and must be renewed if man would be saved. Thus it is said, "*The heart* is deceitful above all things, and desperately wicked," Jer. xvii. 9. That is, the heart of man, as such, without reference to any particular class or condition of men. The fair meaning is, that wherever there is a human heart it has this characteristic—that it is a deceitful heart—more deceitful than all things else in a world full of deceit; and that it has within it the elements of desperate wickedness. The same account of the universal depravity of the human heart is given in Gen. viii. 21: "The imagination of *man's heart* is evil from his youth." This appears also in the form of an universal declaration. It is not that the profligate race which had been just swept away by the deluge was evil, but it is that the heart of man, as such, is evil from his youth.

As these positive declarations settle the question so far as the Bible is concerned, I turn to the other source of evidence in the case—the consciousness of the heart itself. And as the form of direct address will better fall in with the nature of the argument which I wish to urge, you will permit me with plainness to use this form. The argument relates to the following points:

(1.) You are conscious that you have no vital religion; nothing that can be properly called religion. You do not even pretend or profess to have it. You would not consider it a reflection on you at all to have it said that you made no profession of piety, as you would to have it said that you do not profess to be influenced by the laws of honour or honesty. And in your life there is nothing that can be fairly interpreted as showing that you have real religion. You do not truly pray; you do not habitually read the Bible; you do not cherish love to God;

you do not depend on his mercy for salvation; you do not identify yourselves with religious persons. You claim to be moral, upright, faithful to your engagements, kind, courteous; but in your own heart and wishes and intentions you do not claim to be religious men. Possibly you may say that all this is unkind and uncharitable. But I see not how it is so. I will concede all that you claim. I will yield all that you ask on the score of morality. I will even go farther than you will. *I* will yield to a man the claim to be a religious man when he professes to be, even when appearances are much against him—for I am not ignorant how much I must need the exercise of that charity "which suffereth long and is kind;" and I believe that there may be true piety where there is much imperfection, and if *you* make any profession of godliness I will extend the same charity to you. But I have not so read the New Testament, or so learned the character of Christ, or been so taught by any of the rules of urbanity, as to ascribe to a man what he does not himself profess to have; as to go with kind-heartedness beyond what he habitually lays claim to, and to attribute to him what never constituted a part of his own profession. Every man has a right to choose and "define his own position," and to make his own professions; and for myself, I ask no man, either from charity or justice, to attribute to me opinions and sentiments which I do not profess to have. In the same way I shall continue to judge of my neighbour, and shall conclude that I am doing him no injustice in supposing that he has no spiritual life when he asserts no claim to have any, whatever I may think about those who profess to be influenced by it.

(2.) Another consideration is, that every man is conscious that there is much in his heart that is opposed to God and to religion. The depths of depravity indeed in his soul may not have been explored; there may have been no outbreaking wickedness to overwhelm his name and family in disgrace; he may have been neither a scoffer nor an open infidel; and in fact he may never have recorded one sentence in the most confidential letter to a friend, or given utterance to one remark, in the most familiar intercourse, opposed to religion; yet no man can reach a mature period of life without knowing that there is much in his heart that is opposed to God and to religion. Many of the doctrines of religion are unpalatable to the natural heart. Its more spiritual duties are onerous and irksome. Its restraints seem like a violation of freedom. The law of God is laid across the path at times and in a manner that chafes the feelings, and disturbs the plans of life. The claims, rebukes, threatenings, and penalties of both law and gospel are galling and unpleasant to the soul. There is much in the character and government of God that seems to such a man to be not only mysterious, but wrong. In his afflictions, disappointments, and blighted hopes, he has been conscious of murmuring thoughts, and has been obliged to exercise restraint lest they should find their way to his lips. He cannot but be conscious that when God has directed him to love him supremely, he has not done it; when he has required him to form his plans with reference to his glory, he has formed them with reference to ease, pleasure, gain, or ambition; when he has called on him to repent, he has remained impenitent; when he has commanded him to believe, he has continued unbelieving; and when he has counselled him to pray, he has restrained prayer. He cannot but be conscious that he has given indulgence to a roving imagination; that he has delighted to dwell, in his recollections of the past, on the objects fitted to debase and corrupt him; and that he has formed many a plan, and cherished many a wish, on which a pure Being could look only with a frown of indignation. And he cannot but be conscious that he has never found that pleasure in religion of which the Bible speaks, and which Christians declare that they enjoy; and that in the course of his life there has never been one whole day, or one whole hour, in which the mind would have found enjoyment in religion. His mind and heart are not in the course of things which God wishes, and which God is carrying forward. Hear what one says who knew:—

> "Our life is a false nature—'tis not in
> The harmony of things,—this hard decree,
> This uneradicable taint of sin,
> This boundless upas, this all-blasting tree,
> Whose root is earth, whose leaves and branches be
> The skies which rain their plagues on men like dew—
> Disease, death, bondage—all the woes we see—
> And worse, the woes we see not—which throb througn
> The unmedicable soul, with heart-aches ever new."
>
> *Childe Harold*, iv. 126.

(3.) The next remark is, that such a heart is not fitted for the employments and enjoyments of heaven unless it is changed. This is evident, unless the joys and employments of heaven consist in the mere prolongation of the pleasures and business of this life. If commerce, and manufactures, and merchandize, and agriculture were to be the business there, we do not see but they might be happy. If men were to contend there in the forum; if on their lips "listening senates" were to hang; if the pursuits of science were to give employment to the mind; if under the chisel the marble were to breathe, or under the brush the canvas be filled with forms of life; or if pleasure were to open new parks and gardens and banqueting halls, we admit that the unrenewed mind might find happiness in heaven. But we have only one account of heaven that is worth regarding,—that in the Bible. And according to that, heaven is not the prolongation of the employments of this life, as dreamed of by the Swedenborgian; nor a Mohammedan Paradise, where Houries are created to give infinity of duration to sensual joys; nor the Elysian fields of poets; nor such abodes as the scientific and the literary world look for. It is a place of *religion;* a place of adoration and holy love; a place of pure and prolonged thanksgiving and praise; a place where the soul is expanded by the contemplation of religious truth, and where, in his works, God is adored as "first, and last, and midst, and without end." God is there. Christ, the holy, incarnate Saviour, is there. Holy angels are there. The redeemed of all ages and lands are there; and it is a world of religious beings, and not a world of mere sages, or philosophers, or poets, or patriots, or of the winning and the accomplished. And if these things are so, then nothing can be plainer than the declaration of the Saviour in the text, that, "Except a man be born again, he cannot see the kingdom of God."

II. The second general consideration which I urge is, *that no change which man passes through in the present life will fit for heaven except that produced in regeneration.* Men experience many other changes,—some of them sudden and remarkable, and some of them extending their influence far into future years, and even as far as we can follow the dying into the dark valley; but none of them are changes that fit for heaven. We change in our habits, views, opinions, employments, hopes, anticipations, temperament, passions; in the transition from childhood to youth, from youth to manhood, from manhood to old age. At one period, we are blithe, cheerful, merry, playful, thoughtless. At another, we cherish the generous aspirations of youth, when the blood is warm in our veins, and the world is full of allurements. At that time we are generous, open, ardent; full of life, of energy, of promise; laying large plans, and grasping at wealth and honours. Then we settle down into the calmness of sober life; we give place to serious reflection; we allow judgment to preside where passion did; we become less lavish of expenditure, and husband our resources; we feel ourselves pressed down with the cares of the world, and we give ourselves to the serious business of living. Then the "sear and yellow leaf" comes on. The shades grow long, and are chilly. We become fixed in our opinions; staid in our judgments; unchangeable in our views. The fires of youth have all gone out. The business of life has been passed through. We look upon a new generation that has come up with great energy, and is pressing hard on us to elbow us out of our place, and already wishing us gone, and coveting our houses and lands. We settle down into a contented and honoured old age, and look with satisfaction on our "children's children, the crown of old men" (Prov. xvii. 6); or perchance we draw our purse-strings tighter, as we have less use for what we have wasted life in acquiring, and become peevish and fretful, and fancy that the world, since it lost our counsel and influence, is all the while growing worse and worse.

Now one remark which I wish to make is, that in none of these changes, great as they are, is there any one that of necessity fits for heaven. The characteristics which come up in youth no more fit us for heaven than did those of the child; nor in the transition from youth to manhood, or from manhood to old age, is there of necessity a change that fits men for heaven. Not all old men are prepared to enter into the kingdom of God, any more than those in the days of their youth. In none of these changes is there any permanency to reach beyond the tomb; and if there were, in none of them is there a change to fit for heaven. The exchange of playfulness and thoughtlessness for other habits, is not religion; the subjugation of the raging passions of youth, and the coming on of the settled habits of manhood, is not of necessity the love of God; nor is the kind of feeling with which an old man regards the long path which he has trod, filled with many rough places and hills and valleys, the deadness to the world which fits a man for heaven.

Another remark which I make in view of these changes is, that so far from their fitting for heaven, there may be in fact *less* inclination for religion in the succeeding change than there was in the one that went before. The young man often has less tenderness of feeling on the subject of religion, than he had when a child; the man in middle life, than he had when a youth; the old man, least of all. The child put his little hands together every morning and evening, and uttered the language, "Our Father who art in heaven," and wept freely when his mother told him of the woes of that kind-hearted Saviour who died for all. The same child, when he becomes a youth, may be a sceptic at heart; in middle life, an avowed infidel; in old age, a hard-hearted atheist and a scoffer. His advance on the successive stages of life has not been an advance in religion, but a departure from it; and the bright-eyed and lovely boy, who commenced life gladdening a father's heart with the hope that he would be a Christian, ends it with no respect for religion, and no belief in its Divine authority and claims.

Another remark may be made here respecting the changes which occur in men's lives. They often change from vice to virtue; from gross intemperance to soberness of living; from profaneness to outward respect for the name of God; from the love of idle and dissolute companionship to a love for the fellowship of the virtuous and the refined; but there is of necessity no change here that fits men for heaven. The reformed inebriate is not necessarily a man who loves God; nor does one who abandons habits of profligacy of course become a man of prayer. A man may change his business, his profession, his country, his dwelling, his friends; but it does not follow that he has passed through any change that will fit him to dwell with God. He may subdue many of his evil propensities; may humble much of his pride; and cease to be a scoffer or a philosophical foe of the gospel; may forsake his wicked companions, and may become a supporter of the gospel, and a regular and respectful attendant in the house of God on the sabbath,—and still be as decidedly irreligious at heart as he was before. The most decided period of irreligion in his life may be when all these changes have been gone through; the most determined hatred to religion ever expressed in the eye may be in that unnatural and frightful brilliancy with which it is lighted up when told to believe in Christ, just before its light is to be extinguished for ever. All these things are too plain, and too much a matter of common observation, to make it proper to lengthen out the argument which they furnish: and if these things are so, then there is but one change that fits men for heaven; and then nothing can be more true than the declaration of the Saviour, that "Except a man be born again, he cannot see the kingdom of God."

III. The third general consideration which I urge to show the necessity of regeneration is the fact, *that nothing can be substituted in its place*—nothing can be made to answer the same purpose. If this be so—if it be true that men by nature are not fitted for heaven, and that none of the numerous changes which they undergo in the ordinary transitions of life fit them for it, and that they can substitute nothing in the place of the new birth that will answer the same purpose,—then it will follow clearly that there is a necessity that man should be born again. Now, that it is so will be apparent on the slightest reflection. There is *one* doctrine of substitution, or putting one thing in the place of another, that is set forth as a true principle in the government of God, and is that on which the redemption of the whole world is made to turn:—it is the doctrine of the substituted sufferings of the Redeemer in the place of sinners, and the fact that our hope of salvation depends on that. But in the Scriptures the doctrine of substitution is limited to that, nor is there an intimation that the principle can ever be extended. It was only the extraordinary necessity of the case that justified the admission of that one instance into the system; and it was only the fact that immense and eternal good would accrue from that one case to unnumbered millions that made it proper. But the necessity extends no farther. There is no intimation that one man can take the place of another; or that a lack of any one thing required can be compensated by something else which shall be offered in its stead. And the scriptural doctrine on this point is one of common sense. You demand a specific act of obedience from a child. There is no general virtue, and no *other* act of obedience which will supply the place of that, if it is not rendered. You demand love from a friend. If that is withheld, there is no offering of gold or silver, of wine or oil, that will supply its place. A wife demands constancy and fidelity in a husband. If these are not rendered, there is no diamond-ring—no string of orient pearls—no richly-set bracelets—no winning smile of professed affection, that can supply their place. They are all insult and mockery—an infinite aggravation of the offence, when tendered by an unfaithful man; and what *might* in other circumstances be tokens of affection of inestimable value, are now spurned with disdain and loathing.

God demands the heart—the love, the friendship, the confidence of his creature, man; such love, and friendship, and affection as are the fruit of a renovated heart. *With* such a renovated heart, what you could render to him would be an acceptable and a valuable offering. Your moral life and integrity, based on holy principles, would be acceptable; the homage of the bended knee, and the song of praise in appropriate forms of devotion, would be lovely in his view; your acts of fidelity in the transactions of business and in the relations of life, as the expression of love to him, would be pleasing in his sight; your money, offered in charity to the cause of humanity, would be received as a grateful tribute at your hands. But suppose you go and offer these things *without* a renovated heart—without love to him—without having obeyed his first commandment, can they be a substitute for such a renovated heart? Can a moral life, and faithfulness in your dealings with mankind, answer the same purpose as the love which he requires you to render to himself? Can the homage of the bended knee, and the song of praise on the lips, answer the purpose of the offering of the heart before One who looks through all the chambers of the soul? Can wealth hoarded and prized, or scattered among the needy; can beauty or accomplishment; can a graceful exterior, a lively wit, a cultivated intellect, and propriety of manners, be of value to him without the *heart*, or answer the purpose which he contemplates by its change? Just as much as diamond rings, and strings of pearls, answer the place of fidelity and affection to an outraged and injured wife—*and no more.* Go and plead your moral character before God, as a reason why you should be saved. What would be its reception? "All this would be well," might be the response, "but *the heart* was required; the regenerated affections of the soul were demanded. Where *are* the affections of that heart?" Go plead your fidelity to your family; your kindness as a husband, and father, and neighbour; your honesty to men. "All this is well. But where is *the heart for me?*" the Saviour might reply; "where is the evidence of love to your God?" Go plead accomplishment, wit, learning, talent, beauty:—are these what are required to fit men for heaven? Are these proposed to be substituted in the place of what *is* required? Be not deceived. Nor rank, nor wealth, nor talent, nor learning, nor gracefulness of manners, nor eminence in your profession, nor oratory, nor the crown of victory won on the battle-field, nor any other thing, can be a substitute for the renovated heart. They will not answer the same purpose while men live here; they will not extend their influence to a future world when they die. A splendid steamer leaves the wharf to cross the ocean. Youth, and beauty, and rank, crowd on board; age, and middle age, are there; the high, the low, the rich, the poor, the bond, the free, the peasant, the prince, are there. She moves majestically on. Suddenly she strikes an iceberg, and in a moment goes down. There is a tremendous plunge; a heaving of the waves; a boiling, rolling sea for a few moments where she sank. But it is soon over. The sea is again smooth. The deep, dark, blue ocean rolls on; and the ruffled deep becomes calm—

> "A glorious mirror, where the Almighty's form
> Glasses itself."

But those distinctions of age, and beauty, and rank—where are they? Have they attended those who sank, as they went up to the bar of God? Vanished—all vanished—before the sea was made calm where they sank; and alike the prince and the peasant, the master and his slave, make their bed amidst the corals of the ocean. There was but one distinction that lived on. If there was piety in one heart and wickedness in another, they lived on. The distinction that survived the catastrophe, and the only one, was that which was made when the penitent heart yielded itself to God, and was born again.

IV. I suggest one other thought, which will require no time to prove or illustrate it: it is, *that there will be of necessity no such change in death as to fit the soul for heaven.* And if this is so; if man by nature is unfit for heaven; if no change which he ordinarily undergoes fits him for it; if he can substitute nothing in the place of a renovated heart to fit him for heaven; and if death will make no such change as will adapt him to the employments of the skies,—then it follows that there is a necessity for man to be born again. And that it *is* so, assuredly I need not now attempt to prove. What is the change at death? The rose of health fades from the cheek; the brow is "chill, and changeless;" the eye is closed, and in that lifeless form there is "a mild angelic air,"

> "Before decay's effacing fingers
> Have swept the lines where beauty lingers."

But there is no *religion* in that change. At death, we are borne away indeed from the world where we were tempted; the objects that with idolatrous affection we loved; the allurements of wicked companionship; the assembly-room, where, in festive mirth, we forgot God and provoked his wrath;—but there is no *religion* in that. All that is solemn, tender, affecting on the dying bed may be gone through, and still there be not a particle of religious emotion there. And is there some magic power—some potent charm in the grave—in the long slumberings there—in the solemn stillness—in the withdrawment from scenes of gaiety and temptation—to change the heart, to wean the soul from the world—to prepare even the *body* there for the resurrection of the just? Or is there something in the solemn, lonely journey of the departed spirit up to God—some new efficacy of the blood of the atonement to be applied to the soul on its upward way to fit it for the skies? Surely none of these things can be pretended:—and if none of these things are so, then there is a necessity that the sinner should be born again before he dies.

The argument which I proposed to submit to you is now before you. It is not an argument addressed to you as if there were any doubt about the meaning of what the Saviour says in the text, or as if his authority were not a sufficient ground for the truth of a doctrine; or as if the truth of what he says could be confirmed by any reasonings of mine;—but an argument designed simply to show that what he says commends itself to every man's conscience and sober judgment.

The only thought which I would seek to hold before your minds in the application of this subject is, the indispensable necessity of this change for every one of you if you would be saved. Whether it is to be produced by a Divine or human agency; whether you can effect it yourselves or not; whether you can by your own efforts contribute to it, or whether those efforts would be fruitless, are not points which we shall now discuss; nor is their solution necessary in order that the force of the considerations suggested should be properly felt. The single point which is before us now is, that this change is indispensable if you would enter into heaven. Every one; every son and daughter of Adam; every prince and every peasant; every master and every slave; every profligate and every moral man; every one who outrages all the laws of decency and urbanity, and every one who is the charm and glory of the social circle, must experience this change, or he cannot enter into the kingdom of God. He must experience it, unless the Saviour was wrong in his estimate of the human character, and has uttered what is not based on truth. He must experience it, unless he can show that his heart is such by nature that he is fitted for the enjoyments and employments of heaven; or unless some of the transitions through which he passes in life will answer the purpose; or unless he can substitute something else for it at the bar of God; or unless there will be some mysterious process in the grave, or beyond it, by which the body and the spirit shall be fitted for the skies. The language of the Saviour to all is, "Ye must be born again." Reason gives her sanction to that declaration; conscience echoes it in your ears; and pious kindred and friends seek to bear it to the heart. Every man feels and knows it to be true, when he will let conscience speak out, when he has any just view of his own heart, or when from a bed of death he looks out on eternity. The solemn declaration of God our Saviour on this subject, thus seconded by reason and conscience, is laid across the path of every aged man, of every one in middle life, of every youth, and of every child. Of the crowd that you meet in the thronged pathways of a great city, it is true that no one reaches heaven unless he is born again; and of the solitary stroller in a summer's eve on the verge of a babbling stream, or the lonely traveller on the mighty prairie, it is no less true that unless *he* be born again he cannot see the kingdom of God. It is equally true of each and every one of *you* that without this change you will never enter heaven. The heart *must* be changed. The impenitent soul must become contrite; the proud man must be humbled; the unbelieving must put his trust in the Son of God. And if the course of argument now pursued is sound, the subject is one that demands your immediate attention. Few days remain in which this change *can* occur, and then all will be fixed for ever. Soon the time will come in which it will be said of each and all, "He that is unjust, let him be unjust still; and he that is holy, let him be holy still." God grant that before that time—not far distant—shall have arrived, each heart may be so changed that it may convey gladness to the bosom to *hear* it said that all hereafter is to be fixed and unchanging. The line once crossed, which divides time from eternity, all is over for ever; for in the world of despair no one is ever born again.

SERMON XIX.

THE NATURE OF REGENERATION.

2 Cor. v. 17.—"If any man be in Christ, he is a new creature: old things are passed away; behold, all things are become new."

The point which I propose, from these words, to illustrate is, *the nature of regeneration*, or *of the new birth*. The apostle evidently refers to this in the text. He is adverting to the great change which had occurred in his own mind on a particular subject, and then advances the general sentiment, that when one becomes a Christian all his views are changed, or become "new." "We have," says he, "known Christ after the flesh, yet now henceforth know we him no more." That is, "I formerly had carnal and worldly views of the Messiah. In common with my countrymen, I looked for a temporal prince and deliverer. But I entertain these views no longer, and regard him no more as such. My views of him are essentially changed, and I now regard him as a spiritual Saviour, dying to make an atonement for sin." A change resembling this, he says, occurs in the case of all who are converted. If *any man* is in Christ, or becomes a true Christian, his views are in a similar manner changed;—changed to such an extent that it may be said he is a new creature, for the change of view does not pertain merely to his apprehensions about the Saviour, but extends to everything. In reference to all matters, "old things are passed away; behold, all things are become new."

This statement expresses, with perfect accuracy, the change which occurs in regeneration. It is a change of view not merely with reference to one particular point, but to the whole subject of religion; a change so great that it may be properly called a *new creation*, or of such a nature that all things may be said in the view of the mind to be *new*.

It is my object now to illustrate the nature of this change; and, in order to this, it is important that we have clear views on two points. The first is, that we separate from the work certain things which are not essential to it, or in reference to which there may be considerable variety; and the second is, that we understand what is essential to it. These are the two points which I propose now to examine.

I. *There are some things which frequently accompany a change of heart, which are not essential to it.* That is, in the circumstances and feelings attending it, there may be considerable variety in different individuals. This diversity relates to such points as the following, which it is important particularly to specify, because erroneous views have often given great occasion of distress:—

(1.) In regard to the *duration* of the seriousness, or the conviction for sin, which usually precedes a change of heart, or is experienced before evidence is obtained of conversion. Some duration of time, as a season of serious reflection, or of deep and pungent conviction for sin, usually precedes conversion, and seems to be inevitable. The change is a rational change, and occurs in connexion with a serious consideration of our condition as sinners, our danger, and our need of the mercy of God; and indeed the change does not usually occur except as the result of a careful and earnest inquiry into the character of our past lives, and of much solicitude about our final welfare. But no particular duration of time is specified in the Scriptures as necessary to reflect on our condition preparatory to conversion, and in fact there is great diversity. In some instances conversion is preceded by anxiety that has continued without much intermission for months or years; in others, there has been a succession of deep convictions for sin, like successive shocks of an earthquake, each followed by calmness and unconcern; and in others the whole work seems to be accomplished in a few hours or a few moments, and to all appearance it may be as genuine in the one case as in the other. Many causes contribute to this variety. The temperament of the individual as phlegmatic or sanguine; the kind of instruction imparted to him then or before; the circumstances in which he is placed, binding him with greater or less tenacity to the world; the state of religion in the church—as a time of general coldness, or a time of revival; or the want of proper counsel from his friends, or of proper sympathy from those who should help him on to God,—all tend to modify the *time* during which this work is taking place on the soul. Some have been taught, or have somehow imbibed the opinion, that a protracted "law-work" is necessary before they can be converted, and they expect this of course, and would be alarmed at any speedy evidence of a change of heart; and some, better taught, feel that the moment there is genuine

17

conviction for sin, the penitent may go to God for pardon, and they go at once and find peace.

(2.) There is great variety in regard to the intensity of feeling that precedes or attends the new birth. There is always feeling or emotion of some kind, and to some extent. So great a change in a man's opinions, relations, prospects, hopes, plans of life, as occurs in conversion to God, cannot take place without some degree of feeling. No similar change in a man's character and prospects occurs without emotion. But men pass through important changes in life with a great variety of feeling; and the sacred writers have shown their accurate knowledge of man by not attempting to describe any definite amount of feeling as necessary in the work of conversion. This matter is regulated by a great variety of causes, and so regulated that no specific rule could be given. Two brothers lose a much-loved sister. In the bosoms of both there will be a deep sense of the loss; but the amount of the emotion, in its manifestation at the grave, may be very different. In one, it shall be seen in gushing tears; in the other, the emotion is too big for utterance, and not a tear shall moisten the cheek. The one turns away relieved in his anguish by outbreaking sorrow; the other, with a mountain on his heart, and with a universal deadness of sensibility to all that he once loved. A father and mother stand by the grave of a child. They both feel as they never before felt, and as mortals never feel in any other situation. But nature has made a difference between the emotions of the mother and the father, and the difference will find expression at that grave. So when the soul mourns over sin, when it is about to give up the world, when the great question pertaining to the eternal welfare is to be settled for ever, there will be, there must be emotion. But it will be differently manifested. If accompanied with strong crying and tears, in view of past guilt and present danger, nothing should lead us to say that such feeling is inappropriate; or if, in a mind differently moulded, it should be more calm, settled, and uniform *conviction*, let us not say that it cannot be genuine. The sorrow of that mother who never weeps may be as intense and deep as that of her whom the slightest sickness of a child bathes in tears.

(3.) There is great variety in regard to the degree of happiness attendant on the new birth. That there *is* joy in the change of heart, or on becoming a true Christian, is often affirmed in the sacred Scriptures, and results from the nature of the case. Conversion is usually preceded by distress of mind in view of past guilt; by a sense of danger; by solicitude about the final destiny of the soul. It results from the nature of the mind, that when this is removed, it should be followed by peace, calmness, joy. But the *degree* of happiness will be modified by a great variety of causes. It must depend much on the depth of the previous distress; on the degree of clearness attending the evidence of conversion; on the habitual temperament of the mind. Some minds are full of distrust and caution, and scarcely allow themselves to contemplate the *real* grounds of hope which may exist; some are sanguine, in their temperament, and embrace the slightest indications of safety, and often rejoice when there is little occasion for joy. As a matter of fact, therefore, there is in this respect the greatest variety in the minds of those who are truly converted; nor can any certain rule be laid down in regard to the degree of happiness which would be a clear token of a change of heart.

(4.) The same thing is true in regard to the *evidence* of conversion. In some instances the change is so sudden and decided that the convert understands clearly the force of the expressions, "being brought out of darkness into marvellous light," and "being translated from the kingdom of Satan into the kingdom of God's dear Son." So sudden is the transition, so deep was the former conviction of sin, and so undoubted are the evidences of a change, that the day and the hour can be designated with an accuracy little liable to error. In many such cases the whole of the subsequent life shows that the hope thus cherished was well-founded; and that a change of heart did occur that was as decided as was supposed. But I need not say that this does not universally characterize the work of conversion, nor is it usually the case. In most instances, the evidence is of a much less decisive character. Light seems to struggle with darkness; doubt is mingled with hope; clouds hang about the horizon, or even shut in the heavens, with only an occasional lighting up of the sky. Instead of a transition like that which would occur if the sun should rise suddenly at midnight, and appear at once on the meridian, and stand there ever onward without eclipse, and without a cloud, conversion is rather like the dawning of the light in the east, where you can scarcely mark the change from deep night to commencing day, and where it is so gradual that you can select no fixed points, no sudden transitions, till the sun appears. And if the figure thus suggested by the Scriptures themselves (Prov. iv. 18) may be carried a little farther, when the sun *is* up, it is not always clear and unclouded day. He may rise bright and glorious, and send his rays across the landscape, lighting up all with beauty, and then be suddenly buried behind a dark pile of clouds; or he may meet a tempest in his way, and the lightnings may play beneath him; or the moon may cross his path and cover his disk, and a gloom and chillness—the best illustration which nature affords of what the Christian experiences when the light of God's countenance is withdrawn—may come over the world.

(5.) A fifth variety is observable in the different views of *truth* that may be presented to the mind at the time of conversion. This will be determined much by the previous habits of reading, thought, or education; by the things that have occupied the mind most during conviction for sin; or by some casual direction which may have been given to the mind at the time of the change. With one, the attention may be occupied almost entirely with a sense of the great evil of sin, and the depravity of the heart; another shall have the thoughts directed almost exclusively to the Saviour—to the beauty of his character, to the purity of his precepts, or to the glory of his atonement; another shall see a new beauty stealing over the works of God, and to him they shall seem to have come fresh from his hand, stamped with all the proofs of creative power and goodness; while the heart of another shall be charmed with beauties in the Bible which have never met the eye before. Or, perchance, some single truth, or some single duty, shall enchain the affections and the attention; and at the first moment of conversion the mind may be fixed on some duty or Christian enterprise that is to give character to all the subsequent life. A man converted in old age will be likely to have his thoughts turned to the mercy of that God who has so long preserved him in his sins, and to find his heart overflowing with gratitude as the leading emotion; an ingenuous and ardent youth will most likely look onward, and the eye will fix on some plan of benevolence, and he will be likely to hear with singular distinctness the command, "Go ye into all the world, and preach the gospel to every creature." An ardent fancy will dwell on the bright scenes in heaven; a heart of tenderness will melt at the remembrance of the scenes of Calvary. "All these worketh that one and the selfsame Spirit, dividing to every man severally as he will," 1 Cor. xii. 11.

It would be easy to extend these remarks much farther, and to suggest many other differences which occur in the circumstances of the new birth. But what has been said will illustrate the general thought, that there is great variety in the feelings and views attending regeneration. There are two observations which it is proper to make here by way of inference from what has been said, before we proceed to consider the second point proposed. One is, that in examining our own evidences of piety, we should not compare ourselves much with others. Nothing is more common for young converts than to do this; and yet, if the remarks now made are well-founded, nothing is more improper. With the same amount of religion, and with evidences of piety no better or brighter than your own, another person may have had views and feelings to which you may have been almost wholly a stranger. He has a different temperament; he has been differently educated; his past life has been different; the things that arrested his attention were different; and the subjects that have particularly interested his mind at conversion have been different. There can be no certain standard of judging in the case, if you attempt to determine the nature of your own feelings by a comparison with those of others; and there can be no propriety in setting up such a standard. The true question is, whether you have the characteristics of real piety laid down in the Bible; not whether you have experienced all that your neighbour has.

The other remark is, that if these views are correct, there is room for the exercise of large charity on the subject of religion. We should not judge others. We should not infer that because their experience does not accord wholly with ours—that because they have not precisely the same views of sin, or have not been pressed down so long with the anguish of conviction, or have not had the same clearness of evidence on their conversion, or are not able to mark with the same accuracy the moment when the change occurred—that therefore they are not Christians. All this may be true; and yet there may have been a work of conversion in their hearts, genuine and thorough, that shall abide the test of all the trials of this life, and the severer investigations of the final day. We are prepared now to consider,

II. The second point proposed for illustration: it is, *What is essential to a change of heart?* or, What uniformly occurs to distinguish this change from the other revolutions to which the mind is subject?

The short answer to this inquiry is, that it is the commencement of true religion in the soul. It is the moment when real piety commences, and the sinner begins to live to God. Whether that point of time is actually perceived or not, or whether the convert can or cannot fix on the precise moment when the heart is changed, yet there *is* a time—a moment—when religion first begins to be exercised in the soul; and that is the moment of the new birth or regeneration. This single thought—that regeneration is the commencement of true religion in the soul—will aid much in the inquiry whether *we* have ever been born again, and would save much of the perplexity which is usually felt on the subject. I have said that it is this which distinguishes this change from all other changes. Men experience other changes of feeling and character sometimes as sudden, as marked, and as permanent, as the change in regeneration; but there is no true religion in them. A dissipated young man becomes sober and temperate; a bitter foe becomes your friend; a man of a wild and impetuous temper settles down into the staidness and gravity of sober life; economy succeeds to extravagance; the love of the theatre and the ball-room give way to more rational enjoyments; frivolity and vanity are sometimes succeeded by sober attention to the duties of a family or a profession; or a youth spent without promise is sometimes followed by a middle life diligent in an honourable calling, and an old age of respectability; but in any or all of these changes there may be no religion. So we change at the different periods of life. We change, of course, from youth to manhood, and from manhood to age; we exchange that which characterizes the young man for that which becomes the man sustaining the responsibilities of life; and then we put on the peculiar characteristics in temper, and opinions, and prejudices of age; but none of these changes amount to regeneration; for in none of them is there of necessity the commencement of religion in the soul. All may be passed through, and yet there may be no love of God, no preparation for heaven.

Keeping the main thought in view, that the new birth is the beginning of religion in the heart, I propose now briefly to specify a few things which are always manifested in this change.

(1.) The first which I mention is, that there is a new view of the beauty of religion. Religion appears lovely; it has charms which were not before felt or perceived. I do not mean, of course, that there is any new intellectual power, or faculty of perceiving truth, created. I do not mean that the "new man in Christ" becomes different as an intellectual being from what he was before, or that he becomes of necessity intellectually superior to his fellow-men. I know well that it is not so. But while the mental faculties remain unchanged, the mind may acquire a wholly new view of the value of an object, and see a beauty in it unperceived before. This often occurs in other things than in religion, implying a change that may be a good illustration of the nature of regeneration. We are often sensible of some such change of view in regard to the value of objects, and in regard to their beauty also. A young man may have no deep sense of the value of temperance. Driven on by youthful passion, or led on by the solicitation of so-called friends, thrown into circumstances where he may have little time and less opportunity for reflection, he will see no particular beauty in this virtue, and a temperate life will have no charms for him. But his views may be suddenly changed, and *so* changed that a temperate life shall appear lovely in his view, and that no consideration would induce him to return to his former sentiments and practice. So virtue of all kinds may be made to appear lovely to those for whom it had no charms; and a change from vice to virtue may occur that shall characterize the whole of the subsequent life.

A change, of which this is but the feeble illustration, occurs in regard to religion, when a sinner is born again. Religion assumes a different aspect from what it had ever before in the view of the mind. Before, the attention given to it was of a very limited or a very undesirable character. In many cases, it excited positive disgust and hatred; it roused violent opposition; it was made the subject of ridicule and scorn. In other instances, where this violence of opposition was not felt or expressed, the utmost interest that was felt in religion was such as this. It was an interest arising from the belief that it was of value to the community, or because preaching had some intellectual or literary attractions; or because one's friends were members of a particular church; or because there was a general belief that religion was necessary for the salvation of the soul. But when the heart is changed, the interest in religion is of a wholly different kind. It is the interest arising from *love;* an interest in that which is seen to be beautiful, and where it assumes an importance superior to all other things combined. That new beauty, perceived in religion, leads to a corresponding interest in all that pertains to it. There is an interest in the duties and doctrines of religion; in the welfare of the church; in the spread of the gospel; in prayer and praise,—that now seems to find a place in the soul as a matter of course, which nothing before could rouse or create. And this leads me to observe,

(2.) That happiness is now found in the things that were formerly disregarded, and that afforded no pleasure. Particularly there is a new pleasure in the following things: (*a*) In the character of God. He is now seen to be just such a Being as should be adored and loved. Before this change, the views of God in the minds of men are very various. In many cases, there is felt a decided opposition to his character; in others, his laws are regarded as severe; in others, there is entire indifference to his claims; in others, there are strong doubts about the rectitude of his administration:—in none, is there any perceived beauty in his character. But when the heart is changed there is a new view of God, and a happiness felt in him unknown before. The heart is reconciled to him, and acquiesces in his claims. The character of God is such as meets the entire approbation of the soul; and the renewed man feels that it is just such as it is desirable it should be. Were there power to make any change in that character, the Christian would not do it, for God's character in the view of his mind is perfect. The language of the renewed man is, "Whom have I in heaven but thee? and there is none upon earth that I desire besides thee." (*b*) The same thing is true in regard to the plan of salvation through the Redeemer. It is impossible for an unconverted sinner to find happiness in the contemplation of that plan, or perhaps to see much beauty in it, or to feel anything attractive in the idea of depending wholly on the merits of Christ for salvation. The most, perhaps, that can be felt is a cold admiration of the character of the Redeemer; but as to any beauty in the scheme of the atonement, or any happiness in its contemplation, it is unknown to the sinner. But the converted man finds pleasure in the contemplation of that plan of salvation. It meets his case. It provides a way of pardon. It has brought him back to God. It has done for him what he cannot do, and has saved him from errors from which otherwise he could not have been saved; and his happiness now is identified with that scheme of salvation by the Redeemer. Christ becomes "all in all;" and the language of the soul is, "I count all things but loss for the excellency of the knowledge of Christ Jesus my Lord." (*c*) Thus, too, there is pleasure in the Bible. There is a beauty now seen in its pages which man never sees until he is converted; and nothing is more common for the young convert, in speaking of the Bible, than to say that it is to him "a new book;" and his wonder is excited that the same things may have been read, and perhaps from very childhood, with no perception of their beauty. There is no miracle in this; no exertion of any new intellectual faculty or power of mind. The simple fact is, that the statements in the Bible now meet a new condition of his heart, and those beauties are perceived *because* they correspond with the state of the soul. The same thing will continue to occur through life. New circumstances arise; new forms of temptation and trial occur when new beauty is seen in the word of God, and it seems to have been penned just for such an occasion. A closer acquaintance with it only shows more and more with what profound skill it is adapted to the wants of the human soul; and the impression of its beauty and value increases to the end of life. I need not remind you how often the beauty of the sacred Scriptures is commended by the saints of old, nor what exquisite happiness the psalmist represents himself as finding in the volume of revealed truth:—"O how love I thy law! it is my meditation all the day." "More to be desired," said he, speaking of the statutes of the Lord, "are they than gold, yea, than much fine gold; sweeter also than honey and the honeycomb." This is language that would express only the feelings of a heart that is renewed. (*d*) The same thing is true of the happiness found in the worship of God—of the privilege of drawing near to him in the closet and in the sanctuary. "It is good for me to draw near to God." "How amiable are thy tabernacles, O Lord of hosts! My soul longeth, yea, even fainteth for the courts of the Lord; my heart and my flesh crieth out for the living God." "I had rather be a door-keeper in the house of my God than to dwell in the tents of wickedness." This, too, is language which expresses the feelings of a new-born soul. It is not language which expresses *any* feelings which they have who are not renewed. There is no interest which such persons can have, in the pomp of gorgeous religious rites; or in the music of the sanctuary, executed with the utmost power and skill; or in the most eloquent exhibition of truth in the pulpit, that meets the fulness of such declarations about the happiness felt in the worship of God. It is a happiness peculiar to the renovated man; where the heart finds pleasure in communion with God; where the regenerated spirit finds pleasure in those pure services that raise it above the world. And though I do not design to insist on it that these *elevated* joys are *essential* to the evidence of a change of heart, yet I *do* mean to advance the sentiment, that where such a change exists there will be experienced a happiness in God; in the plan of salvation; in the Bible; in public and private worship,—such as was not experienced before, and such as is produced only by the love of religion.

(3.) A third essential feature in this change is, a readiness to forsake all sin, and all pursuits that are inconsistent with a holy life. This enters of course into the change, for it is a change from sin to holiness. The past life is now seen to have been unholy, and it becomes the purpose of the soul to abandon all that is offensive to God. And this love of sin, and of sinful pursuits, is not abandoned now *merely* because it is commanded to be; it is the preference of the heart to do it. The renewed heart renounces these things as a matter of course, and at any sacrifice. Paul gave up at once his career of ambition,—though it required the sacrifice of all his earthly prospects; and the Ephesian converts abandoned a dishonest calling at once, though requiring the sacrifice of their "books" and the destruction of a large amount of property. No proposition can be clearer than that a man who is not willing to forsake his sinful pursuits can have no evidence that he is born again.

The same remarks are applicable to the world, to its pleasures, its gaieties, its vanities. In the case of a true convert to Christ, the theatre is forsaken, not because it is a matter of express injunction in the Bible, but because it ceases to interest the mind. The changed heart becomes interested in other things, and in the superior relish for the pleasures and hopes of religion: the pleasure once found in such amusements is extinguished of course. So to a mind truly converted and made to taste the happiness of communion with God, the pleasures of the ball-room and the brilliant party cease to allure and charm. To such a mind it is not mere *command* which requires the forsaking of "the pride, pomp, and vanity of the world;" it is not mere conscience which keeps from an indulgence in such pleasures; it is not the mere apprehension that pain will be given to the friends of piety, and dishonour reflected on the church—though all of these things will influence the mind; it is, that the relish, the love for such things is lost. The heart has become attached to nobler and more elevated pursuits, and has learned to find pleasure in that which now satisfies the soul. "Old things have passed away, and all things have become new;" and pleasures which a few months since the individual would not have been induced to forsake for any price in gold or diamonds, are now abandoned as a matter of course. The heart has become dead to such pleasures; and to mingle in them now with relish and satisfaction would be far more difficult than it would have been before to forsake them—nay, would be impossible.

(4.) I need only advert to one other essential characteristic of this change: it is, that there is a readiness to devote all to God, and to do his will. The question asked by Paul at his conversion was, "Lord, what wilt thou have me to do?" and the same question substantially is asked by every one who becomes a Christian. Before the heart is renewed, far different principles rule the conduct. Men act with reference to honour, to gain, to office, to amusement, to sensual indulgence. Their time they regard as their own; their talents as their own; their houses, lands, bonds, stocks, books as their own, to be held and disposed of without reference to the will of another. The young man feels at perfect liberty to choose any calling that may gratify his taste, or that holds out alluring prospects of gain, without reference to the will of his Maker, or to the good of men. The plan is laid for a profession which shall give the greatest scope for the display of genius, or which shall conduct most speedily to the temple of fame, or which shall soonest enable him to look round on his possessions with the consciousness of independence. In all these things conversion to God makes a decided, a thorough change. Talent, learning, strength, vigour of body, is felt to belong to God. Though educated for different purposes, as Paul was, the young man feels now that his talents and learning are to be devoted to his Maker; though wealth has been gained for different objects, yet the convert now feels that it all belongs to Him who has redeemed him; and though the young female may have been trained to adorn the social circle, yet it is now felt that these accomplishments should be made tributary to the purpose of doing good in those circles which it was designed only to please, and should be subordinate to the grand purpose of preparation for the society of the skies. "Old things are passed away, and all things are become new;" and talent, and influence, and learning, and wealth, and accomplishments are converted to the new and holy purpose of living to God.

There are, perhaps, other things which might be adduced here, but you will gather, I trust, from what has been said, what is essential to this change. The grand thing, you will understand, is, that it is the commencement of pure religion in the soul. Whether attended with more protracted or briefer preparation; with higher or lower degrees of joy; with more decided or with fainter evidences of conversion; with the contemplation of identical or different truths,—it is the same. It is the beginning of real piety in the heart. Whether it be in the thrilling scenes of a revival of religion, or under the calmer operations of truth, where few are converted; whether the change take place in the ardour of youth, or when age has chilled the sensibilities and awakened the intellect; whether under a ministry holding to Calvinistic or Arminian views, or a ministry of "three orders" or "one;" or whether in a church with multitudinous forms, and with a great zeal for the "apostolic succession," and with great regard for the office of baptism; or where there is no ministry, and no form, and no belief in baptism at all,—there is but one work that is the work of conversion ; there is but one baptism of the Spirit ; there is everywhere essentially the same thing in the change of the heart. It is the beginning of true religion in the soul. It leads to simple dependence on Christ for salvation. It is attended by a new interest in religion ; a new pleasure in its services ; a new relish for the Bible and for prayer ; new love for Christians, new plans of life ; as well as with a readiness to forsake all that God hates, and to devote the life to his service in any sphere to which, by his Spirit and his providence, he shall direct.

SERMON XX.

THE AGENCY OF THE HOLY SPIRIT IN REGENERATION.

Titus iii. 5.—"Not by works of righteousness which we have done, but according to his mercy he saved us, by the washing of regeneration, and renewing of the Holy Ghost."

In the two last discourses I have considered the necessity and the nature of regeneration or the new birth. If the remarks there made are correct, there are various important questions in regard to the subject which at once occur to the mind. The main inquiry is, *By what agency* is this change produced? Is it by our own? Is it by the unassisted effect of truth on the heart? Or is it by a Divine power? It is evident that our views of the agency by which the heart is changed will materially affect our sense of duty and obligation in regard to the change. If the work be accomplished by a Divine Agent, it is clear also that our views of duty and obligation in regard to it will be materially affected by the opinions which we cherish respecting the *nature* of his agency on the soul. I propose, then, at this time, to arrange my remarks under the following heads:—I. I propose to show that the heart is renewed by the agency of the Holy Ghost; and, II. To explain, as far as I may be able, the nature of that agency.

I. *The Holy Spirit is the Agent by whom the work of regeneration is produced.* I mean by this, that it is by his efficient operation that the heart is changed; that without that agency the change would never occur; and that whatever subordinate agencies may be employed, or whatever means used, the fact that the heart is renewed is to be as distinctly traced to him as the creation of the world is to be traced to the power of God. The power of the Holy Ghost on the heart is always indispensable in securing the result; and no heart ever has been changed, or ever will be, except by his power so exerted on the soul. Of all the myriads now in glory redeemed from our world, and of all yet to be redeemed and saved, no one will ever have been brought to heaven in reference to whom there has not been a distinct and special exertion of his power in changing the heart.

What may be the nature of the agency of man himself or of the truth in this change, is a distinct and important subject of inquiry; but whatever may be that agency, it is not such as to exclude the efficient operation of the Holy Ghost in the change, or such of itself as ever to bring one soul to heaven. I am thus particular in the statement of the doctrine because of its importance; because Christians have often vague views in regard to it; and because it is desirable that impenitent sinners should understand it.

There are two sources of evidence in regard to the truth of this doctrine—the Scriptures, and experience. A few remarks on each of these points will show the nature of this evidence. First, the Scriptures. The text furnishes the best proof: "Not by works of righteousness which we have done, but according to his mercy he saved us, *by the washing of regeneration, and renewing of the Holy Ghost.*" Whatever controversy there may have been at any time in the church about the relation of baptism to this change, or whatever support a false interpretation of this passage may have been supposed to give to the doctrine of baptismal regeneration, the main point is abundantly clear. Salvation is accomplished by the renewing of the Holy Ghost. No application of water can answer the purpose of his agency, or can effect the work without it. And even if the doctrine of "baptismal regeneration" be held, and it be maintained that the Holy Spirit is certainly given on the proper administration of that ordinance, still the necessity of that agency is affirmed, and the efficacy in the change is to be traced to him. You will not understand me as conceding even the *possibility* that the doctrine of "baptismal regeneration" is true, or that there is a reference to it in the text. So far from that, I hold that there is no doctrine whatever that more certainly saps the foundation of all true piety in the church, and tends to destroy the souls of men; and, compared with that, all the errors that may be supposed to be held, or not held, in the controversies about the shibboleths of party, and forms in religion, and the apostolical succession, are trifles not worthy to be named. But I am showing that even on the supposition that there be in our text an allusion to such a doctrine, still the main thing is indisputably taught there, that men are saved, if saved at all, by the renewing of the Holy Ghost. The same thing is taught by the Saviour in John iii. 5: "Except a man be born of water, *and of the Spirit,* he cannot enter into the kingdom of God." The same remarks might be made in regard to this passage which have been made of the text. Even on the supposition that there is reference here to the necessity of baptism, still it is explicitly affirmed that the agency of the Holy Spirit is indispensable to salvation. The affirmation is distinct and unequivocal, that unless a man be born or "begotten" of the Spirit, he cannot enter into the kingdom of God. In further confirmation of this doctrine, we might appeal to all those passages of Scripture which affirm that a Divine power is exerted in renewing the heart; that God hath begotten us to a lively hope; that of his own will he hath begotten us through the truth;—to the assurance of the Saviour that the Comforter would come to convince the world of sin, of righteousness, and of judgment;—and to the account of the transactions on the day of Pentecost. All the affirmations in the sacred Scriptures of a Divine agency in renewing the heart are to be understood of the Holy Ghost, because, although *general* where they occur, in other places it is distinctly affirmed that the Holy Ghost is the agent by whom this work is effected. As the texts adduced settle the question about the teachings of the Scripture on the subject, let us look at the other source of evidence—that derived from experience. This is not referred to because it would demonstrate it without the teachings of the Scripture, but to show how plain the account of the matter is in the Bible, and how effectually the belief of this truth is secured among the friends of God.

The nature and strength of this evidence will be perceptible from the following facts, which no one who is acquainted with the subject can deny:—

(1.) Every man who becomes a Christian believes that the change in his heart has been effected by a Divine agency. There is something about the change in his soul which satisfies his mind that it is not by any agency of his own. Whatever may have been his personal efforts in the case; whatever struggles he may have gone through; and whatever views of Christian doctrine he may subsequently embrace, yet he has no doubt that the change is to be traced to a power from above. Such is his view of his own depravity; of the downward, earthly, corrupt tendency of his soul, that he is certain that, if he had been left to himself, he would have been a wretched wanderer still on the dark mountains of sin, and would never have been disposed to turn to God. It becomes his habitual and settled conviction that if he had been left to his own ways he would have continued to walk in the broad road that leads down to death.

(2.) So universal and settled is the belief of the Divine agency in the conversion of men to God, that it has been incorporated into the creed and confession of faith of every Christian church on earth. No exception to this has ever occurred; not a church has ever existed, it is believed, of any denomination, which has not, in its symbols, attributed this change to the power of the Holy Ghost. There is not one that attributes the change to man; not one where it is intimated that man is of himself competent to effect it.

(3.) The same thing is expressed in the writings of theologians. No doctrine of the Scriptures has been more constantly and firmly asserted by writers on theology; and it may be confidently affirmed that there never has been an evangelical writer of respectability who has denied the necessity of a Divine influence in renewing the heart. This sentiment is found in writers of every age and of every form of evangelical theological sentiment;—of men who have entertained different opinions on the will and the ability of man;—of men who have held different sentiments on the nature of Divine and human agency, the forms of worship, the ordinances of religion, and the constitution of the church. All "schools"—old and new; all classes of theologians—Calvinistic and Arminian; all denominations—Presbyterian, Episcopal, Baptist, Methodist, Lutheran; and all evangelical theologians of all countries and ages, maintain it. I have never found the doctrine denied in any theological writings of this kind with which I am acquainted; I have never heard a doubt expressed of its truth among those ministers with whom I am particularly associated, and with whom I am accustomed to act; I am morally certain there is not a Presbyterian minister in this land that would express a doubt about its truth and its vital importance.

(4.) The truth of the same doctrine is expressed in the prayers and thanksgivings of all sincere Christians. They pray *as if* they believed it; as if it were their hope and stay; as if they relied on it as the only ground of encouragement in doing good to others, and as the only basis of calculation in regard to the salvation of men. They pray for themselves, their friends, their families, their country, and the world, *as if* they believed that it is only by the exertion of Divine power that the obstacles to salvation can be overcome in the human heart; and, in forming their plans for doing good to others, they expect success only on the supposition that the Spirit of all grace will attend those efforts, and will crown them with his blessing. And when they think of the foundation of their own hopes of heaven, they attribute it wholly to the agency of the Spirit of God on their hearts. Their thanks are rendered to the God of grace because he was pleased to arrest them when they were in the way to death; to awaken them to see their guilt and danger; to convince them of their sins, and to lead them to God. Whatever effort they themselves have made; whatever profound and patient thought they have bestowed on the subject; and whatever help they have received from ministers and others, yet they feel that their thanks are primarily and chiefly due to God for his mercy; and the language of my text expresses precisely the sentiment of their hearts: "Not by works of righteousness which we have done, but according to his mercy he saved us, by the washing of regeneration, and renewing of the Holy Ghost; which he shed on us abundantly through Jesus Christ our Saviour."

I have been thus particular in this statement for two reasons: first, to show that the doctrine of the Holy Spirit's agency in renewing the heart is so clearly taught in the Scriptures, and is so incorporated in the experience of all true Christians, as to secure its permanent belief in the Church; and, secondly, to repel the charge which is often brought against what are called "New School" Presbyterians of denying it. It is not often that I allude to any such charges. But this has been so wholly gratuitous, and so deeply injurious, that in a discussion of the subject a very distinct avowal of its belief seemed to be demanded. I have had, from my position and relations to the church, an opportunity of a somewhat extensive observation of the kind of doctrines which are held up before men in preaching; and I venture the declaration, that there is no class of ministers in this land that dwell so much on the necessity of the agency of the Holy Spirit to renew the hearts of men as what are called "New School" Presbyterians, and those who sympathize with them. I venture still farther the remark, that the doctrines of "grace"—the stern and rigid doctrines of Calvinism, as they are supposed to be,—the doctrine of decrees, of Divine sovereignty, of election, and kindred doctrines, are nowhere so steadily and so firmly maintained in preaching, and in the affections of the heart, as in the "New School" churches. It is true that our preachers attempt to show how these things are; that they endeavour to prove that these doctrines are not inconsistent with human freedom, and the unlimited offer of the gospel, and the willingness of God to save all, and the ability of man to do his duty, and the doctrine of accountability; but it is also true that there is no shrinking from the avowal, the defence, and the thorough discussion of these doctrines, and from a desire that our congregations should feel and acknowledge their full force in the matter of salvation.

II. Our second inquiry relates to *the nature of the agency of the Holy Spirit in conversion*. Our Saviour has explicitly forbidden us to hope to be able fully to explain the nature of this agency. He says (John iii. 8), "The wind bloweth where it listeth [pleaseth], and thou hearest the sound thereof, but canst not tell whence it cometh, and whither it goeth: so is every one that is born of the Spirit." The meaning is, that his agency is invisible, and is to be known by its effects. We see not the wind; but on a calm summer's eve we see the harvest-field gently wave, or the bosom of the lake gently ruffled; or we see the leaf of the aspen tremble when we feel our own cheeks scarcely fanned;—or in a tempest we see the forest bend, and the ocean lashed into foam, and cloud rolling on cloud, and fences, and trees, and houses, swept along in the tornado; and we judge that there is some efficient agent to do all this, though in both cases invisible. So we see certain effects on the mind and life of man. He is changed. Sometimes the influence that produces the change is gentle as the zephyr that bends the osier on the bank of the rivulet, or that moves over the harvest-field; and sometimes it is as mighty as the tempest that prostrates the oak on the hills. In each case it secures the result. It converts the soul. It inclines the understanding to contemplate Divine truth, personal duty, and obligation; the conscience, to decide in favour of God and his claims; the will, to yield to the motives which prompt to obedience; the soul, to devote itself with all its powers to the service of its Maker. It leads men before of various sentiments, opinions, habits, prejudices, and philosophical views, to *harmony* in the great matter of salvation, and unites them in love to the same object, and in the hope of the same heaven.

Our Saviour has told us, that the agency which does this is unseen; and by a simple illustration, such as he was in the habit of using, he has told us that when we see certain effects produced, we ought to infer that there is an adequate cause. The remark implies, indeed, that there is much in regard to it which is unknown to man, and which he cannot explain. But his observation does not forbid us to look at *facts*, as far as we may be able to observe them—just as we would in regard to the effects of the wind. There are many things, in both instances, which may be known; and nothing forbids us, in either case, to make the observation as extensive as we can, and to record the facts just as they occur. I invite your attention, therefore, to a few statements of facts which have been observed, in respect to the nature of the Holy Spirit's agency in renewing the heart.

(1.) The first which I mention is, that his agency on the mind in conversion is not that of compulsion. It is not such as to destroy the freedom of man, or in any way such as to interfere with the proper exercise of his powers as a moral agent. When a man becomes a Christian he acts as a freeman; and whatever power has been exerted over him, no violation has been done to his liberty, nor has he done anything which has not been to him a matter of preference or choice. This will be made clear by a few remarks. One is, that the agency of God is always according to the nature of the thing on which it is exerted. He created the world by the mere exertion of power without means, or apart from any existing organization or laws. He will raise the dead by the same power. He originally fixed the stars, and preserves their positions by the same power. But when he moves the planets, raises the tides, excites the tempests, causes the seasons to return, congeals the waters in the winter, or dissolves them in the warmth of returning spring, it is by the same power indeed, yet it is in accordance with fixed laws; and he does not, except in miracle, exert his power in a mode that is a departure from those laws. So it is his power that produces the effects we see in the vegetable creation; but it is in accordance with the laws of the vegetable kingdom. He governs the lion of the forest, and controls the whole animal creation; but it is in accordance with the instincts of their nature. And in like manner he governs man, and produces important changes in his views and feelings; yet it is not by miracle, but in accordance with the laws of mind. He does not govern the stars by the "ten commandments;" nor does he control the lion or the leopard by influences such as he would use to form the lily or the rose; nor does he control man by such power as he would use to subdue the lion or the panther. Everything is controlled in accordance with the laws of its own nature; and as man is made a freeman, with the appropriate powers of moral agency, it is certain that the laws of his nature will be consulted and respected in any control that God exerts over him, just as it is that the laws of crystallization will be in forming ice and snow; that the orange and the lemon will be made to grow in accordance with the laws of the vegetable kingdom; and that the lion will "roar and seek his meat at the hand of God" by the instinct of his nature.

We find uniform statements in the sacred Scriptures in accordance with this. When the worlds were made, it is said to have been by the "word of God" (Heb. xi. 3), without any instrumentality. When the dead were raised by the Saviour, it was in the same way. But when man is referred to as converted, though there is a uniform assertion that it is by the Divine power, yet it is said to be by the use of means; by the word of truth; by the preaching of the gospel; by the presentation of motives to induce him to turn to God. Throughout the whole work, he is treated not as stones, or trees, or planets, or the tribes of animals that roam the forest are treated, but as *a man*—as endued with conscience, and reason, and moral powers, and as capable of judging of right and wrong. No power is spoken of except in connexion with the presentation of truth, and of the proper *means* for acting on a free moral agent, and no effect is described but such as could be exerted on the powers of such an agent.

As a matter of fact, it is undeniable that all the changes which occur in regeneration are those connected with conscious freedom. The converted sinner acknowledges the power of God in his change. He is sensible that he has become what he is by an influence from on high. It was some such mysterious power that arrested his attention; that alarmed his conscience; that induced him to give his heart to God. But he has been sensible of no violation of his freedom. He has done nothing which he has not done freely. He was not converted by bringing a deep sleep upon him, as Eve was formed from the side of Adam, nor was an unnatural stupor diffused over his frame benumbing all his faculties, and leaving him to be moulded as the clay; but he was converted in the full exercise of his faculties, and with the entire consciousness of acting as a freeman. He has done nothing which he did not prefer to do; he has abandoned no sin which he did not choose to abandon; he has formed no new plan of living by becoming a Christian which he did not choose to form. One of the most free and unfettered acts of his life was that when he gave himself to God; and he became a Christian with as much conscious freedom, and often with as much of the spirit of rejoicing, as the imprisoned father leaves the gloomy cell where he has been long immured, to visit his children when his prison doors are thrown open, or as the galley-slave exults when the chains fall from his hands. There is no act that man ever performs more freely than that of becoming a Christian. His whole heart is in it; and no matter what sinful course he abandons, what sacrifices he makes, and what friends he is constrained to leave, or what amusements he is required to abjure, he does it most freely. And no matter what trials he may see before him; no matter though his embracing religion may require him to forsake his country and home to preach the gospel in a heathen land, it is all cheerfully done. It is the act of a freeman. He prefers it. He would not, for all the gold and diamonds and coronets and crowns of the earth, have it otherwise. And though he is conscious—for who could not but be so in such a change?—that this has been brought about by the power of God, and will always ascribe it to the agency of the Holy Ghost, yet he feels that no law of his nature has been violated, and that one of the most free acts of his life was then when he gave his heart to God.

The doctrine which I here state is precisely that which is so well expressed in the Westminster Confession of Faith: "Effectual calling is the work of God's almighty power and grace, whereby he doth in his accepted time invite and draw them [his elect] to Jesus Christ, by his word and Spirit; savingly enlightening their minds, renewing and powerfully determining their wills, so that they, although in themselves dead in sin, *are hereby willing and able* FREELY *to answer his call*, and to accept and embrace the grace offered and conveyed therein." "All those whom God hath predestinated unto life, he is pleased in his appointed time effectually to call—renewing their wills, and by his Almighty power determining them to that which is good;—yet so as *they come* MOST FREELY, being made willing by his grace." "God hath endued the will of man with natural liberty, so that it is neither forced, nor by any absolute necessity of nature determined to good or evil." "When God converts a sinner, and translates him into a state of grace, he freeth him from his natural bondage under sin, and by his grace alone enables him *freely* to will and to do that which is spiritually good." These passages from the standard of Presbyterian doctrine state the simple truth in regard to the conversion of the sinner. Whatever *power* is used, the sinner acts freely; *he* chooses life; *he* prefers to be a Christian; *he* is conscious that there is no compulsion, and no violation of the laws of his moral nature. And all this is in exact harmony with the promise made to the Messiah: "Thy people shall be *willing* in the day of thy power," Psa. cx. 3.*

(2.) The agency of the Holy Spirit in regeneration is in entire accordance with the *truth* that is brought to bear on the mind. What may be the exact power of the truth itself in producing this change, whether it may or may not have a power of its own, or an adaptedness to the soul which acts by itself or by "moral suasion," is not material in order to understand the remark which

* This promise possibly may have reference not to conversion, but to the voluntary efforts put forth by the Saviour's people to promote the triumphs of his kingdom. The general principle, however, is such as warrants the above reference to it.

I now make. The idea is, that there is no change produced on the soul in regeneration which *the truth is not fitted to make*, or which the truth, if it secures its proper result, will not make. In repentance, for example, there is no sorrow of the heart in reference to guilt which *the truth* about ourselves is not of itself fitted to excite. In the love of God experienced by a converted man, there is no effect produced which *the truth* about the Divine nature and character is not fitted to secure. There is no love experienced towards God which ought not to be exercised, or of which he is not worthy. In the exercise of faith in the Redeemer, there is no effect produced on the mind which is not in strict accordance with the truth. All the confidence reposed in him *ought* to be reposed in him, from the excellence of his own character; from what he has done for us; from his claims on us. And so when the heart glows with joy in the contemplation of the truths of the Bible; when the mind is filled with peace resulting from reconciliation with God; when the hope of heaven is strongly cherished producing delightful anticipations of future glory,—there is no effect produced which *the truth* is not calculated to work. All the emotions and feelings, the hopes, the joys, the penitent sorrows, the believing acts of trust in Christ, secured in regeneration, are just such as the truth is fitted to produce on the mind. There is no evidence that the Holy Spirit goes beyond this, or that he secures one effect on the soul which the truth, as brought to bear on the mind, is not adapted to induce. That man is a sinner, is a simple and affecting matter of fact. Commonly he does not feel this, or care about it. In regeneration he does; and the proper view of this constitutes repentance. That there is a God who ought to be loved with all the heart and mind and strength, is a simple matter of verity. The sinner does not feel this. At regeneration this *is* felt; and to secure this, is one of the great effects produced by the change. That Christ died for man as the only Saviour, and is every way fitted *to be* a Saviour, is a simple truth. Before regeneration, men do not feel this, or believe it. At regeneration, they do; and the effect on their minds is to lead them to exercise that confidence in the Redeemer which they ought to exercise. That there is a heaven is simple truth, whether men believe it or not. Before conversion, they do not believe it. When the heart is changed, they do; and the effect on the mind is simply that which the *truth* about heaven is adapted to produce. If these are just views, then they are of great importance in understanding the subject. For thus it will follow, that there is encouragement to present the truth to the mind of a sinner;

that it is proper to use means for his conversion; that there is encouragement to appeal to men to love God, to repent of sin, and to believe the gospel. And thus it will follow also, that that mode of preaching which counsels men to "wait" for the agency of the Holy Spirit to convert the heart, is presumption of the most offensive character. It is the same kind of trusting in God which a sick man would exercise who should lie passively on his bed, and use no means for his restoration; or as a farmer manifests who "observes the clouds" without sowing, and who passively and indolently looks to God for a harvest without even ploughing his fields. It will follow, also, that it is no more rational for us to wait for the interposition of God to save us without effort of our own, than it would be for such a farmer to wait for God himself to *create* a waving harvest on the unploughed and unsown field, and to expect that the harvest would spring up before him without any effort on his part. The idea which I wish you to receive is, that you can have no basis of calculation or of hope about your salvation *beyond* the means which you use, and the efforts which you put forth. What hope there would be if you should put forth your highest efforts, is another question. It is *true* of the farmer that his hopes *may be* disappointed after all his efforts. Blight and mildew, or drought, or a tornado, may frustrate all his expectations. But he can have no ground of anticipation or of hope whatever, unless he ploughs and sows his field. And so it is with you in regard to salvation. You can have no warrant whatever for hope or expectation, unless you will make an effort; unless you will pray; unless you will attend to the truth; unless you will use all proper means to secure its due effect on the mind. Look at a farmer. See him go to work, and pull down all his fences around his field; see him then draw on logs and brush, and pile them up everywhere. See him cart on vast masses of stone, and cover up the parts of the field that are most fertile. Then see him go and sow, on the few spots that may remain uncovered, the seed of cockle, and nettles, and thistles, and devoutly stand and wait for God to give him a harvest of wheat. And what think you would be his prospect of such a harvest? I will tell you. Just as much exactly as your prospect of salvation in the way in which you deal with your mind and heart. You take down all the defences of truth, and all the guards against error around your soul, and allow the soul to be like an open common. Then you cover up all the mind, and crush it down, by cares and pleasures of this world; by ambition and unholy indulgences. Then you make the heart hard—like piling vast masses of stone on a fertile soil. And then you fill the mind, not with truth, but with all sorts of error, that take root and grow just as fireweed and thistles do on the farm; and then you pretend to wait on God for his power to clear away all this rubbish, and root up all these thorns and thistles, and to convert the soul; and there is no wonder that the soul is not converted.

(3.) The agency of the Holy Spirit in conversion is in accordance with all the laws of our nature; or is such as to secure the proper action of our mental and moral powers. Man has an understanding; but before regeneration it is darkened by sin; it takes perverted views of the proportionate value of things; its decisions are blinded by prejudice, by passion, and by selfishness, so that it has no just and proper view of things as they are. The Holy Spirit at conversion secures the right action of the understanding, and it looks at things as they are in reality, and the mind acts as if those things were so. Man, before conversion, has *a conscience.* But its decisions are often perverted, dimmed, or resisted. It prompts man to love and obey God, but he does not yield to it; it urges him to pray, and prepare to die, but he resists its promptings; it admonishes him of past guilt, and urges him to repentance, but he refuses to yield; it warns him against passion, and worldliness, and vanity, but he pursues these things in spite of its rebukes. When he is converted, the Holy Spirit secures *this* effect. He leads the man to honour the dictates of conscience—to cease to oppose it—to act in accordance with its verdicts. He no longer attempts to silence its rebukes; to turn a deaf ear to its warnings; to pervert its decisions; or to act in violation of its promptings. Man, before conversion, has *a will.* But it is perverse, obstinate, selfish, blind. Its actings on religious subjects are more likely to be wrong than right;—are always wrong. The unconverted sinner never wills anything, because his Maker wills it, or in accordance with his Maker's will. The Holy Spirit in conversion secures the right action of the will. He leads the man to a readiness to determine his own deeds, plans, and purposes, in accordance with the will of God. There is no new faculty, and no old faculty with new powers; there is simply such an influence exerted over it as to secure its decisions in accordance with the will of God. And the same is true of all the faculties and powers of the mind. The agency of the Holy Ghost is just such as to secure their proper and healthful action. No new power of mind is created, none is directly expanded. Nothing is created as an independent substance and put into the soul at conversion; nor has the man any constitutional powers or propensities *after* conversion which he had not *before.* The effect, to use a figure often employed in the sacred Scriptures to describe the influences of the Holy Spirit, is like that of the rains and dews of heaven. A land is desolate by drought. Its streams are dried up; its harvests have failed; its fields seem to be burned over, and here and there stand but a few stunted shrubs covered with dust, only heightening the desolation. Trees are planted, and seeds of flowers, and fruits, and corn are sown in vain. The trees wither, and the seeds remain in the ground, and not a germ unfolds itself. The sun, small and piercing, rides up a "hot and copper sky," and pours down his scorching beams on panting animals and enfeebled men. A rock, far-projecting, is a most grateful shelter, and night furnishes the only respite and comfort for the smitten inhabitants of the parched land. Clouds then gather; the rain descends, and the whole aspect of the land is changed. Streams and water-falls pour down the valleys; the fields rejoice and smile; the stunted shrub is green again; the seed, long buried, springs up, and the earth is covered with a carpet of beautiful green, and the air is filled with fragrance. In the East, where such things are common, they succeed each other with a rapidity to us unknown, and hence the illustration is so often used in the Scriptures. Such a change comes over a sinner's soul, over a community and a congregation, when the Holy Spirit of God descends with renovating power. Nothing can effect it but the power of God, as nothing can effect the change in the land of drought but the rain and dews that God shall send down;—but, like that, it is *not* a change produced by miracle. It calls forth the inactive and slumbering powers of the soul—as the rain does the sleeping powers of nature. It vivifies and quickens all the faculties of man. It illuminates his understanding; prompts him to just decisions of conscience; leads his will to determine right, and disposes him to devote himself to God. And it diffuses over the soul of the individual, and over the church and people thus blessed, a moral loveliness of which the beauty of the landscape after the fertilizing rain is but the faint and imperfect emblem.

Such, I apprehend, is the truth, as far as it goes, in the explanation of the Holy Spirit's agency in the conversion of the soul. That there is much about that agency which is unexplained, and which it is beyond our power to explain, is not denied, but the same thing is true in regard to every case in which we attempt an elucidation. In the action of the wind, the dew, the rain, the sunbeam in vegetation, there is much beyond any explanation which has been yet suggested; but this throws no obscurity on a multitude of things which *are* clear and intelligible. So it is in regard to the conversion of the soul. That it is by the agency of the Spirit of God is clear beyond dispute; and it is equally clear that it is done in perfect accordance with the freedom of man; that no effect is produced which the truth is not fitted to work out; and that it is in entire accordance with all the powers of our rational nature.

If these things are so, then two conclusions follow from what has been said, of more importance to us than any other which can have relation to this subject; and with a bare allusion to these I shall conclude this discourse. The first is, that of *encouragement*. There *is* one Agent who can accomplish all that is needful to be accomplished in our salvation; and if the sinner perishes, it will not be because he who is entrusted with the work of changing the heart is deficient in power. There is no heart so hard, that it may not be subdued; none so proud, that it may not be humbled; none so wicked, that the Holy Spirit cannot make it holy. What man cannot do, *he* can accomplish; and in our conscious weakness and sinfulness, therefore, we may feel that he has power to effect in our souls all that need be effected to secure our salvation. The other conclusion which follows from the view that has been taken is, that there is an *obligation* resting on *man* in regard to this change. If it were in all respects like creating a world, or like raising the dead; or if, in any sense, the work of the Spirit were of the nature of *miracle*, there would not be any such obligation. Man could be under no more obligation to love God and repent of sin than he is to create a new star or sun, or to lift up the tides of the ocean. But conversion is wholly a different thing. In the whole change man is a freeman. He acts in view of truth, and the effect is in accordance with truth. His own active powers are concerned, for all the change is *on* those powers,—securing their proper action. Hence, there is an ample field for our agency; for our use of means; for our putting forth our efforts in the work. And hence there is true philosophy, as well as an incentive to exertion, to work, and to trust in God, in the remark so often made, that man should make the effort for his own salvation *as if* it were to be secured wholly by his own power; and yet depend on the grace and Spirit of the Lord as if he could do nothing. Or to express the same thing, and to express all, in the better language of an inspired apostle, man should "work out his own salvation with fear and trembling, for it is God that worketh in him both to will and to do of his good pleasure." May God give us all grace to do it, for Christ's sake, and to him be all the praise. Amen.

SERMON XXI.

THE NATURE OF REPENTANCE.

Acts xx. 21.—"Testifying both to the Jews, and also to the Greeks, repentance toward God."

Paul, in the passage before us, refers to the main things on which he insisted in his preaching. As a leading point he "testified" or bore witness to the necessity of exercising repentance toward God. The necessity of this he urged on all of the two great divisions of the human family to whom he had access—the Jews and the Greeks:—that is, he urged it on all classes alike; on every human being. He in reference to whom repentance was to be exercised was God: "repentance toward God." It was *his* law which had been violated. Transgressions in their most important bearings always terminated on him. He had a right to take cognizance of them. He only could pardon those who had committed them. Paul, therefore, in all places laid it down as one of the primary doctrines of religion, and one of the things essential to salvation, that every human being should exercise repentance toward God.

I propose, at this time, to enter on the consideration of the subject of repentance—a subject occupying a primary place in all systems of religion which regard man as in any sense a sinner. It was a primary doctrine in the system of Lord Herbert, the first and the best of British Deists; it was the leading doctrine of John the Baptist—of the Saviour himself—of Paul. "In those days came John the Baptist, preaching in the wilderness of Judea, and saying, Repent ye: for the kingdom of heaven is at hand," Matt. iii. 1, 2. "From that time Jesus began to preach, and to say, Repent: for the kingdom of heaven is at hand," Matt. iv. 17. So Paul here says that he had "taught the Ephesians publicly, and from house to house, testifying repentance toward God."

There are many interesting and important inquiries in regard to repentance which a minister of religion *ought* to be able to answer. What is repentance? What is the reason of its appointment as a condition of salvation? Why could not men be saved without it? What is its efficacy in a system of revealed religion? How is true repentance distinguished from false? Why will not that regret which every man feels when he has done wrong be sufficient for salvation, even though he should not embrace the gospel? These and kindred inquiries always occur to thinking minds when the subject of repentance is suggested; and on these I propose to submit some views which I trust will show the reason of the place assigned to it in a system of revealed religion.

The first question which presents itself is, What *is* repentance? To that inquiry I intend at present to confine my remarks. The views which I entertain of the nature of repentance, I will express in a few propositions, which I trust will make it plain to all.

I. *Repentance, in general, is a state of mind which springs up in view of perceived personal guilt.* I say "in general," because I wish under this head to describe it as a mere mental operation experienced by all men, or as it exists in the mind of every one when he is made sensible of wrong-doing. Every man experiences repentance of some kind. If he did not, you could not define it so that he could understand it, any more than you can define colours to a blind man, or harmony to the deaf. The peculiar nature of *evangelical* repentance will be the subject of a distinct proposition. The inquiry now before us is, What is repentance as a mental operation, distinguished from other mental operations?

The proposition which I have laid down is, that it is a state of mind which springs up in view of perceived personal guilt. Let us analyze this, and see whether we cannot find here all the essential elements of which the mind is conscious when it exercises repentance.

(1.) It is in view of *perceived* guilt. I mean that the mind must *perceive* or *see* that it has done wrong. You must see that something has been done or omitted for which you are blameworthy. The mind cannot repent without this. It never does. You cannot make a man repent for the colour of his hair, or for having a deformed limb, or for a natural impediment in his speech, however much he may regret its existence, or seriously feel its disadvantage. In relation to an *action* which a man performs, you cannot make him repent unless he *perceives* that it is wrong, and that he deserves blame for it. If he esteems what he has done to be *right*, all arguments are vain to induce him to exercise repentance. Your appeals are powerless as long as he does not see that he is blameworthy for what he has done. If he thinks that circumstances justified what he has done, though others may think that it was wrong; if his mind is so little enlightened that he does not know what was right or wrong in the case; if he is so debased by vice, or superstition, or ignorance, that his moral perceptions are blunted and paralyzed, you may labour in vain to awaken in his bosom the feelings which constitute repentance. If, for instance, he has killed a man, and is conscious that he did it in self-defence, however much he may regret the necessity of the act, while he retains the belief that it was justifiable and right you can never excite in his bosom the feelings of repentance.

(2.) The second thing in my statement of what constitutes repentance in general is, that it must be in view of *personal* guilt. I mean by this, that a man cannot repent for the act of another. Repentance always has metes and bounds, and is always limited by what we ourselves deserve. There is no other guilt but that which is personal; and you can never make a man feel any other. The human mind has been so created that it can repent for no other: and every theory formed on the supposition that one man can repent for the sin of another, and every instance in which a man has attempted to persuade himself that he *has* done it, must be false. The soul of man has not been made in a manner so loose, and so regardless of laws, that either of these things is possible. You may regret what another man has done; you may suffer on account of it in person, in property, in health, or in your family; you may weep over it all your life, but you do not *repent* of it. The son of an intemperate father has abundant occasion to regret the career which his father has pursued. It may have deprived him of property which he would otherwise have inherited; it may have made him the early victim of disease; it may have subjected him to the passionate outbreaks of one who has been made a madman by intoxication; it may have separated him from the respectable society which he might otherwise have enjoyed; it may have prevented his acquiring an education, and preparing himself for honourable usefulness; it may have compelled him to enter on life every way under disadvantage, and many a time he may have wept over it, but it is an abuse of language to say that he has ever *repented* of it. Between his feelings, deep and pungent as they may be, and what they would have been if he had been himself the drunkard, there is a line which is never crossed; and God has so made the human soul that it never can be crossed. So of the shame which an erring daughter may bring on a family; so of the deep sorrow which invades the soul when a son is reckless and abandoned. The blood which mantles your cheek then, is made to mount there by a different law from that which diffuses the shame and sorrow of repentance when you yourself have done the wrong.—The principle which I am here laying down is universal. Your our own mind can never exercise repentance for what another has done, nor can repentance with you be connected with any of his acts, except so far as he is your agent, or you have authorized him to act in your place, and then the repentance is not for what *he* does, but for what *you* did in appointing him. That class of theologians who suppose that it is the duty of men to repent of the sin of Adam, advance a dogma which is against all the laws of the human mind; and they who work themselves up into a belief that they *do* repent for what he did thousands of years before they had any being, however amiable their tears may be, and however their sorrows may assume the semblance of piety, must be ignorant of the nature of their own mental operations. That they may regret what he did; that they may mourn over the ravages of sin introduced by his guilty act, no one can doubt;—that they should *repent* of what he or any other man ever did, the laws of our nature render impossible. A man can as properly take to himself credit for the virtuous deeds performed by another, and claim a reward for them, as exercise repentance for his vices and his follies.

(3.) The third thing which is implied in my statement is, that repentance is a state of mind which springs up by a law of our nature when our personal guilt *is* perceived. What I mean is, that when it exists at all, it is originated by this law. I will not say that repentance *always in fact exists* when guilt is perceived, for I know that it is possible for a man by an effort of will, or under the influence of some strong perverted purpose, to oppose the regular operations of the laws of his own mind, and to resist conclusions which the fair exercise of *reason* would reach if there were no perversion and no opposition. Such may be the stubbornness of his will, such the determination *not* to see a certain result in a process of reasoning, that he may set aside the clearest testimony; and evidence, which according to the laws of his nature *ought* to make a deep impression on him, may in fact make none, while evidence which may in fact have no real force, may seem to him "strong as proof of holy writ." So, I admit, it may be in regard to repentance. It is possible that a man may perceive his guilt, and yet may hold his mind in stern resistance to the laws which would lead him to repentance. He may resolve *not* to feel; not to weep; not to make confession; not to allow the usual marks of guilt to be depicted in the eye, the cheek, the frame. He may even tremble under the consciousness of guilt, and yet resolve not to abandon his course, though to persevere in it may require him to drive his purposes over all the finer feelings of his nature.

What I mean is, that where repentance *does* exist, it springs up in accordance with one of the regular laws of our nature. It is not the object of creative power. It is not brought about by the agency of God irrespective of the laws of the mind. It is not the operation of the Divine Mind. It is our own mind that repents; our own eyes that shed forth tears; our own hearts that feel; our own souls that resolve to do wrong no more. God cannot repent for us; nor can he produce repentance in us in any other way than by causing our own minds to perceive their personal guilt, and by some agency securing the proper action of the mental laws which he has ordained.

As this is a point of great importance on the question whether men are bound to exercise repentance, and whether they are able to do it, it is desirable that it should be made as clear as possible. I would observe, then, that this is a matter of plain common sense, and would be clear to all men if it had never been mystified by theologians. All men understand the nature of repentance. All understand how it springs up in the mind. All have experienced it a thousand times. You cannot find a person who at some time has not exercised repentance. You cannot find a child, who, if he should look into his own mind, would need to be told what is meant when he is required to repent for having done a wrong thing; and in the emotions of a child when he feels sorrow that he has done wrong, and resolves to make confession of it and to do so no more, you have the elements of all that God requires of man in repentance as a condition of salvation. You recollect your own feelings when a child. You broke the commands of a father. His law was plain; his will was clear. When the deed was performed, you reflected on what you had done. You saw that his command was right; that you had done wrong by breaking his law, and had incurred his displeasure. He had always treated you kindly; his precepts had never been unreasonable, and you could not justify yourself in what you had done. By a law of your nature—a law which you did not originate, though its operations you might have checked and controlled—you felt pain and distress that you had done the wrong. That feeling of distress sprang up in the mind as a matter of course, and without any perceived foreign agency, and you resolved that you would go and confess the fault, and would be guilty of the wrong no more. This is repentance; and this is the whole of it. You have a friend. He has a thousand times, and in a thousand ways, laid you under obligation. He has helped you in pecuniary distress; shared your losses; attended you in sickness; defended your reputation when attacked. He himself in turn suffers. Wicked men defame his character, and in an evil hour *your* mind is poisoned, and you join in the prevalent suspicion and error in regard to him, and give increased currency to the slanderous reports. Subsequently you reflect that all this was wrong; that you acted an ungrateful part; that you suffered your mind to be too easily influenced in forgetting your benefactor, and that you have done him great and lasting injury. You are pained at the heart. Then spring up in the soul, by a law of your nature, bitter feelings of regret for what you have done; and you resolve that you will go to him and relieve your own mind, and do him justice, by making confession; that you will implore forgiveness; that you will endeavour as far as possible to undo the evil, and that you will never repeat the wrong again. This is repentance; and this is the whole of it. Let these simple elements be transferred to God and to religion, and you have all that is included in repentance. Be as honest toward God as you have been many a time toward a parent or a friend; suffer the laws of your nature to act as freely and with as little obstruction towards your Maker, as you have done in your treatment of your fellow-beings, and you will have no difficulty on the subject. You will see that repentance, as a leading doctrine of all religion, is neither arbitrary nor unreasonable. The difficulty is, that when you approach religion you are determined to find something unintelligible, severe, and harsh, and you at once suppose that God in his arrangement there is arbitrary and unkind.

(4.) If the views thus far exhibited are well-founded, then they will do much in explaining the nature of the Divine agency in producing repentance. It is true that there is an important sense in which he is the Author of it. It was true, as the disciples said when Peter visited Cornelius, and saw the effects of the gospel on his mind, that "*God* had granted to the Gentiles repentance unto life," Acts xi. 18. It is true that the Lord Jesus was exalted "to be a Prince and a Saviour, for to *give repentance* to Israel, and forgiveness of sins," Acts v. 31. But it is also true that the Divine Mind does not repent for us. It is true that repentance is not created by mere physical power. It is true that the nature of the Divine agency is not to produce it independently of the laws of the mind itself, and of the efforts of the soul. It is your own mind that is to repent; your own heart that is to feel; your own tongue that is to make confession; your own soul that is to resolve that you will do wrong no more. The effect of the Divine agency, if I understand it, and if the views already suggested are correct, is to bring truth before the mind; to make the mental vision clear, so that it shall be perceived; to remove the obstructions to the fair operations of the mental laws, and repentance follows as a matter of course. And in like manner when he *commands* men to repent, it is not a command to *create* emotions in their souls by an act of their own will; to originate feeling by merely *resolving* to do it:—it is, to allow their minds to act according to their nature; to permit guilt, when perceived, to produce its legitimate effect on the soul; to be as honest towards him, as they expect their children to be towards themselves. He presumes that every man understands the nature of repentance; and that all that is required is, to secure the fair operation of the mental laws which he has ordained.

II. In the second place, *evangelical repentance, or repentance as connected with true religion in the soul, is a state of mind which arises from the perception that all sin is committed against God.* My meaning is, that when true repentance exists, the primary and main ground of the sorrow is, that the crime has been committed against him; that his law has been violated; that he has been offended. It is not that it is disgraceful in the view of the community; it is not that it will be attended with the loss of favour or popularity among men; it is not that a father, or a child, or a neighbour has been wronged; nor is it that it will be followed by punishment in this world or the next;—but it is that God regards it as an evil thing, and that its chief evil is in the fact that it is a violation of his law. In cases when wrong has been done to a human being—to a neighbour, or relative, or stranger—the chief evil in it, as viewed by a true penitent, is not the injury that has been done to man, but the wrong that has been done to God. In true repentance, the wrong that has been done to man may be comparatively forgotten, and the attention fixed with absorbing and overpowering interest on the crime regarded as an offence against God.

As this is a point of much importance, and one which is not very clear to most persons, I propose to show that it is so, and why it is so.

(*a*) In my text, repentance is spoken of particularly in its relation to God:—"testifying repentance *toward* God." In the parable of the prodigal son, the penitent is represented as saying, "I will arise and go to my father, and will say unto him, Father, I have sinned *against heaven*, and before thee," Luke xv. 18. When he came to his father, he said, "Father, I have sinned against heaven, and in thy sight." The errors and follies of his life appeared to have been primarily against heaven; the sins which he had committed against his father were, in his view, secondary in the magnitude of their evil to the same offences regarded as committed against God. So David, in the fifty-first Psalm, says, "Against *thee, thee only*, have I sinned, and done this evil in thy sight," ver. 4. And so in 2 Sam. xii. 13, where he refers to the same offence, he says, "I have sinned *against the Lord*." We are not to suppose that the prodigal son was not sensible that he had been guilty of a great wrong towards his father; but that it was secondary in the magnitude of the evil as compared with the sin against God. We are not to suppose that David was not sensible of the wrong that he had done to Uriah, or to the laws of the land, or of the injury which his example would do to men. Of all this, he might have had, and probably did have, the deepest conviction; but all this, when compared with the magnitude of the sin as committed against God, was so comparatively trifling, that he said, "Against *thee, thee only*, have I sinned, and done this evil in thy sight." The mind was turned away from everything else, and fixed on the amazing offence regarded as committed against God. In that, the thoughts were absorbed and lost; and it was that which overwhelmed the soul of the penitent monarch.

These instances are evidently set forth in the Bible as examples of true repentance; and the design is to show that in genuine repentance sin is contemplated primarily as committed against God, and as an evil in his sight. It derives its chief aggravation from that fact, and the principal sorrow of the soul is, that *he* has been offended.

(*b*) I proposed to explain to you why this is so, and show that it is reasonable that it should be so. When we attempt to show that this is the nature of repentance, and when we urge you to regard all your sins as deriving their main aggravation from the fact that they are committed against God, there is often a feeling which arises in the mind that this is unjust. You have wronged a neighbour. You see the evil; confess it; ask his forgiveness; obtain it: and why is not that the end of it? The injury was done to him; it has been repaired: why is not that all? Why should it be carried up before God? Above all, why should your main distress of mind be not that your neighbour was wronged, but that God was offended? You violate the command of a parent. You reflect on it; regret it; confess it; are forgiven. Why is not that all? It was in the domestic circle; it was known nowhere else; the wrong has been repaired; the breach has been healed. Why is not that an end of it? Why should you be required to make another "issue" in regard to it, and go over, with all the sorrows of repentance, and the humiliation of a confession, before another being—making a double confession necessary for a single offence, and leaving nothing done till *he* is pacified? What if in childhood you had a quarrel with another boy, and had "made it up," and then another person should come in and should demand that you should make it up with him also?

To explain this, I will submit to you a few remarks:—

(1.) There is a kind of repentance which arises from the contemplation of a wrong regarded as committed against man. That is the common form in which it exists in the world, and that we have all experienced. A neighbour has been wronged by you. You see it, confess it, and obtain his pardon, and the matter between you and him is settled. You have done all that you could to repair the evil; he professes to be satisfied, and it would now be wrong for him to insist on anything further, or to allow this to affect his future treatment of you. But does this do anything towards settling the matter between you and God? That is wholly another thing, and should be made the most important thing. Your neighbour is not in the place of God; nor is he authorized to act for him; nor can he take upon himself to forgive the offence as committed against him. Two boys have a quarrel. One is greatly in the wrong, and greatly injures the other. When the deed is committed, he sees the wrong, regrets his passion, goes and makes humble confession, and is forgiven. That settles the matter so far as they are concerned, and perhaps so far as the entire group of boys are concerned among whom it happened. But there is another view of the case much more important, it may be, than this; and this hushing up of the quarrel does nothing in regard to that. The boy that did the wrong has a father, and the law of that father has been violated. He told him not to go to that place. He commanded him to have nothing to do with that boy. He trained him to be gentle, and kind, and inoffensive; to restrain his passions; to avoid all occasions of brawls; to honour him; to fear God. His law now has been violated; his counsels disregarded; his government despised; himself, as a father, dishonoured. The offence which the boy committed against the other was the act of a moment, produced under the excitement of passion; it was a single act of wrong:—the offence as committed against a father was a sin against long and careful training; it involved the whole question whether the father is to be obeyed or disobeyed, and had a direct bearing on the whole subject of paternal government. Now it is clear that the son, when he has settled the matter with the injured boy, has done nothing to settle it with his own injured father; and that the act, as viewed against him, is a much more serious evil than as viewed against the boy who was directly wronged. If that son now has true repentance, he will not only be affected by the offence viewed as committed against his playmate, but he will feel that there is a much more important matter than this to be adjusted in his own father's house.

(2.) This leads me to observe, that on a similar principle the offences which we commit are to be regarded in their direct relation to those who are immediately wronged, and to their much higher bearing on God. You do wrong to a neighbour, or brother, in the church; a wife, a lover, a stranger. You become sensible of the wrong, confess it, repair it as far as possible, receive forgiveness, and the matter between you and the offended party is settled. You give each other the hand, and are friends again. But that does not affect another and a more important point—the relation of the offence to God. For illustration of this, there has been no better case than that of David. That he had done a great and grievous wrong to Uriah and his family there can be no doubt. But could all that wrong have been repaired, there was another and a much more important light in which it was to be viewed. He had violated two of the positive commands of God. A professor of religion; a prince; the head of the covenant-people; a man signally favoured by God; occupying a most prominent position in the world,—he had disregarded the law of his Maker, and trampled his statutes in the dust. His sin had been public, and of a most aggravated character; and contemplating all its relations, the offence as committed against Uriah, in comparison with the same sin regarded as committed against God, was a trifle; and he, therefore, under the feeling of genuine repentance, cried out, "Against thee, *thee only*, have I sinned, and done this evil in thy sight."

(3.) This suggests, then, another thought in regard to true repentance. It may have been often exercised towards your fellow-creatures whom you have offended, and you may have obtained their forgiveness; and still the great matter pertaining to true repentance may be yet unsettled. You may have violated the commands of a parent, and may have repented of it and obtained his forgiveness; you may have wronged a neighbour, and may have confessed the wrong and obtained pardon; you may have been unfaithful in a public trust, and may then have done all you could to repair the evil considered as an offence against the laws of society; you may have led the innocent into error or sin, and then may have done all you could to repair the wrong so far as they are concerned; and still the most important questions pertaining to those offences are unaffected. They all have a relation to God and his government. They are all to be considered as violations of his law; as so many wrongs done to him. Nothing has been done in regard to that matter, nor do you meet either the primary or the full requirements of repentance until you go and say, "I have sinned *against heaven*;" "against *thee, thee only*, have I sinned, and done this evil in thy sight."

III. In the third place, *true repentance, as a part of religion, involves not only regret for past sin as an evil in the sight of God, but a purpose to abandon it and to do it no more.* This point is so obvious that it will be necessary to dwell on it only for a moment. It is clear that if there be no such purpose to abandon the sin, there can be no genuine repentance. If David had intended to repeat the sin, over which he mourned, as soon as that was forgiven, nothing would be more plain than that all his sorrow for the crime would have been hollow and insincere. His sorrow in that case could have arisen only from an apprehension of punishment, and not from any genuine hatred of transgression. Had the prodigal son made his confession solely with a view to obtain the favour of his father, and acquire another portion of the estate, intending then to repeat his acts of ingratitude and profligacy, it is clear that there could have been no genuine repentance; no regret for his sin as such. In all cases of genuine repentance there must be a purpose to abandon the sin, and not to repeat the wrong. This principle, so familiar to us in our treatment of each other, is not less true in our relations to God. There, also, it is true in its largest, broadest sense—for *all* sin is regarded as committed against him. When one *man* has done wrong to another, all that he who has been injured can require in order to his extending forgiveness is, that the offender should make acknowledgment and restitution for *that* particular offence. He could not demand that there should be an acknowledgment to *him* of *all* his sins, nor even that he should change his conduct in regard to others. But in reference to repentance toward God, it is required that there should be sorrow for *every* sin, and an *universal* purpose to forsake the ways of transgression. He that comes before God professing to exercise repentance, with a purpose to indulge in any one sin of any kind, shows that his repentance is as really false and hollow, as he does who intends to make a confession to his neighbour for any one act of wrong, and yet purposes to repeat the offence as soon as he has an opportunity. No man, therefore, can be a true penitent who does not intend to abandon all sin. No one becomes a true Christian who does not purpose to break away from every form of transgression, and to lead a holy life. Men who become Christians are indeed imperfect. They are liable to fall into sin. They do many things over which they have occasion to mourn. But he who professes to become a Christian, *intending* that this shall be so, *purposing* to repeat any sin and then to repent of it, manifestly knows nothing of true repentance, and can have no evidence of piety. "If I regard iniquity in my heart, the Lord will not hear me," Psa. lxvi. 18.

In view of the thoughts suggested in this discourse, we may remark, in conclusion,—

(1.) That as a mere mental operation repentance in religion does not differ from repentance exercised on other subjects. As a mere act of mind, repentance toward God does not differ from repentance as exercised toward an injured parent or friend. How can it? The difference is in the object towards which repentance is exercised, not in the act of repenting, as a mere exercise of mind. Yet repentance, as a mental operation, is easily understood, and all are familiar with it. Who is there that has never repented of anything that he has done? Who that has not confessed a wrong? Who that does not now feel that he has much to regret in the past, and that there is much which he *ought* to confess? Be as honest toward God as you have been toward a parent, lover, or friend, and you would have no difficulty on the subject of repentance. It would be easy to be understood, and all your difficulties would soon vanish. Religion, if this be so, is not unreal, arbitrary, and impossible; it is a practicable thing, and it accords with all the laws of the human mind.

(2.) It follows from the views presented, that repentance is not beyond the proper exercise of the power of man. Every man practises it. Every child repents. Every one has at different times felt regret for something that he has done; has made confession; has resolved to transgress no more; has turned from the evil course. This is repentance; and no one in such a case has resorted to any plea that it was impossible, or that it was unreasonable. No one who has injured a friend; no child who has violated the command of his father, when he is convinced of the wrong, and when the duty of proper acknowledgment is pressed upon him, ever thinks of taking shelter under the plea that repentance is beyond his power, and that he cannot exercise it. It is only in religion that we ever hear any difficulty suggested on the subject; there only that we are told that it is beyond a man's power, and that we must wait for a Divine influence before it can be exercised. But why should it be beyond a man's power in reference to religion more than anywhere else? Why easy elsewhere; why impossible here? The answer is plain. Men wish to find an excuse for not repenting; and regardless of any reflections on the character of their Maker, rather than forsake their sins they charge him with requiring that which is impossible, and coolly attempt to satisfy themselves by saying that they have no power to obey his commands.

(3.) It follows, from what has been said, that it is the sinner who is to repent. It is not God who is to repent for him—for

God has done no wrong. It is not the Saviour who is to repent for him—for it is not he who has violated the law. It is not the Holy Spirit who is to repent for him—for how can that blessed Agent feel such sorrow, or why should he? My impenitent friend, *it is your own mind* that is to repent; your own heart that is to feel sorrow; your own feet that are to turn from the evil way; your own mouth that is to make confession. I know and am persuaded that, if it is ever done, it will be by the aid of the Holy Ghost; but I know equally well that *you yourself* are to be the penitent, and that this is a work that cannot be done for you by another. The mind that has done the wrong must repent. That very heart that has sinned must feel all the sorrows of repentance that are ever felt in the case; those very eyes that have looked with desire on forbidden objects must weep, and must do all the weeping in the case; and those very lips that have been profane, or false, or impure, must make confession, and the confession can be made by them alone.

(4.) Finally, it is right and proper to call on men to repent of their sins. If they repent when they have wronged a friend, or violated the law of a parent; if repentance is an operation of the mind, with which all are familiar; if it is not beyond the proper reach of the human faculties; and if the sinner himself is actually to feel sorrow, and to make confession,—then it is right to call on men to repent of their sins committed against God. The gospel, in approaching men, commends itself to their common sense, and requires of them only that which they themselves see to be reasonable and proper. It comes to them, and says that they have sinned against God; that all sin may be regarded as terminating on him, and as a violation of his law; that *for* that sin there should be sorrow felt in the heart; that there should be willingness to go to him and make penitent acknowledgment, and implore forgiveness; and that there should be a solemn purpose to repeat the wrong no more. This is what the gospel demands of every sinner as a primary and essential condition of salvation. Is it wrong in its demands? is it unreasonable in its claims? What less *could* it ask? And how could it meet the convictions of your own minds in regard to what may be reasonably required, if it did not demand this? When we summon you, therefore, to repentance, we urge the appeal no less by the conviction in your own minds of what is right, than by the authority of God.

SERMON XXII.

THE RELATION OF REPENTANCE TO PARDON IN THE CHRISTIAN SYSTEM.

Acts iii. 19.—"Repent ye, therefore, and be converted, that your sins may be blotted out."

In the prosecution of the subject of repentance, I proceed now to consider the question *how* repentance is of avail in the procuring of pardon; or the relation of repentance to pardon in the Christian system.

It seems to be admitted on all hands, that repentance under the Divine administration is connected with the pardon of sin. Lord Herbert, the leading British Deist, laid down the necessity of repentance as one of the ten fundamental truths taught by natural religion; and held it to be indisputable that repentance would be effectual in securing forgiveness. This is probably the sentiment of the great mass of mankind, whether they embrace the Christian system or not. As every child feels that if he has done wrong towards a father he ought to repent of it,—and argues, and in general argues justly, that if he truly repents his father will forgive him,—so men seem to reason about their Great Father in heaven. This opinion is held by the Christian in connexion with his belief in the merits of the sacrifice of the Redeemer; in what sense I will endeavour to explain in the sequel of this discourse. By others,—by avowed Deists, and by infidels in every form, and by the mass of men,—the reference to that sacrifice is excluded; and it is held that mere repentance without respect to that will be accepted by God, and will secure the pardon of sin.

The form in which the doctrine is held by those who do not practically embrace Christianity, probably comprises the two following particulars: first, that repentance for a wrong done is, under the Divine administration, enough; that is, that the Divine government is equitable and mild; that God is disposed to pardon; that when one becomes sensible of a wrong done, it is all that the Universal Parent will or can require; and that repentance, therefore, will secure the restoration to Divine favour; —and, secondly, that *in fact* they themselves *do* exercise repentance—all the repentance that can reasonably be demanded.

When they have done wrong, they say, they always regret it. They are pained at heart. They are ready to make confession and restitution as far as is in their power for the wrong done—even though it was unintentional. They do not recollect an instance, perhaps, in which this has not been done; and if such an instance could be referred to in their past lives, they would lay down their book or their pen, or leave their plough standing in the furrow, and go at once and repair the evil. Thus, they trust, the account between them and justice is kept substantially balanced, and they entertain the hope that the Divine mercy will not be withheld from them in the great day.

These are the principles which prevail where the Christian doctrine of seeking forgiveness through the merits of Christ is laid out of view; and the question now is, whether these are sound principles—or in other words, what is the true relation of repentance to pardon? Let us examine the system now referred to, in which there is undoubtedly some mixture of truth, and see what is the correct doctrine on the subject. The inquiry will be conducted by laying down a few connected propositions.

I. It will be agreed on all hands, *that under the Divine administration there is no pardon, in the proper sense of the term, where there is no repentance.* Indeed, if the term *pardon,* or its equivalent *forgiveness,* is ever used, without the correlative *repentance,* it is probably employed in a somewhat lax signification; not in its strict and proper sense. When a man who is in the penitentiary, or who is under sentence of death for murder, is pardoned by the executive, the term means merely that the *penalty* is remitted, or is not executed. There has been in the bosom of the executive no such feeling exactly as is implied in the word *forgiveness.* His feeling in the case is distinct from that which he would have had if he had been personally wronged, and he who had wronged him had come and made penitent confession, and he had forgiven him. So when in your heart you exercise forgiveness towards those who have injured you when they manifest no repentance—as the Saviour prayed for his murderers, "Father, *forgive* them," the feeling is distinct from what it is when you see them truly penitent, and when in view of their repentance you *declare* them forgiven. You use the term in a somewhat lax and indefinite sense, as meaning that you do not harbour malice against them; that you will take no revenge for what they have done; that you will be ready actually to pardon them if they will apply to you for forgiveness.

Repentance and forgiveness, in the proper sense of the terms, have, in the common apprehensions of men, a very close connexion. It is a point on which we will all start together in our inquiry, that there can be no pardon under the Divine government where there is no true repentance. There is no one point probably about which men would be better agreed than this. The Deist supposes this; all men suppose it. The hardened man; the man who never felt one pang of regret that he has done wrong; the man who wholly justifies his own course; the man who knows that he has done evil, and who intends to persevere in it, cannot obtain *forgiveness* in any proper sense of that term. He may remain for a long time unpunished, the sentence of the law may be suspended over him, he may have many comforts and blessings, and his life may be filled with hilarity and joy; but it would be an abuse of language to say that he was *forgiven* or *pardoned*. If he ever obtains pardon, in the proper sense of that term, it must be somehow in connexion with his exercising sorrow for what he has done. This, then, is a fundamental principle in all religions. It is a point on which Christians and all other men must agree. Wherever it leads us, we here start together.

II. My second proposition is, *that mere repentance of itself will not repair an evil which you have done, and on account of which you feel compunction.* Sin, or wrong done, produces evils which no mere *regret* on the part of him who has done it can repair. It is not an universal truth that regret or compunction on the part of the offender will put away the evil, and restore matters to the condition in which they were before the wrong was done.

This truth is perhaps sufficiently plain in itself without any further illustration; but as it is the dividing point between Christianity and other systems; as it is very material in understanding the relation of repentance to pardon; and as it is an important fact in the character of the Divine administration,—it is of moment that it should be further illustrated.

It is an essential position in the view which one takes who rejects the doctrine of the atonement, and who denies its necessity in order that repentance can be of avail, that "when men have transgressed the Divine commands, repentance and amendment of life will place them in the same situation as if they had never offended."*

Now, is this so? Is it a correct principle in regard to the Divine administration? Is it one that is sustained by the course of events? Will repentance and reformation of themselves arrest the course of things consequent on transgression, and prevent

* Magee on the Atonement, p. 19.

any further suffering or punishment on account of it? Let us look a moment at facts in the case, and see what repentance will and will not do.

(*a*) In the common occurrences of life, does the man who by intemperance and voluptuousness has injured his character, his fortune, and his health, find himself instantly restored to the enjoyment of those blessings, on repenting of his past conduct, and resolving on future amendment? The answer plainly is, he does not. Repentance, even the bitterest remorse, will not do it. It will not at once bring back the fortune that has been lost by gambling; nor will it at once restore the bloated and diseased frame of the voluptuary to "the freshness of a child's." Nor will it arrest at once the pain and anguish of body and mind, and the disgrace which may have been engendered by the evil course. These travel on beyond the moments of repentance, and meet a man perhaps far on his way beyond the period when he penitently forsook the path of transgression. It is true, indeed, that repentance is one of the indispensable ways by which these evils are to be arrested, and that, as a consequence of that, a man may be restored to prosperity, to the possession of property, and to honour. But this does not occur at once. It is to be a gradual process. It will be by slow and toilsome steps. Not one cent of lost property will repentance at once bring back; not one pang of disease produced by voluptuous living will it at once arrest. By sober and persevering toil, the man of wrecked and ruined fortune *may* become rich again; by the proper care of his health, the ravages of disease may be arrested, and he may yet be blessed with length of days, but not by any miraculous or sudden effect of repentance.

(*b*) Will repentance repair the wrong that you have done to others, and place things in the same situation in which they were before? In some respects it may. The property which you stole, you may restore; the trespass which you committed may be paid for by a full equivalent. But will it recall a murdered man from the grave? Will it restore innocence to the ruined victim of hellish arts? Will it undo the wrongs which you have done to a mother and her children by making their father an inebriate?

(*c*) Will repentance at once arrest the evils of a youth wasted in folly and vice? It may indeed make you industrious and plodding and virtuous at twenty-one, and ever onward. But will it recall the hours which you have wasted at the card-table, or in the company of the idle and the worthless, or in absolute indolence, or in building castles in the air, or in following after wild and illusive vagaries of the mind? It may enable you to do something hereafter; but it will not repair the past, and through the longest life you will suffer disadvantage from the want of what you might have acquired in the wasted days of your youth.

(*d*) Will repentance obliterate the *pain* which you have caused others by your misconduct? It *may* do much in many cases to effect this; perhaps in some cases it may remove it all. A frank and full confession, the expression of deep and genuine sorrow, *may* in some instances wholly arrest and remove the anguish of heart felt by a father or a mother in view of your ingratitude and disobedience. But will it always do this? Is it the universal law? Alas, that father's locks may have been turned prematurely grey by your misconduct; and no penitence of yours can make one hair black again. Or the broken-hearted parent may be now in the grave, crushed to the earth and consigned to the tomb by the ingratitude and follies of a son; and no penitence of yours can bring him up again to the cheerful light of the living. Look over the past. How small a part of those to whom you have done wrong, who have been injured or pained by you, are now within your reach! To how few of them could you make confession and reparation if you should try! Part are in their graves. Part are in distant lands. Part scattered over your own country. Here, the wrong struck a parent's heart; there, the heart of a sister; there, the heart of a wife—all now dead. Here, it planted a poisoned arrow in the bosom of a friend, and he is now far away. There, it reached a benefactor, and he is gone, you know not where. And there, the memorial of it is seen in the bowed form of a father, and how can you make his frame erect again, and restore to him the lustre of his earlier years?

These are plain principles; and they show us that repentance, however genuine and bitter, will not at once arrest the consequences of an evil course, and restore things to the condition in which they were before. There are things which remain to be adjusted under the operation of God's moral government, which are not affected by the mere fact of repentance. The relation of repentance to pardon, therefore, is *not* that it necessarily arrests the evil, and prevents all future suffering on the account of sin in this world. And how can he who rejects revelation, and the evidence there furnished of pardon, prove that it will arrest all these evils at any period of his existence? What will it do to repair the evils done to a murdered man; to an injured father, mother, or sister; to those inveigled into error or crime who may now be in their graves? The grand principle which I seek to lay down here is, that repentance does not of itself repair the wrong done; and that "indemnity is not a consequence of repentance here." * Can a rejector of revelation *prove* that it will be hereafter? What would be the basis of such an argument? What "counter-facts" to those which have been stated are there to show that it is probable it will be so?

III. My third proposition is, *that when wrong has been done, repentance will not do anything to restore to favour, without some act on the part of him who is offended and injured.* The whole matter lies in his bosom, in his will; in that which no power, or wealth, or influence, or tears, can of necessity control.

Repentance is always in view of a wrong done. But a *wrong* necessarily contemplates two or more persons; for even when there *seems* to be but one, by a species of fiction of language we show that it is essentially supposed there are *two.* We sometimes, indeed, speak of a man's *wronging himself;* doing injustice *to himself,* as if there were two persons concerned, the one acting against the other—the man's baser passions acting against his higher nature:—as when it is often remarked of a man that "the only enemy he has is *himself.*" And so we retain the same fiction of language when we speak of our own follies and faults, and say that "we cannot *forgive ourselves* for what we have done." Even here we keep up the notion, that as a wrong it pertains to *two.* There must be an act of penitence in the one, and of pardon in the other, before it can be adjusted.

In all other instances, it is clear that wrong pertains to two or more parties. A wrong is something *done* to another—to his feelings, character, property, government, family, health, limb, life, or soul. There are two parties—the injurer and the injured; the wrong-doer, and the individual, or the corporation, or the government that has suffered. When a wrong is done, therefore, it becomes at once an affair pertaining to two or more parties.

It follows, therefore, that when a wrong is done, it is not the mere act of the one party that will heal it. There must be a common or joint action in the case. The friend who has been injured must act, as well as he who has injured him; the parent as well as the child; the government as well as the subject.

It is clear, also, that whatever may be the feelings or the action of the one who has done the wrong, there must be some action or expression on the part of the injured before the difficulty is removed. The sacrifice must not only be brought, it must be accepted; the recompense must not only be tendered, it must be received; the confession must not only be made, it must

* Magee.

be admitted to be satisfactory. On the part of the injured and the wronged, there must be some arrangement made in the case; some promise; some expression of a readiness to pardon, and to have the difficulty healed,—and, if he be a moral governor, to have the penalty remitted,—before he who has done the wrong can have evidence that his own arrangement for removing the difficulty will avail. It would not do for a child to disobey a parent, and then to make such an acknowledgment in the case as he *himself* should please, and demand that that should be accepted; and as little would it do for him to do wrong *presuming* on what he supposed to be the clemency of his father in such a case. Such an arrangement on his own part, and such a presumption, would do nothing to heal the breach, or to relieve the difficulty in the case. It will not do to presume on the character of any one too far. A child is making a most hazardous experiment, when he *presumes* on the forbearance of even a parent. He is making a most hazardous as well as wicked experiment, who *presumes* on the kindness and forbearance of a friend, when he provokes or neglects him. A husband is making a most hazardous, as well as wicked experiment, who *presumes* on the patience and forbearance of the most kind and affectionate wife, by treating her with neglect and want of love. There is a point beyond which, even if it were right at all, it will not be safe to *presume* on the kindness and forbearance of any one, however kind, or generous, or noble. How far, then, may a man *presume* on the kindness and forbearance of God, about whom he knows so little? How may he know that he would accept an offering for transgression; that he would receive the confessions of the lips for having done wrong; that he would regard with favour even the tears and sighs that would be the expression of a broken and a contrite heart?

The real question, then, in all cases where wrong has been done is, whether there is any act or declaration, on the part of him to whom the wrong has been done, to which he who has done it could *trust* for the certainty of pardon. If you know enough about his character in any case, *that* might furnish you with some, perhaps with a certain ground of hope. But you want something more even than that. You want some act on his part; some arrangement; some promise.

Now what does the rejector of revelation pretend to here? According to him, what arrangement has there been on the part of God to show that repentance will be connected with pardon? Rejecting as he does, systematically and on principle, *all* revelation, what does he pretend to rely on that will furnish such assurance? That it *may be* so may be true; but does he *know it?* How *can* he know it? How can he know anything about it? The mere *fact* of repentance is certainly no evidence of pardon; for millions have repented of a wrong who never have been forgiven; and the mere fact that a wrong-doer experiences remorse is no evidence that he who has been wronged will be disposed to forgive.

Here then, again, we part with the rejector of revelation. We, who profess to believe in the Christian system, suppose that God *has* made an arrangement on this very subject, and has made it known to us in his word. We not only profess to know what repentance is, and to presume that the injured and the wronged in the case will be disposed to accept of the expressions of penitence, but we profess to have, what the case demands, a *statement* from him on this very point, which relieves the whole difficulty, and which assures us that in connexion with repentance our sins will be blotted out. We have, then, what is requisite when two parties are concerned,—as there always are when wrong is done; we have the statement of the one who is injured, that repentance on the part of the other will be followed by forgiveness. There is but one question which remains to be asked on the subject to fill up the argument, and to give us information of all which it is needful for us to know. It is, in what way it is *consistent* for God to do this; or what *is* the arrangement by which it is done. This is not indeed absolutely necessary for us to know,—since if we offend another it is sufficient to be assured that *he* regards it as consistent for him to forgive, and the fact that he will do it is really all we need; but still there would be an advantage in being made acquainted with the method by which it is done if we could. It might give us some enlarged views of his character; it might enable us more to admire the plan.

IV. This leads me, then, to the statement of a fourth proposition, *that the exercise of repentance is made available and efficacious in the case, through the atonement made by the Saviour*—or in virtue of his death regarded as a sacrifice for sin. The exercise of repentance in connexion with the atonement meets all the necessary conditions of pardon, and is the only plan which does. The meaning is, that the death of Christ as a sacrifice has done so much to *repair* the wrong done by sin, that now pardon may consistently follow repentance. Two or three remarks, I trust, will make this clear.

First, as already observed, in *all* cases where repentance is proper, a *wrong* has been done—an *injury* has been the result of that which causes repentance; since if there is *no* wrong, no injury, there is no occasion of repentance in any case. But mere sorrow or regret on your part, however urgent or protracted, does nothing to remove that wrong, or repair that injury; and the wrong must be in some way repaired before repentance can be satisfactory. A simple *case* will make this clear. A father, in moderate circumstances, sends his son to college, away from home. The father has just the means of maintaining him there by meeting the ordinary and necessary expenses—and no more. He gives his son repeated and solemn charges on the subject of economy in his expenditure, assuring him that he can only meet term-bills and the expenses of living on a prudent scale. In particular, he charges him not to enter a certain house of entertainment, though entirely respectable, and though kept by a man every way respectable. Solely on the score of necessary economy, he enjoins this duty on him, and makes it a point of absolute command. At the end of the year a large bill, wholly beyond his power to meet, is sent to him from that prohibited house. The son confesses the wrong, expresses regret, and asks for pardon. Is there nothing to be done in the case but simply to forgive him on that confession? True, it may be that the worthy man who sent the bill had no authority to trust a minor, and that the father might not be legally bound in the matter; but there is the sentiment of honour strong in the father, and equally strong in this respect in the son;—and what is to be done? It is out of the question for the father to pay; and the existence of that very debt operates to prevent any arrangement between the father and the son on the question what is to be done for his wilful disobedience. Unless the worthy creditor will forgive the debt, which he cannot afford to do, and cannot well be asked to do, it seems to be a barrier in the way of reconciliation between the father and the son, which cannot be overcome. If, however, some friend of ample means, seeing the difficulty, and hoping that a generous act on his part might have a good effect on the young man himself—obviously in danger of being a spendthrift, and ruining himself by dissipation—should volunteer to pay the bill, *that* part of the difficulty would be removed, and the way would be entirely open for the negotiation to proceed between the father and the son. If the evidence of repentance were satisfactory, there would then be no other obstacle to his being forgiven—and it might even be hoped that good would come out of the whole affair—perhaps even more good in the end, than if it had not happened at all. At all events, it would be felt and owned by all parties, that the complete reconciliation consequent on repentance was made effective by the interposition of the friend, and that but for this, there was no way in which it could have occurred so well, if at all. Now it is conceivable that the act of the friend might be known only to the *father*, and that all that the son might know about it might be the mere declaration of the father that he would forgive him, and that *in some way* he had arranged the debt. Still, it would have a better moral influence on his mind that he should know all about it—especially if the friend had been himself at some considerable self-denial in doing what he had done.

Secondly, repentance is connected with pardon, because it is in close connexion with that which is designed to be an expression of the evil of the sin; with that which is done to repair the evil and the wrong. My regret and sorrow show my conviction that the price that was paid, or the suffering that was endured, to repair the wrong, was deserved by me. I express my regret mainly in view of that, and regard that as an *exponent* of the measure of my ill-desert. The ancient penitent led his victim to the altar, laid his hands on his head, confessed his sin, and the victim was slain—the penitent acknowledging that he deserved to die. We approach by faith the Great Victim that was slain for sin; confess our transgressions before him; lay our hands on his head; and confess that the stroke that descended on him was deserved by us; that *his* sufferings were an exponent of our guilt.

Thirdly, in such cases, repentance is connected with a promise, an assurance on the part of God, that he will forgive. We have seen in the former part of this discourse, that a wrong pertains to two parties, and that the action of each is necessary in order to forgiveness. The action of the offended and injured party in this case—God—consists in the arrangement which he has made in order that pardon may be consistent with his justice, and in the assurance that it may be obtained by repentance. The Christian religion is the only one that is characterized by a *promise* or *pledge* on the part of the Deity; and there is no promise of pardon made to men except in connexion with repentance, and none even then except in view of the great Sacrifice made on the cross. Every other kind of religion is conjecture—fancy—poetry—or, if it will be more agreeable to have it dignified with a higher term, the deduction of reason. No other system, however, makes pretensions to a *promise* of the forgiveness of sins. In the Christian scheme, repentance avails to procure pardon because God has himself made all the arrangements on his part to make pardon consistent and proper; and because, in view of these arrangements, he has expressed a willingness to receive the penitent again to his arms.

The conclusions to which we have been conducted by the arguments in this discourse are these:—

(1.) That there is no certainty in regard to the forgiveness of sins in Deism, in Infidelity, in Heathenism. There is no *evidence* that any promise is made in either of them that sins may be forgiven even on the bitterest repentance; there is no evidence that they are so pardoned. No voice from heaven announces the fact that they *may be* forgiven; no voice declares that they *are*. The weeping and broken-hearted penitent is greeted with no assurance that his sins are blotted out; nor can he prove that the paternal arms of the Deity are extended to embrace him. All is conjecture; all is uncertainty; all is destitute of that which we need when we feel that we have done wrong—for then our crushed and suffering hearts cry out for *evidence* that we may be pardoned; for some kind, consoling word that we may be, that we are forgiven.

(2.) The hopes of Infidelity are a violation of the principles which the infidel himself is obliged to hold. He must hold, he does hold, that repentance does not repair the evils which sin makes in the actual course of events; that it does not restore the property of the drunkard, or the gambler, or the spendthrift; that it does not give vigour and length of days to the frame enervated by dissipation; that it does not recall the murdered from the grave; that it does not bring back the hopes of youth wasted in folly; that it does not necessarily secure forgiveness from an injured parent or friend. And yet, in the very face of all these things, he holds that repentance, without anything else, is all that is necessary to turn away the wrath of God, and to arrest the evils caused by the violation of his law. He holds that a sigh, a groan—though on the death-bed—is all that is needful to make it certain that the long, black catalogue will be blotted out, and that his soul will be landed safe in heaven. *Why* does he hold this? What promise has he? Where does the analogy of nature sustain him? Where—where are the *facts* on which he builds such a hope?

(3.) Christianity is the only form of religion that addresses words of consolation to the broken-hearted penitent. It is the only religion that approaches man with a promise from heaven. It accords with the analogy of nature so far as to teach that man *must* be penitent if he would hope for pardon; and then, when nature leaves us as a guide, it takes up the matter and shows us how and why it may be done. It comes to man with an *assurance* that God now will accept the confessions and tears of the contrite in heart, and that the offender may be restored to favour.

It meets us just where we *want* to be met; just at the point where our embarrassment is greatest. We are weeping, suppose, over our sins. We have been led to reflect on them, and to see their evil, and to desire pardon; we are in that state of mind in which the Heathen are, and which the system of the Deist contemplates. But just here is the point of our greatest perplexity. We stand and weep. We have no doubt of the evil of our wrong-doing—of our ill-desert. We cast our eyes around to see what is the effect of repentance; to see what it does to repair evils done, or to arrest the effects of depravity. It does nothing such as we want it to do. It restores no wasted property or health; recalls none from the grave; heals no heart that is broken and crushed; raises up no form that has been bowed down by the ingratitude of a child; makes no hair black and glossy that has been whitened by grief. We stand perplexed, and ask, what evidence is there that repentance will arrest the progress of evil at all, and that it will stay the woes that we fear are coming upon us for our crimes? Just there—where we want it—Christianity approaches us. It tells us that it is true that in the ordinary course of events repentance does not *immediately* arrest the progress of evil, and repair the ravages which it has made; but that an arrangement has been effected by which this shall be *ultimately* done, and that the arrangement shall *commence* at once in regard to *us*, by the assurance of forgiveness, and by the imparting of peace to the soul—a pledge of the truth of its message. Now this is what we want. It meets us at the very point where we need it. It is a beam of light coming down where all is dark; it sheds peace on a soul where all was perplexity and trouble.

It is in accordance, then, with what he needs, when we exhort the penitent to go to God; to confess his sins; to look up to him through the Great Sacrifice made on the cross for man, for pardon. Such an exhortation meets the obvious wants of our nature, and should lead every guilty man at once up to God; and in executing my commission in addressing the guilty and the dying, I would earnestly entreat each one of you in view of what has been said, to go to the God against whom he has sinned, and confess his transgressions, and plead for mercy. "Repent, and be converted, *that your sins may be blotted out.*"

SERMON XXIII.

THE PHILOSOPHICAL NECESSITY OF REPENTANCE.

LUKE xiii. 3, 5.—"Except ye repent, ye shall all likewise perish."

THE reference in this declaration, twice repeated by the Saviour, is to those Galileans who were put to death by Pilate while offering their sacrifices, and to those persons in Jerusalem on whom the tower of Siloam fell. They were supposed, by those who brought their case before the Saviour, to have been punished in this way for their uncommon guilt. He corrects that misapprehension, and takes occasion to state to those who had addressed him, that unless *they* repented, they should all likewise perish. The meaning is, not that they would perish in the same manner, but that they would *as certainly perish.* There was no way of avoiding that which was fairly implied in the word *perish*, but by repentance. The Saviour has, therefore, in this passage, strongly affirmed the necessity of repentance in order that men may be saved from destruction.

In the two previous discourses I have considered the nature of repentance, and its relation to pardon in the Christian system. I enter now on a consideration of its necessity *as a condition of salvation.*

In the Scriptures there are two indispensable conditions of salvation prescribed—repentance and faith. The inquiry is at once suggested to a reflecting mind, why *these two things* are selected as the essential conditions of salvation, or why the question of eternal life and death is made to turn on the fact that they do or do not exist in the mind. Why has God selected these two states of mind, rather than any other two, as constituting the basis on which we are permitted to hope for his favour? The inquiry has more difficulty, perhaps, in reference to *faith* than to *repentance;* but still, no one can help asking why God has made *repentance* indispensable to salvation? Is the appointment arbitrary, or is it demanded by some law of our nature? Is it because he chose to specify *some* condition, though in a manner immaterial what,—like the selection of one tree out of many trees in Paradise,—as a test of man's obedience; or will repentance so meet the evils that are in the soul as to make it proper to demand this as a condition of salvation? Is it the mere appointment of *will* on the part of God, or is there something existing in our own hearts and lives to be affected by it, which makes it impossible that we should be saved, in any proper sense, without it?

In connexion with these questions of a philosophical character, there is another class of a somewhat more practical kind. Why, in reference to salvation, and as a condition of it, has God required us to exercise *sorrow of heart*, rather than insisted on a correct moral character as a condition? Would it not be more worthy of God to make eternal life depend on virtue and benevolence; on honesty and truth; on the faithful discharge of our duties in the family and in public life, than on any mere state of the feelings? And why is it that he requires the man of many years and many virtues, and the youth of great amiableness and purity, to renounce all confidence in these virtues, and all dependence on them, and to approach his throne weeping over the errors of a life? Can he require feigned sorrow? Can there be virtue in forced and affected tears? Can there be that which will commend us to Him when a man of uprightness, a man of honour, a man of truth, shall "bow down his head like a bulrush," and weep like the vilest sinner? Why has he made the path to heaven a path of sorrow at all? Why must we go there with the head bowed down with grief? Why has he made the road a *thorn-hedge*, and not planted it with roses? Are there no joyous emotions that might have been made the conditions of salvation? Is there nothing that would make the eye bright, and the heart cheerful, and the soul glad, that might have been selected, of at least equal value with pensiveness and a heavy heart, with melancholy and tears?

Such are some of the feelings which spring up in the minds of men when we come to urge on them the duty of repentance. My desire is, if possible, to meet those feelings, and to show that they are not well-founded. I shall aim to prove that the requisition of repentance is not arbitrary, but is based on the nature of things, and that a man MUST REPENT, or PERISH. I shall endeavour to vindicate the character of God, alike from his right as a Sovereign to make this a condition, and from the necessity which there is in the nature of things that we should exercise repentance if we would obtain his favour, or enjoy peace.

I. In the first place, *God has a right to appoint terms on which he will bestow his favours on his creatures.* I will endeavour to show you that he has this right.

(1.) It is a common right which *all* exercise when they have favours to confer on others. A charter for a college or a bank is thus conferred. A grant of land to an institution of learning is thus bestowed. A copyright of a book, or a patent for an invention in the arts, is thus secured. A right of way; a privilege to construct a bridge or a draw; a "permit" to build a house or a factory, is thus secured. The right of citizenship, or the freedom of a city, is thus conferred. All such favours are connected with *conditions* expressed or implied; and no one doubts that a government has the right to specify the conditions on which the favour may be enjoyed. It is inherent in the very fact, that we have that to confer which will be regarded as a *favour* or *boon* by others. The only thing to *guard* this, or to prevent its being oppressive, is to be found in the character of the government or of the individual who has the power of conferring the favour; and in the fact that the corporation or individual, on whom it is proposed to confer it, is under no obligation to accept it, if it is regarded as unjust; that is, if it is considered that there would be no advantage in accepting it on these terms.

(2.) God has actually dealt thus with his creatures in the bestowment of his favours. He has never relinquished the right to prescribe to men *in everything* on what terms his favours may be enjoyed. He has actually appointed conditions, by compliance with which alone his favour can be hoped for—conditions as clear as were ever prescribed in a charter for a college or a bank, or a patent of nobility made out by a sovereign to a feudal baron. Life, health, reputation, success in business, are all his gifts; and he has proffered them to men only on certain conditions, and those conditions are clearly specified. Heatlh, for illustration, is in all cases his bestowment; and he has an absolute right—a right which he is constantly exercising—to state to man on what conditions of temperance, prudence, care, and cleanliness it may be enjoyed; and if the man does not choose to comply with those terms, the blessing will be withheld. There is no way in which he can *originate* any other conditions on which the blessing may be secured, or by which he can induce God to depart from these terms in his case by special favour, and confer the gift by miracle. Life is his gift, and he has a right to say on what terms it may be possessed and enjoyed. Property is thus also his gift, and he has a right to say how it may be procured and retained. Heaven is his home, and he has a right to say on what terms man may be permitted to dwell there. It is his to bestow a harvest on the husbandman, and equally his to prescribe the conditions on which it may be done, and to *specify* as the condition that it shall be by industry, and by the cultivation of the earth, in the proper season, and in the proper manner. It is true that man has the power to reject the conditions—just as a company has power to reject a bank-charter; but it is equally true that if it is done, and the man prefers to spend the time of sowing and ingathering in idleness, the favour will be conferred in no other manner. The only appropriate question to be asked in the case is, whether God has *in fact* appointed anything as indispensable conditions of his favour. That settled, every question on the subject may be regarded as at rest.

(3.) These remarks are especially true in regard to an offender. He who violates a law, cuts himself off from any *claim* to favour under that law; and if he obtains any favour, it must be on such conditions as the one who is injured or wronged shall choose to prescribe. You have wronged a friend or a neighbour. It is clearly not *yours* now to prescribe the conditions on which he shall forgive the offence, and receive you to his favour, but *his*. A child violates your commands. Do you not feel that you have a right to prescribe the terms on which he may obtain forgiveness? Do you not feel that it is yours to bestow or withhold pardon as you please? You have a professed friend who has wronged *you*. The offence is undeniable; it is admitted. Do you not feel that you have a right to prescribe the terms on which he may enjoy your friendship again? And if you should require that he should express regret, and confess the wrong, and repair the evil as far as is in his power, would you think that he had a right to complain of you? And would you think it a sufficient answer to such a demand should he say, that such a requirement is arbitrary, and that you might have selected some easier conditions, and that you might have planted the path of return with flowers rather than with thorns? How obvious would be the answer, that it is as easy to make the *confession* as it was to do the *wrong*; that the one really injured in the case is *himself*, and not you; and that as to the *thorns* in the case, *he* planted them in the path, and not *you*.

The whole question, therefore, in regard to the necessity of repentance as a condition of salvation, might be left on this ground. We might come and say to men, that God has great favours to bestow on his creatures, but reserves the right to prescribe the conditions on which they may be received; or that as one whose law has been violated, he retains the right which all who are wronged claim, of specifying the conditions on which pardon may be obtained. But the object which I had particularly in view was not to show that he had a right to prescribe *some* condition of his favour, but to show why *repentance* is one of those conditions. Is there anything in the nature of the case which made it proper that *this* should be selected? This leads me to remark,

II. In the second place, *that repentance is in fact an indispensable condition to restoration to favour when one has done wrong.* It cannot be otherwise. When an offence is committed, when wrong is done, when a law has been violated, there is no way by which the forfeited favour can be regained in any case but by that which is implied in true repentance;—by a process involving all the elements of grief, regret, confession, confusion of face, and purpose to abandon the evil course, which are included in repentance toward God. The place from which the offender fell is never regained but by contrition; the path by which he must ascend to that lost height is a pathway of tears. If this be so, it will be seen that God, by requiring repentance as a condition of his returning favour, is acting in accordance with the great principles on which the world is in fact governed. That it *is* so, will, I trust, be made plain by a few simple illustrations. I shall vary the illustrations, though with some hazard of repetition, because I wish to show you that this is the way in which the affairs of this world are conducted.

Let us return again to the case of a father. Your child violates your law; offends you; is guilty of palpable disobedience. He is so old that he can be treated as a moral agent, and is capable of acting under a moral government. He has done much to forfeit your favour, and to incur your displeasure. He has become the companion of the dissipated and the vile; and with such associates has wasted the fruit of your toil. Towards that son you will cherish still the feelings of a father; but I may appeal to any such unhappy parent to say, whether he could admit him to the same degree of confidence and favour as before, without some evidence of repentance. You demand that he should express regret for his errors and follies; you require evidence, that will be satisfactory to you, that he does not intend to do the same thing again; you expect proof that he will be disposed by a virtuous life to repair, as far as possible, the injury that he has done your name and your honour as a father; and the moment you hear him sincerely say, "Father, I have sinned against heaven, and before thee, and am not worthy to be called thy son," that moment you are ready to go out, and to throw your arms round his neck, and to forgive him—AND NOT TILL THEN. You could not do it consistently with self-respect;

with the good of your own family; with the character which you mean to maintain as a father, *until then.* There is nothing else that can be a substitute for this. He may come back laden with "pearls and barbaric gold;" he may have become eminent in learning; he may have encircled his brow with laurels won in the field of battle,—but these cannot be a substitute for the confession and repentance which you demand as a father. If still proud, and insolent, and disrespectful to you, how *can* you lay your hand on his head and bestow on him a father's blessing?

Let us recur to another illustration. You had a friend. You thought him sincere. But he betrayed you; and in feeling, in property, and in character, you have been made to suffer by him. I ask any man, whether he can receive such a friend again to his bosom, and press him to his heart, without some evidence of regret for what he has done, and some proof that he will not do it again. You cannot do it. You cannot force your nature to do it. The sea might as well break over the iron-bound shore, or the river flow back and again climb up the mountain side down which it had leaped in cascades, as for you to do it. You will satisfy yourself in some way that he *regrets* what he has done, and that he intends not to do it again, or you can NEVER receive him with the confidence of a friend. Your nature, though in other respects you may be gentle and pliant as the osier, is as firm on this point as the everlasting hills, and is, in this respect, but the counterpart and the image of God, who does the same thing. Mind can never do otherwise. You cannot make it do otherwise. It would be worth nothing if it could do otherwise.

Let us take another illustration. It may be drawn from the case of one who has committed an offence against the community —the case of a man who has been guilty of theft, burglary, arson, or forgery. The whole community demands evidence that he has repented of his crime, and that he purposes to do so no more, before it will admit him again to its favour. If you go into his cell and find him alone on his knees before God confessing the sin; if you see evidence in him of regret and sorrow that the deed was done; if you believe that the reformation is entire and sincere, the community will receive him again to its bosom, and will forget and forgive the past, and he may rise again to public confidence, and to affluence and honour. But if none of these things are seen; if he spends the years of his sentence sullen, and hardened, and profane, and without one sigh or tear, he is never forgiven. He may have paid the penalty of the law, but he is not forgiven, and the community is not disposed to receive him to favour; and he goes forth to meet still the suspicions and frowns of an indignant world; to be watched with an eagle eye, and to be excluded all his life from the affections and confidence of mankind.

We will take another instance of the operation of this law. It is that of a man who has wasted his health and property by intemperance. He was once in prosperous circumstances; saw around him a happy family; was respected and beloved; enjoyed health, and was rising to honour and affluence. He yielded to temptation, and all was swept away. Peace fled from his dwelling, and his wife sits in poverty and tears, and his children are growing up in idleness and vice, and he himself is fast hastening to a drunkard's grave. Is there any way now by which health, and domestic peace, and property, and respectability can be regained? There is, if he has not gone too far—if he has not come too near the end of life. But how? By this course:—He will *reflect* on his sin and folly. He will feel deeply pained in view of the evil that he has done. He will lament the course of life which has driven comfort and peace from his dwelling. He will resolve to forsake the ways of sin, and will abandon for ever the intoxicating bowl. He will reform his life, and will become sober, industrious, and kind, will labour to pay his debts, and to establish his credit again; and, if he does these things, health will again revisit his frame, and peace his family, and his farm will again be fenced, and ploughed, and sown, and the rich harvest will again wave in his fields. But this is the very way in which God requires the sinner to come back to himself—the path of repentance. He requires him to reflect on the past; to feel that he has pursued a guilty course; to break off his transgressions, and to lead a different life. Why should it be thought more strange in religion than in the actual course of events?

The same is true, to take one more instance, in the case of a gambler. He has been led on by the arts of temptation till he has lost his all. He had received an inheritance from a wealthy father. Now it is entirely gone. From one step to another he has been drawn into temptation, till he is stripped of all, and is penniless, and is ready to give himself up to despair. Is there now any way by which he can emerge from this depth of woes, and become a man of respectability and of property again? There is one, and but one. It is a strait and a narrow path, like that which leads to heaven. He will *reflect* on the sin and folly of his course. He will feel pain and sorrow at the remembrance of that hour when he yielded to temptation. He will mourn in the bitterness of his soul over that sad day. He will resolve that he will never enter a gambling-room again; that he will seek to repair his fortune, not in that way, but in a better way; that he will devote his life to a course of steady industry and virtue; and if he will do all these things, he may regain the confidence of his fellow-men, and God will bestow on him wealth and respectability. But this is substantially the way in which a sinner is to return to God. This is repentance.

So in respect to indolence, vice, dissipation, crime in all forms. If men ever turn back the evils which result from these sins and follies; if they ever escape from the withering and blighting curse which pursues the wicked, it *must* be in connexion with repentance. If there is no evidence of repentance and reform, that withering and blighting influence will pursue the transgressor over sea and land, to the end of the world, and to the end of life. He can never escape the curse of violating the laws of heaven until he gives evidence of sincere sorrow for his offence. But the moment that is done, the avenger ceases to pursue him; his friends come again around him; he finds peace again in his own bosom; and the winds and the waves, the sunshine and the dew, the sky, the clouds, and the earth, man and his Maker, join to bless him.

III. My third general argument is, *that from the nature of the mind itself, when one has done wrong, there can be no security for permanent peace but by repentance and forgiveness.* I say *permanent* peace. I do not deny that temporary peace may be obtained. I do not deny that men may seem to be happy when wrong has been done. But the question now before us is, whether the guilty can find permanent and substantial happiness, happiness that may be relied on, and that may be made the basis of calculation in regard to the future, without all that is essentially involved in true repentance? Is not this the way which the God of nature has appointed by which the guilty mind is to obtain relief? Is not the certainty of this fact one of the means by which he designs to lead the sinner to the exercise of true repentance?

When a man has done wrong, one of the questions which must occupy his attention is, in what way he can be happy though he *has* done the wrong. How can he avoid the usual effects of guilt in the soul in producing trouble? He has wronged another in dealing with him; he has concealed the defects of an article in trade; he has made a false representation; he has made a wrong entry on his books; he has robbed his employer; he has forged his name to a check; he has left his father's house at night, and visited a scene of revelry and sin. One of the questions which the mind cannot practically evade in such cases is, how can this wrong be done, and yet the wrong-doer be calm and happy? And here is the question which is now before us. Can the mind find permanent happiness without repentance? Or is that the way which nature has provided in order to obtain permanent peace?

Now, I need not pause to detail the ways which men adopt in these cases. They are almost as numerous as the individuals concerned, and as the offences which they commit. There is, of course, in all cases, an attempt to *conceal* the offence, and this calls into requisition all the varied talent and skill with which the guilty may be endowed, and is often done with consummate art. In other cases, there is an effort made to turn away the mind from the recollection of the offence; and thousands of our sins of word, and thought, and deed, are in fact forgotten. In other cases there is an attempt to satisfy the mind, by a process of reasoning, of the correctness of what has been done; and in some sophistical and Jesuitical maxim the mind finds temporary peace. In some cases the conscience becomes gradually insensible, until it is "seared as with a hot iron." In other cases there is an attempt to obliterate the natural marks of guilt in the frame, until the brow is made brass, and a deed of depravity may be performed with an eye and a hand as steady as when one performs the noblest deed of virtue.

Yet there is defect in all this. It does not answer the purpose. It does not meet the demands of the human mind in the case. It does not secure permanent peace. For it furnishes no security in those respects in which security is desirable. (*a*) It furnishes no guarantee that the mind will *remain* in this condition in which you succeed in putting it. What is your security that the offence will always be forgotten by yourself? What is your security that your conscience will always remain untroubled? What is your security that the false and pernicious reasoning will always appear as plausible as it does now? What is your security that some secret power may not undertake a work with your soul; that your memory may not do its office better than you intend; that in the dark night, or when far away, or when on a bed of sickness, you will not think of what you will wish not to think of? (*b*) But again: this furnishes no assurance that the sin will not be detected, and that all your attempts to conceal it may not be brushed away by some invisible hand, like cobwebs. What are bolts, and locks, and false entries, and all the arts of concealment, when *God* means that a thing shall be revealed? What murderer was ever safe when *He* meant that he should be known? What act of fraud in a bank; what scheme of iniquity in robbing poor pensioners of their due; what well-executed forgery; what crime of any kind, was ever concealed when *He* meant that it should be "proclaimed on the house-tops?" In how many ways may an offence be divulged? What a trifle may be a clue to the whole development? No man ever does a wrong thing, however artful may be his attempts to conceal it, who is not apprehensive that it may be revealed. Some eye may have witnessed it, of which he knew nothing; some combination of circumstances may disclose it which he cannot control; some accomplice may prove faithless, though sworn to secrecy; some "bird of the air" may tell a tale that you would not have told in the ear of another for worlds:—and the way to make the mind peaceful, when wrong has been done, is not by *concealment*.

The way which God and nature prescribes is by repentance and confession. For, (1,) there is relief *in repentance itself*. Sorrow for the wrong is that which nature seeks and struggles for; and you do wrong to your own soul when you refuse to indulge it. Every one knows that there is *relief* in repentance—that the mind throws off a burden when the eyes run down with tears on account of wrong which has been done; that that is what nature demands, and *must have*, before the soul is happy. We have all been children. Now, when we had done wrong to a parent or a playmate, did not all the better feelings of our nature urge us to go and confess the wrong? And what violence did we do to all our gentle and pure sensibilities when under the influence of pride and false notions of boyish honour we refused to do it, and braced ourselves in an effort to find happiness without it! But, (2,) there is relief in the act of *confession*, and in *forgiveness*. The very act of confession furnishes relief to a guilty mind; and when we hear the word *forgiveness*, it diffuses peace through the soul. It was with a knowledge of the deepest principles of our nature that the Saviour said to the weeping, guilty female, who washed his feet with her tears, "Thy faith hath saved thee; *go in peace*." Go in peace she would—for in the tears she poured forth on the feet of the Saviour, and in the words of forgiveness which fell from his lips, she had found relief for her guilty conscience—a peace which nothing thenceforward could disturb.

IV. My fourth general argument is, *that in a return to God from a course of sin, repentance would follow as a matter of course, even if it were not prescribed and demanded as a condition of favour*. It would be impossible to come back from a course of depravity to the ways of virtue,—to form and express the intention to lead a virtuous and holy life,—without experiencing in fact all that is essentially involved in repentance. If this be so, then the requirement of repentance as a condition of salvation is not an arbitrary demand, but is in fact a mere statement of what *must* occur in all cases in order that a sinner may be saved.

A return to God is a restoration to love—to obedience—to a purpose to serve him. When one has sinned, can this return occur without the exercise of *sorrow* for the errors and follies of the past? Can it occur without regret more or less poignant that God was forsaken? Can it occur without the formation of a purpose to do so no more? To ask these questions is to answer them—for the answer is at hand in every mind. When an alienated being comes back to God, it will be only by repentance. He will, he must feel regret that his past life has been spent in estrangement from his Maker. He will look with deep feeling on the many mercies his Maker has conferred on him; and with amazement on the fact that to this moment he has abused them all. No man ever yet passed from hatred to love; from alienation to friendship; from disobedience to obedience; from dishonesty to uprightness; from intemperance to temperance; from dissipation to soberness of life,—without experiencing regret, remorse, and sorrow at his former course of life, and without passing through a process similar to that which God requires of the returning sinner. No man ever did or can return to that God from whom he has been alienated, without feeling and expressing regret that he has wandered, and without a purpose to do so no more. At the remembrance of his abused mercies; at a view of the goodness which has kept him in all his wanderings, and especially of the mercy which sought him by the gift of a Saviour, he must feel and he must weep; and he cannot return without bitter regrets that he has abused so much love, and slighted so much mercy, and wasted so large a part of his season of probation. Returning love, and a sense of God's goodness, must be attended with sorrow of heart that he ever transgressed, and with a resolution to do so no more:—and this is repentance. This *must* have occurred in the case of every one who returns to God and virtue; and the demand for repentance, therefore, is not arbitrary, but is laid deep in the laws of the human mind.

If this train of remarks be well-founded, we are conducted to the conclusion which we sought—*the philosophical reason why repentance is required in order to salvation.*

(1.) It follows from the view which has been taken, that in its primary demand the Christian religion has consulted the laws of our nature, and shown respect to those laws. Its Author has shown that the laws of the mind are understood, and has based his demands on a knowledge of those laws. A system of religion adapted to the condition of sinners *could not* have been originated which did not demand repentance, nor is it possible for man now to conceive of any plan by which a sinner could be brought to obedience, and raised up to heaven, without passing substantially through the process demanded by repentance.

(2.) It follows that if men refuse to repent, they are sinning against a great law of their nature, as well as against a positive law of religion. They are constantly making war on themselves—on all the finer feelings of their souls—on all that is noble and generous in the human heart—when they refuse ingenuously to acknowledge the wrong; when they attempt to cloak it; when they resolve to persevere in a career of depravity; when they are unwilling to go and make confession to their Father in heaven. Their whole nature prompts them to do this. It is a course whose propriety is engraven as with the pen of a diamond on their own souls. It is the way which nature prescribes for our relief when we have done wrong. We are to seek it by confession, by tears, and by imploring pardon; and until this is done, there is a want in our soul which is never met—an unchangeable law of our nature which is never gratified. The only solid and permanent peace which a sinner can ever find is when weeping over his transgressions at the feet of his offended God and Saviour, and when *He* smiles benignantly on him, and says, "Son, be of good cheer: thy sins are forgiven thee."

(3.) It follows from the train of thought which we have been considering, that if the sinner will not repent HE MUST PERISH. This is the thought which is suggested in the text:—"Except ye repent, ye shall all likewise perish." It cannot be otherwise. There is no way conceivable by which a sinner can be saved but by repentance. It is a law of our nature that it *must be so*—for there are elements in our souls, which, if we have sinned and are impenitent, *must* sooner or later produce misery, and *must* work out our ruin. No man can have any *security* of happiness who has done wrong, but has done nothing, and will do nothing, to confess and to repair the wrong. No child is happy in these circumstances; no man is; no creature of a moral government can be. God holds a mysterious but absolute power over the soul; and he has only to arrange matters so as to drag your secret sins from their hiding-places, and array them before your minds, to create within you all the elements of hell. There is enough in every man's heart and life to make him miserable for ever and ever, if it be allowed to take its course according to the laws of our nature, and to carry its full desolations through the soul. When a sinner "perishes" it will not be an arbitrary thing; but it will be because, if he will not repent, it cannot be avoided. Then, sinner, in connexion with humble, penitent confession your soul may find permanent and eternal peace; if that is withheld, such peace can never visit your bosom. May God teach you the way of happiness and salvation. Amen.

SERMON XXIV.

THE FOUNDATION OF THE COMMAND TO REPENT LAID IN THE CHARACTER OF MAN.

Acts xvii. 30.—"God now commandeth all men everywhere to repent."

A command addressed to all men requiring repentance, supposes that all men are personally guilty, or that there is some wrong-doing in the life of each individual, which makes it proper that he should be required to repent. God does not demand hypocritical or affected sorrow. He does not require his creatures to repent of that which is right; or which could in no sense have been avoided; or which has been done by another. There can be no repentance where there has been no wrong—no guilt.

The inquiry before us now is, whether it is true that every man is guilty in such a sense that it is proper to command him to repent. This is everywhere assumed in the Bible; it is assumed in my text; it is assumed by every one who preaches the gospel, whether in a Christian or a heathen land. Yet the command is not extensively obeyed. It is addressed to thousands who give themselves no trouble about it, and who do not feel *themselves* particularly called upon to obey it. The *reasons* why they do not may be many; but among them it may be presumed that one of the most prominent is that which I propose now to notice—that they do not suppose themselves to be *guilty* in any such sense as to make the command in their case proper.

In prosecuting, therefore, the general subject of repentance, I propose to call your attention to the simple inquiry, whether it is true that every one is guilty in such a sense that it is needful to call on him to repent? In order to bring this fairly before you, I shall have to consider two points:—I. The estimate which men form of themselves on this question; and, II. What there is in their character and lives which makes it proper to call on them to repent.

I. *The estimate which men form on the question of their own guilt.* When we call on men to repent, we are at once met with certain classes of feelings in regard to their own lives and conduct, which it is necessary to remove or correct before the command will be felt to have any force. A few feel and admit that they are sinners,—such sinners as to make the command appropriate in regard to themselves. But this is by no means the feeling of the mass of those to whom the command of repentance comes; and before that command can be seen to have any weight, it is necessary that there should be produced in their minds in some way the conviction that they are guilty. In order to do as much justice as possible at the same time to the character of my readers and to my subject, I shall, under this head, attempt to describe the views which are commonly entertained on this point, and shall concede what I deem to be correct in regard to those views. The gospel of Christ does not require me to do injustice to any man.

The views, then, which are entertained may be described as comprising the following particulars:—

(1.) You allege that you are not gross and open sinners. You are not idolaters. You are not profane. You are not scoffers. You are not inebriates. You are not debased by sensuality. Many of the heathen were; many in every community now are; and you would readily concede that it would in every way be proper to call on them to repent. It was eminently so in the times of the apostles; it is so now in heathen lands; it is so among the debased and sunken portions of every community. But this, it would be alleged, is not the character of the mass of those to whom the gospel is preached.

This, I admit, is true. No one can deny it; no one should desire to deny it. In declaring the gospel, I am not required or expected to do injustice to any man, or class of men. I am to withhold from none of them the fair praise for what they have and are. I am not to attempt to group and blend all men together, and to represent them as in all respects on the same level. I am to do wrong to no man's amiableness, or integrity, or purity of morals. If I meet a young man amiable and upright, like him whom the Saviour met, I am to "love" him as he did, and not to attempt to rank him with Judas Iscariot; if I see a pure and virtuous female, I am not to represent her as a Mary Magdalene. I am neither to maintain that one man is as bad as another; nor that any man is as bad as he can be;—and if I were required to do this, I should despair of bringing men to repentance.

(2.) You allege that you are not *habitually* a wrong-doer. You aim to do right. You mean faithfully to discharge your duties. Your purpose is to be honest, upright, true. You do not mean to do wrong to your wife, or children, or neighbour, or client, or customer, or the stranger that comes into your dwelling, or that you may meet in your travels. You mean to pay your debts; you mean to tell the truth; you mean to be faithful to your promises. If you fail in regard to any of these things, it is not by design, but it is to be traced to infirmity, inadvertence, want of full information, or circumstances wholly beyond your control. You are conscious to yourself that in the main this *has* been your character. If, in the course of a life, we will now suppose a life somewhat protracted, you have ever been guilty of a falsehood, it has been perhaps but in a single instance—an instance which you have a thousand times regretted—while the *characteristic* by which you are best known is that of a man of unimpeachable veracity. If in the course of such a long life, you have ever done injustice to another man in dealing with him; have taken advantage of him by your superior knowledge; have wronged him out of what was due to him; have overreached him in a bargain,—it has been in perhaps not more than a single instance, when you were younger, and you have a thousand times regretted it; and your prevailing character has been that of an honest man. If, at some time in your life, you have done wrong to the character of another, it was when you were misinformed, or were excited by passion, or were led to suppose that he had injured you. Upon calmer reflection you have a thousand times regretted it, and if he is dead you feel the bitterest compunction that it was done; if he is living, there is nothing which you would not do for his welfare—and your prevailing character has not been that of a calumniator and slanderer.—If at times you have indulged in passion, under sudden provocation, or a nervous temperament, or when off your guard, you have as often regretted it, and you are conscious that it is not your habitual *aim* to do so, and that your deliberate purpose is not to wound the feelings or pain the heart of another. You cherish the hope also that the world will do you justice in this, and that in spite of these sudden and temporary ebullitions you will be regarded as having a kind heart, and as ready to do good to others.

Now I admit that there is much truth also in all this. I admit it because it is undeniable, and because religion does not require us to do injustice to the character of any human being. I think that those of us who trust that we *have* exercised true repentance, deep as may be our conviction of the depravity of the heart, believe this to have been true in regard to ourselves. I think that we can all look over our lives and see that the instances were very few and far between in which we *intentionally* did a wrong thing;—in which we were guilty of falsehood, or fraud, or dishonesty. This will meet the eye of many such men—men who from day to day are not conscious of an intention to do a wrong thing; who are conscious that they would not cheat a man for the brightest diadem that ever a monarch wore, and who go into their office, into the bank, into their counting-rooms, *intending* to do right to all men, and who, when Saturday night comes, whatever sense of imperfection they may have, lie down on their pillows with the reflection, that through the week they have not done *intentional* wrong to any human being.

In what sense, then, you would ask me, are such men called on to repent? Why is the command addressed to all human beings? What is there in their character and life that makes it proper in their case? These are fair questions. They are questions which men cannot help asking. They are questions which the ministers of religion are bound to answer.

II. My second object was to show *what there is in the character and lives of such men which makes it proper to call on them to repent.* My aim will be to state that only of which you are conscious, and to show that there is that in the case of every one which makes it proper for his Maker, through the gospel, to address him in the language of the text.

(1.) I begin with this thought, that with all your conscious integrity and purity, there has not been a day of your life in which you would be willing to have all your thoughts, and plans, and desires, and imaginings for that day made known to the world, or even to your best friends. I mean that you would not be willing to have all these things written down by some attending amanuensis, or by some invention resembling the magnetic telegraph, and made known instantly to those who are around you. In the purest day of your life, you would not be willing to have all these thoughts written in letters of light in some conspicuous place, to be read by every passer-by. The very thoughts which you have had this day, you would not have thus permanently transcribed for all the diamonds of the East. If you were certain that this were to be done, if you should see the mysterious finger coming forth and *beginning* to make the record, shame would *begin* at the same time to cover you, and you would rush from the spot, or cover your face with your hands, and hide it in confusion.

Now there are three reasons why a man would not wish such a revelation of his secret thoughts and feelings. One is, because he has plans which, though not wrong or improper in themselves, he would not desire others to know. They are his plans of business, of study, of inventions; his views of a case in law entrusted to him; his methods of practising the healing art; his tact in his calling, which he would not desire to have every one know, for his living may depend on it, though he may feel that if it *were* known it would be in a high degree creditable to himself. But every man has his own secrets; and they constitute no inconsiderable part of his *capital* in business. At any rate, many of his prospects would be blasted if his views and plans were in the possession of others. A second reason is, that many of our thoughts and imaginings are merely foolish, and trifling, and unprofitable —and we could not desire others to know that our minds *could* be employed on so barren subjects, and in a way so little befitting our dignity and character. We allow the imagination to roam quite at its ease; we amuse ourselves in building up splendid castles, and then in seeing them tumble into gorgeous fragments or vanish:—as children set up bricks, or build houses of blocks to see them fall over; or as the Arabian, in his tales, paints a gorgeous vision, and sees it vanish away. Now we should not feel that in this employment of the mind there was absolutely anything corrupting or wrong; but we should not care to have the world suppose that we are quite so unprofitably employed as we are. There is yet a third reason, of a much more serious character, and extending to many more things. We should be unwilling that our plans and thoughts should be disclosed, because we feel that they are *wrong*. They are the fruits of an evil, a proud, a vain, a sensual, an envious, a corrupt heart. We are dwelling with delight on some sinful pleasures in the past, and trying to live them over again, when they should be forgotten:—thus polluting the mind as much by the memory as by the act. We are dwelling in imagination on some forbidden pleasures, and arranging them to our fancy:—thus corrupting the soul as really as the act itself would do. We are indulging in hateful pride of beauty, or dress, or attainments, or wealth; and suffering a whole deluge of evil thoughts to come in upon the soul in regard to our superiority over others. We are looking on the dress, or the person, or the house, or the equipage of another with envious feelings, and allowing the mind to be filled with *hatred* of them on account of their possessions, and with repining and dissatisfaction at our own lot. We are coveting, it may be, our "neighbour's house, or his wife, or his manservant, or his maidservant, or his ox, or his ass," or something else that is our neighbour's. We are remembering the injury that some one has done us, and thinking how sweet revenge would be. We are maturing some plan for the indulgence of a guilty passion, and are increasingly impatient as it begins to ripen towards its accomplishment. We are running over trains of thought which we know are not pure, and which we feel are polluting—for "the very passage of an impure thought through the mind leaves pollution behind it:"—and if a cherub should approach us in our reverie in the most sylph-like form, and on wings as pure as the northern snows, and with the gentlest whisper of the zephyr, should breathe into our ears that it was *known*—how would it startle us from our reverie, and cover us with confusion! It is probable that either in respect to the desires and plans of the present, or the doings of the past, it would be in the power of such a messenger, by the gentlest whisper in the ear, "*That thing is known!*" to startle us from our seats in wild confusion and horror.

How, then, shall we be pure before God? For, "if our heart condemn us, God is greater than our heart, and knoweth all things," 1 John iii. 20. "Unto me," said an ancient sage, "an oracle was secretly imparted, and mine ear caught a gentle whisper of it. In distracted thoughts among the visions of the night, when profound sleep falleth on men, fear came upon me, and trembling, which made all my bones to quake. Then a spirit glided along before my face; the hair of my flesh stood on end:—it stood, but its form I could not discern; a spectre was before mine eyes:—there was silence, and I heard a voice—Shall feeble man be more just than God? Shall man be more pure than his Maker? Behold, in his servants he putteth no confidence, and his angels he chargeth with folly: how much more true is this of those who dwell in houses of clay, whose foundation is in the dust, and who are crushed before the moth-worm?" Job iv. 12—19.

But, if there are thoughts within us all that could not bear such a revelation, then for these thoughts it is proper to call on the sinner to repent. Say, sinner, if you can conceive that Gabriel should cherish for one day in heaven such thoughts as are the habitual inmates of your bosom, would not all heaven demand the expulsion of the archangel, or his lowly contrition before the throne?

(2.) I refer, secondly, to the sins of which you are conscious in your past life. I have my eye on the concessions which I have made, and shall not depart from them. But with these full in view, it is right to look at the past life, and see whether sins have not been committed which make the demand for repentance proper. There are two classes of these sins to be taken into the account: those which you have carried out and accomplished; and those which you *would* have committed but for the want of opportunity, and by some providential restraint.

(*a*) The first class is made up of those which you *have* committed, or which have been accomplished by some open deed. These may seem to be few in number, but in the aggregate they may not be so few. The question is not how many times you have done *one* wrong thing, but how many times you have done *all* wrong things. It is not exactly whether you have been guilty of one falsehood or more ; of one act of dishonesty or more ; but it is, how many wrong things are fairly chargeable on you when they are *all reckoned together*—when *all* your acts of dishonesty, and passion, and deceit, and prevarication, and unkindness, and disobedience, and improper words, and pride and vanity, and corrupt imaginings, and envy, and jealousy, and every other evil thing remembered and forgotten, are taken together. For many of your sins are forgotten by you, though remembered by Him who has uttered the command in the text. But if such an inventory were taken of our lives, what a catalogue might be made out against us! Who would be willing to be summoned to the bar of his Maker in a strict and impartial trial of all that he has done on all subjects, and at all times, that he has known to be wrong? In such an honest catalogue, if drawn out before our eyes, it may be that we who think ourselves *most* virtuous, would be so overwhelmed that we should see that shame and confusion of face become us.

(*b*) But there is another aspect of the point before us. The sins which we have designed or devised, and which we should have committed, if we had had the opportunity, or if we had not been restrained by some invisible influence, or if we had not been thwarted in the midst of what seemed to promise a successful prosecution of our plans, ought to be taken into the account. For we are answerable before God, not only for what we *have* actually done, but for what we *desired* to do, and what we would have done if we had not been prevented. When a man levels a rifle at another with an intent to murder him, the act is not changed to innocence if the weapon misses fire, or if some one strikes it from his hand, or if God interposes and makes his arm unsteady by fear, or powerless by paralysis. When you laid your plan to defraud a creditor, the guilt is not washed away because the laws are so made that you could not evade them. When you contemplated and desired to lead the innocent astray, you are not rendered guiltless because God in some way interposed and saved your intended victim and a circle of friends from the agony of a broken heart. The grand question is, what has been your *desire*, your aim, your purpose, your wish. For these things you are to answer before God; and when a man looks honestly over his life, and reflects on what he has *wished* to do, and *would have* done, but for some restraint of Providence, who can say that he has no occasion for repentance? Grateful he will be, if he has any just views, that God restrained him from the deep disgrace of the outward act; but he must settle with God yet for the internal plan and desire from the execution of which God so mercifully restrained him.

(*c*) There is still another aspect of the point before us. Who can tell what any of us would have been, but for some steady and constant restraint? Others have fallen into deep depravity; why have we not done it? They have wrecked character, and hope, and happiness; what is the lesson which this fact should teach us about ourselves? Our eyes have seen distinguished clergymen in different denominations fall into gross and open sin; officers in banks and custom-houses, and high public functionaries abuse their trust, and ruin their character; merchants yield to the power of temptation, and ruin themselves and their families. As we heard this, we became alarmed, and trembled for ourselves. We asked, if such men fall, what confidence can we put in other men; what confidence in ourselves? Why did we allow it to come back upon our own souls, and fill us with self-distrust? Because we knew and felt that there was that within us which, placed in the same circumstances, would, for aught that we could see, lead to the same result. Then we asked, to what we owed our preservation, and what we should have been if we had been left in a similar manner? Then we felt that there was a deep foundation of evil in our souls—in the souls of all; and that all that is needful for its development is to throw man into circumstances of temptation without restraint. I admit that the primary effect of this, when others fall, should be to make us *grateful* to God that *we* have been preserved, but it should also show us what is in our own hearts. No virtuous man ever yet witnessed the fall of another who did not feel humbled himself, and who did not feel that there was in his own heart a deep foundation of evil.

The truth is, we owe much more of our virtues to external circumstances—to Providential restraints—to secret checks from an invisible cause—than we are in our pride willing to acknowledge. But how much credit should a man take to himself for these things? Who can tell what he would have been but for those restraints, and if he had had his birth in another land, or in different circumstances? And why should not a man, in his estimate of his own character before God, think of himself not merely as he *is*, but as he would have been without restraint? Why, when he contemplates his virtue and integrity, with the guards and checks which are thrown around him, should he not think of what he might have been, and would have been, *but* for these guards and checks?

If these are just principles, we can see proper foundation for the call to repentance and humiliation before God. Our open deeds of evil scattered along through life, and many of them forgotten; our plans of evil which we formed and cherished, from the accomplishment of which we were providentially prevented; our conscious weakness of principle, which would have made us what others have been if there had been no restraint on us,—all these things show us how we are estimated by Him who knows all things, and who sees all the secrets of the heart, and show us one of the reasons *why* it is that he has called on all men everywhere to repent.

(3.) I refer, thirdly, to your treatment of your Maker. You have been careful in respect to your conduct towards your fellow-men, but no one can deny that our deportment towards God is of much more importance in estimating our own character than our treatment of a fellow-creature. It is mainly, I need hardly remind you, on account of our treatment of himself that he calls on us to exercise repentance—for all sin and wrong ultimately terminate on him.

Now what has been your treatment of your God and Saviour? Has your deportment towards him been such as to satisfy your own conscience; such as to meet his approval? Or has it been such as to make it proper for him to call on you to exercise true repentance; to feel and express regret and sorrow?

I by no means intend to say that the feelings of those for whom I write, and whom I would call to repentance, have been alike; or that any general description would accurately represent them all. But the following specifications, I apprehend, will find a counterpart in the bosoms of most of those whom I thus address, and will be recognised as an accurate account of the course of life of which they are conscious:—

(*a*) You have *neglected* God. You have not lived as if there were a God; you have not rendered to him the homage which is his due. In many cases this neglect has been entire; has been long-continued—perhaps has lasted through a long life. You are not in the habit of praying to him—of acknowledging him in your closet, your family, your plans of life. There has been nothing in your life which has been a proper recognition of his existence and his claims; of the fact that he is your Creator, and that you are dependent on him, and that you sustain any relation to him whatever. Suppose you had neglected a wife, a mother, a father, a child in this manner! What a *wrong* is often done by mere *neglect!* Yet there is no one to whom men sustain important relations who is so much neglected as God.

(*b*) You have *withheld* your affections from *Him*, and transferred them to others. You have loved the creature more than the Creator. You have given that place in your affections, which was due to him, to gold, or pleasure, or honour; to your child, or to your houses and lands. Your supreme love you have fixed not on God, but on these objects; and your strong attachment for *them* has displaced *Him* from the heart. But is there no *wrong* in thus transferring your affections? Suppose you were to transfer to another the affections due to a wife,—is there no wrong done? Is there less when the affections are *all* withheld from God, and concentrated on some one other object, or distributed among a thousand?

(*c*) You have neglected the Bible. There may be among you some who have never read it through in their lives; some who never read the half of it; some who never read twenty chapters in it; some who are in no regular habit of reading it; some who have not looked into it for years. But suppose this Book to be a real revelation from heaven; to contain the true law of God; to disclose the true plan of salvation; to have been given and preserved with great care and interest on the part of God; and to be full of the wisdom in counsel which man needs,—is there no wrong done to him by neglecting it? Hear a parable. A young man embarked for a distant land. He was an only son, greatly beloved by his father. He was young, and inexperienced, and was going among strangers, and was likely to be thrown into circumstances where he would need a counsellor. The father had himself been over all those lands; had encountered all those dangers; and he knew well what kind of instructions would be most useful there. With great pains he sat down and *wrote out* such counsels as became a father in such circumstances, and gave them to his son. The son, confident of his own wisdom, and regardless of his father, resolved to throw himself on his own resources, and coolly folded up the instructions and laid them away at the bottom of his trunk—and never read them. When out of his sight he threw them into the deep, and saw them no more. Was no wrong done to that father? Would he have no occasion to regard himself as treated with neglect and scorn?

(*d*) You have violated his Sabbath. He asked of you to devote the one-seventh portion of your time wholly to him; the remainder he gave to you, under a proper recognition of himself, to pursue your worldly plans. That was the time he gave you to plough your fields, and to do your trading, and to write your letters, and to perform your travelling, and to accomplish your secular reading. But the one portion—the seventh—he deemed not more than a suitable part of your time for the proper recognition of himself in the world, and for securing those spiritual influences on the soul indispensable for your own best good. You took *all* the time to yourself. You worked hard all through the week, filling the mind with worldliness, and then took "the Lord's day" to do up a great number of miscellaneous items that could not be brought into the week, or that the customs of society would not allow you to do. You read novels and newspapers; you wrote letters and adjusted your accounts; you indulged the worldly *thinking* which you could not find time for in the week; you made out briefs, and arranged the testimony in a case preparatory for the morrow; you lounged; you slept; you went abroad for recreation. Is there no wrong in this? "Will a man," says the prophet, "ROB GOD?" There is indeed no wrong on the supposition that the Sabbath is to be like all the other days of the week. But suppose it is not. Suppose there is some meaning and binding force in these words, "Remember the Sabbath day to keep it holy;" and in the declaration that it belongs to "the Lord thy God," and that "in it thou shalt not do any work." May there not be a robbery of *time* as well as money? And may not your Maker be robbed as well as man?

(*e*) You have cherished hard thoughts of God. You have thought that his character was unlovely. You have thought that his laws were stern and severe. You have thought that he has dealt hardly with you when he has taken away your property, your health, or your child. You have thought that he was partial in saving others, and not saving you. You have complained in your spirit that you were to die, and to be judged; and that you were exposed to his endless wrath. Is there no wrong in this? Suppose your child thought thus of you—what would you think of him? Would it be agreeable to you that he should entertain these thoughts of a father?

This catalogue might be indefinitely extended, but I have said enough for my purpose. If these things are so,—if it is true that we have all guilty thoughts and feelings which we would not have disclosed before the world; if we are conscious of many acts of criminality in the past, and admit that there are many more which we may have forgotten, and would have been many more if we had not been restrained; and if it is true that we have been guilty of long-continued wrongs against our Maker,—then the position which was laid down may be regarded as demonstrated, that it is right for God to call on every man to exercise true repentance.

I add but one other remark in conclusion. These sins and wrongs with which vou are chargeable—secret and open, remembered and forgotten—*must in some way be disposed of.* They must either be repented of and forgiven, or they must be recalled to your remembrance hereafter, and enter into the account when you are judged. It is impossible but that they should be noticed in some proper way by your Maker. If they are forgiven, if they are blotted from his book, that ends the matter. But if they are not, they must come into judgment. And who could bear this revelation? Who is there that would not turn pale, and tremble, and call on the rocks and mountains to cover him, if he knew that all that he has ever thought, and said, and done, were about to be disclosed to assembled worlds?

SERMON XXV.

THE EVIDENCES OF TRUE REPENTANCE.

2 Cor. vii. 9—11.—"Now I rejoice, not that ye were made sorry, but that ye sorrowed to repentance; for ye were made sorry after a godly sort, that ye might receive damage by us in nothing. For godly sorrow worketh repentance to salvation not to be repented of; but the sorrow of the world worketh death. For behold this selfsame thing, that ye sorrowed after a godly sort, what carefulness it wrought in you, yea, what clearing of yourselves, yea, what indignation, yea, what fear, yea, what vehement desire, yea, what zeal, yea, what revenge! In all things ye have approved yourselves to be clear in this matter."

This was an instance of genuine repentance, and the things here enumerated are characteristics of true repentance. The case referred to was one in which manifest wrong had been done by the church at Corinth, 1 Cor. v. Paul had written to them respecting the wrong, enjoining on them to take the speediest measures to put it away. This letter had had all the effect which he wished. They had seen the error; they were deeply grieved and pained on account of it; they felt the force of the reproofs of the apostle; and the sorrow which they experienced was such as God approved, and such as was fitted to work salvation. There was deep distress of mind—evinced in their "sorrowing after a godly sort;" there was "carefulness,"—or diligence, effort, forwardness in removing the evil; there was a "clearing of themselves,"—not an apology for the sin, but a desire to state all the mitigating circumstances of the case, and to show that the church was not disposed to be the defender of evil; there was "indignation,"—indignation against the sin, and a cordial hatred of it; there was "fear,"—fear lest the thing should be continued or repeated—a state of mind anxious that the whole evil might be corrected, and that no vestige of it should remain among them; there was "vehement desire,"—a fervent wish to remove all cause of complaint; there was "zeal,"—zeal in putting away the sin, and in producing a reformation; there was "revenge"—that is, they immediately set about the work of punishing the offender. This sorrow, and ardour, and earnestness, and promptness, the apostle regarded as good evidence of the genuineness of their repentance; as a specimen of that "godly sorrow which worketh repentance unto salvation not to be repented of."

The subject which will now be considered is, *the evidences of true repentance*. The inquiry is, What are the evidences of true repentance? What distinguishes true repentance from false? How may we satisfy ourselves that we have truly repented of our sins?

The characteristics of repentance may be arranged under three heads, or three things seem necessary to the *full* and *complete* proof of true repentance. They are these:—the internal feeling of *regret* or *sorrow* which is experienced in view of sin; the *purpose* deliberately formed in the mind to abandon it; and the actual *forsaking* of the evil. I say these are necessary to the *full* and *complete* evidencing of real repentance. It is true that there may be circumstances where the first alone, or the first and second combined, would be indicative of genuine repentance, but there might be no opportunity to *test* them, and the three are necessary to furnish evidence that shall be of the highest kind, or that shall be satisfactory in the highest degree. I propose to illustrate these in their order.

I. The first which I specify is, *the internal feeling;* the regret for the wrong; the sorrow of heart which is experienced. This, of course, will be known only to the individual, except so far as he chooses to make others acquainted with it.

I do not say that mere regret or sorrow, of itself, is *full* evidence of repentance, for it may not be the right kind of sorrow—it may not be such as would bear the application of a test—it may not be permanent in its influence; but regret, or sorrow, enters *always* into true repentance. It results from the laws of the mind that where a wrong which we have done is contemplated in a proper manner, it should produce regret and pain. It enters into the meaning of all the words by which we are accustomed to express repentance. Thus in the text and context, the apostle says that the letter which he had sent to the Corinthians had made them "*sorry* though it were but for a season;" he says that they "sorrowed to repentance;" he speaks of their "mourning;" he speaks of their "sorrowing after a godly sort." There may, indeed, be great diversity in the depth, and pungency, and duration, and external expressions of sorrow experienced by true penitents. This diversity arises much from a difference of temperament; from the previous character; from the extent and aggravation of sin; and, so far as *appearances* are concerned, from the habits of self-control or the want of it in individuals. There is often the most deep and permanent feeling when there are no tears; and the sorrow which is accompanied by loud and boisterous outcries, is often a sorrow which lies very near the surface of the soul, every trace of whose existence soon vanishes. But sorrow of some kind is necessary to repentance; and if we have never had a pang of regret for the past, if we have never felt that we have done wrong, if we have never felt ashamed, and humbled, and confounded in view of our errors and faults, if we have never had anything of the spirit of the publican when he said, "God be merciful to me a sinner," or of the prodigal when he said, "Father, I have sinned against heaven and in thy sight, and am no more worthy to be called thy son," or of David when he said, "I acknowledge my transgression, and my sin is ever before me," we may be sure that we have never truly repented.

Yet we should not suppose that *all* sorrow experienced in view of past sins is necessarily true repentance. "There is a sorrow of the world," in view of sin, "which worketh death." Judas the traitor had deep anguish in view of his crime, and went and added to his guilt another enormous act of transgression. Many a gambler has had the keenest feelings of regret when his money is gone, who had no real penitence; and there is deep sorrow in those "doleful regions" where there is "weeping, and wailing, and gnashing of teeth," but there is no true repentance there.

At this stage of our inquiry, therefore, it is of the highest importance that we should endeavour to lay down some marks by which we may be able to distinguish that sorrow which enters into true repentance from that which constitutes the false;—and this may be done by asking ourselves the simple question, *Why* do we feel sorrow at all in the case? *What is it* that produces it? If it is produced by any of the things which I will now specify, it is clear that the sorrow furnishes no evidence of true repentance:—

(1.) If it is produced by the mere dread of punishment. It is clear that in such a case the sorrow which exists is not in view of the *sin*, but only of the *penalty*. If the apprehension of punishment were taken away, the sorrow also would disappear.

(2.) If it arises from the mere shame of detection. In such a case there is clearly no evidence of true repentance. A man may be greatly ashamed and grieved because some base, or mean, or vile, or detestable act is found out, who would have had no trouble on account of it if it had remained concealed. His grief is, that he has been exposed, not that he has done the *wrong;* and there are none, probably, who have not done many things which would suffuse the cheeks with crimson if they were known, but who have no compunctious visitings as long as they are concealed.

(3.) A similar kind of false repentance or sorrow for the past arises from the idea that a man has made a *mistake*, or is likely to suffer *loss* on account of his conduct. When a man has made a bargain which is likely to involve him in loss, when he has missed an opportunity to make an advantageous bargain, he often experiences regret, and in many cases reflects on himself for his folly. So a man may feel in relation to his past life. He looks at the money which he has squandered, and the time which he has wasted which ought to have been employed in study or in honest industry; at the hours of his life which he has trifled away in foolish conversation, or equally foolish reading; and finds himself now placed at an eminent disadvantage on account of it, and if he has any proper sense of it, will regret it. But still he may regret it, not as having any sense of the wrong, or the sinfulness of his course, but only as a matter of *loss*—and with much the same feeling that the man has who has made a bad bargain. If the *loss* could in any way be made up to him, he would have no trouble on account of his course considered as *sinful*. So a daughter of vanity may exercise the same kind of repentance in view of the waste of time, and the loss of health, in the ball-room. She has allowed her rest to be broken; she has exposed herself unprotected by any suitable dress to the cold of a winter's night after being heated in the dance; and she begins to be alarmed at the paleness of her own cheeks, and then at the slight hectic that she cannot conceal, and then at the cough which will not leave her, and she is sad and sorrowful as she sees that the grave must soon close over her in spite of all that friends and physicians can do. But there is necessarily no genuine repentance here—no sorrow for the sin. She mourns over her faded health and beauty; over her imprudent exposure; over the fact that she has wasted her life;—but there is no sorrow that she has done wrong; that she has offended God; that she has spent her time in the neglect of her Saviour and her soul; and that she has jeoparded her salvation.

(4.) There is often sorrow, and deep sorrow, in view of our conduct considered as a violation of some law of etiquette, when there is no sorrow for the act considered as a violation of the law of God. I apprehend, that some of the deepest pangs that are felt in this world are those which arise from the violation of some social law; from something that may expose you to the censure of so-called "society;" something that may occur to throw you out of the fashionable circle in which you wish to move; something that may forfeit the favour of those distinguished in elevated life, whose "good grace" you would wish to preserve. Many a votary of fashion experiences pangs of this kind keener than ordinarily accompany true repentance towards God; and amidst the ever-varying delusions of the human mind it is *possible* that this may sometimes be mistaken for true repentance. You have offended the world; you have been disappointed in your attempts to secure its favour; you have been thrown out of the circles where you were ambitious to shine; and you turn your attention to religion, and suppose that you come into the church a true penitent. And yet there may be no evidence of repentance at all. You may never have had one real sigh of regret for anything that you have ever done against God; and you come weeping to the altar of Christ, not because you have offended *him*, but because you have been disappointed in your foolish ambition to move in a circle from which you have been excluded.

It would be easy to enumerate many other things of this sort which may be mistaken for sincere repentance. The idea is, that the sorrow which is produced by mere loss, or by the disgrace of exposure, or by disappointed ambition—the sorrow which terminates on *the world*,—has in it necessarily none of the elements of repentance. I will not deny that any one of these things may be the *occasion* of turning the mind to a contemplation of the evil of the course pursued, and that, impressed with the folly of these things in one point of view, you may be led to see their folly and wickedness in a higher sense. But clearly, in the matter as we have contemplated it thus far, there is of necessity no true repentance, and a man may have all these things, and never experience one pang of regret for his conduct regarded as a sin against God.

The sense of what I have said, therefore, is this:—that true repentance is based on the contemplation of an act regarded as in itself evil and wrong; regarded as a sin against God. Whether it exposes to punishment or not; whether it is detected or undetected; whether attended with loss or with gain; whether reputable in the eyes of the world or disreputable; and whether it will continue us within the limits of the clique, or clan, or caste where we have been, or raise us to that to which we have aspired, does not affect the question. It is seen to be evil and wrong in the sight of God, and the sin is loathed, and we loathe ourselves on account of it. Our thoughts are not occupied about the question of exposure or concealment; about the honour or disgrace attending it; but about its intrinsic loathsomeness, and hatefulness, and vileness. It follows, consequently, that the true penitent, in dealing with his own heart, is more concerned with those things that are unknown to the world, and of which there is no danger that they should be known, than he is with the fact that the "secret faults" that have been concealed from every eye are now disclosed, or with those presumptuous sins that every one sees. It is sorrow for the wrong done; the intrinsic evil; the loathsomeness, the vileness, the ingratitude, the corruption of a heart *seen* to be blacker and viler than has ever been suspected by the world. When that sorrow exists, and from these causes, a man may trust that he has exercised true repentance.

II. The second thing which I specified as entering into true repentance is, *the purpose deliberately formed in the mind to abandon the evil.* My meaning in this connexion is, that it is not *enough* to have sorrow for the past, unless there is a purpose corresponding with that sorrow, and co-extensive with it, to forsake the evil course altogether. I will admit, also, in regard to this, as in regard to the former, that even *this* would not be full and complete evidence of the sincerity of repentance—for (1,) the purpose, though formed, might not be adhered to; and, (2,) there might be no opportunity to carry it into effect: but there can be no true repentance, and no satisfactory evidence of repentance, where this purpose is not formed.

To explain this remark still farther, it should be said, that the purpose referred to is not one of distant and future amendment, but is one which contemplates the immediate and entire abandonment of the evil; a direct "breaking off from transgressions by righteousness, and by turning unto the Lord." To resolve to abandon a sinful course at some future period, however solemn and sacred that resolution may be, is no evidence of present repentance. In such a case, the actual state of the mind is seen in the determination to *continue* the wrong-doing, and that state indicates a prevailing love for the sin, and a determination to practise it as long as it will be safe.

It is not difficult to persuade men to form purposes of *future* amendment. Indeed, most men need *no* persuasion on that point, but, however wicked they may be, they have in general made up their minds to it already. The point of difficulty is, when you come to persuade the man to resolve *at once* to give up his habit of profane swearing; to become temperate; to forsake the companionship of the vile; to abandon his dishonest acts in dealing; to commence the habit of family prayer; to begin to serve the Lord. I should have no difficulty in so setting before you the evils of a wicked life as to persuade you to resolve at some future period to reform; my difficulty is in persuading you, in view of a life *perceived to be wrong*, to resolve at once to break off from your evil ways. I wish now to show you that there can be no evidence of repentance without this.

It surely cannot require many words to convince you that this *is* so. In all the appeals that are made to men in the Bible to repent of their sins, it is implied that there should be a resolution at once to forsake the evil. It is nowhere hinted—it would be a mockery of all our conceptions of repentance if it were—that men might resolve to pursue their evil courses a little longer, intending then to return to the Lord. Nothing is more manifest in the Scriptures than the duty of *immediate* repentance; of all that is involved in a purpose to abandon an evil course as soon as it is seen to be evil. We all see at once, that this accords with all the conceptions that we have on the subject of repentance. If a man does *not* thus resolve, whatever may be the expressions of sorrow which he may utter for the past, it is clear that his heart still loves the evil. The purpose, moreover, must relate to entire abandonment of the evil in every form and modification. It will not do, for example, for a man to resolve to abandon the *open* form of the sin, and to practise it in secret. It will not do for him, constrained by public sentiment, to yield so far to that public sentiment as to abandon the sin for the present, and to retain the secret love of it in his heart, and to hope for the time when by a change of public opinion it may be proper for him to resume it. It will not do to resolve to give up one form of the sin, and to practise it under a different name. It would not do to take the capital which public sentiment or the laws should forbid him to employ in one way, and to invest it in a form equally evil. It would not do, for example, for a man who had a large capital invested in the slave-trade, to take that same capital and build a distillery, or to sell out his distillery and become the lessee of a theatre. Where there is true repentance, there must be a deliberate purpose to abandon evil in any and every form, and in every modification. The repentance, if genuine, is not so much for the *form* of the evil, as it is for the *evil itself.*

This is so plain, that it requires no farther remarks to prove, that when there is true repentance there will be a purpose deliberately formed to forsake evil *as* evil; to forsake *all* evil. It is necessary here, as under the former head, only to make a few remarks in order to distinguish true repentance from false, considered in this view. It may be observed, then, that in this aspect, more than in the former, a man may be led to resolve to abandon a course of evil from some motive which may be no indication of sincere repentance. He will be still more likely to resolve to *abandon* a course of conduct from some motive which is no indication of true repentance, than he would be sincerely to *regret* it. He may be induced to resolve to abandon an evil course from any one of the following motives—and when these are the motives, nothing can be inferred as to the genuineness of repentance:—(1.) It may be because the course involves a loss of *property*, and not because he is convinced of the wrong. Thus a man might give up gambling, or horse-racing, because he always loses; or a seller of ardent spirits might abandon the traffic, because it makes so many bad debts; or a man might set his slaves at liberty, because they are unprofitable. Desirable and proper as the course in this and similar instances might be in itself, yet the man should not infer that he has had any true repentance for the *wrong;* for it is clear that if the business had been profitable, he would have had no trouble on the subject. In the same manner a man may resolve not to travel any more on the sabbath, or to withdraw his investments from a sabbath-breaking railway company, not because he exactly sees that it is *wrong*, but because he is apprehensive that in the end it will prove to be unprofitable. (2.) A man may resolve to abandon an evil course, because he is involved by it in *disgrace*. He has become a drunkard, and he resolves to reform, not because he is convinced of the evil and wrong of intemperance in itself considered, but because he has lost his character in the view of the community, and is likely also to lose all his business. It is evident that, in such a case, there would be no true repentance for the cause considered *as an evil*, but only of regret for the dishonour and disadvantage coming on him. (3.) In like manner, a man may resolve to abandon a certain course because the strong current of public sentiment is set against it. Thus multitudes are the friends of temperance,—not because they see any evil in moderate drinking, and especially in wine-drinking; and not because they have any sense of the goodness of God in keeping *them* from the ruin into which others have fallen, who began life in the same way in this respect with themselves; and not because they have any compunction that they ever wasted their own money, and squandered their own time, and jeoparded their own souls, or ruined their sons or others by their own example,—but because the public sentiment is changed. The result is indeed a good one, whatever is the motive—for it is a great point gained when even one, from whatever cause, becomes a warm, practical friend of thorough temperance; but let not the man suppose that there is necessarily any *principle* in this, or that there is any genuine regret for the evil of his own example and life.

The sum of what I have said under this head of my discourse is this:—that in true repentance there will always be a deliberate purpose to abandon every evil; but that so far as this furnishes any *evidence* of true repentance everything depends on the *motive* by which it is done.

III. The third point which I propose to illustrate is, *that in true repentance there will be an actual forsaking of sin;* an endeavour to arrest the progress of the sin at once, and to repair its evils on ourselves and on others. The essential idea here is, that injury has been done by the life of sin, and that there is an actual exertion to stay that injury—a closing up of the plan of evil—a counter-influence of good commenced, to be continued ever afterwards. This occurred in the case mentioned in the text; and it is so manifestly required in every instance of true repentance that it would be improper even to attempt to *prove* it. All that is necessary is to show what is implied in it. This evidence of repentance, then, involves the following things:—

(1.) It involves an honest abandonment of the sin, no matter how lucrative, how alluring, how reputable, or how honourable. The eye in true repentance is fixed on the sin, not on the profit or loss, the honour or dishonour. When there is true repentance for a course of life, there will be an immediate cessation of the wrong, no matter what may be involved in it—even though it may be attended with the sacrifice of any amount of property. At Ephesus there were many persons transacting a lucrative business by a species of magic, employing a considerable investment of capital. Many of those engaged in it became convinced by the preaching of the apostles that the employment was evil, and they "brought their books together, and burned them before all men," amounting in value to fifty thousand pieces of silver, Acts xix. 19. So if a man who has been engaged in the manufacture or sale of ardent spirits becomes convinced that the business is contrary to the word of God, it will be abandoned, no matter what may be the pecuniary loss, or the effect on his business. The consideration of *property* as opposed to the will of God in the case will not affect him for a moment. If he is a true penitent, he will hereafter live an upright and a godly life. He will seek another employment, or he will beg or starve rather than persist in doing wrong. If a man is convinced that slavery is sinful and wrong, no pecuniary consideration will induce him to continue the relation for a moment longer; the only question will be in regard to the welfare of those whom the law has recognised as under his protection. If a man is convinced that it is wrong to run cars, or canal-boats, or stages on the sabbath, and that it is wrong to be the owner of money thus invested, no pecuniary consideration will induce him to retain property thus invested; no pecuniary loss or sacrifice will prevent his withdrawing from the business. The sole question that passes before the mind, when there is true repentance, is in regard to the right and the wrong of any particular course of life; and when *that* is settled, all is settled.

The remark now made may be extended to everything—even to those things where no pecuniary sacrifice is involved. Whatever may be the nature of the *sacrifice* implied in giving up a sinful course, it will be submitted to. For there are often sacrifices, on becoming a true penitent, greater than those of money. If you have loved the gay world; if you have been the patron of vanity and folly; if you have lived, not to honour God, but to find pleasure in the theatre or the ball-room; if your heart has become wedded to a life frivolous in the eyes of mortals, and odious in the eyes of angels and of God, it may require of you a sacrifice which gold could not well measure to give up this course to which you have been devoted. Yet it is of the nature of repentance for the follies of the past that it should be done. What repentance requires, is not that you should come to the altar with streaming eyes and a head bowed down like a bulrush to-day, to mingle in such scenes again to-morrow; but it is that the evidence of your repentance should be manifest in the place where wrong has been done. Your vacated seat at the table of sinful hilarity and song; your vacated place where you have been accustomed to be seen in the dance; your prompt and decided expression of a purpose to lead a different life, when allured to scenes where God is forgotten, and where religion cannot be honoured, is the way, and the only way in respect to this in which you can evince true penitence for the past, and satisfy the world that you mean to live for nobler ends.

(2.) True repentance, as it respects the *conduct*, and as the evidence of it is to be found *in* the conduct, involves a course of life that is fitted to repair the evil which we have done to *ourselves* by our former lives. We cannot, indeed, even in the most thorough repentance, do this entirely. We cannot recall the wasted hours; we cannot recover the money that we have lost by vicious indulgence; we cannot at once restore health to the body enervated by dissipation—perhaps we can *never* do it perfectly,—but we can set about an honest purpose to repair the evil by a different course of life, as far as it may be possible. We cannot, indeed, recover the hours already wasted; but we may resolve that there shall be *no more* wasted, and we may be at such a time of life that the squandered part shall not *materially* affect our ultimate attainments and usefulness. We cannot recover our squandered property; but we can so regulate our lives that there shall be *no more* squandered, and so that we may acquire all that shall be necessary for our own wants and the wants of our families, and so as to furnish us the means of doing extensive good. We may have, indeed, injured our health; but the injury may not be irreparable, and we may resolve that the wrong done shall be carried no farther, and we may yet be enabled to pursue our task of life with restored and invigorated powers. If there *is* such a purpose at once to check and arrest the progress of the evil on ourselves, there is evidence of genuine repentance for the past; if there is not, sighs, and tears, and professions amount to nothing.

(3.) The evidence of repentance implied in our conduct invoves also such a course of life as shall repair, as far as possible, the injury done *to others*. There is much, indeed, here which cannot be repaired. You cannot recall from the grave the man who has been deprived of life; you cannot bring to the cheerful light of the living, the father and the mother whose hearts have been broken by your misconduct, and who have gone down with sorrow to the tomb; you cannot make the hair of a father that has been turned prematurely grey by your ingratitude and folly, black and glossy again; you cannot restore to innocence the deluded victim whom you have ruined by your seductive arts, your example, or your bad principles.

But you may, notwithstanding, do much to repair the evil which you have done to others. A wounded father's heart you may heal by a frank confession, and by a subsequent life of strict propriety and virtue. A wrong which you have done to another by dishonesty and fraud, you may in a great measure repair by confession, and by an honest restoration of all that you have taken from him by fraud. And though in many cases it may be beyond your power to undo the wrong that you have done to *them*, yet you may more than compensate for this to *the world* by the service which you may render to society. In a battle, you have at one moment proved yourself to be a coward, and the battle may be lost; but in a hundred subsequent engagements you may be faithful to your standard, carrying it into the very camp of the enemy. You may have made one infidel by your example or bad principles, and you can never save *him* now from the blighting influence of infidelity; but by a consistent and zealous Christian life you may save hundreds of others from becoming infidels. In the days of your sin and folly you may have led one ingenuous and noble youth to love the intoxicating glass, and no effort of yours can save him from a drunkard's grave; but by becoming now the warm and consistent friend of temperance, you may be the means of saving hundreds of such youths from such a grave; and so far as society is concerned, you may do an hundredfold to repair the wrong. Saul of Tarsus, when he was converted, could never recall to life the martyred Stephen; nor could he bring back to the earth those whom he had imprisoned, and against whom he gave his voice when they were put to death; but he could devote his great talents to the work of propagating the religion which he had persecuted, and save thousands and tens of thousands from a more dreadful death than that of the martyrs. He did it. He set about the great work of repairing the wrongs which he had done to the world as a persecutor; and the sincerity of his repentance was evinced not only by his expressions of deep humiliation and sorrow in view of the past—by his solemn declaration that he was the "least of all the apostles," and was not "fit to be called an apostle, because he persecuted the church of God,"—but by such a life of devotedness to a righteous cause as man never before led, and by a career pursued in repairing the wrong, which was felt to the ends of the earth, and which will continue to be felt to the end of time.

In this abandonment of an evil course; in this struggle against sin; in this solemn purpose to forsake that which has been seen to be wrong, and in this honest and persevering effort to repair the injuries which have been done by our past misconduct, is to be found the evidence of true repentance.

We may learn from our subject,

(1.) That there is much *false* repentance in the world. There is much sorrow that expends itself in sighs and tears and temporary emotion, and that "brings forth no fruit meet for repentance." There is much forsaking of sin for other reasons than because it is seen to be wrong. It is abandoned because it is unprofitable; or because it is unfashionable; or because it does not comport with good breeding and the maintenance of the character of a gentleman; or because the popular sentiment sets strongly against it; or because it is expensive, and cannot well be afforded; and not because there is any deep sense of the evil. The evil is still loved, and you would be ready to practise it again if your own circumstances, or the views of the public, should be changed. So, many men break off from certain sins, not because they hate them, but because they are growing old, and can no longer enjoy them; many do it, not because their views are changed, but because they are laid on a bed of pain, and the hour of death draweth near. It becomes, therefore, obviously a very solemn duty for each one to examine his own heart, to ascertain *why* it is that he has forsaken the paths in which he once so cheerfully walked.

(2.) We may see the reason why a death-bed repentance is of so little value. Jeremy Taylor maintained that a death-bed repentance is impossible. There could not be, he said, *evidence* furnished that it is sincere and genuine. But, whatever may be true on *that* point, our subject teaches us that all the evidence furnished by a death-bed repentance is of very little value. A moment's reflection, it would seem, would satisfy any one of the truth of this remark. Let him think how many regrets are felt by those in health for their past conduct, which never amount to true penitence; how many expressions of sorrow are made, followed by no correspondent action; how many alarms are felt that produce no turning from sin; how many resolutions are formed only to be disregarded; and then let him reflect on the usual condition of the mind on a death-bed:—how incapable of calm reflection; how likely to act from the influence of mere alarm; how often it is wholly or partially delirious,—and he will see how little dependence is to be placed on expressions of penitence in such circumstances. Let him ask himself also how many in the sphere of his observation there have been, who on a sick bed have resolved to forsake their sins and to live to God, but who on their recovery have shown that their repentance was false and hollow, and he will learn what to think of that repentance when there has been no such recovery. It is a common thing for men when they are sick, and suppose that they are about to die, to become apparently penitent and religious;—not common for them when they recover to give evidence that the repentance was genuine. In a ministry now of nearly thirty years, I have had opportunity to see many sick and dying persons. In all that time I cannot now recall a solitary instance of one who became apparently penitent on a sick-bed, who furnished any evidence in his subsequent life that it was genuine. Now, if this be so in the usual cases of restoration to health, I would not say that it would absolutely *prove* that in cases which terminated differently there was no evidence of true repentance; but who can help asking the question, What evidence would they have probably furnished, if they had been restored again to health?

(3.) Finally, the conclusion of the whole matter then is this:—If we would have evidence of repentance that is *worth* anything—that will furnish consolation to our friends when we are gone—that will enable them to go and bend over our graves with the consolation derived from the belief that we are in heaven; if we would have them go and inscribe on the stone which marks the place where we sleep, in an intelligent manner, some simple and sweet passage of the word of God indicating their belief that we are happy, or have them plant there the flower which as it blooms from spring to spring shall be expressive of the hope that we shall be raised to life and glory, *that* evidence must be found in a life of piety so uniform as to show that we hate all the ways of sin. It must be founded on the workings of our minds in their best state, and in their maturest powers. And for myself, I desire to have, and to leave to my friends in that hour when, so far as this world is concerned, I shall give them the parting hand, a hope not derived from the workings of a mind broken and prostrate by age or disease, or from an expression of regret then *wrung* from my dying lips—but a hope derived from the best exercise of my intellect and my heart in my maturest days, employed with prayerful energy, and assisted by the grace of God, on the great subject of religion. No other subject so *demands* the exercise of those powers; nothing else would I desire to have placed on so firm a basis, and so far beyond the danger of deception, as my hope of immortality.

SERMON XXVI.

FAITH A CONDITION OF SALVATION.

MARK xvi. 16.—"He that believeth, and is baptized, shall be saved."

IN illustrating this text, I propose to answer the question, why faith has been demanded as one of the conditions of salvation. The objections to giving such prominence to faith in a system of revealed religion, and to making the whole question of salvation turn on it, are objections more commonly felt than urged; but they are such that it will not do to pass them by as unworthy of notice. They are such as these:—that the rewards which God has to dispense to men are elsewhere bestowed, not according to their faith, but according to their character and conduct; that it would seem to be proper that the retributions of the future state should be according to what a man *does*, and not according to what he *believes;* that it is not probable that the retributions of eternity would be made to turn on *any* mere state of mind, and that if they did, there is no reason why the state of mind implied in *faith* should be selected in preference to any other; and that to make eternal life depend on the exercise of faith is, in fact, to propose a reward for *credulity*, and to justify the remark sneeringly made by the sceptic, that "our holy religion is founded on faith, *not* on reason."* Perhaps to these objections, some would be disposed to add another, that even the Scriptures themselves declare that when the rewards of eternity shall be apportioned on the final trial, the retribution will be "according to the deeds done in the body," and that the grand question which will come up will be, not what a man has *believed*, but what he has *done.*

These objections are worthy of particular consideration. I propose, then, to draw your attention to the inquiry why faith in the Lord Jesus Christ has been made an indispensable condition of salvation. The inquiry will be exhausted if the following points can be made clear:—that it is proper that there should be *some* conditions of salvation; what would be the proper characteristics of such conditions; and whether these characteristics are found in the faith that is required in the gospel.

* Hume.

You will perceive that the argument which I propose to conduct is one that is to be derived very materially from an appeal to the common sense of men, and will rest much on what calm reflection will show to each one to be proper in the case. I regard this mode of argument as legitimate, because I suppose that, in fact, the gospel *makes* its appeal to the common sense of mankind, and is to be kept up by that from age to age.

I. *It is proper that there should be some conditions of salvation;* that is, that there should be something in view of which the rewards of eternal life shall be bestowed, or which will constitute the public reason why they are bestowed. The essential idea here is, that in order to our being saved, there should be something on our part which will indicate our wish to be saved; or which will show that we regard salvation as a great and desirable thing, and that we are willing to be saved in the method proposed. This proposition is so clear, that I suppose it will be admitted by all persons, unless it be held that all men will be saved; and even then it would hardly be maintained that men would be saved without *any* conditions—that is, without anything that would be a public and sufficient reason why they should be admitted into heaven.

That, if men are saved, there are to be some *conditions* on which it is to be done, seems to be clear, because it is the universal law under which we live. There are certain well-understood terms on which we expect that the Divine favours will be bestowed, and the knowledge of these constitutes the basis of all our calculations and efforts. It is true that favours are sometimes conferred without respect to any known conditions; but it is also true that such interpositions are very rare, and that they never enter into a wise man's calculations as a basis of action. Thus, sometimes, a man may, in pulling up a shrub, like Atahualpi, open a vein of silver; sometimes a man may discover a valuable mine of gold or copper on his farm; sometimes he may unexpectedly be found to be heir to a great estate in a distant land; or some one of whom he knows little, and on whom he may have no claim, may, by a mere freak, leave all his property to him by will. But these things occur so rarely, and are regulated by laws so subtle, if regulated by laws at all, that they are not the ordinary rules on which men act, and they can never enter into the calculations of a wise man. As there are no known *conditions* on which they are regulated, we do not form our plans in view of them, and, in fact, our plans are the same as if it were understood that they were never to occur.

The great law under which we act is different. It is, that

there are *conditions* on which all that we hope for depends. There are things appointed by which we are to show our interest in it; our sense of its value; our desire to obtain it. If we are to *have* anything, it is on certain conditions:—if wealth, we are to labour for it; if health, we are to take proper precautions in regard to it; if reputation, we are to show that we deserve it. There is not one thing which we expect under the operation of chance or hap-hazard, or which a wise man would calculate on from that source; and since this is the general law under which we live, no one can complain that the offer of heaven is put on the same footing. In fact, no one *does* complain. Each man supposes that there is some *condition* on which eternal happiness may be obtained. Each one supposes in his heart that he *does* certain things, or that he *believes* certain things, which will be regarded as the ground or reason why he should be made happy hereafter. One man, with this view, maintains a life of strict integrity and honesty; another is kind to his family, to the distressed, to the poor; another is the friend of his country, and glories in the name of a patriot; another is zealous in the outward duties of religion; another puts on a hair cloth, and immures himself in a convent; another makes a pilgrimage to a distant shrine; another believes that there is one God, and that Mohammed is his prophet; and another believes that Jesus is the Christ, the Son of the Blessed, and looks for salvation only through him. In all these, and in all the other methods by which men hope to be saved, there is *something* which they regard as a *condition* of salvation; that is, something which will indicate such a desire for salvation, or such a fitness for it, that it will constitute a public reason why they should be saved, and not lost.

It may be regarded, then, as the common opinion of mankind, that there should be some *conditions* of salvation, and this common opinion evidently accords with the Scriptures.

II. The second inquiry proposed was, *What are the proper characteristics of such conditions?* Making our appeal to the common sense of men, and to their observation in regard to the manner in which the Divine favour on other subjects than religion is bestowed, it will not be difficult to furnish an answer to this question. The following seem to me to be obvious and just principles in the case.

(1.) The conditions of salvation should be as *easy* as possible, consistently with the maintenance of other interests. That is, they should be such as not to put salvation out of the power of any for whom it is designed, and to whom it is proposed. There might be other important interests to be looked at and secured, but evidently this is one, and one which could not be overlooked. If the other interests could not be secured consistently with this, it is clear that no offer of salvation could be made. If a garrison were besieged, and a surrender were proposed and agreed on, it is plain that the conditions of the surrender should be such as could be easily complied with by all who were embraced in the articles; and if women and children were included in the number, it would be the height of injustice to make the terms such that they could be complied with only by armed warriors in their full strength, and that deliverance could be secured only by the highest skill of military discipline. So in salvation. A proposal for salvation should be such as will be adapted to all. It should be such as can be embraced by all. It should therefore be of such a general character that it would be applicable to all, and so easy that all could avail themselves of it. But who *are* the "*all*" embraced in a plan of salvation? Not philosophers merely; not men of learning, and rank, and experience, and wealth, and age only;—but women, children, servants; the poor, the unlettered, the down-trodden; the savage, as well as the freeman and the man of civilized life. It is quite clear that a condition of salvation *might* be conceived of that could be complied with by a man of the intellectual power of Plato or Bacon, which would be entirely beyond the grasp of a child or a savage; and yet it is *as* clear that in a system of religion designed for *man*, there were important reasons why the question of salvation should be made to turn on some one thing that could be complied with by all. It would be very easy to show that the distinctions made in this world by rank, and wealth, and talent are not such as it would be desirable to perpetuate in heaven, and therefore not such as could properly be laid at the foundation of a system of true religion on earth.

(2.) The conditions should, if possible, be such as would meet certain evils which already existed, or which would be likely to exist, if salvation were not provided. Thus, for example, in the methods by which *property* is to be bestowed on men, it would seem to be desirable, and in fact to have been a leading thing in the plan, to meet the evils which would grow out of indolence; and at the same time that property was conferred, to confer a much greater benefit on the *character* by the very method by which it was to be obtained. For, there are great and undeniable evils in indolence. There are great evils which exist when property can be acquired without the necessity of effort. There would be incalculable evils to mankind if their wants were all supplied without the necessity of exertion. The hard soil; the stern climate; the very rocks of New England, are more favourable to good influences on the character than the soil and climate by which all the wants of man may be supplied under the equator; and every blow which man is obliged to strike to secure property, is of more value to him than the property which he obtains. So all the exertions which are necessary to secure health, or honourable reputation, or a comfortable home, are designed to meet certain evils which would exist if these exertions were not necessary, and which *do* exist always when the ends can be reached without those means. It would be an incalculable *evil* for man if God should build houses for him as he creates trees; if he made wheat to grow as he does cockle and clover; if he created flax and hemp as he does nettles and brambles; if he manufactured the robes of princes as he does those in which the lily of the valley is adorned; and if he clothed the daughters of men with rich attire and with brilliant ornaments, as he gives its beauty to the humming-bird or the flamingo. Every exertion which he has made necessary for man or for woman has been designed to meet some *evil* which would exist if such exertion were not required; and every *condition* which he has imposed on which these things are to be obtained, is an arrangement of benevolence. On the same principle, in making arrangements for salvation, if there were any existing evils in the mind of man by nature, or any things which *would* be evils if salvation had not been provided, it might be presumed that there would be an eye to those evils in arranging the terms on which men might be saved. If, for example, there were evils which arose from the want of *faith in God*, it might be presumed that the conditions of salvation would have some reference to those evils, and would be adapted to correct them.

(3.) The conditions of salvation should be such as to show, on the part of him who would obtain it, an *interest* in the thing, and a desire to secure it, which would be in some degree commensurate with its importance. We may argue this because it is actually the condition under which we live. The efforts which men are willing to put forth, the self-denials which they are willing to practise, the perils which they are willing to encounter, furnish the measure of their estimate of the *value* of the object. It seems to have been a general principle of the Divine arrangements not to bestow favours on men unless they showed that they so valued them as to be willing to make efforts to procure them. Thus, the danger encountered by the pearl-diver, shows his sense of the value of the pearl; the labour which a farmer is willing to lay out on his farm, shows his estimate of the value of the harvest; the perils which a merchant will encounter to procure in a far-distant city a stock of goods, show his sense of the value of gain; the willing privations to which the soldier submits in the tented field, show his sense of the worth of glory. The degree of *interest* which we have in anything is expressed in this way, and so expressed as to be intelligible to all men.

It could not be expected that salvation would be conferred on us in any way in which our desire for it should not be expressed, any more than it would be expected that diamonds, or gold, or earthly crowns would be. Accordingly it would be reasonable to suppose that the conditions of salvation would be such that by complying with them there might be the honest indication of a *desire* to be saved. It would be unaccountable, if the matter of salvation should be arranged in this respect in a way unlike anything else; and if we should find that it was bestowed upon men where no desire was expressed, and there was nothing which could be construed into a *wish* to be saved.

(4.) The conditions of salvation should be clearly such as to have a good influence on the character; to enlarge the mind; to elevate the aims; to cultivate the nobler powers of our nature. This may be observed to be the character and tendency of *all* the conditions which God has made necessary, in securing *any* object which he approves. The cultivation of the earth, for example, is in itself adapted to produce a happier effect on the human mind in keeping it pure, and raising the thoughts to God, than any other worldly occupation—for it had more directly the appointment of the Deity. In that appointment, emanating as it did from God, there is nothing in itself that is fitted to enfeeble the mind; to debase the powers; to degrade our nature; to arouse gross and sensual propensities; to excite mad and turbulent passions. So in the appointment respecting salvation, it *cannot* be supposed that the conditions would be such as to debase and degrade our nature; it cannot be believed that anything would be specified that would call forth our sensual propensities, or that would make our views more contracted and narrow. We should look for that which will expand the mind; which will elevate the thoughts to higher objects than those on the earth; which will lead us up to God, and to the contemplation of nobler relations than any which we sustain here below. Whether *faith*, as a condition of salvation, is adapted to open the eyes on other worlds, and to bring higher and more important relations and interests to view than those disclosed by sense, would be a fair and legitimate subject of inquiry.

III. The third inquiry proposed was, *Whether these characteristics are found in the requirement of faith as a condition of salvation?* In answering this question, it would be easy to go over again the points which have been specified, and to show, in regard to faith as a condition of salvation, that it is one of the easiest terms which could be proposed, and that it is adapted to man as such—to all classes of men; that it meets certain great evils in the world which have been originated by the want of faith, and which have always existed where there has been no confidence in God; that it is a condition in which the highest interest may be shown in salvation, and the highest desire to be saved; and that it is fitted eminently to elevate the thoughts, and to purify the heart, and to accomplish just those effects which ought to be accomplished on the mind of a being like man, leading him to act, not under the influence of sense, but with reference to the world to come. But to dwell on these points would be only to go over the ground again which we have already trod; and the subject is capable of illustration in a somewhat different form, and in a manner that shall bear more directly on the question why *faith in Christ* particularly is required in order to salvation.

Bearing in mind the remarks now made—that a restoration to confidence would meet innumerable evils in a family, in a commercial community, between neighbours, and between nations, where it had been disturbed, and that the restoration of confidence in God would meet all the evils under which this world labours now,—I proceed to show why *faith in Christ* particularly is made so important as a condition of salvation. With reference to this, two remarks may be made.

(1.) The first is, that we are to repose faith or confidence in Christ, as authorized to negotiate the terms of reconciliation between God and man. The whole system of revealed religion proceeds on the fact—a fact which is apparent without any revelation—that an *alienation* exists between God and man, or that man is in a state of revolt. It was with reference to this alienation that the Son of God came into the world, to accomplish the most difficult of all undertakings, that of reconciling opposing minds, and of bringing them into harmony. On the one hand, there was the Infinite Mind of God, whose law had been violated, and whose government had been rejected and outraged, and whose threatenings had been disregarded; and on the other, there were countless millions of minds that were or would be wholly alienated from the Creator. To bring the holy Creator and the millions of rebellious created minds to harmony; to propose the terms on which God was willing to pardon; to make such arrangements that he could consistently pardon; and to bring the minds of revolted men to a willingness to be reconciled, and to cease their rebellion,—was the work undertaken by this Great Peacemaker.

But it is evident that this work could not be accomplished by him, unless there were confidence in him on both sides of this unhappy controversy. In infinitely smaller matters, when nations are alienated, and have long been contending, if a mediator should propose arrangements of peace, or if ambassadors are appointed to negotiate a peace, it is clear that the matter could not proceed a step, unless there were confidence on both sides in the mediator or ambassador.

Christ is a great Mediator; a Peacemaker between God and man. On the part of God, there was every reason to repose entire confidence in so great an undertaking; for he was his only-begotten Son, eternally in his bosom, and loved, with an infinite love, before the foundation of the world, John xvii. 24. By him the worlds had been made (John i. 3; Heb. i. 2); by him they had been sustained; and under him, with reference to the work of redemption, their affairs had been administered up to the time when he appeared in the flesh. God the Father reposed unlimited confidence in him when he appointed him to be the Mediator, and entrusted to him the execution of the great purpose of reconciling the world again to the Divine government. This confidence reposed in Christ in the work of mediation is often referred to in the New Testament by the Saviour himself, and by the sacred penmen. "This is my beloved Son," was declared from heaven at his baptism, "in whom I am well pleased," Matt. iii. 17. "Father," said the Saviour, just before his death, "glorify thy name. Then came there a voice from heaven, saying, I have both glorified it, and will glorify it again," John xii. 28. "Thou hast given him power," said he again, "over all flesh, that he should give eternal life to as many as thou hast given him," John xvii. 2. "All power is given unto me in heaven and in earth; go ye therefore and teach all nations," Matt. xxviii. 18, 19. "I am the way," said he, "and the truth, and the life; no man cometh unto the Father but by me," John xiv. 6. So we are told that "there is one God, and one Mediator between God and men, the man Christ Jesus," 1 Tim. ii. 5. These things show the degree of confidence which God reposed in him in the work of mediation—entrusting to him the message of mercy, appointing him to convey it to men, and endowing him *as* Mediator with all the power and authority which were requisite to accomplish so great a work.

But confidence in Christ is not less required in regard to the other party than in respect of Him who had appointed him. It is clear that, unless we have confidence in him as the messenger and ambassador of God ; unless we regard him as sent from heaven and authorized to propose terms of reconciliation ; unless we feel that he can make *a definite arrangement*, and that what he proposes will be sanctioned by God ; unless we feel that he is *authorized* to propose terms of pardon, and to declare our sins forgiven, and to pronounce us accepted and justified, it would be impossible for us to avail ourselves of any arrangement for salvation through him. We should feel that we were trifling with a great subject ; and in our serious moments, and when we think of the great interests at stake, we should be in no humour to trifle. None of *us* would seriously think of embracing *any* terms of reconciliation with God proposed by Mohammed, or Zoroaster, or Confucius ; by Lord Herbert or Mr. Hume ; for we suppose that none of these men were authorized to propose terms of salvation ; we have no faith in them—no confidence in them as ambassadors of God, whatever we may think of them in other respects. We should feel no more *safe* in regard to salvation after such a negotiation than we did before. The primary ground of faith, therefore, in Christ is, that we should have confidence in him as a mediator, an ambassador, a peacemaker ; as authorized to propose to us the *terms* on which peace may be obtained with an offended Creator. All this was involved in the idea of the *Messiahship*, and particularly of his being the "Great Prophet that should come into the world." "If ye believe not that I am he, ye shall die in your sins," John viii. 24.

(2.) The second remark to which I referred, showing specifically why faith in Christ is demanded, is, that he himself is in fact the only Saviour ; it is by his agency and merits only that we can be received into the favour of God. He came not only to *bring* the message of reconciliation, and to *propose* the terms, but to *do* and to *suffer* whatever was necessary to be done and suffered in order that we might be accepted of the Father, or in order that we might be saved consistently with the interests of justice. The case somewhat resembles what it would be in the instance of an ambassador coming to negotiate a peace, who should not only come to propose the *terms*, but should actually have in his possession that which alone could be regarded as a reparation for wrong done by one of the parties to the other, and who should come not only to persuade the party which had done the wrong to be willing to be reconciled, but also to take the benefit of what he was ready to furnish to repair all the evil done, and to satisfy the other party. In such a case, it would not be unreasonable to ask *confidence* in himself, or to make this one of the conditions by which the favour might be available. In fact, it could not be consistently made available in any other way, or on any other condition; and unless there were faith in him, the negotiation could proceed no further.

Thus, we are required to exercise faith in the Lord Jesus. We are destitute of merit. We have violated the law of God, and can do nothing to repair the wrong. We are debtors to an incalculable amount to justice; and we have nothing with which to pay the debt. We can do absolutely nothing to vindicate our own conduct; to repair the past wrong; to undo the evils that we have done; to make up for the dishonour which we have put on the law of God, to atone for our thousands of faults and follies. At this point the Son of God appears, and he comes with the assurance that he has himself perfectly obeyed the law, and has done all the honour to it which can be done by obedience; that he has suffered a most bitter death—a death aggravated by every form of cruelty—as an expiation for our sins; that he will become the guarantee or surety that the law shall suffer no dishonour if we are saved, and that no injury shall result from our pardon; that in fact all the good effects have been secured which *could be* by our being doomed to bear the penalty of the law ourselves; and that all that is needful for us now is to become united to him by an indissoluble bond, to put ourselves under his protection, and to be *so* identified with him that it will be proper to treat us as he is treated—to treat us *as if* we had personally obeyed the law, or borne its penalty. That which will constitute the closest union in the case, and which will do most to render this identity of treatment proper, is *faith;* simple confidence in him as our Saviour, and reliance on his merits. If that exists, we are safe—safe as he is, and destined to the same glorious inheritance in heaven; if that does *not* exist, we are left as we were without a Saviour, and the law is suffered to take its course, and we perish. The primary ground of condemnation is *not* that we *have not believed on him*—but it is, that we were before under condemnation for our sins, and should have been whether he had come to save us or not. That, however, is greatly aggravated, showing at once the justice of the previous ground of condemnation, and greatly enhancing it, that we did not embrace his offered conditions of deliverance:

as when a man is sick, and is likely to die, and certainly *will* die if he does not take a certain medicine, and yet refuses to take it, the primary ground of the difficulty is not that he *will not take* the medicine; the main, the essential difficulty preceded that, and would have existed whether the medicine had been provided or not—but, as a moral being, his case may be greatly aggravated by rejecting the only thing which would save him from the grave.

I have thus stated some of the reasons, as I understand them, why faith in the Redeemer is required as one of the indispensable conditions of salvation. Two remarks may be suggested in conclusion:—

(1.) The gospel is adapted to man. Its conditions are of such a nature as was clearly proper in a system of religion designed for man, *as such*, contemplating the race as made up of a great variety of classes and conditions—the rich and the poor; the high and the low; the free and the bond; the learned and the ignorant. It was plain that the terms should not be such as would be adapted to one class to the exclusion of another, but should have such a reference to what was common to us as men, and what was practicable, that they might be embraced by all. Thus salvation resembles all the arrangements which God has made for the race—and is like the air which we breathe, and the water which we drink at the fountain, and the fruit which we pluck from the tree,—adapted not to kings and philosophers only, but to children and peasants; not to princesses only that shine in courts, and delicate females that "will not adventure the sole of the foot upon the ground," but to her who has her home in the most secluded valley, or who, in the wildest sportiveness of nature, trips lightly over the hills. And to *despise* religion on this account; to pass it by neglected; to deem it unworthy of *our* notice because it has been embraced, and loved, and enjoyed by the poor, the uneducated, the unrefined—is as wise as it would be to refuse to breathe the air of heaven because those of humbler rank breathe it; or to taste the water of the fountain because "one on whom fair science never dawned" stoops down and drinks there; or to refuse to find pleasure in the landscape, or the light of the sun, because some poor slave has seen beauty in the prospect, and felt his soul expand with the feeling that he was a creature of God—or because some poor wretch has looked out from the grated window of a dungeon, and felt a ray of comfort come into his soul as he was permitted to see the beams of the morning illuminate the tops of the distant hills.

(2.) It follows, that if there are *conditions* proposed for salvation, if these conditions are not complied with, then there is no rational ground for hope of eternal life. So we feel and know about other things; and why shall we not about salvation? We avail ourselves of the conditions on which property, health, reputation, may be obtained; and feel that the only rational basis of hope in the case is, that we comply with the terms on which these things are offered to men. If we are unwilling to comply with these conditions, and the favour is withheld, we feel that we have only ourselves to blame. But these terms are not as *easy* as those on which salvation is offered. It is easier for a man to be certain of going to heaven, than it is to be certain of being rich, or of enjoying health, or of being honoured. A very small part of the toil which the merchant or the farmer endures to procure wealth; a very small part of the self-denial which the soldier practises to obtain honour; a very small part of the painstaking which the invalid resorts to when he goes to other lands to restore himself to health—and often in each case in vain—would secure beyond doubt the salvation of the soul. The means appointed are more easy; the result is more certain from the voice of experience; the promise is more sure. But if man will not *employ* those means, why should he not fail of salvation, just as certainly as he must be poor, or sick, or unhonoured, if he gives himself up to indolence, and makes no effort to be rich, vigorous in body, or honoured? And if at last he perishes, when the conditions of salvation were so easy and so available, whom shall he blame but himself? And how can he *avoid* perishing if he will not avail himself of the *only* terms on which God has ever promised eternal life? In view, then, of all these considerations, I repeat once more the solemn declaration of Him who is "the way, the truth, and the life," your final Judge and mine:—"He that believeth, and is baptized, shall be saved; and he that believeth not shall be damned."

SERMON XXVII.

THE VALUE AND IMPORTANCE OF FAITH.

HEB. xi. 6.—"But without faith it is impossible to please him: for he that cometh to God must believe that he is, and that he is a rewarder of them that diligently seek him."

THERE are two points of inquiry respecting faith which I next propose to consider:—one is, the *place* which faith occupies in the system of revealed religion; and the other, the *reason* why such a degree of prominence has been given to it.

I. *The place which faith occupies in the system of revealed religion.*

No one can mistake as to this. It is declared to be indispensable to salvation; the whole question of life or death is made to depend on it; it is necessary in order to avail ourselves of the benefit of the death of Christ; the opposite of faith, *i.e.* unbelief, is condemned in the most unambiguous manner, and it is solemnly declared that the want of it shall for ever exclude from the kingdom of God. It is unequivocally stated in the New Testament, that where there is not faith there is no true religion, and that no one can approach God with any hope of acceptance without it. It is made one of the conditions of salvation which are never dispensed with; and whatever else a man may have, if he have not this, it is declared that he cannot be saved.

The following passages of the New Testament will show the place which faith occupies in the Christian system, and, though familiar, seem necessary to be repeated in order to prepare for the remarks which I have to make in explanation of the subject. "He that believeth, and is baptized, shall be saved; but he that believeth not shall be damned," Mark xvi. 16. "He that believeth on him is not condemned; but he that believeth not is condemned already, because he hath not believed in the name of the only-begotten Son of God," John iii. 18. "He that believeth hath everlasting life, and he that believeth not the Son shall not see life, but the wrath of God abideth on him," John iii. 36. "If ye believe not that I am he, ye shall die in your sins; and where I am, thither ye cannot come," John viii. 24, and vii. 34. So the text:

"Without faith, it is impossible to please him; for he that cometh to God must believe that he is, and that he is a rewarder of them that diligently seek him."

Such passages settle the question in regard to the prominence which faith occupies in the system of revealed religion, and show that, in that system, the whole subject of man's salvation is made to depend on it. It is one of the two indispensable things on which the salvation of any of the race is made to rest.

Now to this view of the importance of faith in a system of religion, I need not say that numerous objections at once occur to many minds. The prominence given in Christianity to faith has been a standing objection urged by infidels against the system; and even in minds not inclined to scepticism there are difficulties which are not easy to be removed. Mr. Hume, in his Essay on Miracles, remarks with a sneer, that "our most holy religion is founded on *faith*, not on reason;" and then proceeds to show that it is not safe to subject it to any severe test of reason.

The most material objections, and those which involve real difficulty in regard to the prominence given to *faith* in the system of Christianity, are the following:—

(1.) That it is an arbitrary arrangement; that faith in itself has no such essential prominency and importance as to make it proper to select this as a condition of salvation; that as a mental exercise it has no peculiar dignity or value over other mental exercises which should have led to its selection; and that, in itself considered, there is no more reason why *faith* should have been selected as a condition of salvation than why, for example, hope, or fear, or love should have been.

(2.) That salvation should not be made to depend on *any* mere mental operation; that the rewards of heaven and hell should be apportioned rather to the character and conduct than to any mere state of mind; that we judge of men, not by what they *believe*, but by what they *do;* that the retributions of this world necessarily, in courts, in families, in holding offices, and in the measure of prosperity which men enjoy, or the reverses which they experience, are not determined by what men believe or do not believe, but by what they *do*, or fail to do; and that there is a propriety that the same rule should be observed in the retributions of the future state.

(3.) That faith, as a mental operation, is beyond our control; that we are so made that we cannot help believing where proper evidence is presented, and cannot make ourselves believe where there is not; and that as men have no control over their faith, they are not responsible for their belief.

(4.) That it is no matter what a man believes, provided his conduct is right; and that one mode of faith can no more affect the interests of society, or a man's own soul, than another; and that the grand question is, not what are a man's *opinions* on speculative matters, but what is his *character*.

(5.) It would probably be added, that *faith* stands in quite strong contrast with *reason*, and that to represent religion as depending on faith is to undervalue the rational nature that God has given us, and that it is in fact making *credulity* a virtue, and diminishing the respect which our Maker has taught us to show to our own rational powers.

I could perhaps make these objections appear stronger by expanding them, but I have not designedly diminished their force, or concealed the point of difficulty. It will be seen at once that they are capable of being made to be weighty objections, and that the public defenders of the Christian system are not at liberty to pass them by unnoticed, or to treat them as though they were worthy of no regard. As interested themselves in the questions of religion, as well as in relation to their office as guides of others, they are bound to meet them in a frank manner, and to inquire whether they can be removed.

II. We are conducted, then, to the second and main point to be considered—*the reason why such prominence has been assigned to faith in the system of revealed religion.*

I begin this part of my subject by observing, that a word, though susceptible of an easy and unobjectionable explanation, may by long usage, or by certain associations, have had certain ideas attached to it which may greatly injure its use in an argument. Instead of suggesting only what is essential in the meaning of the word, it may suggest, either with that or without it, certain other things which may greatly impair its force, and leave a very erroneous impression. Thus the word *faith*, when suggested, may have in many minds a near alliance to *credulity;* in the same minds, or in other minds, it may be understood as something in contradistinction to *reason*, as implying that faith is not based on reason, or would not be sustained by it; and when the word is used, there may be conveyed with it the idea that it is something wholly separate from reason, and that the thing in relation to which faith is exercised is something which could not be supported by reason. This was evidently the aspect in which the word was suggested to Mr. Hume's mind when he said, "Our most holy religion is founded on *faith*, NOT on *reason*."

There will be some advantage, therefore, and no injustice in any way, in conducting the argument, in taking a word which involves all that is essential in *faith*, without the danger to which I have referred. I propose, therefore, to make use of the word *confidence;* a word which expresses all that is essential in the idea of *faith*, and which is not liable to the disadvantage already referred to. *Confidence*, it is clear, may be founded on good and substantial reasons. Indeed, it cannot exist without something that is regarded as a valid reason in any particular case, for we always connect with that word the idea that there is *good reason*, in the instance to which it is applied, why confidence should exist. If a man has confidence in the ability of a mercantile house to meet its engagements, it is supposed to be because he has good reason for it. The same thing may be true indeed of *faith*, and should be in all true faith, but the word does not always suggest that idea. I propose, therefore, in illustrating the value and importance of faith, in a system of religion, to make use, in general, of the word *confidence* instead of the more usual word.

The question then is, What is the value of *confidence* in a community; or, in other words, Is there any such value to be attached to it as to justify the primacy and importance attributed to *faith* in the Bible? What important part does it perform in the world? What evils result from the want of it?

Faith, or confidence, if a virtue at all, or if of value at all, is a social or relative virtue. It is true that we sometimes speak of having *confidence* in ourselves; but it is under the influence of that common fiction of the mind by which we regard ourselves as two persons, or as having antagonist feelings and principles; as when we speak of the reason and the passions as in conflict, and struggling for the mastery, and identify ourselves with one of them as at war with the other, Rom. vii. 17—23. But when we speak of *having confidence*, with strict propriety, it is of confidence in another—another person, a government, a bank, a debtor. Faith, then, might be distinguished, if it were necessary to go further into an examination of this point, from many virtues which terminate on ourselves, and which pertain only to ourselves. The point of examination now is, its value in the *relations* which men sustain, or in social interests. All that I can say will be merely to vary a very simple idea, or to apply one thought to different things; but it will, I trust, conduct us to the conclusion which it is desirable to reach in order to confirm the statement in my text.*

* Some of the remarks and illustrations on the subject of *faith* in this discourse have been made substantially in a different connexion in a previous sermon in this volume, but they seem so appropriate to the design of this discourse that it was not found convenient to omit them.

(1.) I begin with a reference to the value of confidence in a family. It can hardly be necessary to do much more here than simply to refer to the subject. All of us feel that the welfare of a family depends wholly on this; and that if it were destroyed, happiness would at once flee from our dwellings. All the good order, the prosperity, the happiness of a family depends on the confidence that a husband and wife repose in each other; in the confidence that children have in their parents; and perhaps in a not less degree in the confidence which parents have in their children. Every hour that we live in these relations we are dependent on that confidence for our peace of mind; and in relation to our domestic comfort and order there is nothing that could be substituted for it. Every hour of happiness that any of us have had in the marriage relation has been identified with that, and at any moment our happiness would have been destroyed effectually if that had not existed. There could have been no substitute for it. No prosperity abroad; no success in business; no honours lavished upon us in the world; no sudden gains; no pleasures derived from literature, science, or the arts, could have been a substitute for this, or could have mitigated the pangs which would have existed in the bosom at the very idea of "infidelity," or a want of confidence, in this relation. The happiness and success of a parent depend wholly, too, on the confidence which his children repose in him. No parental government can answer the purpose where this is not secured; there can be no domestic peace where this is not found. It is not on *force* that we rely in governing our families and making them happy; it is in the confidence which our children shall have in our wisdom, our integrity, our ability to give them the advice which they need, our qualifications to govern in the little community of which we are the head. If that cannot be secured in a family, there is nothing else that can be permanently substituted in its place. And, as already remarked, perhaps to a not less degree is domestic happiness dependent on the measure of just confidence that we repose in our children. If we have no confidence that they will act rightly; if we cannot trust them out of our sight; if we feel when they go out of the door that they will visit some place of infamy, regardless of our commands, whatever else they may have, whether learning or talent, it is plain that peace will be a stranger to our bosoms, and that slumber will not visit our eyelids.

Now if these things be so, it will be seen that the most effective mischief which any man could do, or could desire to do, in a family, would be simply to destroy this mutual confidence. If I had the power, and wished to strike the most deadly blow at the heart of a family, I should do nothing more. I should go and take away all the confidence of a husband in his wife, and of a wife in her husband, and fill their minds with distrust and jealousy—and by doing this I should take away all peace from their bosoms, and sleep from their pillows. Or I should go and destroy all confidence in the bosom of sons or daughters towards a father; and teach them to feel that he was not worthy of their respect or love—and I should thus introduce insubordination and disobedience into the most peaceful dwelling on earth. Or I should go and destroy all the confidence of a father in his sons or his daughters; and I should make him restless and sad whenever they were out of his sight; and I should fill his bosom with the keenest anguish at the feeling that all his hopes had been blasted, and I should transform all his cherished and happy prospects in regard to their future character into dark and gloomy forebodings, and I should so torment him by a simple want of confidence as to make him wish that neither he nor they had been born, and long for the hour when he should find rest from his mental tortures in the grave.

(2.) Let us apply this remark to the relations sustained in a commercial community. Let a man reflect but for one moment how much the prosperity of such a community depends on mutual confidence, and he cannot be insensible to its value and importance. Let confidence in a commercial house be shaken, and how many interests are affected by it at once! Let confidence in a bank be shaken, and there may not be an interest in that community which is not affected by it. As when the storm shakes an old oak that has stood for generations, the admiration of men, the far-distant fibres of the roots, fine and tender, that run under the ground hidden from human view, shall be torn and rent, so it is when confidence in such an institution is shaken. There are a thousand interests which you would not have supposed would have been affected, that feel the shock. For such a shock affects not merely the commercial world—the men whose business may be dependent on its stability. In that bank shall have been confided the little property of hundreds or thousands of widows and orphans. He who had had the ability to lay up what it was hoped would make old age or the day of sickness comfortable, had entrusted it there. The professional man that had saved from his hard earnings what he felt he should need when the infirmities of age should forbid his longer toil, had felt that he had made competent provision for declining years, and had deposited it there. The father who had a beloved daughter, for whom he would make some provision as an expression of his love, and who had sought to calm his own mind when he reflected that he might be taken away, and be no longer able to be her protector and friend, had deposited what he meant for her there. When confidence fails in such an institution; when it reels, ready to fall; when it comes down a mass of ruins, and no one can tell where the millions entrusted to it are scattered, there are thousands and tens of thousands of hearts that are made to bleed, and a blow is struck that vibrates through a community, reaching remote points that you would not have supposed could be affected by such a shock.

To commercial men, it is needful only to advert to this point. Well do they know that the entire prosperity of the community depends on confidence, and that when that is gone, all is gone. To see this in its full force, all that would be necessary would be to recall to recollection past events in our own community, and in our own land. From the minds of those who then lived, and especially from the minds of the multitudes who were so deeply interested, those scenes will never pass away while life lasts. Confidence in banks, and commercial houses, and in the solvency of distant debtors, seemed almost universally to have failed, and the whole land was agitated and convulsed, not because we were poor, or because our soil had ceased to be fruitful, or our air was pestilential, or our resources had departed, or because "grim-visaged war" frowned upon us, but because *confidence was gone.*

The same remark might be made here which was made respecting the peace of a family. If I had the power, and were disposed to inflict the deepest evil on a community, I should do no more than destroy this universal confidence. I should go into the commercial world and breathe suspicions, and start rumours, and insinuate doubts, and circulate reports, and unsettle the confidence of one commercial house in another, and of one bank in another, and of one part of the country in another, until I produced universal distrust; and just so far as I succeeded, I should spread universal ruin. No foreign war, no spreading pestilence, no change of the seasons, would produce deeper distress in this land; for what commercial operation is there that could be continued for a day, if confidence were gone?

(3.) Let us apply this remark to the intercourse of nations, and see if we can find an illustration of the value of confidence or faith there. Nations never have been entirely independent of each other; as society advances, they are becoming less and less so. They may be independent in their government and laws, and so far as any direct foreign interference is concerned; but they are so in no other sense. They are adjacent to each other, and the prosperity of one affects the prosperity of another; or they are distant, and are dependent for a thousand things which can be produced in the one, but which cannot be produced in the other. Formerly, when men had fewer artificial wants, and when the facilities of commerce were less, they were far more independent; for Assyria, and Persia, and ancient Germany, and Gaul, were far less dependent on other nations, and would feel the effects of any change in other nations, far less than Great Britain and the United States, or even France and Russia, would now. The *tendency* of things is to increase the dependence, and to make the nations of the earth one great brotherhood.

There have been two ways of endeavouring to secure a safe and prosperous intercourse among nations :—by the force of arms, and by treaties of commerce and of peace ; by the dread of the sword, and by mutual faith. The ancients relied mainly on the former ; and seemed to regard a *treaty* as secure only so far as there was dread of the armed legions, or the war-galley. Rome had little confidence in the fidelity of the nations that were reduced to her control as provinces, except as they understood that if they were *not* faithful, the Roman legions would soon thunder at the gates of their cities.

The course of events, the tendency of society, is leading the world to repose on another kind of security in the intercourse between nations. We indeed endeavour to blend the two things still—to intimidate, and to secure confidence, and there is a sort of reliance on both ; but there is a growing sense that the former is unnecessary, and that our main dependence is on the latter. What merchant is there that sends a ship from one of our ports to Calcutta, or Canton, who ever *thinks* of the armed vessels that float in distant seas as a reason why he may commit his property safely to the chances of commerce ? What is it that holds the commercial world together, and renders commerce safe ? Is it our navy, our army, or is it the faith of treaties ? You may say, perhaps, that those treaties would not be regarded if an armed power were not at hand to enforce them ; but that remains to be seen. The truth is, that the nations are depending more and more on what is for their mutual interests, and on the faith of treaties ; and are looking with more and more jealousy on any armed interference, and more aversion on any effort to secure commercial advantages by superior force of arms. The world is to be held together by *confidence*, and not by the terror of arms ; and the sacredness of plighted faith is to take the place of the sword.

Let any intelligent man reflect how much at this moment the commerce of our own country and of the rest of the world is secured by *treaty*, by plighted faith, and he will see the force and the value of the observations which I am making. There is almost no nation—none with whom a treaty would be of value—with whom such a treaty of commerce does not exist. There is almost no land, no port even, where we have not a *consul*—not an armed man at the head of embattled legions; not a man with the emblazonments of war—the epaulette and the sword,—but a simple, plain, unostentatious *citizen*—usually of plain dress and plain manners—the fit representative of a peaceful treaty, and the exponent of the faith of nations. What is right to be done in the land where he is, it is presumed will be done; if wrong has been committed toward any of the citizens of his own land, he presumes there will be a disposition to redress it; and though he may feel indeed, and be assured, that the entire power of his country would be ready to *enforce* what is right if it is denied, yet how rare a thing it is that there is any *allusion* to such power in regulating commercial intercourse.

Suppose, now, all this were to come to an end. Suppose no further reliance could be placed on treaties and international compacts. Is there any form of mischief that could be done in this world so great as to disturb this *confidence* between nations, this faith in compacts? If it were done, if it were felt that there were no reliance to be placed on any treaty hereafter, even with all the armed force that you could send, is there a vessel that would leave this port, or any other part of our land, to bring back the productions of distant climes? Could the commerce of the world survive such a destruction of confidence?

(4.) We may apply the remark respecting the value of confidence, or faith, to the administration of a government. . We have seen its value in a family, in the commercial world, in the intercourse of nations. It is an obvious remark that it is of no less value in the administration of a government, in the enacting and execution of the laws, in a judicial transaction. Peace and harmony, and in connexion with them all forms of prosperity, depend wholly on the degree of confidence that shall be reposed in the administration of a government, or the decision of a court. You may be certain, indeed, that a sheriff or a marshal has power to summon an armed force to his aid, but you are not induced by that to pay your taxes or your custom-house duties, or to submit to the judgment of a court. You calmly acquiesce, because you have confidence in the general working—the equitableness of the institutions of your country. Such confidence may be reposed in a judicial opinion that a nation shall acquiesce in it, though conflicting claims of the highest order may be involved; the laws of states may have come in collision; and property to an amount which no one can estimate may be at stake.

Our whole land is dependent every day on confidence in the government; on confidence in the judges; on confidence in the general virtue of the people; on confidence in the excellence of our institutions. There is not a wheel of the government that could move for a moment if it were not for this. No one of us would entrust a letter to the mail, no one of us would carry a cause before any constituted tribunal, or even submit it to an arbitration.

(5.) We are prepared now to apply the remark to the main thing pertaining to the subject before us—the government of God. The demand in the Bible is, that man shall repose confidence in his Maker, for "without faith it is impossible to please him." The inquiry which we have had in view has been, What is the *reason* why faith under his government has such a primacy, and is of so much value?

Now it is obvious that the value of *confidence* is as great in God's government as in any other, and may be as great in the universal family, embracing all worlds, over which he presides, as in the much smaller families with which we are conversant. But it should also be added, that to an extent elsewhere proportionably unknown the government of God is one of *confidence*, not of *force*. With all power in his arm, and with all resources to bind, and fetter, and restrain, and punish, at his command, still that which he most relies on in his administration is not *force*, but love and confidence. It is in every way probable that that is the *only* thing on which reliance is now placed in heaven in controlling the pure and happy minds there, and that vast as they know the power of God to be, they are not restrained by that, but by the all-controlling influence of affection. They have *confidence* in God—in his wisdom and his goodness—in the equity of his laws and in the principles of his administration; and this is all that is needed to preserve order, and harmony, and peaceful obedience in heaven. For

Love is the golden chain that binds
The happy souls above.

The thing, too, on which reliance was placed in Paradise to secure obedience was *confidence*. There was no force employed there. There were no walls built around it which man could not overleap. There were no cherubim with flaming swords to prevent the egress of man, as there were, after his apostacy, to forbid his return. As long as *confidence in God* remained, man was happy.

When that failed, he was ruined; and the want of confidence in God was there, as it ever has been since, the source of all the woes that man has experienced. With strict philosophical accuracy, all the woes which have come upon the race have arisen from a want of confidence in God as the just moral Governor of the world. Man has no confidence in his law, in his goodness, in his truth, in his promises, in his threatenings, in his qualifications for empire. He has no such confidence in him as to submit to his teachings; to bow reverently to his will where his dealings are mysterious; to resign himself to him in his trials; to embrace his promises, when he offers heaven to him; to feel alarm, and to turn from his sins, when he threatens the punishment of hell. Even now, with all our external sources of trouble and woe, with all the sorrows and ills of poverty, want, sickness, bereavement, and dreaded death, this would be a happy world if man had confidence in God; for the moment you can infuse into the bosom of a sufferer, no matter whether in bereavement, on a sick bed, or in any other form of woe, *confidence in God*, that moment you have soothed the anguish of the soul, and diffused through the bosom peace and joy.

I will ask your attention, in view of the reasoning pursued in this discourse, only to one thought of a practical nature suggested by the subject. It is, that infidelity, or unbelief, as a speculative or practical matter, is not a harmless thing. It is often supposed to be so. It is regarded as a mere matter of speculation; a thing in reference to which the utmost freedom of the mind may be innocently indulged; a thing in which you do others no wrong, for you deprive them of no property by it, and suppose that you do nothing to sap the foundation of their happiness.

But if the views suggested in this discourse are correct, nothing can be more unfounded than this opinion. Is that a harmless system which, if it came into your family, would unsettle all the confidence which you have in your wife, and all the confidence which your children have in you as a father? Is he an innocent man who would unsettle all confidence in a commercial house, in a bank, in a lawyer, in a physician, in a bench of judges? Would that be an innocent system which would breathe suspicion in the community on the character of every minister of the gospel, and every professor in a college, and every teacher in a school? And if you may suppose that a man of capital should establish a system of agencies all over the land, and have them wholly under his control, and that the design should be by a well-arranged scheme of operations to destroy all confidence, say in every merchant, and every monied institution, would you say that that was a harmless system of operations? And suppose that a man should come into your family and unsettle all the confidence of your children in God, and in the principles of virtue and sound morals, and in that holy volume which you regard as the foundation of all just views of morals,—shall we regard *him* as a harmless man, and his opinions as a matter of no consequence? Or suppose, by an extended system of agencies, by the facilities of the press, by his power of scattering pamphlets and books all over the land, he should pursue an extended scheme of operations to destroy all the confidence of man in God as a moral Governor, and in his law, and in the principles of virtue, and in the foundations of morality; that should tend to destroy the confidence which the poor, the afflicted, the oppressed, and the dying repose in God their Saviour; which should leave them to suffer without support, and to feel that they are "in a forsaken and fatherless world," and to die without hope,—will you say that *such* a system is harmless? Why more so than when your malignant agent establishes a system with a view of unsettling the confidence in every merchant and monied institution throughout the land? Is confidence in the foundations of morals, and confidence in God as the righteous moral Governor of the world, of *less* importance than in a man or in a bank? The perpetrator of the deepest mischief in this world is the man who lives to unsettle *confidence.* Let my enemy come, if he wishes, and take the little property which my hands have earned; let him come and strike me on one cheek and on the other; let him take my coat and my cloak also; let him turn me out from my happy and peaceful home, a penniless wanderer on the face of the earth;—but let him *not* come and destroy the confidence which my wife reposes in me, and I in her; let him not come and unsettle the foundations of moral principle in which I have endeavoured to ground my children; let him not seek to alienate our confidence in each other and in our God. Poor, and penniless, and cold, and naked, and with no certain dwelling-place, I should wander with my family with one source of pure happiness, undisturbed, if they trusted in me, and I in them, and all in God; but in the most splendid palace that imperial wealth could build and adorn, I could never be happy if confidence in them, and in my Maker and my Saviour, were blasted and destroyed.

Nor is unbelief, as a practical personal matter, more harmless. Sinner, it is not an innocent thing that you have no confidence, no faith in the God that made you. You wrong him; you wrong your own soul. There is no being that is so worthy of your confidence as he; none that has so high a claim. And how can you "please him" if you have no confidence in him? Can a child—a son—a daughter—though learned, and accomplished, or graced with polished manners, though admired for beauty, or praised for talent, or distinguished for eloquence,—can such a child "please" his father, can he be worthy of his love, if he has no just confidence in him—if he treats him with cold neglect—if he never relies on his promises, or respects his principles? Sinner! the source, the root, the germ of all the evil in your soul, is the want of confidence in God. The evil will be arrested, the ruin which is coming on you will be stayed, the moment you are brought back, through the great Mediator, to exercise faith in him who made you—and not *till* then. Without that, dissociated from him, you are destined to a degree of wretchedness and woe, compared with which all the evils produced by want of confidence in a family, a commercial community, between nations, or under a human government, are trifles not to be named!

SERMON XXVIII.

FAITH AS AN ELEMENTARY PRINCIPLE OF ACTION.

2 Cor. v. 7.—"We walk by faith, not by sight."

In the first discourse on the subject of faith, I illustrated the inquiry why faith is made an indispensable condition of salvation; in the second, I considered the value and importance of faith.

Faith enters so much into the Christian system, is regarded as so essential an element in our conduct as religious beings, and is designed to accomplish so important effects on our character, that, in every point of view in which it can be regarded, it demands our careful and prayerful consideration. It seems to be supposed that there is some foundation for the importance attached to it in our very nature, or that man is so made that it is designed that faith shall be an important element of his conduct, and shall exert an important influence over him. If there were not something in man that laid the foundation for this, the prominence given to faith in the Bible would seem to be unauthorized, and the purpose of making so much out of it would seem to be an attempt to institute an arbitrary arrangement, and to separate religion from all other principles of action. I propose, then, in order to explain the prominence and the value assigned to faith in the Bible, to consider it as an elementary principle of conduct; or to inquire into the influence which it is adapted to exert on man. I shall refer to it, not exclusively as a Christian virtue—for the object is to inquire why it should be incorporated among the Christian virtues at all; but as a state of mind—a principle of conduct—a law of our being. Our aim is to ascertain what place it is designed to occupy in the mind of such a being as man, and placed in the circumstances in which he is; and the bearing of all my remarks will be to illustrate the power of that principle stated in the text, "We walk by faith, not by sight."

In order to illustrate the subject properly, it will be necessary to consider two points:—I. What the principle is; and, II. Its influence as an element of conduct.

I. The first inquiry is, *What is the principle referred to?* It is of the highest importance to settle this, because, either by inadvertence or design, faith is so often confounded with other things, that its value as an element of action is by no means appreciated, and on this account religion is charged with that which, if true, would make it unworthy the serious attention of mankind. A very common impression is, that faith is synonymous with credulity, and that in proportion as we exalt faith as as principle of action, we undervalue reason. Let us then inquire, and see whether we can ascertain precisely what the state of mind is, when we say in any proper sense, that a man "*walks by faith.*" Perhaps we can bring out the state of mind which it is proposed to consider, by placing it in contrast with other things.

(1.) It is to be distinguished from credulity, and indeed in many respects is the opposite of credulity. "Credulity is a weakness of mind by which a person is disposed to believe, or yield his assent to a declaration or proposition without sufficient evidence of the truth of what is said or proposed; a disposition to believe on slight evidence, or no evidence at all."—*Webster.* Credulity relates to the belief of reported or alleged *facts;* believing them when there is no sufficient testimony or evidence, and is the opposite of clear and thorough investigation; faith, as an element of action, refers not so much to what *are now* facts, as to what *may be;* not so much to what has been in the past, as to what may be or will be in the future. Credulous men believe in things which are said to have occurred, or which are alleged to be occurring at the present, which are of little importance in themselves, and which are fitted to exert no good influence on the character; faith has relation, as an element of conduct, to things to come, and to those things which are deeply to affect our character and destiny. Children, in an amiable sense, are credulous—for they act on the principle of our nature, which teaches us, and prompts us to believe, until we *learn* to distrust by painful experience. Whatever is reported to them, they believe—for they have not yet learned to distinguish truth from falsehood, and indeed have hardly learned as yet that there *is* any such thing as falsehood. Men in the infancy of society are credulous—for they are then much like children; and amidst the multitudes of things which are before their minds, and the numerous questions which present themselves, and under the influence of an imagination easily excited, they have not yet learned to separate the true from the false, and believe them all alike: stories of preternatural apparitions, and the influence of the stars, and portents, and omens, and the deeds of demi-gods, all together. Hence, all early history is made up of marvels—like the books with which it has been so much the fashion to entertain children. The dupes of superstition are credulous; for they connect certain things with *religion*, and they have settled it in their minds that *all* that is connected with religion is true. Hence they can believe that the blood of St. Januarius is liquified at certain seasons of the year, and that the "house of the Virgin" was borne miraculously through the air from Palestine to Italy; hence they can believe in the virtue of climbing up the steps on Pilate's staircase, and that the "seamless coat" of Christ was discovered by St. Helena, after lying for centuries unknown, and then again, that it was as marvellously preserved in the cathedral at Treves. Infidels, though it may seem to be a paradox, are credulous men. Lord Herbert, among the best of them, was among the most credulous of men; and I take the liberty to affirm that, as a *body* of men, none have been more distinguished for *credulity* than those who have been reckoned among infidels. Faith, as a principle of action, is wholly distinguished from this. A man who has faith, and is greatly influenced by it, *may* be a credulous man; but his credulity pertains to other things connected with his mental organization, and not to his acting by faith.

(2.) By many, faith is sometimes contrasted in a strange manner with a habit of scepticism and of doubt, and with an implied advantage in favour of the latter. It is supposed by them, that, as a habit of mind, a disposition to doubt, to be cautious, to be slow in admitting evidence, and to refuse assent in cases where so many yield so readily, not only stands in strong contrast with the state of mind required in the gospel, but is a *better* state of mind. Such a man, therefore, supposes that while he retains this disposition of mind to examine *everything* in an impartial manner, and to admit the full influence of all reasonable doubts on his mind in any case, he cannot be a Christian. Yet, if I understand the matter, this is not a just view of the case at all. The faith of the gospel is not opposed to the most candid and thorough investigation of any subject; and the state of mind here referred to, and placed in contrast with it, is not distinguished from the faith of the gospel by a habit of bolder and more independent thinking. The difference between them is not in regard to the freedom of inquiry; it is in regard to the influence of *hope* and of *desire*. Give to a man who is a sceptic the influence of the *hope* which the gospel proposes; create in his heart a *desire* for that on which faith rests, and in view of which it acts, and that same man will be no more cautious and independent than he who lives by faith. It is the absence of this, and not independence of thinking, which distinguishes him; for while he has no desire to know God, to live for ever, to be holy and pure in a future world, he is of course sceptical. He cares nothing about the evidence on the subject. He neither examines it, nor will he allow it to make any impression on his mind. His mind, therefore, is not *better*, in the sense that it is more candid, and cautious, and independent; but *worse*, in the sense that it is a mind that does not feel or appreciate the influence of *hope*, and of *desire* for that which is of the highest value and importance.

(3.) Faith, as an element of conduct, I need hardly say, is distinct from acting under the mere influence of the senses. "We walk by faith, *not* by sight." Most men act only from a reference to the senses, or in the light only which the relations of the senses cast on objects. They say, "Let us eat and drink, for to-morrow we die," 1 Cor. xv. 32. "I shall have peace, though I walk in the imagination of mine heart, to add drunkenness to thirst," Deut. xxix. 19. If they do not live under the influence of the *senses*, in the lowest meaning of the term—that of gross corruption—yet they aim to give what they would regard as the due influence to the information derived from the senses, or the inlets of knowledge from the external world. They become "matter of fact" men; their thoughts range only through the circle of the questions which arise about "profit and loss;" or they make close calculations by measurements of heights and distances, and abide by them. They give no scope to the fancy—to hope—to those generous impulses which would carry them out of the range of mere calculation. Now this is well as far as it goes; and is the basis of many of the excellent rules of economy, and a restrainer of extravagance. But it may make the mind exceedingly narrow, and prevent the development of some of its noblest powers. Man is made to be something else besides a mere creature of sight and of hearing; he is capable of being much more than an ingenious measuring and calculating machine. Faith, as an element of action, does much more—is much more expanding and noble. Even the ancient Greeks and Romans, though heathens, admitting the influence of this principle, furnished a striking illustration of the power of faith. They opened their eyes on distant worlds, and supposed there were many other things than the sight reveals; and though the gods which they *supposed* to have a dwelling-place in the groves, and by the fountains, were the work of imagination, yet they acted out the principle of our nature which *longs* to find other things than the sight reveals, and were under far better influences in many respects, in elevating and expanding the mind, than they would have been if confined to the grovellings of sense. Men who have no principle of *faith* in their nature, who are universally sceptical in regard to its revelations, are like the ancient mariners. In their frail barks they crept along the shore; always kept some headland or promontory in view; anchored in a friendly bay at night; and never put out into the open sea. Columbus, with different feeling, turned his prow boldly to the West, and held it steadily in that direction in the faith of "giving a new world to the kingdoms of Castile and Leon." So faith goes beyond the limits of time and of the senses. It not only believes in the existence of the worlds which the telescope reveals, but *peoples* those worlds; not only believes in the existence of that universe which strikes the outward eye as so glorious, but in the existence of a more glorious God that formed them all; not only believes that there is such an atom in creation as this earth, and such a thing as the "vapour of human life," but that there is a world to come, and that there is life everlasting.

(4.) One thing more may be said in order to distinguish faith as an element of action. It has a very near relation to *hope;* and is, in fact, on the authority of an apostle, the *embodiment* of hope. "Now faith is the *substance* of things hoped for," Heb. xi. 1. It takes hold of things that are not seen, but which may be as *real* as though they were; and of things which are not yet *facts*, but which *may be*. A young man *hopes* for distinction in political life. As a reality, it has as yet no existence. But it *may* have. It is in his mind's eye *as if* it were a reality, and he sets it before him as his hopes and desires would prompt; and though far distant, he studies, and struggles, as if it might be so. Demosthenes, when he went into his cave, and tried the strength of his voice by the raging elements of the deep, doubtless had in his mind's eye an image of what it would be to be the first orator of the world. See what *faith* entered into such a purpose, and into such a conception:—faith in his own powers; faith in the effect of careful culture; faith in believing that formidable obstacles may be overcome; faith in his countrymen, that they would do honour to him who deserved it; faith in history, that it would transmit his name to future times; faith in all coming generations, that they would receive his name with honour, and transmit it onward. So now in higher things:—faith carries the mind upward and onward; fastens on objects of *hope*, and turns them into living forms, and allows them to influence the mind: and the view by faith of those superior realities turns giants here to dwarfs, and mountains to mole-hills, and crowns to baubles, and heaps of hoarded gold to particles of glittering dust, and the palaces of princes to the play-houses of children. Man begins to live for nobler objects; and there comes over the soul the expanding and elevating thought that there is something worth living for, and that he is indeed *immortal.*

II. Having thus endeavoured to state what this principle is, I proceed to consider, in the second place, *its influence as an element of conduct.* With an ultimate view of illustrating its influence in religion, and of showing you that there is much worth living for beyond what the senses reveal, and that it is rational to act in view of that, I will endeavour to illustrate its value under these specifications:—as prompting to action; as expanding and elevating the mind; and as indispensable in all just views of religion.

(1.) We may consider it as an element of our nature leading to *action.* We will look at it now in general, without particular reference to religion. We have seen that it stands in contrast with cold calculation; with what is disclosed by the mere testimony of the senses; with the low and grovelling objects that appeal to the appetites. A man into whose character there enters not the element of faith, is one who has no confidence in the power of truth in meeting and arresting evils; in the elevation and perfectibility of society; in the practicability of correcting errors, or of checking and removing individual or organized wrongs; in himself; in his fellow-men; or in God. His mind never ventures beyond a very limited range—that which has come under his own observation, or which is within the compass of a very rigid calculation. Let us look at such a mind, and see what it would accomplish in such a world as this.

(*a*) A sturdy farmer, trained to the use of the axe, and the hoe, and the plough, and with the advantages of an education in a common school, and with some reading to expand his mind, stands on an eminence in the wilds of the West, and looks over a boundless forest. It waves in the interminable distance, and the sun has never yet been suffered to penetrate through that thick foliage to the earth. There is no city, or town, or even log-cabin to be seen. Not even the smoke of the Indian wigwam reveals that any human being is there. But there, an intelligent eye may see the evidence of as rich a soil as the sun ever shone upon; and those valleys may yet be covered with harvests and with flocks; and houses and mills, villages and towns, may yet spring up there. Winding along, through that forest, may be seen the course of a river—and the opening where it runs shows that it is a *broad* stream—though on its bosom never yet floated anything but the bark-canoe of an Indian. In all that boundless expanse, there is neither road, nor bridge, nor fence; neither church, nor college, nor school-house. Yet that man is possessed of *faith;* faith in his axe, in his arm, in his skill—in himself, in his growing boy, in his neighbours that will unite with him; and he *believes* that all that forest may be felled, and that it may become a fertile field, and that colleges and sanctuaries and cities may smile there; and that on that river the magnificent steamer may glide laden with rich productions from that teeming soil. Many a weary day must indeed be spent, many a hard blow must be struck, before that result shall be reached; but there is more than *hope* that it may be done, to animate and cheer the woodsman; there is *faith* that it *will* be done; and the forest gives way, and the fields are ploughed and fenced, and houses and all the improvements of art appear in what was the interminable wilderness, as if by magic. Yet there is no magic about it. It is all the result of desire, and hope, and faith,—and corresponding toil.

(*b*) A man looks at his country. He greatly loves it—for it is the land of his birth; his interests are there; and in every way he desires its prosperity. But he sees it oppressed. It groans under heavy and unjust burdens. There are evils. The unconstitutional claims of the government, the evils of a deficient representation, may be deeply felt; or foreign troops may be quartered on the citizens to awe them. On these things the patriot looks with deep emotion, and with an earnest desire that they may be removed. The man in whose soul the reigning element is doubt, or who is governed solely by the decisions of his senses, would be prompted to no effort for relief, would venture nothing for it. But not thus did men look upon the wrongs of their country in the times of Hampden; not thus did Patrick Henry and John Hancock look upon the wrongs which our own land endured. In those minds and hearts there were no elements of scepticism. There dwelt there in the strongest degree the element of *faith.* They were moved, not by the love of gain or applause; they not merely felt that their country was suffering wrong; they not merely *hoped* and *desired* that their wrongs might be removed,—but they had strong *faith,* unwavering *confidence,* that it might be done. They had faith in the justice of their cause; in the virtue of their countrymen; in the valour of men that might be summoned to defend the national rights;

in the fathers and mothers of the land, that they would give up their sons to its defence; in the nations of the earth, that they would approve their course; and in God, that he would be the Friend of the oppressed and the wronged—and whatever liberty there is in England or in this land is the result of *such faith*.

(2.) We have considered this principle of our nature as an element leading to action. Let us now, for a moment, consider it as an *expanding* and *elevating* element of conduct. We might here take the very cases which have already been referred to, and perhaps they would furnish all the elucidation which would be required. But we may vary the illustrations, and while we furnish new confirmations of what has been already said, place the point now before us in a more distinct light. John Howard, born to an ample property, and encompassed by all that was necessary to worldly enjoyment, with leisure for literary pursuits, or for the pleasures of the table or the field, or for the refined courtesies of life in England, might have spent his days, as thousands do, with most limited views, and with a heart most selfishly contracted. A sceptic as to the world's improvement; a doubter as to the feasibility of any project to elevate the degraded; a disbeliever in any enterprise that looked to the elevation of the more debased portions of mankind; a man who confined himself to questions of mere calculation,—he might have lived only to improve his estates, and in one narrow circle his ideas might have for ever revolved. But God had endued him with a heart benevolent by nature; and the finger of Providence pointed to an object worthy of its exercise. He was led to look on the prisons of Europe. But how did he look on them? True, there was enough to excite all the compassion of his soul, and such a man would weep over the unpitied wrongs of the prisoner. But he looked on them not only to weep. There was another, and a much higher and more expansive feeling in his bosom than mere compassion. It was *faith*. It was a belief that those woes might be mitigated, that those wrongs might be repaired, that the condition of the sufferer might be alleviated. What was this? It was confidence in human nature; in man,—in his sense of justice and humanity, when roused to it; in princes and lawgivers—that they might be disposed to do right; in society—that its workings might come nearer to perfection; above all, in God, that *he* would show himself the Friend of the oppressed and the wronged;—and this faith expanded the heart of Howard to embrace the world, and made him what he was. So Clarkson and Wilberforce looked upon injured Africa—not merely with the feelings of compassion, but with *faith* in the English heart;

in the justice of their countrymen, if their sentiments were fairly expressed; in the sense of right with which God has endowed man; and in the Great Governor of the nations, that he would ultimately crown with success every effort to break the bonds of oppression.

An American youth, educated at a university, and about to enter upon the theatre of life, looks out over the world. He has a heart filled with love to the Saviour, and is desirous of living to do good. His thoughts are turned to the great West. But how many difficulties may be seen there:—difficulties, not so much of poverty, and privation, and toil, and want of the kind of society to which he has been accustomed—but difficulties in saving that vast region from the evil influences that are setting in upon it from all quarters of the world. Far more formidable are those moral difficulties than were the forests, and the unbridged rivers, to our woodsman; and yet with an eye of faith he may look all over that land, and see it in the future, spiritually, as the "garden of the Lord." He crosses the mountains with no doubt that there the standard of the Cross is everywhere to be erected; that those lands are to be cultivated by a Christian people; that churches are to be reared, and that colleges and schools are to scatter their rich benedictions all over that immense region. He has *faith* that this is all to be a Christian land; and he enters upon his work with a higher and more expansive aim than his own country in any other department can furnish. Long, perhaps, he labours under discouragement, and amidst many trials. Worldliness abounds; error reigns; few give heed to his voice; yet he never doubts that "the wilderness and the solitary place shall be glad, and that the desert shall bud and blossom as the rose."

With similar feelings, and at the same time of life, another young man casts his eyes over the heathen world. How dark and degraded it seems! How many millions, and hundreds of millions of human beings are sunk in idolatry! How sin—most loathsome, and debasing, and revolting—abounds! What scenes of misery open on his view; what cries of distress break on his ear! How long and unbroken has been the reign of death! Who shall elevate the degraded man? Who shall scatter the darkness of the world? It is not in man, he sees, to do it. There is no recuperative energy in the heathen mind to recover it from its low debasement. There are no agencies there at work to bring these evils to an end, and to re-enstamp upon those degraded intellects the effaced image of a holy God. More than in any other department of human action, perhaps, he goes to his work under the influence of *faith*—faith in the simple promise of God—and his bosom, amidst all that discourages and disheartens, is expanded as by faith he sees "afar" the time when "one song shall employ all nations, and the dwellers in the vales and on the rocks shall shout to each other, and the mountain tops from distant mountains shall catch the flying joy;" when "the earth shall be filled with the knowledge of the Lord, as the waters cover the sea." In his benevolence and his faith, he embraces the world; forms, as Paul did, the largest plans for its welfare; and devotes himself to the high and noble enterprise of spreading everywhere the religion of truth and love. He believes that truth has power; that the race may be elevated; that oppression, idolatry, and wrong of every kind may cease; that the gospel is mighty, and will prevail. He has faith even in man—degraded as he seems to be, and is; that there is some chord in his soul that may be struck that will respond to the proffered offer of pardon and of heaven; and much more, he has faith in God and his promises, that this world shall not always be thus sunken and wretched, but that it shall be redeemed and elevated. He may not live to see it in the reality, but he sees it as a bright and glorious object in the distant future; and knowing that many a hardship must be endured before it is realized, that many a youth must give himself to the work and fall in a heathen land before it is accomplished, he is willing to be one of those labourers, that the bright millennial morn may yet dawn upon the world.

(3.) I have endeavoured to illustrate this principle as an element of action, and as elevating and expansive in its nature. There remains but one other thought, the third, to complete the illustration of the subject. It is, that it is an indispensable element in all religion. The error of false religions is not in acting by *faith* when they people the invisible world with divinities; it is, that the *objects* of their faith are not real, but are false. But *all* religion must be a work of faith. It goes beyond the regions of the senses. It pertains to the future, to the distant, and to the invisible. It is designed to bring the invisible, and the future, to bear upon us as realities. If this be not so, there *can* be no religion. The only thing that *reason* asks in the case is, that those objects be *in fact* real, and not the creations of fancy. But if we have religion, we *must* believe that there is an invisible God; that there is a future state, yet unseen, of course; that there are to be rewards hereafter; that we are destined to a higher sphere of being, and that it is rational to act in view of that higher existence. How *can* there be any religion of any kind, unless there is faith in these things? And all religion, of all sorts, is just a work of *faith*, and is designed to influence us *by* faith. We see one world, and we believe that there is another; we see stars and suns, and we believe that there is a God who made them; we see ourselves to be sinners, and we believe that we may be recovered from sin; we see the race sunken and degraded, and we believe that it may be redeemed; we see that we are to die, and we believe that we may live again. Going beyond the limits of the world of sense, we bring before us a world that is invisible, and act as if it were a reality; and in religion, as in all other things, faith, embodying the conceptions of hope, is "the *substance* of things hoped for, the *evidence* of things not seen." The mind is carried from the narrow limits of the world disclosed by the visual organs to other worlds, and the things unseen control and mould the heart.

And now, what practical good shall follow from this discussion? Much *may* every way. It has brought before us one of the laws of our nature, on which religion purposes to engraft itself, and which is destined to work wonders for man. It is that to which the world owes its elevation thus far, and all that has been accomplished for the race. Every field that we see smiling in the harvest is the result of the faith of him who ploughed and sowed it—faith in the seed, and in the fertile earth, and the sun, and the rain, and the Providence of God; every principle of liberty which we enjoy is the result of the faith of gifted minds—of men who *believed* that oppression might be made to cease, and that man might be elevated to a just conception of his own rights; every college in the land, every house of refuge, every asylum for the blind and the deaf, as well as every Christian sanctuary, is a demonstration that those who reared them *believed* that much might be done for the wretched, and that the race *might* be elevated and saved.

We are prone to act under the influence of sense. This arises almost from the necessity of the laws of our being. But our Maker meant that the strong principle of faith should come in to counteract this tendency, and to reveal our own true worth and dignity, not as sensual beings, but as rational and immortal—as capable, unlike other animals, of going beyond the range of the senses, and of acting in view of the distant, the great, the unseen. Hence, we can act in view of the future—of the future liberty and glory of our country, as if it passed before us in a splendid panorama. We can act in view of a world redeemed—as if already the shout were going up from every land, "The kingdoms of this world have become the kingdoms of our God and of his Christ." We can act in view of God—as if we saw him everywhere, and felt that he heard every word, and knew every thought; "enduring," as Moses did, "as *seeing* him who is invisible." We can act in view of heaven—as if we already saw the pearly gates wide unfold themselves, and could look far into distant worlds.

What man needs for his elevation is the acting out of this principle of faith—acting more by faith, and less by sight. He needs a more vivid impression of the presence and the glory of God; of the reality of heaven; of the power of truth; of the wonders of the invisible world—the glittering crowns, and the thrones, and the harps of heaven,—and then indeed the things of this world *would* be baubles and trifles. The religion of this age needs to be expanded that it may become more a religion of faith; the church needs to be taken away from the dominion of the senses, and led to exercise a more simple faith in the truth and the promises of God; and the human mind needs to be elevated and purified by the contemplation of things that are vast and everlasting. Then shall man rise to his true dignity when other worlds shall have to his view the reality of this; and when in their overpowering splendour and glory, as apprehended by the mind, the objects which now seem so vast to us shall dwindle down to nothing, and when all through his brief journey to the grave, man "shall walk by faith, and not by sight:" living by it every day; forming his plans in view of its revelations; consecrating himself and his all, by its power, to the service of a holy Saviour and to the good of the church and the world:—and then, when his work is done, whether sooner or later, under its revelation of brighter worlds, cheerfully going down into the cold river of death—the narrow stream which divides the shadows amidst which he has been moving for a few brief days from the realities of the world which, amidst those shadows, he discerned afar, and where he is now for ever to dwell. Thus let *us* live—thus *may* we die.

SERMON XXIX.

THE IMPORTANCE OF THE INQUIRY, HOW SHALL MAN BE JUST WITH GOD?

JOB xxv. 4.—"How can man be justified with God?"

THESE are the words of Bildad—one of the sages who had entered into controversy with Job in regard to the government of God. They were uttered in view of the majesty and holiness of the Most High; and the meaning is, "When the greatness and glory of God are contemplated, how *can* man be regarded as holy before him?" "Dominion and fear," says the Shuhite, "are with him. Is there any number of his armies? How, then, can man be justified with God? or how can he be clean that is born of a woman? Behold even to the moon, and it shineth not; yea, the stars are not pure in his sight. How much less man, that is a worm?" The same sentiment had been twice before expressed by the speakers in this controversy. It was first uttered by Elihu in perhaps the most sublime account ever given of a vision of God to men:—"A thing was secretly brought unto me, and mine ear received a little thereof. In thoughts from the visions of the night, when deep sleep falleth on men, fear came upon me. and trembling, which made all my bones to shake. Then a spirit passed before my face; the hair of my flesh stood up: it stood still, but I could not discern the form thereof: an image was before mine eyes, there was silence, and I heard a voice, saying, Shall mortal man be more just than God? shall a man be more pure than his Maker? Behold, he put no trust in his servants; and his angels he charged with folly: how much less in them that dwell in houses of clay?" Job iv. 12—19. The same sentiment was expressed also by Job himself as a doctrine by no means new to him, and as one which had received his careful thought, and to which he freely expressed his assent:—"I know it is so of a truth:—how should man be just with God?" Job ix. 2. The question thus propounded by these eastern sages, in the earliest debate among men of which we have any record, may be regarded as an inquiry proposed by *man*—by *human nature*. It expresses the deep workings of the human soul in all ages on one of the most important and difficult of all subjects. The question means, How shall man be regarded and treated as righteous by his Maker? What methods shall he take to secure such treatment? What can he do, if anything, to commend himself to the favourable regards of a holy God? What can he do, if anything, to make amends for the past? What can he do, if anything, to turn away future wrath? Can he vindicate himself before the eternal throne for what he has done? If not, can he see how it is consistent for God to treat him as righteous? This question meets us everywhere, and enters into and moulds all the forms of religion on the earth. Let us contemplate it with the interest which becomes so grave a question, and one which is so identified with our everlasting welfare. The inquiry, as illustrating and expressing the feelings of human nature, may be considered with reference to two points—its importance, and its difficulty.

I. *The importance of the inquiry.*

(1.) Its importance will be seen by this consideration—*No one can be saved unless he is just or righteous in the sight of God.* Unless there is some way by which God can consistently regard and treat us as just or righteous, it is impossible to believe that we can enter heaven when we die. Unless man is personally so holy that he cannot be charged with guilt; or can justify himself by denying or disproving that charge of guilt; or can vindicate himself by showing that his conduct is right; or can appropriate to himself the merit of another as if it were his own, no one can believe—no one does believe—that he can enter heaven. Probably there is no conviction of the human mind more deep and universal than this; and every man, whether conscious to himself of acting on it or not, makes it elementary in his practical belief. If any one is disposed to call this proposition in question, or if he is not conscious of acting on it, he will see that it must be true, by looking at it for a single moment. The proposition is, that no man can be saved unless he is just or righteous in the sight of God. Can God save a wicked man *as such,* and in view of his wickedness? Can he hold him up to the universe as one who ought to be saved? Can he take the profane man, the scoffer, the adulterer, and the murderer to heaven, and proclaim himself as their patron and friend? Can he connect a life of open wickedness with the rewards of eternal glory? Nothing can be more clear than that if a man is made happy for ever in heaven, there will be some good reason for it, and that reason cannot be that he was regarded as an unrighteous person. There will be a fitness and propriety in his being saved; there will be some reason why it will be proper for God to regard and treat him as righteous. This view, which is perhaps sufficiently obvious, may be illustrated by a reference to human government. No just government could become the patron and friend of the pirate and the murderer, or bestow its rewards on one who in all respects deserved to meet the penalty of the laws. On this belief, also, every man acts in reference to his own salvation. Each one has a firm conviction that no man can be saved unless he is just in the sight of God. A man, when he thinks of being saved, always thinks either that he has kept the law of God, or that he has a good excuse for not complying with it, or that he can make reparation by penances, pilgrimages, sacrifices, or fastings, or that he can appropriate to himself the merit of another. He never thinks of finding favour with God *as* a transgressor, or on account of his crimes; he never supposes that his iniquity can be the foundation of his salvation. God made the human soul, and he so made it that it never *could* believe that he would save a man *because* he was wicked, or unless there was some way in which he could be regarded and treated as righteous.

(2.) The importance of the inquiry is seen from the testimony of man everywhere. Man is *apparently* greatly indifferent to religion, and it often seems impossible to arouse his attention to the great and momentous questions connected with it. But taking the race together, he is not so indifferent to the subject as he appears, and could we know all the secret thoughts and feelings of each individual, we should find that his indifference is often in appearance only. There are workings of the soul which are carefully excluded from public view. There are thoughts which every man has, which he would not wish others to know of. There are deep, agitating, protracted inquiries resulting in settled conviction, or tossing the soul upon a restless sea, which men would wish to hide from their best friends. There is often a deep interest in a man's mind on the subject of religion, when his whole soul seems to the world torpid and inactive, or when he would repel your inquiries, or when he would seem as "calm as summer's morning."

A very slight acquaintance with the human mind or with the history of opinions is all that is needful to see the importance which the inquiry on the subject of justification has assumed in the view of man.

(*a*) It was seen in the investigations of ancient philosophers and sages. "How shall man be just with God," was the question which pressed itself on the minds and hearts of the speakers in the book of Job, and was a question which was echoed and re-echoed in the whole heathen philosophic world. Many who are profound and patient inquirers on other subjects, often regard investigations on the subject of religion as unworthy their attention. They think them appropriate inquiries for contending theologians; for disputatious and subtle schoolmen; for the feeble in intellect, or for the dying; but they regard them as having only slight claims on a philosophic mind. Yet were they to go and take lessons of the masters of science and of profound thought, they would think differently. Will such men tell us what points of inquiry have most occupied the attention of the intellects of other times? Will they refer to the volumes which contain the results of the investigations of past ages? Will they let Socrates once more speak, and Plato give utterance to his views, and Cicero and Seneca declare what most engrossed their attention? One thing they will find in all the past—one grand absorbing question they will meet with everywhere—one inquiry to which all physical science was made subservient. It was the subject of religion; the question of man's acceptance with God; the grounds of his hope of future blessedness. The real inquiry among thinking men of all ages and lands has been, "How shall man be just with God?"

(*b*) The same earnestness of inquiry we find still in the heathen world. From the recorded views and religion of the heathen, we may learn much about man when he utters his sentiments without disguise; and what we find universally among *them* we may regard as the language of human nature. Now there is no one thing expressed with more uniformity or more earnestness all over the pagan world than this question, "How may we be just with God?" It was the foundation of all sacrifices, penances, pilgrimages, self-inflicted mortifications. All these things were intended so to make expiation for sin, or so to appease the anger of the gods, that they who thus performed the rites of religion might be regarded and treated as righteous. Take this inquiry away, and their sacrifices and penances would be unmeaning. Take this away, and the earnestness of their religion would soon cease, and degenerating into an empty form, would of itself soon expire.

(*c*) There is another method by which we may learn the views of the human soul about the importance of this inquiry. It is by contemplating the soul when under conviction of sin, and reflecting on its prospects about the future world. Then there is no inquiry so momentous in the view of the mind as this—"How shall a man be just with God?" There are many more persons in this state than is commonly imagined. There is probably no one who reaches the years of mature reflection, before whose mind this inquiry has not at some period assumed an engrossing importance. With almost no danger of error, you may assume of every man whom you meet, that his mind either has been, or is now, deeply interested on the subject of his salvation, and that in his life there are periods when no inquiry appears so momentous as this. In his moments of solitary musing, or in a time of bereavement, or under the preaching of the gospel, or when remembered truth seems to come with new-armed power to his soul, or when the recollection of guilt seems recalled to him by some invisible agency, or when lying on a bed of languishing, this great inquiry has come before him, How may he be justified before his Maker? How may the guilt of his sins be washed away? How may he be regarded and treated as a righteous man? To those who have been in this state (and who has not?) it is needless to say that *then* no inquiry seems more momentous than this. In times of revival of religion, the student in a college loses his relish for his ordinary studies, and almost the capacity to pursue them, absorbed in the more important study respecting salvation; the merchant loses his relish for his gains, engrossed in the greater inquiry how he may obtain everlasting life; the farmer, the mechanic, and the mariner feel that they can hardly pursue their wonted employments, for a more momentous subject has engrossed the soul. The eye may be on a passage in Horace or Livy, but the thoughts shall be elsewhere; and the hands may be employed in labour, but it shall be performed with a heavy heart, and the toil pursued with scarcely any consciousness of what is done. The calm, fixed, steady, contemplative eye of the student, and the readiness of the man of business to leave his counting-room and place himself under religious instruction, show with what intensity this inquiry has seized on the soul. The busy, the studious, and the gay often become absorbed in the great inquiry, and then no honour of scholarship, no amplitude of gain, no brilliancy of pleasure or amusement, seems comparable in value to the solution of the question, "How shall man be just with God?" We need not pause here to consider whether this is a just estimate which the soul thus puts on the magnitude of this inquiry. We are concerned only in getting at the language of man himself when in his sober moments. It will at least be conceded, that in those moments of profound absorbing thought,—those moments when men of all classes are willing to turn aside from their usual pursuits; those times when the great inquiry can make the pleasures of the ball-room and the scenes of splendid amusement tasteless, and can loosen the hold of the votaries of gold on their gains, and cause the ardent student to turn aside from his books, —then it is that the human mind is as likely as ever to judge correctly of the importance of what has come before it. Yet there is but one sentiment then—that this question absorbs and annihilates all others.

(3.) There is another consideration which shows the importance of this inquiry: it is, that the views that are entertained of justification modify and shape our views concerning all the other doctrines of religion. It is the central doctrine in the whole system, and spreads its influence over every other opinion which man holds on the subject of salvation. The opinions entertained on this subject distinguish respectively the Protestant and the Papal communities; divide Protestants themselves into two great parties, evangelical and non-evangelical; separate heathens from Christians; give form to all the systems of infidelity and Deism, and constitute the peculiarity of every man's individual faith. When it is known definitely what a man thinks on this one point, it may be known whether he is a Papist, or a Protestant; a Christian, or an infidel; a heathen, or a friend of the Saviour; a formalist, or a devoted servant of God. Luther did not say too much when he said of this doctrine of justification, that it was the article on which depended the permanency or ruin of the church; and with a sagacity equal to that of Tallyrand, when from a very slight matter he predicted that the throne of France would be overturned, Luther saw that the doctrine of justification would meet every corruption of the Papacy, and eventually overturn the system.

The fabric of the Papacy is an ingenious attempt, originated and arranged under the auspices of a higher than human intellect, though fallen, to delude man with the belief that there is some other way by which he may be justified with God than by faith in the Saviour. The whole system of heathenism is an attempt to answer the question how man may be justified with God. The systems of infidels, and of men who are depending on their own morality, or relying on penances and pilgrimages, are another answer which is given to the question. If the observations now made are correct, it will be conceded that this doctrine has an importance which cannot be over-estimated. If it be so, that no man can be saved who is not justified in the sight of God,—that the race everywhere, in the anxious inquiry of sages, in the systems and sacrifices of the heathen, and in the deep workings of the soul rendering every other pursuit tasteless and valueless, has shown a sense of its importance,—and that it spreads its influence over every form of belief,—the importance of the inquiry will be admitted.

II. The second point proposed to be noticed is, *the difficulty of the inquiry*. By the speaker in our text it was evidently felt that it was not easy to furnish an answer to the question proposed. Bildad, Eliphaz, and Job were agreed in one point: it was, that man could not be pronounced free from sin before a holy God. The evidence of his depravity was too manifest to admit of this. In the sight of God, too, they held that the very heavens were not pure, and that the angels were chargeable with folly, Job iv. 17; xv. 15. So bright was his holiness that the moon was shorn of its beams, and the stars were not pure, ch. xxv. 5. How, then, could man be pure? How could he be just with God?

But what *is* the difficulty? Why has the human mind been so much perplexed in relation to it? Why may not God admit man to heaven, and regard and treat him as if he were righteous? These questions can be answered in a single remark, and the whole difficulty may then be seen at a glance. It is, *that man is in fact not righteous*. The difficulty is, to see *how God can regard and treat him as if he were*. It is easy to see how, *if* he were righteous, God could treat him so; or how he could treat him as a sinner—that is, according to his real character. But how shall he treat him differently from what he deserves, or as if he had a character which it is known he has not? Whatever theories may be embraced by men, or whatever opinions may be entertained on the subject of religion, it is true as a matter of fact that these perplexities have been felt by men,—that they have given rise to grave and agitating questions,—and that man has not felt that he could give a solution that was wholly satisfactory. There is no inquiry which has taken hold on man everywhere, under all forms of government and opinion, and in every climate, and amidst every degree of progress, which has not had some real foundation in the nature of things. The race in its soberest moments does not busy itself with trifles, and especially will not allow itself to be troubled and tortured by inquiries that are of no importance. The difficulty which has been felt on this subject, therefore, is not imaginary; but from the fact that the inquiry has been so universal, and so beyond the human powers satisfactorily to explain, it is clear that God meant it should be regarded by man as a point to be solved only by Divine revelation. The real difficulties in the case, and the state of the human mind in regard to them, may be illustrated by the following observations:—

(1.) There was the impossibility of man's vindicating himself from the charges of guilt brought against him. If he could do this, all would be clear, for God will not condemn the innocent. But it could not be done. These charges were brought in such a way, and enforced in such a manner, that man could not so meet them as to escape the conviction of their truth. They are brought where there is a revelation by God himself in his word; and where there is not, as well as where there is, by conscience. Man is told, in the word of God, that he is a sinner; his recollection of what he has done assures him that it is so; the dealings of God with him convince him that there must be some cause of alienation between himself and his Maker; and every sick bed, and every grave, and every apprehension of future wrath, confirms the conviction. If man were to undertake to convince himself that he is not held to be guilty, the argument could not be derived from the dealings of God with him in this world. It is not easy for a man to satisfy himself that he is not a sinner, when the earth is strewed with the dying and the dead; when his best friends are cut down all around him; when he himself is to die, and when he is so made that he cannot but tremble at the apprehension of the judgment. If any one wished to construct an argument to prove that he is not a sinful man, and that man can be just with God, he would need to be removed to some world where he would not see so many things that seem to be mementoes of human depravity, and so many evidences that his Creator regards him and his fellow-men as guilty. Men have everywhere felt this difficulty. There is no one sentiment in which men more uniformly agree than in this. Every man regards every other man as a sinner, and puts himself on his defence against him, for his locks, and bolts, and notes, and bonds, and securities all demonstrate this; and every man knows that he himself also is a sinner. There is nothing of which he is better apprized, nothing he believes more firmly than this. There is not a living man that could bear the revelation of his thoughts to others for a single day; and that not merely because others have no right to know what is passing in his mind, but because he feels that those thoughts are wrong. Confusion, blushes, shame, and shrinking would diffuse themselves over every assembly, and through every crowded thoroughfare in the streets of a great city, and in every lonely path where stranger should meet stranger, if each one knew that another was surveying closely the thoughts of his heart, and saw what was passing there; and if every man felt that his bosom were so transparent that all the workings of his soul could be observed by others, no one would venture out of his chamber; no one would move along the pathways where he might encounter a fellow-man; the thronged places of business would be deserted, and our great and crowded cities would become like the cities of the dead. No man would venture at midnight on the mountain top, or on the lonely prairie, to stretch out his hands to heaven, and say, "I am pure as the stars that shine upon me, or as the God that made them." So universal is the consciousness of guilt, and so certain does every man feel in his sober moments that he cannot vindicate himself before God. "*How then* SHALL *man be just with God?*"

(2.) It must have been early apparent to men, and any one can see now, that it would involve a difficulty, if the guilty were saved, or if they were regarded and treated as righteous. How could this be done? Man does not do it himself in reference to those who are guilty, and how could God? No father feels that it would be proper to regard and treat an offending child as if he were obedient; no friend acts thus towards one who professes friendship; and no government acts thus towards its subjects. All order and happiness in a family would cease at once, if this were to occur; and government on earth would be unknown. There is a great principle of eternal justice which seems engraved in the convictions of the soul, that every one ought to be treated according to character, and that there *ought* to be a difference in the Divine dealings towards the good and the evil. But what if God treated all alike? What if he made no distinction in regard to character? What if he admitted all to favour, punished no one, and rewarded piety and impiety, fraud and honesty, vice and virtue, reverence and blasphemy alike, with the same immortal crown? What if the murder of the innocent, and the highest deed of benevolence, were equally a passport to his favour? What if he met the licentious, and those of virgin purity of soul, when they came before him, with the same smile of approbation? Would not the universe feel that he was regardless of character? Would it be possible to correct the impression?

But it will be said, perhaps, might he not pardon the guilty, and the fact of pardon constitute a ground of distinction which the universe would understand? True, if it would be *proper* to pardon in this state of things. But are there no difficulties attending the subject of pardon? Can it always be granted? Can it be granted to an unlimited extent? Does a father feel that it is safe and best to adopt it as a universal rule that he will forgive all his children as often as they may choose to offend him, and without any condition? Any one may easily see the difficulty on this subject. There are thousands of men confined in penitentiaries. Many of them are desperate men, regardless of all the laws of heaven and earth. Would it be felt to be safe or proper at once to open their prison doors? Who would wish to be in the neighbourhood, when they should be turned impenitent and unreformed upon the world? If the community is scarcely safe now with all the precautions and guards of justice, what would it be if they were all withdrawn? These difficulties must occur to any one when he asks the question, How can the guilty be justified?

(3.) It is a matter of simple fact that men have felt this difficulty, and the methods which have been resorted to, to devise some way of justification, show how perplexing the subject has been to the human mind. We may learn something of the embarrassments which men feel by the devices to which they resort to overcome them. Look, then, for a moment, at some of the methods to which men have resorted in order to answer the question satisfactorily, How can man be just with God?

(*a*) One class have denied the charge of guilt, and these have endeavoured to convince themselves that they *are* righteous, and that they may safely trust to their own works for salvation. If this could be done, all would be well. But the mass of men have felt that there are insuperable difficulties in the way of doing this. We shall hereafter inquire whether it is practicable.

(*b*) Many have endeavoured to excuse themselves for their conduct, and thus to be justified before God. They are sensible that all is not right; but if they can find a satisfactory excuse, that is, if they can show that they had a right to do what they have done, or could not help it, they feel that they would not be condemned. And they are right in this. To do it they lay the blame on Adam, or on ungovernable passions, or on a fallen nature, or on the power of temptation, or on the government of God. They attempt to show that they could do no otherwise than that they have done; that is, they have a right to do it in the circumstances, and of course are not to blame. We shall inquire hereafter whether this position can be made out.

(*c*) Many have endeavoured to make expiation by blood, and have sought to be justified in this way. Hence the sacrifices of the heathen—the flowing blood and burning bodies of lambs, and goats, and bullocks, and prisoners of war, and slaves, and of children offered to appease the anger of the gods. Thousands of altars smoke in this attempt, and the whole heathen world pants and struggles under the difficulty of the inquiry, How may a guilty man be justified with God?

(*d*) Many have sought the same thing by pilgrimages and penances; by maceration and scourging; by unnatural and painful postures of the body; and by wounds which their own hands have inflicted on themselves. The victim of superstition in India lies down beneath the car of his idol, or fastens hooks in his flesh, or holds his arm in one posture till it is rigid. Simeon, in Syria, on an elevated column, spent his years in misery. Antony, in Egypt, went and lived in a cave; and Benedict originated the monastic system in Italy. Mecca is crowded by pilgrims, to acquire righteousness by a visit to the tomb of the prophet; and the shrines enclosing the bones of the saints are encompassed by throngs in Italy for a similar purpose. The garment of hair frets and tortures the body, and the sound of the lash is heard in the cells of the convent, to gain the same end; and the whole system of penance and self-inflicted torture, all over the world, is just a commentary on the question, How shall man be justified with God?

(*e*) To crown all this, another device has been resorted to. It has been held that there were extraordinary merits of saints who lived in former times; that they performed services beyond what were required; and that these merits were garnered up in a sacred treasure, and are placed at the disposal of the head of the Papal community, to be distributed at his pleasure to those who are conscious of guilt,—and this is the answer some have given to the question, How shall man be justified with God?

From these remarks will be seen what men have thought of the difficulty of this question. In these various ways, human nature speaks out and reveals what is passing in the bosom. They are the methods to which men have resorted, as the best answer which they can give to this inquiry. To see the real difficulty, however, we should be able to go down into the depths of the soul; to gauge all the agonies of guilty consciences; to look at the woes and sorrows which men are willing to endure that they may be justified; and then to see how one and all of these plans utterly fail—how they leave the conscience just as defiled as it was before, the propensities to evil unchecked, the grave as terrific as ever, and the judgment-bar as full of horrors. When we stand and survey these things, we ask with deep concern whether any one of these is the way by which man can be justified with God? If not, is there any other way, or is there none?

I shall have accomplished my object in this discourse if I have secured one thing—if I have been enabled to turn your attention to the subject as a personal matter. I have sought to show you the importance of the inquiry, and the difficulties which encompass it. I have wished to awaken the mind to it—to excite a spirit of inquiry which may be allowed to occupy the mind in hours of leisure. I aim to make an impression which will not pass away like words which vanish in the utterance. Assuredly, I need not say that this inquiry is one in which every man has a personal concern, and is one from which none should turn away. It is clear that unless a man can be justified with God he cannot be saved, and the question then comes up at once whether we know of any way, or whether we have embraced any method by which we can be thus justified. Can any one of us over-estimate the magnitude of this inquiry? Can we attach too great importance to a question which is to throw its influence for ever onward into that vast eternity on which we are soon to enter? Am I asking an unreasonable thing of each one of you, when I ask you to allow the full pressure of this inquiry to come upon your hearts this day, How can *I* be justified with God? Is it unreasonable to entreat you to review the method on which you have been relying, and to ask yourselves whether that method will answer in the great day? I will propose one other question. There is one Book that professes to answer this inquiry. It has a simple object. Its laws, and poetry, and prophecy, and proverbs, and history,—more pure, sweet, and sublime, than can be found in any other book,—all bear on this one subject. It is the scope of the Book—the beginning, the middle, and the end. It proposes to answer the question which human reason cannot answer; to furnish instruction where philosophy fails; to reveal a great sacrifice, where all other oblations are ineffectual; and to give peace to the conscience, when everything else leaves it like the troubled sea. Am I in error in saying that each one of you has that Book in your possession? Am I unreasonable in asking you to open its holy pages, and to kneel down and say to the Father of lights, "Teach me, O my God, how I may be justified with thee?"

SERMON XXX.

MAN CANNOT JUSTIFY HIMSELF BY DENYING OR DISPROVING THE CHARGE OF GUILT.

Rom. iii. 20.—"By the deeds of the law there shall no flesh be justified."

By the "deeds of the law" is denoted conformity to the law, or obedience to the law. The word "*law*" here includes law of all descriptions, moral as well as ceremonial; for the apostle, in the previous part of the chapter, had referred particularly to the violation of the moral law. Having shown that men were universally guilty of such violation, he draws from this argument the conclusion stated in my text, that it is impossible now for any one to be justified by obeying the law of God. The proposition, then, which I derive from the text, and which I propose to defend, is, *that man cannot be justified by his own righteousness.* To see the truth of this proposition, it is necessary to know what is meant by being justified, and then to show that it cannot be secured by a man's personal obedience.

The term *justify* is a legal term, but it is also in common use, and is intelligible to all. An illustration or two will make it plain, and will lay the foundation for the train of thought which will be pursued in this discourse. A man is charged with murder. He may put his defence on one of two grounds. He may either deny the fact of having killed; or admitting that, he may show that he had a right to do it, or is excusable for it. If the charge is not made out against him, of course he is just in the sight of the law, and is acquitted. Or if the fact be made out or admitted, he may take the ground either that he did it in self-defence, or that it was done under such a state of mental derangement as to destroy responsibility—and he is acquitted. He had no "malice prepense." He intended no murder; he committed none; and the law does not hold him guilty of the charge. A man is charged with trespass. He takes a similar ground of defence. He denies the fact, or maintains that he had a right to do what he has done. He sets up a claim to a "right of way" over a field which his neighbour owns, and having established that, he is acquitted, or is held to have done no more than he had a right to do in the case. He is a just man in the eye of the law, and may pursue his own business, enjoy the immunities of a good citizen, the honours of an unsullied name, and protection in his rights unmolested. It may be added here, that there is no other way by which a man can justify himself in the sight of the law. He could not do it by admitting the fact of the trespass, and by paying the fine, or making compensation for the injury done; for though he might be discharged, yet this would be no justification of what was done, and would avail nothing towards showing that he was right in doing it. It does not make a wrong right either to intend beforehand to pay for the mischief, or to make amends for it after the deed is done. This remark will be used hereafter in examining the attempts which men have made to justify themselves.

Now if man attempts to justify himself before his Maker, he must take one of the grounds referred to. He must either deny the charge brought against him; or admitting the facts in the case, he must show that he had a right to do what he has done. If he can do either of these, he will be justified, for God does not condemn the innocent. We will suppose, then, the case of a man arraigned at the bar of his Maker, as we all soon shall be, on trial with reference to eternity. There are two things that occur to us at once. What is the charge against him? What is the defence which he sets up? If there is no charge, he is justified of course. If his defence is valid, he will be acquitted.

It is necessary then, first, to look at the charge which is brought against man. The charge is, that he has violated the law of his Maker, or is a transgressor. It is that of apostacy, or revolt from God; entire failure to keep his laws; a life spent in the constant neglect of acknowledged duty, and the habitual commission of known sins. It may be assumed that every reader is sufficiently familiar with the Bible to know the nature of these charges without their being specified in detail. No one trained in a Christian community can be ignorant of the account of our race which the Bible gives. These charges of guilt do not make the impression which they ought, for these reasons:—because we are so familiar with them; because others are implicated with us; because we do not cordially believe them. Many a man reads the account of human nature in the Bible without supposing there is anything serious in the matter, or much fitted to trouble him. There is many a one who would pass a sleepless night if he knew there was a charge of petty larceny against him, which would bring him into court to-morrow, who has no trouble at the charge of total apostacy and utter revolt brought against him by God. There is many a one who would be in the deepest consternation if he knew that his name was before a grand jury in some such connexion as his conscience could easily suggest, who has no alarm at the thought of the "grand assize," and no dread of the formidable catalogue of crimes drawn up against him in the secrecy of the Divine counsels. A few remarks will demonstrate that these charges against man in the Bible *ought* to make an impression, and that men ought to be willing to look at them. A case or two may therefore be supposed which will show how men ought to be affected in view of such charges brought by the Creator. The case of an officer in a bank may be referred to. He has been long there, or in other stations in public life; and has gained a character, compared with which all the gold that the vaults of the bank could contain would be worthless as the sand. Suddenly, charges are brought against him of unfaithfulness to his trust. They come from quarters worthy of his attention; proceed from such a source as inevitably to gain the ear of the community; are such that his family must know of them; are sustained by such circumstances of actual losses in the bank as to render the charge credible; and are of such a character as to make it necessary for him to leave his post, disgraced perhaps for ever. Now it is not necessary to suppose that these accusations are true. All that is designed is to show the effect which charges of guilt, from a respectable quarter, usually have on a man's mind. But suppose he secretly knew they were all true, how could his conduct be explained, if he were utterly indifferent and unconcerned?

In regard to the charges which are brought against man a few remarks may be made here, to show why they should be allowed to make an impression on the mind. (1.) One consideration respects the source from whence they come. They are professedly the charges of our Maker and final Judge. They are those on which we are to be tried at his bar, and in reference to which our destiny is to be determined. (2.) They are the most fearful of all accusations which can be brought against a creature. No crime can be equal to that of being an enemy of God; and no offence against human society can equal, in enormity and ill-desert, the crimes of which man is charged against his Maker. (3.) The charge extends to every human being. No exception is made in favour of youth, beauty, rank, or blood; none in favour of the amiable, the honest, or the moral; none in favour of those who have endeavoured to wipe away the accusation by their own good conduct. It is not indeed charged that one is as bad as another, or that any one is as bad as he can be; but it *is* that every one is guilty of violating the law of God, and is held to be such a sinner that he cannot save himself. (4.) It is charged that each and every one is of such a character that the eternal pains of hell would be an adequate recompense for his crimes. He is held to be under condemnation, and to be justly exposed to punishment that shall be severe in the extremest degree, unmitigated, and everlasting. Each one is held to be such an evil-doer that it would be wrong for God to admit him to heaven as he is, but not wrong to consign him to unending woe. It is important not to disguise anything about this, or to seek to hide it by soft names. The robber is deemed worthy of the penitentiary; the murderer is regarded as deserving death on the gibbet; and in like manner it is held in the charge brought against man, and the threatenings appended to them, that every man deserves the pains of everlasting death, and that if he should receive what is properly due to him, he would be cast off from God, and punished for ever. Such is the nature of the charges against man. On these he is held guilty; on these he will be arraigned. The Bible has two aspects. It reveals a way of pardon; but it is also the grand instrument of indictment against man. It is designed to reveal his character; to reprove his crimes; to overwhelm him with the conviction of guilt; and to be the standard of judgment on the final day. The question therefore arises, now to be considered, whether if these are the charges against man, he can vindicate or justify himself. It has been already remarked, that there are but two grounds to be taken in such a vindication. One is, to deny the facts charged on man; the other is, if the facts be admitted, for him to show that he had a right to do as he has done. There is nothing else that can be conceived of in the case to be done by him, unless it were to attempt to make expiation or reparation by extraordinary merit, by penance, or by sacrifice; though this would not *justify* him for what he had done, any more than a man's paying a fine could make it right for him to put out his neighbour's eye, or burn his house. If neither of these things can be done, it will follow that man cannot be justified by his own righteousness. These points will now be considered in their order. The first is, that man cannot deny the truth of the charges brought against him. In support of this the following considerations may be urged:—

(1.) The source whence these charges come. They are made by God himself. It is assumed here that the Bible is true, and the argument will be conducted on that assumption. In another part of this volume it is shown that it is equally impossible to deny the main facts, whether the Bible be true or false. The position now is, that the sinner cannot take the ground that God has mistaken the facts about man, or that he has designedly brought a false accusation. It surely cannot be necessary to go into an argument to prove this, but an illustration or two may be allowed. (*a*) One is, that it is impossible for God to mistake on this subject. Men often do mistake in reference to character and conduct. Charges are often falsely brought, and men are often condemned as guilty on false accusations. This may be intentionally done; or judges and jurors may be mistaken; or witnesses may be suborned to sustain the accusation, or those needful for the defence may be absent; or a combination of circumstances which no human sagacity can control, may seem to confirm the charge of guilt against the innocent. But obviously no such mistake can occur in relation to the charges brought in the Bible against man, nor can man set up a vindication of himself on the ground that his Maker has erred in reference to the facts alleged. (*b*) As little can he urge that the accusation has been overdrawn; that a degree of guilt has been charged such as the facts would not justify; or that there has been an intermingling of prejudice or passion which has given a colouring to the charge, and that a calmer view may modify these accusations. We can easily admit that such things may occur among men. Judges and jurors are liable to the same passions as other men, and in a time of popular excitement it may happen that the contagion may reach the bench and the jury-room; and hence the laws are careful that the administration of justice shall proceed with as much calmness and coolness as possible. It may happen, also, that false charges are brought against men, because they are obnoxious to those in power. Many a one who has stood in the way of the purposes of a tyrant has been removed under the forms of law, to gratify the passions of such a man, and many a pure name has been covered with infamy by the malignity of those in authority. But it is not needful to show that none of these things can be alleged by man in regard to the charges brought against him by his Maker. It cannot be pretended that God has been hurried into these charges under the influence of passion; or that man is obnoxious to his purposes, and that he would have him removed. The charges are made with the utmost deliberation. They are made by the most benevolent Being in the universe; by One who can have no pleasure in finding out proofs of guilt; by One who, from his nature, is disposed to make every possible allowance for weakness and infirmity; by One who sees, better than man can state it, everything that can be said in his defence; by One more disposed than any human being ever was to do justice to all that is amiable and pure. If man wishes to find a friend who will be kind to his infirmities, and do justice to him when the world does him wrong, he can find no such friend as God. (*c*) It may be added here, that the charge is one that no denial affects. It has been deliberately made, and is that on which we are to be tried. We may deny it, or disregard it, but it is not thereby affected. Whatever we may choose to think of it does not change the estimate which our Maker affixes to our character, any more than the private views of a prisoner at the bar can modify the estimate of the judge and jury: God will pronounce sentence on us according to his own estimate of our character; and the only security which we can have that we shall not meet with condemnation will be in the fact, that on some grounds he will regard it as not proper to condemn us. But that cannot be by attempting to deny the truth of the charge which he brings against us, or by holding him either to be malignant or mistaken.

(2.) To show that man cannot deny the truth of what is alleged against him as a violator of the law, it may be observed, secondly, that so far from obeying the perfect law of God, he has failed of yielding perfect obedience to the very lowest rules of morality. The standard at which man aims is in general low enough, and might be supposed sufficiently accommodating to satisfy any one who wished to save himself by his own righteousness. That standard is, at any rate, at an immeasurable distance from the holy law of God. Yet let a man take any standard of conduct which he pleases, and he will fail in all attempts to show that he has always been conformed to it. Who would undertake to prove before any tribunal that could take cognizance of the motives, the thoughts, the words, as well as the outward conduct, that he had always been honest, true, kind, chaste, or courteous? Who would attempt to prove that he has on no occasion failed in his duty in the tenderest relations of life? What husband would attempt to prove that he has always had right emotions towards the wife of his youth? Who in this relation would attempt to prove that he had on no occasion forgotten the high trust committed to him when she left her home and friends to be his? What child is there that would undertake to prove that he has never failed in his duty to his father or his mother, that he has always been as respectful obedient, and grateful as he ought to have been? Is there no compunction, when he sees a father die? Is there nothing which he would wish to recall when he stands by a mother's grave? What brother would undertake to vindicate all his conduct towards a sister? or what friend is there that has never had a feeling towards his friend which he ought not to have entertained? Who is there that would undertake to say that he has never failed in the duty of perfect honesty and truth in the transactions of business? Nay, to come down to a lower standard, Who, professing to be governed by the laws of honour, would venture, when he comes to die, to stake his eternal welfare on the fact that he has never failed of perfect conformity to that arbitrary code? Who that professes to be governed by the rules of etiquette would attempt to maintain that those laws have always been perfectly observed? Let a man choose his own standard of action; let him refer to any code by which he professes to regulate his conduct; would he be willing that every thought, and word, and feeling, and action of his life should be brought out to noonday, and that his eternal welfare should be determined by the issue of the question, whether he had or had not been perfectly conformed to that code? If not, how shall he vindicate himself from the charge of sin? And if he cannot vindicate himself in reference to these low and imperfect standards, how shall he stand acquitted of the charge of having violated the high and holy law of God? That, he has never made a standard or rule of life. That, he has never attempted to obey. The love to his Maker which that requires, he has never once attempted to exercise. The holy duties which that enjoins, he has never endeavoured to perform. Its sacred injunctions he has never thought of bearing with him to the relations of life, to the counting-room, to the circles of his friendship, or to the scenes of his amusement. How, then, will he proceed in attempting to show that the charges of guilt brought against him are not true?

(3.) The charges which are brought against man by his Maker are sustained by all the facts of history. What ground would that man take, who should attempt to show that the accusations in the Bible against the race, that it is sinful and prone to evil are unfounded and false? On what would he base his argument? To what part of the world, to what historic monument, to what recorded opinions would he turn? Men often feel that the account in the Bible of the character of man, of the human heart, of the tendency of our nature, is harsh and gloomy. They are inclined to think better of the race, and to suppose that the views in the Bible must have been derived from the observation of man in a peculiarly dark age of the world, or were the result of feelings bordering on misanthropy. They think that man is better than he is there represented; or at least that by certain modifications in society he reaches a state where that description does not apply to him. On this account it is felt that the charge is one that cannot be sustained; and that it is not true now, that all hope of salvation on the ground of an upright life is cut off. But let a few indisputable facts be submitted to candid men. (*a*) One is, that the historic account of human conduct in the Bible is no worse than in other records. The narration of crimes, of wars, of ambition, of carnage, of blood, of sensuality, of venality, of political profligacy or corruption of manners there, is no worse than is to be found in Livy or Suetonius, in Gibbon or Hume. Every crime recorded in the sacred narrative has more than one parallel in the records of profane history; and every sentiment there expressed about man can be confirmed by any number of testimonies that the most sceptical could demand. The world has been many a time in a state like that described by Moses as the cause of the deluge; and the earth now bears up many a city where all the crimes on account of which Sodom was overthrown still have an existence. Herculaneum and Pompeii have been revealed, by the monuments exposed to human view from beneath the ashes that covered them, to have been as corrupt, and corrupt in the same sense, as the cities of the plain; and a single one of the capitals of Europe embosoms probably now more revolting sins than they all. There is not an instance of fraud, corruption, or villany, attributed to man in the Bible, which has not its parallel in the present age of the world. The instances of depravity whose deeds are recorded in the Bible find abundant parallels in profane history; and not one of the men of guilt there referred to surpasses in wickedness the names of Nero, or Tiberius, of Alexander VI., or his wretched son, of Henry VIII., or Charles II.; or of the leaders of the French Revolution. (*b*) The account contained in the Bible of human depravity is sustained by the opinions of the sober and reflecting in all ages. Those who have given themselves to the contemplation of the condition of the world, have seen in it the sad tendency to depravity in human nature, lamented it, and sought to correct it, and yet the current of iniquity has swept over every barrier which man could erect against it, and sweeps on unchecked from age to age. (*c*) The same view of the human character has been taken by wicked men themselves. Byron had no confidence in human virtue; Walpole said that every man had his price; Chesterfield regarded all virtue as false and hollow; Robespierre and Danton acted under the belief that every man deserved the guillotine. And (*d*) every man acts on the presumption that every other man is a sinner, and that no confidence can be placed in him without securities; and expects that every other one will regard himself in the same light. His security is not in human virtue, but in vaults, and bars, and locks, and bonds; and he himself expects to be treated by every other man as if he had the same character. His head neither hangs down with shame, nor do his eyes flash with indignation, when he is asked for security that he will pay an honest debt, or when he is told in a bank, or on exchange, that no individual or corporation will trust him without having some other security besides himself that he is a safe and honest man. In these circumstances, how can man go before God and attempt to justify himself on the pretext that the charges against him are not true? Can he take the ground that his Maker is mistaken, or that he has maliciously brought a false accusation?

(4.) There is but one other observation which it is necessary to make on this part of the subject. It is, that conscience sustains the truth of all the charges which are brought against man. Man exhibits this very strange and remarkable characteristic, that he often frames an argument to show that the race is not as guilty as it is accused of being, and perhaps succeeds in convincing others, but still his argument does nothing to affect the proof as it lies in his own soul. There is that within himself which is to him overpowering demonstration that his arguments are all false, and that the charges against him are true. God has so formed the soul, that he has there at all times what may be summoned forth, at his pleasure, as a living witness that all that he has charged on man is true, and that shall render nugatory in a moment all the reasonings of men about the uprightness of their own hearts. This proof is found in a man's own conscience. This is a device by which man himself is made to coincide with and confirm the views of the Almighty; to approve where he approves, to condemn where he condemns. It stands apart from the deductions of reason; is little affected by the arguments which men may employ; is susceptible of being called up to give judgment at any time; often pronounces sentence against the favourite opinions of the man himself; and when unbiassed, uniformly declares judgment in favour of right, and condemns what is wrong, and is always on the side of God and his claims. This mysterious and wonderful power is wholly under the Divine control. No matter what may be the cherished opinions of man; no matter how he may call in question the correctness of the Divine testimony against human conduct, and no matter how reluctant man may be to admit the impossibility of being saved by his own works; God has power at any moment to summon the mind itself to sustain his own account of the state of the heart, and to put it into such a condition as to leave not a shadow of doubt that all that he has said respecting its depravity is true. It requires all the art of a sinner to keep the voice of conscience silent, and to save himself from its rebukes. Well he knows that if suffered to speak out, it will be in tones of deep condemnation. It often does speak out. In solitude; in the silence of the night; under the preaching of the gospel; when the mind in its lonely musings runs back, by some mysterious law of association, to the past; in a revival of religion; on a bed of sickness, or in the prospect of death,—conscience often utters its voice in tones that are so distinct that they can neither be misunderstood nor suppressed. These are circumstances where man is most likely to judge according to truth; and in such circumstances, he is so made as to feel, without a doubt, that the judgment pronounced by conscience is in accordance with that of the Most High, and that the views pressed upon his conscience then about his own character, are those which will be confirmed by the sentence of the final Judge. "In thoughts from the visions of the night," said an ancient sage, "when deep sleep falleth on men, fear came upon me, and trembling, which made all my bones to shake. Then a spirit passed before my face: the hair of my flesh stood up: it stood still, but I could not discern the form thereof: an image was before mine eyes, there was silence, and I heard a voice saying, Shall mortal man be more just than God? shall a man be more pure than his Maker? Behold, he put no trust in his servants; and his angels he charged with folly: how much less in them that dwell in houses of clay, whose foundation is in the dust, who are crushed before the moth?" Job iv. 13—19.

I have concluded but one part of my argument, having aimed to show that man cannot justify himself before God by taking the ground that the facts are not as charged upon him, or that he has not in fact violated the law of God. This has been shown by these considerations:—that it is impossible to believe that God would bring a false charge against man; that, as a matter of fact, man fails of perfect conformity to the very lowest standard of morals; that the account in the Bible of the human character is confirmed by all the records elsewhere existing of the character of man; and that when man has denied the charges against him, conscience comes in to confirm the accusations and the decisions of the Almighty.

I should be glad to leave a single distinct impression on the minds of my readers. It is, that charges of guilt of a most serious nature are made against every one of us. I should desire that you would consider the source of those accusations, and be willing to look at the evidence that they are true. If, as I believe, they are brought against us by God himself, not one word is needed to show that they demand attention. They are the most serious charges that can be made. They come from a source demanding the ear and the fixed attention of those against whom they are brought. If they are alleged by our Creator, they are true; if true, they should excite alarm. They must somehow, and at some period, be met. It will not do to deny their truth, or to laugh at them, or to forget them, or to regard them with unconcern. There they stand written against us in the word of God. They are recorded in the history of our race. They are engraven on our own souls. They are of such a nature that they can easily be made to meet us on the bed of death. They are such that unless they can be shown to be false, or unless the offences charged on us be forgiven, they must sink us down to everlasting suffering. And can man be unconcerned, where there is the slightest evidence that such allegations are brought against him by his Creator? There are those from whose eyelids, if they had a suspicion that a rumour were breathed abroad in this community respecting their integrity as men of business, sleep would depart to-night. There are others, whose character is to themselves so dear and so sacred, that a whisper about their want of holy virtue would throw them on a restless bed, and drive peace from their bosom. Can you be indifferent when your Creator stoops from his throne and charges you with sin, with open rebellion, with such a character as to exclude you from his favour? Can you suffer all this to pass by you as the idle wind? Oh! could you see all, your eyes would not know the sweets of slumber to-night; your body would be deprived of calm repose; your conscience would be racked with horror; your soul would be overwhelmed with deep and gloomy forebodings. Can it be a slight thing to be charged with damning guilt by the eternal God?

SERMON XXXI.

MAN CANNOT JUSTIFY HIMSELF BY SHOWING THAT HIS CONDUCT IS RIGHT.

Rom. iii. 20.—"By the deeds of the law there shall no flesh be justified."

In the last discourse, I proposed to show from these words, that man cannot be justified by his own righteousness. In doing this, I endeavoured to point out what is meant by justification, and then entered upon an argument to prove that man cannot justify himself before God. I observed that when a man is accused of crime, there are two grounds of defence which he may set up, on either of which, if successfully maintained, he will be acquitted, or will be declared *just* in the sight of the law. He may either deny the fact charged on him, or, admitting the fact, he may urge that he had a right to do as he has done. I showed that man is charged by his Maker with the violation of his law, and that if he will justify himself, he must either deny the truth of the charge, or show that in the circumstances of the case he had a right to do as he has done. The first of these grounds of defence I proceeded to examine at length, and attempted by the following considerations to establish the position that man cannot deny the truth of the charges brought against him:—that God, who brings them, could not be mistaken, and could not have brought them from malignity; that man, in fact, so far from obeying the holy law of God, has failed of perfect conformity to the lowest standard of morality; that the account of man in the Bible is confirmed by all the facts and all the monuments of history; and that the charges in the Bible are sustained by the decisions of conscience.

The only other ground of defence or of justification which man can set up is, that it was right or proper for him to do as he has done; that admitting the facts in the case to be as they are charged—that he does not love his Maker with a perfect heart—that he violates his laws—that he is under the influence of unholy passions—and that he neglects many things which are required of him,—yet that such are the circumstances in which he is placed that it is not wrong for him to do as he has done, or that he has a valid excuse, and ought not to be condemned. His condition, he might be ready to admit, is one that is to be pitied; but his conduct is not such as to deserve blame or punishment. If a man can make this out, he will not be condemned, for God will not condemn the innocent. If man has good and sufficient excuse for what he has done, there is no being in the universe who will look more benignantly on it than God, for there is no one so ready to do justice to the innocent, or to allow its proper weight to all that ought to exculpate. It is necessary, therefore, to examine this ground of defence, or to inquire whether man can set up the plea that he has a right to do as he has done; to live as he is in fact living. Man is soon to stand before his Maker on a high charge of guilt. If he cannot deny the facts charged on him, he must take the ground that he has a right to do as he has done; that he has a valid reason which excuses him; that he ought to be acquitted, and that his deliverance should be hailed everywhere with songs and rejoicing, and that he ought to be received to heaven in triumph. What is this ground of defence? What is its value? Will it avail on the final trial?

Here it may be observed, that man will not set up the plea of insanity, though more insane on the subject charged on him than many who have been acquitted by human tribunals. Man has too much pride, and too much confidence that he is right and that God is wrong, to urge this plea. Nor would he maintain that God has no jurisdiction over the case, for nothing is plainer than that he owes allegiance to the laws of his Maker, and that he cannot go beyond the limits of his empire. The points on which the accused sinner must rely, if he would undertake to show that he is not to blame for what he has done and to justify himself, must be such as the following:—either that the constitution of things under which he is placed is such as to make it inevitable that he should do as he does; or that he is but acting out the nature which God has given him, and that therefore it must be right; or that the law of God is unreasonably severe and stern, and he is excusable for not obeying it; or that the time of preparation for eternity is too short, and that too great interests are made to depend on this brief period of existence; or that the penalty is too severe, and that if a man acts as well as he knows how, though he does not conform to the holy law of God, he ought not to be recompensed with eternal torments. If these points can be made out, man ought to be acquitted. If they cannot, has he any other ground of defence on which he can rely?

I. The first of these grounds of defence is derived from *the constitution of things under which we are placed.* Our minds, when we set up this defence, go back to the arrangement with Adam, and the effect of his sin on his posterity. The form of this defence is, that his fall, by the Divine arrangement, placed us in far more unfavourable circumstances for salvation than those in which we should otherwise have been; that his apostacy made it certain that all his descendants would sin; that it made it certain that the first act of each moral agent on earth would be wrong; that there was a strong probability thus created that all his posterity would be lost; and that all our strong propensities to evil, and our exposure to ruin, are to be traced to this arrangement. If they who rely on this ground of defence were disposed to take shelter under the declarations of Scripture, the defence would be found in the following statements of the apostle Paul:—"Through the offence of one many are dead." "The judgment was by one to condemnation." "By one man's offence, death reigned by one." "By the offence of one, judgment came upon all men to condemnation." "By one man's disobedience, many were made sinners." "The law entered, that the offence might abound," Rom. v. 15—17, 20. If these things are so, how can man be held to be guilty for conduct thus rendered certain and inevitable?

The question now is, whether this can be regarded as a vindication of the undisputed facts in the conduct of man. Will it be admitted as a sufficient reason for what we have done in violation of the holy law of God, when we stand at his bar? The fact is undeniable, that man early goes astray, and that he continues to wander farther and farther unless he is restrained or reclaimed. Is it a sufficient excuse for this that Adam fell, and that we live under such a constitution that his sinning made it certain that we should sin also?

Now in examining this question we may admit two things:—one is, that our circumstances in consequence of his fall are in many respects less favourable than they would otherwise have been; or that incalculable evils have come upon us in consequence of his apostacy; and the other is, that there is much about it which neither revelation nor human philosophy explains. But these are different points from the one before us, whether that act of our first father is a sufficient excuse or apology for our crimes; or, whether we can take shelter under that constitution as a vindication from the charge of guilt. In reply to this, two or three remarks may be made.

The first is, that we are responsible not for his sin, but for our own. The sin which is charged upon us is not his, but ours. The question is, not whether his acting as he did will free us from accountability or ill-desert, on account of *his* act—which is plain enough;—but whether it will free us from ill-desert on account of *our own* sins. We could not be held guilty, that is, blameworthy, for his sin; and if this were the charge, the defence set up must be conclusive. No reasoning has yet shown that man either *is* or *can be* regarded as blameworthy on account of the crime of his first father.

Again, the fall of Adam, and the constitution under which we live, compel no one to sin. All sin is voluntary, and there is nothing in which man more consults his own pleasure than in the course of life which is charged upon him. Every profane man means to be profane; every dishonest man prefers to be dishonest; every sensual man has pleasure in moral corruption. It is a great law of our being that where freedom ends, responsibility ends, and there is nothing more universally true than that a wicked man does only what he prefers to do. Nay, the sins which are charged on him are very often the fruit of long and deliberate plan; and so attached is he to a course of iniquity, that no argument or entreaty is sufficient to induce him to attempt to change his method of life. So voluntary are men in their sins, that there is no argument or topic of persuasion which will induce those living in sin, of themselves, to break off their transgressions and turn to God. A man must take the ground that he is compelled by the act of Adam to do what he would otherwise not do, before that apostacy can be a vindication from the charges alleged against him. Further, this plea would neither be urged nor admitted by man himself in any other case. In all the numerous charges brought against men before human tribunals, in different lands and ages, it is probable that this has never once been alleged as a vindication. To no murderer, thief, pirate, or traitor, has it ever occurred to urge this in his own defence. The state of the world has never been such that it would be tolerated for a moment; nor has the consideration that Adam fell, and that we are under a constitution where all sin, probably ever modified, even in a single instance, the verdict of a jury. There have been men on the bench, and in the jury-box, who have held this as a theological dogma, or as an excuse for their own sins before God; but in a court-room nature speaks out, and no man would venture to apply such a dogma of theology to a decision of the bench. What would it avail on a charge of murder before any court in the world?

One other remark. It remains yet to be shown, that the facilities for obtaining the Divine favour by men in their fallen state are less than they would have been had they entered the world in the condition of their first parents. Are any sent to hell for Adam's sin? That remains yet to be proved. Are any infants lost? Not a particle of evidence has ever yet been furnished of this. Is it beyond the capacity of children to please God? Let the remarks of the Saviour about the hosannas in the temple answer. Is it less easy for *us* to obtain the Divine approbation, and to be saved, than it would have been if Adam had not fallen? That remains to be proved: for if a choice were to be made, it would seem to be easier to believe on Christ, and to trust to him for salvation, than to keep a holy law unbroken for ever. And if these things are so, then man cannot put his defence on the ground that he is brought into the world under a constitution which made it certain that he would be a sinner.

II. A second ground of defence to which man resorts in self-vindication, akin to this—but more common and more plausible —is, *that he is but acting out the propensities of his nature.* He did not make himself. He is as God made him. He is but indulging inclinations which his Creator has implanted in his bosom, and the indulgence of which, therefore, cannot be attended with blame, or followed by his displeasure. Can it be wrong for him to look upon the light of the sun? Can it be wrong for him to be charmed with the beauty of a sweet landscape, or the pleasant music of a waterfall? Can it be wrong for him to allay the demands of hunger and thirst, to protect himself from cold, and to provide a shelter from the storm? The innocence of these things being admitted, as it must be, he applies the concession to *all* the propensities and inclinations within him, to all that has led him to do what is charged upon him as wrong, and says, "I am as God made me, and for that I cannot be held to be guilty: I ought, therefore, to be acquitted of the charge of guilt." Let us inquire whether this will answer as a ground of defence before God.

The most obvious remark in regard to it is, that if it is a valid excuse in reference to religion, it is in reference to human conduct generally. For why may not any man accused of crime urge the same thing in self-defence? Has he done anything more than act out certain propensities which he found in his nature? When Cæsar crossed the Rubicon, Hannibal the Alps, Alexander the Granicus, or when Napoleon poured his armies on Italy, Egypt, Austria, or Russia, did they do anything more than follow out the inclinations of their nature? Did they not find stirring within them a spirit of ambition which urged them on to trample down the liberties of mankind? Did Robespierre or Diderot, Alexander VI. or Cæsar Borgia, do anything more than act out certain propensities in their souls? Did Torquemada in the inquisition, or Cortes in the butcheries of Mexico, do anything but act out what they found within theirs? And the assassin, the duellist, the murderer, what does he do more? Is he not following out his natural impulses, as much as the sinner who urges this plea? And would not this plea be as good for the one as the other?

But further, this plea is contrary to the convictions of common sense, and the universal judgment of right among men. If it were well-founded, then the true course for man, if he would please God, would be to give unrestrained indulgence to every inclination in his bosom. Nay, then it would be wrong for him to check *any* of his passions, and his duty would be to give them the rankest growth, and the broadest indulgence possible; for should not man cultivate all that God has implanted in his bosom? Then all the restraints on the passions of children must be displeasing to God; all the lessons of order, morality, and religion, are a contravening of his wishes; all colleges, schools, and churches, are a nuisance; all court-houses and prisons are a violation of human liberty. Then the great benefactors of the race, and those who have been especially the friends of God, and have obtained the highest seat in heaven, have been those who have proclaimed the innocence of universal licentiousness, or who have furnished the greatest facilities for the indulgence of passion. From the preachers of religion—from pious princes—from the dispensers of justice—from the patrons of order and of law—from Paul, Aurelian, and Hale,—the crown is to be transferred to such moralists as Paine, such princes as Charles II., and such judges as Jeffries. But who is prepared to take this ground? This view goes against the common sense and the common judgments of men. There *are* things in man to be restrained in order that he may be virtuous. It is not sufficient to secure the meed of virtue to say, "I am as God made me, and am but acting out the propensities of my nature." What then is the mistake which is made in this plea? What fallacy is there in it, for it seems to have plausibility and truth? An answer may be readily given to these questions by making a distinction, which the young man may apply through life to the noblest purposes of self-improvement. In the plea set up, two things are confounded, which are wholly distinct, and which are to be dealt with on different principles:—our constitutional propensities as God made them, and our corrupt propensities which have another origin. The former are to be cultivated, and carried to the highest pitch of perfection possible; the latter are to be checked, restrained, subdued. The former are innocent, noble, and ennobling; the latter are debasing and degrading—"corrupt, sensual, devilish." There *are* propensities of our nature, and laws of our being, which God has implanted, and which, if kept within proper limits, are harmless, or which may contribute to our highest elevation in the scale of existence. To eat, to drink, to sleep, are laws of our animal being, harmless if restrained, debasing if indulged in contrariety to the just rules of temperance. To aspire after knowledge, to seek a "good name," to rise to the fellowship of higher intelligences, to bring out and cultivate the benevolent affections, is to follow nature as God has made us, and never betrays or debases us. But to follow out the inclinations of ambition, and pride, and vanity, and lust, and revenge, is a different thing. These debase and sink to a lower level than that of brutes; for in proportion as we may rise, so may we descend. The star that culminates highest, may sink the lowest; and as woman, if vile, sinks lower than man *can*, so man, if debased, sinks beneath the brute.

Men mistake then in this. When they indulge in these things, they are *not* in any proper sense acting out their nature. They are not as God made them. They are sunken, debased, fallen. Let men act according to the great laws which He has impressed upon their being, and they will be noble, holy, godlike. Thus acting, man would have met the approbation of his Maker, and might have pleaded innocent to the charges of guilt. But let him not give indulgence to corruption, and then seek shelter in the plea, "I am as God made me."

III. A third ground of defence would be, *that the law of God is stern and severe, and that his requirements are of such a nature that man has no power to comply with them.* The position which would be taken is, that there is no obligation where there is no ability, and that as man now has no power to yield obedience, he cannot be held to be chargeable with guilt. The principle here stated seems to be one that is based on common sense, and that must ever command the assent of all men who are not blinded by theory or by prejudice. It is impossible for man to feel himself guilty, or blameworthy, for not doing what he had no power to do. He may count it a misfortune, or he may experience calamities and suffer losses, because he has no greater power, but it is not possible for him to feel on this account the compunctions of remorse. With the limited powers of man, it is impossible for him ever to feel himself guilty for not creating a world, or not guiding the stars, or not raising the dead; and he cannot conceive that by any revelation whatever, or any course of reasoning, or any requirement laid on him, he should ever feel himself blameworthy for not doing these things. If then it were so, that God has required of man more than he is in any sense able to perform, the nature which he has given us—and which in that case would be a very strange and unaccountable endowment—would teach us two things: one, that his government was a tyranny; and the other, that man could not be to blame. Such a creature under such a government might be made to suffer, but could not be punished; he might experience pain of body, but he never would know the pangs of remorse. But is this so? The law itself is the best exponent of the views of God on this subject, and that law is clear and explicit. "Thou shalt love the Lord thy God with all thy heart, and with all thy soul, and with all thy mind. This is the first and great commandment. And the second is like unto it, Thou shalt love thy neighbour as thyself. On these two commandments hang all the law and the prophets," Matt. xxii. 37—40. Could anything be more reasonable than this? God asks nothing which we have not; nothing which we have no power to render. He asks "*all*" the heart, the mind, the strength, and he asks no more. He does not require for himself the service claimed of angelic powers, but that adapted to our own; he asks no love for our neighbour which we do not feel that we are abundantly able to show to ourselves. To take shelter from the charges against us, under the plea that our Maker has required services beyond our power to render, is therefore directly in the face of his own requirements; is to charge him with tyranny, where his requirements are as clear as noonday, and as equal as they can be, and where he has expressly told us that the plea cannot, and will not be sustained:—"O house of Israel, are not my ways equal? Are not your ways unequal? Therefore will I judge you, O house of Israel, according to your ways, saith the Lord God. Repent, and turn yourselves from all your transgressions; so iniquity shall not be your ruin," Ezek. xviii. 29, 30.

IV. A fourth ground of defence on which man charged with guilt is secretly relying in self-justification is, *that the penalty of the law of God is unreasonably severe, and that no consideration can make it right to recompense the errors and crimes of this short life with eternal punishment.* The ground here taken is, that it would be *wrong* for God to punish man in this manner, and therefore that man has a claim to eternal life. The inference which the sinner charged with guilt draws is, that if the penalty is unreasonably severe, he cannot be held to be guilty, and has a right to disregard the law of his Maker. Now it is not my design to attempt a defence of the doctrine of eternal punishment, or to show that the impenitent sinner will suffer for ever. It must be admitted that there are mysteries on that subject which the human powers at present cannot explain. All that the subject demands is, to examine this reasoning which the sinner sets up in his defence. Is the severity of a penalty, then, even supposing it to be wholly unreasonable, a valid excuse for violating law, or for doing wrong? It is possible to conceive—for such things have been—that the penalty for the crime of treason may be entirely too severe; that its execution may be attended with barbarous cruelty; and that it may be followed by a taint of blood, and by inflictions on the family of the traitor wholly unjustifiable by any principles of equity. But would this be any justification of the act of treason? Does it make the betrayal of the state a matter of duty or of innocence? Is it such a meritorious act, that he who performs it has a claim on the offices and emoluments which a sovereign has to bestow on deserving subjects? So in the matter before us. If there are things which we cannot explain about future punishment,—if it has a degree of severity which we have no means of vindicating,—is it fair to infer that it is *right* to violate the law of heaven; and has he who does it a *claim* on the crown of glory? Yet this seems to me to be what is involved in this ground of defence which a man charged with sin sets up. Would it be reasonable or proper for him to suppose that God would *admit* a plea drawn from his own alleged injustice and cruelty, as a reason for the habitual violation of his law? But the plea has no force in another respect. Our relations to the administration of justice are not only concerned with the question what the penalty is, but with the question whether it is practicable to avoid it. There may be reasons operating in the appointment of a penalty which we do not understand. All that is necessary for us to know is, what the penalty *is*, and to have such freedom that we can avoid it by a correct life. They who live in England now, or they who lived under the administration of the laws in times of greater severity, can have no reason to complain, so far as appears, of the punishment affixed there to treason. It can be readily seen, indeed, that there would be much that would be painful and disgraceful in being drawn on a hurdle to the place of execution; in being quartered, and publicly exposed; in the confiscation of property, the degradation of a family, and the taint of blood; but why should a good citizen, who did not design to commit treason, complain of it? It would be easy to avoid it, and his knowing the severity of the punishment should only make him the more cautious to do his duty to his country. Least of all, knowing what the penalty was, could he when he had betrayed his country set up a plea of innocence on the ground that the penalty was severe? Without pursuing this reasoning any further, may it not be asked here whether it is not just as applicable to the government of God as to a human administration?

V. There is but one other ground of defence, or self-justification, which the accused sinner can be supposed to set up: it is, *that too great results are made to depend on the present life*; that life is too short, that our days are too few and fleeting, that our continuance here is too uncertain, that we are liable to be too suddenly called away, to make it proper to suspend so great interests on anything that we can do here. The accused sinner would take the ground that eternal consequences demand a longer probation, and that the longevity of the antediluvian patriarchs was a period quite circumscribed enough to make it proper to suspend so great interests upon life. Much might be said in reply to this, but reference might be made to the instances which occur in the life of an individual or in a state, where the most momentous and far-reaching results are made to depend on the action of a moment. But without dwelling on the numerous illustrations which occur on that point, two remarks may be made in reply to this ground of defence. One is, that, as experience has in millions of cases shown, the time allotted to man is ample for a preparation for eternity. Countless hosts before the throne have found it so, and millions are on their way to join them, who find the period of probation abundant to enable them to prepare for heaven. That all others are not with them in the same blissful path is not because life is too short to enter it, but is to be traced to other causes. Men require length of days to amass wealth, or to perfect their schemes of earthly aggrandisement, but the purposes of salvation do not need it. The giving of the heart to God in sincerity through Jesus Christ—an act which may be performed in the briefest period during which a moral agent lives—is enough to secure salvation. Wealth or honour could not be secured in so brief a period, but the salvation of the soul may. The other remark is, that this vindication is set up in circumstances which painfully demonstrate that it cannot be sincere. Not time enough to secure salvation! Too great interests suspended on this brief period of existence! Unreasonable to make eternal results depend on the fleeting hours of this short life! And from whom do these objections come? From those on whom the hours of life hang heavily, and "who are often wishing its different periods at an end;" from those who are impatient for some season of festivity or enjoyment to arrive, and who chide the slow-revolving wheels of time; from those whose days are weariness and sadness, for they have nothing to interest them, nothing to do; from those whose principal study is the art of killing time, and all whose plans have no other end; from those who waste the hours that might be consecrated to prayer in needless slumber, and from whose lips each morning, while they now are locked in repose, there might proceed the earnest breathing of a penitent heart that would ensure salvation; from those who, over worthless or corrupting verse, or in the perusal of romances, or in day-dreams, or at the toilet, waste each day time enough to secure the redemption of the soul. From such lips and hearts, from those who live thus, and to whom life puts on these forms, assuredly the objection should not be heard, that too great results are made to depend on this short life, and that therefore they are blameless in neglecting God.

If these are correct views, then the sinner cannot justify himself. It has been shown that he cannot deny the reality of the facts charged on him, and the grounds of defence which the human heart is disposed to set up in self-vindication have been considered. It is not improper, at this stage of the argument, to make a personal appeal to my readers, and to ask them to look at the ground which we have gone over as a personal matter. To my mind it seems clear beyond the shadow of a doubt, that the position which has been taken is correct as an argument, and that it is clear that man can neither deny the truth of the charges alleged against him, nor vindicate himself for what he has done. But whatever may be thought of the argument, attempted *as* an argument, on one point there can be no difference of opinion—that the conclusion which we have reached is in accordance with the Bible. That conclusion is, that the unpardoned sinner is a lost and ruined being; that he is under condemnation; that he is held to be guilty in the sight of God; that he is soon to be arraigned on charges involving the question of his eternal welfare; and that unless he is in some way acquitted of those charges, they will sink him to ruin. The views which have been thus expressed lie at the foundation of the system of salvation by grace. They are such as when felt lead to the conviction of sin, and to that sense of helplessness which is preparatory to the reception of pardon and salvation by the grace of the gospel. If these views produced the effect they are fitted to work, they would leave the impression of guilt, helplessness, and danger on the mind of every one who is not converted and pardoned. Sooner or later every one will feel this. The sinner may be unwilling to admit the force of these arguments now; for no one, if he can help it, will be overwhelmed with the conviction of guilt, or have his mind unsettled and harassed by apprehensions of danger. But not always can he put this subject far from him. He will lie down and die; and there are sad feelings which the dying sinner has, when he reflects that his life has been spent in sin, and that he is dying under condemnation. He will, from the bed of death, look out tremblingly on the eternal world—on that shoreless and bottomless ocean on which he is about to be launched; and it will be sad to feel that he is about to enter that vast and fearful world an unpardoned sinner. He will tread his way up to the bar of a holy God; and little as he may be concerned about that now, it will be sad to tread that gloomy way alone, and to feel as he goes that he is under condemnation. He will stand and look on the burning throne of Deity, and on his final Judge; he will await, and with what an agony of emotion, the sentence that shall fall from his lips, sealing his eternal doom! Oh, how can he then be just with God? How vindicate his ways before him? How stand there and justify his neglect of the Divine commands, his neglect of prayer, his neglect of the offers of mercy, his neglect of his own soul? How, then, can he show his Maker that it was *right* not to love him; not to pray to him; not to thank him; not to embrace his offers of mercy? How can he show that it was *right* for him to live without hope and without God in the world? How *can* he be saved?

SERMON XXXII.

MAN CANNOT MERIT SALVATION.

JOB xxxv. 5—8. "Look unto the heavens, and see; and behold the clouds, which are higher than thou. If thou sinnest, what doest thou against him? or if thy transgressions be multiplied, what doest thou unto him? If thou be righteous, what givest thou him? or what receiveth he of thine hand? Thy wickedness may hurt a man as thou art; and thy righteousness may profit the son of man."

THESE are the words of Elihu, who, though not inspired, has expressed a sentiment which the Spirit of inspiration has regarded it as important to preserve. The general idea is, that God is so great and independent that the conduct of men can neither injure nor profit him; that though man may be affected in his interests by the treatment which he receives from his fellow-men, no such treatment, whether good or evil, can affect the great and eternal God—the God that made the heavens, and that dwells in regions beyond the clouds. The evil conduct of man cannot mar His happiness, or otherwise injure Him; nor can man's acts of righteousness so benefit Him as to lay Him under obligation. "If thou be righteous, what givest thou him? or what receiveth he of thine hand? Thy wickedness *may* hurt a man as thou art; and thy righteousness may profit the son of man." It is one part of this general sentiment only that I here design to illustrate—that our acts of righteousness cannot so profit God as to lay him under obligation to us.

In the two previous discourses I have endeavoured to prove that man cannot justify himself either by denying the facts charged on him, or by showing that he had a right to do as he has done. The inquiry at once presents itself, How then can he be saved? There are but two ways conceivable—one by his own merits, that is, that he somehow deserves to be saved; the other, by the merits of another or of others. If it be in the latter way, it must either be by the merits of Christ, or it must be because certain eminent saints have done more than was demanded of them, and that their merits, garnered up and deposited in certain hands, can be made over to others. It is not proposed to inquire now whether this latter method be in accordance with truth, but whether men can merit salvation for themselves. They can do it if their lives are such that they deserve to go to heaven, or if it would be wrong for God to punish them for ever, for "God will not do wickedly, neither will the Almighty pervert judgment," Job xxxiv. 12. The importance of this inquiry will be at once perceived; for the great mass of mankind are depending on their own righteousness for salvation, and the grand issue between Christianity and the world lies just in this point. There are two subjects of inquiry, which, if they can be made clear, will conduct to the truth in this case:—I. What is meant by merit? and, II. Can man merit heaven?

I. *What is meant by merit?* The word is in common use, and the common use is the correct one. We speak of merit when a man deserves a reward for something which he has done, or when it would be wrong to withhold it. He renders to him who employs him an equivalent, or what is of as much value as is paid him for his services. Two or three simple illustrations will make the common use of the word plain, and show its bearing on the question before us.

You hire a day-labourer. You make a bargain with him at the outset; he complies with the terms on his part, and at night you pay him. He has earned, deserved, or merited that which you pay. He has been faithful to his part of the agreement, and the service which he has rendered is *worth* as much to you as the wages which you pay him. You *could* have done the work perhaps yourself, but you preferred to hire him, for you might yourself be more profitably or pleasantly employed. At all events, what he has done is worth to you all which you pay him, and it would be wrong on every consideration for you to withhold it. If you choose to give him anything more than was specified in the agreement, it would be a gratuity; but that which you agreed to give him he has a right to demand, and you are not at liberty to withhold it. He has deserved or earned it, for he has rendered you a full equivalent, according to the terms of the contract.

A man enlists to defend his country as a soldier. It is supposed, in the contract which is made with him, that his service will be of equal value to his country with the pay which he receives. By fighting its battles; by guarding its sea-coasts, villages, towns, and hamlets; by keeping its fields from being trod down by an enemy; by protecting the lives of aged men, helpless women, and children; and by defending the flag of the nation from insult, it is supposed that his services are worth full as much to the country as he receives in his pay. The pay is graduated in part by the best estimate which can be made of the value of the service which a man can render in this calling, and the nation would be no *gainer* by dismissing him from its service. He complies with the contract, and when he comes and shows his scars, and tells of his perils and privations, his weary marches, and his risk of life, and his separation from home and friends in the cause of his country, his country will not grudge him the pittance that he receives, for he has earned it, and merited it, and it would not be right to withhold it from him.

You employ a physician; the service which he renders you, you regard a full equivalent for what you pay him. What you receive from him in his care, attention, skill, and sympathy, you consider to be fully equal in value to the compensation which you give him. Your relief from pain, your recovery of the use of your bodily powers, or the restoration to your affectionate embrace in sound health of a wife or child, you consider as an ample equivalent for all which he asks you for his services; and were an election to be made, you would much prefer to pay the amount of the physician's fees to going through those sorrows again. What he receives from you, you feel that on every account he deserves or has earned, and it would be wrong for you to withhold it.

In each of these cases, that is true which the apostle Paul affirms, "To him that worketh, the reward is not reckoned of grace, but of debt." These illustrations will explain the proper sense of the word "merit." In each instance, there is an equivalent for what is paid; in each instance, what is demanded could be enforced as a claim of right. There is no other sense in which the word *merit* or *desert* can be used. All besides this is *favour* or *grace*. If you choose to give the day-labourer, the soldier, or the professional man more than you agreed, or more than his services are worth to you, you have an undoubted right to do so, but you would not put it on the ground of his merit or desert. You would feel that it was a gratuity which could not be enforced by justice, and that no blame would be attached to you if it were withheld. If his perils, or services, or self-denials and sacrifices, were greater than you anticipated when the contract was made, or if the service rendered was really of more value to you than the amount which you are pledged to give him, you may consider yourself bound by equity to give him more, for you feel that he has earned or merited it. Thus you would be glad to compensate, if you could, the wounded soldier who has perilled all in your defence; and on the same principle, if you could do it, you would wish to recompense the man who at the risk of his life should save your child from the devouring flame, or from a watery grave.

II. We come now to apply these principles to the case before us. Keeping this explanation of the nature of merit in view, we approach the inquiry, *whether man can merit heaven?* Can he be saved because he deserves it? Can he be so profitable to God that he can advance a just claim to an admission into the world of glory? If he can, then his salvation follows as a matter of course; if he cannot, he should lose no time in endeavouring to ascertain whether there is any other way by which he may be saved. In reference to this inquiry, the following considerations may be submitted:—

(1.) Man can render no service to his Maker for which the rewards of heaven would be a proper equivalent. Or, in other words, the amount of service which he can render is not such as can be properly measured by the reward of everlasting life. His service to his Maker and to the universe is not of so much value that he can claim eternal life as an equivalent. We have seen that this does exist in the case of the day-labourer, the soldier, and the physician. We can see a correspondence between the service rendered and the compensation in these cases, which makes us feel that there is propriety and equity in the reward. But in reference to any connexion or correspondence between the service which man can render his Maker and the rewards of heaven, we can see no such propriety and equity. The one does not measure the other. The universe is not so much benefited by the service of man, that everlasting life and infinite happiness would be only a fair equivalent, or such that wrong would be done if that reward should be withheld. Yet is it not a fair principle, that this must be the case if man deserves or merits salvation? Must there not have been such an amount or value of service rendered that it would be injustice to withhold the reward—injustice such as would occur in the case of the faithful day-labourer, the soldier, the physician, if their pay were withheld? That must be extraordinary service rendered to the universe, or to God, which deserves the glories of an eternal heaven as its reward. That is extraordinary service rendered to you if a stranger rescues a child from impending death, and restores him to your transported bosom, and you feel that no compensation which you can make would be more than an equivalent. That was extraordinary service which was rendered to their country by the heroes of the American Revolution; and as the results of their patriotism and perils are seen in the unexampled prosperity of the land which they rescued, we feel that the pension of the old soldier is a very inadequate recompense. That was extraordinary virtue which led the father of his country through the trials, perplexities, and perils of that time, and which he evinced when, having laid the foundation of our liberty, he voluntarily retired to private life, leaving the people in the enjoyment of freedom; and we feel that no wealth which the nation had to offer, no monument of marble or of brass which art could rear, would equal the measure of his praise. But has man any such extraordinary service to render to his Maker and to the universe? Has he done anything, can he do anything for God, and for the empire which he rules, which would make the wealth of heaven and its everlasting glories only an equitable recompense? Obviously, there is no congruity, no fitness, no correspondence between the one and the other; and when men talk about *meriting* heaven, or when they feel that they *deserve* to be saved, they have not well considered the import of language. They use it correctly in common life. Is it not right to ask that it may be used with the same exactness in religion?

(2.) This general principle, which appears so obvious, may be illustrated with particular reference to the *religious* services which men render to their Maker. If man merits heaven, and is to be saved on account of his own deservings, it will be conceded that the service must be in some way connected with religion, or of such a nature that it can be regarded as the service of God. You would not feel yourself bound to pay a day-labourer if, instead of working for you, he worked all day for your neighbour, or were idle; you would not think of recompensing a soldier if he slept at his post, or fought under the standard of the enemy.

There *are* religious men upon the earth—men who are honestly engaged in the service of God, and who, in connexion with their religious services, are looking for the rewards of heaven. Our subject, in its progress, demands that we inquire just here whether the service which they render is of such a nature that they merit eternal life? Is it because they are so profitable to God and his cause that the rewards of heaven would be only an equivalent for the services which they render? Let us look a moment at this matter.

A man who is truly religious renders a real and a valuable service to the cause of virtue and of God. His existence is a blessing, and not a curse. The universe is made better and happier because he lives. It would be a loss to society and to the universe, if his example, his conversation, his plans of wisdom, his experience, and his generous deeds, were annihilated or had not been. When the "rewards" of heaven are bestowed upon him, it will not be without some reference to a fitness or propriety that they should be so bestowed. There will be a sense in which every man will be "rewarded according to his works." But in reference to the bearing of this indisputable fact on the case before us, there are two or three things that deserve to be considered.

(*a*) One is, that your individual existence is not necessary to secure the service which is now actually rendered. God is not so dependent on you that he could not accomplish his purposes without you, or that if you should be removed, service of equal value might not be secured in some other way. By the great law of his kingdom, the agency of man is to be employed in the accomplishment of his purposes, but your individual agency is not indispensable. The services of a minister of the gospel who is eminently useful, and who is at a time of life, and has a measure of experience and learning, that seems to fit him for an important station, can be supplied by some one that God can place in his stead. When he is taken away, a mighty chasm indeed seems to be made; but his withdrawal soon ceases to be felt, for others rush in to fill his place: as the surface of the ocean soon becomes smooth, and it seems to be as full as it was before, though the waterspout has lifted up and carries away a portion of the mighty deep, or the sun has caused it to ascend in vapours; for streams and rivers all the while pour into that ocean, and keep up a constant supply. The man that was so learned and wise that it seemed as if no one else could supply his place at the head of a college, or so sagacious and prudent that it seemed as if some vast plan of benevolence depended on him, is removed; but the chasm is soon filled up—just as in storming a city, when the leader falls, some subaltern steps into his place, and leads on the conquest with the freshness of youth, and with wisdom and valour that had been in training for this very breach which God foresaw would occur. Let us not, then, suppose that *our* services are indispensable to God. Let us not imagine that he is dependent on us, or is under obligation to us. In the bosom of society, there are undeveloped powers, which will more than fill our places; in the church, there is piety maturing which can do more than we can do: and the very purposes of human advancement cherished in the Divine Mind may demand our removal.

(*b*) The religious man will reflect, further, that his best services do not *deserve* heaven. A man who is truly pious, and who has any proper sense of his own imperfections, and of the glory to which he is looking forward, never feels that there is any proportion between the services which he renders to God here, and the immortal blessedness to which he hopes to be elevated hereafter. He renders no service to the cause of truth and virtue which in his own estimation is an equivalent for the rewards which he trusts are in reserve for him; and after all his toils he feels that those rewards will be not of "debt," but of grace, and that he is an "unprofitable servant." God has taken effectual care of this in his plan of salvation; and whoever he may be that expects heaven on the ground of his own merit, it will not be he who gives evidence that he is truly a devoted and faithful servant of God.

(*c*) If, however, at any time this feeling of *merit* or claim should arise in the mind of a truly pious man, it is effectually checked by a moment's reflection on the way in which he has been disposed to engage in the service of God at all. It is not by any native inclination or tendency of mind; it has been solely by grace. Whatever service he may render, the origin of it is to be traced back to that distinguishing mercy which led him to seek after God, when he was disposed to pursue his own ways; which recalled him, when he was a wretched wanderer from the paths of truth and salvation. The case is like this:—You go into a "market place," and find a man "idle," and inclined to be idle. You reason and remonstrate with him, and by persevering entreaty, and the offer of reward, arouse him from his indolence, and induce him to spend his time in your service. Now, however faithful he may be, or however valuable may be the services which he may render you, he will never feel that any merit is to be attributed to himself. He owes to you his industrious habits, and all which he can ever secure by his labour. Or to take a case more in point:—You go into a miserable hovel, and find a wretch in the lowest stages of vice and misery. He was once a man in heart as well as in form, but now he has wholly lost the manhood of the one, and almost of the other. He is loathsome by vice and disease, and is a wretched outcast. He has no wish *to be* a man again; he has no energy to arouse him from his condition; he has no friend to take him by the hand, or even to pity him in his vices and woes. You take compassion on him. You clothe him in decent apparel. You remonstrate with him on his evil course. You remind him of what he was, and tell him of what he may be still. You rekindle the dying spark of self-respect; show him that he may yet forsake the paths of vice and again be respectable; breathe into him gradually the wish to be virtuous and pure and happy; give him a comfortable home to dwell in, and a piece of land to cultivate as his own. You speak kindly to him when he is discouraged; shield him when he is tempted by his old companions; offer him ample rewards for any services which he may render you,—and he returns to the ways of industry, and rises to a condition of competency and respectability. Perchance, doing this, you have lighted on a "gem of purest ray serene" in that rubbish, and the unhappy wretch whom you have rescued had a genius which takes its place among the brightest constellations of talent, and its light beams afar on the nations. Yet how will he feel in these circumstances? Will he feel that this is to be traced to his own merit, and that the wealth or honour which may gather around him is the measure of his desert? He will feel that but for you he would even now have been occupying that wretched hovel, or more likely would have been in the drunkard's grave. Whatever he has of moral worth, influence, or reputation, is to be traced to you. Thus it is with the Christian; and feeling this, he cannot regard himself as so profitable to God as to merit the rewards of heaven.

(3.) If it were conceded that the rewards of heaven were a proper recompense for the religious services which man can render to God, yet they would not be the suitable reward of those who are commonly expecting heaven on the ground of their own merits. The truly religious man, as we have seen, expects heaven, not on the ground of his own deserts, but through the grace of God. We may therefore lay the case of such out of the question in the inquiry whether men can deserve salvation by their own merits. The other class, embracing the mass of mankind, expect to be saved because they deserve to be saved, or, which amounts to the same thing, because they do not deserve to be damned. The ground of their claim is not that they are religious —for that they do not profess to be; and not that they render such service to the cause of God that the rewards of heaven would be an *equivalent* for their services—for they do not profess to be engaged in his service at all. What, then, is it? It is, that they are honest, true, faithful to their contracts, honourable in their dealings, disposed to aid others in their distress, and courteous in their treatment of their fellow-men. One who leads such a life, they suppose, does not *deserve* to be cast off and made miserable for ever; or, what is the same thing, they suppose that in all justice and equity he *ought* to be made happy in a future state—that is, that he may be saved on the ground of his own merits. What is now the value of this claim? With the principles before us which have been laid down, let us endeavour to answer this question. The inquiry is, Is heaven the appropriate reward of such a life? An illustration or two will make this plainer than abstract reasoning would do. You hire a man as a day-labourer. He comes to you at night for his pay. If he has been industrious according to the contract, and faithful to your interests, the case is a plain one, and you do not hesitate. But you put the interrogatory to him, "Did you go into my vineyard, and spend the day in cultivating it for me, and in a careful regard to my interests?" "No," is the honest reply; "but I *have* spent the day diligently. I have not been an idle man. I have attended to the cultivation of my own vineyard, and been faithful to my family, and I may appeal to all my neighbours for my general courtesy and honesty of life." If you now say that this is a case which is so palpably absurd that it never could occur, it may be replied, that it has been made absurd on purpose. Such a man would be only speaking out in the honesty of his heart what is the secret claim of every one who is not engaged in the service of God, and who yet feels that he ought to be saved. He does not even profess to be attending to the interests of his Creator, or engaged in his service.—You send a clerk to some distant town to collect your debts. He returns. "Have you been diligent and successful in the duty assigned you?" "I *was* diligent. I travelled much. In all my journey I injured no one; I treated no one roughly; I addressed no one in any other manner than in the language required in refined life. I also acquired valuable lands for myself, and have a prospect of rising to affluence and respectability." "But what has this to do with the reward which would be appropriate for one employed in *my* service?" "Nothing," a child would reply. But has it not just as much to do with it as the claim of a man who does not profess to serve his Maker, and who lives only to regard his own interests, has to do with the rewards of heaven?—You have a servant or an apprentice, whom you have a right to punish if he does wrong. You enjoin on him a specific duty—a duty of much importance to yourself, and one that is clearly reasonable in its nature. At the proper time you call him to account. The duty is not discharged; the service is not rendered. He pleads, however, that he does not deserve punishment. He has been steadily engaged all the while; he has been entirely honest and upright in his dealings with his fellow-servants; he has treated them with perfect courtesy, and has even acquired an enviable reputation for amiableness of manners; nay, he has more than once relieved a fellow-servant that was poor and sick and dying. All this is very well, it would be said in reply, but how can this constitute a claim for the particular reward which was offered? How can it show that he who has wholly omitted a known and specific duty does not deserve the punishment which was threatened? With what face could such a servant claim the reward due to faithful service in the cause of his master?

These plain and obvious principles are as applicable to religion as they are to the common transactions of life. God requires of us a specific service. It is not general and indefinite, or left to our choice as to what it shall be. It is, that we shall serve *him;* that we shall obey his commands; that we shall seek his glory; that we shall love him, honour him, and treat him as our God; that we shall be penitent for our past sins, and be willing to accept his favour on his own terms; that we shall be serious, religious, prayerful, believing, holy. If this is done, he promises heaven. But it is *not* done. Those now referred to do not even lay claim to *any* of these things. One of the last things that they would claim, or that their friends would think of claiming for them, is, that they are religious, or that they act habitually from reference to the will of their Creator. They claim to be moral, honest, true, urbane, kind; but how can this lay the foundation of a claim to the appropriate rewards of piety? How in these things, when they do not even intend it, can they render *any* service to God which would be the proper basis of his rewarding them in heaven? No more than the day-labourer, the clerk, and the servant, carefully attentive to their *own* interests, but wholly regardless of the interests of their employer, can expect a reward.

Having thus stated these arguments to show that man cannot by any services which he can render make himself so profitable to God as to merit salvation, or be of so much advantage to His cause as to render an equivalent for the rewards of heaven, it remains only to remark,

(4.) That if he cannot do this by a life of obedient holiness, he cannot by any offering which he has it in his power to make. The reasons for this are so obvious as to make it needless to dwell on them. One is, that no offering which we can make can be of any advantage or profit to God. He is made no richer by any oblation of silver and gold which we can bring him; he has no unsatisfied wants which can be supplied by our ministrations? "If I were hungry," says he, "I would not tell thee; for the world is mine and the fulness thereof. Will I eat the flesh of bulls, or drink the blood of goats?" Psa. l. 12, 13. Another reason is, that all that we possess is his, and we can give to him nothing to which he has not already a prior and supreme right. "Every beast of the forest," says he, "is mine, and the cattle upon a thousand hills. I know all the fowls of the mountains, and the wild beasts of the field are mine," Psa. l. 10, 11. Another reason is, that nothing that we could offer would be a compensation for our past offences, or repair the evils which we have done by our neglect of duty and by our open sins. "Wherewith shall I come before the Lord, and bow myself before the high God? Shall I come before him with burnt-offerings, with calves of a year old? Will the Lord be pleased with thousands of rams, or with ten thousands of rivers of oil? shall I give my first-born for my transgression, the fruit of my body for the sin of my soul?" Micah vi. 6, 7. And how shall a man profit God; how lay him under obligation to save him; how render such service as to be an equivalent for heaven? Shall he flagellate his own body? Yet how will that profit God? Shall he gird sackcloth on his loins, or wear an irritating haircloth garment to torment himself? Yet how will that benefit his Maker? Shall he go on a pilgrimage to some distant shrine? How will his Maker be advantaged by that? Shall he shut himself up in a gloomy cell, and withdraw from the light of the sun and the moon and the stars, and from the society of living men, and doom himself to wretchedness and woe? But will his God be made more rich or more happy by his austerities? Shall he seize upon the objects dearest to his heart, and destroy before bloody altars the lives which his Creator has given? But will it profit God if we kill his own creatures, and pour out their blood before him? If none of these things will do, with what plea of merit can we come before him? How can we render such service as to have a claim on heaven?

In view of this train of thought, two additional observations may be made:—

(1.) We see the falsehood of that system of religion which speaks of human merit, of the treasured and garnered merits of the saints of former times. If the principles now suggested are correct, how can there have been any such extraordinary and superabounding merit in past times that it may be available now for men? If there were such treasured merit left by the saints of other days, it might still be a question what claim of right any man has now to distribute it to others; but any such claim of superabounding merit is alike at variance with the Bible and with every just principle of reason. Yet this doctrine is one of the principal supports of the Papacy, and is one of the dogmas that demand credence in our land and of this generation. It will be shown, hereafter, that in Him who died to atone for our sins there *is* ample merit to supply all our deficiencies, and that the results of his atonement may be ours. The claim that superabounding merit has been wrought out by the saints, derogates from and almost annihilates this; and the claim that his merits and theirs are lodged in human hands, to be dispensed or withheld at pleasure by a priesthood, is one of the chief supports of the most appalling and terrific systems of spiritual despotism that have ever tyrannized over man. Thanks to Him who has bought us our pardon—the disposal of the merits of his sacrifice is committed to no human hands, and can be interrupted by no human power!

(2.) This subject is one of direct practical interest to all. If we are ever saved, there will be a good reason for it; for nothing is merely arbitrary in the matter of salvation. There are but two ways possible of being saved—the one by our own merits, the other by the merits of another. If in regard to the latter there are no merits of the "saints" on which we can rely; no merits of parents or pious friends of which we can avail ourselves, then the merits of the Lord Jesus constitute the only foreign dependence which we can have. The whole question is then just this:—Do we rely on our own merits for salvation, or the merits of the Redeemer? Here the world is divided; the Christian, on the one side—the Pagan, the Mohammedan, the infidel, the moralist, on the other. This single question separates the inhabitants of the globe into two great parties never to be united. But if the principles in this discourse are correct, the question may be put to every man—to his reason, his conscience, his heart—whether he *has* any merit on which he can rely as a ground of salvation. Has he done anything for which the equivalent is to be found in the rewards of an eternal heaven? Has he so deserved the rewards of life, has he rendered such service to his Maker, that he can stand at the final bar, where we all must soon stand, and claim an admission to heaven? Can he demand it as a right that heaven's portal should be thrown open to him, and he be welcomed there? If so, on what ground? What is the basis of the claim? Religion? The unconverted sinner makes no pretension to it. Repentance? He has never shed a tear over his sins. The love of God? He has no spark of love to that glorious Being in his heart. Sacrifices in his service? He has made none. An honest endeavour to do his will? He has never made this the rule of his life. What *is* the service which he has rendered? What has been the life which he has led? What is the state of his account with God? What is the condition of his heart? Oh, let him look at the broken law of God, His violated sabbaths, His rejected gospel, His grieved Spirit, His neglected word; let him look at his own life of thoughtlessness, selfishness, and vanity, his neglect of prayer, his pride and opposition to God; let him look at the sins of childhood and the worldliness and wickedness of riper years; let him look at the times when God has called and he has refused, when the Saviour has stretched out his hands and he would not regard it; let him look at his broken vows and promises—the times when he resolved that he would be a Christian if he reached a certain period of life, the solemn covenant which he made when he was sick, that if God would spare him he would be His;—let him look at these things, and then see whether he has a claim to an admission to heaven, and whether he can be received there because he has been profitable to God. Oh, if you saw these things aright, you would hail with transports of unspeakable joy the announcement which we make to you, that there *is* One whose merits can cancel all your sins, and give you a title to salvation. Then, oh! with what joy would you, as thousands have done before you, cast away the "rags of your own righteousness," that you might be clothed in the robe that is "made white in the blood of the Lamb!"

SERMON XXXIII.

WHAT IS MEANT BY THE MERITS OF CHRIST.

JOHN i. 16.—"And of his fulness have all we received, and grace for grace."

THAT is, all we who are Christians, or who are Christ's real followers. In the fourteenth verse of this chapter it is said of the Lord Jesus, that he was "full of grace and truth." In the Epistle to the Colossians (ch. i. 19), the apostle Paul says of him that "it pleased the Father that in him should all fulness dwell:" that is, with particular reference to the salvation of men, for he immediately adds (ver. 20), "And having made peace through the blood of his cross, by him to reconcile all things unto himself." These expressions all refer to an *abundance* or *fulness* of grace in the Lord Jesus as sufficient for all that would be saved by him, or such as would supply all their want of personal merit when they appear before God; and as there is in us a *total* want of merit towards God, the sense of the whole must be, that we can be saved only by the merits of Christ. I propose to endeavour to explain what that merit is.

In the previous discourses on the subject of justification, I have endeavoured to demonstrate that man cannot justify himself before God. In the last discourse I aimed to prove that man has no merit of his own on which he can rely for salvation, or that he can do nothing which will make eternal life a fair equivalent or compensation for his service, or which will bring the Almighty under an obligation of justice or equity to save him. I propose now to show that there is One who *has* ample merit which can supply all our defect, and which may be so available to us as to secure our salvation.

There are few phrases in more common use than the merits of Christ; few declarations that are repeated more frequently by ministers of the gospel and others, than that men can be saved only by His merits; and few things that are more frequently uttered in prayer than that we plead His merits only for our salvation. The frequency with which this expression occurs, and the bearing which it has on the general subject now under consideration, makes it proper that we should attempt an explanation of it. Common as the use of it is, a formal attempt to explain it is not often made, and it is to be feared that it is often used without an intelligent apprehension of its meaning.

The phrase does not occur in the Bible, but the idea which is intended to be conveyed by it exists there as a vital and central thought in the whole plan of justification by faith. In the prosecution of this subject it will be proper, I. To explain what is meant when we speak of the merits of Christ; and, II. To show in what his merits consisted.

I. *What is meant by the merits of Christ?* The general idea is expressed in the text:—"And of his fulness have all we received, and grace for grace." There was an *abundance* or *fulness* in him of which we might partake; that is, there was a completeness—πλήρωμα—which in our conscious want or deficiency, could meet all our necessities, so that we could receive "grace" corresponding with that which was in him. When we speak of the merits of Christ in connexion with our salvation, it is meant that there was an amount of merit in his services which he did not need for any personal advantage or for himself; which had been secured with a special purpose to supply the great and undisputed deficiency of man; and which can be made available to us, on certain conditions, and in the way which God has revealed as the ground of our acceptance. The main object is not now to prove that there *are* such merits treasured up in Christ, but to explain the language. Whether the doctrine be true, and if there is such merit in him how it may be available to us, will be the topics of future inquiry.

(1.) In the explanation of the subject I would then advert, first, to the doctrine respecting *merit* laid down in the last discourse. A man merits a reward when he has earned or deserved it; when he has fully complied with the terms of the bargain; when his services are worth as much to you as you pay him. We may recall the illustrations of the day-labourer, the soldier, the physician, in each of which cases it was said that the service rendered was fully equal in value to the pay which was given. The service measures the pay; the one is equal, or is supposed to be equal, to the other. To withhold the compensation is injustice, or is palpably wrong. This is the ordinary and proper sense in which the word *merit* is used among men, and it was in this sense that I endeavoured to show that man cannot merit salvation.

(2.) I observe, secondly, that cases may arise where much more may be done for you than one who is in your employ is strictly bound to perform. A reference to some of these cases will enable us to explain the subject before us.

(*a*) You have a man in your employ engaged under the ordinary conditions of service as a labourer, or clerk. Without any special agreement with him, or without anything being said about it in your contract, he is to do what is commonly understood to be required in that condition of life; what is usually done by those in the same employment. He is to be at his post at a certain hour in the morning, and to remain until a certain hour in the evening, and is to be faithful to his employer's interests, and diligent in the prosecution of the business entrusted to him. On these conditions, without anything more specific, the contract is usually made with clerks, and bookkeepers, and day-labourers, and journeymen-mechanics, and lawyers, and ministers of the gospel. It is not deemed necessary to be any more specific than that they shall be faithful to the interests of their employers, and render the amount of service which is usually expected in their occupation. But it is very possible to conceive that one may go much beyond that. He may be engaged at a much earlier hour than is usual, and may prolong his toils far into the shades of night. He may evince uncommon tact and sagacity in the management of affairs entrusted to him, and such may be his skill and success, that his services may have a value far beyond anything which you had anticipated in the contract. You would not feel yourself at liberty to turn him off or to complain if he had *not* done this. You would not feel that he has a legal claim on you for anything *more* than you promised to pay him, for you did not contract with him for this special service; but you would be likely to feel that he has a claim of honour on you, and if, when he leaves your service, you know of any situation of special advantage that can be obtained, you would feel yourself under a sort of moral obligation to endeavour to secure it for him. Here is something *merited*, since more has been done than he was *bound* to do.

(*b*) A second case:—A man in your employ may be placed in circumstances where he may have an opportunity of doing something for your *special advantage*, though of a nature which was not distinctly specified in your contract with him. He may have great sagacity, and may watch the changes and chances in the market, and enable you to make important and advantageous purchases; he may be in possession of intelligence respecting coming changes in the markets, which may be of great service to you; or he may, by uncommon tact in business, be enabled to save you from inextricable bankruptcy. Now if he is a mere bookkeeper, or salesman, you could hardly *claim* as a matter of right that he should bring his sagacity in these things into your service; perhaps you would hardly blame him if he took advantage of it to advance his own interests, provided he did not injure you. His specific business is to keep your books correctly, or to sell your goods in the manner in which you shall direct him, and his sagacity and tact in *these* departments you have a right to require should be employed in your service. But your contract and your claim extend no farther. Yet if he *chooses* to go beyond this, and actually, while he incurs no possible risk, is the means of great advantage to you, as an honourable man you would feel that he *deserved* an appropriate acknowledgment. Many instances of this kind might be referred to, but these will illustrate the point under consideration.

(3.) It is necessary to make but one other remark in order to see the bearing of these illustrations on the case before us. Reference has been made to "*abounding merit;*" to cases in which service is rendered *beyond* what was in the contract; to that which was wholly voluntary, and yet where there would be a claim *in honour* at least for a suitable acknowledgment, or where an honourable man would feel himself under obligation to bestow a reward. The remark which is now to be made is, that he who has this extra claim on you may do what he pleases with the reward which you may feel willing to give. It may not be needful for him, or he may not choose to make use of it for himself; but he may be disposed to make another use of it which will develope some trait of mind that will by no means diminish your respect for his character. Suppose some such cases as the following in the application of the instances referred to:—that he should ask you to aid a younger brother of his who was just beginning business, and who was greatly in need of credit; or, in the event of his death, to show kindness to his aged father or mother; or to appropriate the gratuity which you designed for him to some young man who was struggling to obtain an education. Or suppose that the faithful servant should ask you to release from bondage his wife or child, in consideration of the extra and quite equivalent services which he had rendered to you. Or to take another case:—Suppose a friend of his had, in an unhappy moment, defrauded you, might he not ask you to "set that to his account?" In either case, would you not feel that what he asked he had a right to ask? And would you not be the more deeply affected with respect for his character by this request? He did not perform the extra service for reward. He did not expect it. He did not mention it to you. He did not claim *any* reward. But when *you* felt that he had a claim to it, and pressed it upon him, and would not be refused, he looked not for gorgeous or gay apparel for himself, or for a purse of gold, or a splendid house, nor did he ask you to trumpet his fame; but he looked round on those struggling with poverty, crushed and enfeebled by age, bound in affliction and iron, or burdened with debts which they could never discharge, and asked you to forget him and to remember them. The developments of such a character would fill your mind with new conceptions of its beauty, and your heart would be insensibly knit with his.

It will be perceived that these illustrations bear on the explanation of what is meant by the merits of Christ. His merit was of this extraordinary or superabundant kind. It was beyond what could have been demanded of him, and was such that, if he chose to ask it, or so designed it, it could be made available to others. This leads us to the second general inquiry—

II. *In what did His merits consist?* Keeping in view the remarks already made, it will be necessary to show that all that he did when on earth was of this extraordinary character; that he rendered real service to the universe for which the rewards given him will be no more than an equivalent; and that his merits were of such a nature that they may be made available to others.

(1.) All that he did was of an extraordinary character, or was service which could not have been demanded of him. This remark is based on the fact that he was Divine, and has no pertinency except on that supposition. When it is said that his service or work was such as could not be demanded, it is meant that there was no law or obligation which could bind the Divinity to become incarnate, to be an humble teacher of mankind, to minister to their wants with his own hands, or to make an atonement for their transgressions. The entire transaction was of a kind which could be enforced by no law. If he was equal to the Father and one with him, he was under no law but the infinite and eternal law of his own Divine nature. There was no obligation on him to become a man, a priest, a sacrifice; to toil, to weep, to die.—Another illustration may be introduced here. There is an heir-apparent to a crown. Every consideration of propriety, (and perhaps a statute-law of the realm,) requires him to perform the duties of a son in the palace, and to appear and act on all occasions as becomes the first man in the realm next to the throne. But there is no law which requires him to become a day-labourer, or a menial, or that makes it his duty to go into some peasant's cottage and watch the long night by the cradle of a dying child. There may possibly be no law against it, if he chooses to do it; but it *cannot* be demanded of him. The Son of God in heaven would appear there always in a manner appropriate to his unequalled relation to the Father; but what law was there requiring him to come down to earth, to be a man of sorrows, to take part in our sadnesses and woes, and to die? If he did this, the service was altogether of an extraordinary character, and was entirely a work of merit. This remark is obvious. Its bearings, if conceded to be true, are of great importance. The force and pertinence of this reasoning, as has been already remarked, proceeds on the supposition that he is Divine. If he is not, however exalted as a created being he may be, it does not appear how he could have *any* extra merit, and consequently how the doctrine of justification by his righteousness could be held. If Christ be a mere man, or an angel, or an archangel, or creature of any rank, no such extraordinary service could be rendered—none could be made available to us.

We have seen that man may acquire extra merit from his fellow-man, merit which may be made available to others. The question is, why a creature may not do this in reference to the service of God; and why, if the Saviour were less than Divine, he might not do the same thing for us? The answer to this question is obvious. When you employ a man, you contract for a certain amount of service or of time. You do not contract for *all* that he has. You contract for what is usual, or what you specify. All beyond the limits of that contract remains his. But there is no such contract, understanding, or stipulation, expressed or understood, between a creature and God. *All* a man's powers, his time, his talents, his service, his skill, his learning, his influence, belong to his Maker. Of every creature God demands "all the heart, the mind, the might, the strength." There is not a moment of time in which a creature can feel that he is released from the claim of his Maker; there is not a power or faculty of mind or body which he possesses which is beyond the range of the demand of the Divine law; there is not a service of prayer, or praise, or sacrifice which he could render, which is beyond the limits of his duty; there is not an act of benevolence to the poor, the needy, the sinful, or the dying, which he can perform, which is beyond the all-comprehensive grasp of the Divine command to do good. Can a creature of the Almighty put himself into the midst of a service acceptable to God which he may feel was not required of him? Can he love with an ardour beyond what God requires? Can he maintain a degree of fidelity in temptation beyond what is demanded? Can he stoop to some scene of woe, and do good to a sufferer in a way which the law that binds him to God did not make his duty? Can he evince compassion for the sinful and the sad beyond what the law of his nature and the commandment of his Maker demand? If he cannot, how can there be such extra merit that it can be made available to others? And if the Lord Jesus were a mere man, as one class of Socinians tells us; or an angel of exalted rank, as another class assures us; or the highest created intelligence, as the Arian affirms,—how could he have wrought out any merit which can be available to us? How could he have done anything beyond what he was bound as a creature to do? How could he so have stepped beyond the limits of the Divine law as by abounding merits to save a world? It is difficult to see, therefore, how he who denies the Divinity of the Lord Jesus can hold to the doctrine of a meritorious sacrifice on his part, or to the doctrine of justification through his merits at all: and there is a melancholy consistency in the philosophy and practical faith of those who deny his Divinity, in yielding up the doctrine of the atonement, and then the whole doctrine of justification by faith. But admit that Christ is God, equal with the Father, and all is clear. Then, being under no obligations to become incarnate, being bound by no law to leave the throne of heaven, and seek a home in a manger, a lodging-place without a pillow, a death on a cross, and a burial in the grave destined for another, all this is the work of extra merit, and may all be available for others. We see him in our world, not as a mere man, and thus bound by law to render every service to the cause of God; but as Immanuel—God with us—the voluntary messenger from heaven—the equal with God—performing a service to which no law bound him, and to which no other powers were adequate, and which therefore may constitute a fulness of merit that may be available for those who have none.

(2.) The second remark is, that Christ rendered real service to the universe by his work. His coming, his teaching, his death, his resurrection, were an advantage to the cause of God and of virtue, to the full extent of the reward which he will receive. The universe has been so much profited by his voluntary and wonderful service in the cause of virtue and salvation, that there is a propriety that he should be rewarded for it; and the reward which he will receive is no more than an equivalent for the value of the service rendered. It will be asked, What has been the advantage of his work to the universe? In what way is it to be measured or estimated? It may be replied, We do not know fully yet, nor are our minds in a condition now, if they will ever be, to estimate what is appropriate to "satisfy" him for the "travail of his soul." But the general answer, whoever can appreciate its meaning, will be, that the value or worth of his voluntary services is to be estimated by *all the evils which his coming has arrested or prevented, and by all the happiness in this world and in heaven of which it has been the cause.* If we could ascertain this, we could estimate the amount of his services to the universe, and of course the amount of the reward which is due to him, or the amount of his merit. No attempt can be made by us to gauge the amount of this merit. All that can be done is to submit a few hints to illustrate the real nature of the service which he rendered.

(*a*) He did voluntary good through his life. He healed the sick, gave sight to the blind, hearing to the deaf, and vigour to the lame; he restored the maniac to his right mind, and brought back the poor outcast who "dwelt among the tombs" to the comforts of home. All this was doing good to the world, which, if he had not come, would not have been done.

(*b*) He set a most holy example of virtue to mankind. He showed what true virtue is—how man should live, and how he should meet the temptations of the great enemy of the soul. All this is so much gained to the cause of virtue, above what would have been if he had not come; and the value of having one perfect example in a world where there had been no such standard, and amidst the conflicting opinions of men on the subject of morals, cannot be estimated.

(*c*) He taught man by his example how to bear trials. He himself went through all the usual forms of woe and grief, and showed in each one of them how man ought to endure calamities, and how in them consolation might be found. But who in a suffering and dying world can estimate the value of such an example?

(*d*) He taught man the true character of God; the nature of his law; the kind of worship that would be acceptable to him, and the way in which the throne of mercy may be approached. But who can estimate the value to a sinful world of the knowledge of the way of pardon?

(*e*) He introduced a religion which has contributed everywhere to the promotion of industry, purity, chastity, truth, honesty, intelligence, and liberty; which has raised one sex from the deepest degradation, and softened the asperities and removed the tyranny of the other; which has led to the founding of hospitals and asylums, and which will ultimately put an end to all the forms of evil and vice that tyrannize over man:—and who can gauge the amount of service which He has thus rendered to man and to the universe?

(*f*) He made an atonement for sin—his greatest, noblest work. He vindicated by his death the honour and the law of God, and solved the question which has everywhere confounded the human intellect, how justice and mercy can meet together, and how righteousness can be maintained, and yet the sinner go free. He secured to the universe by his death all the advantages which could have been secured by the everlasting punishment of the sinner himself, and all the advantages which now result from admitting to heaven countless millions who but for his sacrifice would have been eternally wretched:—and what finite mind can estimate the value of His service rendered to the universe?

(*g*) He checks evil by his gospel and his grace, and turns the disobedient to the paths of virtue. Take one single example as an illustration of the amount of service thus rendered,—the case of Saul of Tarsus. Think of what he would have been with his extraordinary talents, his uncommon learning, his vast energy of character, and his restless ambition, and his proud and self-confident heart, if there had been no atonement; and then of what he *was* after he was converted to the cause of truth. Think of his influence, while he lived, in meeting the evils and corruptions of idolatry; in closing temples of polluted worship; in purifying the fountains of morals; and in diffusing abroad the principles of pure religion. Think of the good which has been done since his time, by his incomparable writings, in maintaining the truth, and imparting consolation in a world of sorrow; and see in the conversion of that man an instance of the kind of service which the Lord Jesus rendered to the universe. Then reflect that the case of Saul of Tarsus is but one of many hundreds of millions—individually less bright, but in the aggregate outshining his,—as the mingled light of the galaxy is of greater glory than the twinkling of a single star,—and then ask, Who can estimate the amount of service which the Son of God has rendered to the universe? All that has been done by His holy life and example; all that has been accomplished on earth by the influence of His religion; all that His death did to honour the Divine law; all that has been or will be done by arresting evil and staying the desolations of sin; all the additions which have been or will be made by redemption to the numbers of the heavenly host; and all the immortal songs and joys of the redeemed in heaven,—all these things are to be taken into this estimate, and will be the measure of the voluntary service rendered to the universe by the Son of God. It remains only, in order to a complete explanation of the subject, to add—

(3.) That all the merit of Christ's work—all the reward which he deserved—is available to others. It is that superabounding service which has been before referred to, which can be appropriated in any way that he shall ask. Not needing it for himself, for he dwells in "the glory which he had with the Father before the world was," it can be appropriated to those who are poor, and needy, and destitute of any claim of merit. The reward for all his extraordinary services may be such as he shall wish, and his heart will not ask augmented glory for himself in heaven as Divine, but will seek it in the elevation and immortal felicity of the poor and lost upon the earth for whom he died. By such a reward the universe will *lose* nothing, but will on every account be a gainer; and the benevolent heart which rendered these extraordinary services may be abundantly satisfied by asking that the "lost may be saved." It was on grounds like these that it was said in the promise, "Ask of me, and I shall give thee the heathen for thine inheritance, and the uttermost parts of the earth for thy possession," Psa. ii. 8. Thus too the promise was, "He shall see of the travail of his soul"—the fruit of his wearisome sorrow—"and shall be satisfied," Isa. liii. 11. Thus too, in asking in his parting prayer that his work on earth might be remembered, he could use with propriety the strong language, "Father, I *will* that they also whom thou hast given me be with me where I am, that they may behold my glory which thou hast given me," John xvii. 24. To secure their salvation, and the universal spread of his gospel, he can urge the extraordinary claim of the service which he has rendered by his life of spotless virtue; his pure example; his relief of human woes; and the sorrows which he voluntarily endured in order that the law of God might be maintained, and eternal justice asserted, even when salvation was offered to men.

If these views are correct, then it follows,

(1.) That we are to look nowhere else than to Christ as the meritorious cause of salvation. Had it been possible for any mere created being to have wrought out sufficient merit to save the soul, the incarnation of the Son of God, and his death on Calvary, would never have occurred. The moment it is maintained that man may merit salvation for himself, or for others, the doctrine of the atonement is denied, and the work of Christ dishonoured; and the doctrine that there are anywhere, or in any hands, garnered up the merits of holy men of which we can avail ourselves, derogates, to just the extent in which it is held, from the Great Sacrifice, and is an attack on the fundamental doctrines of the gospel. In our hopes of salvation we have but one place to which to look. It is not what our own hands have done, or what has been done by holy men of other times; it is the infinite merit of the Son of God.

(2.) The merits of the Saviour are sufficient for the salvation of all mankind. If the view which has been taken is correct, it is clear that the benefits which he has rendered to the universe, by his holy obedience and death, are commensurate with any rewards which he may receive in connexion with the salvation of men. "It pleased the Father that in him," in every respect, "should all fulness dwell;" and alike in his power, his benevolence, his willingness to save, and the merits of his work, there is an ample sufficiency for the wants of all mankind. Needing none of the results of his great work on earth for the promotion of his own happiness, all that he did may be made available to others, and all men may come with equal freeness and confidence. He had the promise of an ample and satisfactory reward, when it was said that he "should see of the travail of his soul, and should be satisfied;" and on the basis of that promise he himself uses such language as this: "If any man thirst, let him come unto me and drink." "Come unto me, all ye that are weary and heavy laden, and I will give you rest;" and "whosoever will, let him come and take the water of life freely." There was no original deficiency in the merits of the Saviour for human salvation, nor has his merit been exhausted by the numbers that have already been saved. Salvation in him is like a copious fountain breaking out in a desert. Such a fountain is free for all who may come. It stands in the pathway where the multitudes move, where the caravans pass along —and no one has a right to appropriate it exclusively to himself. No tribe of men may enclose it, or may obstruct its waters. One company of weary travellers has as much right there as another, and to no one particularly appertains the office of dispensing it to the fainting pilgrim. Any one who will come and kneel down there, may drink freely. And it will never be exhausted. The fountain will pour out its waters from age to age. The present company of thirsty travellers will soon pass on. They will pursue their journey, and go off to die; but there the stream will flow on, unexhausted and inexhaustible, to the end of time. So it is with the fountain of salvation. As many of the present generation as choose may come and partake, and then as many of the next and the next, and still the fountain will flow on, unexhausted and inexhaustible. It will flow just as fresh and just as full in the last generation that lives, as it did in the days of the Saviour's personal residence on earth—as it does now; and the last sinner that is to be saved will find it as pure and as life-giving to his soul as it is to ours.

(3.) Finally, let no one then say that he is so great a sinner that he cannot be saved. I know how the troubled sinner feels. I know that his guilt often presses him down as a mighty burden, and that he feels he has no claim to salvation. We do not ask you to come depending on your own merits. We believe that you never will find eternal life, if you make your own deeds your plea. But the sinner sometimes has another feeling. He not only feels that he has no merit and no claim to salvation, but he feels that his sins are so great that not even the merit of the Lord Jesus will be sufficient to cancel his guilt. Here, fellow-sinner, you err. Here you do injustice to his holy life, to his benevolent heart, to his death. That infinite merit which he secured by his work on earth, he is willing should be available for your salvation. And that is like the illimitable ocean. It is always full; and no matter how many have sought and found salvation there, there will be countless millions more. Come, then, thou who art conscious that thou hast no merit of thine own, and be one of that blessed number who receive of his fulness, grace for grace. "Ho, *every one* that thirsteth, come ye to the waters, and he that hath no money; come ye, buy and eat; yea, come, buy wine and milk without money and without price," Isa. lv. 1.

SERMON XXXIV.

IN WHAT SENSE WE ARE JUSTIFIED BY THE MERITS OF CHRIST.

ROM. iii. 24.—"Being justified freely by his grace, through the redemption that is in Christ Jesus."

THERE are several things affirmed in this text. One is, that the persons referred to—that is, Christians—are *justified*, or that there is a sense in which they are regarded as righteous. A second is, that this is done *freely*—δωρεάν: that is, that it is not by purchase or merit on our part, but that it has on the part of God *the freeness of a gift*. A third is, that it is by the grace of God; that is, that it is regarded as a proof of his favour *to be* justified. A fourth is, that this is through the redemption that is in Christ Jesus, or is in virtue of his merits.

In the previous discourses, I have endeavoured to show that man cannot justify himself, and that he has no claim of merit before God; but that there is in the Lord Jesus infinite merit, of such a nature that it may be made available to us. In the prosecution of this general subject, it is proposed now to illustrate two points:—I. What is meant by justification in the gospel; and, II. In what way we are justified by the merits of Christ.

I. *What is meant by justification in the gospel?* My object here is to state what is the exact condition of a man who is justified. In what respect does he differ from what he was before? What change has taken place in reference to him? How is he regarded by his Maker differently from what he was before? What new relation does he sustain to God, to his law, and to his plan of providential dealings? These, it will be seen, are important questions, which probably every one is disposed to ask who attentively considers this subject. They are questions, also, on which serious mistakes are sometimes made, as well by those who attempt to explain the subject, as by individual Christians in reflecting on this new relation. A few remarks, showing what is *not* meant, and what *is*, will make the subject clear.

(1.) It is not meant that a man who is justified on the gospel-plan is justified in a *legal* sense. What it is to be so justified has been before explained. It is when a man is accused of a crime, and is able to vindicate himself, either by showing that he did not do the act charged on him, or that he had a right to do it. If he can do either of these things, or, which is the same thing, if the charge is not proved against him, he is acquitted by the law, or is held to be righteous in regard to the offence charged. I have endeavoured, in the former discourses, to show that in a legal sense man cannot be justified before God; and whatever may be thought of the argument in the case, it is certain that this is not the kind of justification described in the gospel. It is needful here to remark only, that Christ did not come to aid man in justifying himself in this sense. He did not come to take the part of the sinner against God, and to enable him to make out his cause. He did not come to be his advocate in the sense of assisting him in rebutting the charges made against him; in showing that the charges had been falsely laid; in explaining his conduct so that it might not appear to be wrong; or in offering palliations for admitted criminality. Whatever be the nature of the work which the Lord Jesus came to perform, and however he may aid us in our salvation, it is all done with the concession, on his part, that we are guilty to the full extent which the law charges on us.

(2.) It is not in any proper sense a *legal* transaction. Justification by the law is known only in one way—by perfect and uniform obedience. The law of God, in conformity with the general principle of law, knows no other mode. It makes no provision for the pardon or justification of those who violate it, any more than a human law does. The plan of justification in the gospel is a departure from the regular process of law; and whatever inferences may follow from this, either against the system or in favour of it, the fact is not to be denied. "But now," says the apostle Paul, "the righteousness of God without the law is manifested;" that is, the method of justification in a way different from that known in the law, Rom. iii. 21. All attempts to show that the plan of justification in the gospel is a legal transaction, or is in accordance with legal principles, have been signal failures; and if there can be no other justification than that which is properly legal, the whole effort to be saved must be given up in despair.

(3.) Nor does it mean that the man who is justified ceases to be ill-deserving or guilty in the proper sense of the word. When a man is justified by law, he is declared to be *not* guilty or ill-deserving. But it is not so when a man is justified by the gospel. It is expressly said respecting this plan that God "justifies the ungodly," Rom. iv. 5: meaning that it is admitted they *are* ungodly at the time, or that they are personally guilty. The act of justification does not change the nature of the offence, or prove that to be right which is in itself wrong. Crime is what it is in its own nature, and is not modified by the manner in which he who commits it is treated. To pardon a man out of the penitentiary does not prove that the act of burglary or theft for which he was committed was innocent. To forgive a man under the gallows does not prove that he is not ill-deserving for the act of murder. To be led, from any consideration, to treat a man who has injured us as if he had not done it, does not prove that the act was not wrong; or that he should not regard himself as blameworthy for having done it. Our kind treatment of him will not be likely in any degree to diminish his sense of his criminality; and the act of pardon with which an offender against God is met, when penitent, will not lessen his sense of his own guilt. God never comes in the act of justification to convince him that he has not done wrong, but to save him though it is admitted that he *is* a great sinner; and the consciousness that he is a sinner will attend him and humble him through life. He will lift up his eyes and his heart with thankfulness that he is a pardoned man; not with pride and self-complacency that he is an innocent man. He will have the spirit of the publican, not of the Pharisee. The publican that went down to his house justified would not go feeling that he was innocent; he would be filled with gratitude that so great a sinner might be forgiven.

(4.) Justification in the gospel does not mean mere pardon. It has been supposed by many that this is all that is denoted by it. But there are insuperable objections to this opinion. One is, that it is a departure from the common use of language. When a man who has been sentenced to the penitentiary is pardoned before the term of his sentence is expired, we never think of saying that he is justified. The offence is forgiven, and the penalty is remitted; but the use of the word *justify* in his case would convey a very different idea from the word *pardon*. Another objection is, that the sacred writers have so carefully and so constantly used the word "justify." If mere pardon or forgiveness were all that is intended, it is difficult to see why another word has been constantly employed, and a word so different in its signification. And another objection is, that mere forgiveness is *not* all which the case seems to demand. There was required a reinstating in the favour of God; a restoration to forfeited immunities and privileges; and a purpose in regard to future treatment which is not necessarily involved in the word pardon. It may be conceived that, in cases of pardon for high offences, there would be required, in order to meet all the circumstances of the case, not only a remission of the penalty, but a distinct act restoring to the offender or his family his title, his hereditary honours, and his place in civil relations. The pardon of Lord Bacon would not have restored him at once to the bench, nor the forgiveness of Raleigh to his station in the court of Elizabeth. In the case of a sinner against God, pardon respects mainly the *past;* justification, the purpose of God in reference *to the future.* Forgiveness remits past crimes; justification respects the purpose of God to treat the offender *as if* he had not sinned: and though these may be simultaneous, yet they may be separated in conception as distinct things. The one forgives the past; the other reinstates the offender in the lost favour of God.

(5.) It is not meant that in the act of justification the merits of the Lord Jesus become so transferred to us that they can be regarded as *literally ours*, or that his righteousness is in any proper sense our *own.* This is not true, and cannot be made to be true. Moral character is not capable of being transferred from one individual to another; and however the benefits of what one does may be conveyed to another, it will always be true that the character of an individual is what it is in itself. It will always be true that Christ, and not we, obeyed perfectly the law of God; that Christ, and not his people, died on the cross; and that the merit of his life and death is strictly his, and not theirs. It will always be true, also, that they violated the law of God, that their characters were sinful, and that they deserved not the mercy of God. No man can really believe that the moral character of one individual can be transferred to another, and no one should charge the Bible with inculcating any such doctrine, either with respect to the effect of Adam's transgression on his posterity, or the righteousness of the Redeemer in the salvation of his people.

(6.) We are prepared now to remark positively, that justification on the gospel-plan denotes a purpose on the part of God to treat a sinner *as if he were righteous.* It implies an intention not to punish him for his sins; not to regard him as any longer under condemnation; not to treat him as an alien, an apostate, and an outcast;—but to regard and treat him in the future in all his important relations as if he had never sinned. It involves the purpose to shield him from the condemning sentence of the law, and the wrath that shall come upon the guilty; to admit him to the fellowship of unfallen beings; to regard him as entitled to all the privileges of a child of God, *as if* he had not fallen; to throw around him the ægis of the Divine protection and favour to the end of the present life, and then to admit him to immortal life in heaven. These things would have been his if he had not fallen; and these things are now made his in virtue of the merits of the Redeemer. In all his great relations, in all the most permanent and important things that affect him, he *is*, and is to be, *as if* he had not sinned. The main evils of the apostacy in his case are arrested, and it is the Divine purpose to regard and to treat him as a child of God.

It is important to remark, that in these statements it is not designed to affirm that in *all* respects the act of justification places a man in precisely the same situation in which he would have been if he had not sinned. It is, indeed, designed to teach that in the direct Divine dealings with him he will be regarded and treated as if he were personally righteous. But why, then, it will be asked, does he suffer and die? Why is he not removed to heaven, as Enoch and Elijah were, without seeing death? Why does the justified man ever pass through severe bodily trials, like Job or Hezekiah; or experience the evils of poverty and want, like Lazarus; or why is he called to part with beloved children, or to be thrown into prison, or to lie down in the sorrows of the most painful form of death, as thousands have already done, and as the children of God now often do?

It is necessary to make such exceptions or qualifications as these in explaining the nature of justification. Though justified, man is not *in fact* treated in this world in all respects as he would have been if he had not sinned. In the life to come he will be. But nothing is plainer than that in the present life things occur in reference to the treatment of those who are justified, which would not have occurred if man had not sinned, and which will not occur in heaven. Poverty, sickness, bereavement, death, and kindred evils, come upon the righteous and the wicked, the saint and the sinner, the man who is justified and the man who is not. These evils are indeed softened and mitigated by religion, and may be among the means by which the justified man is better prepared for heaven; but still they exist *as* evils, and are to be regarded as among the fruits of sin not removed by the act of justification, and as furnishing the exceptions or qualifications alluded to when it is said that in this life the justified man is not treated in *all* respects as if he had not sinned. The *reasons* why the evils of sin are not entirely arrested by the act of justification, and why the believer is not treated in this life in all respects as if he had not sinned, seem to be principally two:—(*a*) One is, that it is not the nature of religion to arrest or change the operation of physical laws. It will have an indirect and gradual effect in checking some of those laws, but to have made that effect direct and immediate would have required a constant miracle. It is not the design of religion to restore health or property which has been wasted by dissipation; to check the results of vice in those who have been led astray by evil example, or to stay the effects of a life of guilt on our physical frame. A life of virtue will ultimately do much to accomplish this; but to do it at once would require the physical power of a miracle. For the same reason, to be justified does not save from temporal death, from death in accordance with the laws of our physical being. No one can doubt that God *could* have saved us from this, but it would be easy to suggest reasons why it has not been done. (*b*) Another reason why the act of justification does not secure the same treatment in all respects here as if man had never sinned, is that he who is justified, and who is at heart a true believer, is often in circumstances where he needs the discipline of the hand of God. He is not at once made perfect; and his imperfections, his wanderings, his neglect of duty, his worldliness, often demand the interposition of God for his own good in a way which would neither be necessary nor proper in the case of one who had never sinned. Hence, if the Christian sins, he may be recalled even by stripes. Hence he comes under the regular physical laws of the Divine administration in the world. Hence he is sick or bereaved. Hence, like other men, he may be cut off by the pestilence, may be swallowed up in the promiscuous ruins of an earthquake, or lie down on a bed of long and lingering disease, and die. Here, he is subject to the physical laws of our being, and to the administration of a wise discipline; in the world to come, he will be treated altogether as if he had never sinned. No distinction will be made between him and unfallen beings, nor will there be any such remembrance of his own former guilt as that he shall occupy a less elevated position, or have less ready access to the throne than if he had never been a transgressor.

II. It was proposed, in the second place, to show *how justification is accomplished through the merits of Christ*,—or how his merits become available to us for this purpose. It is not uncommon to say, in explaining this, that His "righteousness is imputed to us," or that it becomes ours. But as this language, to many minds, does not convey a very definite conception, and as, to other minds, it often conveys erroneous impressions, and seems to be irreconcileable with the common notions of men about moral character, it is necessary to explain in what sense we become justified by the merits of Christ. Perhaps in doing this, also, it may be shown that so far from being contrary to the common notions of men about what is right and proper, it is in fact but carrying out, on the most elevated scale possible, what is practically occurring every day in the common relations and transactions of life. It is to be observed, then,

(1.) That we are often benefited by what others have done. The meaning is, that what they have done is of the same advantage to us, for certain ends, as if we had done it ourselves. A case or two taken from familiar transactions will illustrate what is meant, and help to a proper explanation of the subject. Take the case of a father and a son. The reputation of the one is often a passport or recommendation to the other, of very great value, as he enters on life. The son has as yet no known character, no acquaintance with the world, no credit. The father has all these. He is widely known as a man of virtue; he has an extensive and honoured circle of acquaintance; he has ample credit in the business in which he is engaged. Now while it is true that this character and credit belong to the father as his own, and cannot be literally transferred to the son, it is also true that, for certain purposes, it may be made to answer the same ends for the latter as if it were his own. Unless, by his own misconduct, he shall forfeit the advantage which he might derive from it, it will be a passport to him in starting on his career; it will go before him, preparing many hearts to greet him with kindness; it will obtain for him the confidence of others; it may be the means of securing for him many a friend and helper when calamities come, even when his father lies in the grave. While it will always be true that all the merit and the credit appertain to his father, and while, whatever may be his own subsequent worth, he will cherish a deep and abiding impression of that, it is also true that, for certain purposes, he could have derived no higher advantages in the case if the character and the credit had been his own. It would not indeed to *all* intents and purposes be the same, but there are great and valuable ends in his passage through the world which could be no better secured if all this *had* been his own. The influence of his father's name and character, unless he forfeits the advantage, will attend him far on, perhaps entirely through, the journey of life.

Take another common case. A young man embarks in business without capital. He has acquired already, it may be, a character for industry, talent, and honesty; but he has no means by which he can commence the enterprise of his life. What he wants now is *credit*. If he had that, he would be sure of success. But he has none as yet of his own. He has had no opportunity to make himself known, so as to secure the extensive confidence of his fellow-men. You have had such an opportunity, and have reaped its result. To a certain extent, and for certain purposes, you allow him to make use of your name. You endorse his papers, and agree to be responsible for him. Now this to him, in the case referred to, is of just as much value as though the credit attached to your name were his. It will be, in the particular matter referred to, worth as much to him as though he himself had earned all the influence attached to that name, and secured by a long and upright life the credit which it conveys. There will be indeed, in other respects, important points of difference, but not in the immediate use which he designs to make of the name. He will have a very lively sense of the truth that he himself has *not* this credit, that he is unknown, and that he is under the deepest obligations to you. He will never so far mistake the matter as to suppose that your moral character is transferred to him, or that he can regard it as in any proper sense his own; but he *will* consider that it is available for just the purposes for which he wants it. It is all he needs to secure the grand object of his life, and is as good to him *as if* it were his own.

Further: if we would look over society we should find that this arrangement prevails everywhere, and that we are indebted to it every day. It may be doubted whether we live a single hour, or execute a single plan of life, without being more or less indebted to it. It is an influence diffused around us like the air we breathe, or the sun which shines on our way; or it is like the tissues of the human frame, where each part derives benefits in its functions from the numerous other parts with which it is more or less closely interwoven. It enters into the very texture of society, that we avail ourselves of the toils, the sacrifices, the virtues, and the honoured names of those with whom we are connected. No man acquires a reputation for virtue who does not do much to benefit his children and friends in this way; and one of the chief stimulants to effort in parents is, that they may place their children on as high vantage-ground as possible when they embark on life. That youth enters on life under great disadvantages who cannot encircle himself with this influence, and who is constrained to "cut his way" to respectability or to wealth alone. As a matter of fact, however, there are few that do this. The name and influence of a father or a friend, a letter of commendation from those who are known and loved, will be a passport to us in distant climes and among strangers; will meet us with its benign influence on the Rhine or the Ganges; will help us when we should otherwise fall into the hands of freebooters in a foreign land, or when we should otherwise sink under poverty and want; or on a distant shore will raise up for us a friend on the bed of death. He enters life under the best auspices who can avail himself most of this, without sacrificing his independence, or being a sycophant or parasite; and he is the most foolish and ungrateful of mankind who would willingly renounce all this advantage, and choose to weather the storms of life, and make his way through the world friendless and alone.

(2.) The second remark in explaining the way in which we are justified by the merits of Christ is, that there are two methods by which we avail ourselves of the benefit accruing from the character and virtues of others. The one is, by natural relationship. This occurs in the case of a child, who, as a matter of course, derives advantage from the industry, the character, and the credit of a parent. The other is, by an arrangement made for that end. Instances of this latter kind occur everywhere. The case of an adopted child is one—a case where there is no natural relation, and no natural claim, but where one chooses, for any reasons, that the child of another should be received into his family, and treated *as if* he were his own. It occurs not unfrequently in the case of a matrimonial alliance, where the one party makes use of the name and influence and rank of the other, and on that account has a degree of respect to which otherwise there would be no claim. It occurs in the cases already referred to, where the use of a name is conceded. The name of the missionary Schwartz was thus the means of saving from starvation the whole of a British garrison; and many a man owes his subsequent elevation in life to assistance furnished him at the outset. Cases have arisen where the signet or the ring of a prince has been placed in the hand of another, conveying to him, if danger should befall him, all the influence and security which would be possessed by the owner himself; nor is it very uncommon to give a *carte blanche* to a friend to be filled up at pleasure.

(3.) It only remains now, in view of these illustrations, to make a third remark, in explanation of the way in which we are justified through the merits of Christ. The gospel-plan is, that we are permitted to avail ourselves of his abounding merits, so that we may be treated as if those merits were our own. It is not that His merits are transferred to us, or that his moral character or righteousness becomes properly ours, or that we cease to deserve punishment, or that an apology is made for our sins, or that Christ takes our part against justice; but that his merits are so ample, his life and death have accomplished so much, and his work has been so meritorious, that we may, by a suitable connexion with him, be regarded and treated *as if* we were truly righteous before God, so that " God can be just, and the justifier of him that believeth in Jesus ;" just and true, " while he justifies the ungodly."

This connexion between the Saviour and those who are benefited by his merits is not a natural connexion, for no such relation by nature subsists as would entitle any one to be regarded and treated as righteous on his account; but it is a relation which is constituted entirely by faith. The influence of faith in forming it, and in making it proper that they who are united to him should be treated as righteous, will be explained hereafter. It is sufficient now to remark, that the relation which is sustained is one that is *formed*, not one that exists by nature. It is formed by a personal union of the soul to Christ, and by the gracious concession on his part, in accordance with the Divine arrangement, that we may avail ourselves of his infinite and inexhaustible merits, so that we may be treated *as if* they were our own. There are two additional thoughts which may be suggested to illustrate this :—

(*a*) The one is, that his merit is inexhaustible. There is no diminution or exhaustion of the merit of his work by the numbers that avail themselves of it. This makes the plan of redemption wholly different from anything which occurs among men. A man of the widest credit and highest standing may be conceived to allow his name to be so often used by those who have no claim to it, or who turn out to be worthless and abuse his claim, as to *exhaust* his credit and make his name good for nothing. Not so the Saviour. No numbers that apply exhaust his credit, or diminish at all the merit of that blood by which they are saved. That blood is as efficacious now, and that holy name of our Advocate is as much honoured in heaven now, as when the first sinner was justified, and when the gates of glory were first thrown open to receive a ransomed soul.

(*b*) The other remark is, that the Lord Jesus becomes the Surety that the universe shall suffer no wrong by our being admitted to heaven. So far as we are concerned, he pledges himself to meet all the claims of the law and of justice upon us. That is, he becomes the Surety, that, under this arrangement, as great good shall result to the universe from our being saved as would be attained by our punishment for ever. By such punishment, nothing would have been gained in regard to the honour of the law, the truth of God, and the interests of justice, which are not secured under the present arrangement by the substituted sorrows of the Son of God in making the atonement. Thus he becomes the "Surety of a better covenant" (Heb. vii. 22), and stands before the universe as the public pledge that no harm is done to any interest of truth and justice by the admission of one who is an acknowledged sinner into heaven. Thus the publican was justified; thus Paul, the persecutor and blasphemer, "won Christ and was found in him, not having his own righteousness, which was of the law, but that which was through the faith of Christ" (Phil. iii.

8, 9); and thus multitudes of the profane and the sensual, by believing on Christ, have entered heaven and been blessed. There stands the Great Advocate, not for their *sins*, but for *them;* and there stands the security that no injury shall be done by treating even *such* sinners for ever *as if* they were righteous, and that all that law or justice could ask, all that could be secured either by their own personal perfect obedience, or by their enduring the eternal penalty of the law, has been secured by *his* holy life and meritorious death. When, therefore, they enter heaven, it is not over prostrated law; over an humbled government; over disregarded threatenings; by a changeful policy; or by partiality in the administration; it is because their Great Surety has himself secured the honour of the law, and because in their conscious destitution of merit he has enough for them all. His name is the guarantee to justice and to God; his inexhaustible merits, the reason why they may be treated *as if* his righteousness were their own.

This is what is properly meant by *imputation.* The true doctrine implies no transfer of moral character; no infusion of righteousness into the soul; no physical identity between the Redeemer and his people; no such charging of their sins to him as that he became in any proper sense a sinner, or deserved to be put to death,—nothing but the purpose on the part of God, in virtue of what he has done, to treat those who are themselves guilty as if they were righteous. "By that righteousness being *imputed* to us," says President Edwards, "is meant no other than this, that the righteousness of Christ is accepted for us, and admitted instead of that perfect inherent righteousness which ought to be in ourselves. Christ's perfect obedience shall be reckoned to our account, so that we shall have the benefit of it, as though we had performed it ourselves." *

I have thus submitted to you some views on perhaps the most important subject of religion. They pertain to that great doctrine which separates Christianity from every other system of religion, and to the answer which Christianity furnishes to the question, asked with so much solicitude in every age, "How shall man be justified with God?" The answer is, that we are "justified freely by his grace through the redemption that is in Christ Jesus." It is this doctrine which divides the religion of the gospel from other systems; which makes it what it is; which gives it whatever influence or power it has in speaking peace to the troubled conscience, and bidding the spirit that is captive under sin go free. It is this which will enable man to appear

* Works, vol. v. p. 394.

before his final Judge justified, not by any miserable attempt to deny the fact that he is a sinner, to apologize for his errors and follies, and found a claim to favour on such apology, to substitute an external morality for that holiness of heart which the law of God requires, or to present as a ground of acceptance the vain oblation of outward forms.

I have endeavoured also to show, that though this method of justification is entirely peculiar to Christianity, and separates it from all other religious systems, yet that it accords with principles prevailing everywhere in society, and on which men act every day and in every land. It is the embodiment and concentration of these principles, and shows their operation on the highest scale possible. Thus, as already remarked, in matters pertaining to this life, we owe to the name, and standing, and credit of others, an introduction to the world, facilities for doing business, valued friends who may succour us in trouble :—and on substantially the same principles, though on an infinitely higher scale, we owe to the merits of another—the Son of God—an introduction to the Divine favour; the friendship of angelic beings; the peace of pardon; the calmness of the Christian death; a passport to heaven, and the crown incorruptible beyond the grave. Whatever of joy or peace, of honour or favour, we shall have in the long ages of eternity, is to be traced to the operation, on the highest scale possible, of this principle—that we may be benefited by the sacrifice and toils, the name and merit, the righteousness and sufferings of Another.

In common affairs we do not disregard or undervalue this. Those who enter on life regard it as a felicitous circumstance in their condition, if they may go forth with such passports and commendations to the esteem of the world. That young man would justly regard himself as destitute of every manly and generous feeling, as well as every principle of self-respect, who should discard and spurn this advantage, and prefer to go forth to the world without the commendation or the patronage of a single friend. *We* are going to a more important theatre of being than is this narrow world. We shall soon pass beyond its outer bounds, and move through other regions. We are to go up and meet our Maker; to enter on a mode of existence that shall have no end; to be associated with orders of beings now to us unknown;—and there are great interests at stake, compared with which all the concerns of earth are trifles. We go to a royal court—the court of heaven—where we have no claim or right to appear. We go up to obtain, if admitted there, the favour of a Being whose law we have violated, and whose displeasure we have incurred. We go where we can take no wealth with us; and where, if we could, it would avail nothing;—where we shall be disrobed of all in a graceful exterior, or in fascinating manners, that may commend us to others here; and where, if it should accompany us, it would be valueless;—where the name of a father, or the powerful influence of a friend that might recommend us to the favour of men, would be of no avail;—where no earthly thing on which we here rely as a passport to others could be a commendation. But there *is* One in human flesh that dwells there. He once lived among men. He was most holy, and lovely, and pure; but He died. He rose from the tomb, and the everlasting gates were opened, and He entered his native skies. To the very interior of the court of heaven, to the sacred seat of Deity, to the throne itself He has been admitted, and is seated there. With all that heaven He is familiar, for He is there at home. With all its streets of gold, with all its far-distant mansions, with all its many departments fitted up for the abodes of the blessed, He is familiar. His powerful aid He proffers us in our sin and ignorance and helplessness, and assures us of his willingness that we should plead *his* name, and make mention of his merits *as if* they were our own, as a reason why we should be welcome there. In heaven, his plea has never been denied; the claim of his merits has never been dishonoured. Shall we refuse his offer? Shall we spurn his name? Shall we turn away from that Friend, and Advocate, and Patron, and go there friendless and alone? Shall we seek to commend ourselves to a holy God by our own doings, and to stand there in our own attempts to vindicate our ways? Shall we spurn the robes of salvation which he proffers, so white, so pure, so full and flowing, and gird ourselves with the rags of our own righteousness?—How you, my hearers, may feel on this point, I know not. But for one, I, who expect to stand soon before that holy throne of Deity, desire to have some better righteousness than any which I have been able to work out myself. I wish to have something which I may plead in the place of that which I have failed to render. I would have some better passport to the skies than can be furnished by my poor prayers and services in the cause of God. I *must* have some Friend there whose name is all-prevalent, whose petition is never denied, and about acceptance through whose merits there cannot be the shadow of a doubt.

SERMON XXXV.

THE INFLUENCE OF FAITH IN JUSTIFICATION.

ROM. i. 16, 17.—"For I am not ashamed of the gospel of Christ: for it is the power of God unto salvation to every one that believeth; to the Jew first, and also to the Greek. For therein is the righteousness of God revealed from faith to faith: as it is written, The just shall live by faith."

IN the last discourse, when showing how we are saved through the merits of Christ, it was remarked, that the means by which we become interested in his merits, or by which they are made available to us, is *faith*. I propose now to show the influence of *faith* in our justification. The doctrine of the text is, that a man is considered just before God, and treated as such, not in virtue of his own works, but in virtue of his exercising faith in Christ. "For therein," that is, in the gospel, "the righteousness of God," or God's plan of regarding and treating men as righteous, "is revealed from faith to faith;" that is, by faith unto those who have faith, or who believe; "as it is written, The just shall live by faith," or those justified by faith shall have everlasting life. It is needless to prove at length that this is the settled doctrine of the New Testament. "Therefore we conclude," says the apostle in the third chapter of this epistle (ver. 28), "that a man is justified by faith without the deeds of the law." Again, "By the deeds of the law, there shall no flesh be justified in his sight. But now the righteousness of God without the law is manifested, being witnessed by the law and the prophets; even the righteousness of God which is by faith of Jesus Christ unto all and upon all them that believe: for there is no difference," Rom. iii. 20—22. So the apostle Paul says again, "A man is not justified by the works of the law, but by the faith of Jesus Christ," Gal. ii. 16. In accordance with this, is the great doctrine which the Saviour taught his disciples to promulgate, as comprising *all* that he designed them to preach: "Go ye into all the world, and preach the gospel to every creature. He that believeth, and is baptized, shall be saved; but he that believeth not, shall be damned," Mark xvi. 15, 16. That is, there is no other method of being saved but by believing, or by faith; and if a man has not this, he must be lost.

Probably every one who has ever read these passages has been disposed to ask, Why is so much stress laid on *faith* in the plan of redemption? Why is it made so central, and so indispensable in the salvation of the soul? What inherent virtue is there in this act that has given it such a pre-eminence over all other virtues? What is there in this that should make it a substitute for all the good works that men can perform? Perhaps some will be disposed to add, that the system of Christianity is thus removed from all other systems, and is different from all the laws and principles on which men act in other things. Merit, in other cases, is not in accordance with a man's *belief*, but according to his virtues—his moral worth; and why should *faith* have such special eminence in the eye of God? The rewards of this life are not distributed according to a man's faith or credulity; and why should the rewards of heaven be? We judge of the excellency of a man's character, not according to the readiness with which he embraces what is proposed to him for his credence, but usually somewhat in proportion to his caution and the slowness of his belief; and why does religion require a man to hasten to believe that which is proposed to him, as if this were the chief of virtues? When also a man is put on trial, he is acquitted, not because he exhibits an example of trusting in his judge or his advocate, but because he is able to vindicate his conduct; and why shall we not look for something analogous in religion? Why are pardon and hope, life and joy, heaven and glory, peace here and bliss hereafter, all made to depend on *faith*—the centre and the circumference, the beginning, the middle, and the end, according to the gospel, of every virtue? These are inquiries which it is natural to make; they are inquiries which the friend of Christianity should feel it to be a part of his vocation to answer. The *relation* or *connexion* which these questions bear to the subject before us is this:—Supposing that man has no merit of his own, as has been shown, and that there are infinite merits in the Redeemer through which we may be saved; why is it proper that we should avail ourselves of those merits only through faith? Why should faith be the instrument by which we may be treated *as if* those merits were ours?

The answer to these questions is, that, in the circumstances of the case, faith constitutes a union with the Redeemer of such a nature as to make it proper to treat us substantially as he claims to be treated—that is, as righteous; to make it proper that we should share his happiness, his favour, his protection on earth, and his glory in heaven; and that the union formed by faith between the soul and the Redeemer is so tender, so close, and so strong, as to imply an identity of interest, and to make it certain and proper that the blessings descending on him should, according to their capacity and wants, descend on those who believe. It is evident that the particular *reason* why faith has been selected as the means of this is, that it constitutes a union more close, firm, and enduring than any other virtue; and that it meets more evils in the world than any other act of the mind would do. On this account, it is singled out from all other acts of the mind in the plan of justifying men.

To many, these remarks may appear abstract and obscure. It is proposed therefore, in a series of observations, to show *why* faith is so important; why it is the very *cardo rerum*—the hinge of salvation. One other preliminary remark should be made: it is, that there is a great and essential difference between *faith* and *credulity*. We distinguish them accurately in common life; but we fear that they are sometimes confounded when men think of religion.

(1.) As we have already seen, faith acts an important part in the affairs of the world. Using the word in the sense of *confidence*, there is nothing else on which the welfare of society more depends, or which is more indispensable to its prosperous and harmonious relations. It enters into everything, and we are every day and every hour acting under its influence, and depending on it as essential to all that we hold dear. It is the cement of families, of neighbourhoods, of governments, of nations. The faith of treaties, of compacts, of promises, of friendships, of affection, is that which holds the world together, and without which society would go to pieces. To loosen it at once would be like loosening every rope in a ship, or unscrewing every fastening and bolt in a machine. It is by faith, or mutual confidence, that the relations of domestic life are maintained; that the harmony of a family is secured; that business in a mercantile community is carried on; that a banking institution effects the purpose for which it was chartered; or that a government can secure the ends for which it was instituted. It is by faith only that we derive lessons of valuable instruction from history, or that we act with reference to what is yet to come. If we had no more confidence in any of the testimonies of history than we have in the fabulous details of the dynasties of India, the mythological periods of Grecian history, or the legends of the saints, all past history would be utterly useless, for it would convey no certain lessons. If we had no faith in the stability of the course of events,—the rising of the sun, the moon, and the stars—the return of the seasons—the continuance of the laws of magnetism, of gravitation, or of vegetation,—we should form no plan for the future; we should neither plant a field, nor build a ship, nor venture out on the ocean, where we might soon be without sun, or star, or compass. We confide in our teachers, in a physician, a counsellor, a clergyman; and it would be impossible that the cause of education, jurisprudence, or religion, could be maintained if there were no such confidence. The farmer of the Eastern States believes in the vast fertility of the West, of which he has heard, but which he has never seen, and with his wife and children leaves the graves of his fathers to seek that land on the strength of his faith. The merchant believes that there is such a place as Canton or Calcutta, though he has seen neither, and on the strength of that faith would embark all his property in the same vessel, and stake the whole question about making a fortune in this world on his strong confidence that such places, of which he has heard, have an existence. In like manner, we are exercising confidence in everything. We believe the testimony of the historians, though we never saw Xenophon, or Thucydides, or witnessed the events of which they wrote; we vote for the man whom we have never seen; we confide in the bankers across the waters, whom we never expect to behold. Were it not for this unceasing confidence, and its varied operations, we could not get along for a single day or hour. The affairs of the world would at once stand still; the bands of society would at once become loosened; and everything would fall into irretrievable confusion.

It is true, there is much credulity in the world, and multitudes in all professions and relations in life are imposed on. But so also there is much counterfeit money, and many may be injured or ruined by it. But the existence of a circulating medium is indispensable, and there is by far more genuine than false coin at any time in the world, and any quantity of spurious coin does not render that valueless which is genuine. So, any amount of credulity does not prove that it is improper for men ever to repose confidence in one another, or that all faith is valueless.

(2.) The second observation illustrating the importance of faith with reference to the subject before us is, that faith is the strongest conceivable bond of union between minds and hearts. It is, in fact, the cement of *all* unions, and without which all else is valueless. In friendships, in treaties, in national compacts, in social intercourse, in the tender domestic relations, it is *the* very bond of union, and there is nothing else that can be a substitute for it. The seal, which is affixed to a letter that is sent to a friend, makes it secure, not because no one has power to break it, but because there is confidence in each post-master through whose hands it may pass, and in each stranger or friend into whose hands it may happen to fall, that he will respect the seal, and will not break it. The piece of wax or wafer, that is appended to a written compact, makes it secure, not because neither of the contracting parties has *power* to break it, but because it is a pledge of mutual confidence. The seal, which is appended to a will, renders it secure, not because no one has *power* to break it, but because the testator has confidence that his friends and that the courts of his country will respect his wishes, when his mouth is for ever closed against the possibility of his declaring his desires, and his hand powerless to assert his rights. A treaty between nations is secure, not by any inherent power in the parchment on which it is drawn, nor because the seal cannot be broken, but because this is the expression of the *confidence* which now subsists, the belief that both will regard it.

Look into the relations of life. What is it that forms and preserves those numerous unions on which the very existence of society depends? What is the basis of the union of husband and wife, of parent and child, of brother and sister, of friend and friend? What but mutual confidence? And is it asked, What is the strength of that? In answer to these questions, an illustration may be employed taken from the most tender relation in life. This illustration is used because it is the very one more than once referred to on this subject in the Bible, and because it enters so vitally into the welfare of society. Here is a young man just entering on life. His character is fair; his profession is honourable; his person and standing are liable to no objection, and no suspicion;—but what he *may* yet be no one earthly can tell, for no one can certainly predict what a man will be till he is tried. Here is a youthful female,—the joy of her mother, and the pride of her father's heart. She has been delicately trained; has a home that has every attraction; is secure there of unfailing friends as long as her father and mother shall live; and has ample means of support. She breaks all these ties; leaves the home of her childhood; bids adieu to father, mother, brothers, and sisters, and commits herself into the hands of this comparative stranger. A father's and a mother's and a brother's love she exchanges for his. Her hand, her heart, her property, she gives to him. She pledges herself to go where he goes; to suffer what he suffers; to make his friends hers; to love him with an ardour with which she loves no other human being; to break away from every tie of country and home, if he shall will it; and, in a sense more absolute than exists in any other case, to commit her happiness into his hands. Every day and every hour that they will live, she is dependent on his prosperity, his virtue, and his smiles for her happiness; and the moment his affections are withdrawn, or he ceases to be a virtuous man, her happiness is dead. If he is virtuous, faithful, and kind, she regrets not the act of confidence with which she gave him her heart and hand. But what if he trifles with her happiness? What if he always meets her with a frown? What if he proves false to his vows? What if he becomes a wretched drunkard?—Now what has been the foundation, and the source, and the strength of this union? Confidence; and when that is gone, domestic peace dies. She has made a sacrifice of her happiness, and her earthly felicity is a wreck.

Let another thought be suggested here: it is, that this union of confidence secures an *identity* in their destiny. They are one—"one flesh," said the Saviour—and the same event will now affect both. Before this union, the storm might have beat on one of them, and sunshine gladdened the path of the other. Now, the storm and the sunshine come on both alike. The light that gladdens the eyes of the one, is also a pleasant thing to the other; the star that rises propitiously on one, rises propitiously also on the path of the other. The blessings of peace and joy that greet the one, greet the other also. There is one heart, one pulsation, one breathing, one soul made up of the two. And so, if calamity comes. If, under the roof where they are to abide, the pale destroyer shall come with stealthy foot-tread, and change the rose on the cheek of a smiling babe to the lily of death, it will be a scene in which both their hearts will bleed alike, and they will weep together over the open grave. If one is sad, both are sad; if one is poor, both are poor; if around one the storms of life beat heavily, the tempest will beat on both. Their union, one pre-eminently of mutual faith plighted before the altar, constitutes an identity in all the great events of life, and secures to both substantially the same treatment from the Great Disposer of all things. They share the same fortune—the same honour or disgrace—the same sorrows and the same joys; they are wafted on to a port of bliss, or are wrecked in the same vessel; they are greeted with the same welcome in life, they are buried in the same grave. It is easy to apply this illustration to the matter in hand.

(3.) The third illustration is, that faith is of such a nature that it is adapted to meet all the evils of the world. The idea is, that it has been made the hinge or turning-point of salvation, because the want of it has been the source of all the calamities which man has suffered, and because, if this is restored, the evils of the world would be at an end.

The grand evil on earth, and the source of all subordinate evils, is *a want of confidence in God.* This was the evil at the start, that man reposed more confidence in the teachings of the tempter than in the law of the Creator; and this has been the source of all our woe. Man has no confidence in his God; does not believe that He is qualified for universal empire; that He manages the affairs of the universe well; that His law is equal and just; that His dispensations are in accordance with equity; that His plan of salvation is wise;—he does not show confidence in Him by yielding implicit obedience to His laws, or by submitting to His dispensations;—he does not go to Him and ask counsel of Him in the darknesses and perplexities of life; he does not seek support from His arm in times of calamity; he does not commit his great interests to Him, believing that He will be his guide through life, and that He will yet make "all things work together for good." But he confides in other things;—he confides in his own strength, till his strength fails; in his philosophy, till it deludes and deceives him; in his fellow-men, till they all betray him; in friends and kindred, till they drop into the grave; in his skill and sagacity, till he comes to a place in life where the "right hand forgets its cunning." He confides in stocks and stones, in graven images, and four-footed beasts, and creeping things; but by nature he has no confidence in God.

This is the grand evil of the world, this the source of all our woes; for, a want of confidence here produces the same kind of evils, though on a larger scale, as a want of confidence everywhere. We have seen that the welfare of society depends on mutual confidence. Now, to see how wretched any society can possibly be, we have only to suppose the existence there of the same want of confidence which subsists in man toward his Maker. What would be the result? No man would know in whom to trust; no one could form a plan dependent in any manner on the fidelity of others; no one could be certain that any of his purposes of life could be effected. The scene at Babel would be re-acted again all over the world, and worse disorder than that which followed from confounding the languages of the people there, would pervade all classes and conditions of mankind. The remedy for such a state of things would be the restoration of mutual confidence. In such a condition of ill, nothing would have so far-reaching an effect. It would, in fact, *meet all* those ills, and make society harmonious and happy. The wheels of commerce, of government, of domestic peace, of public improvement, of education, would again roll on harmoniously, and happiness would again bless the world. The want of faith or confidence in God has produced all the ills on earth of which those just supposed are but an emblem; the restoration of confidence in God would strike at the root of all those ills, and make this a happy world. It is this which makes heaven happy, where every being has confidence in God, and in all that dwell there; and, with all our wants and sadnesses, this too would be a happy world if there were universal confidence in God. In our sorrows, we should then have peace, for we should believe that all is well-ordered; under our heavy burdens of life, we should find support, for we should go and roll all on his arm; in all the dark and perplexing questions that now agitate us about the introduction of moral evil and the prevalence of iniquity, our minds would be calm, for we should feel that there was a reason for it all; and in the prospect of death—that which now makes us so sad—our hearts would find more than peace, we should utter the language of joy and triumph, for it would be only the coming of a messenger to bear us to a much-loved Father's arms. The grand thing that needs to be done on earth to make this a happy world, is to restore universal confidence in God; and this is the whole aim of religion—this the object of the scheme of redemption. Hence the necessity of faith is laid at the foundation of the whole scheme; it is the cardinal thing in the plan of salvation. This restored, what a happy world, after all, would this be! For it is a beautiful world. It is full of the proofs of God's goodness and love. There are a thousand comforts that meet us every day and every night, and a thousand tender cords that should bind us to our Creator. If we confided in Him as qualified for universal empire; if we felt that He is *fit* to manage the affairs of his own world; if we believed that He will yet bring order out of confusion, and light out of darkness; if we trusted that his law is good and his commandment holy; and if we would go to Him with the confiding spirit with which a little child goes and tells all his troubles to his father, this would be still a happy world. For that grand undertaking of the Almighty Father of us all to restore unwavering confidence in himself, manifested in the gospel, the world should be unfeignedly thankful; and one of the principal topics of praise on earth should be, that He has required faith as the very elementary principle of his religion.

(4.) A fourth remark in explanation of the subject is, that faith is required, or is made the condition of justification, for this reason:—there is an obvious propriety that, where salvation is provided and offered, there should be some act on our part signifying our *acceptance* of it. If we are to be saved through the merits of Christ, there should be some act indicating our wish or our will; some expression of our desire in the case; something that shall serve to distinguish us from those who are not saved.

It evidently would not be proper, it would not be consulting the nature which God has given us, to receive the human race indiscriminately into heaven without any intimation of a wish to be saved; nor would it be fitting to save one part and leave the other, unless there were something that would indicate in the one a desire to be saved, which did not exist in the case of the other. What would better show this than faith? What would be a better expression of a desire to be saved? What act would be more appropriate in *accepting* salvation, in the intimating of a wish that the benefits of the death of Christ might be ours? What would constitute a stronger bond between the soul and Him than this? What would come nearer towards constituting that identity on which it is proper that those who are united should be treated alike? You are a father. You have two sons. They both become disobedient. They leave your house at their pleasure; go where they choose; are out at such hours as suit their convenience; keep such company as they desire; and are wholly regardless of your laws. They heed neither your promises nor your threats, and they have gone so far that they have now no confidence in you. You have favours which you are willing to bestow on them. You would be willing to receive them to your house, and to treat them as sons, alike in your lifetime and in your will. But would you think it unreasonable, that as a condition of their being received and treated *as* sons they should evince returning *confidence* in you? And if one of them *should* return, and should ever onward manifest the confidence due from a son to a father, and the other should not, would you think it improper to make a distinction between them in your lifetime and at your death? And would they and the world be at a loss for a *reason* why it was done? The remark here is, that faith in Christ is the appropriate *act* by which we *accept* of the benefits of his work, and that this constitutes a difference between him who accepts of salvation and him who does not accept it; and that this is a *reason* why the one should be treated *as if* he were interested in those benefits and the other not—that is, a reason why the one is justified and the other not.

(5.) The fifth remark necessary to explain the subject, or to show why faith in Christ is made the turning-point of justification and salvation, is, that the act of believing on Christ is made in circumstances and in a manner indicating *confidence* of the highest kind that ever exists in the human bosom, constituting a union of the closest conceivable nature. It is an act so identifying the soul and the Saviour that it is proper that the same treatment which the Redeemer receives should in their measure be received by his people, or that, in the Divine treatment, they should be practically regarded as *one*. The circumstances are these :—

(*a*) The sinner feels that he is lost and ruined. He is made sensible that he is guilty before God, and that he has no claim to Divine mercy. His heart is evil; his life has been evil; his whole soul is evil. If justice were done him, he feels that he should be for ever banished from God and heaven. Yet he feels that he has a soul of infinite value. It is to endure for ever. It is capable, in the long eternity before it, of suffering more than the aggregate of all the sorrows that have yet been endured on earth and in hell. It is capable, also, in that infinite duration, of enjoying more than the aggregate bliss of all that has been experienced on earth, united with all that has been known in heaven. A boundless eternity is before the trembling sinner, and infinite interests are at stake.

(*b*) He despairs of salvation for himself. He feels now that he has no power to rescue his soul from death. He cannot confide in his own arm, or in the arm of any mortal. He has tried every method of salvation, every way of obtaining peace of conscience, every plan that proposed security to his soul,—but in vain. He stands now a lost and ruined being, trembling on the shores of eternity. The boundless ocean spreads out before him. Clouds and darkness rest upon it. He has deserved no mercy; he has no claim on God to be his guide and protector; he can urge no reason why he should be admitted to a world of peace.

(*c*) In these sad and perilous circumstances, he commits his soul, with all its infinite and eternal interests, into the hands of the Lord Jesus. By a simple act of faith he embraces Him as his Saviour, his Friend, his Sacrifice, his Advocate. Renouncing all confidence in his own merit, he resolves to rely on the merit of Christ; abandoning every plea on the ground of what he has himself done, he resolves to urge the merits of the Saviour as his plea; and forsaking for ever all reliance for salvation on birth or blood, on moral virtues or intellectual attainments, on rank in life or the commendation of friends, on the goodness of his own heart or on forms in religion, he stakes his own everlasting interest, and the question of his final salvation, on the belief that there *is* a Saviour, and that Jesus is the Son of God, and that He is able and willing to save him. He is willing to risk the issue on this belief; and he who was a moment before trembling on the verge of hell as if there were no hope, now calmly turns the eye to heaven, and smiles through his tears, and says, "I know whom I have believed, and am persuaded that he is able to keep that which I have committed unto him against that day."

(*d*) This is a wonderful act of confidence. That is great confidence which is evinced when a drowning man seizes a rope that is thrown to him, and suspends the question of his safety on the belief that you can draw him to the shore. That would be great confidence which the man who was shipwrecked, and who had clambered up a projecting rock above the reach of the waves, would evince, if he should fasten around his body a rope let down from above, and swing off over the raging billows, trusting to the rope and the strength of those above to draw him up. And that is great confidence, in a case already referred to, where a delicately-trained youthful female leaves her mother and father, and commits herself, for weal or woe, into the hands of a comparative stranger. But such acts are not equal to that by which the dying soul commits itself to the Saviour. They will hardly do for an illustration. For what are the raging waves of the ocean compared with the rolling fires of the world of despair? What is the perilled death of the body compared with the death of the soul? What are all the temporal interests which youth, or beauty, or virtue can commit to another here, compared with those eternal interests which are entrusted to the Son of God?

(*e*) It remains, then, only to add, that in virtue of such a union there *should be* identity of treatment. So we saw in the illustration of the husband and wife, where the union between them led on to common sorrows and common joys; common successes and common reverses; common sunshine and common shade. Much more should it be so in the more tender and close union of the soul to the Saviour by the act of faith. They become one. He is the "Vine," they are the "branches;" he the "Head," they the "members;" he lives in them, and dwells in them. He is "Christ in us, the hope of glory." "We are members of his body, of his flesh, and of his bones." "I live," says the apostle, "yet not I, but Christ liveth in me." "Because I live," said the Saviour, "ye shall live also." Through all life's future scenes his people will be treated as one with him; and the union is so close that it introduces them to common joys and triumphs with him for ever. They will be made happy, because the same blessings that descend on the "Head" will flow to all the "members."

In view of these remarks, the following thoughts may be suggested in conclusion:—

(1.) The simplicity and ease of the way of salvation in the gospel are remarkable. The leading thing required of him who would be saved, is faith, or confidence, in the Redeemer. Thus Paul said to the trembling jailer at Philippi, "Believe on the Lord Jesus Christ, and thou shalt be saved," Acts xvi. 31. So again in the Epistle to the Romans, "If thou shalt confess with thy mouth the Lord Jesus, and shalt believe in thine heart that God hath raised him from the dead, thou shalt be saved. For with the heart man believeth unto righteousness, and with the mouth confession is made unto salvation," Rom. x. 9, 10. Here, as everywhere in the New Testament, salvation is represented as easy. The terms are as simple as possible. There is no requisition of our attempting to obey the whole law of God as a condition of salvation; no demand on us to offer costly sacrifices, or to make pilgrimages to a distant shrine, or to practise penances and fastings, or to lacerate the body, or to attempt to work out a righteousness by conformity to external forms, or by union to a particular church. The simple, the single thing demanded is, faith on the Son of God. If man has this, he is safe. No matter what his past life has been; no matter what his complexion, rank, or apparel; no matter where he lives or dies; no matter whether he worships in a splendid temple or under the open vault of heaven; and no matter whether his body rests in consecrated ground or amid the corals of the ocean,—he is a child of God, and an heir of the kingdom. Whatever may be said of this plan of salvation, it cannot be said that it is not sufficiently simple, and that it does not breathe a spirit of benignity towards the lost and ruined children of men. The infidel cannot object that God has not adapted it to the condition of human nature as it is—made up, for the most part, of the ignorant, of the down-trodden, and of children; nor that it has required more of any man than the human powers can render. Yet,

(2.) While thus simple and easy, it is on the great principles which we see everywhere prevail. There is required in salvation that which keeps the social world together, and causes human things to move on in harmony—that without which all the interests of man would be a wreck. There is required that which would arrest all human ills, and make this still a happy world—*confidence in our God.* Man wants but this to make him a happy being here; he will want but this to make him happy for ever. As confidence is the great principle which cements society, so it was indispensable in religion that confidence in God should be restored. We cannot conceive that a human being could be saved without faith. Even if it had not been distinctly and formally *required in the plan*, it is impossible to conceive that there could have been salvation without it. The very process of returning to God from our wanderings implies returning confidence—for how or why should the sinners return to him if they have no confidence in him? And how could they be happy in heaven if they had no confidence in God? What would heaven be, if there were there the same distrust of the Deity, and the same rebellion against him, and the same alienation from him, and the same doubt of his being, his justice, and his goodness, which exist on earth? The plan of salvation by faith is laid in the deepest philosophy, and is based on the irreversible nature of things.

(3.) The subject suggests a remark on the nature and aims of infidelity. Men often think that unbelief is a harmless thing. They sometimes regard it as a special proof of meritorious independence to be an infidel. They pride themselves on their philosophy and their freedom from vulgar prejudices and priestcraft—perhaps on their freedom from the prejudices instilled by a pious parent, a pastor, or a Sunday-school teacher. They consider the denunciation of unbelief in the gospel as singularly harsh, and use no measured terms in expressing their abhorrence of a system which denounces the eternal pains of hell on a man because he will not believe. The want of faith, say they, is a harmless or a meritorious thing. But are you connected with a bank? Would you think *that* a harmless effort in a daily paper which should attempt to unsettle the confidence of the community in your institution?—Have you a character for virtue, which you have secured by years of toil and of upright deportment? Is that a harmless report in the community which tends to destroy all confidence in that character?—Are you a father? Is it a harmless effort of your neighbour when he attempts to unsettle the confidence of your own children in your virtue?—Are you a husband? Is he a harmless man who shall aim to unsettle your faith in the wife of your bosom, and produce between you and her an utter want of confidence?—And is there no evil in that state of mind where there is no confidence in God that rules on high; the God that made us, and that holds our destiny in his hands? Is it nothing to unsettle the faith of men in God, and to introduce universal distrust in his government? Is it nothing to inculcate or cherish the thought that the Governor of the world is a dark, malignant, harsh, and severe Being, and to alienate the affections of creation from its Maker? Let the history of the earth answer. All our evils began in that unhappy moment when our first parents lost their confidence in their God. "Loss of Eden," toil, sweat, despair, perplexity, and death, tell what the evil was. Calamities have rolled along in black and angry surges, and the dark flood still swells and heaves upon the earth.

Peace will be restored, and Paradise regained, only when man is restored to confidence in his God; and this is the grand and glorious work of the gospel. This done in any heart, and its "peace becomes as a river, and its righteousness as the waves of the sea." This done all over the earth, and millennial joy will visit the nations. This done, as successive individuals or generations leave the world, and death is disarmed of his sting, for the departing soul leans with full assurance of faith on the Saviour.

SERMON XXXVI.

THE BEARING AND IMPORTANCE OF THE DOCTRINE OF JUSTIFICATION BY FAITH.

Rom. i. 17.—"The just shall live by faith."

From these words I desire to illustrate the bearing and the importance of the doctrine of justification by faith. The points which have been illustrated in the previous discourses are the following:—The importance of the inquiry, How man can be justified with God; the fact that man cannot justify or vindicate himself by denying the truth of the charges against him; the fact that he cannot do it by showing that he had a right to do as he has done; the fact that he cannot merit salvation; the consideration of what is to be understood by the merits of Christ; the sense in which we are justified by the merits of Christ; and the agency of faith in our justification. It is proposed now, in the conclusion of the subject, to refer to some historical illustrations of the value and influence of the doctrine of justification by faith, and to show why it has the place which history has assigned it.

I. In illustrating *the value and influence of the doctrine as shown by history,* three periods of the world may be briefly referred to.

(1.) The first is, the age of the apostles—when, perhaps, the effect of the doctrine of justification by faith was more vividly seen than it has ever been since. That this was the doctrine which Paul preached, which he made prominent in his writings, and which he everywhere defended, no one acquainted with his history can for a moment doubt. It would be needless here to transcribe the passages of his writings which declare his views on this point, or which show how earnestly he expressed his convictions of its truth and importance. Everywhere he maintained that a man is not justified by the deeds of the law, but by the righteousness of faith; that we are saved, not by works of righteousness which we have done; that they that are under the law, are under the curse; and that they who are justified by faith, have peace with God through the Lord Jesus Christ. In the most earnest and emphatic manner he abjured all dependence on his own merits for salvation; disclaimed all reliance on the extraordinary zeal for religion which he had manifested in early life, and on his own blameless outward deportment; and declared it now to be the grand purpose of his soul to "know Christ, and to be found in him, not having his own righteousness, which was of the law, but the righteousness which is of God by faith," Phil. iii. 9. In this, he coincided with all the other apostles, who taught as he did, that no reliance was to be placed on outward forms of religion, on good works, on an amiable character, or on alms, as the ground of salvation. It was *then* that the doctrine of simple dependence on Christ for salvation went forth with freshness and with power. It was unencumbered by any attending doctrine of a different character to fetter its movements, or to hinder its progress through the world. There was no necessity proclaimed of depending on rites or forms of religion; no reverence for sacred places was inculcated as necessary to salvation; no connexion with a particular church, organized under a peculiar ministry, was declared to be essential; no saving efficacy was attributed to sacraments and to alms; no merits of the holy men of other ages could be looked to, to make up the deficiency of those who sought to be saved; no promise was held out that the dead might be saved through the extraordinary sacrifices and benevolence of the living. The naked doctrine of justification by faith in Christ stood out before the world, fresh in its youthful vigour, with no trappings or ornaments to hide and obscure it; a simple, solemn, sublime truth, that all might appreciate, and that might be available to all. This was then the sword of the Spirit, slaying human pride; cutting down the self-righteousness of men; prostrating the great and the mean, the learned and the unlearned, the patrician and the plebeian, the master and the slave, the man in purple and the man in rags, alike—a sword, whose keenness was not rendered useless *then* by being hid in a gorgeous scabbard.

The doctrine thus promulgated by the apostles stood opposed to the prevailing views of all the world. It was opposed to all the aims of the Pharisees—the essential tenet of whose religion was expressed graphically and honestly by one of their own number—"God, I thank thee that I am not as other men are." It stood opposed to all the views of the Sadducees, who held to the necessity of *no* kind of religion, denying the whole doctrine of the future state. It stood opposed to the Essenes. the remaining Jewish sect, who sought to work out their salvation by extraordinary fastings and privations, and by exclusion from contact with the world. It stood opposed to the whole system of sacrifices among the heathen, who sought to propitiate the gods, and to render themselves accepted, by dependence on the forms of religion; and it was at variance with all the views of philosophy—the pride of the Stoic, confident in his own righteousness; the licentiousness of the Epicurean, justifying his own voluptuousness; and the self-complacency of the sage, relying on his own wisdom. An apostle could go nowhere, where this doctrine would not come in conflict with all the prevailing views in regard to the way in which men might be saved. Yet no one now can be ignorant of the effect of this doctrine, as promulgated by the apostles. This it was which changed the religion of the world; for Christianity made no other advances than as it taught men to renounce every other ground of dependence, and to rely for salvation solely on the merits of the Lord Jesus Christ. It had no martial power by which to make its way; it had no influence derived from name and rank to enforce its claims; it had no authority derived from a venerable antiquity on which to rely; it had no gorgeous and imposing forms to enable it to command the respect of those who had worshipped in the Parthenon or the Pantheon; it had no claims to any new discoveries in philosophy. It had but *one* thing that was new, great, improving, commanding; and that was the announcement of Christ crucified, and the fact that men everywhere might now be justified by the merits of His atoning blood. Never has any truth on any subject stood more by itself, to make its own way without adventitious aid, than this did in the hands of the Christian apostles; and never before had any simple truth on any subject produced such changes in the world.

(2.) The second fact to which reference will be made, is the state of the world when the doctrine of justification by faith was obscured and almost extinguished in the Church. It soon began to be obscured. Very early the professed friends of religion began to lose sight of it. So strong in the human mind is the love of pomp and ceremony and form, so attached is man to splendour and show in religion as in everything else, so prone is the heart to rely on its own doings, and so reluctant is the sinner everywhere to depend for salvation on the righteousness of another, that this doctrine gradually died away, and almost ceased to be remembered in the church. Then arose the system which spread night all over the Christian world—the night of ignorance, error, superstition, and crime,—a night deepening for ages, till it terminated in the consummate depravity of the Papacy under Alexander VI. Amid this forgetfulness of the doctrine of justification by faith, or of salvation by simple dependence on Christ crucified, arose the universal respect for sacred places and orders of men; zeal for splendid temples of worship, and for gorgeous ceremonies; extraordinary veneration for the sepulchres of saints, and for their holy remains; pilgrimages to the Holy Land; the doctrine of baptismal regeneration, and of absolution of sins by the imposition of holy hands; the belief that grace was imparted by sacraments, administered by a priesthood; the doctrine that the merits of the saints of other days were garnered up for the benefit of future ages, and placed at the disposal of the Church; the multiplication of sacraments, with saving efficacy attributed to them all; and the belief of a peculiar sacredness attached to ground consecrated to the burial of the dead. All these were features of one great system. They had *some* relation to Christianity, and had grown in part out of the abuse of its doctrines. But though various, they were arranged evidently under the auspices of one master-mind, and with the same end in view. That was to render nugatory the doctrine of justification by faith, and to substitute in its place the doctrine of salvation by works. It was, indeed, salvation by works connected with the religion of Christ, and was a different system from that of the Pharisee, who expected to be saved by conformity to the law of Moses,—or the Grecian philosopher, who hoped to reach heaven by the purity of his doctrine and his morals,—or the degraded Pagan, who relied on the blood of sacrifices,—or the man now who relies on his own honesty and fidelity in the various relations of life; but it was essentially the same system. It excluded the simple dependence of the soul on the Lord Jesus for salvation, and substituted in its stead a reliance on human merit.

The effect was seen in the darkness, sin, and corruption of Europe before the Reformation. Every feature of the state of things in the "dark ages" can be traced to an obscuring of the great doctrine of justification by faith. Every advance of society into that deep and deepening gloom was connected with some loosening of its hold on that doctrine, and the substitution of something else in its place, until the hold was entirely gone, and Europe was plunged in total night.

(3.) The third historical fact, therefore, to be referred to, is the effect which the recovery and restoration of this doctrine had on the church and the world at the period of the Reformation. To those who have studied the history of that period, as all Protestants should do, it is unnecessary to say that this was the elementary doctrine—the central view—the starting-point in the whole of that glorious revolution. This was the great truth which dawned on the mind of Luther, and which led to all that he attempted and accomplished for the restoration of the Church to its primitive purity; and it occupied an equally central position in the view of all his fellow-labourers. Three times was the doctrine of justification by faith brought before the mind of Luther, with the same sort of power which it had when promulgated by the apostles, and with such energy as to rouse all that was great in his soul into life. The first was when he was a monk in his cell. He had found a copy of the Bible, and he began to study it, and to lecture on it. He commenced with the Psalms, but soon passed to the Epistle to the Romans. One day, having proceeded as far as the seventeenth verse of the first chapter, the words quoted from Habakkuk, "The just shall live by faith," arrested his attention. A new thought struck him. A new way of salvation opened before his mind. A new light shone upon his heart; and the words, "The just shall live by faith," seemed never to leave him. The second instance was when he first visited Rome. These words followed him, and lingered on his ear. One of his first impressions was, that he was now in the very place to which Paul had addressed these words in his epistle. Yet in that city how were they obscured and unknown! On every hand were arrangements for being justified by works—by forms and ceremonies, by pomp and pageantry, by the merits of the saints, and by penance. What a total obscuration of the great doctrine which Paul had taught in the letter to the church there, and which he had himself doubtless taught when he had dwelt in that city! The third instance in which these words were brought to the heart of Luther was more impressive still. "One day, wishing to obtain an indulgence promised by the pope to any one who should ascend on his knees what is called '*Pilate's Staircase*,' the poor Saxon monk was slowly climbing the steps, which they told him had been miraculously transported from Jerusalem to Rome. But while he was going through this meritorious work, he thought he heard a voice like thunder speaking from the depth of his heart—'*The just shall live by faith!*' He started up in terror on the steps up which he had been crawling; he was horrified at himself; and struck with shame for the degradation to which superstition had debased him, he fled from the scene of his folly. This powerful text had a mysterious influence on the life of Luther. It was a creative word for the Reformer and for the Reformation."* It was this truth that wrought out the Reformation;—and whatever there was in that work that is valuable and precious, whatever there was to shed a benign

* D'Aubigné.

influence on literature, liberty, and morals, whatever there was to spread pure religion over Switzerland, or Germany, or England, or ultimately over our own land, and then by a reflex influence on Asia Minor, on Palestine, on the palmy East, on dark Africa, and on the islands of the sea, is to be traced to those moments when this text broke with so much living power on the soul of Luther—"The just shall live by faith." It became with him an elementary truth, that the doctrine of justification by faith was the "article of the standing or the falling Church"—the very *joint* or *hinge* (*articulus*) on which the whole depended.* To that doctrine we owe, in its various developments, all that we value in this Protestant land, and all that distinguishes us in religion from what Europe was in the days of Alexander VI. and Leo X.; and there is not an interest of religion, liberty, or learning, which has not been moulded by it more than by any other single cause. Our modes of worship; our readiness to spread the Bible; our freedom of discussion; our general diffusion of intelligence; our untrammelled press; our separation of religion from the state; our societies for the spread of the gospel; our blessed and glorious revivals; our deliverance from superstition, and from the tyranny of a priesthood, and from the corruptions and abominations of the monastic system, and from the debasement of penances and pilgrimages, are all to be traced to the power of this single truth that blazed with such an intensity on the soul of the poor Saxon monk. Such being some of the facts in the case, let us,

II. In the second place, inquire *why this doctrine has this importance and power*. This will be seen if we can trace its connexion with what undeniably it has been everywhere united to:—a religion of deep spirituality, of simplicity of worship, of deadness to the world, of freedom of opinion, of liberal views, and of great and cheerful sacrifices for the good of mankind. There are but two systems of religion on the earth: the one is that of self-righteousness; the other, that of salvation by the merits of Christ;—the one, that of men who attempt, in various ways, to justify themselves before God; the other, that of those who seek to be justified through the righteousness of the Redeemer. The bearing and importance of the latter, in contrast with the former, is the point now before us.

(1.) This doctrine of justification by faith has a power of reaching the soul, and of calling forth every active energy of our nature, which the other system never can have. It leaves the impression, that the soul is of vast value; that religion is of

* "Articulus stantis vel cadentis ecclesiæ."

inestimable importance; that the grand purpose of living should be religion. The reason of this, which may not at once be apparent, is, that it finds the soul in such a state, wherever it is embraced, that it arouses all that is thrilling, and vast, and momentous in the soul itself, and in its hopes and relations. The language which the doctrine of justification by faith addresses to each individual is this:—"You are a lost sinner. You have no righteousness of your own. You never will have any. Your heart is by nature depraved, and your whole past life has been evil. In all that you have done, you have done nothing to merit the favour of God, or even to commend yourself to his approbation. All your righteousness is as filthy rags. All your outward forms of religion—your fastings, penances, and vows, your amiableness of character, your honesty, your integrity, your pride of birth and station, are all to pass for nothing before God in the matter of justification. Nor can you hope of yourself to do anything more in the future that will commend you to God than you have done in the past. No form of religion, no flood of tears, no framing of the life by an outward law, no acts of self-denial, no fastings, prayers, or almsgivings, can wipe away the deep stains of past guilt on the soul, or constitute an expiation for what you have done. In this state you are near the grave, and just over the world of woe. A moment might cut you off from the land of the living, and from the possibility of being saved. In this state you are wholly dependent on the sovereign mercy of God. You *may* be saved, but not by works of righteousness of your own. You *may* be saved, but it must be by renouncing all dependence on your own righteousness for ever. You *may* be saved, but it must be wholly by the merits of another. Kings, sages, philosophers, priests, poets, warriors, knights, senators, judges; the gay, the accomplished, the rich, the poor, the vile, the bond, the free,—all lie on a level before God. You *may* be saved, but it will only be by making up the mind to a willingness to be saved in the same way as the vilest of the species, and to stand before the throne clothed in the same robes of salvation that shall adorn the most debased and down-trodden of the human race." Now it is easy to conceive, even for those who have not experienced this, that such a religion must have the elements of great *power* of some kind. It can make its way only by sufficient power to crush the pride of man; to bring down his lofty thoughts; to humble him in the dust; and then to impart life where there has been none. There is nothing negative and tame about it. It has living energy through all this process. No man reaches the position of self-abasement and self-renunciation, where this doctrine finds him, without a struggle with his own pride. To come down there, and to lie thus low before God, is the result of mighty power on a proud man's soul, and is no neutral or unmeaning thing. It is not the work of ease, and of effeminacy, and the business of a holiday, for a man to renounce all his own righteousness, and to be willing to acknowledge before heaven, and earth, and hell, that he is so great a sinner that he ought to be excluded from heaven, and banished from the earth, and be doomed to unspeakable torments for ever in the world of woe. And it is not an unmeaning thing, when in this state a voice from heaven bids him rise from the dust, and go forth a pardoned man, a renovated being, a child of God, an heir of heaven.

Accordingly, this *is* the doctrine which arouses the world. It was this which produced the commotions in the apostolic times, when it was said, "These that have turned the world upside down are come hither also." It was this which produced so much excitement at Jerusalem, at Antioch, at Philippi. It was this which aroused Europe in the Reformation. It is this whose power is seen in every revival of religion. It is this whose energy is felt in the efforts made to carry religion around the globe.

To illustrate what has been now said, reference may be made to the case of two individuals, who have stated the effect of this doctrine on their own minds. The first is that of the apostle Paul. It is found in the Epistle to the Philippians:—"If any other man thinketh that he hath whereof he might trust in the flesh, I more: circumcised the eighth day, of the stock of Israel, of the tribe of Benjamin, an Hebrew of the Hebrews; as touching the law, a Pharisee; concerning zeal, persecuting the church; touching the righteousness which is in the law, blameless. *But what things were gain to me, those I counted loss for Christ. Yea, doubtless, and I count all things but loss, for the excellency of the knowledge of Christ Jesus my Lord,*" ch. iii. 4—8. The other is Luther's record of his own feelings when he was first made to understand this doctrine. "Though as a monk," says he, "I was holy and irreproachable, my conscience was still filled with trouble and torment. I could not endure the expression—'The righteous justice of God.' I did not love that just and holy Being who punishes sinners. I felt a secret anger against him; I hated him, because, not satisfied with terrifying by his law and by the miseries of life poor creatures already ruined by original sin, he aggravated our sufferings by the gospel. But when by the Spirit of God I understood these words—when

I learned how the justification of the sinner proceeds from God's mere mercy by the way of faith—then I felt myself born again as a new man, and I entered by an open door into the very paradise of God. From that hour I saw the precious and holy Scriptures with new eyes. I went through the whole Bible. I collected a multitude of passages which taught me what the work of God was. And as I had before heartily hated the expression, 'the righteousness of God,' I began from that time to value and to love it as the sweetest and most consolatory truth. Truly this text of St. Paul was to me as the very gate of heaven." *

To a soul thus lost and ruined this doctrine always has this power. To others it has neither power nor beauty; nor can we hope that it will make its way among men except where the soul is deeply aroused on the subject of religion. Then it is what it is so often said to be in the Scriptures, "the power of God:" it is His mighty energy quickening the soul that was dead in sin to newness of life.

(2.) The second remark illustrating its bearing and importance will be drawn from the contrast of this doctrine with the opposite. It has already been observed, that there are in fact but two kinds of religion on the earth—that of self-righteousness, and that of dependence on another for salvation; that in which man attempts to justify himself, and that in which he relies for justification on the merits of the Son of God. These systems divide the world; for, however numerous may be the methods by which men attempt to save themselves, they all have this essential characteristic, that they are systems of self-righteousness. What are the characteristics of these two systems? What would be the tendency of each of them? Let them be put in contrast, and what must be their respective effects? The effect of the one—of the plan of justification by faith—we have already in part seen. Its obvious tendency must be to produce humility, penitence, gratitude, a simple reliance on the Saviour, a disposition to make him all in all in religion. What are the effects of the opposite system? They must be such as these:—

(*a*) Pride. "God, I thank thee that I am not as other men are," is its language all over the world.

(*b*) A multiplication of forms, and a reliance on them. Religion becomes an *outward* thing, not a work of the heart. So it was with the Pharisees, the Greeks, the Romans; so it is now in the Pagan world, among Mussulmans, and in all the perverted forms of Christianity. It matters little what the outward system

* D'Aubigné.

is; where the doctrine of justification is obscured or unknown, religion *must* degenerate into heartless forms. It makes up for its want of vital power by the multiplication of rites and ceremonies. It adds a new ceremony for every step of departure from the doctrine of justification by faith; it attaches an additional sacredness to externals as this doctrine is obscured; and where this is wholly lost out of view, religion becomes merely a punctilious performance of imposing rites, a careful observance of forms. A man, when he thinks of death and the judgment, *must* have *some* righteousness on which to rely. If it be not that of the Saviour, and if there be the pretence of religion at all, it must be that consisting of a sacred reverence for forms.

(*c*) The denial of the doctrine of justification by faith will be always attended with superstition. There will be an attempt to merit heaven by reverencing dead men's bones, by pilgrimages, by bodily tortures, by seclusion from the world, by garnishing the sepulchres of the righteous, and by imploring the intercession of departed saints. The world must make up its mind to have the doctrine of justification by faith held in its purity, or to have a religion of superstition substituted in its place. One or the other has prevailed always; one has always excluded the other; the suppression of the one has been the occasion of the introduction of the other; and one or the other will live to the end of time. The question is now before this country, whether we shall hold on to the great doctrine of justification by faith, or whether we shall go abroad and import all the superstitions of heathenism, either original or baptized at Rome; whether we shall adhere to the grand truth which was the element in the Reformation, or take Christianity, so called, as it was in the days of Alexander VI. and Leo X.

(*d*) The system which denies this doctrine has been from some cause an exclusive and a persecuting system. To whatever this fact may be traced, of the fact itself there can be no doubt. The history of the world has confirmed it, and that history has taught us that if we would be free from the evils of an exclusive and a persecuting system, we must hold in its simplicity and its purity the great doctrine of justification by faith.

(3.) A third thing illustrating its bearing and importance is its connexion with freedom of thought and the advancement of society. The fact here is more apparent than the reason of it. No one acquainted with history will dispute the position, that the doctrine of justification by faith has been held with the most simplicity and purity in the times when freedom of thought has most prevailed, and in the lands most characterized for it. And no one can doubt that the denial of the doctrine, and the denial of the right of free inquiry, have gone together. It was the same system that by all its arrangements denied the doctrine of justification by faith, which imprisoned Galileo. The Inquisition grew up in lands where this doctrine was rejected, and has flourished there only, and could live nowhere else. The proclamation of this doctrine in Europe by Luther and his fellow-labourers unfettered the human mind, and abolished the Inquisition; and nothing can be clearer than that no circumstances could ever arise in any land in which the doctrine of justification by simple faith in Christ is held, under which the Inquisition could be established; and we may be certain that, as long as we can assert this doctrine in its purity throughout all our borders, we shall be free from thumb-screws, and racks, and *auto-da-fés*, and dark dungeons made to incarcerate the advocates of any religious belief. Whatever *else* we may be subjected to, this doctrine will be a palladium to us of far more value than the image of Minerva was to Troy, to secure for us the protection of Heaven.

The *reasons* of the fact which is now adverted to would be found in such considerations as these:—that in this doctrine there is nothing which we wish to conceal; that it depends for its support on nothing which may not be fully examined; that it recognises everywhere the equality of men; that it asks no patronage from the State; that it relies for its advancement on its own simple power *as truth*—as commending itself to the conscience and the reason of mankind, and as finding a response in the soul of every man who feels that he is a sinner. The support of the other system is to be found in just the opposite of these things. It cloaks itself in mystery. It seeks to establish the claims of a priesthood composed of a superior order of men—and this *must* be based on arguments that will not bear the light. It is, and must be, sustained by the power of the State. It loves a *teaching* rather than a *reasoning* religion. It is identified with all that human ingenuity can devise to substitute a righteousness in the place of that by faith in the Saviour. It is identified with interest—where the procuring of absolution becomes a matter of bargain and sale. And it is conscious that the free examination of its claims would show how baseless is the fabric on which it stands, and how worthless all the devices which have been originated to enable man to work out a righteousness of his own. Without pursuing these thoughts further, one other remark may be added:—

(4.) It is the fourth in order, and is this, that the doctrine of justification by faith is connected with liberality in religion. We have seen what is the character, in this respect, of the opposite system. It is essential to every other system that it *be* illiberal and exclusive. The reason is this:—According to every such system, grace is conveyed only through a certain channel. There are certain men who alone are appointed to dispense it; it is to be obtained only in union with a certain ecclesiastical connexion, and in the performance of certain specified rites and ceremonies. But none of these things are essential to the doctrine of justification by faith. It is a direct concern between the soul and its Saviour. It practically removes every human being from any participation in obtaining for the sinner the favour of God. However the ministers of religion may have been instrumental in arousing the attention of the soul to its guilt and danger, or in pointing the way to the Cross, yet the transaction is one where all foreign agency and all human holiness of office are excluded. It matters not whether the minister officiates with or without a surplice; whether in a plain "meeting-house" or a magnificent cathedral; whether he can trace his commission through the apostolic succession or not; whether his doctrines can or cannot be sustained by synods and councils; nay, whether there *be* any minister of religion at all;—the soul may be justified by simple faith in the Lord Jesus. The worshipper may be a Cameronian on the hills of Scotland under the open heaven; or a man who has strayed somehow into a conventicle; or a wandering savage who is made to listen, to attend, to be enraptured, till his eyes pour forth tears under the preaching of some humble missionary on whose head the hands of a mitred prelate have never been laid,—and there shall be all the elements of the doctrine of justification. What has occurred to him on the hills, or in the woods, or in a school-house, or in a church, he feels may occur anywhere else in the same way. It will not then become *essential*, in his view, that the doctrines of religion should be preached on a hill, or in a valley; that the minister stand in front of a tent, or that he serve at a particular altar; that he wear a certain vestment, or be able to trace his spiritual genealogy back to far-distant times. That which he wishes to know is, whether a man has experienced in his own soul what he has in his—the power of the doctrine of justification by faith in the blood of Jesus. If so, that is enough. It is to him a question of comparatively no moment whether such an one thinks that baptism by immersion is the only method; or whether he regards John Wesley as the greatest and the best of men; or whether he believes that all human wisdom was embodied in the Westminster assembly of divines; or whether he thinks that the ministry exists only in three orders. All these will be comparative trifles. The grand matter is, that the lost and guilty soul is justified by the blood of the "everlasting covenant;" and this settles everything that is truly valuable in his view in regard to the salvation of the soul. Such a system, it is clear, must be essentially liberal. It cannot be a system which will be primarily concerned in "questions and strifes of words" about the externals of religion. It will recognise in every man, who has ever felt the efficacy of the blood of Christ, a Christian brother. It will regard all men by nature as essentially on the same level in reference to salvation. There will be, in the matter of religion, no favoured class, no holy order; none by nature nearer heaven than others, and none who shall have a right to prescribe to others what they are to believe or to do. One point, one grand doctrine distinguishes them,—no matter of what sect, or country, or complexion they may be,—that they are redeemed by the blood of the same Saviour. They are of the same family. They have the same rights in the kingdom of grace. No one has a right, in virtue of blood, or name, or connexion with outward forms of religion, to claim a superior nearness to heaven; nor, if the soul is justified by the blood of Jesus, has any believer the right or the disposition to withhold the name of Christian, or to say that a soul thus justified is left to "the uncovenanted mercies of God."

The doctrine which has been considered constitutes the peculiarity of the Protestant religion. Protestantism began in the restoration of the doctrine of justification by faith. This, more than anything else, distinguishes the system. All there *is* of Protestantism that is of value, is in this doctrine; and all that we have of liberality in religion, and freedom from persecution, and purity of doctrine, is to be traced to this.

The whole discussion on the doctrine of justification may be closed by a personal appeal. There are but two ways conceivable in which you can be saved. One is, on the ground of your own righteousness; the other is, on the ground of the righteousness of the Lord Jesus. There is no middle way. The grand question, then, and one in which every individual has the deepest interest, is, What *is* the ground of your reliance? On which of these do you depend, when you think of being admitted to heaven? If you rely on the former,—on your own righteousness,—it must be either because you can disprove *the facts* which are charged on you as sin; or because, if the facts are undeniable, you will be able to vindicate your conduct before the bar of the Almighty. Here, then, it may be solemnly asked, whether you are willing to rest your soul's interests on such a foundation? Are you prepared to abide the issue of such a trial? Can you calmly look forward to such an investigation of your life before God's bar, and feel secure when you think how tremendous the interests of the soul that are at stake? Are you prepared to go up to meet your Maker with the feeling that your only hope there is self-vindication? I AM NOT. I turn to the other system which I have endeavoured to set before you. I look away from all that I have done,—the miserable rags of my own righteousness,—to the white robe of salvation wrought out by my great Redeemer, and seek to wrap that robe around my guilty soul; and I feel that, if justified by faith in his blood, I shall be safe.

A guilty, weak, and helpless worm,
  On Thy kind arms I fall;
Be Thou my strength and righteousness,
  My Saviour and my all.

THE END.

www.ingramcontent.com/pod-product-compliance
Lightning Source LLC
LaVergne TN
LVHW020922110826
845150LV00004B/737

* 9 7 8 1 4 2 5 5 5 4 5 7 6 *